International Encyclopedia of
Women's Suffrage

International Encyclopedia of
Women's
Suffrage

June Hannam, Mitzi Auchterlonie,
and Katherine Holden

ABC-CLIO

Santa Barbara, California
Denver, Colorado
Oxford, England

Library of Congress Cataloging-in-Publication Data
Hannam, June, 1947–
    International encyclopedia of women's suffrage / June Hannam, Mitzi
Auchterlonie, and Katherine Holden.
        p.   cm.
    Includes bibliographical references and index.
    ISBN 1–57607–064–6
    1. Women—Suffrage—Encyclopedias.   2. Feminism—Encyclopedias.   I.
Auchterlonie, Mitzi.   II. Holden, Katherine.   III. Title.
JF851.H28 2000
324.6'23'03—dc21
00–011032

06 05 04 03 02 01 00   10 9 8 7 6 5 4 3 2 1

ABC-CLIO, Inc.
130 Cremona Drive, P.O. Box 1911
Santa Barbara, California 93116-1911

This book is printed on acid-free paper ∞ .

Manufactured in the United States of America

Contents

Preface

The main aim of this encyclopedia is to demonstrate the international dimensions of the demand for women's right to vote. It seeks to shift the focus of attention away from the suffrage movements in the United States and Britain, which have long been used by historians as a model through which to view and understand the achievement of women's enfranchisement in other countries. Entries, therefore, have been selected to ensure that a sample of countries are included from all five continents. Specific countries have been chosen either because they had an active suffrage movement or because they provide examples of particular circumstances under which women achieved the vote, such as the relationship between suffrage and nationalism, war, or decolonization. The countries chosen also illustrate the different time periods in which women achieved the vote, from the late nineteenth century up to the present day. Individual countries form a significant proportion of the entries; it is important to examine the specific national contexts in which women gained the right to vote, but we argue that a full understanding of the nature and timing of the granting of suffrage can only come from a comparison between those individual countries.

Individuals who played an important role in the suffrage movement form a second significant category of entries. Wherever possible one or two key figures have been chosen for each of the countries covered. The largest number have been drawn from Britain and the United States where the organized suffrage movements were strong and active for more than half a century. So much biographical material is available for those countries that only a fraction of active participants are included in the encyclopedia. As well as the recognized leaders of national organizations, entries have been chosen to represent the class, race, and ethnic diversity of suffrage activists and the range of political perspectives that they held.

We have also emphasized international suffrage organizations and individuals who sought to develop international links. A further category of entries covers themes that represent more recent interpretations and approaches in the writing of suffrage history, such as the imagery, advertising, drama, poetry, and novels of the movement, while attention is also given to the involvement in the suffrage campaign of neglected groups such as socialists.

The extent to which material is available in the English language has undoubtedly had a significant impact on the selection of the entries in the encyclopedia. Moreover, for some countries, work on the history of women's suffrage has only just begun. The encyclopedia should be seen, therefore, as a starting point for understanding the international dimensions of the campaign for women's suffrage, but by no means the end of the story.

June Hannam, Mitzi Auchterlonie,
and Katherine Holden

Acknowledgments

We would like to thank Paul Auchterlonie and Margaret Ward for providing some of the entries on the Middle East and Ireland, and Ruth Sayers for her help with administration. The Humanities Faculty, University of the West of England, Bristol, has been very generous in allowing us the use of its facilities. Colleagues in the library have been particularly helpful in obtaining material as quickly as possible. A very special thank-you to Arthur, Helen, and Paul for all their support at home over all those weeks and weekends when we were preparing the manuscript.

Introduction

"Although Nearly Strangers We Are Friends"[1]—The International Dimensions of the Women's Suffrage Movement

The movement for women's suffrage was a nineteenth- and twentieth-century phenomenon that arose in a context of increasing demand from a wide range of groups for more representative government. In most countries of the world, women did not gain the right to vote at the same time as men and their sex became a key factor in determining who should be excluded from political representation. Although struggles to extend male suffrage tended to be fought out between men in different social groups, the struggle for women's right to vote often led to conflict between men and women in the same social groups (Blom, 1980, 5). In no country did women have the vote before men, and when women were finally granted the franchise, in most countries it was initially more restricted than male suffrage. Only in Finland did both sexes achieve universal suffrage simultaneously. Women's inclusion in the franchise had to be debated and campaigned for, and in many countries this turned into a lengthy conflict. Ida Blom suggests that this reveals the value of the vote as an agent of power in political democracies in the nineteenth and twentieth centuries (Blom, 1980).

The story of women's struggle to achieve the vote has attracted a great deal of attention from historians, but they have in the main focused on the campaigns waged in Britain and the United States. This can partly be explained by the length and size of those movements, and the fact that participants there, as members of economically and politically powerful nations, saw themselves as providing leadership for the rest of the world. The International Woman Suffrage Alliance, for instance, prided itself on its mission to convert non-Western women to the suffrage, and its president, Carrie Chapman Catt, expressed surprise when, as a result of her travels in 1911–1912, she found that women in Asia already had a movement of considerable strength. The emphasis on Britain and the United States can also be explained by the growth and strength of women's history in those countries since the 1960s, which has led to detailed studies of the women's movement. Women's history has been slower to develop in other countries, even in Europe. In France, for example, the strength of social history has reduced interest in political history, including that of women, and therefore histories of the French suffrage movement have tended to be produced by scholars outside the country (Offen, 1994). These developments have reinforced the view that feminist movements, including the struggle for the vote, were largely a Western European and American phenomenon and that where such movements developed in Asia or Africa, they were imitative of Western models. And yet as Kumari Jayawardena suggests, movements for women's social and political emancipation in China, India, and other parts of Asia can be traced back to the nineteenth century, but have been "hidden from history" (Jayawardena, 1986; Burton, 1991).

Despite increasing interest in the women's suffrage movement throughout the world, there are no texts that provide a comprehensive coverage of the international dimensions of the campaign. Histories of the suffrage struggle in individual countries are often hidden away in journals or books that are not necessarily accessible to the general reader, and the variety of languages in which they are written can create a barrier for readers. It is our intention in this encyclopedia, therefore, to redress this imbalance. We examine the enfranchisement of women in a wide range of countries and bring them together in the same text. This should make it possible for the reader to make comparisons in a number of key areas, such as people involved in the suffrage struggle, tactics that were used, and the timing of the achievement of the vote. By exploring the suffrage struggle from the perspective of countries other than Britain and the United States, it will be possible to challenge conventional wisdoms that have been derived from an Anglo-American model.

This work of reference does not claim to be comprehensive, and size limits alone have required us to be selective. The choice and length of entries have at times been affected by the extent to which material is available in English. Nonetheless, we have attempted to ensure that examples of women's enfranchisement have been drawn from as many different countries as possible, spanning all five continents. The material included in the entries provides a starting point for comparisons, and the extensive bibliography should enable the reader to follow up on specific issues in greater depth.

This encyclopedia sets out to examine the process by which women have gained the right to vote. A large number of entries examine the enfranchisement of women in individual countries, which enables comparisons and contrasts to be drawn. In entries that examine countries with a strong organized suffrage movement, the emphasis might be on women's struggle for the vote; in others, greater attention is paid to the broader political context, which might either have hampered or facilitated women's enfranchisement. There are also biographical sketches of a variety of suffrage activists and entries on selected suffrage organizations—together these entries reveal the breadth, complexity, and different characteristics of the movement as well as some common patterns. An emphasis is placed on the international links between suffragists, whether at an organizational or at a personal level, and on the texts that had an influence on the campaign across national boundaries. Some of the more thematic entries, such as autobiographical sketches and the entries on citizenship and imagery, introduce the reader to recent topics of interest and new approaches in the writing of suffrage history.

The encyclopedia concentrates on suffrage campaigns, although these were usually only part of a broader movement that sought changes in women's social, political, and economic position. Contemporaries in the nineteenth century used various terms to describe this, such as the "women's rights movement" or the "woman question." The word *feminism* was rarely used until the twentieth century. Nonetheless, it has been employed throughout this study as a way to identify a perspective or a movement that recognized that women were discriminated against on account of their sex and that sought to challenge their subordinate position. We acknowledge, however, that the term can have a range of meanings and that definitions of feminism have been strongly contested (Lerner, 1979; Cott, 1987; Offen, 1988).

Suffrage History: New Interpretations

The recent revival of interest in the suffrage movement has produced new questions about suffrage history and a reinterpretation of familiar narratives. In the United States, suffrage studies have shown that the movement was more broadly based than previously thought, and detailed accounts of local suffrage activities provide an insight into the specific concerns of suffragists and the alliances they made with various political groups, which varied from state to state (DuBois, 1997; Gullett, 2000). In Britain in particular, several publications, produced in the last five years, have taken a fresh look at the campaign there (Holton, 1996; Joannou and Purvis, 1998; Eustance, Ryan, and Ugolini, 2000; Purvis and Holton, 2000). One new area that these studies explore is the way in which suffrage activists represented themselves, both to contemporaries and to subsequent generations. Suffrage campaigners constructed their own history of the movement, through autobiographies and other writings, which have had a long-lasting impact on the framework of analysis adopted by historians. It was also important for suffrage campaigners to use imagery, art, and literature in order to present their struggle in positive ways and to counter the negative stereotypes so often put forward by their opponents. Maroula Joannou and June Purvis conclude that "artists and intellectuals had a key role to play in bringing about cultural change, and that cultural change in itself was in the long term no less significant than political change in helping to reshape the possibilities of what might be understood by being fully human" (Joannou and Purvis, 1998, 11).

On the one hand, the histories of the British and American suffrage movements, by continuing to raise new questions, have added a great deal to our understanding of the complexity of the suffrage campaign and have led to the development of new approaches and areas of inquiry. On the other hand, an Anglo-American focus can distort perspectives on the worldwide suffrage movement. This focus has produced a model in which the achievement of women's suffrage is associated with a militant, mass campaign, and yet women gained the vote much earlier in some countries where there was a smaller suffrage movement, such as New Zealand and Finland. Melanie Nolan and Caroline Daley also point out that the Anglo-American model affects the chronological framework through which women's suffrage is viewed and assessed. This model equates the end of the "first wave of feminism" with the achievement of universal suffrage in Britain and the United States in the 1920s, when the movement is thought to have fragmented. And yet in 1940 at least half of the female population of the world still lived in countries with no female suffrage (Nolan and Daley, 1994, 9).

Nonetheless, recent studies have begun to recognize the distortions that can arise if the movement is always looked at through the experience of British and American campaigners. The collection of articles edited by Daley and Nolan is a particularly important antidote here in that it draws our attention to the characteristics and strength of the suffrage movement in a variety of countries, including Australia, New Zealand, Japan, and the South American nations of Argentina, Chile, Colombia, and Uruguay, and exemplifies the benefits for the historian of adopting a comparative approach. The authors note, for example, that although it is frequently mentioned in standard texts that Australia and New Zealand enfranchised women much earlier than other countries, this is rarely discussed in any depth. And yet the success of the quiet, peaceful suffrage movements in these colonial farming societies could lead us to revise the standard account of how and when women's suffrage was achieved. Moreover, Leila Rupp's study of women's international organizations, Ellen Carol DuBois's article on the involvement of socialist women in the suffrage struggle throughout the world, and Antoinette Burton's analysis of the relationship between British imperial suffragists and women in the colonies all emphasize the international dimensions of the suffrage movement and the need to think critically about the ethnocentrism of American and Western European suffragists (Rupp, 1997; DuBois, 1991; Burton, 1994).

Thus we now have a greater understanding of the complexities of the suffrage movement. These include the relationship between suffrage activity at a local level and the strategies of the national leadership, the nature of militancy, the links with other political organizations, and the ideas that underpinned the movement. Attention has been drawn to the complex and often contradictory ways in which women developed a political identity as they worked their way through conflicting loyalties based on class, gender, and political party. Of particular importance for this study has been the growing recognition of the ethnocentric assumptions underlying the suffrage movement in Europe, Australasia, and North America. White women's strong sense of national and imperial identity provided a way for them to justify their demand for the vote, while at the same time valuing the sense of sisterhood that came from international links, yet this identity also worked to exclude women of color. This new work, set alongside the history of women's emancipation in a variety of different countries throughout the world, enables us, therefore, to take a fresh look at key features of the women's suffrage movement and to question conventional wisdoms.

Separate Spheres and the Women's Movement

Women's exclusion from the franchise was only one of many ways in which they suffered from inequalities because of their sex. With the development of urbanization and industrialization in Europe and North America in the nineteenth century, middle-class women in particular were increasingly identified with the private, domestic sphere of the home and with the moral guardianship of the family. Although their legal, economic, and social position varied in different countries, middle-class women increasingly found that they were denied access to education and to the professions and that once they were married, they had few legal rights. Indeed their inequality under the law was strengthened in the nineteenth century. In France, for example, the Code Napoléon (Napoleonic Code), a civil law code promulgated by Napoleon I in 1804, consolidated revolutionary gains for men but was a setback for women, who were classified with children, criminals, and the insane as legal incompetents (Anderson and Zinsser, 1988). The Code Napoléon gave the husband full legal powers over his wife, her property, and her children. A wife had to obey her husband and there were harsh penalties if she committed adultery. The code was influential throughout Europe and adopted in countries such as Italy, Belgium, and Holland.

Further, there were many contradictions in women's position. For example, they were economically dependent but did not always have a male relative to support them; they were expected to educate their children, while lacking a broad education themselves. In this context, a minority of middle-class women began to challenge aspects of their social position, but their exclusion from the franchise was not necessarily at the forefront of their concerns. Women tended to concentrate on educational reforms, changes in property laws, philanthropic issues, and moral reforms such as temperance or campaigns against the state regulation of prostitution. Many women were reluctant to challenge contemporary definitions of femininity and notions of what was appropriate behavior for a woman and therefore felt more comfortable in pursuing moral issues. Moreover, in authoritarian regimes such as Russia, political activities were subject to repression by the authorities, and in Germany women were legally barred from forming political societies.

In countries subject to colonial rule, women's traditional precolonial roles could be adversely affected because women were associated by colonial officials with domesticity and the private sphere of the home. In parts of precolonial Africa, for instance, women had a broad role in decision making and were often responsible for women's affairs. Thus, among the Igbo of what is now eastern Nigeria, an official called the Omu looked after women's interests, including the regulation of market trade, and among the Yoruba of western Nigeria, the Iyalode represented women on the king's council. In general, colonial powers simply ignored such positions or bypassed them and therefore deprived women of their power (O'Barr, 1984).

On the other hand, colonial rule could also lead to the growth of women's movements and to their participation in formal politics. In the Middle East and East Asia, for example, in countries such as Egypt, Sri Lanka, and India, both women and men were influenced by Western ideas about education, monogamy, and personal freedoms for women and saw these as a sign of progress. Middle-class women, many of whom were educated in England, sought to adopt the concept of the "new woman," which involved copying European styles of dress, education, and freedom of movement. New ideas were expressed in women's magazines and in some instances gave an impetus to the demand for suffrage. Nonetheless, Western ideas about women were themselves ambiguous in that they rested on a notion of separate spheres between the sexes in which only men were seen as having a major role to play in the world of public affairs. These ideas could also conflict with movements for national independence, which drew on indigenous religious and family traditions (Jayawardena, 1986). Women were often encouraged to take part in these nationalist, anticolonial struggles, although the nature of their participation varied between countries, as did the extent to which they retained political influence after independence was won.

Suffrage Ideas and Citizenship

Suffrage movements, therefore, were often slow to develop, even among women who had already begun to organize to achieve change in their position. The demand for the vote was often voiced when more general franchise reforms were under discussion, which made it easier to highlight the exclusion of women. Involvement in other campaigns such as temperance also drew women's attention to the need for the vote because these campaigns assumed that they could use suffrage to achieve social reforms. When women did begin to campaign for suffrage, they used a range of arguments to support their position. They drew on the ideas of the French Revolution and of nineteenth-century liberalism to argue that women should have the vote as a natural right based on their common humanity with men. Indeed it was suggested that women could not be fully human unless they had citizenship rights. Women also argued that they should have the vote because of their *difference* from men. They claimed that women were characterized by moral and caring qualities, developed in the family, which they should use for the benefit of society more generally. It was frequently suggested that women would "purify" politics and that their influence would lead to the moral regeneration of society. This argument was increasingly used in the British and American suffrage movements toward the end of the nineteenth century and formed the basis of the demand in other parts of the world, such as South America.

Historians have tended to see a dichotomy between prosuffrage arguments that were based on equal rights and those that emphasized women's difference from men. In his study of feminism in Europe, America, and Australasia, Richard Evans argues that feminism generally, and the suffrage movement in particular, were rooted in classical liberalism and were radical in their emphasis on the rights of the rational individual regardless of social origins and position. By the end of the nineteenth century, however, liberalism itself changed to adopt a collectivist solution to social problems. Evans suggests that suffrage campaigners became more conservative in outlook as they accepted that there were innate differences between the sexes and used these as a basis for their demands (Evans, 1977).

Recent studies, which draw on reinterpretations of liberalism itself, have challenged these assumptions by suggesting that from the beginning, suffrage campaigners used a complex set of ideas that were not mutually exclusive (Scott, 1988; Caine, 1992). These studies argue that the same woman could weave together different sets of arguments, demanding that women should be equal to men in areas such as the law and politics, while asserting that the sexes could also be different. Barbara Caine in particular draws attention to the way in which feminists were bound up with the preoccupations of the society in which they lived, and that the ideas of contemporaries shaped their own discussion of women's position. In her study of four Victorian British feminists, she argues that if they had not "accepted and addressed the ideal of womanhood articulated in Victorian domestic ideology, they would not have been able to speak to their contemporaries at all" (Caine, 1992,

17). Once feminists engaged with the notion that women had special qualities that were developed in the domestic sphere and could be used for the good of society, then it was hardly surprising that they adopted the moral imperative of the ideal of womanhood as a central part of their own outlook.

This raises the issue of what citizenship meant to suffrage campaigners and how they sought to justify their claims to the vote. A new interest in the "languages of suffragism" has revealed different shades of meaning that are far more subtle and complex than a simple dichotomy between equality and difference. Jane Rendall's study of British suffragists in the mid-nineteenth century shows how they were influenced by liberal ideology, but also reworked it. Although some argued that women should be able to exercise the vote because they owned property or were taxpayers, others, such as Lydia Becker, believed that citizenship should rest on humanity alone, although qualifications for voting should be rooted in "intelligence, rationality and responsibility" (Rendall, 1994, 134). Becker, along with Millicent Fawcett and other leaders, not only thought the individual's right to vote would contribute to women's self-development, but also argued that enfranchisement would lead to an unselfish public spirit in which women could help those less fortunate than themselves. By the twentieth century, the latter view came to predominate in the arguments of suffragists, both in Europe and elsewhere, as they claimed that women should be able to influence legislation from their specific perspective as wives and mothers.

The ethnocentric and racist dimensions of the suffrage movement have become increasingly apparent. For example, when Black men were enfranchised before women in the United States, the suffrage movement split and some of its leaders were subsequently drawn into using both racist and elitist arguments to justify their demands for suffrage. Likewise, the ethnocentrism of many white women suffragists in Australia and Canada excluded Aboriginal women and women of African and Asian origins from the rights to citizenship. Work by Jane Rendall, Antoinette Burton, Barbara Ramusack, and others has also made us far more aware of the extent to which suffragists in Western Europe were ethnocentric and racist in their outlook and in the terms that they used to demand the vote (Rendall, 1994; Burton, 1994; Ramusack, 1990). Suffragists came to political maturity in the context of liberal notions, both of progress and also of imperialism, and they saw themselves as part of a "progressive movement of civilization" that could be measured by the improvements that had occurred in the condition of women. They shared the generally held view that in "oriental societies," which were associated with white slavery, women were little more than "beasts of burden," and they believed that their mission was to take the lead in encouraging women's emancipation and therefore progress (Rendall, 1994). As Burton notes, British suffragists also used women's potential for strengthening the Empire as a way to counter the arguments of antisuffragists that women had no understanding of foreign and imperial affairs. Suffragists claimed, on the contrary, that women could make a distinctive contribution to the imperial state both by feminizing the harsher side of imperial rule and by their unique ability to appeal to women who might take part in anticolonial unrest.

In other contexts, women's citizenship was identified far more closely with nationalist and revolutionary struggles in which their enfranchisement or their active participation in politics was seen as crucial for the good of the nation or a particular class. Evans emphasizes the importance of liberal nationalist movements as a vehicle for feminism and suffragism in small European nations dominated by foreign powers, as in Scandinavian countries and parts of the Habsburg Empire in the late nineteenth and early twentieth centuries. Similarly, in countries of the East, such as Sri Lanka, China, Japan, Indonesia, and Vietnam, women took part in anticolonial and nationalist struggles as well as demanding rights for themselves. In her study of the Czech suffrage movement, Katherine David suggests that feminists adopted the rhetoric and arguments of Czech nationalism to justify their own goals. They constantly referred to the democratic traditions of their own country, which, if allowed to flourish, would benefit women, and they contrasted this with "German aristocratism" and "racialism" (David, 1991, 33).

Socialist women also derived a specific set of arguments from their broader politics to explain why women should be enfranchised. Although they accepted that the suffrage was an integral human right, they did not dwell on its importance for the development of the individual but rather emphasized that it would enable women to more easily take part in struggles that would benefit the working class as a collective group and would lead to the achievement of a new society. They also claimed that women's increasingly public role in production meant that they should also have a public political role (DuBois, 1991).

Social Backgrounds of Suffragists

Concepts of citizenship were closely related to the backgrounds of those who took part in the suffrage campaign. A small number of aristocratic and upper-class women were committed suffragists, including Lady Betty Balfour in Britain, the Norwegian Baroness Alexandra Gripenberg, and Hudá Sha'rawi, the daughter of an Egyptian landowner (Bush, 2000). However, the leaders and rank-and-file members of suffrage organizations were largely drawn from the educated, urban middle class—and not simply in Western Europe and the United States. Bertha Lutz from Brazil, for example, was the daughter of a pioneer of tropical medicine, and Sarojini Naidu was from a Brahmin family in India, was educated in England at Cambridge University, and married a doctor. This was a common pattern. Suffrage leaders in Latin America and elsewhere frequently had links with Europe through birth and education and tended to use European suffrage movements, especially in Britain, as models to be either emulated or avoided, according to their political perspective.

Nonetheless, the term *middle class* could cover a wide variety of different backgrounds, ranging from upper-middle-class women from very wealthy families to those who earned a living in some form of professional work—a category that increased in size over time as employment opportunities opened up for women. Schoolteachers and journalists were an important group within the suffrage movement and could form a bridge between middle-class and working-class women. Although some women from solid middle-class backgrounds became schoolteachers, it was also possible for working-class women to enter this occupation. The Spanish suffragist Clara Campoamor Rodríguez and the British suffragette Mary Gawthorpe were both teachers from working-class backgrounds, and Madeleine Pelletier, the daughter of a vegetable seller, became France's first female doctor. There are also examples of individual working-class women who became active in the suffrage movement, including Hannah Mitchell, Selina Cooper, and Annie Kenney in Britain. Their numbers increased when suffrage organizations developed closer links with the labor movement. In New York, for example, Rose Schneiderman, a cap maker, Leonora O'Reilly, a shirtworker, and Maggie Hinchey, a laundry worker,

who were leading members of the Women's Trade Union League, became active in the suffrage campaign just before World War I. Working-class women, such as Adelheid Popp in Austria, also became involved in the suffrage movement through their membership in socialist women's organizations that campaigned separately for the franchise in many countries. In some instances, as in Puerto Rico and Austria, socialist and working-class women took the lead in the campaign (Azize-Vargas, 2000).

Suffrage Demands and Party Politics

The suffrage movement has often been characterized as a solid middle-class movement whose members, drawing on mainstream liberalism, were moderate or even conservative in their political outlook and their methods. But as we have seen, this description can serve to obscure the very real differences in background, political ideas, and aims of those who took part, in particular if the involvement of radical liberal and socialist women is considered. One major point of conflict among suffrage campaigners was the type of demands that they should make. In those countries where the male vote was subject to property or other qualifications, suffragists tended to demand votes for women on the same terms as men, which would have led to enfranchisement for only a small proportion of women. For most campaigners this was a tactical issue, since it was believed that there was no possibility of women achieving the vote on more favorable terms than men. Yet for some conservative, upper-class women, a restricted franchise represented a bulwark against mass democracy. This was particularly the case in countries, such as Australia, where there was a system of plural voting, which enabled individual citizens to cast multiple votes in an election. Here even conservative men sometimes gave their support to suffrage in order to gain the extra votes propertied women would provide. There were also arguments among suffragists about just how restricted women's voting rights should be. In nineteenth-century Britain, for instance, there were differences of opinion over whether the demand for the vote should include married women, while in Norway Gina Krog was prepared to continue to support the demand for a limited franchise for women, even after men had achieved adult suffrage, on the grounds that gradualism would be the most effective policy.

The support of the "bourgeois" suffrage movement for a limited franchise was a major cause of the breach with socialist women, who demanded a universal franchise for both sexes on the grounds that votes for propertied women alone would not help the working class. However, the majority of suffrage campaigners did hope for the achievement of a universal franchise, whether in the long term or the short term. Individual socialist women often took part in suffrage campaigns because they believed that the principle of women's enfranchisement was the key issue and that, tactically, this would only be achieved in the short term if women demanded the vote on the same terms as men. In Britain there was a long, ongoing debate within socialist groups and in the Labour Party about the merits of supporting an adult franchise as opposed to a limited franchise, and this debate was accompanied by an unusual degree of interaction, involving both individuals and organizations, between the labor movement and the women's suffrage movement. Elsewhere, socialist groups affiliated with the Second International followed the official policy of support for a universal franchise. Where there were large, separate organizations of socialist women, as in Germany, that saw the "bourgeois" women's movement as a competitor for the allegiance of working-class women, there was little cooperation

between the two groups. Yet, alliances were sometimes made between "bourgeois" and socialist working women's organizations that had previously been hostile to one another. For instance, in Mexico in the 1930s, an umbrella organization called Frente Único Pro-Derechos de la Mujer (Sole Front for Women's Rights) was formed, which at its height recruited 50,000 members, uniting women from widely varying class and political backgrounds in the fight for the vote.

Suffrage campaigners' links with other political movements also affected the methods and tactics they used. Suffragists adopted techniques that were very familiar in any kind of pressure-group politics. The most common approach was to lobby, petition, or send letters to politicians while at the same time spreading propaganda through meetings and newspapers or other written material. As early as the nineteenth century, women were prepared to use more confrontational techniques, such as refusing to pay their taxes. However, it was not until the early twentieth century that the British movement adopted the militant actions that were to inspire the rest of the world and influence the actions of women's groups as far away as China. It has been argued that in developing their own brand of civil disobedience, members of the British Women's Social and Political Union (WSPU) learned their tactics from the socialist movement and from Irish nationalism (DuBois, 1991). The actions of WSPU members also influenced the constitutionalist groups in Britain, who began to organize large demonstrations and public meetings, and suffrage campaigners from abroad who attended these events attempted to introduce more direct action methods into their own campaigns upon returning home. In many European countries, however, women were still reluctant to demonstrate on the streets, and some suffrage movements, as in South America, sought to distance themselves from militancy to avoid being accused of being "unwomanly" or too radical.

A further source of dissension between suffrage campaigners was their link with other political movements and political parties. The women's suffrage movement did not operate in a vacuum; each national movement was part of the political context in its own country. Moreover, its members were not necessarily interested only in the vote, and they might take part in other political campaigns as well. Biographical studies have shown that individual women could have complex political loyalties and identities, which were subject to negotiation and change over time. As Burton notes, British suffragists were not feminists first, British second, and bourgeois third, but were at the crossroads of several interlocking identities (Burton, 1991, 69). Although some women were prepared to put suffrage before all else, others attempted to achieve their goals through party politics or were not necessarily always willing to subsume their party loyalties in favor of suffrage politics. In Britain, for example, many suffragists were also active in the Women's Liberal Federation (WLF) and saw both movements as inextricably linked together. They attempted to persuade the WLF to refuse to support Liberal candidates who did not come out in favor of votes for women, but when they were at first unsuccessful, they were reluctant to leave the WLF because they were committed to other aspects of Liberal politics, such as Home Rule for Ireland.

Suffragists throughout the world usually looked to liberal and socialist parties for support, but the extent to which they could rely on this support depended on their specific political context. Socialist and liberal rhetoric of sexual equality was not always put into practice if the interests of men, or those of a particular political party, seemed threatened. Liberal parties perceived women as conservative in outlook and feared that they would vote for their opponents, and socialist groups were unwilling to support women's suffrage if they felt this might jeopardize the extension of men's voting rights. In Austria, for example, the Social Democrats campaigned for manhood suffrage despite the policy of the Second International. Yet during times of nationalist, anticolonial, or revolutionary struggles, women were often encouraged to take an active role. The need to strengthen the revolutionary movement in Vietnam, for example, led the Communist Party in 1937 and 1938 to pass resolutions emphasizing the importance of women's participation in politics. Party branches formed special women's committees and at a May Day Rally in Hanoi in 1938, thousands of women marched through the streets (Jayawardena, 1986). In her speech to the rally, Bao Tam demanded the "progressive eradication of barriers differentiating men and women" (Jayawardena, 1986, 210).

Thus women faced a dilemma when they took part in mixed-sex movements at the same time they participated in the suffrage struggle. There could be a tension between their solidarity with other women—as they struggled against a shared disability on account of their sex—and their loyalty to nation, party, or class. Individual women had to juggle these competing loyalties and identities, and they had to make difficult choices over the course of a lifetime. Similar difficulties confronted suffragists as they tried to make links with other women across national boundaries. They adopted a rhetoric of internationalism, peace, and sisterhood, but identification with nation and, in the case of Western women, with imperialist and racist assumptions cut across and conflicted with their shared experiences as women. For example, it has been argued that, during her tour of Latin America in the 1920s, Carrie Chapman

Catt, the leader of the International Woman Suffrage Alliance (IWSA), was primarily interested in strengthening the image of the United States and that she did not consider feminists in the countries she visited to be her equals.

Opposition

One area in which women could feel solidarity with each other was in dealing with the fierce opposition to their demand for the vote. Given that women were excluded from political power, they had to persuade male legislatures to support their case. The arguments used against them were very similar, regardless of the country being considered, although the emphases and the intensity of the opposition varied according to the political context of different countries. In Britain and the United States, for example, resistance was strong enough to explain why it took so long to achieve the vote, whereas in Australia and New Zealand there was far less opposition. Yet even in Australia, the state with the strongest antisuffrage movement, Victoria, refused to allow women to vote in state elections for six years after they had been granted the national franchise.

In most countries, politicians opposed women's suffrage on the grounds of political tactics and expediency, fearing that women voters, as an unknown quantity, might benefit particular political parties. Often both the right and the left feared women's participation in the political process, but for contradictory reasons. Liberal, radical, and socialist groups, which claimed to support women's suffrage on principle, feared that a franchise for women based on property qualifications would benefit their opponents. It was assumed that because of their identification with the domestic world of home and family, most women would lean toward conservatism. In France, for instance, republicans believed that women would vote for Catholicism and the restoration of the monarchy, and therefore they were ambivalent in their attitude toward women's suffrage. On the other hand, conservatives often characterized women as likely to support progressive reform movements; the liquor interest and big business in the United States, for example, were long-standing opponents of women's right to vote because of women's association with the temperance movement and with social legislation to protect women and child workers.

There were others who opposed women's right to vote altogether. In countries where the suffrage movement was strong, as in Britain and the United States, antisuffrage organizations were formed that included both men and women. Their opposition to women's suffrage went far deeper than tactical considerations, resting on a fear that the franchise would pose a challenge to men's privileged position. Carole Pateman argues that antisuffragists gave sexual difference a political meaning, which made womanhood itself a disqualification for citizenship (Pateman, 1992). A common argument was that women's role within the home and their feminine qualities did not equip them to take part in foreign policy or affairs of state. There was far less opposition, therefore, to the local or municipal franchise because the management of local questions such as education or public health was seen as more suited to a woman's sphere of interest and expertise. Female antisuffragists shared the fears of many men that women's enfranchisement would disrupt the family, and they also believed that women might lose men's economic and social protection. In non-European countries, suffragists could also face opposition because their movement was associated with Western ideas and values.

Why Did Women Achieve the Vote?

Nowhere are the benefits of a comparative approach revealed more clearly than in attempts to explain why women achieved the vote when they did, and under what conditions. Some commonly held assumptions, for instance that women in a number of European nations achieved the vote after World War I as a reward for their war work, do not stand up to close scrutiny. Although women in Britain, the United States, Canada, and Germany were enfranchised, women in Italy and France were not. One factor differentiating the former group from the latter appears to be the presence of a strong, organized suffrage movement that continued to apply pressure for the vote, rather than whether women contributed to the war effort. Other general patterns that have been previously identified appear, however, to have more validity. Patricia Grimshaw has suggested that a common feature among places where women were enfranchised at an early date, including the American states of the Midwest, New Zealand, South Australia, West Australia, and New South Wales, is that they were colonial farming societies with a preponderance of men (Grimshaw, 1994). Men in such new societies may have felt less threatened by women's enfranchisement, and therefore, Grimshaw argues, it is important to explore the attitudes of male legislators as well as women campaigners.

In explaining the comparatively late enfranchisement of women in Latin American countries like Chile, Argentina, Uruguay, and Colombia in the mid-twentieth century, Asunción Lavrin points to the tenacity of the opposition in machismo societies and the difficulties of encouraging women to give their support in societies steeped in traditional gender relations (Lavrin, 1994). Evans suggests that Catholic countries were more resistant to women's suffrage than Protestant countries, and that involvement by women in nationalist struggles could delay their own enfranchisement (Evans, 1977). Such general patterns, however, should not be allowed to obscure differences between countries that might, on the surface, appear to be very similar. David's work on Czechoslovakia, for example, suggests that women's involvement in the nationalist cause did not hamper the achievement of suffrage, and that men rallied behind women's issues more fully than they did in other central European countries. She also notes that although predominantly Catholic, the Czechs associated the Habsburgs with loyalty to Rome and tended to be anticlerical in their outlook (David, 1991). Likewise, it has been suggested that the development of a liberal-feminist suffrage movement in Uruguay was in part due to the fact that the influence of the Catholic Church was not as strong there as it was in Chile (where the suffrage movement was less successful) (Ehrick, 1998).

One of the key questions for debate is to what extent did women's agency, that is their organized struggle to achieve the vote, affect the achievement and timing of their enfranchisement? Those who emphasize that women received the vote as a reward, either for war work or for their participation in nationalist or anticolonial movements, or simply because it was thought to be expedient when political structures changed, tend to downplay women's active role in their own emancipation. Recent studies of the suffrage movement, however, have reasserted the importance of women's agency, also recognizing the limits and constraints on that agency in particular contexts. They also explore the complex relationship between women's actions and the political and social structures in which they had to operate (Nolan and Daley, 1994).

The existence of a strong suffrage movement was clearly not enough, on its own, to guarantee success; other conditions were also necessary. In Switzerland, for example, women were not enfranchised until long after other Western European countries, but there had been an active Swiss suffrage movement since the early twentieth century. Britain and the United States also had strong movements, but in both countries, women had to wait over half a century before they achieved the vote. On the other hand, there was no automatic guarantee that women would have been included in the Franchise Bill in Britain in 1918 if they had not continued to lobby the government and to make their presence felt. Moreover, in the United States it was women's hard work at a national and at a state level that ensured that the Senate would ratify the Nineteenth Amendment, albeit by the narrowest of margins.

Moderate women's suffrage campaigns can often be overlooked. In Australia and New Zealand, for example, women and men worked together in quiet and peaceful movements that ensured that the vote for women was placed on the political agenda. Although the women's suffrage movement was weak in many areas, the involvement of women in some form of protest about their exclusion from the political process ensured that their enfranchisement received publicity and could not simply be ignored. There are also examples of countries, in particular in Africa, where women were concerned about education, marriage practices, food and water shortages, and other issues of political significance but took little interest in the vote. Very often universal suffrage came as a matter of course with decolonization and independence, which in many countries came after World War II.

After the Vote

Despite the growing interest in women's suffrage history, far less attention has been paid to what happened after women achieved the vote. And yet here, too, there have been considerable differences from country to country. Too often suffrage histories focus on the point at which women first gained the franchise, but in many countries women's suffrage was still restricted in some way. In Belgium, for example, mothers and widows of soldiers who died in World War I were enfranchised in 1920, but a full suffrage for women was not accepted until 1948. In India a limited suffrage for women based on education and income was won in 1935, with full voting rights being introduced only in 1949; in South Africa, only white women were enfranchised in 1930, whereas black women had to wait until 1994. And there could be losses as well as gains. In Spain women were enfranchised in 1931 but lost the right to vote when Franco came to power in 1936 and did not regain the franchise until 1976. In Syria full suffrage was achieved in 1953, but after a coup d'état the same year, a limited franchise was reintroduced.

Women's achievement of the franchise usually brought with it the right to stand for election as candidates, although the Netherlands was unusual in giving women that right *before* they had the vote, and in New Zealand, women were denied the right to enter Parliament for more than 25 years after they had achieved the vote. Nonetheless, the removal of formal barriers to political participation did not mean that women were elected to either local or national assemblies on equal terms with men. Although women had the right to vote and stand as candidates in South Australia by the late nineteenth century, the first woman was not elected to Parliament until 1959. In all countries, it has been common for only a very small number of women to gain election to representative institutions; as late as 1990, only 3.5 percent of the world's cabinet ministers were women and in 93 countries, women held no ministerial positions (Nolan and Daley, 1994, 19). Nonetheless, there have been differences between countries in terms of women's representation in government. In Norway, for example, until World War II women never constituted more than 2.5 percent of those who held seats in local assemblies, and only 3 out of the 150 members of the Storting, the national parliament, were women. In the 1970s, however, women's participation in politics increased so that by 1979, 22 percent of members of local assemblies and 23.9 percent of members of the Storting were women (Blom, 1980, 21). In Malaysia, where women received the suffrage in 1957, only 7.8 percent of the total number of legislators were female in 1995 (Ariffin, 1999).

Suffrage campaigners were full of optimism about what women could achieve and how their lives would change once they had the vote. One of their key arguments was that women would be able to have a say in legislation that affected women and children, and in a number of countries women fought for equal rights legislation aimed at improving all areas of women's lives. In many cases, the movement emphasized "social citizenship," the idea that women have a specific contribution to make to the community as wives and mothers who take an interest in welfare measures. Thus women's citizenship was still defined in terms of their difference from men. This was a far cry from those suffragists who argued that women's enfranchisement meant more than the ability to influence legislation, since the vote also affected women's social and economic status and the relationship between the sexes in the family. Writing in 1934, Winifred Holtby, a British novelist and feminist, claimed that the significance of women's struggle for the vote lay in the way it had helped to shift public perceptions of women. It had enfranchised women "from more than their lack of citizenship. It had disproved those theories about their own nature that had hitherto constituted an obstacle to women's advancement" (Joannou and Purvis, 1998, 1).

Looking back over half a century, this optimism seems misplaced. In all countries, women faced formidable obstacles to their full political participation; the political world was still defined in masculine terms, and the structure of power within political parties could make it difficult for women to gain selection as candidates or to influence policy. Women's achievement of voting rights highlighted even more starkly the ways in which men continued to exercise power and privileges at work, in the family, and through other social structures. This has led to a degree of skepticism about the importance of women's suffrage and perhaps explains why little attention has been paid to its effects. It has been argued, for example, that in the United States, women gained the vote when the "influence of parties and electoral politics on public policy was declining" and when interest groups and the formation of public opinion were seen as "more effective ways to influence government" (Baker, 1994, 104). Indeed, women had always sought other ways to bring about political change—through voluntary work, protest movements, and lobbying—or, as in many African societies, through indirect methods such as using male relatives to ensure a desired outcome or the use of female gossip (O'Barr, 1984). Pateman, however, argues that women's votes have helped to bring legal and policy changes that have contributed toward a transformation of women's lives, but that it is difficult to assess precisely what part the vote played compared with other influences on social and economic change. She calls, therefore, for far more research on the political significance and consequences of women's enfranchisement, with specific attention to the comparative approach. Such research is necessary to determine whether, for instance, it has made a difference that women in Australia and New Zealand have had the vote for over a century, but in Switzerland only since 1971, and whether women's exclusion or inclusion in the franchise has affected their social position and relationships between the sexes (Pateman, 1994, 345–346).

It appears, therefore, that there is a great deal still to be discovered about the suffrage movement—whether this means more in-depth work on suffrage movements in those countries that have been neglected by historians, or a reassessment of movements that have received a great deal of attention. We need to explore and to test out the assumptions made by contemporaries about the importance of the vote for women and the changes it would bring to their lives. In such a project, it is important to examine the characteristics of suffrage history in the specific political and social context of individual countries, while at the same time using a comparative approach to explore and modify the explanations and interpretations made.

References Anderson, Bonnie S., and Judith P. Zinsser. *A History of Their Own: Women in Europe from Prehistory to the Present.* Vol. 2 (1988); Azize-Vargas, Yamila. "The Emergence of Feminism in Puerto Rico, 1870–1930" (2000); Baker, Paula. "The Domestication of Politics: Women and American Political Society, 1780–1920" (1994); Blom, Ida. "The Struggle for Women's Suffrage in Norway, 1885–1913" (1980); Burton, Antoinette. "The Feminist Quest for Identity: British Imperial Suffragism and 'Global Sisterhood,' 1900–1915" (1991); Burton, Antoinette. *Burdens of History: British Feminists, Indian Women and Imperial Culture, 1865–1914* (1994); Bush, Julia. *Edwardian Ladies and Imperial Power* (2000); Caine, Barbara. *Victorian Feminists* (1992); Cott, Nancy. *The Grounding of Modern Feminism* (1987); Daley, Caroline, and Melanie Nolan, eds. *Suffrage and Beyond: International Feminist Perspectives* (1994); David, Katherine. "Czech Feminists and Nationalism in the Late Hapsburg Monarchy: 'The First in Austria'" (1991); DuBois, Ellen Carol. "Woman Suffrage and the Left: An International Socialist-Feminist Perspective" (1991); DuBois, Ellen Carol.

Harriot Stanton Blatch and the Winning of Woman Suffrage (1997); Ehrick, Christine. "*Madrinas* and Missionaries: Uruguay and the Pan-American Women's Movement" (1998); Eustance, Claire, Joan Ryan, and Laura Ugolini. *A Suffrage Reader: Charting Directions in British Suffrage History* (2000); Evans, Richard J. *The Feminists: Women's Emancipation Movements in Europe, America and Australasia, 1840–1920* (1977); Grimshaw, Patricia. "Presenting the Enfranchisement of New Zealand Women Abroad" (1994); Gullett, Gayle. *Becoming Citizens: The Emergence and Development of the California Women's Movement, 1880–1911* (2000); Holton, Sandra Stanley. *Suffrage Days: Stories from the Women's Suffrage Movement* (1996); Jayawardena, Kumari. *Feminism and Nationalism in the Third World* (1986); Joannou, Maroula, and June Purvis, eds. *The Women's Suffrage Movement: New Feminist Perspectives* (1998); Lavrin, Asunción. "Suffrage in South America: Arguing a Difficult Cause" (1994); Lerner, Gerda. *The Majority Finds Its Past: Placing Women in History* (1979); Nolan, Melanie, and Caroline Daley. "International Feminist Perspectives on Suffrage: An Introduction" (1994); O'Barr, Jean. "African Women in Politics" (1984); Offen, Karen. "Defining Feminism: A Comparative Historical Approach" (1988); Offen, Karen. "Women, Citizenship and Suffrage with a French Twist, 1789–1993" (1994); Pateman, Carole. "Equality, Difference, Subordination: The Politics of Motherhood and Women's Citizenship" (1992); Pateman, Carole. "Three Questions about Womanhood Suffrage" (1994); Purvis, June, and Sandra Stanley Holton, eds. *Votes for Women* (2000); Ramusack, Barbara. "Cultural Missionaries, Maternal Imperialists, Feminist Allies: British Women Activists in India, 1865–1945" (1990); Rendall, Jane. "Citizenship, Culture and Civilisation: The Languages of British Suffragists, 1866–1874" (1994); Rupp, Leila J. *Worlds of Women: The Making of an International Women's Movement* (1997); Scott, Joan. "Deconstructing Equality-versus-Difference: Or the Uses of Post-Structuralist Theory for Feminism" (1988).

Notes

1. May Wright Sewall to Marie Stritt, 22 January 1901, quoted in Leila Rupp, *Worlds of Women: The Making of an International Women's Movement* (Princeton, NJ: Princeton University Press, 1997), 203.

International Encyclopedia of
Women's Suffrage

Actresses' Franchise League

The Actresses' Franchise League (AFL) was formed in 1908 and became a significant force in the British women's suffrage movement. The theater was one of the few places where women could not only carve out an existence that was independent from men but also gain wealth and recognition in their own right. It is therefore not surprising that women working in the theater should have demanded the right to participate in selecting their country's government.

The AFL had a high profile in many suffrage marches and demonstrations, and because many of its members were well-known actresses and glamorous figures, they attracted large crowds of onlookers. The league also raised funds for other suffrage societies by writing and producing plays and sketches, usually either farce or melodrama, on the theme of women's oppression and the need for the vote. These were often performed at the end of public meetings in order to attract larger audiences, and were also offered as fund-raising matinees open to the public in some of the London theaters and later also in provincial venues.

By 1912 the AFL had become extremely successful, with a membership of 750, and was raising large sums of money for the suffrage movement. However, in 1913 the league was left in disarray by a rift between rival factions supporting either the militant Women's Social and Political Union (WSPU) or the moderate constitutionalists. A vacuum in the AFL leadership enabled the Play Department, led by Inez Bensusan, to step in and launch a women's theater at the Coronet Theater in London's Notting Hill Gate. Suffrage plays were performed there until 1914, after which AFL members, in common with other suffragists, moved to support the war effort, offering entertainment to the troops in their camps. Although the AFL survived into the 1920s with 900 members at the end of the war, it lost its political edge after most women in Britain gained the vote in 1918.

See also Britain; Drama, Novels, Poetry, and Film; Women's Social and Political Union.
Reference Hirschfield, Claire. "The Woman's Theatre in England 1913–1918" (1995).

Acuña, Angela, and La Liga Feminista

Angela Acuña was the most prominent supporter of women's suffrage in Costa Rica and founder of La Liga Feminista (the Feminist League), which she led for more than two decades.

Acuña, whose mother was half German, attended private school in England during one of the most turbulent periods of suffrage activity and had attended suffragette meetings. On her return to Costa Rica in 1910, she became the first woman to enroll in a secondary school for boys in order to gain entrance to university. She trained as a lawyer but had to appeal to the Legislative Assembly in 1916 to exercise her profession because women at that time were not allowed to witness wills or other legal documents. Although Acuña was given permission to practice as a lawyer, she was barred from being a notary; this was a right given only to voting citizens until 1922.

In 1920 Acuña turned her attention to the subject of women's rights but decided not to follow the confrontational path of the suffragettes she had encountered in England, seeking rather to minimize conflict with her opponents. This was a policy that, though successful within its own terms, probably slowed down the achievements of the women's rights movement. She was anxious not to discard her femininity and was flattered by the inscription on a gift from a male friend: "To the most feminine of feminists."

Acuña had distanced herself from the prodemocracy demonstrations against the dictatorship of General Federico Tinaco on the grounds that he was a family friend, but after he was removed in 1920, she began to petition the legislature to make changes in the constitution. In 1920 she led a group of women from the Colegio Superior de Señoritas who confronted members of the Legislative Assembly, asking them to support a limited suffrage motion put forward by the new president, Julio Acosta García.

Acuña went on to represent Costa Rica at the Pan-American Women's Conference in Baltimore in 1922 and returned to form the first official Costa Rican suffrage organization, La Liga Feminista, in 1923, becoming its first president. She began sending petitions to the Legislative Assembly in 1924, and in 1925 she made a formal demand to take women off the list of people prevented from voting. This demand was made on the grounds that the 1871 Constitution did not specifically exclude women.

None of Acuña's attempts at changing the ideas of a very traditionally minded legislature were successful, and in 1927 she returned to Europe for three years. During her absence, Liga Feminista became noticeably less interested in women's rights and more involved in traditional female activities. In 1929 it changed its name to La Sociedad Cultural (the Cultural Society) and no longer focused on suffrage as a key goal. After Acuña returned to Costa Rica in 1931, she held the presidency of La Liga Feminista once again, now restored to its original name and direction. Under her leadership, further proposals were made to amend the constitution in 1931, 1932, 1934, and 1939. However, in an attempt to counter the arguments of her opponents, Acuña now restricted her goals, concentrating only on achieving a limited suffrage for educated and professional women. Yet all her attempts still failed.

In 1943 the league became involved in grassroots campaigns to prevent the government from making antidemocratic electoral reforms. Acuña favored the move by conservative opposition candidate Léon Cortés to court women by reforming electoral law in their favor. She and the league organized against the countercampaign, which mocked women's attempts to secure political rights. For example, the league managed to prevent the performance of a new play, *Las Candidatas,* in which suffragists were ridiculed.

Yet despite all their efforts, none of the league's attempts at electoral reform were taken seriously by the legislature. By 1947 Acuña had moved to Los Angeles and the league had withdrawn from organized political activities, leaving other women's groups to carry on the struggle. However, when Costa Rican women finally achieved the vote in 1949, Acuña sent a congratulatory letter to the legislature, and she went on to become the first woman ambassador to the Organización de Estados Americanos (Organization of American States).

See also Britain; Citizenship; Costa Rica; Pan-American Women's Conference.
References González-Suárez, Mirta. "With Patience and Without Blood: The Political Struggles of Costa Rican Women" (1994);

Sharratt, Sara. "The Suffragist Movement in Costa Rica 1889–1949: Centennial of Democracy?" (1997).

Addams, Jane

Jane Addams (1860–1935), an American who gained an international reputation for her settlement work and peace activities, also put her weight behind the suffrage cause. Born in Cedarville, Illinois, the daughter of a senator, she founded Hull House, a social settlement in Chicago, in 1889, and in 1903 she became vice president of the Women's Trade Union League. She lectured all over the country on her social work activities and wrote a large number of books and articles on the subject. She also became increasingly involved in the politics of the Progressive Party and seconded Theodore Roosevelt's nomination as presidential candidate at the 1912 convention. In 1911 she became vice president of the National American Woman Suffrage Association, and in 1913 she attended the Congress of the International Woman Suffrage Alliance (IWSA), held in Budapest, Hungary. She argued that the vote would enable women to act as an influence for reform and social improvement and that it would help them to preserve their homes as well as to contribute to the life of the community. These views were expressed in an article, "Why Women Should Vote," published in the *Ladies Home Journal* in 1910.

In 1915 Jane Addams presided at the International Congress of Women at The Hague, Netherlands, a gathering dominated by IWSA members active in the peace movement. She then put most of her energies into the peace movement, acting as president of the Women's International League for Peace and Freedom from 1919 to 1929. She was honored for this work when she became the first American woman to receive the Nobel peace prize in 1931. Although suffrage was only one among many political and social causes that she championed throughout her life,

Jane Addams was such a prestigious international figure that her belief that women should have a voice in legislation helped to give added weight to the suffrage movement at a crucial time.

See also International Congress of Women, The Hague; International Woman Suffrage Alliance; National American Woman Suffrage Association; United States of America; Women's Trade Union League.
Reference Tims, Margaret. *Jane Addams of Hull House, 1860–1935* (1961).

Adult Suffrage

See Universal Suffrage.

Advertising

Women's suffrage campaigners, particularly in Britain and the United States, used commodities to advertise their cause. At the same time, businesses saw the potential of a mass suffrage movement to provide a market for their goods and began to use suffrage imagery in their own advertising campaigns. The militant British group, the Women's Social and Political Union (WSPU), was among the first to realize the importance of spectacle in drawing attention to its demands. The WSPU urged women to wear its colors of purple, white, and green during public demonstrations, and it was soon selling commodities in these colors, ranging from badges and ribbons to jewelry, dresses, hats, and board games.

In the United States, women's suffrage groups in the nineteenth century sold an array of goods at bazaars in the local colors, but these products were often homemade. After 1910, however, the National American Woman Suffrage Association (NAWSA) stocked a wide range of manufactured suffrage goods, including pencils, stationery, cups, playing cards, and fans. Suffrage goods were advertised in the women's press, and the NAWSA published a regular catalogue of "Women's Suffrage Literature and Supplies." Before World War I, goods were

VOTES FOR WOMEN,

For the work of a day,
For the taxes we pay,
For the Laws we obey,
We want something to say.

6342

Suffrage campaigners used many products to advertise their cause. This postcard distributed in the United States outlines the rationale of suffrage for women. (Library of Congress)

gests that novelty goods "brought the movement to a mass audience of non-suffragists and allowed them to participate in suffragists' infectious spectacles" (Finnegan, 1999, 124). In 1915, for example, New York City suffragists distributed 1 million suffrage buttons, 200,000 cards of matches inscribed "Vote Yes on the Suffrage Amendment," and 35,000 paper fans advertising votes for women.

The suffrage campaign had increasingly close and complicated links with the fashion industry and with commercial enterprise. Many manufacturers and retailers advertised their goods in the suffrage press, using slogans that made reference to the vote. Others made goods that tied in directly with the campaign. In Britain, for example, the WSPU informed its members about shops that stocked dresses in their colors, and one firm, Swan and Edgar, advertised dresses that were suitable to be worn on the NUWSS Suffrage Pilgrimage in 1913. Selfridge's of Oxford Street, London, sold a wide range of suffrage goods and when Emmeline Pankhurst was released from prison in 1909, the shop flew a flag in WSPU colors. Some firms, including Selfridge's, continued to advertise in the WSPU press even after the escalation of militancy caused many businesses to withdraw support. Some of those who offered goods and services to the suffrage movement were themselves active supporters of the campaign. For example, art photographer Annie Bell offered special terms to WSPU members, and Rose O'Neill, an artist, gave her time and skill to drawing "Kewpie" doll postcards for the NAWSA.

Although many advertisers were using the rhetoric of women's suffrage for their own purposes, Finnegan suggests that suffragists were willing to accept this because they believed that it was a sign of their movement's growing importance and status. Presenting women in domesticated or romantic ways could cause tensions between commercial advertisers and the

sold in the many suffrage shops established by the major suffrage organizations, which also advertised meetings, distributed suffrage literature, and provided a focus for activists in the campaign.

The production of suffrage commodities fulfilled a number of different purposes. It raised money for the movement and also played a part in drawing attention to the campaign and enabling women to demonstrate their political commitment. The British group, the National Union of Women's Suffrage Societies (NUWSS), urged its members to wear the union's colors of red, white, and green so that they could develop a clear constitutionalist identity in the face of the challenge from the militants. Margaret Finnegan also sug-

women's suffrage movement, although in the United States at least, such images fit with the uncontroversial views of women's citizenship held by the less radical suffragists.

Extensive use of advertising—both by suffragists and by businesses who saw an advantage in making suffrage goods or in adding references to the vote to existing commodities—went hand in hand with the development of a mass suffrage movement in the early twentieth century, which increasingly sought to draw attention to itself through spectacle and large demonstrations.

See also Citizenship; Imagery; National American Woman Suffrage Association; National Union of Women's Suffrage Societies; Pankhurst, Emmeline; Propaganda; Women's Social and Political Union.
References Atkinson, Diane. *The Purple, White and Green: Suffragettes in London, 1906–14* (1992); Finnegan, Margaret. *Selling Suffrage: Consumer Culture and Votes for Women* (1999); Tickner, Lisa. *The Spectacle of Women: Imagery of the Suffrage Campaign, 1907–1914* (1987).

Africa South of the Sahara

In the past, most African women were more concerned with issues such as marriage practices, access to education, and food shortages than with suffrage, and they sought other ways to influence politics. In the precolonial period, African women often had power within the family and the community, but they lacked official political authority. Despite this, there are numerous examples of female chiefs and women's collective organizations playing a vital role in politics at the local level. In addition, many women were able to exercise political influence because of the crucial economic role they played in market trading and agricultural production. By putting pressure on males in authority and by refusing to accept communal decisions, women were often able to reverse unpopular local laws and taxes.

In the colonial period, women's power became seriously eroded because most colonial officials, whatever the dominant power, shared the fundamental belief that women belonged in the home and that the realm of politics was of no concern to them. Many women resisted their marginalization by participating in collective action, such as the tax resistance campaigns in Nigeria and Tanzania, and by playing an active role in nationalist and liberation movements, for example, in Eritrea, Guinea-Bissau, Namibia, South Africa, and Zimbabwe. Some well-educated women, including Funmilayo Ransome-Kuti of Nigeria and Constance Cummings-John of Sierra Leone, were active in the political arena and were able to align emerging women's movements with particular political parties, while at the same time calling for women's enfranchisement.

With the creation of the nation state in the postcolonial period and the increasing centralization of authority, political life has tended to become alienated from its local and communal roots, with the result that it remains difficult for women to enter the public sphere, with some notable exceptions such as South Africa. The keys to political success are high levels of education and salaried employment, and as many African women remain illiterate, this is, in some ways, the most important hurdle for women to overcome. The rise of military and other dictatorships has tended to make the situation worse, but women are continuing the struggle to play a role in African politics, and there are many notable examples of African women who have achieved positions of authority in their respective governments.

Central Africa

The administration of what is now Burundi, the Democratic Republic of the Congo (formerly the Belgian Congo, then Zaire), and Rwanda remained in the hands of the Belgian colonial authorities

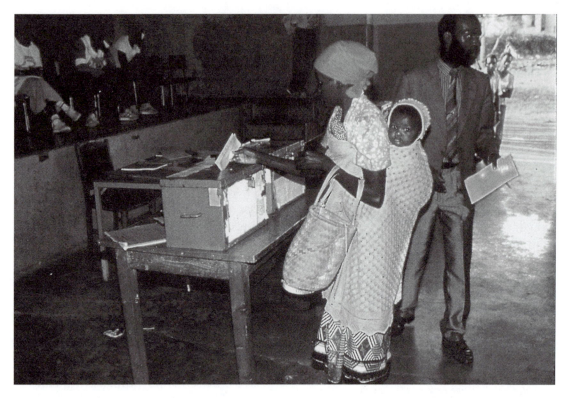

Women first cast their votes under a system of universal suffrage in Zambia in 1964. (Gamma)

until independence, with only limited African representation in the late 1950s. Burundi and Rwanda were granted full suffrage for the communal elections of 1960 and the legislative elections of 1961. Universal adult suffrage was confirmed on independence in 1962. The Democratic Republic of the Congo was initially administered as the Belgian Congo by a legislative council and regional assemblies, which contained only Europeans appointed by the colonial authorities. There was greater African representation toward the end of the 1950s, but no full suffrage until independence in 1960, when the colony became known as Zaire.

East Africa

The British colonies of Kenya, Malawi, Tanzania, Uganda, Zambia, and Zimbabwe followed a pattern of representation established by Britain in most of its African territories. White voters, including women, were usually given precedence, and African voters were subject to a variety of educational, fiscal, and property qualifications, all of which disadvantaged women. Universal adult suffrage was introduced only on independence.

In Kenya a legislative council had been in existence since 1907, and European women were given the vote in 1919, followed by Asian men and women in 1923. (The European women, led by a Mrs. McGregor Ross, had formed the East Africa Women's League in 1917 in order to obtain the franchise.) Black African voters had to wait until 1957 before their electoral rights were recognized, when a wider franchise, although one still restricted by property and educational qualifications, was introduced. Around 60 percent of the population, including black African women, gained the vote then, although Arab women from Mombasa had to petition the colonial government to protest that the legislation had denied them the franchise. Their petition succeeded, and they spent the following year registering other Arab women as voters and persuading them to exercise their electoral rights. Finally, upon independence in 1963, universal adult suffrage was introduced.

In what is now Malawi (formerly Nyasaland) and Zambia (formerly Northern Rhodesia), the colonial authorities allowed a limited franchise to Blacks, with educational and property qualifications, before granting independence. In both countries, many women were active in the nationalist movements and made a considerable contribution to the success of the nationalist political campaigns prior to independence, in the expectation of gaining political rights. In Malawi, voters in the elections of 1961 included women who fulfilled the necessary property and educational qualifications, which meant that all European women and around 10,000 Black women were enfranchised. Universal adult suffrage was introduced on independence in 1964. In Zambia the 1959 Constitution granted European, Indian, and Black African men and women the vote, subject to stringent citizenship, residential, educational, and property qualifications, which weighted the electoral rolls heavily in favor of the white population. The first direct elections were held in 1962 on a much wider franchise, and in October 1964, universal adult suffrage was gained on independence.

Zimbabwe (formerly Southern Rhodesia, then Rhodesia) was joined in a federation with Malawi and Zambia between 1953 and 1964, and during this period the franchise in Zimbabwe was widened to include Black women for the first time, by means of a special roll incorporating educational and property qualifications (some European women had already obtained the vote as early as 1919). These complex franchise requirements were included in the 1961 Constitution, which allowed around 50,000 Blacks to exercise limited political power by giving them 15 reserved parliamentary seats. In 1965 the white-dominated Rhodesian Front Party of Ian Smith unilaterally declared independence from Britain, introducing its own constitution in 1969. This reduced the role of Black voters, particularly women, because half the seats reserved for Blacks were elected by male electoral colleges. When the Smith regime fell in 1980, the modern state of Zimbabwe was born, and the new constitution granted universal adult suffrage.

Tanzania (formerly Tanganyika, and including Zanzibar) followed a similar pattern of gradual expansion of the electorate prior to independence. The first general elections were held in Tanzania in 1958 and 1959, with a franchise based on educational and economic qualifications. This meant that all Europeans, most Asians, and a small number of Blacks were able to vote. The 1960 elections were held on a much wider franchise and included the participation of women, both as candidates and as voters, but universal adult suffrage was not achieved until independence in 1961. In Zanzibar, women first gained the vote in 1961, and the two countries united in 1964 as Tanzania.

Uganda held its first direct elections in 1958, with a franchise based on property and educational qualifications. The elections of 1961 were held on a wider franchise, which allowed more women to participate, but they did not obtain full voting rights until independence in 1962, when universal adult suffrage was introduced. In the British island colony of Mauritius, representation had been limited to the elite, until the Constitution of 1947 widened the franchise to include all men and women over 21 years of age who were literate. A new constitution provided for universal adult suffrage in 1959, and in 1968, the island became independent. The islands of the Seychelles gained universal adult suffrage on independence in 1976.

The French colonies in East Africa (Comoros, Djibouti, Madagascar, and Ré-union), in common with all other French overseas territories, were the subject of central control by the French government, with an emphasis on the "indivisibility" of the French Republic and her colonies and an insistence that every country follow the same pattern of constitutional development. The early franchise was usually severely limited, but was gradually expanded until the *loi-cadre* (framework law) of 1956 granted virtually universal suffrage and a considerable degree of self-government. In Madagascar (formerly the Malagasy Republic) and the Comoro Islands, the *loi-cadre* was introduced in 1956, followed by independence and universal adult suffrage in 1960, and Djibouti obtained universal adult suffrage on independence in 1977. Réunion has remained a department of France and has universal adult suffrage under French electoral law.

Ethiopia became independent in 1954, after Italian rule between 1936 and 1941, and British administration from 1941. The 1955 Constitution guaranteed universal adult suffrage. Originally an Italian colony, Eritrea became a federal part of Ethiopia in 1952 and voted in the Ethiopian elections of 1957 on the basis of universal adult suffrage. After a long military struggle, in which women played an important part, the country gained its independence in 1993. A new constitution adopted in 1997 granted an element of universal adult suffrage for the elections to the National Assembly and full suffrage for presidential elections.

Somalia was formed in 1960 from the union of British Somaliland in the north and Italian Somalia in the south. Women in Somalia first participated on equal terms with men in the 1958 municipal elections, and universal adult suffrage was gained in 1961. However, although women in both territories voted in the 1961 referendum on the constitution, the

people of former British Somaliland did not obtain universal adult suffrage until 1963. In 1991 the northern half broke away and declared itself the independent Republic of Somaliland, but as yet there is no agreed-upon constitution.

Southern Africa

The British possessions of Botswana, Lesotho, and Swaziland were subject to the usual complicated and variable constitutional arrangements that the British authorities imposed on each individual colony.

Botswana (formerly Bechuanaland) held its first elections in 1961, with Botswana's Europeans electing 10 members to the Legislative Council. The Black population, including women, was allowed 10 indirectly chosen members, plus 2 nominated from each ethnic group and 10 colonial officials. Universal adult suffrage was granted under a preindependence constitution in 1965, and this was confirmed in 1966 when Botswana gained independence.

In Lesotho (formerly Basutoland), women had no right to vote representatives onto the Legislative Council that was introduced in 1956, and even the new Constitution of 1960 virtually disenfranchised them by restricting voting rights for district councils to taxpayers (district councils then elected members onto the Legislative Council). However, all the female chiefs who addressed the Constitutional Commission in 1962 spoke in favor of women's right to vote, and universal adult suffrage was granted on independence in 1965.

In Swaziland's first elections for its Legislative Council, held in 1964, there were two voters' rolls, one for Europeans and one for the rest of the population. Only those paying direct taxes could vote, although the wives of taxpaying men were also included in the franchise (in the case of polygamous marriages, only one designated wife could vote). On independence in 1967, all women were granted the vote for elections to the House of Assembly, but the Swazi National Council, which advises the king on all matters regulated by Swazi law and custom, is restricted to male Swazis, the only exception being the Swazi Queen Mother.

The Portuguese colonies in Southern Africa (Angola and Mozambique) had a restricted franchise for electing representatives both to the Portuguese Parliament and the various colonial legislative assemblies, and the vote was confined mainly to "non-natives" or *não-indígenas*. In 1961 all colonial citizens, including women, received Portuguese citizenship and could vote in metropolitan and local elections, although Europeans continued to enjoy more civil rights than the Black African population. Angola and Mozambique both achieved independence in 1975, when universal adult suffrage was introduced.

Namibia (formerly South-West Africa) was a former German colony administered from South Africa between 1919 and 1946, which gradually became incorporated into that country, despite opposition from the United Nations. Namibia's white voters, including women, were granted representation in the South African parliament from 1947 to 1977, when, under great pressure, South Africa sponsored elections for a Constituent Assembly to be held in 1978, in which Black Africans (including women) were allowed to vote. However, the main opposition group, the South-West Africa People's Organization (SWAPO), which had a very active women's section, boycotted the elections, and in 1983 South Africa resumed direct rule. After a period of considerable instability and intense diplomatic pressure, South Africa agreed to withdraw its troops from the country in preparation for independence. In the elections held in 1989, all were able to vote, and in 1990, Namibia became independent, adopting universal adult suffrage as part of its constitution. There is a separate entry for South Africa.

West Africa
The British colonies in West Africa (Gambia, Ghana, Nigeria, and Sierra Leone), some of the oldest of Britain's overseas possessions, were of great trading importance. Ghana, Nigeria, and Sierra Leone have separate entries.

In Gambia (Britain's smallest West African colony), universal suffrage was granted in 1960, and this was confirmed on independence in 1965.

The French had considerable colonial interests in West Africa (Benin, Burkina Faso, Central African Republic, Chad, Gabon, Guinea, Ivory Coast, Mali, Niger, Republic of the Congo, and Senegal). As in most of their overseas territories, the French followed the same pattern of central control followed by the gradual widening of the franchise and increased self-government before independence.

In all the French colonies of Benin (formerly Dahomey), Burkina Faso (formerly Upper Volta), Central African Republic (formerly Ubangi-Shari), Chad, Gabon, Guinea (formerly French Guinea), Ivory Coast (Côte d'Ivoire), Mali (formerly French Sudan), Niger, Republic of the Congo, and Senegal, the *loi-cadre* (framework law) was introduced in 1956, granting virtually universal adult suffrage, and this was confirmed in 1960, when all these territories became independent. Women played a very limited role in the political development of French West Africa, particularly in the predominantly Muslim territories bordering the Sahara. However, on the coast, women were active as market traders and in communal organizations, and their political potential was harnessed by several francophone African leaders, notably Sékou Touré of Guinea. The socialist nationalist movement in Guinea was more committed to greater political roles for women, and women became actively involved in the struggle for independence. Touré, the nationalist leader, encouraged female participation, and the women responded by giving money and support and becoming involved in the formation of political policy. After independence, women continued to play a part in the government of Guinea.

Cameroon was a former German colony, which was split administratively between Britain and France after World War I. The French territory followed the pattern of other French West African colonies, adopting the *loi-cadre* in 1956, achieving autonomy in 1958, and gaining universal adult suffrage on independence in 1960. The British territory was administered from Nigeria until 1954, when the Southern Cameroons House of Assembly was created, which granted full regional suffrage in 1959. In 1961 the southern part of the British territory joined the newly independent Federal Republic of Cameroon, and the northern area joined the predominantly Muslim Northern Region of Nigeria, which meant that women did not receive the vote until 1976.

Togo was another former German colony that was divided between Britain and France after World War I. Following a plebiscite in 1956 in which women voted, the British-administered territory became part of independent Ghana in 1957 and therefore adopted universal adult suffrage. In the French territory, most women had participated in local Conseil de Circonscription (regional assembly) elections since 1951, and in 1958 universal adult suffrage was introduced before independence was gained in 1960.

The Portuguese territories in West Africa (Cape Verde Islands, Guinea-Bissau, São Tomé, and Principé) were administered in the same way as the Portuguese colonies in Southern Africa, with the franchise being restricted to non-natives (*não-indígenas*) until 1961, when all members of the community were given Portuguese citizenship and could vote in local and metropolitan elections.

Cape Verde Islands and São Tomé and Principé became independent in 1975, when universal adult suffrage was introduced, and Guinea-Bissau (formerly Portuguese Guinea) gained universal adult suffrage on independence in 1974, after a liberation struggle in which women actively participated.

The Spanish colony of Equatorial Guinea was made an integral part of the Spanish Republic in 1959, electing representatives to the Spanish Parliament in accordance with Spanish electoral law, which at that time granted women only limited suffrage. The country adopted universal adult suffrage on independence in 1960.

In the independent republic of Liberia, in 1947, the Eighth Amendment to the Constitution gave the franchise to all Liberian citizens, provided they held real estate or other property or owned a hut and paid taxes on it—a law that tended to discriminate against women. This property qualification was removed in the 1970s, and the Constitution of 1986 granted universal adult suffrage.

See also Citizenship; Ghana; Imperialism; Nationalism; Nigeria; Ransome-Kuti, Funmilayo; Sierra Leone; South Africa.
References Crowder, Michael, ed. *The Cambridge History of Africa*, Vol. 8 (1984); Nelson, Barbara J., and Najma Chowdhury, eds. *Women and Politics Worldwide* (1994); O'Barr, Jean. "African Women in Politics" (1984).

All-Asian Women's Conference (1931)

The All-Asian Women's Conference, organized by the Irish women's rights leader Margaret Cousins, was held from 19 to 25 January 1931 in Lahore. Delegates were present from Afghanistan, Burma (Myanmar), Ceylon (Sri Lanka), Japan, and Persia (Iran) with observers from Britain, New Zealand, the United States, and Java (Indonesia). The key resolutions at the conference were all concerned with the achievement of equality of status for women and included the adult franchise. The Javanese women refused to participate as delegates because of the involvement of European women. This view was apparently not shared by other delegates who applauded Margaret Cousins's role in initiating and organizing the conference.

See also Cousins, Margaret; Indonesia; Japan; Sri Lanka.
Reference Jayawardena, Kumari. *The White Woman's Other Burden: Western Woman and South Asia during Colonial Rule* (1995).

All-Russian Women's Congress (1908)

The All-Russian Women's Congress was held during a period of active suffrage campaigning in Russia. During 1907, both the suffrage section of the Russian Women's Mutual Philanthropic Society (RZhVBO) and the Union of Equal Rights expressed an interest in calling a national congress that would discuss the "woman question." In 1908 the two organizations managed to collaborate, and it was decided that the Mutual Philanthropic Society should take responsibility for organizing the congress. Some members of the society thought that the program should concentrate on ethical and cultural questions, but the majority agreed that it should be wider in scope and include a debate on civil and political rights. The Ministry of the Interior agreed that the congress should be held but sought to prohibit discussion of political rights. After pressure from the organizers this subject was reinstated, although in an altered form. The organizers sought to bring together women from different social and political groups to debate four main topics: women in the economy, society, and the family; women's role in philanthropy; civil and political rights; and women's education. The 1,053 ticket holders who attended were drawn largely from the middle class, but there was a small group of factory women, the Workers' Group, under the leadership of Alexandra Kollontai, who made an impact on proceedings that was disproportionate to their numbers.

The labor delegation wished to concentrate on economic and social problems, emphasizing their solidarity with proletarian men rather than with "bourgeois feminists," and in this context the debate on women's political rights proved to be particularly divisive. Kollontai, for example, argued that bourgeois women always limited their demands to a property-based franchise that not only excluded working-class women but also helped to reinforce the class interests of the bourgeoisie. Suffragists refused to accept this argument and claimed that a limited franchise would be a first step toward suffrage for all women. Nonetheless, there were also divisions among the "bourgeois feminists" themselves over the extent to which collaboration across classes was possible, and whether campaigns for women's issues distracted from the broader movement for social emancipation.

There were considerable disagreements over the wording of the suffrage resolution, which stated that the establishment of a democratic system based on universal suffrage should be the "principal goal" of women. This led the Workers' Group of delegates to walk out of the congress, although the resolution was passed by those who remained. The congress had failed, therefore, to heal the many divisions among Russian women and also did little to stimulate discussion on the "woman question" in society at large. On the other hand, it demonstrated that women were capable of organizing a major event and also helped to keep the women's suffrage movement alive at a time of increasing government repression.

See also Russia.
Reference Edmondson, Linda Harriet. *Feminism in Russia, 1900–1917* (1984).

American Woman Suffrage Association

The American Woman Suffrage Association (AWSA) was founded in 1869 by Lucy Stone and her husband Henry Blackwell. Stone and Blackwell had been members of the American Equal Rights Association, launched by feminists in 1866 to call for universal suffrage following the ending of slavery. When the Fifteenth Amendment to the Constitution offered Blacks but not women the vote, Stone and other abolitionists, such as Henry Ward Beecher and Mary Livermore, supported it, believing that the women's vote would follow later. They did this in the face of strong opposition by Elizabeth Cady Stanton and Susan B. Anthony, who subsequently withdrew to form a new woman-only group, the National Woman Suffrage Association (NWSA).

The AWSA was formed shortly thereafter, as a rival to the NWSA. The AWSA endorsed the Fifteenth Amendment while at the same time working for the vote for women. The leaders of this group, who included several men, concentrated their efforts chiefly on forming state-based organizations, promoted through their publication, the *Woman's Journal.* In an effort to attract a broader base of members, they tried to make suffrage appear less radical and in tune with American values. They emphasized respectability, giving support only to indirect action and distancing themselves from potentially damaging causes such as divorce or prostitution.

The AWSA put its main energies into state referendum campaigns, of which there were 17 between 1870 and 1900. They had considerable success in achieving municipal suffrage and voting rights for women on school boards, but few of their state campaigns were successful. In 1890 the AWSA merged with the NWSA to form the National American Woman Suffrage Association. The main factors behind the unification of the two groups

Members of the American Woman Suffrage Association campaigning for their cause (Ann Ronan Picture Library)

were the entry of many professional women into the movement and the increasingly more moderate stance of the NWSA.

See also Anthony, Susan B.; Fourteenth and Fifteenth Amendments; National American Woman Suffrage Association; National Woman Suffrage Association; Stanton, Elizabeth Cady; Stone, Lucy; United States of America.
References Evans, Richard J. *The Feminists: Women's Emancipation Movements in Europe, America and Australasia, 1840–1920* (1977); Flexner, Eleanor. *Century of Struggle: The Woman's Rights Movement in the United States* ([1959] 1975).

Anthony, Susan B.

Susan B. Anthony (1820–1906) was a leading figure in the American women's suffrage movement and founder, with Elizabeth Cady Stanton, of the National Woman Suffrage Association. The daughter of a cotton mill owner, Anthony was

Susan B. Anthony's study in Rochester, New York, is full of photos demonstrating how well connected she was with suffragists around the world. (Library of Congress)

born in Massachusetts into a Quaker abolitionist family that supported the temperance movement. The Quakers were one of the few religious groups to practice equality between men and women, but on reaching adulthood, Anthony soon gained firsthand experience of gender inequalities. As a teacher, she received much lower pay than her male colleagues, and in her work for the temperance movement, she was barred from speaking in public. This experience led her to form the first women's temperance group.

Anthony made contact with the emerging women's suffrage movement through Amelia Bloomer, editor of the first woman-owned newspaper, the *Lily*. When Anthony met Stanton in 1851, it was the start of a lifelong association and close

friendship. From this time onward, Anthony dedicated herself to working for women's rights. Regarding the vote as the key to women's emancipation, she traveled around the country on speaking tours, building the movement. In 1869 Stanton and Anthony set up the National Woman Suffrage Association, an organization that excluded men. The woman-only membership policy was in response to what they saw as a betrayal by the abolitionist movement, which supported the Fifteenth Amendment, giving the vote to Black men but denying it to women.

In 1872 Anthony and 16 other women registered to vote in the presidential election on the grounds that the Fourteenth Amendment, which granted legal privileges to all U.S.-born citizens, did not specifically exclude women from citizenship. The women were arrested after casting their votes, but only Anthony was brought to trial. The judge refused her the right to testify and ordered the jury to find her guilty. Yet when Anthony refused to pay the fine, no further action was taken. She continued to work for the suffrage cause, and during the 1880s she and Stanton published a history of the women's suffrage movement in four volumes. In 1890 the NWSA joined with the rival American Woman Suffrage Association, led by Lucy Stone, to form the National American Woman Suffrage Association. Anthony soon took command of the new group. Initially vice president, she took on the presidency after Stanton retired in 1892, a post she held until 1900. Yet despite Anthony's dedication to the suffrage cause, by 1906, when she died at the age of 86, only four American states had granted women the vote.

See also American Woman Suffrage Association; Antislavery Movement; Citizenship; National American Woman Suffrage Association; National Woman Suffrage Association; Protestantism; Stanton, Elizabeth Cady; Stone, Lucy; United States of America.
References Dubois, Ellen, and Susan Kearns. *Votes for Women: A 75th Anniversary Album* (1995); Kraditor, Aileen S. *The Ideas of the Woman Suffrage Movement* (1965).

Antislavery Movement

Women's involvement in the antislavery movement in the mid-nineteenth century has been seen as inseparable from the development of the women's rights movement in the United States and as an important influence on the development of British feminism.

In the earlier part of the nineteenth century, leaders of the American women's suffrage movement such as Elizabeth Cady Stanton, Susan B. Anthony, and Lucy Stone had gained valuable experience in public speaking and running political organizations through their work in the abolitionist movement. During this period, women were generally discouraged from taking an active part in public life and expected to join women-only groups in support of male organizations. At the World Anti-Slavery Convention in London in 1840, women delegates from the United States, who were followers of abolitionist William Garrison, were not allowed to participate in the proceedings. This experience had a profound effect on Stanton and another abolitionist, Lucretia Coffin Mott, leading them to organize a convention for women's rights at Seneca Falls in 1848. It was at this meeting that Stanton made the first formal demand for woman suffrage.

Garrisonian abolitionism also provided the early suffrage movement with a theory of social change. Suffrage activists adopted the Garrisonian principle that legal and political reforms must be preceded by a change in people's views, and they saw their task as bringing about a shift in public thinking through feminist agitation.

In Britain the links between antislavery principles and the ideas of the suffrage movement are less clearly established. However, it appears that the developing women's movement in the latter half of the century made use of antislavery networks, many of which were Quaker or Unitarian, to create its own networks of supporters. The most powerful local women's suffrage societies in London, Bristol, Manchester, and Edinburgh were led by women who had previously been the leaders of antislavery societies and who, like their American sisters, had gained valuable experience in running political organizations and campaigns.

See also Anthony, Susan B.; Britain; Mott, Lucretia Coffin; Protestantism; Stanton, Elizabeth Cady; Stone, Lucy; United States of America; Women's Rights Convention, Seneca Falls.
References DuBois, Carol Ellen. *Feminism and Suffrage. The Emergence of an Independent Women's Suffrage Movement in Amer-*

ica, 1848–1869 (1978); Midgley, Clare. *Women against Slavery: The British Campaigns, 1780–1870* (1992).

Antisuffrage Campaign, British

From the time that the first women's suffrage petition was presented to the House of Commons by John Stuart Mill in 1866, there was some form of antisuffrage agitation, if only at a parliamentary level. In 1875 a short-lived opposition group was set up, calling itself "A committee for maintaining the integrity of the franchise" and consisting mainly of Conservative members of parliament with some Liberals. The first clear extraparliamentary statement on the matter came in June 1889, when women antisuffragists published their "Appeal against the Extension of the Parliamentary Franchise to Women" in the periodical *Nineteenth Century.* The arguments had already been rehearsed, but they were clearly stated in the article—women's legitimate influence was in the private world of home and family and in the philanthropic sphere, but they did not possess the judgment or experience of men when it came to matters of foreign or imperial policy. Furthermore, it was alleged that the weaker physical constitution of women prevented them from playing a full role in political life.

In July 1908 the Women's National Anti-Suffrage League was established to campaign against the vote for women. The Conservative Lady Jersey chaired the executive committee, but Mrs. Humphry (Mary Augusta) Ward was the driving force behind the league's campaign, and it was she who began the league's journal, the *Anti-Suffrage Review.* The league attracted a number of aristocratic and intellectual women, many of whom already had considerable influence without needing a vote, and it was joined shortly afterwards by the Men's League for Opposing Women's Suffrage, led by Lord Cromer. Both organizations had been formed in re-

sponse to the rapid growth of the women's suffrage movement and were based on a fear that the franchise might be extended to women by the Liberal government.

Toward the end of 1910, the two organizations merged to form the National League for Opposing Women's Suffrage (NLOWS), with Lord Cromer as president and Lady Jersey as his deputy. In 1912 Cromer left, and he was replaced by the joint presidency of the former viceroy of India, Lord Curzon, and the Liberal Lord Weardale. The new organization's low-key campaign of petitions and parliamentary deputations contrasted unfavorably with the vigor of the prosuffrage societies, but the NLOWS could always rely on a favorable airing in the press, particularly from the *Times,* and was able to call on influential supporters in the Liberal government such as the prime minister, Herbert Asquith, and Lewis Harcourt. From the outset, the NLOWS challenged the authority of the women's suffrage organizations to represent the views of all women, but both sides of the argument found it extremely difficult to prove their point one way or another. Support for the NLOWS expanded quite rapidly, the number of branches increasing from 140 in April 1911 to 286 by April 1914.

The increasingly militant campaign conducted by the Women's Social and Political Union was successful in turning many would-be sympathizers away from the suffrage cause, and by 1914 the antisuffrage campaign appeared to have achieved its goal—women seemed no nearer to gaining the vote. However, the 1914–1918 war changed attitudes toward mass democracy, and in January 1918 women were enfranchised, although there were still many who did not qualify for the vote. Lord Curzon admitted defeat, and shortly afterwards the league was dissolved.

See also Antisuffrage Movements; Britain; Imperialism; Mill, John Stuart; Representa-

tion of the People Act; Ward, Mary Augusta; Women's Social and Political Union.
Reference Harrison, Brian. *Separate Spheres: The Opposition to Women's Suffrage in Britain* (1978).

Antisuffrage Movements

The demand for women's suffrage was strongly contested. The depth of hostility it evoked in its opponents helps to explain why the enfranchisement of women took so long to achieve in most countries of the world. Antisuffragist ideas were put forward not only by writers, journalists, politicians, and political parties but also by ordinary citizens who made their feelings known at meetings and demonstrations. Opponents of women's suffrage sometimes joined together to give an organizational expression to their antisuffragism, in particular when suffrage movements appeared to be getting stronger. In the United States there were numerous antisuffrage groups at the state level, but after the vote was won in California in 1911, these groups joined together to form the National Association Opposed to Woman Suffrage. In Britain the Women's National Anti-Suffrage League and the Men's League for Opposing Women's Suffrage were established in 1908; two years later, these merged to form a new group, the National League for Opposing Women's Suffrage. Clearly, women could show as much hostility to the enfranchisement of their sex as men. In the United States, as early as 1882, women took the lead in establishing a Boston Committee of Remonstrance to oppose women's suffrage in Massachusetts.

Authoritarian regimes, for example in Central and Eastern Europe, and Conservative parties in most countries tended to be opposed to democratization or to the extension of voting rights in general. There were also interest groups, such as the liquor interest and big business in the United States, that feared that women's enfranchisement would lead to moral and social reforms. On the other hand, liberal and socialist groups, whose political philosophy was based on the rhetoric of equality, could also be found opposing women's suffrage on the grounds of political expediency. In some instances, as in Austria, it was argued that men's universal suffrage could be jeopardized if votes for women were included in the demands for franchise reform. Elsewhere, it was feared that women's conservatism, which supposedly arose from their identification with domesticity, could benefit the opponents of liberal or socialist parties.

In Russia, for example, Pavel Milyukov, leader of the Kadets, argued that peasant men would desert those parties that gave their female relatives the vote. Likewise, members of the Third French Republic were afraid that women's clerical sympathies would work against their interests and similar fears were expressed in Chile. Even committed feminists, such as Amanda Labarca and Paulina Luisi, were unsure about the appropriateness of campaigning for women's suffrage if it meant that the size and power of the clerical-Conservative party would be strengthened. In parts of South America and in Asia, where nationalist movements were strong, women's suffrage could be opposed as a foreign idea.

Nonetheless, opposition to women's suffrage cannot simply be explained by political expediency alone; indeed, it was based on far more deep-seated fears. Antisuffragism was closely bound up with the ideology of "separate spheres," which was reinforced by the political philosophers of the Enlightenment. Women were thought to be naturally suited to the domestic world and lacking in the qualities of liberty and independence needed to exercise citizenship. Thus William Gladstone, the British Liberal Party leader and prime minister throughout much of the latter half of the nineteenth century, claimed that women wanted chivalrous protection rather than votes and that their womanli-

Opposition to women's suffrage was an organized movement in many countries. In the United States, it was strongest in urban areas such as New York City. (Library of Congress)

ness would be jeopardized by voting. The view that women were unsuited to take part in imperial affairs or foreign policy explains why they often achieved local voting rights while being denied the franchise at a national level. There were also widespread fears that women's suffrage would challenge traditional gender relationships and male authority.

Ridicule was often used to undermine suffrage supporters. In Uruguay, for example, one opponent invented a new term, *machonismo,* to describe the desire to copy men and to divert women from the path nature had intended. In Syria and Lebanon, men who "followed women" were subject to ridicule, and in many countries, cartoonists, such as the French

Jules Félix Grandjouan, used their drawings to show that the vote would bring domestic chaos and to depict suffragists as unsexed, mannish creatures. Such fears could seem especially well founded when there was concern about population questions and motherhood, as in Western European countries in the first half of the twentieth century, or when colonial struggles brought social upheaval, as in the Middle East and Asia. Many female opponents of women's suffrage shared these views and feared the disruption to family life and the loss of male protection that women's suffrage might cause.

The strength of political opposition to women's suffrage succeeded in delaying the success of the movement because women needed male support in the representative institutions of their various countries in order to bring about constitutional change. Neither should the importance of the ideas put forward by antisuffragists be underestimated. A great deal of the propaganda of suffrage campaigners was aimed at countering the arguments of their opponents, in particular the negative representations of suffragists. In responding to these arguments and images, suffragists were themselves influenced by the prevailing framework of ideas, such as the idea of natural differences between the sexes. In attempting to use these ideas to their own advantage, they made only a partial challenge to existing gender divisions.

See also Antisuffrage Campaign, British; Citizenship; Imperialism.
References Flexner, Eleanor. *Century of Struggle: The Woman's Rights Movement in the United States* ([1959] 1975); Harrison, Brian. *Separate Spheres: The Opposition to Women's Suffrage in Britain* (1978); Lavrin, Asunción. *Women, Feminism and Social Change in Argentina, Chile and Uruguay, 1890–1940* (1995); Pateman, Carole. "Three Questions about Womanhood Suffrage" (1994); Thompson, Elizabeth. *Colonial Citizens: Republican Rights, Paternal Privilege and Gender in French Syria and Lebanon* (1999).

Appeal of One-Half the Human Race . . . (1825)

The critical feminist document *Appeal of One-Half the Human Race, Women, against the Pretensions of the Other Half, Men, to retain them in Political and thence Civil and Domestic Slavery . . .* was published in London in 1825. The author, William Thompson (1775–1833), an Irish Protestant landowner, was a follower of the utopian socialist Robert Owen, but in his introduction, Thompson acknowledged the contribution that his friend, Anna Doyle Wheeler (1785–1848), had made to the work. Wheeler was an Irish Protestant who had met the French utopian socialists Charles Fourier and

Claude-Henri Saint-Simon, and was deeply influenced by their schemes for social progress. In later years, Wheeler translated Saint-Simonian feminist periodicals, like *Tribune des femmes* (1832–1833), and occasionally gave lectures in the Unitarian South Place Chapel, where advocates of women's rights like Harriet Taylor and John Stuart Mill often met.

The *Appeal* was written to refute philosopher James Mill's argument that women were not entitled to any political rights, as their interests could be adequately represented by their fathers and husbands. In their reply, Thompson and Wheeler asserted that, far from not requiring any rights of their own, all women "having been reduced to a state of helplessness, slavery, and of consequent unequal enjoyments, pains and privations, are more in need of political rights than any other portion of human beings" (Thompson [1825] 1983, 107). The *Appeal* argued for an end to the legal, political, educational, and economic disabilities of women and for an end to the "double standard" of sexual morality, which allowed men sexual license while women were expected to remain chaste pillars of respectability. Thompson and Wheeler suggested that only a society based on cooperation and collective property would remedy women's grievances, because such a society could provide the economic relationships and social conditions that would allow women equal rights.

Although it has always been the least known, the *Appeal* was one of the most important feminist texts of the early nineteenth century, and it raised many of the questions about the social construction of femininity that were to be discussed by John Stuart Mill in his book *On the Subjection of Women*, published in 1869.

See also On the Subjection of Women; Sexuality; Socialism in Europe.
References Pankhurst, Richard. "Anna Wheeler: A Pioneer Socialist and Feminist"

(1954); Taylor, Barbara. *Eve and the New Jerusalem: Socialism and Feminism in the Nineteenth Century* (1983); Thompson, William. *Appeal of One-Half the Human Race . . .* ([1825] 1983).

Argentina

Argentina was one of the later Latin American countries to grant women the vote. Despite several decades of feminist activity, it was not until 1947, under the populist revival of General Juan Domingo Perón and the decisive influence of his wife, Eva Perón, that Argentine women were finally enfranchised.

Early women's organizations in Argentina, such as the Argentine National Council of Women founded in 1900, tended to be conservative in outlook. Their leaders were unwilling to challenge the gendered social and economic order that situated women within the family, concentrating on educational and moral objectives rather than the achievement of political rights. Women's groups that formed during the first two decades of the century held a variety of views on political rights. Some, such as La Liga Nacional de Mujeres Librepensadores (the National League of Women Freethinkers) led by María Abella de Ramírez and Julieta Lanteri, did embrace suffrage as an objective. Others, such as Unión y Labor (Union and Labor), felt suffrage should be postponed until women had achieved their mission to moralize and educate society in civil ethics.

Socialist and anarchist groups, which had been actively mobilizing women in Argentina since the 1890s, also varied in their views on women's citizenship. After 1910, anarchist women disowned feminism and refused to discuss women's suffrage. The Socialist Party's main interest was in seeking protective legislation for working women in order that their maternal role should not be endangered. However, after the passage of male suffrage leg-islation in 1912, the socialists embraced female suffrage as party policy. In 1911 Alice Moreau, representing women on the Left in an article for *Revista Socialista Internacional* (*International Socialist Review*), argued that women should be organizing and working for suffrage rather than leaving the task to legislators.

During the 1920s and 1930s, Moreau and other socialist feminist leaders joined with nonsocialist feminist groups in order to pursue legal and social equality. No other major political party favored suffrage, although the issue was thoroughly debated over the next two decades. In 1916 a bill seeking the vote for native-born women in municipal elections was the first of many unsuccessful national and municipal suffrage bills during the next 30 years. In the face of conservative opposition, news of women's wartime activities and of suffrage debates in Europe and the United States helped women's suffrage to remain a live issue.

A major obstacle for women in Argentina appeared in 1916, with a law requiring anyone who wanted to qualify for citizenship to register for military service. In order to take up an appointment as a lecturer in the Faculty of Medicine, Italian-born Lanteri had to be naturalized as a citizen. Since citizens were entitled to vote, to test the legal restrictions on citizenship, Lateri claimed this entitlement. The federal judge who reviewed the case upheld her claim. He declared that under constitutional law, in principle women had the same political rights as men, although in practice such rights were negated by cultural factors. This important principle was confirmed by the federal capital deputies and by a federal attorney in 1921. It was on this basis that arguments for women's suffrage were made over the next quarter of a century.

The 1920s saw the formation of a range of feminist groups, both socialist and nonsocialist, with a considerable degree of

Argentine women gained suffrage in 1947; a mother exercises her right to vote. (ILA—Gamma)

cross-fertilization and cooperation among them. Although suffrage was not their only concern, these groups were willing to act on a variety of fronts to put pressure on politicians for reform. This included holding mock elections for women, the inclusion of a woman candidate on the Socialist Party list, extensive lobbying of influential men at different levels, and the presentation of petitions signed by thousands of women. In 1926 the Civil Code was reformed to recognize new civil rights for women, but the women's suffrage movement continued to struggle against traditionalists who saw the vote as undermining femininity and the home. After a crisis in 1930, which deposed the Radical government and ended with the election in 1931 of a "liberal" general, Augustín Justo, politics in Argentina were dominated by the Right.

Yet feminist hopes for a victory against the forces of traditionalism remained high. Feminists' arguments for the vote at this time were based upon what they saw as the government's neglect of vitally important social and economic problems and an attitude on the part of legislators that denigrated women, forcing them into humiliating dependency. They were concerned at the neglect of the virtues and duties of citizenship by men who denied women these rights and who placed personal and party ambition above the interests of the nation.

A breakthrough seemed imminent in 1932, when the Chamber of Deputies approved a bill granting suffrage to all Argentine women over 18, regardless of literacy, and eliminating military conscription. However, this victory proved short-lived, as passage of the bill required Senate approval; voting against a debate, the Senate shelved the bill until the next session and it was never recalled. Feminist groups kept suffrage on the agenda throughout the 1930s, provoked by schemes to subvert some of the reforms already in place. Attempts to revive the 1932 suffrage bill (still officially under scrutiny in the Senate) failed repeatedly until 1942, when it was finally freed for discussion by the Senate. However, raised hopes that the bill might finally be passed evaporated in 1943, when a military coup deposed President Ramón Castillo, leaving the nation dominated by a right-wing military cadre with open disaffection for women.

When, in 1946, General Perón gained sufficient support from working-class men to be elected to the presidency, Eva (popularly known as Evita) mobilized the support of working-class women in favor of the vote. Her campaign, which argued that political participation would make women more feminine and attractive, enraged virtually all feminist groups, who formed a National Assembly of Women to oppose the Peróns. Despite feminist opposition, Evita achieved her goal on 27 September 1947. Women's suffrage, the primary objective of feminists for so long, had at last been achieved. Yet many Argentine feminists felt hurt and betrayed. Eva Perón's ability to attract and mobilize those women who had ignored or rejected feminist pleas and arguments for so many years was a bitter blow.

See also Citizenship; Lanteri, Julieta; Latin America and the Caribbean.
References Carlson, Manifran. *Feminismo! The Woman's Movement in Argentina from Its Beginnings to Eva Perón* (1988); Lavrin, Asunción. *Women, Feminism and Social Change in Argentina, Chile and Uruguay, 1890–1940* (1995).

Artists' Suffrage League

The Artists' Suffrage League (ASL) was founded in London in January 1907 by the artist Mary Lowndes. Its purpose was to assist the National Union of Women's Suffrage Societies (NUWSS) in organizing a public demonstration to be held the following month, an event that later became known as the Mud March. The motto of the ASL was "Alliance Not Defiance," and the object of the organization was "to further the case of Women's Enfranchisement by the work and professional help of artists" (Tickner, 1987, 16). To this end it produced posters, postcards, and illustrative leaflets that were used in both Britain and the United States. The ASL also produced two humorous illustrated rhyme books, *Beware! A Warning to Suffragists* (c. 1909), written by Cicely Hamilton, and *A.B.C. of Politics for Women Politicians* (c. 1910). Other women who, like Lowndes, made important artistic contributions to the work of the ASL were Emily Ford (sister of the suffragist Isabella Ford) and Dora Meeson Coates, a member of the Women's Franchise League.

The ASL produced thousands of leaflets and posters for the two general elections of 1910 and for numerous by-elections held after 1907. For the general election held in January 1910, the league sent out 2,708 posters, 6,488 postcards, and 65,000 pic-

This poster by Emily Harding Andrews, published by the Artists' Suffrage League c. 1908, illustrates the concern of the suffragists that women had no more rights than convicts, lunatics, or children. (Library of Congress)

torial leaflets on behalf of the NUWSS. The ASL also designed and executed an enormous number of embroidered banners for NUWSS branches and other suffrage groups, and it organized the decorative schemes for important meetings and major demonstrations. One of the most important of these was the NUWSS procession of 13 June 1908, in which about 10,000–15,000 women participated; for this event the ASL designed about 80 banners, with a red-and-white color scheme for the sashes, badges, and flowers, all of which made a great impression on spectators and press alike.

By 1913 the organization felt able to claim that it had "done much to popularize the cause of Women's Suffrage by bringing in an attractive manner before the public eye the long-continued demand for the vote" (Tickner, 1987, 16). The outbreak of war in 1914 ended the activities of the ASL, but members came out of retirement on 13 March 1918, when they brought their banners from earlier campaigns to the Queen's Hall in London, to celebrate the passing of a limited measure of women's suffrage in the Representation of the People Act.

See also Britain; Imagery; Mud March; National Union of Women's Suffrage Societies; Representation of the People Act; Suffrage Atelier.
Reference Tickner, Lisa. *The Spectacle of Women: Imagery of the Suffrage Campaign, 1907–1914* (1987).

Auclert, Hubertine

Hubertine Auclert (1848–1914) was a leading French suffrage campaigner. Born into a moderately wealthy provincial family, she left home for Paris in the 1870s in order to join the feminist activities of Léon Richer and Marie Deraismes. She was soon disillusioned with their failure to prioritize women's political rights and founded her own group, Suffrage des femmes (Women's Suffrage). She demanded equality in all areas of life and attempted to link with the socialist movement, arguing that women and the working class suffered from a common oppression. Auclert was a prolific writer. In 1881 she launched her own newspaper, *La Citoyenne* (the Citizeness), but she also expressed her ideas in other newspapers and gathered together these columns into a publication, *Le Vote des femmes* (The Women's Vote) (1908).

Auclert was an early advocate of civil disobedience. In 1880–1881 she went on a tax strike because she did not have political representation. She was advised in her strategy by a lawyer friend, Antonin Levrier, whom she married in 1881. They lived in Algeria until his death in 1892, when she returned to France. By this time she had lost the leadership of the suffrage movement and was unable to maintain

her newspaper. Nonetheless, she continued to work with single-minded determination for the vote, petitioning the government, lobbying political parties, and writing to the press.

Auclert was one of the minority of French feminists who were influenced by the militancy of British suffragettes, and she joined with Madeleine Pelletier and others in 1908 in support of Jeanne Laloë, a young journalist who ran as a candidate during the municipal elections in Paris. She gained notoriety when she entered a polling booth, smashed the ballot box on the ground, stamped on the ballots, and denounced "unisexual suffrage." This led to her arrest, a fine, and the nickname "the French suffragette." Her actions were condemned, however, by moderate feminists, and she later renounced violent actions. Her militancy and domineering personality isolated her from the mainstream of the suffrage campaign, but she continued to remain active in the movement until her death.

See also France; Pelletier, Madeleine.
References Gordon, Felicia. *The Integral Feminist: Madeleine Pelletier, 1874–1939* (1990); Hause, Steven C., with Anne R. Kenney. *Women's Suffrage and Social Politics in the French Third Republic* (1984).

Augspurg, Anita, and Lida Gustava Heymann

Anita Augspurg (1857–1943) and Lida Heymann (1868–1943) were leading members of the radical wing of the German suffrage movement. They not only shared a political life but also lived together as a couple after meeting at an international women's conference in Berlin in 1896. Augspurg was born in the small town of Verden an der Aller, the daughter of liberal-minded parents. She studied as a teacher in Berlin before moving to Munich, where she opened a photo studio and became involved in the women's movement. Realizing how difficult it was for women to achieve legal reforms, she studied law in Zurich and became Germany's first woman lawyer. Heymann, who came from a wealthy family in Hamburg, attended a teacher training institute in Dresden and then taught in a school for the poor after returning to her hometown. She gave lectures to women, espoused clothing reform, and became involved in trade union organization.

After 1896 the two women always worked together in the women's movement. They were members of the moderate women's group Bund Deutscher Frauenvereine (BDF) [The Federation of German Women's Associations], but their politics developed in a more radical direction when they took part in the campaign against the Civil Law Code, passed in 1896, and in the movement against the state regulation of prostitution. In the same period, they attended the annual congress of the International Council of Women in 1899. When the leadership agreed that antisuffragists should be able to express their point of view, Heymann and Augspurg called an alternative meeting that advocated the establishment of an international women's suffrage organization. The result was the founding of the International Woman Suffrage Alliance in 1904.

In 1902 Heymann and Augspurg established the Deutscher Verband für Frauenstimmrecht (German Union for Women's Suffrage). The union grew slowly and had only 2,500 members by 1908, but when the ban on women's participation in politics was lifted in that year, its membership expanded rapidly and reached 9,000 by 1913. In the period before World War I, however, Augspurg and Heymann were increasingly at odds with others in the organization. They disapproved of the decision of left-wing liberals to support the government in 1907–1908 and adopted a policy of independent militancy on the lines of the British suffragette movement. The two women planned a march through the streets of Munich, although most

women remained in their carriages rather than walking. Heymann also declared that she was unwilling to pay taxes while she was denied the right to vote. Augspurg and Heymann were unable to gain the support of the majority of the union's members, however, and this contributed to growing dissension within the larger suffrage movement. In 1913 they left the union when it moved toward support for a property-based franchise.

During World War I, Anita Augspurg and Lida Heymann put most of their energies into work for peace, helping to form the Women's International League for Peace and Freedom. They continued to be active in the international women's peace movement during the interwar years in an increasingly dangerous climate. In 1933 they were forced to flee Germany, leaving their property behind, and had to rely on friends in other countries for support. They died within a few months of each other in 1943.

See also Germany; International Congress of Women, The Hague; International Council of Women; International Woman Suffrage Alliance; Peace Movement; Suffragette.
References Braker, Regina. "Bertha Von Suttner's Spiritual Daughters: The Feminist Pacifism of Anita Augspurg, Lida Gustava Heymann, and Helene Stöcker at the International Congress of Women at the Hague, 1915" (1995); Evans, Richard J. *The Feminists: Women's Emancipation Movements in Europe, America and Australasia, 1840–1920* (1977); Rupp, Leila J. *Worlds of Women: The Making of an International Women's Movement* (1997).

Australia

Australia was one of the first countries to grant the majority of its female citizens the vote, second only to New Zealand. In 1902 the first Commonwealth Parliament enfranchised women by proclaiming adult suffrage for all future federal elections in the newly formed nation. In fact, the vote had already been granted to women in South Australia in 1894 and Western Australia in 1899, and New South Wales followed suit for state elections in 1902 and Tasmania in 1903.

Some historians have argued that women in Australia were handed the vote on a plate. But winning enfranchisement was not that easy. Although all women, except Aboriginal women in Queensland and Western Australia, could now vote in federal elections, Queensland continued to deny its white female citizens representation in its parliament until 1905, and Victoria was even later, finally giving way in 1908. Australia's claims to be ahead of most other Western countries were also compromised by the failure of Queensland and Western Australia to give Aboriginal men and women either the federal or state vote until 1962.

From the 1880s, suffrage campaigns were fought in every colony, lasting 28 years in total. The main argument underlying suffragists' demand that every person should have a say in government was based upon liberal Enlightenment ideals of justice, natural rights, and individual equality. These ideals had been imported to Australia through European immigration. However, the colonial government was modeled on the British system; with the exception of the South Australian constitution, the constitutions of the Australian colonies were based upon the representation of property. As in Britain, married women in Australia were unlikely to own property, with the result that they were not entitled to vote.

The earliest attempts to get votes for women were therefore based not upon women's claims as individuals, but upon the idea that the property of a minority of single and widowed women should be represented, irrespective of their sex. In Western Australia and Queensland, this demand stemmed in part from conservative interest in reducing the growing political power of gold miners. However, once attempts to give propertied women the vote failed, conservatives in most Australian parliaments aggressively opposed women's suffrage. This was partly on the grounds that the high numbers of women living in cities would give greater weight to urban parliamentary interests and lessen the power of the rural land-owning classes.

The abolition of property qualifications and the plural vote were the principal object of the working-class movement in every colony except South Australia, and these goals complicated the women's suffrage campaigns. Although many working-class men were sympathetic to women's claims, they generally refused to give them their support until the principle of one man, one vote had been achieved. Suffragists were themselves divided on this issue. Some demanded the vote for women on the same grounds as it had been or would be granted to men. Others refused to countenance anything other than adult suffrage. These differing perspectives led to tensions between women suffrage supporters and, in Queensland, between rival suffrage societies, similar to conflicts in the British movement.

The first formal women's suffrage organization in Australia, the Victorian Women's Suffrage Society, was established in 1884 by Henrietta Dugdale and Annie Lowe, and other colonies soon followed suit by establishing their own organizations. These generally crossed party lines, with many suffragists owing no allegiance to any political party. There was no umbrella group, the Australian Women's Suffrage Society being national in name only. Although some suffragists, such as Victorian feminist Vida Goldstein and Elizabeth Nicholls of the Woman's Christian Temperance Union (WCTU), became involved in more than one campaign, few had national reputations.

The WCTU was an important national and international body that supported the suffrage movement. It acted as a unifying force across classes and between conservative women and those on the far Left. In Tasmania, the WCTU was the only organization supporting the vote. However, the Temperance Union's aggressive support for suffrage was based on the assumption that women would vote for prohibition, and this aroused the opposition of the liquor interest to women's suffrage.

In addition to the natural rights arguments, suffragists stressed the advantages politically active women would bring to the nation as morally superior beings and as wives and mothers. Because there was a high percentage of men in the population, most women in Australia married after only a short period in the workforce. The movement was therefore particularly concerned with achieving the vote in order to improve women's unequal position in marriage. Suffrage activists also worked to allay fears and rebut stereotypes of suffragists as masculine women who were undermining the family and stressed the importance of women's role as homemakers who were improving moral standards within society. Suffrage activities were generally fairly conventional, including issuing propaganda leaflets, holding public debates and meetings, sending deputations to parliament, and lobbying parliamentary candidates before suffrage bills were introduced. The early achievement of the vote in many colonies meant that the militant tactics of the British and U.S. movements were avoided.

Although there were many common features among Australian suffrage campaigns, the circumstances under which the vote was granted in the various colonies and states differed. The first colony to give women the vote was South Australia in 1894. This early victory can be explained partly by the fact that unlike other colonies, and indeed unlike Britain, South Australia had gained manhood suffrage and one man, one vote in 1856. Woman suffrage bills had been regularly introduced into the South Australian parliament since 1885. However, it was not until the proposed legislation dropped property limitations for women that the United Labour Party and the United Trades and Labour Council gave women's suffrage their full support. The support of labor for woman suffrage can also be explained by the efforts of suffrage leader Mary Lee to forge links between the suffrage and labor movements. South Australia was equally at odds with other colonies in granting Aboriginal women the vote. South Australian representatives protested when the Federal Convention of 1897 ruled that Aboriginal Australians should not be counted in the census that led to their exclusion from the federal franchise.

Women's enfranchisement in Western Australia, which in 1899 became the second colony to give women the vote, was achieved under political conditions very different from those in South Australia. Here the Labour Party was not formed until 1901, two years after the Conservative Party suddenly changed its views on suffrage and granted women the vote under the system of plural voting. This system remained in operation until it was abolished in 1907. As explained above, Conservative interest in giving women the vote aimed mainly to strengthen Conservative support in the towns and to counter the movement for democratization, which was growing in influence as more male workers moved into the goldfields. There were very few women in the goldfields, and there were no Labour women suffragists. In Western Australia the movement for women's suffrage was confined to middle-class and upper-class women. Campaigning was organized by the WCTU, which formed a Woman's Franchise League shortly before the vote was achieved to broaden support for the cause.

In 1900 Western Australian women voted in the referendum by which the colony agreed to join the Australian Com-

Women in Australia were some of the earliest in the world to gain suffrage in 1902. (Gamma)

tution that stated, "No Aboriginal native of Australia, Africa, or the Islands of the Pacific, except New Zealand, shall be entitled to have his name placed on the electoral roll unless entitled under section forty-one." This section stipulated that the Commonwealth must give a vote to all adults who held state votes. What this meant in practice was that in 1902 only in South Australia (where there were very few Aboriginals left) did Aboriginal women receive the federal vote. Tasmania, New South Wales, and Victoria gave Aboriginal women the right to vote in the Commonwealth at the same time as they granted all women the right to vote in state legislatures. However, Queensland and Western Australia failed to follow their example until the 1960s, mainly because they had nothing to fear in the way of protest from an uneducated and marginalized Black population.

It was in New South Wales that the first published demand for suffrage appeared in 1842. However, women in this colony did not start to organize a suffrage campaign until 1888, when the WCTU began to canvass for support and Louisa Lawson started publishing a suffrage journal, the *Dawn*. The main campaigning group here was led by Rose Scott, who started the Womanhood Suffrage League (WSL) in 1891. Both the WSL and the WCTU put pressure on the Liberal government and the Labour Party to give women the vote, but the latter was willing to consider supporting womanhood suffrage only after the abolition of the plural vote in 1893. It was not until 1899 that the Labour Party put serious pressure on the Liberals to institute women's suffrage. However, campaigners still had to wait a further three years until, in August 1902, a few months after the Commonwealth vote was achieved, women won the right to vote in state elections.

Tasmania followed suit in 1904 after a campaign that was organized entirely by the WCTU. The campaign for the vote in

monwealth. Similar results had been achieved in South Australia, Victoria, New South Wales, and Tasmania in 1898 and Queensland in 1899, but suffragists were angered by the fact that only in Western and South Australia were women involved in the decision-making process. Suffrage campaigners were also unsuccessful in having women's suffrage written into the constitution and had to rely on canvassing for candidates who would support their cause in the first Commonwealth election in 1901. In this they were successful, although it took another year before all white women, irrespective of whether they could vote in their own state elections, were granted the Commonwealth vote and were allowed to stand for election.

Aboriginal women were not so fortunate. A clause was written into the consti-

Tasmania was linked to two main objectives—control of the liquor laws and the repeal of the Contagious Diseases Acts—and was invigorated by visits from WCTU leaders such as Elizabeth Nicholls, who toured the island in 1898 and collected more than 12,000 signatures. The political climate against universal suffrage changed in Tasmania during the 1890s, as Liberals in parliament began to challenge the Conservatives who had long been in power. In 1895 the property qualifications for male votes were reduced, although this still left 10 percent of Tasmanian men without a vote. By 1898, most of the lower house was in theory in favor of woman suffrage, but as in other states, woman suffrage was expendable if it conflicted with other goals. Thus in 1902, when a bill was introduced abolishing plural voting and giving full manhood suffrage—a move that would give Tasmania more bargaining power in the Federal Assembly—the lower house voted against including woman suffrage in the bill. It was not until after the achievement of the Commonwealth vote in 1902 and the formation of a Liberal-Labour alliance in 1903 that victory was in sight. Suffrage was granted to women in Tasmania as part of a program of Liberal reforms, although women were still debarred from taking seats in parliament.

In Queensland the issue of the plural vote once more came to the fore in 1891. Here the Labour Party held a firm position: that women should not be granted the vote until plural votes had been abolished. The suffrage movement was split between three rival groups—the WCTU, the Woman's Equal Franchise Association, and the Woman's Suffrage League—who were unable to agree on whether the plural vote should be retained, although, as in other states, none of them campaigned for Aboriginal women to be included. As in Tasmania, it was not until after women were given the Commonwealth vote that the political climate in Queensland shifted. In the 1904 election, enough Labour members were returned to enable them to form a coalition government with the Liberals, and many enemies of woman suffrage were defeated. In 1905 the Assembly passed an Electoral Franchise Bill establishing a one-adult, one-vote system, including women. The upper house yielded, well aware that if it did not, the Assembly had the power to bring in nominees who might decide to abolish a second legislative chamber.

The last state to give women the vote was Victoria. One of the key factors in this delay was that although manhood suffrage had been granted for the Assembly by the first Victorian Parliament in 1856, plural voting had been introduced for both houses and the upper house had an extremely high property qualification. This led to inevitable opposition between the two houses. In Victoria the fight for the vote was also set in a broader context of women's rights than it was in other states. More concern was expressed about the destabilizing effect of the "new woman" in society, and this led to the formation of a strong antisuffrage movement.

Propertied women were given the municipal vote in Victoria in 1863 and, by an oversight, their names were transferred to the state electoral roles, enabling a few women to cast their vote in the 1864 elections. Although this anomaly was removed in 1865 by changing the term *persons* to *male persons,* it enabled Victorian suffragists in later decades to claim that they had once held the vote and that it had been taken away from them. From its beginnings in 1884, the suffrage movement in Victoria expanded rapidly. In 1894 Annette Bear-Crawford formed an umbrella group, the United Council for Woman Suffrage, which by 1900 had 32 affiliated associations. For two years the council was led by Vida Goldstein, who remained a key figure in the movement until the end of the campaigns.

Although the Labour Party supported

votes for women after plural voting was abolished in 1899, it had little political clout in Parliament. The Liberal-Conservative coalition government continued to block votes for women in Victoria, in part because it was believed that Labour had done well nationally because women had voted in federal elections. The government was concerned that giving women the state vote would strengthen the Victorian Labour Party. Thus, although most Liberals believed in suffrage, they were willing to allow the Conservative upper house to obstruct suffrage bills. They changed their minds in 1908, partly because they no longer believed women's votes would be radical and partly because they believed that continued resistance might push a largely peaceful suffrage movement to follow the British example, turning to militancy. If this were to happen, Victoria would be condemned by the rest of Australia. Thus in 1908, Victoria fell into line with most other states and granted all women the state and federal vote.

Despite Australia's early achievement of the female vote, very few women participated in government in the years following their enfranchisement. None of the parties were willing to consider women as parliamentary candidates, and women, like Goldstein, who stood as independent candidates failed to be elected.

See also Citizenship; Dugdale, Henrietta, and Annie Lowe; Goldstein, Vida; Imperialism; Lawson, Louisa; Lee, Mary; New Zealand; Nicholls, Elizabeth; Plural Vote; Race and Ethnicity; Scott, Rose; Sexuality; Woman's Christian Temperance Union.
References Oldfield, Audrey. *Woman Suffrage in Australia, A Gift or a Struggle?* (1992); Margarey, Susan. "Why didn't they want to be members of Parliament? Suffragists in South Australia" (1994); Spearitt, Katie. "New Dawns: First Wave Feminism, 1880–1914" (1992).

Austria

For many years, Austria's political and social context made it very difficult for a liberal feminist movement to develop and thrive. It was not until the years immediately preceding World War I that a campaign in favor of women's suffrage was organized and, unlike its counterparts in the rest of Europe, the Austrian suffrage movement was led by socialist women. Austria was part of the Habsburg Empire and considered itself part of the German Confederation until the war of 1866 led to a united Germany under Prussian leadership. Because Vienna was the administrative center of the empire, the middle class in Austria was largely composed of civil servants, and the identification of Austrians with the Habsburgs meant that there was little basis for a nationalist movement to develop. Austria was also predominantly Catholic and it was in Protestant countries that feminism made the most headway.

Political structures also militated against the development of either a feminist movement or a suffrage movement. The Austrian parliament, the Reichsrat, had little real power and was weakened by conflicts between different nationalities. Women were unable, therefore, to use tactics familiar elsewhere, such as lobbying representative institutions and seeking allies among existing political parties. In 1867 women were banned from joining or forming political associations, which deterred feminists from touching on anything that might be construed as a "political" question. Women's groups that were formed in the late nineteenth century, therefore, concentrated on employment, education, and welfare issues.

Despite all these restrictions, some Austrian women were able to vote in local elections because, in the reaction following the 1848 revolution, property franchises that included women had been established in parts of the empire. In Austria this enfranchised more women than elsewhere because married women in Austria had greater opportunities to retain control of their property on marriage than did their counterparts in places such as Germany. In the late nineteenth century, under pressure from the Liberals and Social Democrats, who were growing in influence as Austria industrialized, the government attempted to remove property qualifications and in the process disenfranchised women. It was this threat to remove existing rights that led women to take action. The Allgemeiner Österreichischer Frauenverein (General Austrian Women's Association) was founded in 1893 by schoolteacher Auguste Fickert (1855–1910), who had held a meeting in 1890 to protest when the government removed women's right to vote in local elections in Vienna. The association had a wide range of "non political" aims and therefore escaped police repression, but it also sought to preserve existing voting rights.

It was socialist women, however, who were to lead the campaign for an extension of women's voting rights, rather than accepting a defensive struggle to maintain what already existed. The Austrian socialist women's movement was one of the largest and best organized outside Germany. Although the Social Democrats had held large meetings to demand votes for women in the early 1890s and their leader, Victor Adler, confirmed his commitment to women's suffrage in 1903, it did not become a major issue for the party until 1906, when the Social Democrats launched a campaign for manhood suffrage. This caused considerable controversy at the meeting of the Second International at Stuttgart in 1907 because it went against the party policy of supporting universal suffrage for both sexes. Adler argued, however, that manhood suffrage was the only realistic demand in the context of Austrian politics, and he was supported by Adelheid Popp, the leader of the country's socialist women and editor of their magazine, *Arbeiterinnenzeitung* (Working Women's Newspaper).

In 1907, in order to preserve the unity of the empire, manhood suffrage was granted in Austria. This prompted a reorganization of the Social Democratic Party, in which women were able, for the first time, to form a separate organization with considerable autonomy that received a grudging official recognition. In 1908 Austrian women held a conference in which they agreed that women's suffrage was an inalienable right, and activists concentrated in the prewar years on campaigning for women's right to vote as a means for achieving a wide range of other reforms. The movement grew rapidly, and by 1913 there were 28,058 members in 312 local branches, and the circulation of the movement's newspaper stood at 29,000. Nonetheless, it was not until the downfall of the Habsburg Empire in 1918 and the establishment of a republic that Austrian women finally gained the vote from the provisional National Assembly.

See also Germany; Nationalism; Popp, Adelheid; Socialism in Europe; Stuttgart Congress of the Second International.
References Evans, Richard J. *The Feminists: Women's Emancipation Movements in Europe, America and Australasia, 1840–1920* (1977); Sowerwine, Charles. "The Socialist Women's Movement from 1850–1940" (1998).

Autobiography

Many of those who had been involved in the women's movement, in particular the struggle for the suffrage, decided to record their experiences in autobiographies and memoirs. The identification of women with the home and the private sphere, in particular during the nineteenth century, meant that women rarely wrote autobiographies, which were associated with men who wished to publicize their achievements in politics, religion, or warfare. However, the suffrage campaign, with its focus on the public world of politics, inspired participants to celebrate the active part that women had played in many countries in the achievement of the vote by writing autobiographies and other personal reminiscences. Hilda Kean has suggested that in doing so, women sought to challenge their marginalization from history as well as from political life, determined that their struggles would not be forgotten by future generations. In a study of the numerous autobiographies produced by British suffrage activists in the 1920s and 1930s, Kean argues that these women chose the genre of autobiography, rather than history, because the suffrage campaign had transformed their individual lives and they identified the achievement of political goals with personal goals. Their sense of exhilaration can be seen in the titles of their autobiographies, such as Mary Richardson's *Laugh a Defiance* (1953) and Emmeline Pethick-Lawrence's *My Part in a Changing World* (1938).

Suffrage autobiographies provide colorful firsthand accounts of and valuable insights into a political struggle. They enable the historian to ask questions about aspects of the campaign that are rarely revealed in the records of organizations or in newspapers, such as the meaning of suffrage for women, how women developed a feminist consciousness, and the ways in which they reconciled political activities with their personal lives. These narratives highlight the complexities of the ideas and methods of suffrage campaigners and demonstrate the relationships between individuals and organizations that are often seen as separate in mainstream histories. They also show differences between women. Although the bulk of autobiographies were produced by middle-class women, some were written by working-class activists such as British socialist and suffragette Hannah Mitchell (*The Hard Way Up,* 1968) and American trade unionist Rose Schneiderman (*All for One,* 1967).

Nonetheless, historians need to handle such sources with care. Autobiographers from the suffrage movement tended to emphasize their own role in the events they described and were selective about what to include. Dutch suffragist Aletta Jacobs, for example, valued female friendships very much, but these are rarely explored in any depth in her autobiography because her story is organized around events, journeys, and struggles. Moreover, as Kean suggests, autobiographies must be seen as a "representation of experience within the suffrage movement rather than as a quasi objective historical account" (Kean, 1994, 61), a representation in which women who were affected by the present as well as the past sought to construct a very particular version of events. In the interwar years in Britain, for example, the Suffragette Fellowship, established in 1926, encouraged former suffragettes to "perpetuate the memory of the pioneers" by writing their autobiographies. Laura E. Mayhall argues that these authors created a particular version of events in which the "suffragette spirit" was equated with a particular type of militancy, evinced by imprisonment, hunger strikes, and forcible feedings, and that this rendering of suffrage history has since had a long-lasting influence on the interpretations of historians.

As long as they are used with care, however, autobiographies can enrich our understanding of suffrage history. They were written by women suffrage campaigners from all parts of the world and from different classes, and they provided an important means for women authors to relate their experiences in their own voices.

See also Jacobs, Aletta; Mitchell, Hannah; Pethick-Lawrence, Emmeline; Schneiderman, Rose.

References Davis, T., et al. "'The Public Face of Feminism': Early Twentieth Century Writings on Women's Suffrage" (1982); Jacobs, Aletta, *Memories* (1996 [1924]); Kean, Hilda. "Searching for the Past in Present Defeat: The Construction of Historical and Political Identity in British Feminism in the 1920s and 1930s" (1994); Mayhall, Laura E. Nym. "Creating the 'Suffragette Spirit': British Feminism and the Historical Imagination" (1995).

Becker, Lydia Ernestine

A leader of the early British suffrage movement, Lydia Ernestine Becker (1827–1890) was born in Manchester, England, into a middle-class manufacturing family of German origins. In October 1866, she attended a meeting of the National Association for the Promotion of Social Science in Manchester, where she heard Barbara Bodichon of the Langham Place Circle give a paper on the women's franchise. From that moment she became involved in the campaign for women's suffrage.

In January 1867, Becker became the secretary of the Manchester Women's Suffrage Committee, which shortly afterwards became the Manchester National Society for Women's Suffrage. In the same year, she published an influential article in the *Contemporary Review* entitled "Female Suffrage." In 1868 she helped to prepare the test case, *Chorlton v. Lings,* claiming that women had the right to vote under ancient English law under the generic term *men,* but the case was rejected by the Court of Common Pleas. At a time when women rarely appeared on public platforms, Becker was an excellent public speaker, and she undertook many lecture tours for the suffrage cause. In March 1870, she started the *Women's Suffrage Journal,* editing it until her death in 1890, and it remains a valuable record of the early campaigns for the vote. Becker became secretary of the Central Committee of the National Society for Women's Suffrage in 1880 and was appointed its

AN "UGLY RUSH!"

This cartoon lampoons the persistence of Lydia Ernestine Becker, editor of the Women's Suffrage Journal, *and other suffragists. (Ann Ronan Picture Library)*

parliamentary agent, acting as liaison with MPs of all parties who were favorable to the cause of women's suffrage.

Becker always took a cautious approach in framing her demands. At first she was in favor of including married women in the franchise, but by 1873 she had changed her position and, despite protests from other suffragists, insisted on the exclusion of married women from any franchise proposal. Together with Millicent Fawcett, who was her natural successor as leader of the moderate suffragists, Becker believed that the campaign should not be attached to any political party, and this led to a temporary split in the suffrage movement in 1888. Despite her conservative stance, Becker was an important pioneer-

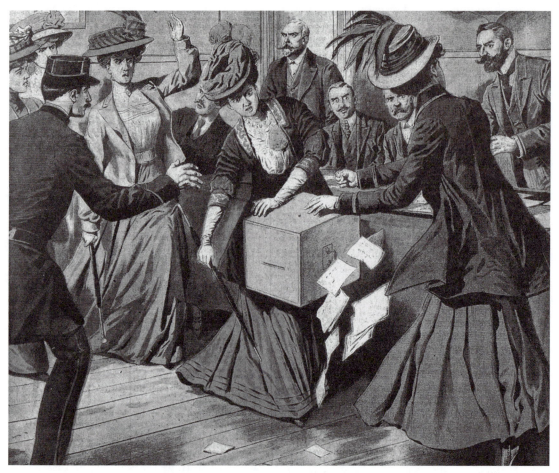

This illustration published in a Paris newspaper depicts Belgian suffragettes upsetting ballot boxes. (Ann Ronan Picture Library)

ing figure in the fight for women's suffrage in Britain; it was mainly her efforts that ensured that the cause was brought to the attention of Parliament and the public during the late nineteenth century.

> **See also** Britain; Fawcett, Millicent Garrett; Langham Place Circle; Newspapers and Journals.
> **References** Blackburn, Helen. *Women's Suffrage: A Record of the Women's Suffrage Movement in the British Isles with Biographical Sketches of Miss Becker* (1902); Spender, Dale. *Women of Ideas (and what men have done to them)* (1983).

Belgium

Although Belgium had a constitutional government in the early twentieth century and was an urban industrial society with a strong middle class, the movement for women's suffrage was weak and women did not achieve the vote in significant numbers until after World War II. The enfranchisement of women was hampered by the predominance of Catholicism; both the Liberals and the Social Democrats feared that women voters, who were the mainstay of the church, would support conservatism. In 1901, the Belgian Socialist Party appeared to be within sight of achieving universal manhood suffrage instead of a propertied franchise when a conservative member of Parliament put forward an amendment to enfranchise both sexes. This was a deliberate tactic to ensure the loss of Liberal support, and therefore socialist women dropped their campaign for women's suffrage in order that the bill for manhood suffrage would not be jeopardized. In doing so, they went against the policy of the European socialist umbrella group, the Second International, to which the Belgian socialists were affiliated, which supported voting rights for both sexes.

In subsequent years, the women's suffrage group, Union feministe pour le suffrage (Feminist Union for the Vote), founded in 1907, provided little pressure for the inclusion of women in the franchise, and by 1910 the union had only just over 100 members in three cities. Women gave considerable support to the war effort during World War I and played an important part in resisting the German occupation, but most women were not enfranchised after the war. Again it was the opposition of the Social Democrats that proved decisive. The Catholic party came to power, along with the Socialists and the Liberals, in 1919 and was sympathetic to the idea of women's suffrage because it would have strengthened its position. For the same reason, the Socialists opposed the measure, except at a local level. In any event, a very small number of women were enfranchised on the basis of war service; the right to vote was given to war widows who did not remarry, widowed mothers of sons killed in the war, and women who had been imprisoned by the Germans. It was not until after the upheavals of World War II that all women finally achieved the suffrage in 1948.

See also Catholicism; Socialism in Europe.
References Anderson, Bonnie S., and Judith P. Zinsser. *A History of Their Own: Women in Europe from Prehistory to the Present,* Vol. 2 (1990); Evans, Richard J. *The Feminists: Women's Emancipation Movements in Europe, America and Australasia, 1840–1920* (1977).

Bennett, Louie

Louie Bennett (1870–1956) was born in Temple Hill, Dublin, to a prosperous merchant family of Protestant descent, and she was educated at Alexandra College, Dublin, the first institution in Ireland to provide a university education to women. She published two novels, *The Proving of Priscilla* (1902) and *A Prisoner of His Word* (1908), before becoming active in the suffrage movement.

With her lifelong partner, Helen Chenevix, Bennett founded the Irish Women's Reform League in 1911 in order to publicize the deplorable conditions suffered by working-class women in Ireland. That same year, they established the Irish Women's Suffrage Federation, a nonparty and nonmilitant umbrella organization that provided much needed coordination to the small suffrage groups active throughout the country. On the outbreak of World War I, Bennett achieved prominence as a pacifist opponent of the war. She was one of the women chosen to represent Ireland at the 1915 Hague Congress. Although unable to reach The Hague because of the British blockade of the North Sea, Bennett joined what was to become the Women's International League for Peace and Freedom, becoming a member of its international executive, in which role she remained active for several decades.

Following the Easter Uprising of 1916, the execution of James Connolly, and the murder of Francis Sheehy Skeffington, pacifist editor of the suffrage paper the *Irish Citizen,* Bennett's views became more sympathetic to Irish nationalism. Skeffington's widow, Hanna, was in the United States publicizing the cause of Irish nationalism, and Bennett, now secretary of the Irish Women Workers' Union (IWWU), took over editorship of the paper. From 1918 onward, both women worked for the paper, which became a vehicle for the IWWU until it ceased publication in 1920, during the War of Independence. Bennett died in Dublin in 1956.

See also International Congress of Women, Ireland; Nationalism; Peace Movement; Skeffington, Hanna Sheehy; The Hague, 1915.

References Fox, R. M. *Louie Bennett* (1958); Hazlekorn, Ellen. "The Social and Political Views of Louie Bennett, 1870–1965" (1988); Jones, Mary. *These Obstreperous Lassies, a History of the Irish Women Workers' Union.* (1988).

Billington-Greig, Teresa

Teresa Billington-Greig (1877–1964) was one of the founders and leaders of the militant British suffrage group the Women's Freedom League (WFL). Born in Preston, Lancashire, England, the daughter of a shipping clerk, Teresa Billington became a schoolteacher in Manchester. Here she first met Emmeline Pankhurst, who persuaded her to join the Manchester branch of the socialist group the Independent Labour Party (ILP). Billington also became active in the suffrage organization the Women's Social and Political Union (WSPU), which in its early years drew members largely from the Manchester ILP. In 1905 Teresa Billington became the first woman organizer for the ILP, but she soon began to devote more of her time to women's suffrage and in 1906 was sent by the WSPU to Scotland to gather members and form branches. In October 1906 she was among WSPU members who created a disturbance at the opening of Parliament in London, and she was arrested and imprisoned for a short period in Holloway prison. Her friendship with the Pankhursts, however, came under increasing strain. Teresa Billington was critical of the lack of democratic decision making in the WSPU, and the Pankhursts were jealous of her success in Scotland.

In October 1907 she helped to form a breakaway suffrage organization, the Women's Freedom League. She was responsible for the league's work in Scotland, where, also in 1907, she had made her home after marrying a Scot, Frederick Greig. The couple adopted the name Billington-Greig. Teresa Billington-Greig was an influential figure in the Scottish suffrage movement, forming a lasting im-

Teresa Billington-Greig, WSPU organizer, was known as the "woman with the whip" for disrupting Liberal party meetings carrying a whip to keep the stewards from ejecting her. (Museum of London)

pression on those who heard her speak. In 1911, however, she left the WFL and launched a bitter attack on the militant movement as a whole, both in the press and in her book, *The Militant Suffrage Movement* (1911). She played no further part in the suffrage struggle but, after World War I, became active again in the Women's Freedom League. In the last years of her life, from 1946 to 1949, she served as honorary director of Women for Westminster, a group that campaigned for women to participate more fully in parliamentary politics.

See also Independent Labour Party; Pankhurst, Emmeline; Scotland; Women's Freedom League; Women's Social and Political Union.
References Leneman, Leah. *A Guid Cause: The Women's Suffrage Movement in Scotland* (1991); Rosen, Andrew. *Rise Up Women! The Militant Campaign of the Women's Social and Political Union* (1974).

Blatch, Harriot Stanton

Harriot Stanton Blatch (1856–1940), the daughter of Elizabeth Cady Stanton, one of the best known of the first generation of suffrage activists in the United States, played an important part in reviving the suffrage campaign and broadening its base in the early twentieth century. After marrying into a wealthy British family, Blatch spent 20 years in England, where she met Emmeline Pankhurst and participated in the work of the Equal Franchise Committee. Widowhood and the ill health of her mother, however, brought her back to live in the United States in 1902.

Blatch had already become involved in suffrage activities in New York during the 1890s, when she stayed in the city for extensive periods. Her skills as an orator made her a favorite for parlor meetings, but she was increasingly disenchanted by the elitist nature of the campaign. She expressed her ideas in a public debate with her mother in the *Woman's Journal,* where she challenged the view that the demand for women's suffrage should contain an educational qualification, arguing that working-class women were perfectly able to engage in political activity and, indeed, that their voice would add a new dimension to American politics.

When she lived in England, Blatch had joined the socialist group the Fabian Society, and she shared that group's views about the importance of women's wage-earning work and economic independence. When she returned to New York in 1902, she became involved in the movement for municipal political reform, a broadly based campaign against corruption, and she joined the Women's Trade Union League (WTUL), a coalition of wealthy and working-class women who aimed to organize women into trade unions. This experience, coupled with the militancy of the British group the Women's Social and Political Union (WSPU), convinced Blatch that the American women's suffrage movement needed to take a different direction.

In 1907 she formed a new suffrage group, the Equality League of Self-Supporting Women, which drew its membership from professional women and working-class leaders of the WTUL and instituted a more aggressive brand of suffrage campaigning. Soon after the Equality League's establishment, for example, Blatch arranged for trade union women to testify before the New York legislature on behalf of women's suffrage. At the end of the year she invited British WSPU member Annie Cobden Sanderson to talk about her experiences in prison. In her remarks, Sanderson emphasized the involvement of working-class women in the British movement. Sanderson's visit, and that of Emmeline Pankhurst a few months later, inspired more militant activities in the United States. In 1910, helped by her colleagues Mrs. (Alva Erskine Smith Vanderbilt) O. H. P. Belmont and Mary Beard, Blatch launched a new group, the Women's Political Union. Unlike its counterpart in Britain, this organization omitted the word *social* from its title so that it would not appear to have connections with socialism or left-wing politics. Blatch also organized a number of suffrage parades and set up silent pickets around the New York State legislature when it debated a suffrage proposal in 1912.

While she still had influence in the National American Woman Suffrage Association (NAWSA), Blatch helped Alice Paul to become the chairwoman of its Congressional Committee. The two women were to develop different political strategies; Alice Paul attacked the Democrats because they were in power, whereas Blatch sought their support in New York. Nonetheless, finding it difficult to get along with Carrie Chapman Catt when she became president of NAWSA, Blatch merged her own organization with Alice Paul's National Woman's Party in 1916.

During World War I, Blatch headed the Food Administration Speaker's Bureau and wrote a book, *Mobilizing Woman Power*. She remained committed to the suffrage movement and in 1926 stood as a candidate for the United States Senate. Although she was not one of the leading figures in the national suffrage movement, Blatch was important for the links that she made with the British suffrage agitation, for her local leadership in New York, and for her attempts to develop new methods of campaigning.

See also Catt, Carrie Chapman; National American Woman Suffrage Association; National Woman's Party; Paul, Alice; Stanton, Elizabeth Cady; United States of America; Women's Social and Political Union; Women's Trade Union League.
References DuBois, Ellen Carol. *Harriot Stanton Blatch and the Winning of Woman Suffrage* (1997); Morgan, David. "Woman Suffrage in Britain and America in the Early Twentieth Century" (1984).

Bolivia

Women in Bolivia gained the vote in 1953 after a successful revolution by the Movimiento Nacionalista Revolucionario (MNR) [National Revolutionary Movement] in 1952. The MNR was a popular movement for democracy, led by a coalition of workers and middle-class reformers, which transformed the system of government and challenged the narrow oligarchy of mining and capitalist landholders who controlled the state. Women's enfranchisement was part of a wider package of reforms that included universal suffrage and the expansion of education and social security.

Earlier in the century, upper- and middle-class urban women had called for the right to vote through autonomous women's groups such as the Ateneo Femenino (Woman's Club). However, it was not until the 1940s, when the MNR became the first political party to include women in its rank and file, that women began to play an active role in national politics. The often clandestine work that women did for the party was not aimed at achieving political rights for themselves, but rather at helping to overthrow the oligarchical regime in power. Even after the revolution and the achievement of women's suffrage, women continued to subordinate their interests to those of the male-dominated party and were not expected to participate in the redistribution of political power.

See also Latin America and the Caribbean.
Reference Ardaya, Gloria Salinas. "Women and Politics: Gender Relations in Bolivian Political Organizations and Labour Unions" (1994).

Brazil

Brazilian women were granted the right to vote by the electoral code of 24 February 1932. Within Latin America, Brazil was second in extending the franchise only to Ecuador, where women won a limited franchise in 1929. Brazil was unusual in the Latin American context in that the women's suffrage movement did not involve working-class women. It was initially led by a small group of upper- and middle-class urban women who had benefited from advances in female education in the late nineteenth century. However, it was not until after World War I that women's suffrage became a widespread and formally organized movement. Its leaders were aided in their efforts by their personal links with leading suffragists abroad and by the achievement of the vote for women in the United States and several leading European countries, which helped to make it an acceptable cause in elite circles.

Both of these factors encouraged the formation of women's rights organizations through which Brazilian women could channel their demands. The best known of these was the Federação Brasileira pelo Progresso Feminino (FBPF) [Brazilian Federation for the Advancement of Women], formed by Bertha Lutz in 1922 and affiliated with the International Woman Suffrage Alliance. At its first well-publicized women's congress in December 1922, which coincided with the centenary of Brazilian independence, the FBPF sought the support of prominent statesmen such as Senator Lauro Muller of Santa Catarina, who presided over the final session on women's suffrage.

It has been argued that the early enfranchisement of Brazilian women was achieved by its leaders' close ties with the political elite, although the movement was not directly linked to any political party. During the 1920s, when women had no direct access to the political process, these activists employed a combination of publicity and personal contacts within government as their main political devices. They also expanded their organizations into most states, mobilizing more and more women. Tactics included manifestos, letter campaigns, press releases, interviews, petitions, and public forums, and several women tried unsuccessfully to register for the vote.

Although there were some breakaway groups in the final years of the campaign, the FBPF remained the preeminent suffrage organization in Brazil. Its leaders sought to reform rather than restructure the political system. They sought political equality on the basis of their desire to improve society and, as in many other countries, allayed their opponents' fears about the breakdown of the family by arguing that the achievement of the vote would enhance women's role as mothers and would not detract from their position in the home. They did this by granting the home a broader significance. For example, they maintained that legislative halls where child protection laws were debated were "nothing but appurtenances of the home" (*Rio Jornal*, 13 December 1921; Hahner, 1990, 149).

Suffragists also linked the vote to women's qualities of morality and altruism, which they believed could be harnessed to social purposes, and they denied that they were trying to compete with men. Such tactics were intended partly to counter antisuffragist propaganda that portrayed them as ugly, sexless manhaters whom no man would marry. The influence of the Catholic Church was also significant in moderating the suffragist outlook in Brazil. Unlike the Mexican church hierarchy, which discouraged even the most moderate feminism, the clergy in Brazil did not object when women educated in religious institutions joined the FBPF. But the church was able to prevent the feminist movement from linking woman's political disadvantages with her subordinate position within the family.

The first breakthrough came in 1927, when the poor northeastern state of Rio Grande do Norte granted women the vote. Previous to this, there had been no feminist activity in this state. Then the incoming governor, Juvenal Lamartine de Faria, had pushed through an amendment of the state voting law that read "without distinction of sex." Although he was a longtime supporter of women's suffrage, he did this partly to enhance his political image. During 1928 some women were elected to municipal councils, and in 1929 the wife of a landowner, Alziro Soriano, was elected as mayor.

The national repercussions of this episode were less positive. When women from Rio Grande do Norte voted in a federal election in 1928, their votes were deducted from the total cast (their votes in local elections within the state still counted). The FBPF responded to this setback in May 1928 with a manifesto that was couched as a National Declaration of Women's Rights, asserting that the right to vote was the principal means for women to defend their freedoms. Yet little real progress was made until after the October 1930 revolution.

The regime of the new president, Getúlio

Dornelles Vargas, sought to present the appearance of reform and seemed willing to listen to dissident groups who had been previously neglected or repressed. The re-drafting of the electoral code gave the FBPF an opportunity to push for change, and it simultaneously kept the issue of suffrage in the public eye by organizing an international convention in Rio. Although José Francisco, the president of the committee drafting the electoral code, was in favor of women's suffrage, the committee's draft proposals restricted the women's franchise to single women, widows with their own income, and married women who had their husbands' permission. When the FBPF protested that this was insufficient and presented the president with a delegation, Vargas gave way. The decree of 24 February 1932 established a secret proportional ballot and gave women the vote on the same terms as men.

The first elections in which women participated were held in 1933. It was estimated that women made up about 20 percent of the electorate, but neither Lutz nor the other FBPF candidate was elected. At first the Vargas regime appeared broadly sympathetic to women's political participation, but by the time Lutz managed to gain a seat in the Congress in 1936, the liberal political climate was giving way to right-wing extremism. The establishment of the Estado Nôvo by Vargas in a coup against his own government in 1937 ended electoral politics and women's political participation until after World War II.

See also Daltro, Leolinda De Figuereido; Latin America and the Caribbean; Lutz, Bertha.
References Hahner, June E. *Emancipating the Female Sex, The Struggle for Women's Rights in Brazil, 1850–1940* (1990); Rachum, Ilan. "Feminism, Woman Suffrage, and National Politics in Brazil, 1922–1937" (1977).

Britain

Britain had one of the strongest suffrage movements in the world, but it took over 50 years before some women at last gained the right to vote. The campaign must be understood in terms of its political context: voting rights were linked to property ownership or taxpaying status, and only some men had the vote. During the nineteenth century, successive Reform Acts in 1832, 1867, and 1884 extended the franchise, so that by the end of the nineteenth century two thirds of adult males had the right to vote in parliamentary elections, but all women were excluded.

It was at times of more general agitation to extend the franchise that women pushed forward their own demands. The issue of women's suffrage was first raised during debates around the 1832 Reform Bill, which explicitly excluded women from voting by the use of the term *male* rather than *person*. Women's suffrage was also one of the early aims of Chartism—a working-class movement in the late 1830s and 1840s that sought to extend the franchise and to gain other political reforms—but the demand for the women's vote was soon dropped so that Chartists could concentrate on the male worker. Nonetheless, it was a middle-class Quaker and supporter of Chartism, Anne Knight, who wrote the first leaflet on women's suffrage in 1847 and then, with other female Chartists, helped to establish a women's suffrage society in Sheffield. This society was short-lived, however, and it was not until the 1860s that an organized movement for women's suffrage began to develop.

The impetus for this movement came from a group of women, including Barbara Leigh Smith (Bodichon), Anna Jameson, and Bessie Rayner Parkes, who had already begun to take an interest in improving women's social position. They had formed committees to expand education for girls, to promote women's employment, and to protect the rights of

Suffrage protest outside the British Parliament, c. 1910. (Library of Congress)

married women under the law. These activities gained focus when the women began to meet in rooms in Langham Place and, in 1857, established the *English Woman's Journal* as a forum for debate and communication between like-minded women. In the early 1860s, they formed the Kensington Society as a debating group, and it was here that the question of women's suffrage was first supported by this circle of friends.

Barbara Bodichon and Elizabeth Garrett, who was to become the first woman doctor to qualify in Britain, helped John Stuart Mill in his election campaign on the understanding that he would present a petition on their behalf to Parliament. A petition was circulated demanding the enfranchisement of all householders, regardless of sex, and 1,499 signatures were collected. The petition was presented in 1866, but the 1867 Reform Act failed to include women. Despite this setback, the suffrage movement continued to grow, and between 1866 and 1868 suffrage committees were established in London, Manchester, Birmingham, Bristol, and Edinburgh. In 1868 they joined together in a loose federation called the National Society for Women's Suffrage (NSWS).

Women argued for the vote on the grounds of universal human rights, pointing out that their exclusion from the franchise only underlined their second-class status. They demanded the vote on the same terms as men and claimed that as property owners and property taxpayers, they should be able to exercise some influence over how their money was spent and over laws that affected women. To underpin their claims, they used texts such as John Stuart Mill's pamphlet, *On the Subjection of Women* (1869), which soon gained an international reputation. Influenced by his wife, Harriet Taylor, Mill argued that women's subordination, including the denial of political opportunities, was the greatest barrier to human improvement.

Over the next decade, women's suffrage campaigners used a variety of methods to publicize their cause. They collected signatures for petitions, lobbied members of Parliament, and spoke at public meetings. In 1870 Lydia Becker, secretary of the Manchester National Society for Women's Suffrage, established and edited the first paper devoted to suffrage, the *Women's Suffrage Journal,* which was soon available in at least a few public libraries. Women also sought to test their rights under the law. In 1868 a number of women tried to register to vote, but they were defeated by the courts; others refused to pay taxes on property while still unenfranchised.

The return of a Liberal government in 1880 raised the possibility of a new Reform Bill to enfranchise men who were still excluded, such as agricultural laborers and miners. A series of large public meetings on behalf of women's enfranchisement were held throughout the country in an attempt to gain more popular support, but once again in 1884 women were excluded from the Reform Act. In the late nineteenth century, therefore, the campaign for women's suffrage was in the doldrums, and the movement was weakened by splits and divisions in its own ranks.

Although the majority of suffrage campaigners in the nineteenth century were drawn from a similar middle-class and upper-middle-class background and gave each other mutual support through a network of friendship and family ties, there had been numerous disagreements among them from the beginning. Women disagreed about how far to extend the franchise, in particular, whether married women should be included. The London Society for Women's Suffrage, in which

conservatives such as Emily Davies and Frances Power Cobbe predominated, argued that married women should be excluded. The Manchester group, including Lydia Becker and the radical liberals Elizabeth Wolstenholme (Elmy), Richard Pankhurst, and Jacob and Ursula Bright, took the opposite view, although by 1873 Lydia Becker had modified her position and demanded the vote only for single women and widows. There were also disagreements about whether support should be given to other movements, such as the campaign for the repeal of the Contagious Diseases Acts, and about whether suffrage campaigners should link their cause to particular political parties. (The Contagious Diseases Acts, which mandated the medical inspection of prostitutes, had been passed in the 1860s. Many argued that they violated the civil rights of women.)

Tensions came to a head in the 1880s when it was suggested that groups including women's suffrage within their broader aims should be allowed affiliate status within the NSWS. Some suffragists, such as Millicent Garrett Fawcett, feared that this was just a ploy to enable women with party political loyalties, such as members of local Women's Liberal Associations, female auxiliaries of the Liberal Party, to take over the movement. As a result of the disagreement, the NSWS split. Fawcett remained with the Central Committee of the National Society for Women's Suffrage, to uphold the "old" rules, and the Central National Society for Women's Suffrage was established under the "new" rules about affiliation.

Although the nineteenth-century suffrage movement has been characterized as moderate in its outlook and cautious in its methods, Sandra Stanley Holton has suggested that if attention is shifted away from the familiar leaders to a network of women centered on the Bright family and other radical liberals, then an alternative, more radical approach can be identified that stretches back to the abolition movement, the Anti–Corn Law League, and Chartism. For instance, the sisters Mary and Anna Maria Priestman, who were related to the Brights by marriage, refused to pay their property taxes and had their goods seized by bailiffs. They were interested in trade unionism among working women and linked women's suffrage to their broader politics through their active membership in the Bristol Women's Liberal Association.

This radical strain was given organizational expression in the late nineteenth century with the formation of two new groups. The Women's Franchise League was established in 1889 under the leadership of Elizabeth Wolstenholme-Elmy, Ursula Bright, and Emmeline Pankhurst. It aimed to include married women in the franchise and worked for a broad program of civil rights for women, such as equal pay. The Women's Emancipation Union was formed by Elmy in 1892 after she had been ousted from the leadership of the Women's Franchise League. Both groups sought to develop links with the labor movement and with international suffrage groups and campaigned for a range of radical causes.

Although the suffrage movement was weakened by divisions in its ranks in the late nineteenth century and had moved no closer to its goal of achieving the parliamentary franchise, there was greater success at a local level. In 1869 women with appropriate property qualifications were able to vote in municipal elections and to stand and vote for Boards of Guardians that ran the Poor Law. A year later they were able to vote and stand for newly created school boards. The property qualification effectively excluded married women from these elections; however, a further change was introduced by the 1894 Local Government Act, which enabled married women to exercise all the voting rights already open to single women and widows. This meant that any demand for suffrage

on the same terms as men would now include married women, a development that made it easier for suffrage campaigners to work together. The same act also enabled women to stand for election to Parish Councils, and this right was extended to County and Borough Councils in 1907, although Ireland was excluded.

At the turn of the century, the suffrage movement underwent a revival and changed in character. It became far more of a mass movement, developing new political strategies and methods that brought it from the periphery into the center of national politics. In 1897 the National Union of Women's Suffrage Societies (NUWSS) was formed, under the leadership of Millicent Fawcett, to bring together the provincial suffrage societies under one organization. One of these groups, the North of England Society, led by Esther Roper and Eva Gore Booth, was sympathetic to the labor movement and attempted to involve working-class women, in particular Lancashire textile workers, in the suffrage campaign. New methods were used, including open-air meetings and public demonstrations, and in 1900 a petition was organized that collected 29,300 signatures from textile workers. This renewed activity prompted Emmeline Pankhurst and her daughter Christabel, along with other members of the Manchester branch of the socialist Independent Labour Party, to form the Women's Social and Political Union (WSPU) in 1903 to carry out propaganda for socialism and women's suffrage. When the WSPU severed its ties with the labor movement in 1907, Teresa Billington-Greig and Charlotte Despard formed a third group, the Women's Freedom League (WFL).

The NUWSS, the WSPU, and the WFL were the largest and most influential groups in the prewar years, and they were joined by numerous smaller organizations that were usually linked to religious or professional groups, such as the Catholic Women's Suffrage Society and the Actresses' Franchise League. Women from a wide range of backgrounds became involved in the movement, including teachers, nurses, clerks, and textile workers, and links were strengthened with women in other countries through the International Woman Suffrage Alliance. All the groups shared the same aim: votes for women on the same terms as men. This was known as a limited suffrage because the property basis of the franchise would have enabled only selected groups of women to vote.

Women's suffrage campaigners argued that what mattered was ending sex inequalities in voting rights before going on to demand votes for all women, but the Labour Party and the Liberal Party both feared that propertied women's votes would strengthen the Conservative Party. Despite support from individual male members, therefore, neither "reform" party would give an official backing to the women's cause. The political tactics of the women's suffrage groups therefore varied. The NUWSS sought to gain the endorsement of individual MPs no matter which party they belonged to, whereas the WSPU opposed all members of the Liberal government, which had come to power in 1906, regardless of their individual views.

The WSPU also developed new, militant tactics. At first these involved relatively moderate "constitutional protests." During the general election campaign in October 1905, for instance, Christabel Pankhurst and Annie Kenney disrupted a meeting by waving flags and shouting "Votes for women!" which led to their arrest. Subsequent actions included heckling speakers, distributing leaflets at places of entertainment, and mass lobbying of Parliament. Eventually, WSPU members adopted the name *suffragettes*, a term coined by the press, to distinguish them from the more constitutionalist suffragists in the NUWSS. As frustration mounted after 1910, when Prime Minister H. H. Asquith failed to in-

troduce a women's suffrage measure, the WSPU launched a new campaign that involved large-scale smashing of windows, setting fire to empty buildings, and destroying mail in mailboxes. From 1905 to 1914 approximately 1,000 women were imprisoned for suffrage activities. After 1909 many of these prisoners went on hunger strikes to protest being denied the status of political prisoners; many of these women were then forcibly fed. A 1913 act, popularly known as the Cat and Mouse Act, enabled the government to release hunger strikers until they had regained their strength, when they could be rearrested.

The militancy of the WSPU inspired other groups to change tactics. The WFL carried out acts that it termed "constitutional militancy," such as tax resistance and a boycott of the 1911 census, and altogether 142 of its members were imprisoned. The NUWSS avoided illegal activities but began to hold large demonstrations that culminated in the Suffrage Pilgrimage, in which women marched from different areas of the country to attend a mass rally in London in 1913. New ways to spread ideas were found, such as the suffrage caravan, in which speakers toured through towns and villages, spreading the word.

Publicity was important for all the groups; posters and postcards presented ideas in a different form and were often sold in suffrage shops, and demonstrations were full of drama and spectacle. Each group had its own newspaper—for example, the *Common Cause* (NUWSS), the *Vote* (WFL), and *Votes for Women* and the *Suffragette* (WSPU). The publicity given to the suffrage campaign boosted the membership of suffrage groups, in particular the NUWSS, which by 1909 had 70 affiliated societies with 13,161 members and by 1914 had 380 societies with over 53,000 members. The militant groups were smaller. The WSPU did not divulge membership figures, but it had 88 branches in 1913 and its newspaper had a circulation of 30,000–40,000. The WFL had 4,000 members.

It is difficult to understand the growth of support for suffrage in the Edwardian period without recognizing how much was due to the enthusiasm and hard work of provincial branches. Moreover, a study of the campaign outside London provides a different perspective on the characteristics of the suffrage movement. For instance, the relationships between individual suffrage organizations, and between them and other political groups, could be far more fluid on a local level than nationally. In Scotland and parts of Yorkshire, for example, there was a close relationship between branches of the WSPU and the socialist group, the Independent Labour Party, right up to the outbreak of World War I, whereas nationally there was hostility between the leaders of both organizations. In Scotland, Ireland, and Wales, local traditions and a sense of national identity could help to shape the movement. In Ireland, the independence question led to the formation of separate suffrage organizations, whereas in Scotland and Wales, although national pride was expressed in the imagery and concepts used, all suffrage groups were affiliated with either the WSPU, the NUWSS, or the WFL.

A study of the political journeys of individual women, at both a local and a national level, also gives a more complex picture of suffrage politics. Women moved between groups at different times, but there was no consistent pattern to this. The WSPU did lose members because of its escalating militancy, although individual women had different views about what was unacceptable to them. Helen Fraser, for example, was the first Scottish WSPU organizer in 1906, and a year later she was arrested when she attempted to enter the House of Commons. But in 1908 she resigned as soon as the WSPU began to throw stones. Other women, such as Mary Blathwayt from Bath, did not resign until 1913,

when the WSPU started to destroy property. On the other hand, escalating militancy could actually attract women such as Dr. Alice Ker, a member of the Birkenhead Women's Suffrage Society, who switched to the WSPU in 1912 and was subsequently arrested for breaking shop windows. Others left the WSPU as a result of splits in the leadership. Emmeline and Frederick Pethick-Lawrence were expelled in 1912, when they questioned the emphasis on individual acts of militancy, and they went on to help form a new body, the United Suffragists, in 1914. Sylvia Pankhurst was also informed that her group, the East London Federation of Suffragettes, could no longer form part of the WSPU because of its close links with the labor movement, and she then campaigned independently. Several WSPU members then left the WSPU to join these other organizations.

The continued failure of Private Members' Bills, including a series of Conciliation Bills, 1910–1912, which had the backing of sympathizers from all parties, led the NUWSS to revise its strategy of seeking support from individual MPs. Instead, in 1912 an alliance for electoral purposes was formed with the Labour Party, which now had a small group of MPs in Parliament. An Election Fighting Fund Committee was established to support Labour candidates at by-elections. Although no victories resulted, the alliance encouraged the NUWSS to give greater attention to the needs of working women and to begin to redefine its campaign as part of a wider democratic movement.

And yet by 1914 the suffrage movement appeared to have reached an impasse. The views of MPs were mixed, with some supporting the suffrage and others still considering that it was inappropriate, if not dangerous, for women to have a say in choosing a government that dealt with imperial and foreign affairs. Asquith was hostile to the movement and had become more obdurate when faced with an escalation of militancy. It was the declaration of war in August 1914 that ended the deadlock and brought suffrage campaigning to a standstill. The Pankhursts gave their wholehearted support to the war effort, while Millicent Fawcett encouraged NUWSS members to concentrate on relief work. In 1915 several members of the NUWSS executive committee resigned to commit themselves to the peace movement.

After so many years of campaigning, women finally achieved the vote at the end of the war as part of a general reform of the franchise, designed to enable servicemen who had fought abroad, and therefore had lost their residency qualification, to vote in the first postwar election. In 1918 the Representation of the People Act enfranchised women over 30 who were on the local government register or who were married to men on the register. The age restriction was intended to prevent women voters from outnumbering men.

It has been suggested that women received the vote as a reward for their services to the war effort, but the reasons are likely to have been more complex than that. Even before the war, a majority of MPs were in favor of granting women the vote, and when the political climate changed, including the suspension of militancy and the replacement of Asquith as prime minister by Lloyd George in December 1916, the way was clear for a new policy. The suffrage groups continued to lobby members of the government during the war, and given that an extension of the general franchise would result in more women voters than under the limited franchises proposed earlier, the main political parties no longer feared that women's suffrage would automatically benefit their rivals. It was to be another 10 years of campaigning by feminist groups, however, before in 1928 all women over the age of 21 finally gained the vote, putting them at last on an equal footing with men.

See also Becker, Lydia Ernestine; Billington-

Greig, Teresa; Cat and Mouse Act; Conciliation Bill; Despard, Charlotte; Drama, Novels, Poetry, and Film; Fawcett, Millicent Garrett; Hunger Strikes; Imperialism; Independent Labour Party; International Woman Suffrage Alliance; Ireland; Langham Place Circle; Militancy; Mill, John Stuart; National Union of Women's Suffrage Societies; Newspapers and Journals; *On the Subjection of Women;* Pankhurst, Christabel; Pankhurst, Emmeline; Pankhurst, Sylvia; Pethick-Lawrence, Emmeline; Pethick-Lawrence, Frederick; Pilgrimage, Suffrage; Representation of the People Act; Representation of the People (Equal Franchise) Act; Scotland; Wales; Women's Freedom League; Women's Social and Political Union.
References Bartley, Paula. *Votes for Women, 1860–1928* (1998); Garner, Les. *Stepping Stones to Women's Liberty: Feminist Ideas in the Women's Suffrage Movement, 1900–1918* (1984); Hannam, June. "'I had not been to London': Women's Suffrage—A View from the Regions" (2000); Holton, Sandra Stanley. "Women and the Vote" (1995); Holton, Sandra Stanley. *Suffrage Days: Stories from the Women's Suffrage Movement* (1996); Leneman, Leah. *A Guid Cause: The Women's Suffrage Movement in Scotland* (1991); Pugh, Martin. *The March of the Women* (2000).

British Antisuffrage Campaign
See Antisuffrage Campaign, British.

Brunschwicg, Cecile
Cecile Brunschwicg (1877–1946) was a leader of the moderate French suffrage organization Union française pour le suffrage des femmes (UFSF) [French Union for Women's Suffrage]. The daughter of a Jewish industrialist and wife of a well-known philosopher at the Sorbonne, Brunschwicg became interested in the demand for women's suffrage after working in the women's trade union movement. She joined the moderate feminist group Conseil national des femmes françaises (National Council of French Women), attended the 1908 International Woman Suffrage Alliance (IWSA) Congress at Amsterdam, and participated in the formation of the UFSF.

Brunschwicg persuaded the UFSF executive committee to establish a membership and propaganda committee with herself as the head, and her enthusiasm and administrative ability were responsible for an increase in the union's membership, in particular in the provinces. Brunschwicg's activities were perceived as a threat by Jeanne Schmahl, the leader of the UFSF, who also disliked her political views. Matters came to a head in December 1910, when Brunschwicg was supported by the executive committee and appointed as secretary-general of the union.

Under her leadership, the UFSF adopted a moderate republican position. Brunschwicg continued as a leader of the UFSF during the interwar years and became a member of the Radical Party in order to influence its views on women's suffrage. At the suggestion of the radical leader, Edouard Daladier, she was asked in 1936 by Léon Blum, leader of the Popular Front, to be one of three women co-opted into junior ministerial positions, although this meant she had to give up her presidency of the UFSF. Throughout her years of campaigning she had adopted a moderate and pragmatic approach and operated both in the formal political sphere and informally as a hostess to Parisian academic society. She remained optimistic, despite political opposition, that the strength of her views and her personal example would prevail.

See also France; International Woman Suffrage Alliance; Union française pour le suffrage des femmes.
References Hause, Steven C., with Anne R. Kenney. *Women's Suffrage and Social Politics in the French Third Republic* (1984); Reynolds, Siân. *France between the Wars: Gender and Politics* (1996).

Bulgaria

In common with many other Balkan states, Bulgaria did not give full voting rights to women until after the upheavals of World War II, when the constitutional monarchy was replaced by a Communist govern-ment. Bulgaria was a predominantly agricultural society characterized by a high degree of gender segregation in public life and the legacy of centuries of Ottoman rule, which ended in 1878. Nonetheless, a feminist group, Bulgarski Zhenski Suiuz (BZhS) [Bulgarian Women's Union], was established in 1901 by women who had been educated in Western Europe. Most of the membership was drawn from urban, well-educated women, and by the 1930s there were 77 member-societies with over 12,000 individual members.

To begin with, the BZhS concentrated on achieving educational and professional equality. By 1903 a split developed, as socialist women sought to emphasize the importance of the class struggle for the achievement of women's full emancipation. As a result of this split, socialist women worked separately in organizations of the Left and were usually hostile to "bourgeois feminism." Nonetheless, it was the Social Democrats who were the first to demand women's suffrage when they launched a campaign for full political and economic equality for women in 1908 as part of a drive to recruit female members.

It was only after World War I that women's suffrage became acceptable to a wider group of political organizations. The BZhS and almost all the other political parties in the 1920s included women's voting rights in their manifestos. In 1937 women achieved a limited measure of enfranchisement when married, widowed, and divorced women were granted the right to elect deputies to the National Assembly, and they were able to vote in the elections of the following year. The undemocratic nature of the government in this period made this a hollow victory; women had to wait until after World War II for universal suffrage to be introduced.

Reference Nestorova, Tatyana. "Between Tradition and Modernity: Bulgarian Women during the Development of Modern Sisterhood and Society, 1878–1945" (1996).

Campoamor Rodríguez, Clara

Clara Campoamor was a leading feminist in Spain during the early part of the twentieth century and the most important single figure in ensuring that Spanish women obtained the vote in 1931.

Campoamor was born in Madrid in 1888, into a poor but respectable family. Her father died when she was very young, and she was obliged to go out to work when she was 13 to support her family. She continued to study part-time, obtaining her Bachillerato (school-leaving certificate) in 1922 and graduating in law in 1924 from the University of Madrid. At the same time, she published occasional articles in newspapers and around 1922 joined the Asociación Nacional de Mujeres Españolas (ANME) [National Association of Spanish Women], the most important feminist organization in Spain, which was dedicated to obtaining political rights for women, including the vote. Campoamor worked hard at her legal career and was active in the women's section of the Ateneo, the men's literary and debating club in Madrid, and in the Real Academia de Jurisprudencia y Legislación (Royal Academy of Jurisprudence and Legislation), in both of which she honed her debating skills and made valuable political contacts. She also played a prominent role in the Lyceum Club, the leading intellectual meeting place for the women of Madrid.

With the fall of the Spanish dictator Miguel Primo de Rivera in 1930, the Ateneo and the Colegio de Abogados de Madrid (Lawyers' Association of Madrid) became hotbeds of political activity. Campoamor, who was a member of both groups, launched herself energetically into the political fray, founding with her friend Matilde Huici the short-lived Agrupación Liberal Socialista (Socialist Liberal Alliance). When this dissolved, she became part of Acción Republicana (Republican Action), at that time a grouping of likeminded democrats. When Acción Republicana became a political party, Campoamor transferred her allegiance to the Partido Radical (Radical Party), and was elected to the first Parliament of the Second Republic in June 1931. By an ironic twist of fate, although women still had not obtained the vote, the electoral decree of 8 May 1931 had removed the statute banning women, priests, and public employees from becoming members of Parliament.

Campoamor was appointed to two parliamentary committees; she was vice-chair of the committee on labor and social security and a member of the constitutional committee, which was especially important because the first task of the new Parliament was to draw up a new constitution for the Second Republic. The issue of votes for women was a highly contentious one. The liberals and their allies saw in the enfranchisement of women an increase in the power of the clergy, whereas the socialists and the Catholic parties in general supported women's suffrage, though for entirely different motives (the socialists supported it on ideological grounds, while the Catholics counted on the support of the majority of women in any election); in either case, many more deputies voted according to their conscience rather than the party line or else abstained.

Campoamor was a wholehearted suffragist and argued clearly and intelligently in favor of women's enfranchisement. In her speeches, she claimed many times that the new Spain was a shining example of democracy, arguing that its proposed constitution was "the most free, the most advanced, and the best that now exists in the world" and that Spain's was "the first chamber in a Latin country to have raised the women's voice." Attacked by her fellow advocate and MP, Victoria Kent, who claimed that Spanish women were too ill-educated to understand political issues, Campoamor replied that Spanish women had participated in the great days of the republic in the past, and that they would be bringing into the world children who should be future republicans. She avoided the question of clerical influence skillfully, by playing on a favorite theme of the anticlericals in the Parliament, namely, the need for civil marriage and divorce. She was continually heckled in Parliament and attacked in private, and through it all she never lost her dignity, although she admitted in her autobiography later (*Mi pecado mortal*—My mortal sin) that she was frequently overcome by "moral fatigue." Finally, in October 1931, Article 36, guaranteeing women the vote as a constitutional right, was passed by 40 votes. Even then, she was forced to defend her position because at the last minute, Victoria Kent introduced an amendment that would have required women to vote in two municipal elections before receiving the right to vote for national representatives. In the meantime, the Catholic parties had withdrawn from the Parliament, so it required all Campoamor's persuasive powers to ensure that the amendment was defeated, by the narrow margin of four votes. Eight days later, on 8 December 1931, the new constitution passed into law, and all women over the age of 23 received the vote.

Judith Keene has argued forcefully that Campoamor made all the difference between the success and failure of Article 36, and that without her passionate and lucid defense of women's right to the franchise, the argument would have been lost. Certainly she paid heavily for her outspoken defense of women's rights. Many of her Radical Party colleagues no longer trusted her, feeling that she had betrayed their anticlericalism; she was denied preselection by the party in the 1933 elections, and her application to join the Izquierda Republicana (Republican Left) in 1935 was rejected. In the same year, her attempt to have the loose political grouping Unión Republicana Femenina (Women's Republican Union), which she had founded, incorporated into the electoral lists of the Popular Front was thwarted. Embittered, she left Spain at the outbreak of the Civil War and emigrated to France, and then Argentina. Her attempts to return to settle in Spain after World War II were frustrated by the claim that she had been a freemason, and having left Argentina in 1955 to settle in Switzerland, she died in Lausanne in 1972.

See also Spain.
References Campoamor Rodríguez, Clara. *Mi pecado mortal: El voto feminino y yo* (My Mortal Sin: The Woman's Vote and Me) ([1936] 1981); Fagoaga, Concha, and Paloma Saavedra. *Clara Campoamor: La Sufragista Española* (Clara Campoamor: The Spanish Suffragist) (1986); Keene, Judith. "'Into the Clean Air of the Plaza': Spanish Women Achieve the Vote in 1931" (1999).

Canada

The Canadian women's suffrage movement began in the 1880s and paralleled closely the British and American movements, achieving its goal during and immediately after World War I. Because

Canada was a federation of provinces, established by the British Parliament in the North American Act (1867) as the Dominion of Canada, women's suffrage had to be fought for at both the provincial and federal levels, the latter being achieved in 1918. However, it is important to remember that members of certain religious groups, many Canadians of Asian heritage, the Inuit, and the registered aboriginals of Canada did not receive the vote until after World War II.

The "prairie" provinces of Manitoba, Alberta, and Saskatchewan were the first to achieve women's suffrage, after relatively short campaigns. The pioneering spirit that opened up the prairies was shared by men and women alike, and this meant that many men were supportive of women's suffrage—the Grain Growers' Associations of Manitoba and Saskatchewan and the United Farmers of Alberta all supported the cause from early on. The first province of Canada to grant full political rights to women was Manitoba. Propertied women had been given the municipal vote in 1887, and in the early 1890s a group of Icelandic women founded the first suffrage association in the province. The first English-speaking organization to support the suffrage cause in Manitoba was the influential Woman's Christian Temperance Union (WCTU) through its committee on legislation and the franchise, and in 1893 the WCTU presented a petition to the provincial legislature asking for the right to vote. A bill asking for women's enfranchisement was presented to the legislature in 1894, but it came to nothing, and this ended any serious suffrage activity in Manitoba for more than a decade.

The campaign was revived in 1912 when the Winnipeg Equality League was founded by Lillian Thomas, and this organization, together with the WCTU and the Grain Growers' Association, worked toward the goal of women's enfranchise-ment. The name of the league was changed to the Manitoba Political Equality League in 1913, and a paid organizer was appointed to undertake an educational campaign that included putting banners on Winnipeg streetcars. However, the provincial government continued to oppose women's suffrage and rejected the arguments of a delegation led by the prominent suffragist Nellie McClung, who went to meet the Conservative premier on 27 January 1914. Despite this setback, the campaign continued unabated until 1915, when a new Liberal government sympathetic to women's suffrage was elected. A measure to enfranchise the women of Manitoba was introduced on 10 January 1916, and after passing its third reading, the bill received royal assent on 28 January 1916. For the first time in Canadian history women had a provincial vote.

The provinces of Alberta and Saskatchewan quickly followed Manitoba's example after relatively straightforward campaigns. The Alberta legislature, always sympathetic to women's equality, had granted unmarried women the municipal vote in 1894. The movement to obtain the provincial franchise for women in Alberta got under way in 1910, and once again the crusade was begun by the women of the WCTU. They were soon joined by the Local Councils of Women (branches of the National Council of Women of Canada), the United Farmers of Alberta, and the Edmonton Equal Franchise League, an association founded in 1913, one of whose members was the indefatigable Nellie McClung. A sympathetic Liberal premier, Arthur Sifton, pledged in September 1915 to bring in a suffrage bill, but, leaving nothing to chance, the suffragists presented a petition containing 40,000 signatures to the premier early in 1916. An equal franchise measure was introduced on 25 February 1916, giving the women of Alberta political equality with men in school, municipal, and provincial elections. The bill gained royal assent on 19 April 1916.

The campaign for equal voting rights followed a similar pattern in Saskatchewan, where once again the farmers played a part in the struggle. The Saskatchewan Grain Growers' Association supported women's suffrage, and in 1913 the wives of its members formed a separate auxiliary group that immediately began to campaign for the vote. Combined with these associations were the local franchise leagues that began appearing during 1914 and the Homemakers' Clubs, founded in 1910 under the leadership of Lillian Thomas, which were committed to political equality for women. All these suffrage organizations, including the WCTU and other sympathetic groups, came together in a federation, and in February 1915 the Provincial Suffrage Board was created. This new Suffrage Board decided to press for the parliamentary franchise immediately and organized a delegation to petition the government in May 1915. Although the administration was sympathetic and the legislature granted propertied, married women the municipal vote during 1915, further petitioning and campaigning were required before a women's suffrage bill was introduced early the following year, receiving royal assent on 14 March 1916.

The movement to obtain women's suffrage in British Columbia began in the 1880s and was largely isolationist in its approach. The campaign was led for more than 30 years by Mrs. Gordon Grant, a pioneer Canadian feminist and member of the WCTU who had helped to found the Victoria Local Council of Women. Mrs. Grant headed a delegation to the provincial legislature every year throughout the struggle, and it was she who drew up the women's suffrage petition that was presented to the legislature in 1885. Propertied women had gained the municipal vote in 1873, but the 11 bills asking for the provincial franchise for women that were introduced between 1884 and 1899 all failed, and after these setbacks the suffrage campaign went into decline. A revival of interest came in May 1911, when local suffrage organizations came together to form the nucleus of a provincial Political Equality League, which was led by Mrs. Grant from 1911 until 1917. In 1913 the league organized a substantial petition, attracted increased membership, and on 14 February sent a delegation to see the Conservative premier, but the government continued to be opposed to women's suffrage. However, the success of the suffrage campaigns in the prairie provinces—together with the promise of support from the Liberal Party, which, sensing an opportunity for political advantage, pledged to bring in an equal franchise bill if elected to government—all combined to turn the tide for the suffrage movement during 1916. The Conservative government, in response to this new alliance, promised to bring in a women's suffrage measure, but only if voters approved it in a referendum to be held at the same time as the general election, in September 1916. The Political Equality League, led by Mrs. Grant, quickly organized a Women's Suffrage Referendum League to campaign for a Liberal victory and an affirmative vote on the referendum, and on 14 September 1916 they achieved both goals. A women's suffrage bill was introduced by the new government of British Columbia on 27 March 1917 and received royal assent on 5 April the same year.

The campaign for women's suffrage in Ontario could be said to have begun with the founding of the Toronto Women's Literary Club in November 1876. More political than literary, the club was founded by Dr. Emily Howard Stowe, a pioneering woman doctor, and its aim was to educate women about their economic and political rights. In 1881, a deputation went to the provincial government to put the case for women's suffrage, and the following year the activists persuaded the Ontario legislature to pass a law giving unmarried women with property the right to vote on municipal bylaws. Because of its increasing success, the club decided to disband and change itself into an organization overtly committed to women's suffrage, and in 1883 the Toronto Women's Suffrage Association was formed. There followed a brief bombardment of the provincial government with women's suffrage petitions, but nine successive bills asking for the municipal and provincial vote, sponsored by the Liberal John Waters between 1885 and 1893, were all turned down by the legislature. After a temporary decline, the suffrage campaign was revived in 1889 when the Dominion Women's Enfranchisement Association (DWEA) was founded. Under the presidency of Dr. Stowe, the DWEA hoped to form the basis of a national network of suffrage societies. In 1891 the local branches of the DWEA received the help of the Ontario WCTU, but despite this powerful alliance, only limited progress was made by the suffrage campaign until 1907, when the DWEA changed its name to the Canadian Suffrage Association.

Successive suffrage bills that were introduced between 1905 and 1908 all failed, but in March 1909 the WCTU and the Canadian Suffrage Association joined forces to organize a huge delegation to the provincial government, where a petition containing 100,000 signatures was handed in by Dr. Augusta Stowe-Gullen, who had succeeded her mother as the president of the DWEA. That same year not only did the influential International Council of Women hold its meeting in Toronto, where its members reaffirmed their support for women's suffrage, but the city also welcomed Emmeline Pankhurst, the prominent English suffragette, who arrived on a lecture tour in November. Despite such publicity for the suffrage movement, that

year another franchise bill was defeated, as were two further bills introduced in 1910 and 1911. Early in 1910 the Toronto Local Council of Women had endorsed women's suffrage, and this meant that by 1912 Toronto had a considerable number of suffrage societies and sympathetic organizations. These included the newly formed Political Equality League, which became the National Union of Suffrage Societies of Canada in 1914, and then the National Equal Franchise Union, formed in 1915 in an only partly successful attempt to create an umbrella organization for all the provincial societies. Between 1912 and 1914, women's suffrage organizations throughout the province saw the failure of a further succession of suffrage bills asking for both the provincial franchise and the municipal franchise for married women, despite the successful efforts of Dr. Margaret Gordon of the local Toronto Suffrage Association (and later the president of the Canadian Suffrage Association) to persuade local councils to support a municipal franchise measure. The Conservative government continued to oppose further suffrage bills introduced in 1915 and 1916; however, early in 1917 the Liberal Party officially endorsed women's suffrage, and the Conservative premier appeared to experience a dramatic conversion to the cause (which he attributed to women's heroic war work) during the hearing of provincial franchise bills in February 1917. Bills to grant all women the provincial franchise and married women the municipal franchise were rushed through the Ontario legislature, and received royal assent on 12 April 1917.

Traditionally, the maritime provinces of New Brunswick, Nova Scotia, Prince Edward Island, and Newfoundland were politically and socially conservative, and this was reflected in attitudes toward the enfranchisement of women. The campaign in Nova Scotia began in 1887 when a bill to allow unmarried, propertied women to vote in municipal elections was passed, but this reform did not originate from women's groups but from the legislature itself. This was followed by a number of petitions asking for women's suffrage, most of them organized by the WCTU as part of their campaign for prohibition, and these activities resulted in six unsuccessful attempts to bring in suffrage bills between 1891 and 1897, the last one being decisively rejected by a 26 to 6 vote. These setbacks meant that involvement in the women's suffrage issue declined in both the legislature and the women's organizations until 1916, when the successful campaigns in the prairie provinces revived interest in the subject. Early in 1917 the Social Service Congress national convention held in Halifax passed a resolution urging the government of Nova Scotia to grant women the vote, and at the same time the Halifax Local Council of Women, which represented 41 women's organizations, voted unanimously for the extension of the parliamentary franchise to all duly qualified adults, regardless of sex. On 14 March 1917 a bill was introduced to give women the provincial franchise on either their own or their husband's property qualifications, but despite tremendous pressure from the WCTU and the Halifax Local Council of Women, the bill was blocked by the Liberal premier of the legislature. The failure of this bill produced the only genuine suffrage organization that Nova Scotia ever had when Dr. Eliza Ritchie formed the Nova Scotia Equal Franchise League in the late spring of 1917. At the first annual meeting of the league, held in Halifax in January 1918, it was decided to hold a house-to-house canvass, and to organize a petition to present to the legislature, which had decided to introduce an equal franchise bill in response to the victories for women's suffrage that had been achieved, not only in some of the other Canadian provinces, but also in Britain on 6 February 1918. The bill was introduced on 28 February and received royal assent on 26 April 1918.

The campaign to achieve the provincial franchise for women throughout Canada was given a valuable boost in 1918, when a bill to give women the federal vote received royal assent on 24 May. But the drive to obtain the women's franchise at the federal level had began much earlier, with the introduction of successive bills between 1883 and 1885 by the suffragist Conservative prime minister, Sir John Macdonald, in an attempt to establish a uniform federal franchise that would include propertied widows and unmarried women. Despite a favorable response to the women's suffrage proposal, Macdonald's efforts failed, and when control of the federal franchise passed to the provinces in the Franchise Act of 1898, interest in the subject waned because it was no longer the responsibility of the federal Parliament. There was no further serious discussion of the federal women's suffrage question until February 1916, when an amendment to the Dominion Elections Act was introduced to give the federal franchise to women who had the provincial vote (Manitoba had granted equal voting rights the month before). The amendment was defeated, but the question had returned to the agenda. On 16 May 1917 the federal parliament held a debate on the women's suffrage question, in which there was agreement about the justice of the women's demands. The Liberal opposition leader, Sir Wilfrid Laurier, suggested that the federal franchise law should be amended to include those women who had the provincial vote, and, unexpectedly, Prime Minister Sir Robert Borden agreed on the need to enfranchise women.

However, no action was taken until an opportunity was provided for women to obtain the federal vote during World War I. The controversial Military Voters Act and the Wartime Elections Act of 1917 enfranchised all women who were serving in the armed forces, mainly nurses, and some 500,000 women who had close relatives in the armed services, provided they possessed the same provincial voting qualifications as men. These measures were followed by the successful introduction of a Women's Franchise Bill, which was given royal assent on 24 May 1918. This bill extended the federal vote to those women who were British subjects, at least 21 years of age, and possessed the same qualifications for provincial voting required for the male voters in their province or in the Yukon and Northwest Territories. In 1920 the Dominion Elections Act freed federal voting from provincial voting qualifications by establishing a separate federal voting list, with voting requirements that were the same for men and women—they had to be 21 years of age or older and have British citizenship and residence qualifications. However, it was not until after World War II that universal suffrage existed in Canada, for until then, Canadians of Chinese, Japanese, and East Indian parentage had no vote unless they had served in the armed forces. Members of certain religious sects that were exempt from military service were enfranchised shortly afterwards, and in 1950 the federal franchise was extended to the Inuit, followed by a final group, the registered Indians of Canada, on 1 July 1960.

When women received the federal vote in May 1918, there were still some provinces where women did not have the provincial vote. Nova Scotia had granted women the provincial vote in April 1918, but the other maritime provinces still lagged behind. In 1886 unmarried, propertied women in New Brunswick had received the municipal vote after women's groups and town councils had petitioned the provincial legislature. However, little further action was taken until 1894, when 18 women in Saint John formed the New Brunswick Women's Enfranchisement As-

sociation, voting at their second meeting to become a branch of the DWEA. This small group of women continued with their campaign throughout the 1890s, organizing petitions and hosting the prominent American suffragist Julia Ward Howe, who spoke at a public meeting in Saint John in 1896. The WCTU also played a part, helping to petition the provincial legislature whenever a women's suffrage bill or resolution was being introduced, which happened every year from 1894 until 1899, with the exception of 1896 and 1898. Although these bills were rejected, the women of the New Brunswick Enfranchisement Association continued to meet. Also disappointing was the lack of support from the Local Council of Women in Saint John, at least until it changed its policy in 1910.

The struggle continued after the turn of the century. Although women activists continued to present petitions, sent two delegations to see the Conservative premier, and lobbied the provincial legislature, the three suffrage bills that were introduced in 1909, 1912, and 1913 all failed. Finally, in January 1917, inspired by the progress made on women's suffrage in other provinces, the New Brunswick Enfranchisement Association began to plan a new campaign, which included distributing literature, gathering further petitions, and holding public meetings. Despite these efforts, a suffrage bill introduced in May 1917 was killed at the committee stage. The women had to wait until 1919, when the Liberal government, influenced by the suffrage legislation passed in Nova Scotia a year earlier, introduced a women's suffrage bill on 21 March. Sadly, the New Brunswick Enfranchisement Association had ceased operating by January 1919, just three months before the bill received royal assent on 17 April 1919.

Prince Edward Island was the only province in which women appeared to show little interest in the question of women's suffrage. Apart from a brief debate in the provincial legislature in March 1893 and a women's suffrage petition presented by the local WCTU in May 1894, the issue was not seriously discussed until 24 April 1918, when the legislature gave unanimous support to a resolution asking for the introduction of a suffrage measure. However, no women's suffrage bill was introduced, despite the fact that women had received the federal vote a month after the resolution was passed. In September 1919 the Liberals were returned to power after promising to introduce a suffrage measure, but again nothing happened. At this point, the Women's Liberal Club launched a campaign that involved lobbying the legislature and holding women's meetings, and these activities stirred the government into action. In April 1922 a bill was introduced giving women the provincial vote, and on 3 May 1922 it received royal assent.

The small-scale campaign for women's suffrage in the self-governing colony of Newfoundland achieved success in a comparatively short time. After World War I, spurred on by the suffrage victories in the other maritime provinces, the women of the Old Colony Club, led by Mrs. A. G. Gosling, decided to form a group dedicated to achieving political equality for women. The new group was successful in achieving the municipal franchise in 1921 but found it more difficult to persuade the government to support a wider franchise. On 20 May 1920 they presented a petition of 1,700 signatures to the legislature, but a suffrage bill presented later that year was defeated. The women presented a further petition in 1921, this time containing the signatures of 7,485 women, an amazing total for an island with so many remote settlements. The Liberal government was resistant to any change in the legislation, and the bill was thrown out. However, with the support of the island's two newspapers, the women persisted with

their campaign, and when a new Conservative government came into office in 1924, a suffrage bill giving the vote to women aged 25 years of age and over was introduced into the legislature and became law on 13 April 1925. When Newfoundland renounced self-government and became part of Canada by the Terms of Union in 1948, the age limit was reduced to 21 years for women voters.

The women of Quebec had to wait until 1940 to receive the vote, mainly because of the political and social history of the province. One of the main factors that influenced the women's suffrage campaign was the fact that Quebec was a French-speaking colony acquired by Britain in 1763, which meant that long-standing religious and cultural differences between the English-speaking and French-speaking populations had always been a source of tension. Interestingly, some women had voted in Quebec up until 1849, when the word *male* was inserted into the franchise legislation. After this, no provincial suffrage bill was introduced into the legislature until 1927, but women had been campaigning for their enfranchisement for some time before that. Some progress had been made in 1892, when the municipal vote had been granted to unmarried women taxpayers (although a local town or city council could choose not to implement the measure).

The campaign for the provincial vote began in earnest in 1909, when the Montreal Local Council of Women officially approved the principle of equal political rights for women. Later that same year they inaugurated a lecture series, bringing prominent suffrage speakers from England, including, in December 1911, Emmeline Pankhurst. As a result of these activities, the Montreal Suffrage Association was formed in April 1913, and there began a campaign that included the distribution of suffrage literature, the organization of petitions, and interviews with the leaders of both the federal and provincial governments. After women received the federal vote in May 1918, the predominantly English-speaking membership of the Montreal Suffrage Association came to the conclusion that the campaign would only succeed if English- and French-speaking women formed a united front. With that aim in mind, they disbanded their association on 22 May 1919, but the new suffrage organization they had hoped for did not emerge until January 1922. The new Provincial Franchise Committee, under the dual leadership of Mme. Gérin-Lajoie and Mrs. Walter Lyman, decided to initiate an educational campaign and to send a delegation to Quebec on 9 February 1922 to lobby the new Liberal premier, Louis Taschereau. His complete opposition to women's suffrage was disheartening, and the Provincial Franchise Committee wound down its activities until 1927, when the introduction of the province's first suffrage bill spurred them into action. Unfortunately, this revival coincided with a split in the committee, which resulted in the resignation of one of its most active members, Idola Saint Jean, who then formed a new group, L'Alliance canadienne pour le vote des femmes du Québec (the Canadian Alliance for the Quebec Women's Vote), a more militant grassroots organization. In 1928 Thérèse Casgrain became the sole president of the Provincial Franchise Committee, and for the next 12 years she led the suffrage movement in Quebec during a period that saw innumerable provincial women's franchise measures fail before victory was achieved in 1940. In November 1929 the Franchise Committee changed its name to the League for Women's Rights, and during the 1930s its activities included sending delegations to the legislature, distributing leaflets, and conducting an imaginative sandwich-board campaign. The league also tried to reach rural women, most notably by using the radio—under Casgrain's

direction a weekly program called *Femina* was broadcast to women all over the province.

The debate on the women's suffrage bill introduced by Dr. Anatole Plant in February 1933 highlighted most of the arguments against women's enfranchisement that persisted in the legislature during the 1930s—that it was against the teaching of the Roman Catholic Church, that it would overturn the social order, and that where women already had the vote, it had brought no apparent benefit. Like all the others, this bill failed, but both Casgrain and Saint Jean believed that their educational campaign was beginning to succeed. Further publicity was achieved when a petition of 10,000 signatures was sent to Britain to be presented to King George V on the occasion of his silver jubilee in 1935. However, any hopes that a change of government might help their cause were dashed when, after defeating the Liberals in the provincial elections of 1936, the Union Nationale came to power under an antisuffrage premier, Maurice Duplessis. The League for Women's Rights decided to launch a further publicity drive to attract the interest of rural women, and it also put considerable pressure on the Liberal opposition to take up the suffrage cause. These efforts succeeded when the Liberal Party adopted women's suffrage as part of its program in June 1938, and when the Duplessis government was defeated in the 1939 elections, the women's organizations felt that a successful end to their campaigning was in sight. Despite further opposition from the Roman Catholic hierarchy, the new Liberal premier introduced a suffrage bill on 9 April 1940, and after a successful third reading it was given immediate royal assent on 25 April 1940. Quebec was the last province to grant women the provincial vote, and this was the final achievement of the women's suffrage campaign in Canada.

The Canadian women's suffrage movement started late compared to those of other English-speaking countries, but success came relatively swiftly and without the use of violence. Although most Canadian suffragists came from middle-class backgrounds, there was support for the suffrage cause from the Women's Labour League (WLL), a working-class organization that was essentially an extension of the male trade union movement. By 1910, the WLL had branches in several cities, including Toronto and Winnipeg, working to protect women's employment rights and to win equal pay for equal work. The WLL came into conflict with the suffrage societies over issues like prohibition, which they opposed for fear of the imposition of a middle-class morality, but they continued to support the principle of female enfranchisement as a means to achieve their aims. The majority of Canadian suffragists were Anglo-Saxon, Protestant, middle-class, well-educated women, committed to social and moral reform. As a result, most politicians came to accept their enfranchisement as inevitable, and even potentially beneficial to the community.

See also Casgrain, Thérèse; Catholicism; Local Franchise; McClung, Nellie; National Council of Women of Canada; Pankhurst, Emmeline; Protestantism; Stowe, Emily Howard; Woman's Christian Temperance Union.
References Bacchi, Carol Lee. *Liberation Deferred? The Ideas of the English-Canadian Suffragists, 1877–1918* (1983); Cleverdon, Catherine L. *The Woman Suffrage Movement in Canada* (1974).

Casgrain, Thérèse

A prominent leader of the women's suffrage movement in Quebec, Thérèse Forget (1896–1981) was born in Montreal into a wealthy family. In 1916 she married Liberal lawyer and politician Pierre-François Casgrain.

Thérèse Casgrain was a founding member of the Provincial Franchise Committee, which was formed in Quebec in 1922. She campaigned for women's suffrage throughout the 1920s and 1930s at a time when numerous suffrage bills met with failure. After a split in the Provincial Franchise Committee in 1927, when Idola Saint Jean left to form L'Alliance canadienne pour le vote des femmes du Québec (the Canadian Alliance for the Quebec Women's Vote), Casgrain became the sole president of the committee, which changed its name in 1929 to the League for Women's Rights.

Casgrain was particularly anxious to reach out to the rural women of Quebec, and with that aim in mind she hosted a popular radio program called *Femina*, which was broadcast to women all over the province during the 1930s. Casgrain and her colleagues continued to lobby the legislature on the question of women's suffrage until, on 25 April 1940, the women of Quebec won their battle for the vote. Casgrain went on to become a prominent politician and antinuclear campaigner, and in 1970, after a distinguished career, she was appointed to the Senate.

See also Canada.
References Casgrain, Thérèse. *A Woman in a Man's World* (1972); Cleverdon, Catherine L. *The Woman Suffrage Movement in Canada* (1974).

Cat and Mouse Act

The Cat and Mouse Act (officially the Prisoner's Temporary Discharge for Ill Health Act) was passed in Britain by a Liberal government in 1913 to counter hunger strikes by suffragettes imprisoned for militant action. It empowered Home Secretary Reginald McKenna to release a hunger-striking prisoner until she had recovered her health, after which she could be rearrested and returned to prison with no remission on her sentence.

The act was dubbed the Cat and Mouse Act by Frederick Pethick-Lawrence and it received a lot of publicity, becoming the

Emmeline Pankhurst and Christabel Pankhurst in prison dress; Christabel Pankhurst spoke out against the Cat and Mouse Act in 1913. (Ann Ronan Picture Library)

subject of numerous cartoons. Its terms were much debated. The *Daily Mail* pointed out that the act enabled a month's sentence to be prolonged to "a sentence of unbearable torment" (Tickner, 1987, 136), and Christabel Pankhurst described it as an "unprecedented measure of repression," preferred by the Liberal government to giving women the vote. However, McKenna argued that it would be both inhumane and tactically unsound to allow women to martyr themselves for crimes such as breaking windows and burning empty houses. On the other hand, he maintained, neither should they be allowed to shorten their sentences by going on a hunger strike.

The Cat and Mouse Act was never en-

forced in Ireland, partly because popular opinion there was against it, seeing it as a "dangerous weapon of political oppression in the hands of any Government" (Ward, 1982). Perhaps more importantly, the British government wished to avoid too much controversy while the issue of Home Rule for Ireland remained unresolved.

See also Britain; Imagery; Ireland; Militancy; Pankhurst, Christabel; Pethick-Lawrence, Frederick.
References Liddington, Jill, and Jill Norris. *One Hand Tied behind Us: The Rise of the Woman's Suffrage Movement* (1978); Tickner, Lisa, *The Spectacle of Women: Imagery of the Suffrage Campaign, 1907–1914* (1987); Ward, Margaret. "'Suffrage First—Above All Else!': An Account of the Irish Suffrage Movement" (1982).

Catholicism

Many historians have argued that Catholicism formed a major block to the progress of women's suffrage in certain countries and that most supporters of feminism were of a Protestant or anticlerical persuasion. They point out that the Catholic Church offered fulfilling roles for middle-class, unmarried women within the ranks of the clergy as nuns, while encouraging married women to direct their energies inwardly toward spiritual goals and discouraging them from involvement in public affairs. Although the influence of the Church was apparent in some antisuffrage campaigns, the relationship between Catholicism and the fight for the vote was often more complex than such a conclusion suggests.

In European countries with large Catholic populations such as France, Italy, and Belgium, where the vote was achieved much later than in most Protestant countries, feminists saw the Catholic Church as one of the main obstacles to the achievement of women's rights. Yet paradoxically, their own anticlericalism also blocked the progress of the suffrage movement. For example, in France, two leaders of the women's movement, Léon Richer and Marie Deraismes, initially opposed giving women the vote on the grounds that it would lead to political Catholicism and a return to monarchical rule. Deraismes later changed her mind, but Richer, founder in 1882 of the moderate feminist group the French League for Women's Rights, continued to oppose radical measures that would endanger the republic. He argued that the woman's vote must wait until women had received a secular education that would liberate them from the influence of the Church. Similarly, in Belgium in 1902, fear of the religious fanaticism of Catholic women led both Socialists and Liberals to drop women's suffrage from their program. In Italy, the suffrage movement recruited very few women and gained support only from socialist politicians and a few liberal intellectuals. Most other politicians were put off by the fact that women would in the main vote Catholic, and the rise of a mass Catholic political party after World War I reduced support for the suffrage still further.

In areas of North America with strong Catholic communities, the Church gave its support to antisuffrage movements. For example, in 1915 a suffrage referendum in Massachusetts, where there were many Catholic voters, won just over 35 percent in favor of the vote. Although the Catholic Church was officially neutral, leading clerics had made powerful statements to antisuffrage associations against the proposed bill. During the 1930s, opposition to the vote was also encouraged by the Catholic Church hierarchy in Quebec, which in 1940 became the last province in Canada to grant women the vote. Countries in South America, such as Peru, Chile, and Colombia, where the power of the Catholic Church was particularly strong, were also among the last to grant women the vote. In Peru, women joining an early feminist group in the 1920s were shamed

by being called Protestant. In Colombia, the Catholic Church organized confessional unions in order to limit the influence of leftist organizations over women in the labor force. In Chile, as in France, concern that women were controlled by parish priests also explains the reluctance of liberal feminists there to push too hard for the vote. For example, in 1922 in a letter to the Uruguayan feminist leader Paulina Luisi, pioneering Chilean feminist Amanda Labarca wondered "if women's suffrage in Chile would favor liberal evolution of the country or would set it back by strengthening the size and power of the clerical-conservative party" (Ehrick, 1998, 412).

Yet in some Catholic countries the influence of the Church is less clearly established. In Ireland, Catholicism did little to prevent a strong militant suffrage movement. It is also unclear how far ordinary Catholics necessarily supported the views of their religious leaders. For example, in Australia some (though not all) Catholic priests spoke out against the vote, yet Victorian suffrage leader Vida Goldstein maintained that in a secret ballot taken at a Catholic fête in 1900, a majority favored woman suffrage, with a vote of 328 to 281.

See also Australia; Belgium; Canada; Chile; Colombia; France; Goldstein, Vida; Ireland; Latin America and the Caribbean; Liberalism; Luisi, Paulina; Peru; United States of America.

References Chaney, Elsa M. *Supermadre: Women in Politics in Latin America* (1979); DuBois, Ellen. "Woman Suffrage around the World: Three Phases of Internationalism" (1994); Ehrick, Christine. "*Madrinas* and Missionaries: Uruguay and the Pan-American Women's Movement" (1998); Evans, Richard J. *The Feminists, Women's Emancipation Movement in Europe, America and Australasia, 1840–1920* (1977); Flexner, Eleanor. *Century of Struggle: The Woman's Rights Movement in the United States* (1975); Lavrin, Asunción. "Suffrage in South America: Arguing a Difficult Cause" (1994); Oldfield, Audrey. *Woman Suffrage in Australia, A Gift or a Struggle?* (1992).

Catt, Carrie Chapman

Carrie Chapman Catt (1859–1947) was a leading member of both the American and international women's suffrage movements. She was elected twice as president of the National American Woman Suffrage Association (NAWSA), went on to found the League of Women Voters in 1920, and also worked tirelessly to develop the International Woman Suffrage Alliance (IWSA). In the years before World War I, she became one of the most influential speakers on women's suffrage in the world.

Born in Wisconsin, Catt grew up in Iowa, becoming in 1880 the only woman, out of a class of 17, to graduate from Iowa State University. Following the death of her first husband in 1886, she married George Catt in 1890. At around the same time, she decided to dedicate her life to the women's suffrage movement, emerging as a full-time activist in 1889. After successfully leading the NAWSA campaign in Colorado, she was promoted in 1895 to the chair of the new National Organization Committee, where she demonstrated her organizational and leadership skills. Catt's achievements were small in her first term as NAWSA president between 1900 and 1904 and she also faced difficulties after power struggles in the organization, so she gave up the post on the grounds of her own and her husband's ill health. She then gave most of her time to the IWSA and was impressed by the energy of the British militants. When she returned from the alliance's congress in London in 1909, she was determined to introduce new life into the American movement without undertaking militant activities. In New York, she formed the Woman Suffrage Party as an affiliate of NAWSA and encouraged women in other states to do the same and to begin to campaign more vigorously for the vote at state level. Her experience proved invaluable for her second term as president of NAWSA from 1915 to 1920.

Carrie Chapman Catt, president of the National American Woman Suffrage Association, finally witnessed suffrage for U.S. women in 1920 (photo 1914). (Library of Congress)

Catt was an inspirational figure in both the national and local state campaigns, particularly in the battle for the women's vote in New York State. Following this important victory in 1917, Catt maintained pressure on the Senate to obtain the approval of three quarters of the states to amend the federal Constitution. In 1920, after 30 years of campaigning, she led the movement to victory.

Catt's role was equally important in the international movement; she was the leading founder of the International Woman Suffrage Alliance in 1904 and its first president. She was repeatedly reelected to this post until 1923, when she requested to be elevated to the position of honorary chair. She formed close friendships with other leading women activists, in particular the Dutch suffragists Aletta Jacobs and Rosa Manus, and helped to inspire younger women with enthusiasm for the cause. Catt traveled widely, inspired by the progressive assumption that American values should be exported to the rest of the world. She made contact with suffrage leaders throughout the world and offered inspiration for many widely dispersed suffrage movements—from South America to Japan—both before and after the U.S. federal vote was won. In 1911–1912, for example, she went on a world tour with Aletta Jacobs in order to stimulate interest in the suffrage movement. The tour did have some positive results; for instance, in South Africa local societies came together for the first time in a national convention, and in Egypt an effort was made to form a suffrage committee. The tour also helped to give the IWSA a new perspective. At the 1913 congress in Budapest, Jacobs presented a banner from Chinese suffragists to demonstrate their recent affiliation with the alliance. Some scholars have accused Catt of cultural imperialism, and she did tend to see herself as a missionary to countries with less developed suffrage movements. On the other hand, her strong leadership and dedication to the suffrage campaign were an inspiration to women, in particular up to the end of World War I.

See also Friendship Networks; Imperialism; International Links; International Woman Suffrage Alliance; Jacobs, Aletta; Japan; Latin America and the Caribbean; National American Woman Suffrage Association; Pan-American Women's Conference; Pan-American Women's Movement; Peru.
References Bosch, Mineke, with Annemarie Kloosterman. *Politics and Friendship: Letters from the International Woman Suffrage Alliance, 1902–1942* (1990); Ehrick, Christine. "*Madrinas* and Missionaries: Uruguay and the Pan-American Women's Movement" (1998); Fowler, Robert Booth. *Carrie Catt: Feminist Politician* (1986).

The Cause

The Cause, written by Ray Strachey (1887–1940) and published in 1928, is one of the best known and most exten-sively cited early histories of the British women's movement. Written mainly as a biographical history of outstanding women, the book analyzes women's un-equal social position and how they chal-lenged it from the late eighteenth century up to the achievement of an equal fran-chise in 1928. Ray Strachey (née Costel-loe) was born into a distinguished Ameri-can Quaker family, the Pearsall Smiths, and was educated at Newnham College, Cambridge, where she studied mathemat-ics, and then at Bryn Mawr in the United States. While she was still a student at Cambridge, Strachey became involved in suffrage politics and worked closely with Millicent Fawcett, who was the leader of the constitutionalist group the National Union of Women's Suffrage Societies (NUWSS). After the vote was won, Stra-chey remained interested in politics, stand-ing three times for Parliament as an Inde-pendent candidate and, after 1921, working for the League of Nations.

The book provides a lively account of the women's movement that is full of in-sights drawn from personal experience, but as Kathryn Dodd argues, it needs to be seen in the context of liberal and feminist politics in the 1920s, in which it was pro-duced. Thus, the book emphasizes "ex-ceptional, civilized and rational women," who used constitutional means to achieve their goals, and especially the leadership of Millicent Fawcett. Members of the NUWSS who failed to support Fawcett, in particular the peace campaigners during World War I, receive little attention, and the militant movement and the involve-ment of working-class women, along with their specific needs, tend to be marginal-ized from the story. Dodd suggests, there-fore, that rather than using *The Cause* as a repository of facts, historians need to read the text in more complex ways, tak-ing account of the moment in which it was produced in order to understand its signif-icance as historical evidence.

See also Britain; Fawcett, Millicent Garrett; National Union of Women's Suffrage Societies.
References Dodd, Kathryn. "Cultural Politics and Women's Historical Writing: The Case of Ray Strachey's *The Cause*" (1990); Strachey, Ray. *The Cause: A Short History of the Women's Movement in Great Britain* (1928).

Chile

Although literate women over 21 were allowed to vote in local municipal elections in Chile from 1934, it was to be another 14 years before all women were granted the national franchise in 1948.

As in many other countries, in Chile the constitution of 1837, which granted the vote to literate citizens over 21, did not specifically exclude women. In 1875 several women attempted unsuccessfully to register as voters, but the issue was not taken up in Congress until 1917. In that year, young members of the Conservative Party sponsored a bill to reform the franchise in which the phrase "of both sexes" was added to the article entitling citizens to vote. This bill, which took most Chileans by surprise, is believed to have been influenced by a newly formed middle-class women's organization, the Club de Señoras, and this attempt at reform became a source of inspiration to women seeking greater political representation during the 1920s.

There was much discussion and debate about how changes in women's economic and social roles would influence the nation's future, and this encouraged the formation of a number of women's organizations during the 1920s. However, many of these groups had a moderate program of reform, believing that women should be preparing to take a greater part in national public life by first performing civic duties at a municipal level. There was also some concern by liberal feminists, such as Amanda Labarca, that women in Chile were too dominated by the influence of Catholic priests and that a successful suffrage campaign would result in a conservative government dominated by the Church. Some groups, such as the Partido Cívico Femenino, saw political emancipation as part of women's social and moral mission, as mothers and educators, to look after the interests of the family. Indeed, this position remained central to mainstream Chilean feminism. Interest in women's suffrage declined during the latter half of the 1920s, when a constitutional crisis resulted in the military control of government under President General Carlos Ibáñez del Campo.

Economic and political instability in Chile spurred women's wider mobilization during the 1930s, as more educated professional women became involved in social work and social reform. During the early 1930s, suffrage became the main issue for most feminist groups motivated by concern about the loss of a constitutional framework and military manipulation. In 1931 women activists marched to protest the Ibáñez regime and, after his fall in July of that year, expanded their political program and gained more support from men. The leading women's group at this time was Unión Femenina de Chile, which attempted to unite all classes and by 1932 had the support of 1,000 women of varying backgrounds. Leaders such as Delia Ducoing maintained links with feminist leaders in North America and in Argentina, Cuba, Peru, Colombia, and Mexico, but they also distanced themselves from Anglo-American feminism, preferring to adopt a softer, more overtly feminine persona.

The municipal suffrage was gained for women in 1934 in a political climate of reconstruction. The literacy qualification was applied to male as well as female voters, reducing the numbers of men and women eligible to vote to an educated elite. Women remained excluded from national elections, but most Chilean feminists were satisfied with this limited achievement. However, by the second municipal election, some more politically conscious women began to campaign for full political rights in order to influence national policy making. By the 1940s full suffrage had become their main objective.

Women's new role in political life was marked by the formation of women's branches within existing political parties. Equally significant was the revival of middle-class feminist organizations, most notably the Partido Femenino and a new umbrella group, the Movimiento Pro-Emancipación de las Mujeres de Chile (MEMCH) [Pro-emancipation Movement for the Women of Chile], which aimed to appeal to women of all social classes, especially working women. Feminist organizations promoted their policies mainly through their publications, but they also gained support through provincial branches, annual assemblies, speaking tours, and the establishment of facilities for working mothers.

The 1930s were a decade of growth, mobilization, and activity for feminist groups. In the 1938 elections, MEMCH supported the Popular Front candidate, Pedro Aguirre Cerda, who was elected as president and promised to give women greater participation in educational, economic, and administrative affairs. However, the bill he introduced that would have enabled women to participate in national elections was dropped after his death and the dissolution of the Popular Front in late 1941.

Women's organizations struggled to survive and keep focused on obtaining the national franchise during the 1940s, but although women were elected as mayors and councillors, a common front was not revived until 1944. In 1945 a new group, the Federación Chilena de Instituciones Femeninas, which had the support of prewar suffrage leaders, joined with the revived MEMCH in a new suffrage project. Chilean deputies influenced by a wider postwar trend recommended national suffrage in 1946, but it took a further two years of debate and pressure from the president before full female enfranchisement became law on 15 December 1948.

See also Catholicism; Citizenship; Ducoing, Delia; Latin America and the Caribbean.
References Ehrick, Christine. "*Madrinas* and Missionaries: Uruguay and the Pan-American Women's Movement" (1998); Lavrin, Asunción. *Women, Feminism and Social Change in Argentina, Chile and Uruguay, 1890–1940* (1995).

China

Chinese women were granted the vote in 1949 soon after the Communist revolution had proclaimed a People's Republic of China under Mao Ze-dong. Article 6 of the Common Program, adopted by the People's Political Consultative Conference, offered women full emancipation, stating that "women shall enjoy equal rights with men in political, economic, cultural, educational, and social life" (Croll, 1978, 223). The right to vote, already exercised by women in some regions before the revolution, was now guaranteed to all, although the extent to which it could be exercised thereafter remained limited by Communist Party ideology and regulations.

An organized and militant women's suffrage movement had existed in China during the first part of the century, although its history is not well known. This movement grew out of early feminist initiatives in the 1900s. These were initially concerned with such issues as foot binding and female education and were led by upper-class and foreign women. However, Chinese women also joined the revolutionary movement to overthrow the Manchu dynasty in 1911 and formed women's military fighting corps. Once a republic had been formed, with a constitution that aimed to introduce democratic practices, women began organizing to assert their rights to elect and be represented

In February 1927 in Wuham, Soong Ching Ling founded a women's political training institute and was photographed with trainees at the opening-day ceremony. (Ann Ronan Picture Library)

on the new legislative bodies. Women's military organizations were disbanded and many were turned into associations whose primary aim was to fight for the vote. Among the new organizations were the Chinese Women's Franchise Association, the Chinese Women's Cooperative Association, in Shanghai, and the Women's Suffragette Association, in Beijing. Some of these groups, such as the Chinese Suffragette Society, led by Tang Junying, modeled themselves on the British movement and published magazines containing translations of foreign articles and stories about Western suffrage activities. In 1912 women's groups from 18 provinces met in Nanking to establish the Woman's Suffrage Alliance, which lobbied the National Legislature to grant women equal rights with men.

Women in some of these groups made militant attacks on provincial and national legislative assemblies. For example, in 1912 Tang Junying led women in a three-day attack on the National Assembly in Nanking. Arming themselves with pistols, they attacked constables and broke windows in imitation of the British Women's Social and Political Union. The *North China Herald* reported that parties of suffragettes had also besieged the Pro-

visional Assembly in Beijing and were threatening violence if women were not granted the vote. In Canton, the Provisional Provincial Assembly had originally recognized women as voters and members but soon changed its mind. Suffragettes protested, holding meetings of up to 1,000 women and sending deputations to the Assembly, citing the examples of Queen Victoria and the last empress, Cixi, as exemplary women citizens. They, too, eventually resorted to violent invasions of the legislature, but with little success. The Permanent Assembly in Canton, elected in 1913, had no women members.

Giving women the vote was perceived by many people as a threat to the traditional family, one that would upset the balance of power within the home and in wider society. One government official stated: "If one recognizes the importance of the bond between husband and wife, then the doctrine of legal rights between men and women is impractical" (Croll, 1978, 75).

The suffrage movement was the first collective expression of feminist ideas in China, but although its activities attracted considerable publicity, its members came from a fairly narrow class and regional base. The great majority were from an educated elite based in urban schools in the cities of Beijing, Shanghai, Canton, and Tientsin, where students were being exposed to radical ideas from the West. Neither urban working women nor the rural peasantry joined the movement. It was also a short-lived phenomenon. By 1913 a military government had displaced the ruling Guomindang under Sun Yat-sen, and suffragette activities were crushed by the forces of conservatism. Women were banned from publishing magazines, joining political groups, and attending political meetings.

Interest in the role and status of women revived toward the end of the decade, stimulated partly by a Western intellectual emphasis on the rights and obligations of the individual. An explosion of new periodicals identified "the woman question" as a major issue of debate. From 1920, women began to enter institutions of higher education and the professions and some started running their own businesses. The focus of feminist activities in this period was now less upon gaining the vote than on participating in the life of the nation through patriotic activities. For example, in 1919 thousands of women mobilized in mass demonstrations and boycotted Japanese goods to protest the persecution of China by the Japanese.

Women's rights associations reappeared in the early 1920s; the vote was one of their main demands and they achieved victories in some areas. For example, the Hunan Women's Association, founded in 1921, sent a delegate to the committee that was debating the new provincial constitution to state their case for the right to vote and be elected. Their efforts were rewarded, as Hunan became the first province to recognize equal rights for women in its constitution. After public demonstrations by suffrage groups, some of which involved violence, women in Canton, Guangdong, and Zhejiang Provinces also won the right to vote for and be elected to their provincial assemblies.

In Beijing, two women's rights organizations were formed at this time. The Women's Suffrage Association, started by students in 1921, identified suffrage as its main goal and the other group, the Women's Rights League, saw suffrage as part of a wider program of rights to be achieved. In 1924, Sun Yat-sen called a National Congress in Beijing to prepare a permanent national constitution, but he denied women the right to attend or send representatives. This exclusion prompted the two groups to form a new organization to fight for women's representation and rights at a national level. They strongly opposed the provision on suffrage written into the draft regulations of the National Congress, confining the vote to men over 25 with a proper education. However, when women began to march in support of their demands, military forces were called in once again and public meetings were prohibited, heralding another period of feminist suppression.

As in the earlier period of suffragette activity, the 1920s suffrage movement never succeeded in attracting a following beyond an educated intellectual elite, and their demands seemed irrelevant to the majority of women. This was particularly true of the growing numbers of urban working women, whose interests were mainly in improving their economic conditions through the trade union movement and the newly formed Communist Party. The disparity between the class and economic interests of the two groups of women made it difficult for them to fight for a common goal. By 1925 Western influence in China was waning and women activists had turned to the Nationalist and Communist Parties, which were mobilizing increasing numbers of working women.

The newly formed Chinese Communist Party had made the emancipation of women one of its policy platforms, and in 1923 it had formally recognized the unlimited right of all to vote regardless of sex. But Xiang Jingyu, leader of the women's section, was also critical of the isolated "feminist only" tendencies of the woman's movement and argued that the vote was irrelevant to women under the current social system. She recommended that women instead join working men in overthrowing imperialist rule as a first step to their emancipation and criticized suffragettes for ignoring the revolutionary movement that should, she argued, be a prerequisite to suffrage.

In 1923 the Nationalist Guomindang government under Sun Yat-sen had entered into an alliance with the Communist Party, and both parties encouraged the growth of a women's movement that would support the nationalist revolution. However, by 1927, when the alliance broke down, the right-wing element of the Guomindang under Chiang Kai-Shek launched an offensive against women's groups suspected of Communist sympathies. Women with bobbed hair (which symbolized the liberated woman) were persecuted, and many were killed.

Despite this repression, the Guomindang government still claimed to champion women's emancipation, and in 1930 it issued a new civil code that gave women equal civil, political, and property rights. Although this was celebrated as a victory by leading feminists and the position of urban educated women did improve, in practice, political activity was discouraged and few women in the countryside knew they had any rights. Moreover, women were urged to concern themselves only with matters pertaining to social welfare, education, and the family. They were excluded from the Congress of Representatives and in the Draft of a Constitution for China, published in May 1936, no provision was made for their representation in the National Congress of the Representatives of the People. Furthermore, no woman was elected in any of the elections that were held throughout the country.

However, by the 1940s the Guomindang government did begin to offer women a limited involvement in national politics. A few women were present among the 220 members of the People's Political Council, a forum for public opinion set up in 1939 that was seen as a step toward constitutional government. By 1942 their number had risen to 14.

The Communist Party also supported the theoretical equality of women, but it continued to see the women's movement as divisive and bourgeois, taking second place to, rather than being an intrinsic aspect of, the revolutionary struggle. After the Japanese invasion in 1931, women's groups focused once again on patriotic activities, and in 1937, after the two parties had formed a second alliance against the Japanese, women's organizations united to support the war effort. Some writers have argued that both parties prevented the women's movement from becoming a vehicle for gaining equality with men. Others have maintained that the Communist Party did support women's liberation, claiming that women in areas under Communist control enjoyed political equality. In liberated areas, women were given full suffrage rights and encouraged to vote for and take part in the administration of their villages. For example, in Fuping county in Hebei Province, 11 villages had women heads, 30 women were elected to the county government, and women comprised 40 percent of those standing for election.

In some villages, women were still excluded from participating in elections and their women's associations were relegated to a secondary position. Yet the women's associations, which expanded rapidly in the 1940s, were involving more and more women and giving them a power base. In one village, women were initially excluded from elections. But after the women's associations refused to recognize the elected head and encouraged their members not to sleep with their husbands in protest, this decision was reversed. In the next election a woman was elected deputy head.

In 1949, after the Communists had gained control of the whole country, the women's movement, with the support of the party, called a nationwide congress with representatives from all the local women's associations to establish the All-China Democratic Women's Federation as its central organizing body. The right to vote was now extended to all women and written into the law.

See also Militancy; Nationalism; Suffragette; Tang Junying and the Chinese Suffragette Society.

References Croll, Elizabeth. *Feminism and Socialism in China* (1978); DuBois, Ellen. "Woman Suffrage around the World: Three Phases of Internationalism" (1994); Yihong, Pan. "Feminism and Nationalism in China's War of Resistance against Japan" (1997).

Chinese Suffragette Society

See Tang Junying and the Chinese Suffragette Society.

Citizenship

Women's struggle for the suffrage has usually been couched in terms of their right to be full citizens of the state. It has been commonplace to suggest that suffragists have based their claims to citizenship either on their equal right to participate with men in public life or on their difference from men, a difference that gives them special qualities to bring to politics. More recent interpretations, however, have challenged the view that these were competing perspectives. Carole Pateman, for example, argues that most twentieth-century suffragists "demanded both equal civil and political rights, and that their difference from men should be acknowledged in their citizenship" (Pateman, 1992, 19). Jane Rendall explores this further in her analysis of the ideas of British suffragists in the nineteenth century. She suggests that most campaigners were influenced by liberal no-

tions of equality and saw women's citizenship as a matter of natural justice and human rights. For some, however, the claim of political rights was rooted in property ownership, whereas for others, such as Lydia Becker, it rested on humanity alone, that is on the individual's ability to reason rather than on their sex. On the other hand, Rendall also argues that suffragists were uncomfortable with the notion of individual rights alone and combined these with arguments based on the language of duty, responsibility, and public service. She also draws attention to the ethnocentric outlook of British suffragists who believed that their participation in politics was part of the inexorable progress toward civilization, in contrast with other parts of the world still "dominated by savage brutality" (Rendall, 1994, 141).

Thus, the meaning that suffragists gave to the concept of citizenship was complex and varied, both between individual women and between suffrage movements in different countries. South American women, for example, linked their demand for the suffrage with a nationalist perspective that valued working for social reforms to solve social problems, thereby ensuring the development of the nation, as well as achieving civic rights for women. Asunción Lavrin argues that this "pushed the understanding of citizenship beyond politics and into a service frame" (Lavrin, 1995, 357). Suffragists in South America argued that women needed to recognize the connection between home and the public world and that once they understood maternal responsibility, they would also seek to influence collective action. This in turn would "give them respect for themselves and for their role in the nation" (Lavrin, 1995, 361). In other countries where women were involved in nationalist and anticolonial struggles, they often framed their demand for the vote in patriotic terms as well as in terms of their own rights, whereas socialist women argued that the vote would

A drawing from The Brooklyn Magazine, *November 10, 1917, argues that if women serve their country as citizens, they deserve to vote. (Library of Congress)*

enable women to play an equal role with men in achieving a new society. They also saw the vote as an instrument of class power and argued that if women could take part in the public world as wage earners, then they should also be entitled to the suffrage. It is important, therefore, to recognize the complex and different ways in which suffragists understood the meaning of citizenship since their definition could influence their politics once the vote was won.

See also Becker, Lydia Ernestine; Latin America and the Caribbean; Nationalism.
References DuBois, Ellen Carol. "Woman Suffrage and the Left: An International Socialist-Feminist Perspective" (1991); Ehrick, Christine. "Madrinas and Missionaries: Uruguay and the Pan-American Women's Movement" (1998); Jayawardena, Kumari. Feminism and Nationalism in the Third World (1986); Lavrin, Asunción. Women, Feminism and Social Change in Argentina, Chile and Uruguay, 1890–1940 (1995); Pateman, Carole. "Equality, Difference, Subordination: The Politics of Motherhood and Women's Citizenship" (1992); Rendall, Jane. "Citizenship, Culture and Civilization: The Languages of British Suffragists, 1866–1874" (1994).

Colombia

One of the more traditionalist countries in Latin America, Colombia was among the latest to give women the vote. Colombian women were granted the franchise in 1954 and first went to the polls in 1957.

Suffrage did not become a topic of debate in the Colombian press until the 1930s, when basic changes were made to the civil code, loosening the restrictions on women's civil rights. Yet in 1936, when a constitutional reform granted universal male suffrage, women were explicitly excluded, although as nonvoting citizens they were allowed the right to take public jobs. During most of the next decade very few people openly committed themselves to women's suffrage, and it was discussed but not strongly promoted in women's magazines.

An organized campaign began in 1944, after a suffrage bill was introduced by a reformist liberal government. This bill stated that the Congress should be allowed to set rules for women's participation in politics. It was attacked by conservatives from both the main parties and, although approved by the House of Deputies, was defeated by the Senate in 1945. Women were declared citizens but were denied the power to vote, and for the next few years all other suffrage bills were stalled.

The suffrage campaign was conducted by three women's groups: Unión Femenina de Colombia (Colombian Women's Union), founded in 1944; Alianza Femenina de Colombia (Colombian Women's Alliance), formed in 1946; and Organización Nacional Femenina (National Women's Organization), founded in 1954. Unión Femenina de Colombia argued that only when women were granted the rights to full citizenship would they be able to argue for equal pay. They were ridiculed by their opponents as unfeminine solteranas, the derogatory term for spinsters.

In 1948 the ninth International Conference of American States, held in Bogotá, restated its support for women's suffrage. However, the civil war fought between 1948 and 1954 gave ample justification for antisuffragists to argue that it was too dangerous to give women the vote during this violent conflict. Ironically, Colombian legislators finally approved women's suffrage just as Gustavo Rojas Pinilla's military regime came to power, and all citizens were barred from voting until he was deposed at the end of 1957.

See also Citizenship; Latin America and the Caribbean.
References Lavrin, Asunción. "Suffrage in South America: Arguing a Difficult Cause" (1994).

The Common Cause

The Common Cause, published between 1909 and 1920, was for most of that time the official newspaper of the British constitutional suffrage group, the National Union of Women's Suffrage Societies (NUWSS). The NUWSS had contributed to the *Women's Franchise,* published from 1907 to 1911 by John Francis, a member of the Men's League for Women's Suffrage, who wanted the paper to represent all shades of suffrage opinion. But the growth of the union, along with a disagreement with the editor, who refused to exclude reports about the activities of the militant Women's Freedom League, led the NUWSS to establish its own paper. The title, the *Common Cause,* was ambiguous; it implied that the "cause" was common not only to women, but also to men, and it reflected a cooperation between the sexes that epitomized the approach of the NUWSS. The *Common Cause* was at first published by an independent company, financed by NUWSS member Margaret Ashton, but it was taken over by the union toward the end of 1909, when it was edited by Helena Swanwick on a salary of £200 a year. Subsequent editors included Clementina Black, between 1912 and 1913, and Agnes Maude Royden, from 1913 to 1914. The NUWSS raised capital for the paper by issuing shares from time to time and also by encouraging branches to take and distribute more copies. It was hoped that the paper would spread suffrage propaganda to a wider audience, although NUWSS members were reluctant to sell the newspaper on the street.

The *Common Cause* played an important role in informing members about local, national, and international suffrage activities and from the beginning had a foreign news column. It contained articles that debated all the latest issues and expressed a variety of opinions, although the paper reflected the official policy of the executive on controversial questions such as militancy or attitudes toward World War I. The *Common Cause* helped to strengthen the alliance made between the NUWSS and the Labour Party in 1912, carrying numerous articles about the problems faced by working-class women and their need for the vote. Although its main aim was to promote the suffrage campaign, the *Common Cause* did contain material on a wide range of issues that affected women's social position, such as marriage, motherhood, and women's work. In 1920 it was succeeded by the *Woman's Leader.* The paper demonstrates how valuable it was for women's suffrage groups to have their own publication at a time when there were considerable differences between organizations on tactics and political strategies. The *Common Cause* is an invaluable source for understanding the attitudes of the constitutionalist wing of the British suffrage movement.

See also Britain; Imperialism; National Union of Women's Suffrage Societies; Newspapers and Journals; Women's Freedom League.
References Burton, Antoinette. "The Feminist Quest for Identity: British Imperial Suffragism and 'Global Sisterhood,' 1900–1915" (1991); Crawford, Elizabeth. *The Women's Suffrage Movement: A Reference Guide, 1866–1928* (1999); Garner, Les. *Stepping Stones to Women's Liberty: Feminist Ideas in the Women's Suffrage Movement, 1900–1918* (1984).

Conciliation Bill

In February 1910 the journalist and suffragist Henry Brailsford, in consultation with Millicent Fawcett of the National Union of Women's Suffrage Societies (NUWSS), gathered together a group of members of Parliament from all the political parties to form the Conciliation Committee for Women's Suffrage. Brailsford believed that such a committee would be the right forum for undertaking the diplomatic work of promoting a nonpartisan solution to the suffrage question.

The Conciliation Committee was headed by the Conservative suffragist Lord Lytton, and by March 1910, 20 MPs had agreed to join, their number rising to 45 by August. Despite their determination to keep the goodwill of all parties, the committee encountered the same problem that had consistently prevented widespread parliamentary support for a women's suffrage bill: whereas the Conservative Party was only willing to consider a limited measure that was based on a property qualification, the Liberal government feared that adding propertied women to the electorate would only serve to increase the Conservative vote, so many Liberals were inclined to favor adult suffrage, which would include a greater proportion of working men and women. The Conciliation Committee decided on a compromise measure, drafting a limited bill that would give the vote to those women who already qualified as local government electors. This meant that about 1 million women, predominantly single householders, would be enfranchised.

On 12 July 1910 the Conciliation Bill passed its second reading in the House of Commons by a majority of 110, but no further facilities were granted for the bill in that parliamentary session. On 5 May 1911 a modified Conciliation Bill was introduced and was carried at the second reading by 167 votes, a significantly larger majority than in 1910. On this occasion, Liberal Chancellor of the Exchequer Lloyd George intimated that the government intended to bring in a new Reform Bill that would introduce manhood suffrage and that it would be possible for a women's suffrage amendment to be added to it. He advised the Conciliation Committee to drop their bill and accept the new proposal. The committee felt they had little choice but to agree, but members of the Women's Social and Political Union (WSPU), who had temporarily suspended their lawbreaking activities during the hearings of the Conciliation Bill, felt betrayed by the Liberal government and determined to step up their militant campaign. At the same time, a deputation from the National League for Opposing Women's Suffrage (NLOWS) found Prime Minister H. H. Asquith sympathetic to their views, and this confirmed the worst fears of the suffrage campaigners. Believing that Lloyd George was not to be trusted, the constitutional suffragists (NUWSS) persisted with the Conciliation Bill, and on 28 March 1912 it was heard in the House of Commons for a third time. On this occasion it was defeated by 14 votes. One reason for this reversal was the increasingly violent campaign of the WSPU, which turned many sympathetic MPs against the bill. The women's suffrage cause suffered a further setback when the promised Reform Bill collapsed in January 1913.

The defeat of the Conciliation Bill destroyed the chance of a nonparty solution to the women's suffrage question and led to the breakup of the Conciliation Committee. The Liberal government's obstruction of the bill caused disillusion and frustration among women's suffrage campaigners and eventually led to the electoral alliance between the NUWSS and the Labour Party.

See also Antisuffrage Campaign, British; Britain; Fawcett, Millicent Garrett; National Union of Women's Suffrage Societies; Women's Social and Political Union.
Reference Hume, Leslie Parker. *The National Union of Women's Suffrage Societies, 1897–1914* (1982).

Conservatism

Conservatism has always been a difficult concept to define, and some writers on the subject have come to the conclusion that there is no clear set of ideological beliefs attached to the term. Nor has the relation between "Conservatism" as party politics and "conservatism" as a set of attitudes and beliefs been written about in very much detail; indeed, there is often an assumption that the term speaks for itself.

Alison Light has observed that those who are political Conservatives are often

THE LADIES OF THE CREATION!

No. I.

THE PARLIAMENTARY FEMALE.

Father of the Family. "COME, DEAR; WE SO SELDOM GO OUT TOGETHER NOW—CAN'T YOU TAKE US ALL TO THE PLAY TO-NIGHT?"

Mistress of the House and M.P. "HOW YOU TALK, CHARLES! DON'T YOU SEE THAT I AM TOO BUSY. I HAVE A COMMITTEE TO-MORROW MORNING, AND I HAVE MY SPEECH ON THE GREAT CROCHET QUESTION TO PREPARE FOR THE EVENING."

"The dreadful consequence of the emancipation of women!" This John Leech cartoon for Punch *between 1842 and 1864 lampoons the idea of gender role reversal between men and women, something traditionally threatening to conservatives. (Ann Ronan Picture Library)*

the first to acknowledge that conservatism is best understood "not as a force that is simply 'anti-change' so much as a species of restraint or 'brake' . . . holding progress back on the leash of caution but allowing it none the less to advance" (Light, 1991, 17). It is, perhaps, this understanding of conservatism that can be related to certain attitudes toward the idea of women's suffrage that were widespread during the nineteenth and twentieth centuries.

Members of the British Conservative Party who were sympathetic to women's suffrage insisted on limited suffrage measures that imposed various conditions such as property qualifications, age limitations, or the woman voter being unmarried or a widow. At the same time, the middle- and upper-class women of the Conservative and Unionist Women's Franchise Association, founded in 1908, insisted that they were working to oppose universal suffrage in any form. Many men and women with conservative instincts tended to be dismissive of the reforming movements and progressive causes that typified liberalism, and conservative views were often combined with an anti-intellectualism, which manifested itself in the criticism of liberal writers like the philosopher and Liberal politician John Stuart Mill, who supported women's enfranchisement in his book, *On the Subjection of Women* (1869). A fear of socialism and a desire to protect property

and maintain established religion and social hierarchies were at the forefront of
conservative thinking, and these attitudes
could be found in the Conservative Parties
of many countries.

In Britain, however, it was sometimes
difficult to identify those who were likely
to be for or against women's suffrage. It is
important to remember that it was not
only the Conservative Party that opposed
the enfranchisement of women; feminist
campaigns and crusades could be equally
objectionable to centrist Liberals. Many
Liberal politicians took the view that any
property qualification would attract votes
to the party of property, which was traditionally the Conservative Party, but they
also greatly feared the implications of adult
suffrage. In Britain the establishment of a
campaign for women's suffrage was mainly
the achievement of Liberal women, with
some Liberal and Radical parliamentary
support. It is therefore ironic that the fight
by the suffragettes was carried out against
a Liberal government, whereas it was a
Conservative administration that waited
until the granting of full suffrage to women
became inevitable and then implemented it.
The Conservative Prime Minister Stanley
Baldwin was simply responding to a shift
in public opinion when he brought in the
Representation of the People (Equal Franchise) Act that gave all British women the
vote in 1928, and this, perhaps, was a typical conservative reaction.

One of the main reasons that some liberals and socialists would deny women the
vote was the fear of what was believed to
be the "innate" conservatism of women,
which implied that they would always vote
for conservative political parties. This supposed "natural conservatism" of women
has sometimes been accepted as a given,
arising from a belief in their natural domesticity, religiosity, or love of tradition,
and it is generally part of any discussion
about why so many women have voted for
right-wing parties until comparatively re-

cently. The rejection of feminism as an idea
has often characterized the response of
more conservative women, who prefer to
see the security of a traditional and respected role—that of homemaker—as a
position of strength rather than weakness.
Women's conservatism can often be a pragmatic response to a more welcoming and
less intimidating stance adopted toward
women by the churches, whereas socialism
and trade unionism have sometimes appeared to be too "masculine" in their approach. Raffael Scheck has discussed this
issue in the context of what happened to
women in Germany at the beginning of the
twentieth century, when German conservatives had rejected the participation of
women in politics but went on to benefit
from the introduction of women's suffrage
in 1918. Throughout the Weimar Republic, the proportion of women voting for the
predominant right-wing party, the German
Nationalist People's Party (DNVP), was
higher than that of men. The DNVP had
attracted right-wing women's groups,
whose members (many of whom were
Protestants) had rejected the feminist aims
of the women's movement and linked nationalist and conservative goals with the
extension of women's moral role from the
home to the whole nation.

In the Catholic countries of Europe, the
Church was usually linked with political
conservatism, and this combination has
made it extremely difficult for women to
get the vote in countries like Belgium,
France, and Italy, where female enfranchisement did not arrive until after World
War II. In Canada, the women of predominantly Catholic Quebec did not obtain the
provincial franchise until 1940, about 20
years after women had gained the vote in
the rest of Canada. Spain and Portugal
were not only Catholic, but endured long
periods of right-wing dictatorship, during
which time any progress women had made
was often reversed, and it was not until
democracy was restored that women ob-

tained full political rights. In France, women were in a double bind. A belief in the "innate" conservatism of women prevented Republicans from supporting female suffrage, for fear that they would be subjected to clerical influence, while the ultraconservative Catholic Church believed that giving women the vote would destroy the sanctity of family life. The ideology of "separate spheres" remained a potent force in French society, and not just among conservative sections of the community. In Muslim countries, members of the conservative clergy have often taken an antisuffragist stand for the same reasons as in other religious faiths and have tried to hold back legislation to enfranchise women—for example, in Iran and Pakistan.

Conservatism has often acted as an antisuffrage force, with many women and men anxious to hold on to the traditional roles for women in the home and in the local sphere of municipal government, where the domestic expertise of women, together with their moral influence for good, can be brought to bear on society. Where conservatives have supported women's enfranchisement, it has usually been on the condition that the vote is limited to propertied women only. Religious authorities often take a conservative view of women's role in society and resist the idea of their involvement in political life. Conservative forces in society can embrace a broad brush of political allegiances, all of which need to be taken into account in any discussion of the women's suffrage movement.

See also Britain; Canada; Conservative and Unionist Women's Franchise Association; France; Germany; Iran; Nationalism; Pakistan and Bangladesh; Portugal; Spain.
References Campbell, Beatrix. *The Iron Ladies: Why Do Women Vote Tory?* (1987); Harrison, Brian. *Separate Spheres: The Opposition to Women's Suffrage in Britain* (1978); Light, Alison. *Forever England: Femininity, Literature and Conservatism between the Wars* (1991); Scheck, Raffael. "German Conservatism and Female Political Activism in the Early Weimar Republic" (1997).

Conservative and Unionist Women's Franchise Association

The Conservative and Unionist Women's Franchise Association (CUWFA) was an organization of suffragists who supported the British Conservative Party. It was founded in November 1908 in response to the overwhelming predominance of Liberal women in the National Union of Women's Suffrage Societies (NUWSS), and its goal was to capitalize on the divisions within the Liberal Party over the question of women's suffrage. There was also increasing unease among Conservative suffragists at the change in tactics of the militant suffragettes of the Women's Social and Political Union (WSPU), which involved threats to public order such as stone throwing and the storming of government buildings. The first president of the CUWFA was Lady Louisa Knightley, who was succeeded by the Countess of Selborne in 1910, and from 1909 to 1916 a quarterly journal was published called the *Conservative and Unionist Women's Franchise Review.*

The association campaigned for the parliamentary vote for those women who owned, occupied, or lodged in a property above a certain value, and it was opposed to universal suffrage in any form. It was agreed that the CUWFA would not oppose any official Unionist candidate but would not actively work for a candidate opposed to women's suffrage. The association was prominent during the campaign for the Conciliation Bill between 1910 and 1912 and was actively represented in Parliament by supporters such as Lord Lytton, Lord Robert Cecil, and the Earl of Selborne. Like many other suffrage organizations, its campaigning ground to a halt shortly after the outbreak of World War I, when it was decided that in the interests of patriotism, the war effort should come first.

See also Britain; Conciliation Bill; National Union of Women's Suffrage Societies; Universal Suffrage; Women's Social and Political Union.

Reference Maguire, G. E. *Conservative Women: A History of Women and the Conservative Party, 1874–1997* (1998).

The Convert

The Convert (1907) was a suffragette novel written by the former actress Elizabeth Robins, who was to become a leading member of the British militant group the Women's Social and Political Union (WSPU). It was one of a number of novels written by suffragette activists out of their own experience and which sought to challenge negative images of the suffragette militant that were to be found in novels and in the press. The novels were pieces of propaganda as well as literary creations, and they often aimed to influence a specific political debate. Therefore, their content should be understood in the context of the moment in which they were produced.

Robins initially wrote a play, *Votes for Women* (1906), that was later turned into her novel, *The Convert*. The novel is based on Robins's assessment of the situation in 1906–1907, and she attended eight suffrage meetings to provide material for some of the chapters. The fictional speakers are based on real people; for example, Ernestine Blunt is drawn from either Teresa Billington-Greig or Mary Gawthorpe, and Lothian Scott is Keir Hardie, one of the leaders of the socialist Independent Labour Party. The novel aims both to show that working-class women supported the demand for the vote and to argue that these women would benefit from even a limited franchise. Working-class women appear as speakers and as members of the audience in the meetings described in *The Convert*; one, dressed in brown serge, is very like Hannah Mitchell, the Lancashire suffragette who met Robins at a by-election in 1906 and later recalled that one or two incidents that she told to the author appeared in the novel. Robins also linked the vote to the solution of a wide range of problems facing working-class women and raised

broader issues like work, sexuality, and motherhood. Finally, the novel also raised the problems posed by upper-class women who were antagonistic to the suffrage campaign because they thought it would undermine their own power to influence events.

Elizabeth Robins's novel, in common with other suffragette fiction, was read avidly by activists who sought a sympathetic portrayal of suffragettes and who enjoyed trying to recognize familiar events and people. It was also, however, written in a style that was accessible to a popular readership and helped to ensure that a wide audience gained a more positive impression of the "militant woman."

See also Actresses' Franchise League; Billington-Greig, Teresa; Britain; Gawthorpe, Mary; Mitchell, Hannah; Robins, Elizabeth; *Votes for Women*; Women Writers' Suffrage League; Women's Social and Political Union. *References* Joannou, Maroula. "Suffragette Fiction and the Fictions of Suffrage" (1998); John, Angela V. "Radical Reflections? Elizabeth Robins: The Making of Suffragette History and the Representation of Working-Class Women" (1995).

Costa Rica

The first proposal for women's suffrage in Costa Rica was made in 1890, but it was to be nearly 60 years before, in 1949, women were enfranchised and a further 4 years before they first went to the polls in a presidential election in 1953.

Arguments voiced against suffrage were closely connected with women's social role and were often presented by male journalists in a humorous guise. In 1913 news of the radical suffragist movement in Britain had a strong impact in Costa Rica. The newspaper *La Información* proclaimed: "How ugly and bothersome to see women meddling in political campaigns" (Sharratt, 1997, 71). Press reports represented women's role as primarily domestic, and expressed fears that if the women were granted the vote, they would neglect their duties as wives and mothers. These views were bolstered by the Catholic Church and the educational system, which reinforced traditional male and female roles and restricted women's access to higher education. Women's enfranchisement also contradicted the civil code, which obliged women to obey their husbands and kept them from positions of power where they could made independent decisions.

Women's aspirations to gain the vote were viewed in isolation, with no connections to any other social struggle. Yet this did not mean that all men ignored the suffrage issue. Indeed, members of the legislature made regular proposals to enfranchise women. One of these, in 1920, followed the restoration of democracy after two years of dictatorship under Federico Tinaco. During Tinaco's regime, women teachers led by the feminist Maria Isabel Carvajal (who wrote under the pseudonym Carmen Lyra) had participated actively in violent demonstrations against Federico Tinaco's regime and were frequently beaten or hosed down.

Tinaco's successor, Julio Acosta García, was a supporter of women's rights but limited his 1920 proposal to municipal suffrage for taxpaying women. On this occasion, a group of women from the Colegio Superior de Señoritas confronted the Legislative Assembly, without using male intermediaries, and asked them to support the measure. The deputation was led by Angela Acuña, who although one of the earliest advocates of women's suffrage, had distanced herself from the violent demonstrations because she was a family friend of Tinaco. However, the women's arguments were not taken seriously. Women's political action during the dictatorship was now dismissed as exceptional, having taken place under extreme circumstances. President Acosta's proposal was defeated on 15 August 1920.

The typical woman pioneer of the Costa

Rican suffrage movement was middle-class, self-supporting, and professionally trained. She often had one European immigrant parent, had studied abroad, and had become involved in international women's organizations. Acuña fits this description. She went on to represent Costa Rica at the Pan-American Women's Conference in 1922 with the support of Carrie Chapman Catt, president of the International Woman Suffrage Alliance.

The Pan-American Conference served to spur many Latin American countries into forming suffrage organizations. In the case of Costa Rica, the first formal suffrage group, La Liga Feminista (the Feminist League), was set up in 1923 by the staff of Colegio Superior de Señoritas, with Acuña as president. It remained active for the next three decades. In 1924 the league sent signed petitions to the Legislative Assembly and, in 1925, demanded that women be removed from the categories of people ineligible to vote (which also included minors, mental defectives, and prisoners) on the grounds that the 1871 Constitution did not specifically exclude women. The main argument used by their opponents was women's subordinate status under the law, which stated that a woman could not confer citizenship directly on a foreign-born husband and must obey and follow her husband if he changed residence. Once again, the women's demands were overruled, but to placate them, the Legislative Assembly suggested that suffrage might one day be granted to educated women.

After a period of decline during the late 1920s, the league was restored in 1931 and Acuña was joined by other leaders, such as Esther de Mezerville, principal of the Colegio Superior de Señoritas. This time the league avoided the more radical proposal of enfranchising all women. Rather it proposed an amendment to the constitution that would give the vote to women who had professional training or were white-collar workers or landowners. Graduates of private school and those who could speak foreign languages were also included. However, despite repeated requests over several years and amendments such as one that would delete women graduates from private schools from the list of women qualified to vote, the motion was never even discussed by a plenary session in the assembly.

The issue of women's suffrage was raised once again in 1943, during the presidency of President Rafael Angel Calderón Guardia. On 15 May 1943, large numbers of women, including members of Acuña's Feminist League, supported a major demonstration in the capital, San José. This demonstration helped to defeat an amendment giving too much power to the executive in overseeing elections. It was followed in August by a meeting, attended by 8,000 women, where demonstrators held white flags to symbolize a request for fairness in the coming elections. The conservative opposition tried to court women's support by pushing an amendment of the Electoral Law to read "the right to vote is essentially a political right and must be exercised by citizens, male or female, for whom it is a right and obligation." Yet as with earlier amendments, this reform was never seriously discussed. Neither party had any real commitment to enfranchising women, and both were still anxious to avoid alienating the Catholic Church.

Despite feminist activism over three decades, women were not fully enfranchised and able to stand for election until 1949, after the Partido Liberación Nacional had come to power and male members of the Assembly of Representatives had drafted a new constitution. On 20 June 1949, a bill was introduced that had been proposed by the predominantly female National Teachers' Association. It redefined citizenship as "an aggregate of duties and political rights to which all Costa Rican citizens of either sex who are eighteen years or older are entitled." Following a debate in which one assembly member maintained that in his own personal poll, the majority of women were against the vote, the amendment was carried by a vote of 33 to 8.

See also Catt, Carrie Chapman; Citizenship; Latin America and the Caribbean; Pan-American Women's Conference.
References González-Suárez, Mirta. "With Patience and Without Blood: The Political Struggles of Costa Rican Women" (1994); Sharratt, Sara. "The Suffragist Movement in Costa Rica, 1889–1949: Centennial of Democracy?" (1997).

Cousins, Margaret (Gretta)

Margaret Cousins (1878–1954) was co-founder of the Irish Women's Franchise League. Born Margaret Gillespie in Boyle, County Roscommon, into a middle-class Methodist family, she won a scholarship to Victoria High School, Derry, and later studied at the Royal Irish Academy of Music, receiving a bachelor of music degree from the Royal University of Ireland. While teaching music part-time, she married the Belfast-born James Cousins, who was to share her interest in theosophy and her commitment to feminism.

Following attendance at a women's franchise meeting in Manchester, Cousins joined the Irish Women's Suffrage and Local Government Association in 1905. After she and her husband met Hanna and Francis Sheehy Skeffington, the four decided to form an Irish suffrage society along the same lines as the British Women's Social and Political Union (WSPU). In 1908 Cousins became treasurer of the Irish Women's Franchise League (IWFL) and one of its most effective organizers. In 1910 she organized an Irish tour for Emmeline Pankhurst and was one of the Irish delegates invited by Pankhurst to attend the Parliament of Women in Caxton Hall in London. Cousins was one of six Irish women arrested following the protest that resulted from the parliament, receiving a sentence of one month in Holloway Jail. In 1912 James Cousins became coeditor (with Francis Sheehy Skeffington) of the suffrage paper the *Irish Citizen*. The IWFL embarked on a campaign of militancy in protest against the failure of the Irish Parliamentary Party to support measures for women's suffrage, and in January 1913 Gretta Cousins received another one-month prison sentence for window breaking following the party's failure to vote for the Snowden Amendment. She and the other two IWFL prisoners were sent to Tullamore Jail, 60 miles from Dublin, instead of Mountjoy Jail, the usual place of detention for suffrage prisoners. The prisoners were, for the first time in the Irish experience, denied first-class status, and they embarked on a hunger strike in protest, winning considerable public sympathy.

Economic circumstances, combined with their theosophical beliefs and friendship with Annie Besant, persuaded the Cousins to leave Ireland in May 1913. A Cousins's Presentation Committee, its members coming from suffrage, vegetarian, theosophical, and dramatic groups, presented them with £1,200 in recognition of the sacrifices both had made. For the next two years they remained in Liverpool, waiting for a position in India to materialize. During that time, Cousins visited Ireland often, continuing her work for the IWFL and also undertaking work in Britain for the WSPU and the Women's Freedom League.

In 1915 the couple emigrated to Madras, where James became subeditor of the *New India,* a journal published by the theosophists, and Gretta started the National Girls School in Mangalore, becoming its headmistress. She became the first non-Indian member of the Indian Women's University at Poona. In 1917 she helped to found the Women's Indian Association (WIA), which, four years later, succeeded in convincing members of the Madras leg-

islature to support women's suffrage. In 1923 she became the first woman magistrate in India, and in 1926 she helped to found the All-India Women's Conference, a women's rights movement that remains active today. She was imprisoned for a year in 1932, after speaking in protest against an emergency powers act. Her former colleagues of the IWFL sent her a message of support from Ireland. She suffered a stroke in 1943 after a two-mile walk to a mother and child welfare center, and died in Adyar, Tamil Nadu, in 1954.

See also Hunger Strikes; Imperialism; India; Ireland; Irish Women's Franchise League; Militancy; Nationalism; Skeffington, Hanna Sheehy; Women's Social and Political Union. *References* Candy, Catherine. "Relating Feminisms, Nationalisms and Imperialisms: Ireland, India and Margaret Cousins' Sexual Politics" (1994); Cousins, James H., and Margaret E. Cousins. *We Two Together* (1950); Ward, Margaret. *Hanna Sheehy Skeffington: A Life* (1997).

Cuba

Cuba was the fourth Latin American country to grant women the vote when, on 3 February 1934, women's suffrage was written into the provisional constitution. As in other Latin American countries, such as Uruguay and Brazil, Cuba had a well-established women's movement that began to organize seriously around suffrage in the 1920s. They achieved their goal in just over 10 years.

A formal demand for suffrage was first made during the Cuban War of Independence, when a clause in the revolutionary manifesto of 1897 sought equal rights for women, including limited suffrage for single and widowed women over the age of 25. However, after the war was ended, the Constitution of 1901, which made Cuba nominally independent but still subject to U.S. intervention, ignored the issue of women's rights. The emerging women's movements hoped that the new republic would consider making changes in the law to improve women's legal and political status.

Woman suffrage was first discussed seriously at the National Women's Congress in 1923, where representatives from 31 women's organizations from a wide range of political orientations debated a full spectrum of women's rights issues. However, suffrage was the issue that drew support from most women, and believing they could use the vote to influence electoral politics, all women's groups embraced it. At the second congress in 1925, political differences emerged between radical and conservative feminists, leaving the latter in control of the congress resolutions. These reinforced the traditional institution of the family, revering women's role as mother while still attempting to enhance women's power in the democratic process. As the congress concluded, recently elected President General Gerardo Machado y Morales pledged to introduce the vote for women during his presidential term.

However, it soon became apparent that Machado's regime was turning into a near dictatorship in which dissident elements were repressed and opponents were arrested and imprisoned without trial. These developments split the women's movement, with moderates hoping that once women had the vote, corruption and repression would come to an end, and radicals believing that only a revolution could redistribute power away from the privileged classes. While Machado was terrorizing his opponents and making constitutional changes that increased his term of office and allowed him to seek reelection, he used the issue of women's suffrage as evidence of his democratic credentials by claiming that all Cubans would be able to vote in the next election in 1934.

By 1928 feminist groups were beginning to fracture along class lines. The most active and influential group, Alianza Nacional Feminista (National Women's Alliance), had a strong middle- and upper-class leadership that resisted making alliances with socialist groups and lacked sympathy with working women. In 1930 tensions came to a head and the more radical elements of the group withdrew under the leadership of Ofelia Domínguez. One of the new groups formed out of this division, Unión Laborista de Mujeres (Women's Labor Union), initially included the vote in its aims, but by 1931, when opposition to Machado was more openly defiant, they broke with other feminist groups and denounced women's suffrage as collusion with the Machado regime. The union's strongest opponent was the Partido Demócrata Sufragista (Democratic Suffrage Party) under María Collado, which pledged support for Machado, believing that he offered the best route to democratic participation and, in the long term, to social justice. Yet despite their divisions, feminists often found common cause. When Domínguez was arrested in 1931, many moderate suffragists, who had been her opponents, strongly protested.

Lynn Stoner has argued that U.S. feminists failed to give Cuban women the support they needed at this important period. For example, in 1929 Carrie Chapman Catt saw some Latin American women as a threat to peaceful relations between North and South America and considered that "they had not fought long enough to appreciate the responsibilities of an elected public" (Stoner, 1991, 13). Yet Francesca Miller points to the fact that in 1928, when women from outside Cuba were attending the International Conference of American States in Havana, they joined the local groups in a parade to demand the suffrage. Cuban women's groups also received international support when members of the Inter-American Commission of Women, which had been formed at the 1928 conference, held their first meeting in Havana in 1930.

Meanwhile, despite Machado's promises, his proposed suffrage amendment failed to gain the two-thirds majority in the assembly required by the Constitution of 1928. By 1930 the political situation had deteriorated into a national crisis. Most feminists chose to oppose Machado and turn the campaign against him into a drive to obtain the vote. After a student who was protesting at the University of Havana was shot dead by police, women who had previously eschewed violence took to the streets to express their outrage. Only Collado and her followers stuck by the president and discredited the students as being "out of hand." Machado attempted to placate the women by reminding them of his constitutional resolution to bring in the vote. But, with the exception of the Partido Demócrata Sufragista, all other suffrage groups rejected his overtures and united to express their opposition. This unleashed further acts of aggression from the regime, this time directed against women. From 1932 Cuba fell into political chaos until Machado was eventually ousted in August 1933.

After Machado's demise, women were provisionally granted the vote by presidential decree during a series of unstable regimes. Suffrage groups maintained their solidarity, leading politicians to view them as a force for stability. Presidents seeking to establish the legitimacy of their regimes promised to comply with feminist demands in order to gain their support, seeing the value of bringing women into the political system. The rapid passage of a Suffrage Act in 1934, endorsing the presidential decree, can be explained by the desire of the new president, Carlos Mendieta, to legitimize his authority. Suffragists took advantage of political unrest to press their cause and increase their status. They became a respected political group and presented themselves as a legitimizing force that few men dared to oppose openly. In 1936, in the first election that followed their enfranchisement, six women were elected to the House of Rep-resentatives, with a number of others taking up posts at the local government level.

See also Brazil; Latin America and the Caribbean; Pan-American Women's Movement; Uruguay.
References: Miller, Francesca. *Latin American Women and the Search for Social Justice* (1991); Stoner, Lynn. *From the House to the Streets: The Cuban Women's Movement for Legal Change, 1898–1940* (1991).

Czechoslovakia

Women achieved the vote in Czechoslovakia in the Constitution of 1919–1920 that followed the establishment of an independent republic in 1918. Before this time, Czech lands (largely in Bohemia) and Slovakia were part of the Habsburg Empire ruled by the Emperor Franz Josef. The constituent parts of the empire had their own legislatures, but these had only limited powers. Women's political activities, as in other parts of the empire, were closely tied up with nationalist movements or with the struggle for socialism. Women were introduced to feminist ideas, however, through the American Ladies' Club, founded in Prague in 1865 by Vojta Náprstek, who admired American women's involvement in public affairs. The club had a library and it organized lectures on topics related to British and American feminism. Women could also find out about developments abroad by reading *Zenske Listy* (Women's Journal), edited after 1874 by the women's rights activist and nationalist author Eliska Krásnohorská. She was responsible for encouraging the first political action undertaken by Czech women on behalf of their sex. Through her journal she organized a petition to the Reichsrat that called for women's right to be admitted to the medical and philosophical faculties of Austrian universities. It gathered 5,000 signatures and was supported by deputies in the Young Czech (National Liberal) Party.

The nationalist movement grew stronger during the 1890s, with demands being made for Bohemian autonomy and parity for the Czech language in the civil service. Women took part in this movement and a small group began to raise demands on behalf of their sex. Krásnohorská ensured that her journal became more of a campaigning paper and organized petitions for women's suffrage and civil rights. Tomas Masaryk, a professor at the university in Prague and a deputy in the Reichsrat, also played a part in stimulating interest in feminist questions, and his wife, the American Charlotte Garrigue Masaryková, translated John Stuart Mill's *On the Subjection of Women* into Czech. After the turn of the century, two feminist groups were organized, the Women's Club of Prague, in 1901, and the Committee for Women's Suffrage, in 1905, both founded by Františka Plamínková. They were strongly nationalist in their views and used arguments that linked together Czech traditions and the improvement of women's social and political position. In 1909, for example, these groups demanded that the International Woman Suffrage Alliance should use Czech as the fourth language alongside English, French, and German in its proceedings.

In contrast to women in many other countries, Czech women were successful in gaining support from a wide range of political parties, including the Social Democrats, the National Socialists, and the Progressives, all of whom welcomed female members and advocated full legal and political equality for women. The Agrarian Party also agreed that women should not lose any of their existing voting rights. Since 1861 women and men who were taxpayers or members of learned professions were able to vote in elections to the Bohemian Diet and in municipal elections, except in Prague and Liberec. Qualified women were also eligible to stand for election to the Diet. In 1908 and 1909 suffragists ran their own female candidate for the Diet and in the next few

years managed to persuade progressive parties to also put forward female candidates, although none were successful. In 1912, however, the Habsburg government ruled that women were not eligible for election and announced its intention of removing any voting rights that women enjoyed in Bohemia. Suffragists issued a "Women's Appeal to the Bohemian Nation" in the newspapers that challenged this decision, even though it meant support for a property-based franchise. They persuaded a number of parties to jointly support a female candidate, and the nationalist author Božena Viková-Kunětická was elected. The governor refused to recognize her election and the Diet was dissolved in 1913, but the event attracted interest from all over Europe.

Women had to wait until the fall of the Habsburg Empire and the creation of a new republic before they achieved equal voting rights. The close links between the suffrage campaign and the nationalist movement appear to have strengthened the women's cause. Katherine David suggests that suffragists expected men to sympathize with their views because of democratic Czech traditions and because men also experienced oppression under foreign rule. Women also benefited from the support of the liberal nationalist leader Masaryk, who was to become president of the republic. Czech women had been able to play a larger role in the struggle for women's rights than their counterparts in Slovakia. Czech territory was less agricultural and had a sizable middle class and a stronger Protestant heritage. Moreover, while Austrians attempted to extend political rights to national groups in their territories, the Hungarians who ruled Slovakia tried to repress ethnic identities and strictly controlled political life. These differences continued once women were enfranchised, with Czech women playing a larger role in formal politics than Slovak women, although even so, only a small number of women were elected to political office and there were no women in the cabinet.

See also International Woman Suffrage Alliance; Masaryk, Tomas; Mill, John Stuart; Nationalism; *On the Subjection of Women;* Plamínková, Frantiska F.

References David, Katherine. "Czech Feminists and Nationalism in the Late Habsburg Monarchy: 'The First in Austria'" (1991). Evans, Richard J. *The Feminists: Women's Emancipation Movements in Europe, America and Australasia, 1840–1920* (1977); Wolchik, Sharon J. "Czech and Slovak Women and Political Leadership" (1996).

Daltro, Leolinda De Figuereido

Leolinda De Figuereido Daltro, a Bahian-born schoolteacher and journalist, was one of the earliest advocates of women's suffrage in Brazil. In 1910 she founded and became president of a small feminist organization, the Partido Republicano Feminino (Women's Republican Party), based in Rio. Her party, which recruited mainly schoolteachers as members, sought to carry the suffrage issue into a Congress that had not taken it up since 1891. In addition to the vote, Daltro called for the emancipation of Brazilian women more generally, including the admission of women to all public service positions.

In 1917 she attempted to register for the vote and organized a public demonstration in favor of women's suffrage. She also tried, unsuccessfully, to gain public office on a number of occasions, including standing for election to the Rio City Council in 1919. She attracted some fame for her work in educating Brazilian Indians and was satirized by antifeminist Lima Baretto. Yet unlike the better-known Bertha Lutz, Daltro never succeeded in creating an effective, broad-based suffrage organization. She had no real political allies in government after 1914, but she continued to work for women's rights through the 1920s. After women gained the vote in 1932, Daltro stood for election to Congress on the grounds that her campaigns had preceded that of all others who called themselves feminist leaders. However, like the other women candidates in that election, she was unsuccessful in gaining national office.

See also Brazil; Lutz, Bertha.
Reference Hahner, June, E. *Emancipating the Female Sex: The Struggle for Women's Rights in Brazil, 1850–1940* (1990).

Davison, Emily Wilding

British suffragette Emily Wilding Davison was born in 1872, the daughter of a Northumbrian family. After graduating from London University, she was briefly a teacher, but she became increasingly interested in the women's suffrage movement and joined the Women's Social and Political Union (WSPU) in 1906. Davison quickly became involved in acts of militancy such as window breaking and arson and was imprisoned many times, the first occasion being in March 1909. She undertook numerous hunger strikes and was forcibly fed, and in 1911 she attempted suicide in Holloway Prison to draw attention to the brutal treatment many suffragettes received during their imprisonment.

Davison is chiefly remembered for the dramatic gesture she made for the cause of women's suffrage on 4 June 1913. Acting on her own initiative, she went to the Derby horse race at Epsom and rushed out onto the course in the middle of the race in an attempt to grab the reins of the King's horse. She was very seriously injured and died in the hospital a few days later. The WSPU organized a spectacular funeral procession for Davison, with 2,000 suffragettes marching behind her

The climax of the suffragettes' efforts to obtain recognition occurred when Emily Davison, a prominent member of the movement, threw herself under the King's horse, Anmer, at the Derby. She died as a result of her injuries. (Ann Ronan Picture Library)

coffin. It has never been entirely clear whether Davison intended to die for the cause or simply carried out a militant protest that went tragically wrong. However, she had written about the prospect of martyrdom for the suffrage cause, and it is for her act of self-sacrifice that Emily Davison will always be remembered.

> *See also* Britain; Drama, Novels, Poetry, and Film; Women's Social and Political Union.
> *Reference* Stanley, Liz, with A. Morley. *The Life and Death of Emily Wilding Davison* (1988).

De Silva, Agnes

Agnes De Silva (née Nell) was the leading activist in the Sri Lankan women's suffrage movement. She was the niece of a pioneer woman doctor, Winifred Nell, and granddaughter of colonial Solicitor General Louis Nell, an early follower of Darwin. In 1908 she married George De Silva, a leading liberal who later campaigned for universal suffrage.

In 1925 Agnes proposed a resolution to the Congress on behalf of the Mallika Kulangana Samitiya (Women's Society) for a limited franchise. She went on to become the secretary of the Women's Franchise Union, founded by middle-class women in 1927. In 1928 she led a delegation from this organization to give evidence to the Donoughmore Committee on constitutional reform, requesting the vote for women. In the same year, she went to Britain with her husband George, who was campaigning for universal suffrage among other reforms, and while she was there, she restated the importance of obtaining the female franchise for Sri Lankan women. After the vote was won in 1931 for all women over 21, Agnes put up as a candidate at the first general election held under universal suffrage. Although she herself failed to gain a seat, she saw two other Sri Lankan women candidates succeed in that election to become the first women legislators.

See also Sri Lanka.
Reference Jayawardena, Kumari. *Feminism and Nationalism in the Third World* (1986).

Declaration of Sentiments
See Women's Rights Convention, Seneca Falls (1848).

Denmark
A movement for women's suffrage did not develop in Denmark until the end of the nineteenth century, but it soon became one of the strongest in Europe—in 1911, for example, Denmark was one of only seven countries in the International Woman Suffrage Alliance that had over 2,500 members. Throughout the nineteenth century there were struggles in Denmark to reduce the power of the absolutist monarchy and to introduce more representative government. In 1866 a wide suffrage, freedom of assembly, and numerous civil rights were conceded, but ministerial responsibility and parliamentary government were still not introduced. Therefore, liberal, middle-class political groups joined with organizations of small farmers to demand further constitutional reforms. This provided the context for the development of a women's movement. A Danish version of John Stuart Mill's *On the Subjection of Women* had been published in 1869, but it was not until 1871 that a women's rights group, Dansk Kvindesamfund (DK) [Danish Women's Association], was established by Fredrik Bajer (1837–1922) and his wife, Mathilde Bajer (1840–1934).

The association was moderate in outlook and concentrated on economic rights for women. By the early 1880s it had only 124 members, but the victory of radical Liberals and Social Democrats in the elections of 1884, along with controversies over the state regulation of prostitution, led to a rapid growth in membership, which stood at 500 by the end of 1883. The DK also established its own journal in 1885, *Women and Society*, edited by Elisabeth Grundtvig. Under the leadership of a new president, Marie Rovsing, the DK campaigned to end the state regulation of prostitution and demanded stricter codes of morality for men. A growing minority within the organization, however, felt that too little was being done about the vote, which many thought was necessary before moral reforms could be achieved. Led by the association's founder, Mathilde Bajer, they established the Dansk Kvindelig Fremskridtsforening (Danish Women's Progress Association) in 1886 and two years later another group, Dansk Kvindelig Valgretsforening (Danish Women's Suffrage Society), was also formed. Both groups emphasized the importance of moral reform and improvements in the work and social lives of working-class women, as well as the vote. They influenced the outlook of the more moderate DK, which in 1888 petitioned the Danish Parliament for the municipal vote.

Nonetheless, the DK remained moderate in its outlook. It did not work for the full enfranchisement of women and tended to support the work of other suffragist groups rather than seeking the vote directly. Yet, the DK gained strength from its membership in the International Council of Women and from the victory of conservatism in Danish politics in the 1890s, and the suffrage groups founded in the 1880s failed to survive. The situation changed in 1898 with the introduction of an electoral reform bill that made no reference to women. When the DK failed to make an immediate response, some of its members joined with other feminists to form the Dansk Kvindeforeningers Valgrets Forbund (DVKVF) [Danish Women's Associations' Suffrage Federation]. Nonetheless, the DVKVF continued to retain links with the DK and with the moderate Liberal Party and restricted its demands to the municipal suffrage. Those who supported the more radical Reform Liberal Party, therefore, broke away in 1900 to form their own group, Landsforbundet for Kvinders Valgret (LKV) [National League for Women's Suffrage], which campaigned for women's suffrage at all levels.

In the early 1900s the LKV was helped by developments in national politics. Moderate Liberals formed a government in 1901, and in 1905 the radicals in the party left to form an alliance with the Social Democrats, who came to power in 1913. These years were filled with debates about constitutional reform that helped the growth of women's suffrage organizations. By 1910 the LKV had 11,000 members, and the more moderate DVKVF had 12,000 members, a significant proportion of the small female population of 1.5 million. The granting of the municipal franchise in 1908 to women who fulfilled a property qualification gave a further impetus to the suffrage movement and meant that more moderate campaigners now put their energies into the achievement of a full franchise. Two years earlier the DK had voted to give equal attention to municipal and parliamentary voting rights, and from 1908 it held an annual Women's Suffrage Day in June. Meetings and speeches were organized, although the group stopped short of the mass processions and lobbying that were associated with the methods of the British suffrage campaigners and were considered inappropriate for Danish women.

In 1912 the government introduced a suffrage bill to enfranchise all men and women over the age of 28. This passed the lower house but was rejected by the upper house in 1913, partly because the bill contained clauses affecting the composition of the upper house itself. This precipitated a constitutional crisis that was still not resolved when war was declared. The domination of the lower house by radical Liberals and Social Democrats, however, ensured that it was not long before the bill was passed, and women finally received the vote in June 1915.

See also International Council of Women; International Woman Suffrage Alliance; Mill, John Stuart; *On the Subjection of Women.*
Reference Evans, Richard, J. *The Feminists: Women's Emancipation Movements in Europe, America and Australasia, 1840–1920* (1977).

Despard, Charlotte

An important figure in the British suffrage movement, Charlotte Despard (née French) (1844–1939) was born in Ripple Vale, Kent, into a prosperous family. In 1870 she married Maximilian Despard, and after being widowed in 1890, she dedicated herself to helping the poor, working in the slums of Battersea, and serving as a Poor Law Guardian, an elected position in a group that administered relief for the poor at local levels. Despard's work among the disadvantaged led her into radical politics, and she became a member of the socialist group Social Democratic Federation and later the Independent Labour Party.

In 1906 Despard joined the militant suffrage organization run by the Pankhursts, the Women's Social and Political Union (WSPU), and in 1907 she was arrested and imprisoned for her militant activities. Although she was a committed member of the WSPU, Despard disliked the dictatorial and undemocratic leadership of Emmeline and Christabel Pankhurst, and she deplored the organization's move away from its roots in the Labour Party. In 1907 there was a serious split within the WSPU over these issues, and Despard, Teresa Billington-Greig, Edith How Martyn, and

Under Charlotte Despard's leadership, members of the Women's Freedom League engaged in nonviolent resistance such as evading the census and refusing to pay taxes until women were given the vote. (Museum of London)

a substantial number of other members left to form the Women's Freedom League (WFL).

With Despard as its president, the new organization embarked on a campaign of constitutional militancy and carried out a number of nonviolent protest actions, such as tax resistance and a boycott of the census held in 1911. Despard was influential in fostering the WFL's progressive image, and her encouragement of links with the Labour Party meant that the organization broadened its interests beyond the vote to include wider economic and social issues that affected women. However, Despard's autocratic style of leadership was resented by some members, and this led to an unsuccessful attempt to oust her from the presidency in 1912.

Despard was a pacifist, and on the outbreak of World War I she refused to join the war effort, preferring instead to lead the WFL in a campaign to secure better conditions for the women and children at home by forming the Women's Suffrage National Aid Corps. After limited women's suffrage had been granted in 1918, Despard resigned from the WFL to stand as a parliamentary candidate, but she was defeated, probably because of her pacifist views. Her last years were spent supporting the Sinn Fein campaign for a united Ireland and speaking out publicly against fascism. She died in Belfast in 1939.

See also Billington-Greig, Teresa; Britain; Pankhurst, Christabel; Pankhurst, Emmeline; Representation of the People Act; Women's Freedom League; Women's Social and Political Union.
Reference Mulvihill, Margaret. *Charlotte Despard: A Biography* (1989).

Drama, Novels, Poetry, and Film

Women writers who became involved in suffrage movements were often inspired to compose plays, poems, novels, and screenplays that debated suffrage issues and promoted the cause to a wider audience. Writing prosuffrage fiction was also a way of countering negative stereotypes and caricatures of suffragists, commonly used to denigrate the movement. These negative images often also appeared in fictional form, in plays, sketches, or novels. Fictional forms were often interchangeable, crossing the boundaries of every type of popular culture. Thus songs and poems might become tableaux; short stories or articles might become plays; plays might become novels or films; and cartoons and images were often accompanied by poems. Women writers and actors, by being seen or heard in public, were also making a political statement, challenging the view that their place should be only in the home. Because most research in this area has concentrated on Britain and the United States, the majority of our examples are from these countries. However, there is evidence that suffrage movements in other countries also used fiction in similar ways.

Poetry is seldom mentioned in discussions of radical suffrage texts, yet in Britain a number of leading suffragists, such as Sylvia Pankhurst, Emily Wilding Davison, and Eva Gore Booth, used poetry to give strong messages to women readers. Poems by anonymous or unknown writers, such as *The Holloway Jingles,* written by hunger strikers in 1912, are equally significant. These drew upon popular lyric forms such as light opera or college songs to create a sense of solidarity with readers, making solitary confinement a collective experience. In China, women's poetry aimed to arouse both feminist and patriotic sentiments, using historical imagery that crossed national and religious boundaries. For example, the early Chinese feminist Jiu Jin, writing in the 1900s, used the image of Joan of Arc in a poem that urged Chinese women to demand their emancipation. Joan of Arc was popular, too, with British and American suffragists.

Poems could also be used to address debates about women's nature and role in society. In New Zealand, the antisuffragist poet and member of parliament Thomas Bracken published a sketch in 1891 called *the Triumph of Women's Rights.* It describes a newly elected Parliament with a majority of women members where the business of the House includes such trivia as the Afternoon Tea Bill. A married woman MP tells other members:

Noo Jock maun nurse the weans an
  wash
Bak a' the bannocks—dinna fash
While I as a member cut a dash.
(Now Jock must care for the children
  and wash
Bake all the barley cakes—don't you
  worry

While I as a member make a show of
  myself.)

However, to counter such accusations that the women's vote would disrupt the home and invert traditional gender roles, a satirical suffrage poem pointed out that middle-class women already spent time on activities outside the home:

No, it isn't home neglecting
If you spend your time selecting
Seven blouses and a jacket and a hat;
or to give your day to paying
Needless visits, or to playing
Auction bridge. What critic could
  object to that?
But to spend two precious hours
At a lecture! Oh my powers!
The house is all a woman needs to
  learn;
And an hour, or a quarter,
Spent in voting! Why my daughter,
The home would not be there on your
  return.

Suffragists in the United States saw public performances of plays, pageants, and films as one of the most powerful ways of putting across their message. Public performances enabled them to create a positive image, reach a mass audience from a wide range of backgrounds, and also associate their cause with modern values, making it appear more dynamic and exciting. In the United States, pageants were a particularly popular dramatic form that made a strong emotional appeal to audiences. In the suffrage pageant *The Allegory,* held in Washington, D.C., in 1913, a series of pantomimes performed by professionals on the steps of the federal treasury building held thousands of spectators spellbound. Other pageants used imagery of shackled women to dramatize what it meant to be denied the vote by comparing women with criminals and slaves, whereas women with votes were associated with the powerful symbol of liberty. Suffrage theater, pageantry, and film also played on the cult of the individual, making suffrage leaders and suffrage actresses into star personalities. In Britain, well-known actresses joined the Actresses' Franchise League, which had a high profile in suffrage marches and demonstrations, attracting big followings. Onlookers often came to marches simply to see their favorite actresses at close range.

To encourage people to see women's enfranchisement as a positive goal, American plays and films often represented women suffragists as attractive, stylish, and charming but also as dignified and virtuous. This also served to counter antisuffragist images of them as embittered, selfish, man-hating spinsters. For example, in Selina Solomons' play *The Girl from Colorado or the Conversion of Aunty Suffridge,* the heroine is a "womanly voter": young, attractive, and sensible but also able to win a man's heart; Aunt Jane in the suffrage film *Your Girl and Mine* links her love of home and family with her goal of improving society and the condition of women. However, suffrage writers in Britain were less interested in presenting positive images of the womanly woman and mother as voter. Indeed, it has been argued that some rejected this image as being associated with the antisuffrage movement. For example, in Cicely Hamilton's very popular play, *How the Vote Was Won,* all the women characters go on strike, but the "womanly woman" character is exposed as devious, unwilling to support the vote if it will affect her financial investments. Such plays had a tremendous impact on audiences and were often performed in other countries. However, antisuffrage plays could be equally damaging to the movement and had to be contested. In 1940s Costa Rica, members of the official suffrage organization La Liga Feminista were successful in stopping the performance of a play, *Las Candidatas,* that ridiculed suffragists.

Women writers also wrote suffrage novels that enabled them to debate suffrage issues at greater length than was possible in plays or poems. As with other literary forms, novels were written partly to challenge the long-standing popular prejudice against the suffrage movement, typified by the British antisuffragist novelist Eliza Lynn Linton's portrayal of them as a "shrieking sisterhood." This term had been coined in the 1880s and was still in currency in 1907. Women who had been accustomed to negative portrayals of suffragettes welcomed the chance to see their cause represented as important, heroic, and exciting.

As with poetry, novels were often written by well-known activists and frequently reviewed by suffrage leaders in their journals. Their style was usually polemical, aiming to rouse readers' passions, and they were accessible to less sophisticated readers. Plots often included events in the suffrage calendar, sometimes mixing fact and fiction. The style and tone of suffrage fiction changed over time. Late nineteenth-century suffrage novels tended to stress the virtue and moral rectitude of suffragists. For example, in the short story "The Women's Duty," published in Britain by the National Society for Women's Suffrage, women voters oust the drunken local councillor, Mr. Boozey, returning instead a candidate who supports the temperance movement. However, fiction written during the suffrage movement's later militant phase is less concerned with preserving the niceties of Victorian respectability and exposes the sexual double standard. For example, in Annie Tibbit's *At What Sacrifice?* the heroine's advocacy of the suffrage cause is explained by her experiences of marital abuse and sweated labor as a single breadwinner. Novels such as Elizabeth Robins's *The Convert* (1907) and Gertrude Colmore's *Suffragette Sally* (1911) also counter the idea that the suffrage movement was of interest only to middle-class women. They portray work-ing women's involvement in the move-ment and try to forge a sense of sisterhood across class lines.

> *See also* Actresses' Franchise League; Anti-suffrage Movements; Britain; China; *The Convert;* Costa Rica; Davison, Emily Wild-ing; *How the Vote Was Won;* Hunger Strikes; Imagery; Militancy; New Zealand; Pankhurst, (Estelle) Sylvia; Robins, Elizabeth; Sexuality; United States of America; *Votes for Women;* Woman's Christian Temperance Union; Women Writers' Suffrage League.
> *References* Cockburn, Katharine. "Woman's Suffrage Drama" (1998); Croll, Elizabeth. *Feminism and Socialism in China* (1978); Finnegan, Margaret. *Selling Suffrage: Con-sumer Culture and Votes for Women* (1999); Hirschfield, Claire. "The Woman's Theatre in England, 1913–1918" (1995); Joannou, Maroula. "Suffragette Fiction and the Fiction of Suffrage" (1998); Sharratt, Sara. "The Suffragist Movement in Costa Rica, 1889–1949: Centennial of Democracy?" (1997); Showalter, Elaine. *Sexual Anarchy: Gender and Culture at the Fin de Siècle* (1992); Tyler-Bennett, Deborah. "Suffrage and Poetry: Radical Women's Voices" (1998).

Ducoing, Delia

Delia Ducoing was the editor and director of *Nosotras,* journal of the Unión Fe-menina de Chile (Women's Union of Chile). This was one of the leading femi-nist organizations in Chile during the early 1930s that aimed to appeal to both working- and middle-class women. Duco-ing's significance lies chiefly in the fact that her views typify a brand of feminism that was widespread in the countries of the Southern Cone (Chile, Argentina, and Uruguay) in this period.

Ducoing consistently advocated women's suffrage because without it women would have no influence on legislation that re-stricted their rights. However, she was anx-ious to reassure her readers that the social order would not be overturned as a result of the female franchise. Rather, women would use their feminine and maternal sen-sibilities to support men and promote peace

and harmony among all social classes. She believed the work of women should be so-cially oriented and gender-specific, such as the promotion of child welfare.

Ducoing's views, expounded in a book published in 1930 entitled *Charlas Fe-meninas,* had an element of racial stereo-typing. She claimed that the influence of Latin culture had given Chilean feminism an ideal of "conscious order," and she was anxious that Chilean women should not imitate Anglo-Saxon feminists in England and the United States. Ducoing's views were derived partly from firsthand contact with U.S. feminists on a visit to the United States in the late 1920s, where she met Doris Stevens and visited the headquarters of the National Woman's Party. After Ducoing split from Unión Femenina in 1933, she kept control of the magazine *Nosotras* and maintained international links with the International Woman's Suf-frage Alliance in the United States and with other Latin American feminists in Argentina, Peru, Colombia, and Mexico.

> *See also* Chile; Latin America and the Caribbean; National Woman's Party.
> *Reference* Lavrin, Asunción. *Women, Femi-nism and Social Change in Argentina, Chile and Uruguay, 1890–1940* (1995).

Dugdale, Henrietta, and Annie Lowe

Annie Lowe (1834–1908) and Henrietta Dugdale (1826–1908) were leading figures in the campaign for women's suffrage in the state of Victoria in Australia. Dugdale claimed to be the first female suffragist when, in 1869, she began agitating for the vote 16 years before the establishment of the first formal suffrage society. She had emigrated to Australia in 1852 with vivid memories of the Chartist riots for univer-sal male suffrage in England in the 1840s, and she maintained her stance as a radical and a freethinker. In 1883 she published *A Few Hours in Far Off Age,* a utopian vi-sion of the future after women had gained the vote. Dugdale's friend and close associate, Annie Lowe, was born in New South Wales to a father with liberal views who believed in equality between the sexes. On her arrival in Melbourne, she was immediately attracted to the suffrage cause.

In 1884, when both women were in their fifties, Lowe and Dugdale set up the first suffrage organization, the Victorian Women's Suffrage Society. They were moved to take this step by an increase in violent crimes against women, which the authorities were largely ignoring or condoning. Dugdale became president of the society the following year. Both women lived through and beyond the organized suffrage movement's 24-year history in Victoria. Lowe held office in several suffrage societies and was a much valued speaker. Though overshadowed in her latter years by the more famous Vida Gold-stein, she continued to work for the movement until the vote was won two years before her death in 1910. Sadly, she never had the opportunity to cast her own vote. She was described as a broadminded, warm, and likable person with a delightful wit. Dugdale, as a freethinker, placed much of the blame for women's subjection on the Christian church, a position that placed her at odds with most other suffragists, yet she was still accepted within the movement. She married for the third time at the age of 77 and lived to cast her vote on a number of occasions before dying in 1918 at the age of 92.

See also Australia; Drama, Novels, Poetry, and Film; Goldstein, Vida.
Reference Oldfield, Audrey. *Woman Suffrage in Australia: A Gift or a Struggle?* (1992).

Egypt

Egypt experienced its first stirrings of feminist debate at the end of the nineteenth century, when the first women's periodicals were founded (1892) and Qasim Amin published his two major works on the emancipation of women (1899 and 1901). The writings of this early period, however, tended to see women only in functional terms, as members of a social unit, the family, rather than as individual beings with political rights, including the right to vote. It took the 1919 revolution, in which women participated in large numbers, to create a feminist movement with political demands.

In 1920, Nur al-Hudá Sha'rawi (Huda Shaarawi), an upper-class Egyptian married to an important politician, founded the Lajnat al-Wafd al-Markaziyah lil-Sayyidat, or Ladies' Central Committee of the Wafd (Egyptian Nationalist) Party (LCC), which gave Egyptian women their first political, mainly nationalist, voice. Egypt was formally declared an independent state in 1922, and the new constitution of March 1923 granted equality of rights and duties and also universal suffrage. However, the election law of April 1923 restricted suffrage to men alone. In March the same year, Hudá Sha'rawi founded the Jam'iyat al-Ittihad al-Nisa'i al-Misri, or Egyptian Feminist Union (EFU), and in May she led a delegation to the 1923 Congress of the International Woman Suffrage Alliance in Rome, where the Egyptian women were warmly re-

ceived. In 1924, when the new Egyptian Parliament opened, the EFU, the WCC, and members of the Jam'iyat al-Mar'ah al-Jadidah (New Woman Society), founded in 1919, all demonstrated in favor of women's right to vote, presenting a list of 32 demands to members of Parliament and government officials. The demand was not for unconditional female suffrage but, consonant with the upper-class membership of the EFU, proposed an educational qualification for female voters. The Wafd Party, which was in government, attempted to defuse the situation by founding a women's newspaper, *Al-Amal* (Hope), whose editor, Munirah Thabit (Mounira Sabet), was an avowed advocate of the enfranchisement of women. The EFU, however, aligned itself with the opposition Liberal Constitutional Party and in 1926 temporarily suspended the quest for female suffrage to concentrate on legal reform and the promotion of women's education.

The granting of the right to vote to women in Turkey in 1934 persuaded the EFU to bring the suffrage cause to center stage once more, and the organization brought a large delegation to the IAW Congress in Istanbul in 1935, led by Hudá Sha'rawi. In Egypt, they pressed the prime minister for the right to vote for and be elected to municipal boards and provincial councils. Munirah Thabit represented the EFU at the IAW Congress in Copenhagen in 1939, calling on governments to enfranchise women to promote peace, and in 1944, Sha'rawi and other delegates de-

On the Egyptian flag is written, "Islam is the solution"; Egyptian women show their patriotism as they register to vote. (Gamma)

manded political rights for all Arab women at the Arab Women's Congress in Cairo.

During the same period, the EFU faced a challenge to its authority as the voice of Egyptian feminism. Fatimah Ni'mat Rashid founded al-Hizb al-Nisa'i al-Watani (the National Feminist Party) in 1944, and Durriyah Shafiq (Doria Shafik) founded the Ittihad Bint al-Nil (Bint al-Nil Union) in 1948; together they attracted middle-class women into political activity. Although the three organizations could form a broad coalition on nationalist issues, they were unable to present a united front in the struggle for the franchise. Hudá Sha'rawi died in 1947, and it was the younger Durriyah Shafiq who led the demands for the vote in the aftermath of World War II. In 1951, she led an invasion of Parliament, in 1952 she published an important white paper on the vote, and in 1954 she went on a hunger strike. The po-

litical climate of liberalism, which had allowed debate on suffrage in the 1920s and 1930s, was replaced in the 1950s both by an increasingly vocal Islamic conservatism and by the authoritarian rule of President Gamal Abdel Nasser. Despite these changes, the activities of Shafiq and her colleagues and the demands of a modernizing state persuaded Nasser to grant women the vote in 1956. However, although all men who qualified for the franchise were automatically registered for the vote, women had to make a special request to exercise their political rights, and as late as 1972, only 12 percent had been registered. Finally, in an ironic epilogue, having just won the vote, both the EFU and the Bint al-Nil Union were forced to disband in 1957, following a political clampdown by the Egyptian government.

See also Nationalism; Shafiq, Durriyah; Sha'rawi, Nur al-Hudá.

References Abdel-Kader, Soha. *Egyptian Women in a Changing Society, 1899–1987* (1987); Amin, Qasim. *The Liberation of Woman: A Document in the History of Egyptian Feminism* (1992). Badran, Margot. *Feminists, Islam and Nation: Gender and the Making of Modern Egypt* (1995); Philipp, Thomas. "Feminism and Nationalist Politics in Egypt" (1978).

Fawcett, Millicent Garrett

The recognized leader of the British constitutional suffragist movement, Millicent Garrett (1847–1929) was born in Suffolk, the daughter of Newson Garrett, a successful, Liberal, middle-class businessman. In 1867 she married the blind member of Parliament and academic Henry Fawcett (1833–1884), who was a friend of the Liberal philosopher and keen advocate of women's suffrage, John Stuart Mill.

Millicent Fawcett was involved in the women's movement from early on—her sister Elizabeth knew the women of the Langham Place Circle, and through her numerous contacts Fawcett met many prominent suffragists. Fawcett became increasingly involved in writing and speaking on the subject of the emancipation of women, campaigning for the Married Women's Property Bill, leading the National Vigilance Association's campaign against the exploitation of children, and becoming a member of the executive committee of the London National Society for Women's Suffrage, which was set up in 1867. Later, Fawcett joined the Central Committee of the National Society for Women's Suffrage, which had been established in 1872 to coordinate the activities of the various suffrage societies.

In 1888 Fawcett, together with pioneer suffragist Lydia Becker, were among those women who left the Central Committee because they did not believe that Women's Liberal Associations (local auxiliaries of the Liberal party) should be allowed to affiliate with an organization that had always maintained a nonparty stance. Members who disagreed with them decided to accept affiliations and formed a new group, called the Central National Society for Women's Suffrage, while Fawcett and her colleagues retained the name of the Central Committee of the National Society for Women's Suffrage. Fawcett's fervent belief that the women's suffrage movement should campaign from a nonparty position was to dominate the constitutional suffrage movement for almost a quarter of a century.

When Lydia Becker died in 1890, Fawcett was already recognized as a leading proponent of women's suffrage with considerable experience in political matters, which included speaking on public platforms against Irish Home Rule (she left the Liberal Party temporarily to join the Liberal Unionists over the issue). It was this wealth of experience that led suffragists to ask her to head the new umbrella organization for the 17 most important suffrage societies in Britain, the National Union of Women's Suffrage Societies (NUWSS), on its formation in 1897. She was formally elected as president in 1907.

During her years as president of the NUWSS, Fawcett saw a considerable growth in the size and influence of the British suffrage movement as a whole. She was responsible for nonviolent campaigning, and she shaped the organization's successful strategy of working within the parliamentary system to achieve its aims. At

Millicent Garrett Fawcett was a leader of the woman's suffrage movement in England for 50 years. (Ann Ronan Picture Library)

cett began to correspond with a sympathetic journalist, Henry N. Brailsford, about the possibility of forming an all-party Conciliation Committee for Women's Suffrage, which would draw up a moderate women's suffrage measure that would be acceptable to a majority of MPs. Fawcett agreed to the plan, and the resulting Conciliation Bill was based on the municipal franchise, which would give the vote, predominantly, to single women who were occupiers and householders. After three unsuccessful attempts between 1910 and 1912 to get the Conciliation Bill passed by the House of Commons, Fawcett became completely disillusioned with the Liberal government, despite her personal sympathies for the Liberal cause. She also blamed the WSPU and its increasingly militant campaign for the unexpected increase in the antisuffrage vote on the Conciliation Bill in March 1912. Reluctantly, she agreed to break the nonparty position of the NUWSS and enter into an alliance with the Labour Party, which was committed to advancing the cause of women's suffrage. This alliance, agreed upon by the NUWSS in May 1912, caused a considerable rift amongst the membership and led to the resignation of Eleanor Rathbone from the executive committee.

There were further disagreements among the NUWSS membership when, on the outbreak of World War I in 1914, Fawcett urged support for the war effort, despite the opposition of many of her colleagues. Fawcett believed that if the NUWSS adopted a peace policy, the chances of gaining the vote would be greatly damaged, and she suffered the loss of half of her executive committee for the sake of her principles. The remaining members of the NUWSS backed Fawcett, and it was agreed to suspend all political activity for the duration of the war.

However, toward the end of the war, the question of electoral reform was revived, and Fawcett and the NUWSS played a

first, Fawcett had admired the more flamboyant tactics of the suffragettes of the Women's Social and Political Union (WSPU), but as militancy increased after 1908, she expressed the fear that such tactics would cause the suffrage movement to lose potential support in the House of Commons. She herself preferred to use traditional campaigning methods such as presenting petitions, lobbying MPs, and organizing meetings and marches.

The women's suffrage campaign made considerable progress during the first decade of the twentieth century, and although successive private members' bills attracted the support of many MPs, they continued to be unsuccessful, mainly because the political parties disagreed as to the form that any enlargement of the franchise should take. In January 1910 Faw-

considerable part in the negotiations over the form any proposed franchise extension should take. Many members of the government had come to believe that some measure of women's suffrage was inevitable, and as a result, in 1918 the Representation of the People Act granted the parliamentary vote to all women over the age of 30 who were on the local government register, or who were wives of men on that register. Fawcett could claim much of the credit for this victory, for she had worked consistently for the women's suffrage cause for more than 50 years of her life. She resigned the presidency of the NUWSS in 1919, and Eleanor Rathbone became the head of a renamed group, the National Union of Societies for Equal Citizenship, which was to continue the struggle for equal franchise reform, with Fawcett's full support. In recognition of her work on behalf of women, Fawcett was made a Dame Grand Cross Order of the British Empire (DBE) in 1925.

Millicent Fawcett was dedicated to the liberal principles of progress and improvement, which she used in her argument for the expansion of the legal and political rights of women. She believed that granting women the vote would serve to confirm their rights of citizenship and give them the opportunity to bring their domestic experience to bear on the decisions of government. Fawcett was a pragmatic campaigner who worked within the political system to achieve her ends, and she lived long enough to witness the granting of parliamentary suffrage to all women in 1928.

See also Becker, Lydia Ernestine; Britain; Citizenship; Conciliation Bill; Langham Place Circle; Liberalism; Mill, John Stuart; National Union of Women's Suffrage Societies; Rathbone, Eleanor; Representation of the People Act; Women's Social and Political Union.
References Caine, Barbara. *Victorian Feminists* (1992); Rubinstein, David. *A Different World for Women: The Life of Millicent Garrett Fawcett* (1991).

Finland

In 1906, Finland became the first European country to give women the vote. As in Norway, in Finland the achievement of women's enfranchisement was closely linked to nationalism. Until the early nineteenth century, Finland had been part of Sweden, from which it derived its political institutions. Only a minority of the population in Finland were able to vote for the legislature, the Diet. Swedish was the official language for politics, business, and the law and was spoken by approximately 10 percent of the population, mostly members of the upper classes. In 1809 Finland came under the rule of Russia but retained a separate status as a Grand Duchy. It was guaranteed its own constitution, but the decisions of the Diet had to be ratified by the Tsar, which was used by the Finns to undermine the power of the Swedish-speaking minority. In the 1880s, after Finnish nationalists pressured the Tsar, they achieved official equality for the Finnish language. Middle-class women played an important role in the movement to ensure that Finnish language and literature were taught in schools.

It was not, however, until equality in public affairs between the Swedes and the Finns had been achieved in the early 1880s that women began to raise their own issues. In 1884, Suomen Naisyhdistys (the Finnish Women's Association), led by Elizabeth Löfgren, was founded by a group of women in Helsinki who had met to discuss John Stuart Mill's *On the Subjection of Women*. They demanded equal rights in education and employment and sought legislation to end the double standard of morality between the sexes. Support was also given to votes for women, and in 1884 a debate was held in the Diet on the question of women's suffrage based on a tax-paying qualification. This prompted the Women's Association to organize a petition on the subject. Nonetheless, women's suffrage was never the main concern of the association, which took far more interest in nationalist politics and in moral reform and philanthropy. Löfgren was married to the editor of the nationalist newspaper *Uusi Suometar,* and other leading figures in the organization, including Alexandra Gripenberg, also had family links with the Finnish nationalist cause.

In 1892 a new group, Naisasialitto Unioni (the Feminist Union), led by the teacher Lucina Hagman, was formed to concentrate on women's suffrage, but even this development was linked to changes in nationalist politics. Now that equality with the Swedes had been achieved, radical nationalists, called the Young Finns, sought freedom from Russia. Hagman's group, mostly supported by younger women who had been born in the 1860s, supported these aims, in contrast to more moderate leaders of the Women's Association who were prepared to compromise with the Russians.

The importance of nationalism and the large size of the agricultural sector militated against the development of a strong women's movement. Throughout this period, feminist groups remained small in size and their memberships were largely comprised of upper-class women, although the Women's Association did attempt to interest peasant women by establishing reading and lecture groups in the countryside. There was also conflict between the "bourgeois" feminist movement, which demanded votes for women within the existing framework of representation based on class and property ownership, and female members of the labor movement, who viewed the suffrage as a working-class issue, rather than as a women's issue, and demanded universal voting rights for both sexes. By 1904 women, drawn from urban areas and centers of rural industry, formed nearly a quarter of the membership of the Finnish Social Democratic Party and were instrumental in ensuring that the party would demand an unrestricted franchise for women as well as men. Thus, in 1904 feminist groups held a mass demonstration of 1,000 women to demand voting rights equal with the existing rights of men, and in the same year the Social Democrats, supported by the nationalist liberals, held demonstrations in favor of universal and equal suffrage.

The increasing repression by the Russian government in the early twentieth century, however, and the attempt to introduce a program of Russification in education and administration led to greater cooperation between Finnish liberals and socialists. Nonetheless, it was the Russian Revolution of 1905 that provided the main catalyst for franchise reform. Unrest in Russia spread to Finland, where there were widespread general strikes. In an attempt to reestablish law and order, the Tsar acceded to the demands of the working class for the reform of voting rights. This was confirmed in the November manifesto of 1905. In the following year, universal and equal suffrage was ratified by the Diet and a unicameral parliament was established.

It has been suggested that the close working relationship between men and women on farms in this predominantly agricultural society and the cooperation between the sexes in the nationalist movement made it easier to accept the idea that political rights should be extended to women. Nineteen women were successful in the first elections for the new parliament, but the reimposition of Russian control after 1906 meant that enfranchisement had little real meaning until after the demise of the Tsar in 1917.

See also Gripenberg, Alexandra; Mill, John Stuart; Nationalism; *On the Subjection of Women.*
References Evans, Richard J. *The Feminists: Women's Emancipation Movements in Europe, America and Australasia, 1840–1920* (1977); Jallinoja, Riitta. "The Women's Liberation Movement in Finland" (1980).

First International Women's Congress, Buenos Aires (1910)

The First International Women's Congress (Primero Congreso Femenino Internacional) held in Buenos Aires in 1910 offered the earliest opportunity for Latin American suffragists to make a united case for the woman's vote. This conference brought together more than 200 women representing Argentina, Uruguay, Peru, Paraguay, and Chile. It enabled emerging feminist leaders, such as Paulina Luisi from Uruguay, to make international contacts and friendships that would endure during the long struggle to achieve the vote in Latin American countries.

Although the majority of papers at this conference did not focus on suffrage, four speakers did discuss it in some depth: J. Maria Samae from Peru and Ann Amontlavo, Raquel Messina, and Maria Josefa González, all from Argentina. Samae linked the rise of the labor movement to new opportunities for women's political participation. Amontlavo argued from a nineteenth-century liberal perspective, invoking ideas of justice and equality. She claimed that women should have the vote both as workers who paid taxes and as mothers who sacrificed their children to war. Messina, who represented the Socialist Women's Center, also spoke on behalf of working women, arguing that because they had no direct representation, working women had to beg men to make social reforms. Finally, González from the National League of Women Freethinkers laid down a challenge to women to end their legal subordination to men, arguing that this liberation could only occur if they got the vote.

Together these women offered an important set of arguments upon which suffragists could draw and expand in future decades to gain a wider audience. Latin American suffragists also participated in pan-American and inter-European conferences. These meetings enabled suffragist leaders to refine their ideas and strengthen their beliefs, which in turn helped them recruit more supporters in their home countries. They also made important international contacts and gained the sense that they were part of a broader movement.

See also Argentina; International Woman Suffrage Alliance; Latin America and the Caribbean; Pan-American Women's Conference; Peru.

References Ehrick, Christine. "*Madrinas* and Missionaries: Uruguay and the Pan-American Women's Movement" (1998); Lavrin, Asunción. "Suffrage in South America: Arguing a Difficult Cause" (1994).

Flapper Vote

"Flapper vote" was a popular phrase used in Britain during the 1920s to indicate the potential voting power of the 2 million

"WELL, SO YOU'RE GOING TO HAVE THE VOTE AT LAST."

"OH, ONLY WOMEN OVER THIRTY, YOU KNOW."

"Votes for women—the first step." This cartoon from Punch, *London, 11 April 1917 illustrates the concern over young women, or "flappers," gaining suffrage. (Ann Ronan Picture Library)*

adult women under 30 who had not been enfranchised by the 1918 Representation of the People Act. The word *flapper* had connotations of youthful irresponsibility. In 1927 the humorous journal *Punch* noted that "Flapper is the popular press catchword for an adult woman worker aged 18–21, when it is a question of giving her a vote under the same condition as men." It was used derogatorily in articles run by the popular press, especially the *Daily Mail* and the *Evening Standard,* in the period leading up to the 1928 Representation of the People (Equal Franchise) Act, which finally gave women in the United Kingdom the vote on equal terms with men.

See also Britain; Representation of the People Act; Representation of the People (Equal Franchise) Act.
References Beddoe, Deirdre. *Back to Home and Duty: Women between the Wars, 1918–1939* (1989); Graves, Robert, and Alan Hodge. *The Long Weekend: A Social History of Great Britain, 1918–1939* (1941).

Ford, Isabella

Isabella Ford (1855–1924) was a socialist and a leading member of the British constitutionalist suffrage group, the National Union of Women's Suffrage Societies (NUWSS). Born in Leeds, England, she was the youngest of eight children of the Quaker solicitor Robert Lawson Ford and his wife Hannah (née Pease), who encouraged all their children to take an interest in social and political questions, including women's rights. During the 1880s and 1890s Isabella Ford became involved in the trade union organization of textile workers and tailoresses in Leeds. Her support for women on strike in this period led her away from the radical liberal politics of her family. With her two closest sisters, Bessie and Emily, she became a member of a socialist group, the Independent Labour Party, in 1893. She was also a member of the Leeds Women's Suffrage Society. She believed that women should have the right to vote not only on the grounds of natural

justice, but also so that they could work for socialism alongside men and therefore help to shape the new society and improve the position of working women. An able and witty platform speaker, Isabella Ford spent the next few years carrying out propaganda for socialism, for trade union organization, and for women's suffrage. She also expressed her ideas in numerous articles in socialist and feminist newspapers and in her three novels. Between 1903 and 1907 she served on the National Administrative Council of the ILP and went from there as a delegate to Labour Party conferences, where she was the first woman to speak when she supported a motion that women should be given the vote on the same terms as men.

After 1906, when the increased vigor of the suffrage campaign convinced her that all other issues should take second place, Isabella Ford directed her energies more fully to the agitation for the vote. She was elected to the executive committee of the NUWSS in 1907 and worked tirelessly for the cause, speaking at meetings all over the country including large demonstrations in London, taking part in deputations to the government, and attending international congresses. She also played a part in helping to bring the labor and socialist movements closer to the suffrage movement and was overjoyed when the Labour Party formed an alliance with the NUWSS in 1912. After war was declared, Isabella became increasingly convinced that suffragists should work for peace. Along with a number of other women she resigned from the executive committee of the NUWSS in 1915, which caused a temporary rift with her close friend, the union's president, Millicent Fawcett. When it became clear toward the end of the war that the government intended to introduce a franchise bill, Isabella renewed her suffrage activities, although she argued that the proposal to enfranchise only women over 30 was an insult. She was asked to stand as a Labour Party candidate in the 1918 election but refused on the grounds of ill health. Nonetheless, she continued to attend international conferences on peace and women's rights and to campaign for the Labour Party until her death in 1924.

Isabella Ford was an example of a well-educated middle-class woman who devoted her life to socialist and feminist causes and to improving the lives of working women. She had a wide circle of male and female friends in the labor and women's movements at home and abroad. Her commitment to socialism, peace, and women's rights often brought her into conflict with one or other of these friends, but her even-tempered personality, her desire to reach agreement by consensus, and her ability to laugh at herself enabled these friendships to survive. Contemporaries acknowledged her considerable influence on the leaders of the socialist ILP, which helped to ensure that the needs of working-class women and the importance of women's suffrage were not forgotten.

See also Britain; Fawcett, Millicent Garrett; National Union of Women's Suffrage Societies; Socialism in Europe.
Reference Hannam, June. *Isabella Ford, 1855–1924* (1989).

Fourteenth and Fifteenth Amendments

The Fourteenth Amendment to the United States Constitution (1868), which sought to secure black voting rights, caused controversy among women suffrage supporters because it introduced the word *male* into the Constitution for the first time. Until then, women's right to vote had been seen as a matter for individual states to decide, but the Fourteenth Amendment would require another amendment to the Constitution to enable women to vote in federal elections. Moreover, the Fourteenth Amendment made an explicit connection between citizenship and the exercise of the franchise. In this context Elizabeth Cady Stanton, Susan B. Anthony, and their followers opposed the Fourteenth Amendment when it was introduced to Congress in 1866, with Stanton in particular making derogatory remarks about the enfranchisement of black and immigrant males when educated white women were excluded.

The opponents of the amendment argued that women had subordinated their own interests during the Civil War for the cause of abolition and should now be rewarded. Stanton and her supporters organized a petition to prevent the states from disenfranchising any of their citizens on the basis of sex, but they gathered a smaller number of signatures than expected. They also failed to receive the backing of the Republicans, who hoped to gain from loyal black voters but felt less secure about the female vote. Other suffragists, including Lucy Stone, Frances Harper, and Julia Ward Howe, were not prepared to endanger the passage of the amendment, even if they disagreed with the precise wording.

The Fourteenth Amendment was ratified in July 1868, and six months later Radical Republicans introduced a Fifteenth Amendment into Congress that read "the right of citizens of the United States to vote shall not be denied or abridged by the United States or any state on account of race, or color, or previous condition of servitude." This caused further dissension among supporters of women's suffrage. Stanton and her followers again decided to oppose this amendment unless women were included, and they further alienated feminist abolitionists by accepting the backing of George Train, a Democrat, a railroad promoter, and a known racist, to launch a newspaper, the *Revolution*.

The women's movement finally split in 1869. At a convention held in January, Elizabeth Cady Stanton had called for a women's suffrage amendment to the Constitution, leading to a fierce debate within the American Equal Rights Association, a group established after the Civil War to pursue the interests of blacks and women. Stanton and Anthony believed that the association, with its predominantly male leadership, was emphasizing black rights and neglecting the needs of women. They therefore formed a new organization, the National Woman Suffrage Association, which aimed to secure women's suffrage and other reforms and was open to women only. A few months later, a second group, the American Woman Suffrage Association, was established in Cleveland. It concentrated on women's suffrage and drew its membership from both sexes.

The Fifteenth Amendment was finally passed in 1870. The issues raised by both amendments had provided the occasion for a split in the women's suffrage movement that was to last for 20 years. It also ensured that in the future, the supporters of women's enfranchisement would have to seek a constitutional amendment of their own rather than relying on securing voting rights simply at the level of the individual states.

> *See also* American Woman Suffrage Association; Anthony, Susan B.; Citizenship; National Woman Suffrage Association; Race and Ethnicity; The *Revolution;* Stanton, Elizabeth Cady; Stone, Lucy; United States of America.
> *Reference* Flexner, Eleanor. *Century of Struggle: The Woman's Rights Movement in the United States* ([1959] 1975).

France

An organized movement for women's suffrage was slow to develop in France, despite the fact that the demand for women's political rights was voiced as early as the French Revolution, when Olympe de Gouges produced *Declaration of the Rights of Woman and of the Female Citizen* (1791). There was a revival of activity on behalf of women's suffrage during the upheavals of 1848, when adult men received the vote. Women from diverse backgrounds, including Eugénie Niboyet, a middle-class philanthropist from Lyons; Desirée Gay, a dressmaker; and the socialist teachers Jeanne Deroin and Pauline Roland, called for political and civil equality. They were unsuccessful, however, and during the early years of the Second Empire of Louis Napoléon Bonaparte, the possibility of any political activity was limited.

An organized movement for women's rights did not develop until the 1860s and 1870s, when a number of feminist groups were formed, including Société pour l'amélioration du sort de la femme, established in 1871 by Léon Richer and Marie Deraismes. The main aim of these groups, however, was to achieve educational and legal reforms rather than the vote. The demand for women's suffrage was raised in the 1870s by Hubertine Auclert, who established her own group, Suffrage des femmes (Women's Suffrage). She criticized the moderate outlook of other feminist organizations and aimed to attract support from women of all social classes. She used radical tactics, organizing street demonstrations and an "unofficial" shadow election, and founded a magazine, *La Citoyenne* (the Citizeness), which lasted from 1881 to 1891. Her suffrage society never had more than a few hundred members and was weakened in the 1890s by internal quarrels that led to the establishment of a rival group, La Solidarité des femmes (Women's Solidarity).

Although the demand for women's suffrage was well established by the 1890s, the movement was weakened by splits between secular republicans, Catholics, and socialists that reflected more general divisions in French politics. The suffrage movement did gain a new momentum, however, after the turn of the century. Inspired by the establishment of the International Woman Suffrage Alliance, Auclert, along with Madeleine Pelletier and Caroline Kauffmann, engaged in militant acts such as showering the Chamber of Deputies with suffragist handbills in 1906 and organizing small parades (rarely attracting more than 50 participants). In that same year, Marie Maugeret, a Catholic suffragist, managed to persuade the annual congress of the Catholic women's movement to debate women's suffrage, and a resolution endorsing full political rights for women was passed by a narrow margin, although the majority of delegates abstained.

The most important group on the moderate wing of the suffrage movement, however, was the Union française pour le suffrage des femmes (UFSF) [French Union for Women's Suffrage], formed in 1909 with the intention of bringing republican and Catholic women together. Active members were drawn largely from the liberal professions, and between 1910 and 1914 the UFSF was led by Cecile Brunschwicg, the wife of a professor. The union had a membership of 10,000, although the affiliated societies sought a range of reforms and not only the vote. In 1914 the UFSF managed to organize an outdoor assembly that attracted 6,000 participants, far fewer than the 25,000 to 50,000 who turned up to suffrage demonstrations in London.

In contrast to women in most other European countries, French women did not receive the vote in the period following World War I. Although the Chamber of Deputies voted in favor of women's right to vote and stand for election in the same way as men, this was overturned by the Senate in 1922.

The women's suffrage movement in France had an uphill struggle. Suffragists were divided among themselves and had to deal with a republican tradition that was masculine in both theory and practice. Suffragists faced opposition from politicians who feared that if women had

the vote they would support Catholicism and monarchism and therefore endanger the Third Republic. This view may have been reinforced by the establishment in 1920 of the first Catholic organization whose only objective was women's suffrage, the Union nationale pour le vote des femmes (National Union for Women's Votes). The persistence of these fears during the interwar years hampered the success of the suffrage movement. Although the movement had extended its organization beyond Paris and into the provinces, so that by 1929 the UFSF alone had 100,000 members, during this period the Radical Party in the Senate joined with conservatives time and again to defeat women's suffrage bills that were passed in the lower house. It was not until the upheaval of World War II provided the conditions for a thorough reorganization of the institutions of the republic that an ordinance enfranchising women, supported by General de Gaulle, was finally passed on 21 April 1944. In 1945 women were able to vote and to stand for election at a local and national level for the first time.

See also Auclert, Hubertine; Brunschwicg, Cecile; Citizenship; French Revolution; International Woman Suffrage Alliance; Kauffmann, Caroline; Pelletier, Madeleine; Union française pour le suffrage des femmes.
References Hause, Steven C., with Anne R. Kenney. *Women's Suffrage and Social Politics in the Third French Republic* (1984); Reynolds, Siân. "Marianne's Citizens? Women, the Republic and Universal Suffrage in France" (1986); Smith, Paul. "Political Parties, Parliament and Women's Suffrage in France, 1919–39" (1997).

French Revolution

The mid-eighteenth-century European philosophical movement known as the Enlightenment produced considerable debate on the issues of women's nature and role in society, so it was natural that the intellectual ferment of the French Revolution of 1789 should give an impetus to the ideas of those writers, like the philosopher

Condorcet, who had written sympathetically about women's claims to political and legal equality.

Women participated in the revolution from the beginning, when they marched from Paris to Versailles in October 1789 to protest to King Louis XVI about bread shortages, and they continued to be actively involved as revolutionary citizens until 1793. It was during their confrontation with the king at Versailles that they forced him to agree to the Declaration of the Rights of Man and of the Citizen, which had been accepted by the National Assembly on 26 August 1789. The Declaration of Rights did not apply to women, and during the National Assembly's debate on the new constitution, this discrimination was reaffirmed when the limits of the franchise were defined. "Active" citizens were defined as male taxpayers—women, foreigners, and servants were among those considered to be "passive" citizens.

In 1791, as the new revolutionary constitution was about to be completed, Olympe de Gouges wrote the feminist document *Déclaration des droits de la femme et de la citoyenne* (Declaration of the rights of woman and of the female citizen). She had adopted the form and language of the Declaration of the Rights of Man, calling for full political equality for women, together with laws that would protect women's property and inheritance rights and children's legitimacy. De Gouges was joined by the Dutch-born revolutionary Etta Palm d'Aelders, who addressed the National Assembly on the question of equal rights for women, especially in the areas of marriage and education. These ideas were disseminated through pamphlets, journals, and petitions and in the numerous women's clubs and societies that had been set up in the early days of the revolution.

De Gouges supported the constitutional monarchy, and at about the same time that the Jacobins began to close down the women's clubs in a move to restrict the public activities of women, she was arrested, tried, and guillotined in November 1783. Revolutionary women like de Gouges became forgotten and neglected in the prolonged reaction against the participation of women in political life that lasted well into the nineteenth century.

Despite these setbacks, the vocabulary of rights contained in the ideas of the Enlightenment and the French Revolution was appropriated and used by the American feminist Abigail Adams (1744–1818), and later, by the leaders of the American women's suffrage movement. In Britain, the writer Mary Wollstonecraft was influenced by the initial idealism of the revolutionaries when she wrote her classic text, *A Vindication of the Rights of Woman* (1792)—a book that was to have a profound influence on liberal feminism.

See also Citizenship; France; Wollstonecraft, Mary.
Reference Levy, Darlene Gay, and Harriet B. Applewhite. "Women and Political Revolution in Paris" (1977).

Frente Único Pro-Derechos de la Mujer (Sole Front for Women's Rights)

Frente Único Pro-Derechos de la Mujer was formed by feminists in Mexico in 1935. It was set up in the wake of three national congresses for women, peasants, and workers held between 1931 and 1934. Although these congresses had revealed the difficulties of uniting these groups in a program for women's rights, it had become apparent that women's suffrage was the one issue on which all feminists agreed, regardless of ideological persuasion.

Frente Único's chief organizer and strategist was María del Refugio García. She concentrated her efforts on achieving the vote in order to gain the support of all Mexican feminists. She was also encouraged by the election in 1934 of President

Lázaro Cárdenas, who had raised hopes that a women's suffrage campaign might be successful. Refugio García created a genuinely popular union embracing 800 women's groups with 50,000 members, many of whom were native women. Suffrage was placed at the top of Frente Único's list of goals.

In July 1937 Refugio García ran for a seat in the Chamber of Deputies. Like Hermila Galindo and Elvia Carrillo Puerto before her, she justified this step on the grounds that the constitution did not specify that women were excluded from citizenship. Although votes cast indicated that Refugio García had won the election, the National Executive Committee refused to seat her on the grounds that it would be necessary to amend the constitution before women could vote or hold office at the national level. When Refugio García and her followers in Frente Único staged a hunger strike, President Cárdenas agreed to submit a bill to amend Article 34 of the constitution.

As a result of strong pressure on the government by Frente Único and other feminist organizations, Mexican women came very near to gaining the vote in the late 1930s. They were betrayed by the Senate, which in 1939 refused to complete the ratification process of the amendment to Article 34, even though it had been passed by the Chamber of Deputies and all 28 Mexican states. Mexican women did not achieve full political rights until 1958, by which time Frente Único's meetings, demonstrations, marches, and hunger strikes were barely remembered.

See also Citizenship; Galindo, Hermila; Mexico.
Reference Macías, Anna. *Against All Odds: The Feminist Movement in Mexico to 1940* (1982).

Friendship Networks

Friendship links between women played a crucial role in the development of the women's suffrage movement, both at a national and at an international level. Indeed, it has been suggested that the dynamic of women's political activity cannot be fully understood through a study of organizations and institutions alone but must be seen as rooted in "personal value systems and in the bonds of family, friendship and community" (Holton, 1994, 213). The suffrage movement, in particular in the nineteenth century, drew the bulk of its membership from well-educated, urban, middle-class women, many of whom, such as members of the Bright family in Britain, already had family and friendship ties that were based on shared political and intellectual values. These networks formed the basis of women's commitment to the suffrage campaign and continued to reinforce that commitment. Conversely, friendship links, such as those of Elizabeth Cady Stanton and Susan B. Anthony from the United States, could also grow *out of* involvement in the suffrage struggle and help to contribute to its success. Family and friendship networks were closely intertwined; marriages were welcomed when they promised to extend the circle of women's suffrage friendships, and there are numerous examples of women who influenced their female relatives across the generations. Elizabeth Cady Stanton and Emmeline Pankhurst are two of the best-known examples of mothers whose daughters joined them in the suffrage campaign.

Women who struggled to challenge their exclusion from politics faced ridicule, hostility, and potential social ostracism at a time when they were identified with the private sphere, and therefore friendship from like-minded women offered much needed emotional support. Political activism affected all areas of women's lives and became inextricably linked with the development of close friendships between suffragists. They maintained their relationships through an extensive correspondence and by meeting at social gatherings, where they could combine relaxation with more formal aims, as well as by getting together at organized events such as conferences or demonstrations. In Australia, for example, Rose Scott used her network of contacts with feminists, writers, and journalists to build up the suffrage movement in New South Wales and maintained her friendships by writing copious letters. She also had a passionate interest in the work of women in other countries and kept in touch through a network of overseas correspondents.

Friendships that developed between suffragists across national boundaries helped to strengthen international ties and understanding. Members of the Bright family in Britain, for example, formed a close friendship with Elizabeth Cady Stanton and Lucretia Mott when they attended the World Anti-Slavery Convention in London in 1840; Sandra Stanley Holton argues that their relationship formed the basis for links between the British and U.S. women's movements that continued into subsequent generations. She suggests that an understanding of such friendship networks can change our view of suffrage history, in particular, our view of militancy, which she believes had its roots in the nineteenth-century abolitionist movement, the British Anti-Corn Law League, and nonconformist opposition to the established church. Thus, militancy was not just a British initiative that was imported to the United States, but it also grew out of "a cross national impulse, one that Elizabeth Cady Stanton and Harriot Stanton Blatch helped foster in Britain" (Holton, 1994, 229).

International leaders such as Carrie Chapman Catt could inspire great devotion in their followers, and intense friendships developed within the International Woman Suffrage Alliance, such as that between Aletta Jacobs, Carrie Chapman Catt, and Rosika Schwimmer. Leila Rupp suggests that women's friendships "cemented their international collective identity," and that they expressed their commitment to internationalism "by forming attachments across national borders" (Rupp, 1997, 203–204). Similarly, she points to the use of family metaphors to describe the nature of women's relationships with each other; Carrie Chapman Catt and Jane Addams described themselves, and were seen by others, as mothers. Bertha Lutz, for example, addressed Catt as "My dear mother" and signed herself "your Brazilian daughter" (Rupp, 1997, 199–200). Rupp argues, then, that women who organized internationally were challenging the view that families are only biological or national, and therefore that they were making another step toward internationalism.

By encouraging women to share experiences and aims, friendship networks among suffragists helped to reinforce their commitment to a common political cause. On the other hand, these networks did not necessarily overcome the many divisions that existed between women. There could be great bitterness, for example, when intense friendships, such as that between Rosika Schwimmer and Aletta Jacobs, broke down. Moreover, friendship circles could reinforce divisions over approach and strategy; the Bright circle, for instance, represented a more radical outlook on women's suffrage than did that of Millicent Fawcett and the London Society, and the Brights used their friendship with Elizabeth Cady Stanton to gain her support in 1882 for their argument that any proposal for women's suffrage should include married women. Friendship networks could also be exclusive as well as inclusive. Friendships develop most easily between women from similar backgrounds, and they did not necessarily extend very easily, therefore, to working-class women or to women from outside

Europe and North America, and seldom took place between Black and white women in the United States and Australia. Suffragists who were involved in mixed-sex politics, such as the socialist movement, were also ambivalent about the emphasis on a separate women's culture. By intertwining personal feelings with political aims, friendship networks, whatever their limitations, helped to ensure that women had a passionate commitment to the suffrage cause and sustained them over long years of campaigning.

See also Anthony, Susan B.; Catt, Carrie Chapman; Fawcett, Millicent Garrett; Jacobs, Aletta; Lutz, Bertha; Mott, Lucretia Coffin; Pankhurst, Emmeline; Schwimmer, Rosika; Scott, Rose; Stanton, Elizabeth Cady.
References Holton, Sandra Stanley. "From Anti-Slavery to Suffrage Militancy: The Bright Circle, Elizabeth Cady Stanton and the British Women's Movement" (1994); Levine, Philippa. "Love, Feminism and Friendship in Later Nineteenth-Century England" (1990); Rupp, Leila. *Worlds of Women: The Making of an International Women's Movement* (1997).

Fusen Kakutôku Dômei (League for Woman's Suffrage)

Fusen Kakutôku Dômei (FKD) [League for Woman's Suffrage], formed in 1924 by the well-known feminist leader Ichikawa Fusae, was the most prominent Japanese woman's organization to place suffrage as its principal goal. It attracted mainly middle-class women and never succeeded in recruiting a large membership. At the height of its campaign for a local suffrage bill in 1930, it had only 1,511 members, mainly from the Tokyo area.

The FKD concentrated its efforts on lobbying members of the Diet. At every Diet session following the granting of universal manhood suffrage in 1925, the FKD sponsored bills for women's suffrage, women's political rights, and the right to join political parties. It was frequently criticized for this policy by the larger, better-organized Federation of Japanese Women's Organizations, who derided FKD members as being merely a few Tokyo-based intellectuals who were "just content to put up golden signs." In 1928 the FKD announced a position of political neutrality: it would support only candidates from parties that had woman suffrage as part of their platform. This policy attracted violent criticism from left-wing women's groups, aimed especially at the FKD leader, Ichikawa, who was accused of ignoring other issues of equal importance to women.

In 1931 the FKD was one of only two groups to offer active opposition to the limited women's civil rights bill that had been introduced by the government and to press for a complete women's civil rights bill. After the failure of the 1931 Suffrage Bill, support for suffrage waned. However, the FKD maintained its focus on the suffrage until 1933, when it turned its attention to women's involvement in municipal government and other community issues. In 1937 the FKD, together with 35 other organizations that supported women's suffrage, formed the Senkyo Shukusei Fujin Rengôkai (Joint Women's Committee for Impartial Elections), which campaigned for voting rights for women and fixed election expenses. The FKD endured a government clampdown in 1940, continuing to produce its journal until forced to cease publication in 1941.

See also Ichikawa Fusae; Japan; Local Franchise.
References Garon, Sheldon. "Women's Groups and the Japanese State: Contending Approaches to Political Integration" (1993); Murray, Patricia. "Ichikawa Fusae and the Lonely Red Carpet" (1975); Vavich, Dee Ann. "The Japan Woman's Suffrage Movement: Ichikawa Fusae: A Pioneer in Woman's Suffrage" (1967).

Galindo, Hermila

Hermila Galindo (1896–1954) was the most prominent feminist in Mexico between 1915 and 1919 and one of the first women to campaign actively for women's suffrage in that country. Born in northern Mexico in 1896, Galindo moved to Mexico City in 1911. Here her skills as orator for the liberal Abraham Gonzales Club soon attracted the attention of the revolutionary leader Venustiano Carranza. She was invited to join his government in 1914, and over the next five years she combined strong support for the Carranza regime with a radical feminist program promoting political, legal, and sexual equality for women. She expressed her views in the journal she edited, *Mujer Moderna* (Modern Woman).

Galindo argued that, because women had to pay taxes and were liable to the same penalties under the law as men, there were no rational grounds for denying them the right to vote and stand for election. When in 1917 Carranza called a convention to revise Mexico's 1857 Constitution, Galindo, with other radical feminists, petitioned its members to include women's suffrage, but they were largely ignored or ridiculed. Soon after this, Galindo put herself up for election to the Chamber of Deputies. Although she had no hope of success, her object was to draw the nation's attention to the number of women who wanted the vote and to set a precedent for future feminist activity. Galindo also set a precedent in her opposition to the Catholic Church's control over the press and Catholic women's organizations. She saw this power as a major block to the progress of women's rights.

Galindo alienated moderate feminists with her radical views. After 1919 she was ousted from her favored position with the government, giving up all feminist activity thereafter. Yet her ideas and tactics, especially her endurance and willingness to express unpopular views in the face of ridicule and hostility, were influential both to her contemporaries and to the next generation of feminists and suffragists during the 1920s.

See also Latin America and the Caribbean; Mexico.
Reference Macías, Anna. *Against All Odds: The Feminist Movement in Mexico to 1940* (1982).

Gawthorpe, Mary

Mary Gawthorpe (1881–1973) was a socialist and a militant suffrage campaigner in Britain before World War I. She was born in Leeds, Yorkshire, and was one of five children of working-class parents. Her mother had been a millworker and then a dressmaker before marriage, and her father had worked in a tannery before becoming a political agent for his employer, a Conservative member of Parliament. Her father's economic support for his family became increasingly erratic, but Mary Gawthorpe was able to train as a pupil teacher, and this offered her the possibility of greater independence. As the relationship between her parents deteriorated, Gawthorpe refused a scholarship to study full-time at the local college and continued to earn money as a pupil teacher before she became fully qualified to teach at the age of 21. In 1901 her parents separated and Gawthorpe and her younger brother had to support the family.

It was at this point that Gawthorpe became engaged to T. B. Garrs, a typesetter on the *Yorkshire Post,* whom she refers to in her memoirs as F. L. He introduced her to the socialist movement, and she became vice president of the Leeds Independent Labour Party (ILP). Gawthorpe gained valuable political experience in the ILP; she wrote a women's column in its local journal, took part in campaigns for free school meals, and gained a reputation as a platform speaker. Although she had heard Christabel Pankhurst speak at the local Labour Church, it was not until Pankhurst's arrest with Annie Kenney in 1905 that Gawthorpe took a direct interest in women's suffrage. She wrote to the local press offering to go to prison herself, and then she joined the Leeds branch of the National Union of Women's Suffrage Societies (NUWSS), a constitutionalist group. Her decision may have been based on the fact that one of the local NUWSS leaders, Isabella Ford, was also a member of the ILP.

During the first part of 1906, Gawthorpe spoke tirelessly at meetings of teachers, trade unions, socialist societies, and suffrage groups. Despite her open support for the actions of militants, she was elected onto the executive of the Leeds NUWSS and took part in "camp stool" meetings in Leeds public parks that were jointly organized by the ILP, the Women's Social and Political Union (WSPU), and the NUWSS. In March she gave up her teaching job and became a paid secretary of the Leeds branch of the Women's Labour League, an auxiliary of the Labour Party. She worked on behalf of

the Labour candidate at the Cockermouth by-election, where she again encountered members of the WSPU. Shortly afterwards she was invited to spend a week with the Pethick-Lawrences in London, where she met Emmeline Pankhurst and was persuaded to accept a paid appointment as a WSPU organizer.

Gawthorpe was imprisoned on several occasions and was one of the most popular speakers and organizers in the WSPU. She spoke at major rallies and demonstrations throughout the country, becoming a national figure in the movement. In May 1909 she helped to organize the Women's Exhibition in London for the WSPU and further enhanced her reputation as a speaker. Her growing popularity and her independence of mind may have caused tensions with the leadership of the union, for her name virtually disappears from the WSPU newspaper over the next few months. In late 1909 she was badly injured when she tried to break up an election meeting. Although she continued as a speaker, failing health led her to withdraw from WSPU activities. For a brief period she edited a feminist journal, *Freewoman,* but she had to give this up because of ill health, which also led her to resign from the Central Committee of the WSPU. She retained her interest in women's suffrage, however, and in 1912 broke a window at the Home Office to protest forcible feeding.

Gawthorpe's involvement with the suffrage movement illustrates the complex relationship between socialist and suffrage politics, in particular at a local level. It also demonstrates the independence of thought and action of many WSPU members, despite the leadership's increasing attempts to control the organization from above. Around the time of World War I, Mary Gawthorpe moved to the United States, where she took part in the suffrage movement until 1917. She then worked in a variety of radical and labor organizations until she married an American, John

Sanders, in 1921. She wrote a short memoir for the Suffragette Fellowship in 1931 and then expanded this into a longer account that was published in 1962 as *Up Hill to Holloway.*

See also Ford, Isabella; Independent Labour Party; Kenney, Annie; Militancy; National Union of Women's Suffrage Societies; Pankhurst, Christabel; Pankhurst, Emmeline; Pethick-Lawrence, Emmeline; Pethick-Lawrence, Frederick; Women's Social and Political Union.
References Gawthorpe, Mary. *Up Hill to Holloway* (1962); Holton, Sandra Stanley. *Suffrage Days: Stories from the Women's Suffrage Movement* (1996).

Germany

It was difficult for a strong women's movement to develop in Germany in the nineteenth century, given the country's authoritarian political system. Like women in other European countries, German women were inspired to voice their own demands by the liberal ideas of the revolutions of 1848. Feminist activist Louise Otto Peters argued that women should have greater access to education and the right to participate in the life of the state, and female political associations were formed in towns such as Frankfurt and Mainz. These initiatives were difficult to sustain in the reaction that followed 1848, and an organized women's movement did not emerge until the establishment in 1865 of the Allgemeiner Deutscher Frauenverein (General German Women's Association), led by Peters. The association was extremely moderate in outlook and limited its concerns to education, philanthropy, and economic issues. In 1876 the association refused to be involved when Hedwig Dohm, a literary feminist, called on German women to take up the cause of women's suffrage. This reluctance to campaign for the vote must be seen in its context: it was illegal for women to take part in political meetings or to join political associations. Moreover, liberalism was in decline in Otto Bis-

Luise Zietz, of Berlin, led the women's section of the German Social Democratic Party with Clara Zetkin. (Ann Ronan Picture Library)

marck's unified Germany, and Prussian militarism predominated.

It was not until the 1890s that the women's movement became more radical in outlook. The departure of Bismarck in 1890 created an atmosphere that encouraged the growth of pressure groups and political parties that sought political and social reforms. In 1894 the General German Women's Association sought to bring together all of the philanthropic women's groups that had been formed in the late nineteenth century in a new organization, the Bund Deutscher Frauenvereine (BDF) [Federation of German Women's Associations]. The BDF grew rapidly and had 70,000 members by 1901. Under the leadership of Marie Stritt, who became president in 1899, women's suffrage was pushed higher on the agenda, and in 1907 the federation's new program of demands included full and equal suffrage rights.

The campaign for women's suffrage was also strengthened by the formation in Hamburg in 1902 of the Deutscher Verband für Frauenstimmrecht (DVF) [German Union for Women's Suffrage], led by the radicals Anita Augspurg and Lida Gustava Heymann. Nonetheless, the DVF was very small and by 1908 had fewer than 2,500 members.

Some of the strongest supporters of women's suffrage were to be found in the women's section of the Sozialdemokratische Partei Deutschlands (SPD) [German Social Democratic Party], led by the gifted speaker and theorist Clara Zetkin and organizer Luise Zietz. As early as 1895, the Social Democrats had tried to get the Reichstag to discuss women's suffrage by seeking an amendment to government franchise bills. The women's section, which numbered 175,000 in 1914, continued to support universal suffrage. In March 1911 it organized the first International Proletarian Women's Day, when demonstrations in favor of women's suffrage were held throughout Germany, with 41 mass meetings organized in Berlin alone. Spontaneous street marches, with women carrying banners and placards, took place in a number of cities and provided a contrast to the methods of the liberal feminist DVF, which had held only one street demonstration, in which women stayed in their carriages rather than walking. Street marches, although common in Britain, were seen as almost revolutionary in Germany and in many instances were broken up by the police. Although never quite so well attended as this first, further Women's Days were held each year up to 1914, enabling socialist women to assert their independence, their right to participate in politics, and their solidarity with women in other countries.

When women's participation in politics was legalized throughout Germany in 1908, new suffrage societies were formed in Berlin and Munich and the movement for women's suffrage expanded rapidly. Augspurg and Heymann adopted a policy of independent militancy, copying some of their techniques from the British suffragette movement, and by 1913 the DVF had 9,000 members. In the following year, the membership of all suffrage societies stood at 14,000. Nonetheless, given the size of the female population, these figures were not very impressive. In the period before the outbreak of World War I, the suffrage movement was weakened by disagreements and antagonism between the main suffrage groups. They not only differed about whether or not to support the Wilhelmine government but also disagreed about the basis on which to demand votes for women. Although all adult men could vote for the Reichstag, most of the parliaments of the federal states had a restricted property franchise. Moreover, faced with the growing power and influence of the SPD in the decade before World War I, the majority of states made their property qualifications even more stringent. In this context it was highly unlikely that the campaign for women's suffrage would be successful, and the suffrage groups became obsessed by their own internal struggles. Only the Deutscher Frauenstimmrechtsbund (German Women's Suffrage League) and the women's section of the SPD supported a universal franchise, whereas the right-wing Deutsche Vereinigung für Frauenstimmrecht (German Alliance for Women's Suffrage) and the older DVF, at least after 1913, supported a propertied franchise.

Despite their weak position in 1914, German women, along with their counterparts in a number of other European countries, obtained the suffrage on the same basis as German men just after World War I, through the decree of 30 November 1918. Although women were acknowledged as having played a vital part in the war effort, it appears unlikely that this was the reason they achieved the vote. Kaiser Wilhelm II had not promised that women would be enfranchised after the war and on a number of occasions gave his opinion that women's role should remain within the home. Rather, the impetus for the introduction of women's suffrage was the German Revolution of 1918, which replaced the kaiser's imperial government with the Weimar Republic. Richard Evans argues that women's suffrage was deemed important, not only because of the democratic nature of the new regime, but also because the moderate leadership of the Social Democrats believed that it would act as an antidote to revolution and would be a way to stabilize the new parliamentary government.

See also Augspurg, Anita, and Lida Gustava Heymann; International Proletarian Women's Day; Socialism in Europe; Suffragette; Zetkin, Clara.
References Evans, Richard J. *The Feminists: Women's Emancipation Movements in Europe, America and Australasia, 1840–1920* (1977); Evans, Richard J. *Comrades and Sisters: Feminism, Socialism and Pacifism in Europe, 1870–1945* (1987).

Ghana (formerly the Gold Coast)

The southern region of the Gold Coast was occupied by the British as early as 1874, and by 1901 British authority had extended throughout the country, thus establishing formal colonial rule. In the precolonial period, women had been active in associations and groups formed for social and ritual purposes, but the British brought European attitudes toward women to their colonial administration, which meant that women were expected to stay in the private sphere of home and family. During the colonial period, women did set up many mutual associations, credit unions, and market women's voluntary groups, and they were also active in the anticolonial struggle, using their power as traders to protest the British authorities.

In 1953 the National Federation of Gold Coast Women was founded, which claimed to be a nonpolitical body, working through church organizations, benevolent societies, and market associations to improve the position of women. The federation sent many petitions to the colonial authorities about discriminatory practices affecting women in employment, marriage, and social life, and it published a journal, the *Gold Coast Woman*. The federation was recognized by the colonial government, but its influence was limited, and it failed to become a national women's movement.

Some of these women activists had joined the nationalist Convention People's Party (CPP), which had been founded in 1949 by Kwame Nkrumah. A woman's section of the CPP was started almost immediately, and Hannah Cudjoe was one of the earliest organizers of women's groups for the party, while women like Mabel Dove Danquah and Akua Asabea Ayisi worked with Nkrumah on the newspaper *Evening News*, writing articles demanding independence. The CPP's agenda of national self-determination appealed to many women, who saw the chance of achieving equal political rights.

Even with the attainment of limited self-government (except in the north) in 1951, the complicated electoral provisions placed barriers in the way of women, and only Mabel Dove Danquah managed to get elected on a CPP ticket to the colonial legislature. Women like Danquah did become involved in preindependence discussions, and in 1957 Ghana gained independence, together with universal adult suffrage.

See also Africa South of the Sahara; Nationalism.
References Arhin, Kwame, ed. *The Life and Work of Kwame Nkrumah* (1991); Hansen, Emmanuel, and Kwame A. Ninsin, eds. *The State, Development and Politics in Ghana* (1989); Klingshirn, Agnes. *The Changing Position of Women in Ghana* (1971); Nelson, Barbara J., and Najma Chowdhury, eds. *Women and Politics Worldwide* (1994).

Gilman, Charlotte Perkins

Charlotte Perkins Gilman (1860–1935) was one of the most influential thinkers in the U.S. women's rights movement in the first two decades of the twentieth century. Descendant of the famous reforming family the Beechers, Gilman was born in Hartford, Connecticut, in 1860 and was married in 1884. After separating and later divorcing from her first husband Charles Walter Stetson, under whose name she initially wrote, she lived for years close to poverty, maintaining herself and her only daughter independently through her work as a novelist, journalist, poet, and lecturer. She was later married again to a distant cousin, George Houghton Gilman.

Gilman promoted her ideas through books, lecture tours, and a monthly magazine, the *Forerunner,* that she edited and published between 1909 and 1916. She was one of the few thinkers to make explicit links between women's economic dependence on men and their subordinate status, an idea propounded in her book *Women and Economics* (1898). Although a strong supporter of women's suffrage, she did not see the vote as an end in itself. Rather it was a means to women's independence, enabling them to become men's equals, capable of exercising the powers of citizenship wisely. Her acknowledgment of the current inferiority of American women, a view she shared with Elizabeth Cady Stanton, went against the prevailing beliefs of suffragists who argued in the main that, despite generations of oppression, women were as capable as men in the political arena.

Gilman opposed the view, held by most suffragists, that women's labor in the home made them their husband's equal. Rather she argued that they should be given the vote precisely because they *were* supported and that gaining the suffrage would be a step toward economic independence. When she argued this belief in a debate sponsored by the Women's Trade Union League in 1909, the overwhelming majority of working-class women who attended voted against her. Their wholesale rejection of her position indicated that as working women, they were already aware of their economic importance within the family.

Gilman was also controversial in her opposition to an educational qualification for the vote. Most suffragists supported this measure, taking the view that it was wrong for uneducated Black and immigrant men to have the vote while it was denied to educated white women. In a debate on the educational qualification at the National American Woman Suffrage Association convention in 1903, Gilman was the only person to speak against the motion, and only five delegates supported her. Gilman led an active life into old age. After cancer finally curtailed her activities, she committed suicide in 1935.

See also Citizenship; National American Woman Suffrage Association; Stanton, Elizabeth Cady; United States of America; Women's Trade Union League.
References Banks, Olive. *Faces of Feminism: A Study of Feminism as a Social Movement* (1981); Flexner, Eleanor. *Century of Struggle: The Woman's Rights Movement in the United States* ([1959] 1975); Kraditor, Aileen S. *The Ideas of the Woman Suffrage Movement* (1965).

Goldstein, Vida

Vida Goldstein (1869–1949) was an Australian socialist feminist and leader of the women's suffrage campaign in Victoria. She was educated at Melbourne Presbyterian College and took an interest in politics from an early age. She became the first paid organizer of the United Council for Women's Suffrage and, from 1899, edited a monthly journal, the *Woman's Sphere,* that combined coverage of local and international issues. In 1903 she founded the Women's Federal Political Association.

After the federal vote was achieved for women in 1902, Goldstein stood unsuccessfully as an independent candidate in

Victoria, but her popularity with voters aroused much hostile criticism from the press. Women in Victoria finally got the vote in 1908, and in the wake of this success, in 1909, she launched a new journal, the *Woman Voter.*

Goldstein believed the women's movement and the labor movement should advance together and stressed the importance of support from working-class men for the women's vote in Victoria. Her feminism also had an international dimension. In 1902 she attended the first meeting of the International Woman Suffrage Alliance in Chicago, where she was elected corresponding secretary. In 1911 a visit to England, instigated by the militant Women's Social and Political Union, increased her recognition of antagonism between the sexes. This is indicated by the more hostile stance of the *Woman Voter* to male sexual behavior after her return from England in 1912. She also encountered male hostility in response to her commitment to peace during World War I.

After the war Goldstein changed direction again, reemphasizing sexual and social harmony between the sexes, and her growing interest in spiritual issues led her to connect the suffrage movement with her religious and pacifist visions.

See also Australia; Britain; Dugdale, Henrietta, and Annie Lowe; International Woman Suffrage Alliance; Militancy; Peace Movement; Women's Social and Political Union.
References Caine, Barbara. "Vida Goldstein and the English Militant Campaign" (1993); Uglow, Jennifer. *Macmillan Dictionary of Women's Biography* (1989); Weiner, Gaby. "Vida Goldstein: The Woman's Candidate" (1993).

Gripenberg, Alexandra

Baroness Alexandra Gripenberg (1859–1913) was one of the leaders of the moderate feminist group the Finnish Women's Association (FWA), established in 1884. She was the second chairwoman of the association, which had a broad set of aims, including equal access for women to higher education, the abolition of state-regulated prostitution, equal pay, and women's suffrage. Along with the group's other leaders, she had close personal ties with the Finnish nationalist movement. Her father was a nationalist and her sister, Elisabeth Stenius, was, with her husband, one of the leading figures of the nationalist movement in Kuopio, where a branch of the Finnish Women's Association was also set up. After the death of her mother, Alexandra lived in Kuopio for two years, where she established close links with the nationalist cause. She remained a member of the FWA when feminists associated with the Young Finns, who sought a closer relationship with Swedish-speaking politicians and thus more freedom from Russia, left to form a rival organization, the Feminist Union.

Gripenberg was not simply a political activist but also had a literary career. She wrote several novels, edited a children's magazine, and produced articles and pamphlets that covered feminist and nationalist themes. She took part in the women's movement at an international level, acting as treasurer of the International Council of Women from 1893 to 1899 and then as its honorary vice president. In 1906, when Finnish women were given the right to vote and to stand for national elections, the political parties established their own women's organizations. Gripenberg became the chairwoman of the Finnish Party's Women's Association and left the FWA because she argued that the party was all-important. She served in the Diet from 1907 to 1908 and shortly before her death was nominated to the presidency of the International Council of Women.

See also Finland; International Council of Women; Nationalism.
References Hurwitz, Edith F. "The International Sisterhood" (1977); Jallinoja, Riitta. "The Women's Liberation Movement in Finland" (1980).

Hall, Sir John

John Hall (1852–1907) was the leader of the prosuffrage politicians in the New Zealand Parliament and worked in partnership with the suffrage movement until the woman's vote was achieved in 1893. Born into a Yorkshire shipbuilding family, he emigrated to New Zealand in 1852, where he acquired land, taking on the status of an English country gentleman. His liberal humanitarian beliefs and support for feminist causes, influenced by John Stuart Mill, made him the perfect parliamentary ally for the leading feminist organization, the Woman's Christian Temperance Union (WCTU). From 1888, when he was recruited by WCTU leader Kate Sheppard, he kept WCTU members informed, advised them on tactics, and voiced their views in Parliament.

Hall had been leader of the government in 1879 when one of the earliest suffrage bills, which he supported, failed. In 1888 he once again took up the cause in Parliament when he presented a petition on behalf of the WCTU and argued for the removal of a clause in the Electoral Bill: "*persons* does not include female." Yet despite his advocacy, women's suffrage was excluded from the bill. Although the WCTU had accepted his suggestion that partial enfranchisement of women taxpayers might be a sensible first step, it was not taken up by Parliament. Over the next few years, Hall continued to introduce women's suffrage bills into Parliament and to propose suffrage amendments to government bills, all without success.

Although the complexities of party allegiances led to occasional lapses in his loyalty, in 1893 Hall renewed his efforts in support of the cause. During the second reading of his own suffrage bill, he unrolled a petition of signatures 300 yards long on the floor of the house, shaming most of his opponents into leaving when a vote was taken. After the third reading of the government Electoral Bill that finally gave women the vote, Hall showed his genuine pleasure by sending a telegram to Sheppard saying, "Politically I can now die happy."

See also Mill, John Stuart; New Zealand; Sheppard, Kate; Woman's Christian Temperance Union.
Reference Grimshaw, Patricia. *Women's Suffrage in New Zealand* (1972).

Haslam, Anna

Born at Youghal, County Cork, Ireland, into a middle-class Quaker family of 17 children, Anna Maria Fisher (1829–1922) attended Quaker boarding schools in County Waterford and in Yorkshire, England. In 1853, while teaching at Ackworth School, Yorkshire, Anna Fisher met another Irish Quaker, Thomas Haslam. The pair returned to Ireland and married in 1854. They settled in Dublin. Due to ill health, Thomas Haslam was unable to work after 1866 and his wife opened a stationer's business, which she continued for the next 40 years.

Haslam began her long career as a campaigner for women by helping Anne Jellicoe to found the Irish Society for the Training and Employment of Educated Women in 1861. This was to lead to the founding of Alexandra College in 1866. Haslam was involved in many feminist campaigns to improve women's access to higher education, as well as campaigns on behalf of working women. Her involvement with suffrage began with the 1866 petition to the British Parliament, demanding the vote for all householders regardless of sex. She was one of 15 women petitioners with Irish addresses. Haslam was also present at the first public suffrage meeting in Dublin in 1870, addressed by the English suffragist leader, Millicent Fawcett. She was also one of the organizers of a suffrage meeting in Dublin in 1872, at which pioneer suffragist from Belfast Isabella Tod was one of the speakers.

During 1874 Thomas Haslam published three issues of the *Women's Advocate,* arguing the case for women's suffrage and advocating the organization of local groups for effective political action. In 1876 the Haslams founded the Dublin Women's Suffrage Association (DWSA). Anna Haslam was secretary of the DWSA from its foundation until 1913, when she stood down and was elected president-for-life. She was reputed to have never missed a meeting and was recognized as the driving force behind the movement. The DWSA was predominantly Quaker, working by publicizing the demand for female suffrage through letter writing and holding drawing-room meetings. The DWSA maintained contact with the English movement and regularly sent delegates to conferences and demonstrations, but its numbers remained small.

During the Land War of 1879–1882, when nationalist women were organized in the Ladies' Land League, the DWSA, unsympathetic to the cause of Irish independence, suspended its meetings. In the late 1880s Haslam was active in the anti–Home Rule movement, fearing for the political and civil liberties of unionists

under a Home Rule parliament. Despite this, she encouraged nationalist and Catholic women to become members of the DWSA and was always regarded with respect and affection by suffragists who held views very different from hers. The 1896 Women Poor Law Guardian Act, passed as a result of DWSA lobbying, was a great success for Irish women, who had failed to benefit from reforms won by women in England. By 1900 there were nearly 100 women elected as Poor Law Guardians who administered relief funds for the poor and this achievement was soon followed by the achievement of all remaining local government franchises.

The 1898 Local Government (Ireland) Act provided the impetus for the expansion of the DWSA, which soon had five branches in the south and west of the country. The organization changed its name to reflect the changing times and finally became the Irish Women's Suffrage and Local Government Association (IWSLGA). Many of the new generation of Irish suffragists were introduced to the movement through their membership of the IWSLGA. Although that organization disapproved of militancy, Haslam herself visited imprisoned members of the militant Irish Women's Franchise League and retained her friendships with the members of the different groups that now developed. The IWSLGA supported the British war effort and helped to initiate women's patrols on the streets of Dublin as part of the campaign for professional women police.

Neither Haslam nor the IWSLGA made any comment on the 1916 Easter Uprising or on nationalist determination to use the war as a leverage to press for Irish independence. The association continued to emphasize the opportunities the situation posed for women's suffrage. Thomas Haslam died in 1917. In November 1918 Anna Haslam led a victory procession of women in Dublin as she cast her vote for the first time. Her support for the Conservative candidate did not diminish the accolade she received from the assembled suffrage organizations. Anna Haslam died at the age of 93 in November 1922, the same year in which the constitution of the Irish Free State gave full citizenship to all women and men over 21. The fact that her organization, renamed as the Irish Women Citizens and Local Government Association, continued in existence until 1947 is testimony to her ability to inspire women to work collectively to further their interests.

See also Citizenship; Fawcett, Millicent Garrett; Ireland; Irish Women's Franchise League; Militancy; Nationalism; Protestantism; Representation of the People Act. *Reference* Cullen, Mary. "Anna Maria Haslam" (1995).

Heymann, Lida Gustava

See Augspurg, Anita, and Lida Gustava Heymann.

History of Woman Suffrage (1881–1922)

This six-volume history, published between 1881 and 1922, is the best-known publication on the American women's suffrage movement and a pioneering study of its kind. The first three volumes, which were produced between 1881 and 1886, were an impressive effort to document the achievements of American women by Elizabeth Cady Stanton, Susan B. Anthony, and Matilda Joslyn Gage—all suffragists themselves. The rest of the project was completed by Anthony and Ida Husted Harper, a professional writer, between 1902 and 1922.

The idea behind the *History of Woman Suffrage* was to present a comprehensive account of the campaign to achieve women's rights, and it is interesting to note that the project was begun many years before the vote was finally won for all American women of voting age in 1920. The authors were anxious to educate and inspire those who were to continue the fight for women's suffrage, as well as to leave an account of the movement for future generations. The project was also intended to record the leadership of the international suffrage movement by American women and to give accounts of women's suffrage campaigns in other countries.

The authors and numerous other women who participated in the project conducted extensive searches of archives and libraries and found articles, letters, speeches, minutes of meetings, newspaper cuttings, and pictures, all of which contributed to the substantial volumes of the *History*. The project was funded by voluntary contributions and bequests that went toward the cost of producing the books, as well as enabling copies to be given free to many schools and libraries.

The *History of Woman Suffrage* was a significant undertaking that not only preserved important historical material that would otherwise have been lost but also recorded the activities of countless women whose contribution to the women's suffrage movement might never have been acknowledged.

See also Anthony, Susan B.; Stanton, Elizabeth Cady; United States of America. *References* Rossi, Alice S., ed. *The Feminist Papers: From Adams to de Beauvoir* (1974); Stanton, E. Cady, et al., eds. *History of Woman Suffrage*. 6 vols. ([1881–1922] 1985).

How the Vote Was Won

The play *How the Vote Was Won*, first produced in 1909, was one of the most successful pieces of suffrage propaganda in Britain. Its first incarnation was as an illustrated pamphlet published by the Women Writers' Suffrage League in 1908. Its author, Cicely Hamilton, founder of the league, had started her career as an actress. An experienced playwright, generally writing under a male pseudonym to avoid bad reviews, Hamilton soon saw the piece's theatrical potential and sought the assistance of novelist Christopher St. John (Christabel Marshall) to turn it into a play.

The play was first performed at the Royalty Theater in London and was produced by Edith Craig, daughter of the famous British actress Ellen Terry. It was an immediate success and after initial casting problems, had a run of its own with a permanent cast. The plot centered around a woman's strike in which women everywhere went to their nearest male relative for support. It concluded with the desperate men converging on Parliament, demanding that women be given the vote immediately. This emphasis on the economic arguments for giving women the vote echoes Hamilton's other works, particularly her best-selling book *Marriage as a Trade,* which analyzed women's economic exploitation within marriage and called for female independence. Critics praised the play's humor and clever lines—regarding its controversial subject and propagandistic motives to be virtues rather than faults. It played to crowded houses and achieved great popular acclaim.

See also Actresses' Franchise League; Britain; Drama, Novels, Poetry, and Film; Women Writers' Suffrage League.
Reference Spender, Dale, and Carol Hayman, eds. *How the Vote Was Won and Other Suffrage Plays* (1985).

Hungary

The development of women's suffrage in Hungary, which at the time was part of the Habsburg Empire, was hampered by conflicts between national and racial groups and by the authoritarianism of the government. In the early nineteenth century, a movement to gain more national autonomy was led by the nobility and the lesser gentry, the Magyars, the Hungarian middle class being mostly made up of Germans and Jews, and it was the Magyars who came to power when Hungary achieved a measure of self-government in 1867. The constitution that was finally adopted that year gave Hungary considerable autonomy, although the ruling bureaucracy and army were based in Vienna and were dominated by German speakers.

Women had taken an active part in the Hungarian nationalist movement since the late eighteenth century. In addition, after 1867 a women's movement developed with the objective of improving access to higher education, and in 1904, a National Council of Women was established to bring together a number of existing societies that concentrated on the achievement of moral reforms. Women's suffrage did not form part of the council's demands at first because franchise questions in Hungary were complicated by nationalist and racial tensions. Only a small proportion of men (less than 10 percent) could vote in Hungary, most of whom were Magyars, and therefore the government feared any extension of the franchise that might enable non-Magyars to vote. The leaders of the National Council of Women, including its first two presidents, Countess Batthyány and, after 1910, Countess Andrássy, were married to leading Magyar politicians and shared their nationalist views.

A group that did have women's suffrage as one of its aims, the Feministák Egyesülete (FE) [Hungarian Feminist Association], was also established in 1904 by Rosika Schwimmer, a Jewish woman from an upper-middle-class family who was president of the National Association of Women Office Workers, and her friend Vilma Glücklich, a teacher. Schwimmer had just returned from the inaugural meeting of the International Woman Suffrage Alliance, which had inspired her to fight for women's suffrage in her own country. The FE campaigned for a range of reforms, including equal education, birth control, and the abolition of child labor, as well as women's suffrage. Schwimmer was the driving force behind the FE and was influenced in her outlook and methods by her friendship with the German suffragists Anita Augspurg and Lida Gustava Heymann. FE members made speeches from the floor at political meetings, distributed leaflets, questioned candidates at elections, and sent a deputation to the Chamber of Deputies.

The political structure of Hungary and competition between national groups meant that the women's suffrage movement had few allies. Some aristocratic nationalists, including 150 deputies who formed a parliamentary Women's Suffrage League in 1908, did support a limited franchise for women, assuming that propertied women would strengthen Magyar rule. The Jewish Liberal Democratic Party supported full female suffrage, and its leader, V. Vászonyi, presented a feminist petition for women's suffrage to the Hungarian Diet in 1913. The Social Democrats, however, were actively opposed to women's suffrage. Not only did they fear that it would hamper the achievement of manhood suffrage, but they also believed that it would be used as a means to bolster aristocratic rule. The violence that accompanied demonstrations for manhood suffrage in 1912, in which many demonstrators were killed or wounded, served to increase suspicions about bourgeois demands for the enfranchisement of propertied women. The views of the Social Democrats were also supported by the Liberals, led by Gyula Justh, who made the demand for manhood suffrage a top priority.

A glimmer of hope for suffragists was provided in 1912 when Prime Minister László Lukács—after receiving deputations from women's groups, including one for a limited franchise from the National Council of Women—declared that a bill would be introduced to this effect. The bill was greeted with such hostility, in particular from the Social Democrats and the Liberals, that it was withdrawn. In the disturbances that followed, suffrage campaigning reached its height. The FE staged a large meeting in September 1912 that was attended by 10,000 people, and Schwimmer organized a demonstration outside the Diet and entered the gallery with other suffragists. Campaigners also tried to strengthen their position by inviting the International Woman Suffrage Alliance to hold its congress in Budapest in 1913. Nonetheless, the conservative nature of Magyar nationalism; the hostility of Social Democrats and Liberals, who were usually allies of women's suffrage in other countries; the limited power of the legislature; and police repression made it difficult for suffragists to make any headway.

It was not until after World War I, when the Habsburg Empire had been overthrown, that women finally received the vote. The government, led by Count Mihály Károlyi, who had personally become converted to women's suffrage before the war, included some members of the Jewish Liberal Democratic Party that had been most sympathetic to Schwimmer's suffrage group before 1914. In common with other countries that had established new, liberal constitutions after the war, women in Hungary received the vote on equal terms with men despite the fact that the suffrage movement had been weak. This victory was short-lived. When the conservative wing of the nationalist movement replaced Károlyi in a counterrevolution, women were disenfranchised. They were granted the suffrage again in 1920, but after 1921 the franchise was restricted to women over 30 who fulfilled educational and economic qualifications. In 1945, at the end of World War II, full suffrage was regained.

See also Augspurg, Anita, and Lida Gustava Heymann; International Woman Suffrage Alliance; Nationalism; Schwimmer, Rosika.
References Evans, Richard, J. *The Feminists: Women's Emancipation Movements in Europe, America and Australasia, 1840–1920* (1977); Wiltsher, Anne. *Most Dangerous Women: Feminist Peace Campaigners in the Great War* (1985).

Hunger Strikes

A hunger strike was first used in the suffrage movement by Marion Wallace Dunlop, a member of the British Women's Social and Political Union (WSPU), in July 1909. She had been sentenced to one month in prison for stenciling a quotation on a wall in the House of Commons. Since 1908, imprisoned suffragettes had been regarded as criminals and were therefore denied privileges that they had once enjoyed, such as wearing their own clothes. Dunlop asked that she be treated as a political prisoner, and when her request was turned down, she began a hunger strike and was eventually released after refusing food for 91 hours. This method of protest was quickly taken up by other suffrage prisoners and was endorsed by the WSPU as a way to gain sympathy for the cause.

Although at first women who went on hunger strike were released, the government changed its policy by the autumn of 1909 and women were forcibly fed. This was a painful procedure that permanently damaged the health of some of those who endured it. *Votes for Women,* the official newspaper of the WSPU, drew attention to the harsh treatment meted out to hunger strikers and also to the class differences that affected women in prison. When working-class women were forcibly fed, for example, they were not given any medical help or examined to see if they were fit. In order to expose this, Lady Constance Lytton, who had a weak heart and in previous hunger strikes had always been medically examined before being forcibly fed, disguised herself as a working woman. She called herself Jane Wharton and deliberately made sure that she was arrested and imprisoned in 1911. She received no medical attention and was forcibly fed with great brutality seven times. She never fully recovered from this experience and had a stroke in the following year. After adverse publicity surrounding forcible feeding, the Prisoner's Temporary Discharge for Ill Health Act, commonly known as the Cat and Mouse Act, was passed in 1913. Under its provisions, hunger strikers could be released from prison and then rearrested once their health had improved.

Hunger strikers gained considerable sympathy from many members of the public, and *Votes for Women* repeatedly portrayed them as martyrs. Nonetheless, their actions also aroused hostility in others, including members of the government who were placed in a difficult position by this tactic. Historians have been divided in their judgment of the effectiveness of the hunger strikes. Some justify forcible feeding on the grounds that it saved women's lives and suggest that hunger strikes were counterproductive in that the government could not be seen to give in to such a threat. More recent studies, however, have been more sympathetic to the hunger strikers. They point to the brutality of forcible feeding and claim that the prison authorities sought to undermine women by invading their bodies, humiliating them, and taking away their sense of self. Although women had to suffer this treatment as individuals in their own private space, the experience of forcible feeding also reinforced their sense of solidarity with others.

In Britain hunger strikes came to an end in 1914, when suffrage prisoners were released at the outbreak of war. Hunger strikes were used later, however, by women in other countries who were still trying to gain the right to vote. In the United States, for example, members of the National Woman's Party who picketed the White House in 1917 were arrested and imprisoned in harsh conditions in Occoquan Workhouse in Virginia and in the District of Columbia Jail. Women claimed that their arrests were illegal, and in protest at the brutal treatment, they went on hunger strike. They demanded the status of political prisoners, but the government was reluctant to establish such a precedent in wartime. Those on hunger strike were forcibly fed. A public outcry following publicity about their treatment finally led to their unconditional release in November 1918. It is difficult to assess how effective these hunger strikes and other acts of militancy were in affecting the attitudes of government officials toward women's enfranchisement. In Mexico, however, it was after María García and her followers had staged a hunger strike that the president agreed to submit a bill to amend the constitution to enable women to vote and to hold office.

See also Cat and Mouse Act; National Woman's Party; *Votes for Women;* Women's Social and Political Union.
References Bartley, Paula. *Votes for Women, 1860–1928* (1998); Flexner, Eleanor. *Century of Struggle: The Woman's Rights Movement in the United States* ([1959] 1975); Purvis, June. "The Prison Experiences of the Suffragettes in Britain" (1995).

Iceland

In 1915 women were enfranchised in the small country of Iceland, where, in common with many other Scandinavian countries, women's suffrage was closely linked to nationalism. Iceland was ruled under the Danish Crown until 1944, and women played an important part in the movement to establish native educational institutions. This, along with their role in the temperance movement, radicalized women, who began to raise issues relating to the position of their sex. The Kvenfélag Islands (Icelandic Women's Association), for example, which was founded in 1894 to gain women's support for an Icelandic university, then went on to collect signatures for a petition in 1895 to gain equal economic and educational rights for women.

The feminist movement began to emerge with the industrialization of the fishing industry and the establishment of Reykjavik as a major urban center, which modernized society as well. In 1907 Kvenréttindafélag Islands (KI) [the Icelandic Women's Rights Association] was formed by Briét Bjarnhédinsdóttir, the editor of a women's magazine. She toured the country and by 1908, five KI branches had been established with a membership of 400. The KI was able to present women's suffrage as a nationalist issue because bills such as the 1882 measure to enfranchise widows and spinsters for municipal elections had been held up by the Danish king's veto until 1902. In the 1900s nationalists lobbied for manhood suffrage, and feminists were able to gather 12,000 signatures out of a population of less than 50,000 for a women's suffrage petition. In 1908 women gained equal voting rights with men in municipal elections, and in 1913 the Icelandic Parliament, the Althing, passed a measure to enfranchise women for all elections as part of a more general reform of the franchise. A worsening of the relationship with Denmark, however, meant that the legislation was not ratified until June 1915, when women finally received the vote.

See also Nationalism
Reference Evans, Richard J. *The Feminists: Women's Emancipation Movements in Europe, America and Australasia, 1840–1920* (1977).

Ichikawa Fusae

The story of the women's suffrage movement in Japan has sometimes been seen as synonymous with the career of its most famous leader, Ichikawa Fusae. She was born in Nagoya in 1893, six years after the Peace Preservation Law of 1887 had barred women in Japan from participating in any political activities, including attending meetings or rallies. From 1919 she saw her primary work as achieving the vote and joined with Hiratsuka Raichō to reorganize the Shin Fujin Kyōkai (New Woman's Association) into an organization committed to political rights for women. This group worked to revise Article 5 of the Peace Preservation Law to allow women to participate in and sponsor political meetings, a measure they achieved in 1922. However, before the reform was passed, tensions in her relationship with Hiratsuka had prompted Ichikawa to leave the country in 1921 on an extended visit to the United States. Here she was strongly influenced by suffrage leaders Carrie Chapman Catt and Alice Paul, and she became determined to educate women in Japan politically.

On her return in 1924, Ichikawa organized a new group, Fusen Kakutoku Domei (League for Women's Suffrage), which was more directly focused on women's suffrage. In 1928 her hopes for a successful women's civil rights bill were high and she again left the country to attend the first Pan-Pacific Women's Conference in Hawaii, but the bill was blocked during her four-month absence. After the failure of the 1931 Suffrage Bill, interest in women's suffrage waned. Ichikawa developed an abiding concern with the management of the electoral process, which she saw as the first step to freeing women to enter politics. She saw women's participation in government as having a "purifying" effect, arguing that "municipal government can be considered as an extension of the household." However, her hopes faded as government control over all organizations increased. By January 1934, when she wrote her article for Fusen Kakutôku Dômei entitled "The Spirit of the Woman's Vote," few others were openly calling for women's suffrage.

During the 1930s she and other women leaders cooperated with the increasingly authoritarian state, making tactical alliances with civil servants at local and national levels. This policy has attracted criticism from a later generation of Japanese feminists. Her justification for her cooperation with military authorities after 1937 was that in her efforts to lessen the disasters of war, she would be aiding the suffrage movement by demonstrating the importance of women's social action. In

1942, after Fusen Kakutoku Domei had been closed down and all women's groups were controlled by the Imperial Rule Assistance Association, Ichikawa was made leader of the Dai Nihon Fujinkai (Greater Japan Women's Association). However, she was asked to resign in 1944 for refusing to support government policies. By the time the war ended in August 1945, Ichikawa had formed another group, putting pressure on the first postwar government to give women the vote before it was ordered by the Allied forces. In December 1945 an act was passed giving both men and women the vote at the age of 20 and eligibility to run for office at 25.

In 1947 Ichikawa was purged by the Allied forces on the grounds that she had collaborated with wartime governments, resulting in her temporary removal from public life. However, in 1949 she was honored at the Second National Women's Day conference as one of the three women to contribute most to woman's suffrage. She returned to politics in 1950 and in 1953 was elected to the House of Councillors. Between then and 1974, when she was awarded the prestigious Magasaya Award for outstanding achievement, she only once failed to be reelected.

See also Catt, Carrie Chapman; Imperialism; Japan; Paul, Alice; United States of America.
References Garon, Sheldon. "Women's Groups and the Japanese State Contending: Approaches to Political Integration" (1993); Murray, Patricia. "Ichikawa Fusae and the Lonely Red Carpet" (1975); Vavich, Dee Ann. "The Japan Woman's Suffrage Movement: Ichikawa Fusae: A Pioneer in Woman's Suffrage" (1967).

Imagery

In some countries the women's suffrage movement used visual propaganda extensively, and with great effect. The purpose of the propaganda was to educate the public about the suffrage cause and to bring pressure to bear on government through the mobilization of public opinion. To challenge a domestic ideology that decreed that women's natural role was in the home as wife and mother, the suffragists introduced new representations of women as active citizens, often paying taxes as property owners, and involved in the business of economic, social, and moral reform. At the same time, the antisuffragists responded to these arguments by using images that supported the domestic ideal, together with crude caricatures that were designed to ridicule the idea of the political woman.

In Britain, the suffrage movement used visual material with great imagination and effect. The Artists' Suffrage League (1907) and the Suffrage Atelier (1909) both produced banners, posters, postcards, and leaflets for the suffrage movement, as well as decorative themes and displays for processions and public meetings. The National League for Opposing Women's Suffrage (NLOWS) attempted to counter this wealth of suffrage propaganda by employing artists to produce a variety of printed material that put their case across to the general public.

A great deal of British suffrage imagery was in the form of postcards and posters, the latter designed to reach "the homes, the halls, and hoardings throughout the land" (Tickner, 1987, 45), and these offered a number of different representations of women to support the suffrage argument. The suffrage societies often used images of impoverished working women on their posters, suggesting that their economic and sexual oppression could only be remedied by giving women the vote, which would enable them to press for reform through the ballot box. Women's responsibility to look after the more vulnerable of their sex was an argument commonly used by the suffrage movement, and the image of the oppressed working woman was a powerful symbol of male exploitation. However, it can also be argued that she was being portrayed as a victim who could only be saved by the middle-class suffragist.

The British suffrage artists also appropriated women from history, such as Joan of Arc and Boadicea, as representations of strong, powerful women operating in a political context. For the women of the militant Women's Social and Political Union (WSPU), the French heroine Joan of Arc was a highly potent symbol, a maiden warrior who had transcended the limitations of her sex, yet retained her virtue, and whose crusade had brought her martyrdom and sainthood. The nonmilitant National Union of Women's Suffrage Societies (NUWSS) used a subdued version of this image in their well-known poster, designed for the suffrage procession held in June 1908. "The Bugler Girl," designed by Caroline Watts of the Artists' Suffrage League, shows a heroic female figure dressed in "spiritual" armor and carrying a bugle, banner, and sheathed sword, with a new dawn rising up behind her in the background. These images were often subverted by antisuffragists, who suggested through their visual propaganda that the politicized female was no heroine, but a woman with a masculine appearance and the unfulfilled life of a frustrated spinster, a view that reflected some of the medical literature of the period.

However, the most common representation used by the British suffrage artists was the "womanly" woman, which was a highly contested image in Edwardian society. The womanly woman of the suffrage movement was usually shown as a mythical female figure, goddess-like and dressed in classical robes, who was used to suggest that a suffragist could retain her femininity and still be active in the political sphere. Behind this matronly figure were often the images of downtrodden, working-class women and children, who needed her maternal, domestic values to be represented in government in order to

This image of the bugler girl published by the Artists' Suffrage League was one of many examples of visual material used by the suffrage movement. (Schlesinger Library, Radcliffe College)

bring them out of their situations of poverty and exploitation. The antisuffragists were able to use the same classical figure in their posters to show the contrast between the dignified model of respectable womanhood and the "hysterical," mannish female who wanted the vote.

Perhaps the most imaginative image of the womanly woman model was used by the Austrian suffragists in the logo of their *Zeitschrift für Frauenstimmrecht* (Journal for Women's Suffrage). In a complex image clearly derived from the expressionist art of Gustav Klimt, one of the founders of the Vienna Secession, an artistic movement that broke away from traditional restrictions in 1897, a woman is shown being liberated from her silence as she breaks the chains that symbolically lock her lips together, so that a new "womanly" woman arises, endowed with the vote and a political voice. Using motifs from the new art of the twentieth century gave suffrage imagery a dynamic, "modern" look, while at the same time the traditional model of womanhood was retained to reassure the more conservative viewer.

The British women's suffrage societies also used the spectacle of the procession as a way to attract publicity and involve their supporters in a collective endeavor that would give them confidence and a spirit of unity. The procession organized by the NUWSS on 13 June 1908, for example, had an impressive display of embroidered banners that celebrated all aspects of women's life and history, many of them designed by members of the Artists' Suffrage League and their founder, Mary Lowndes. The colors of the sashes, badges, and flowers worn in the procession were predominantly red and white, and the overall visual effect of the march received a great deal of coverage in the press.

Visiting suffragists from the United States were impressed by the British suffrage movement's use of spectacle and pictorial propaganda, adopting some of the ideas for their own campaigns. In 1913 the National American Woman Suffrage Association (NAWSA), led by Alice Paul, staged a grand procession with banners and bands in Washington, D.C., taking their model from similar British demonstrations. The NAWSA suffrage parade attracted an estimated 5,000 marchers and was carefully choreographed to place women in the political space, while at the same time reassuring the public that they would always retain their feminine characteristics. The radical suffragist and lawyer Inez Milholland led the parade as the herald of women's suffrage, "carrying the trumpet that is to herald the dawn of a new day of heroic endeavor for womanhood" (Moore, 1997, 93). Along with the procession, the suffragists staged a series of allegorical tableaux on the steps of the Treasury Building, with Columbia, dressed as the goddess Minerva, together with the five virtues associated with womanhood—Justice, Charity, Liberty, Peace, and Hope. The 1913 NAWSA suffrage procession marked a turning point in the American women's suffrage movement, convincing many onlookers of the justice of their cause. As the suffragist paper the *Woman's Journal* observed, "to see was to be forever convinced."

British suffrage posters were used extensively by the American suffrage societies, but American suffragists did produce their own campaign material, often using the same iconography as their British counterparts. In 1913, Alice Paul and Lucy Burns formed the Congressional Union for Woman Suffrage (CU), and this organization produced posters with the image of the womanly woman in classical robes, designed to appeal to women who already had a state vote and encourage them to use it to obtain a suffrage amendment to the Constitution. The model of Joan of Arc combined with the womanly woman image was used very effectively in a poster showing the suffragist Inez Milholland in flowing robes, seated on a horse and holding an unfurled banner. Milholland, an active and well-known participant in the women's suffrage campaign, had died in 1916, while she was speaking at a suffrage rally in Los Angeles. Martyrdom for the suffrage cause was a powerful idea, and the image of Milholland as a kind of Joan of Arc was used as a symbol of sacrifice, reinforced by the wording on the poster that stated that she had "died for the freedom of women."

Alice Park, a Californian journalist, advocated modern advertising methods to enliven women's suffrage campaign materials. Park had noticed the use of color by the WSPU in Britain, where the militant suffragettes had used purple, white, and green in their campaigns and processions, so the California suffragists decided to use yellow to represent "the golden state" in their suffrage propaganda. Park also encouraged the use of "personal advertising," which required the mass production of lapel buttons, suffrage stationery, calendars, postcards, playing cards, ink blotters, and baggage stickers. At the same time, commercial enterprises sought to attract women consumers by identifying their products with the suffrage cause. Breakfast foods and clothing were among the products advertised in this way in both the United States and Britain.

A distinctive kind of suffrage imagery that was used in a number of English-speaking countries was the newspaper cartoon that portrayed a stereotypical view of the "political" woman. Newspapers and journals in Australia, New Zealand, and Britain usually depicted the female suffragist as either an embittered, masculine spinster or a large, domineering wife who has her husband under her thumb. The WSPU periodical *Votes for Women* described a typical caricature of a suffragist in 1907—"a gaunt, unprepossessing female of uncertain age, with a raucous voice, and truculent demeanour, who invariably seems to wear elastic-sided boots,

and to carry a big 'gampy' umbrella . . ." (Tickner, 1987, 169). In Australia, the *Melbourne Punch* carried a number of cartoons along these lines during the period of the Australian women's suffrage campaign, while in Britain *Punch* lampooned the suffragists from the 1870s onwards. These stereotypes were repeated in the commercially produced postcards that were enormously popular in Britain during the Edwardian period.

The women's suffrage movement found few completely new images for their propaganda campaign, preferring instead to use the dominant representations of femininity—most often those associated with motherhood and domesticity. They invested these images with a new dimension—that of the political woman, involved in the world through her commitment to social and moral reform, yet still retaining her womanly qualities. The design and production of thousands of posters, postcards, leaflets, and banners, together with the organization and choreography of pageants and processions, all combined to produce a distinctive iconography that became a powerful contributor to the arguments for women's suffrage.

See also Advertising; Artists' Suffrage League; Australia; Britain; Citizenship; National American Woman Suffrage Association; New Zealand; Propaganda; Suffrage Atelier; United States of America; Women's Social and Political Union.
References DuBois, Ellen, and Karen Kearns. *Votes for Women: A 75th Anniversary Album* (1995); Finnegan, Margaret. *Selling Suffrage: Consumer Culture and Votes for Women* (1999); Moore, Sarah J. "Making a Spectacle of Suffrage: The National Woman Suffrage Pageant, 1913" (1997); Sheppard, Alice. *Cartooning for Suffrage* (1994); Tickner, Lisa. *The Spectacle of Women: Imagery of the Suffrage Campaign, 1907–1914* (1987).

Imperialism

For many European women, participation in the colonial project gave them status and power that they did not have in their own countries. There were opportunities to do work they were not normally allowed to carry out in their own male-dominated societies, as doctors, nurses, and teachers, and they could exercise a kind of authority over the colonized that would not be possible in their home environment. They had come from a society where male authority circumscribed their lives, but they rarely came to understand that it was the same paternalist ideology that underpinned the imperial project. The "cultural imperialism" they brought to the colonized in the shape of Christian missionary work, which involved the "reform" and "conversion" of indigenous peoples, and anthropological study, which brought with it connotations of racial superiority, all helped women to feel that they were part of an imperial "civilizing" mission. However, the marginalization that European women experienced in their own societies could also give them a unique perception of the needs of colonized women. A few used their position to cross the social boundaries between the rulers and the ruled, becoming involved in indigenous movements for political reform and self-determination: for example, the participation of Margaret Cousins in the campaign for Indian independence.

The main colonial powers of Britain, France, the Netherlands, Belgium, and Portugal all had very different approaches to the government of their empires, and the participation of women in the colonial project also varied significantly. There is no doubt that British women were the most actively involved in their empire, as Christian missionaries, teachers, doctors, and reformers, as well as the wives and daughters of colonial officials. Women from predominantly Catholic colonial powers often gained their colonial experience as nuns setting up convents, schools, and orphanages, particularly in South Asia and the Far East.

Britain had begun to extend its influence over India, Canada, and the West Indies during the course of the eighteenth century, and colonies of settlement were promoted in New South Wales from the 1780s, in the African Cape from the 1800s, and in New Zealand from the 1840s. Throughout the nineteenth century, muscular diplomacy combined with the use of force was used to make territories submit to Britain's authority, but it was British expansion over Africa and Asia that was the most far-reaching of all imperial projects, reaching its height between 1850 and 1914. This imperial expansion coincided with the beginning of the organized British women's suffrage campaign in the 1860s, which had taken much of its thinking from the antislavery movements of the 1820s and 1830s. The antislavery discourse constructed by British women campaigners, which centered on the fact of white British women's relative liberty compared to the suffering of the enslaved women, had a subversive subtext of identification with the oppressed slaves, and these two ideas combined into the argument of the British suffragists for the vote.

The extension of the suffrage argument from a purely domestic debate about the benefits that the emancipation of women would bring to British society to an assertion that these benefits could be extended to the lives of the non-European women of the empire characterized much of the campaign for the "imperial" franchise during the late nineteenth and early twentieth centuries. Antisuffrage criticism often centered on the unsuitability of women to exercise this imperial vote; it was argued that governing the empire was a man's job, and that Britain would lose the respect of the indigenous populations of the empire if British rule was "feminized" through women's suffrage. However, the response of suffrage societies was to defend feminine influence as a positive force for good, and in numerous articles about the empire in their suffrage periodicals, they saw the relief of what they believed was the suffering of Indian women as part of their imperial mission. In the *Common Cause,* the journal of the National Union of Women's Suffrage Societies, the British suffragist Helena Swanwick observed that "if it were only for our responsibilities in India, we women must not rest until we have the vote" (Burton, 1994, 191). For British feminists, the quest for an imperial identity that would justify their demand for imperial citizenship was bound up with the construction of Indian women as helpless victims of oppression.

However, far from being passive victims, Indian women had been involved in political and social organizations since the late nineteenth century. Sarojini Naidu, the Indian suffragist, had been politically active since the founding of the Indian National Congress in 1885 and was one of the earliest members of the Women's Indian Association, which was formed in 1917. In the same year, Naidu led a deputation of women to ask the British authorities for the vote for Indian women. British suffragists like Eleanor Rathbone were often unable to admit that Indian women were more than able to run their own suffrage campaign, and this led to some tension between the two groups of women during the 1930s, when new provisions for Indian enfranchisement were being drawn up by the colonial authorities. There were other countries under British rule where women had begun to ask for political rights without the assistance of British suffragists. In Ceylon (now Sri Lanka) women had asked Congress for limited suffrage in 1925, and in Egypt feminist writings had been published as early as the 1890s.

France had an empire that encompassed territories in the West Indies, North and West Africa, and the Far East, and according to the assimilation policy of the French government, the indigenous populations were expected to absorb the language and culture of France—in other words, to become good French citizens. The attitude of French women toward the non-European women of their empire is more clearly revealed in their anthropological studies than in their suffragist polemic. There had been a number of French women travelers in Egypt during the nineteenth century, one of whom was Suzanne Voilquin, who was a member of the Saint-Simonians, an early utopian socialist group who advocated the emancipation of women. Jehan d'Ivray married an Egyptian and lived there for many years, writing a number of books about the country and joining with the Egyptian feminist and suffragist Hudá Sha'rawi to produce the Egyptian feminist journal *L'Egyptienne.* However, the subject of most interest to French women writers was the position of women in Algeria, a French colony since 1830. In what were mostly anthropological studies, they expressed considerable ambivalence toward Muslim society in Algeria, specifically the effect that religion had on the life of women. Hubertine Auclert, the French suffragist, wrote *Les Femmes Arabes en Algérie* (Arab women in Algeria), published in 1900, in which she saw Algerian women as secluded victims of their Islamic religion, who should be guided toward an ideal of French womanhood. She did admit that French women were far from equal in their own society in that they lacked the right to vote. Mathéa Gaudry, a lawyer and anthropologist, echoed these sentiments when she wrote in 1929 that the typical Algerian woman from the Aurès Mountains was "worthy of some education; what I mean is that we could teach her French, how to sew and run a home" (Lazreg, 1990, 334).

However, while the French women's suffrage movement was encountering the opposition of republicans and the Catholic Church to their arguments for the vote, which they did not achieve until 1945, women in Syria and Lebanon, two of the territories under a French mandate, were inspired by nationalism to begin campaigns for women's political rights. As early as 1924, the question of educated women's enfranchisement was raised in Lebanon, while in Syria the issue of female suffrage appeared in women's magazines in the 1920s. When a limited suffrage measure was proposed in the Syrian Congress, French sympathizers put pressure on the assembly to refuse on the grounds that it would disrupt traditional gender divisions in society.

One of the main organizations that brought suffragists together from all parts of the world was the International Woman Suffrage Alliance (IWSA), founded in 1904 and led by the American suffragist Carrie Chapman Catt. The alliance was an important forum for women from different countries to forge links across national and imperial boundaries, encouraging female solidarity in the campaign for the vote. However, despite this emphasis on women's unity, the IWSA was a hierarchical organization that often employed imperial rhetoric to argue its case. In 1911 Catt and Dutch suffragist Aletta Jacobs toured India, Egypt, Palestine, Turkey, Persia, Japan, Sumatra, Java, and the Philippines, and they discovered to their surprise that there was "a serious women's movement in Asia" (Burton, 1994, 192). Although Catt admired what many women from colonized countries had achieved, she believed that it was up to women like the British suffragists to inspire and awaken the longings for emancipation among women in the larger world beyond Europe and the United States.

It is important to mention the serious omissions in the debate about imperial citizenship put forward by British suffragists. For example, they had almost nothing to say on the position of indigenous women in Africa, Australia, and Canada, while their approach to Irish feminism was seen as culturally imperialist by many Irish

women. Nationalist and imperial rhetoric dominated much of the suffrage argument, and the assumption of imperial predominance was present at the international level of the suffrage movement, where the struggle of European and U.S. women was given a greater significance because of the position they occupied in relation to women in the colonized countries. British women, according to the radical suffragist Elizabeth Wolstenholme-Elmy in 1897, were fighting for the vote "to hasten the enfranchisement of the women of all civilised nations," which would lead, she claimed, "to the development of a higher social and political morality all the world over" (Caine, 1997, 168). Although Western feminists liked to link this notion of the beneficial effects of their own enfranchisement with the ideal of a shared sisterhood, the vast majority of them did not develop a critique of imperialism, and they failed to perceive how the paternalist ideology of empire was the very thing that hindered their own progress toward emancipation.

See also Catt, Carrie Chapman; Citizenship; Cousins, Margaret; Egypt; India; International Links; International Woman Suffrage Alliance; Jacobs, Aletta; Lebanon; National Union of Women's Suffrage Societies; Nationalism; Race and Ethnicity; Sha'rawi, Nur al-Hudá; Sri Lanka; Syria; Wolstenholme-Elmy, Elizabeth.

References Burton, Antoinette. *Burdens of History: British Feminists, Indian Women and Imperial Culture, 1865–1914* (1994); Caine, Barbara. *English Feminism, 1780–1980* (1997); Jayawardena, Kumari. *The White Woman's Other Burden: Western Women and South Asia during British Colonial Rule* (1995); Lazreg, Marnia. "Feminism and Difference: The Perils of Writing as a Woman on Women in Algeria" (1990); Midgley, Clare, ed. *Gender and Imperialism* (1998); Ragan, John David. "French Women Travellers in Egypt: Discourse Marginal to Orientalism?" (1998); Strobel, Margaret. "Gender and Race in the Nineteenth and Twentieth-Century British Empire" (1987).

Independent Labour Party

The Independent Labour Party (ILP), a British socialist group established in 1893, was unusual among European socialist parties that were affiliated with the Second International in that it gave support to a limited franchise for women rather than emphasizing the demand for a universal or adult suffrage. As early as 1894, the ILP annual conference, after pressure from the Glasgow Women's Labour Party, made a commitment to women's suffrage when a proposal that "the ILP is in favour of every proposal for extending electoral rights and democratising the system of government" was amended to include "to both men and women" (ILP Conference Report, 1894). Some of the leading female propagandists of the ILP, including Enid Stacy, Isabella Ford, and Emmeline Pankhurst, were supporters of women's suffrage, and at various times sat on the National Administrative Council of the ILP, while Keir Hardie, a key figure in the leadership of the party, was also committed to the women's cause.

While they were still members of the party, Emmeline and Christabel Pankhurst, along with other female members of the Manchester ILP, established the Women's Social and Political Union (WSPU) with the aim of using direct action to publicize their claim for the vote. They received financial and moral support from the local ILP and for the next four years carried out propaganda both for socialism and for votes for women in the north of England. In 1904 the ILP took a different stand from that of the Labour Party, with which it was affiliated, when its annual conference supported a resolution in favor of a limited franchise. Hardie, in particular, argued that priority should be given to removing "sex disability" in voting rights as a matter of principle. Nonetheless, this position was contested from within the ILP, with some leaders and members of the rank and file arguing that a socialist party should be demanding nothing less than adult suffrage.

There was considerable support within the ILP for methods of direct action used by the WSPU in its early years, in particular the disruption of political meetings; these were tactics that women had become familiar with in socialist campaigns. As the WSPU became more disillusioned with the Labour Party's stand on women's suffrage, however, it changed political tactics and at a by-election in 1906 carried out propaganda against the Labour as well as the Liberal candidate. This caused considerable controversy within the ILP and brought to a head the question of political loyalties. Although the Annual Conference of 1907 drew back from calling for the resignation of members of the WSPU and elected Emmeline Pankhurst as one of its delegates to the Labour Party conference, the leaders of the WSPU had already decided to cut their ties with the labor movement.

After 1907 even those women who retained their membership in the ILP, such as Isabella Ford, decided to give a full-time commitment to the women's suffrage struggle and exerted less influence within the party. Adult suffragists held positions of power within the National Administrative Council, and many of the leaders of the ILP became critical of the escalation of WSPU militancy. Between 1907 and 1909, therefore, the ILP appeared to give only lukewarm support to women's suffrage, although Keir Hardie, Philip Snowden, and other ILP MPs who had been elected to Parliament in 1906 continued to champion the women's cause in the House of Commons.

ILP women who were also suffragists worked hard in these years to bring the labor movement and the women's movement together. They tried to persuade local branches of trade unions and labor groups to pass resolutions in support of women's suffrage, and in 1911 the ILP launched a political equality campaign, spearheaded by its newspaper, the *Labour Leader,* which was now edited by women's suffrage supporter Fenner Brockway. This helped prepare the ground for the alliance that was formed in 1912 between the Labour Party and the constitutionalist group, the National Union of Women's Suffrage Societies, which at last identified the Labour Party with the cause of political equality.

Although the ILP did not always give priority to issues of franchise reform, its official support for a limited suffrage demand meant that socialist women who were also suffragists could use the organization as a vehicle to pursue women's enfranchisement. Many of its leading members were committed suffrage campaigners, and a study of their policies and activities reveals the complex relationship between socialist, labor, and suffrage politics in the prewar years.

See also Britain; Ford, Isabella; National Union of Women's Suffrage Societies; Pankhurst, Christabel; Pankhurst, Emmeline; Socialism in Europe; Universal Suffrage; Women's Social and Political Union.
Reference Hannam, June. "Women and the ILP, 1890–1914" (1992).

India

The demand for women's suffrage in India can be said to have begun in 1917, when the subcontinent was under British rule. A delegation of women, organized by the Women's Indian Association (WIA), which had been founded the same year, went to ask the Montagu-Chelmsford Committee on Constitutional Reform for equal voting rights with men. The delegation, which had been organized by Margaret Cousins, an Irish suffragist, was led by Sarojini Naidu, who was already active in the nationalist movement through her work for the Indian National Congress.

The Montagu-Chelmsford Committee had been set up by the British to encour-age progress toward Indian self-government, and as part of an information-gathering exercise, the Southborough Franchise Committee, appointed by the Montagu-Chelmsford Committee to seek out views on representation, was sent to tour India in 1918. Despite extensive petitioning from Indian women suffragists, the Southborough Committee ignored their views on the grounds that the twin problems of hostility to female education and the enforcement of *purdah* would prevent women being able to exercise any entitlement to vote. Indian women suffragists, most of whom were from an educated, urban elite, recognized the problems that women faced in striving to achieve full citizenship, but they always based their argument (as many British women had done) on the special contribution that women could make to the social and moral life of the country and to the education of their children.

The omission of women in the final recommendations of the Montagu-Chelmsford Committee led to protests from the WIA and the Indian National Congress, and both the Home Rule League (founded by an Englishwoman, Annie Besant) and the Muslim League added their call for women to be granted the vote on the same terms as men. In 1919 Naidu and Besant, on behalf of the WIA, together with delegates from the Bombay Committee for Women's Suffrage, went to London to present evidence to the Joint Parliamentary Committee dealing with the forthcoming constitutional reforms. Although this committee also ignored their representations and all the prosuffrage memoranda from numerous Indian and British women's organizations, its final report did contain a proviso that provincial legislative councils might add qualified women to their lists of registered voters. In 1919 the final recommendations were incorporated into the Government of India Act, which established an electorate of 5 million, based on

Indian suffragettes at the Women's Coronation Procession, part of the Empire Pageant, 17 June 1911. (Museum of London)

education and property qualifications, who could vote for representatives on the provincial legislatures. From 1921 onwards, these legislatures, which had been given power over such areas as education and public health, did begin to extend the vote to women, and although their numbers were small, the principle of female suffrage had been conceded. Soon afterward, women began to enter political life as members of provincial councils, as well as becoming magistrates and municipal councillors. During this period, Mohandas Gandhi, the charismatic leader of the independence movement, began his policy of noncooperation, including the boycott campaigns against the British, and nationalist women were expected to put the cause of Indian independence before their fight for the vote. Although this did not stop their suffrage campaigning, it did

lead to continual problems for women, whose loyalty was divided between the two causes.

In 1927 the Simon Commission was appointed by the British to review the working of the 1919 Government of India Act and to recommend further constitutional reforms. Because the members of the commission were exclusively British, all the major Indian political parties boycotted it, and the women of the WIA and the newly formed prosuffrage All-India Women's Conference (AIWC) joined the protest. However, some women, acting independently, met the commission and suggested a limited vote for literate women or reserved seats—ideas that were not publicly approved of by the main women's organizations.

Throughout the series of three Round Table Conferences that were held in London between 1930 and 1932 to discuss how to proceed toward dominion status for India, the Indian women's organizations stuck to their claim for universal adult suffrage, in support of the nationalist agenda. However, some women, particularly those from the Muslim community like Jahanara Shah Nawaz, believed that separate electorates and nominated seats might have to be accepted in order to ensure that women had a chance of being elected. At the same time, in 1932, a franchise committee that had been set up under Lord Lothian delivered its final report, which rejected adult suffrage but agreed that more women should be included in the franchise. The committee suggested that the ratio of female to male voters should be increased from 1:20 to 1:5.

However, there was a setback to the women's case when, in the same year, the British government made a communal award that confirmed separate electorates and reserved seats for Muslims and other minorities, together with special groups such as women. In addition, Gandhi agreed to reserved seats within the Hindu constituency for the untouchables, despite his strong belief in the importance of a unified electorate. Because of this precedent, it was unlikely that the women's demand for universal suffrage would be met.

The final stage of consultation, before the introduction of the new Government of India Act, was the establishment of the Linlithgow Joint Select Committee, and in June 1933 representatives from the three most important women's organizations in India went to London to give evidence before this group. The delegation, consisting of Dr. Muthulakshmi Reddy of the WIA, Rajkumari Amrit Kaur of the AIWC, and Sharifah Hamid Ali of the National Council of Women in India (NCWI), reiterated their demand for universal adult suffrage and their rejection of the various proposals that included wifehood suffrage, separate electorates, and reserved seats for women. They did not agree with the views of their British women supporters who advocated a compromise solution, but argued that they spoke for all Indian women, a claim that was disputed by some of their colleagues who felt that adult suffrage was now a dead issue.

The final Government of India Act of 1935 was a mixture of compromise measures to widen female enfranchisement, including special electorates. As a result, 6 million women with educational or property qualifications became eligible to vote out of a total electorate of 36 million. These women could also stand for election either to general seats or to seats reserved for women in the central and provincial legislatures.

In 1947 India gained its independence, and the new constitution adopted in 1949 provided for universal adult suffrage. However, as a result of partition, many women became citizens of the newly created state of Pakistan, and they had to wait for a number of years before they were fully enfranchised.

See also Citizenship; Cousins, Margaret; Naidu, Sarojini; Nationalism; Pakistan and Bangladesh; Shah Nawaz, Jahanara.
Reference Forbes, Geraldine. *Women in Modern India* (1996).

Indonesia

Women in Indonesia first became involved in politics through the nationalist movement in the early years of the twentieth century, but their interests were initially limited to issues such as opposition to polygamy, child marriage, and forced marriages. The vote did not become a live issue until 1918, when the Dutch established a Volksraad (People's Council), which included both Dutch and Indonesian members, and several reformers argued unsuccessfully for the female franchise. During the 1920s, women's organizations became more political in focus and the main nationalist organizations formed women's branches. However, the primary aim of these groups was to achieve independence from colonial rule, and women were told they should give priority to nationalist rather than women's issues. Religious differences between secular and Muslim women's groups over female education and marriage reform also helped to divide the feminist movement and to retard its progress.

Nevertheless, in 1938 suffrage was the main subject debated at the third conference of the Federation of Indonesian Women's Associations. This body had been set up in 1929 to campaign more widely for women's rights. In 1938, women activists protested against the election of a Dutch woman resident to the People's Council, rather than Mara Ulfah Santoso, the candidate sponsored by the Federation of Indonesian Women's Associations who was a law graduate of Leiden University. Objections were made again when Dutch national but not Indonesian women were offered the municipal vote in 1941, forcing the proposal to be withdrawn.

After the end of the Japanese occupation of Indonesia in 1945, the Dutch sought a return to colonial rule despite the Indonesian Declaration of Independence. Under the new constitution of 1945, women were given legal equality with men and were finally granted the national franchise. Still, Indonesia was unable to establish an independent government until after the Dutch had left in 1948. In 1955, 18 women were elected to the 257-member parliament, but progress since then has been slow. Women have been discouraged from involvement in politics and their level of political activism remains low.

See also Nationalism; The Netherlands.
Reference Jayawardena, Kumari. *Feminism and Nationalism in the Third World* (1986).

International Congress of Women, The Hague (1915)

The International Congress of Women held at The Hague during World War I at-

tempted to bring together women representatives of all nations to try to negotiate a peace. The congress was planned by suffrage leaders from four European countries: Lida Gustava Heymann and Anita Augspurg from Germany, Chrystal Macmillan from Britain, Eugenie Hamer and Marguerite Sarter from Belgium, and Aletta Jacobs, the first woman doctor in the Netherlands. Jacobs, in whose country the congress was held, sent out invitations and was the main organizer. Jane Addams, a leading pacifist feminist from the United States, was asked to preside over the congress.

The congress was attended by women from 12 neutral and warring nations including Britain, Germany, Belgium, the United States, Austria, Hungary, Brazil, Norway, Sweden, Italy, Poland, and the Netherlands. Expressions of sympathy were received from 10 countries who could not attend, including South Africa, Argentina, and India. Twenty-eight German women attended and a delegation of 47 women was sent from the United States accompanied by the British suffragist and peace campaigner Emily Pethick-Lawrence, who had been touring the United States. However, only two other British women, Kathleen Courtney and Chrystal Macmillan, who had arrived early, were able to reach the Netherlands. Twenty-four others arrived at the port of Tilbury, England, but were refused permission to sail on the grounds that the North Sea was closed to shipping. Women invitees from France, Canada, and Russia were unsympathetic to the cause of peace and refused their invitations.

Some sessions of the congress attracted as many as 2,000 visitors in the galleries. Among the resolutions passed by the congress was a commitment to "democratic control of foreign policy with equal representation of men and women; equal political rights and the enfranchisement of women." This conference marked an important shift in radical European suffragists' thinking. Close connections were made between male militarism and female subjection, and the argument that woman suffrage would have a civilizing influence on public affairs was now brought to the center of their agenda. No longer should women's role as peacemakers be confined to the private sphere. Rather, they were demanding political equality in order to participate in foreign affairs and decision making about war and peace at a national and international level.

The final resolution approved by the congress, presented by the well-known Hungarian international suffragist Rosika Schwimmer, stated that envoys should take all of its resolutions directly to heads of state of warring and neutral countries. The women envoys were generally treated with respect, but no government was prepared to accede to their demands.

See also Addams, Jane; Augspurg, Anita, and Lida Gustava Heymann; Jacobs, Aletta; Peace Movement; Pethick-Lawrence, Emmeline; Schwimmer, Rosika.
References Costin, Lela B. "Feminism, Pacifism, Internationalism and the 1915 International Congress of Women" (1982); Evans, Richard J. *Comrades and Sisters: Feminism, Socialism and Pacifism in Europe, 1870–1945* (1987); Vellacott Newbury, Jo. "Anti-War Suffragists" (1977).

International Council of Women

The International Council of Women (ICW) was founded in Washington, D.C., in 1888 with the aim of fostering international solidarity among women. It grew out of an initiative of American suffrage leaders Elizabeth Cady Stanton and Susan B. Anthony, who after meeting women reformers on their travels in Europe in 1882–1883, set up a committee of correspondence to form an international suffrage association. Nothing concrete emerged from this in the short run, and it was not until 1888 that the National Woman Suffrage Association (NWSA),

under Anthony's influence as president, invited women from other countries to attend the group's annual conference. This was to be a celebration of the fortieth anniversary of the Seneca Falls Convention of 1848, where the first organized demand for women's suffrage had been made. Stanton had originally planned to invite only women from suffrage groups, but the NWSA supported Anthony's view that as many different organizations as possible should be represented in the interest of unity among women, including literary clubs, temperance societies, and peace groups. Nine foreign delegations attended, most of which were from Europe, and at the end of the conference a new group, the ICW, was formed to be an umbrella group for all women's organizations. It was agreed that policies needed to be accepted unanimously, which meant that women's suffrage, always a controversial question, was not one of the three issues accepted by the conference. Although a national council of women was formed in the United States after the meeting, other countries were slow to follow suit until Lady Aberdeen, selected as president in 1893, sent her private secretary to Europe to encourage the formation of national councils. Groups were established in Britain, Germany, Sweden, the Netherlands, Denmark, Australia, and Canada and by 1914 the ICW had formed affiliations with 23 national councils, mostly representing European countries.

Suffrage was always a difficult issue for the ICW. Although most members agreed that women should be able at some point to exercise the vote, they held a wide variety of views about how it should be achieved and what emphasis should be given to the demand. In 1899, at the Third Congress of the ICW held in London, any semblance of unity was undermined by the suffrage question. The coordinating committee agreed that antisuffragists should have access to a suffrage meeting

The International Council of Women Executive Committee, 1888. (Library of Congress)

that had been planned. Their attendance was opposed by the organizers of the meeting, the German radicals Anita Augspurg and Lida Gustava Heymann. They convened an alternative meeting that advocated that an international alliance of women involved in suffrage should be formed. In 1902 an international meeting was organized by Carrie Chapman Catt in Washington, D.C., in conjunction with the annual congress of the National American Woman Suffrage Association. Susan B. Anthony was in the chair and Vida Goldstein from Australia was the recording secretary. It was decided to set up a permanent organization at the next meeting of the ICW, to be held in Berlin in 1904, which would pursue suffrage as a matter of human rights and justice. This was a radical demand at a time when the U.S. suffrage movement, for one, had begun to argue that women needed the vote because of their special qualities, derived from the domestic sphere.

With the establishment of the more radical International Woman Suffrage Alliance (IWSA) in 1904, the ICW was positioned on the conservative wing of the international women's movement. This was partly a result of its attempt to bring together a broad range of women's groups and interests, which meant that it avoided controversial questions, and partly because its leaders, Lady Aberdeen and Baroness Alexandra Gripenburg, gave it a reputation as an aristocratic body. Nonetheless, the formation of the IWSA did lead the ICW, in the face of considerable opposition, to establish a Standing Committee on Suffrage and Rights of Citizenship. Anna Howard Shaw, who was responsible for the council's suffrage work, found it difficult to make progress when member groups had such diverse attitudes toward suffrage and the issue remained a contentious one. At the 1909 congress held in Toronto, it was proposed that the name of the Committee on Suffrage should be changed to the Committee on Citizenship so that women from conservative countries would not face difficulties. At the Rome congress in 1914, a resolution that would have allowed the host country to veto the program of a congress—such as a program that included suffrage demands—was heavily defeated, while a suffrage resolution received enthusiastic support. This finally settled the question of whether suffrage should form part of the program of the ICW.

From the beginning the ICW had tried to accommodate women with very different interests, including antisuffragists alongside suffrage supporters, which limited its effectiveness as a campaigning group for women's suffrage. On the other hand, it did seek greater power for women in politics and played a part in bringing women together across national boundaries on a broad range of issues.

See also Anthony, Susan B.; Augspurg, Anita, and Lida Gustava Heymann; Catt, Carrie Chapman; Citizenship; Gripenberg, Alexandra; International Woman Suffrage Alliance; National American Woman Suffrage Association; National Council of Women of Canada; National Woman Suffrage Association; Women's Rights Convention, Seneca Falls. *References* Bosch, Mineke, with Annemarie Kloosterman, eds. *Politics and Friendship: Letters from the International Woman Suffrage Alliance, 1902–1942* (1990); Rupp, Leila J. *Worlds of Women: The Making of an International Women's Movement* (1997).

International Links

The struggle for women's suffrage was a worldwide movement in which women made links with each other across national boundaries. The campaign in one country, therefore, could influence the development and character of the suffrage movement elsewhere. Transnational organizations such as the International Woman Suffrage Alliance (IWSA) enabled women to meet in a formal setting, but of even greater importance were the informal contacts between individuals that had often preceded,

and laid the basis for, the formation of the transnational groups. Women corresponded with each other and used their suffrage journals to publicize the progress of the suffrage campaign in other countries. They also traveled widely, either in an attempt to gain direct experience of suffrage movements elsewhere, or to stimulate the development of the campaign. For example, the U.S. envoy of the Woman's Christian Temperance Union, Mary Leavitt, traveled throughout the world and left behind 86 women's organizations that aimed to gain the vote for women.

In the nineteenth century the United States, with its strong and long-standing women's movement, attracted many visitors from abroad and American suffrage leaders were greatly admired. In the years immediately preceding World War I, however, it was the militancy of the British suffragettes that inspired others. It has been suggested that the experience of militancy in Britain helped to revitalize the suffrage movements of France and the United States. Madeleine Pelletier and Caroline Kauffmann from France, for example, took part in demonstrations in Britain and attempted to introduce more direct action methods into their own country, and Harriot Stanton Blatch, an American friend of Emmeline Pankhurst, invited Annie Cobden-Sanderson, the British suffragette who had been imprisoned, to New York to speak about her experiences. This stimulated a more aggressive style of campaigning in the U.S. movement, which was reinforced when Alice Paul and Lucy Burns, who had both been arrested in London when campaigning on behalf of the Women's Social and Political Union, returned to the United States. Several younger women from South America, including the Brazilian Bertha Lutz, also visited Britain before 1914. The actions of the suffragettes stimulated their interest in women's suffrage, but they were reluctant to import militant methods into their own countries, where they feared that this would increase opposition to their cause.

Women from countries that already had the vote were also in demand as speakers. Kate Sheppard of New Zealand visited the United States and Britain, and the Australian Vida Goldstein was invited to Britain in 1911 by the WSPU. She spoke to numerous meetings and met all the main leaders of the British suffrage movement. She was there to offer help and support— a reversal of the usual relationship between a former colonial and the imperial power, but participation in the militant campaign also challenged her own ideas about cooperation between male and female socialists in a common struggle.

Before World War I, such contacts were largely between women from Europe, North America, and the former colonies of New Zealand and Australia. However, IWSA members Carrie Chapman Catt and Aletta Jacobs did travel to a wide range of countries in 1911–1912, including Palestine, Burma, and Indonesia. There is little evidence that their tour was successful in leading to the establishment of permanent suffrage organizations, but in the Philippines they did give new momentum to the movement and four women's suffrage bills were introduced to the House of Representatives between 1912 and 1918. During the interwar years, far more links were made with women from developing countries, in particular through the IWSA. Bertha Lutz, for example, attended several international congresses in the 1920s and 1930s and had a very close relationship with Carrie Chapman Catt. The Egyptian suffragists Saiza Nabarawi and Hudá Sha'rawi also attended congresses regularly and developed friendships with the leaders of the IWSA.

There is also evidence that, in the context of growing nationalism in the interwar years, women from outside Europe and North America sought to assert their independence. Paulina Luisi from Uruguay, along with other women suffrage campaigners in South America, grew increasingly critical of the domination of North America in the pan-American women's movement, specifically of Carrie Chapman Catt's self-proclaimed role as a missionary to countries with less developed suffrage movements. Consequently, some Latin American liberal feminists joined with their Iberian counterparts to form a new international organization, Liga Internacional de Mujeres Ibéricas e Hispanoamericanas (International League of Iberian and Hispanic-American Women), led by Luisi. Similarly, in the late 1920s women came together from Pacific Rim countries, including Australia, New Zealand, Manila, Japan, the Philippines, and China, in the Pan-Pacific Women's Association, which shifted the center of international links away from Britain. Women from outside Europe and North America also made links with each other. Sarojini Naidu of the Indian National Congress, a campaigner for women's suffrage, inspired Sri Lankan middle-class women when she visited their country in 1922, and feminists in Uruguay, Mexico, Brazil, and Argentina carried out an extensive correspondence in which they began to value their own methods and autonomy.

It must be remembered, however, that these international links tended to reinforce the role of educated, middle-class women in the suffrage movement, since they had both the means and the time to travel. Moreover, notions of sisterhood could break down when national or religious differences came to the surface, as when Hudá Sha'rawi at meetings of the IWSA voiced the concerns of the Muslim women of Palestine against Jewish immigration and challenged the Christian assumptions that lay behind transnational women's groups (Rupp, 1997, 60). Antoinette Burton describes how British feminists thought that they could reach out to Indian women because of their shared womanhood, while at the same time expressing Western imperialist assumptions about Indian culture. Thus, the relationships between suffrage campaigners of different nationalities were complex, but they did attempt to give each other support and to foster international links.

See also Anthony, Susan B.; Blatch, Harriot Stanton; Catt, Carrie Chapman; Ducoing, Delia; Goldstein, Vida; Imperialism; Jacobs, Aletta; Kauffmann, Caroline; Luisi, Paulina; Lutz, Bertha; Naidu, Sarojini; National Woman Suffrage Association; Nationalism; Pankhurst, Emmeline; Paul, Alice; Pelletier, Madeleine; Sha'rawi, Nur al-Hudá; Sheppard, Kate; Stanton, Elizabeth Cady; Woman's Christian Temperance Union; Women's Social and Political Union.
References Bosch, Mineke, with Annemarie Kloosterman, eds. *Politics and Friendship: Letters from the International Woman Suffrage Alliance, 1902–1942* (1990); Burton, Antoinette. *Burdens of History: British Feminists, Indian Women and Imperial Culture, 1865–1914* (1994); Daley, Caroline, and Melanie Nolan, eds. *Suffrage and Beyond. International Feminist Perspectives* (1994); Ehrick, Christine. "*Madrinas* and Missionaries: Uruguay and the Pan-American Women's Movement" (1998); Rupp, Leila. *Worlds of Women: The Making of an International Women's Movement* (1997); Woollacott, Angela. "Inventing Commonwealth and Pan-Pacific Feminisms: Australian Women's Internationalist Activism in the 1920s–30s" (1998).

International Proletarian Women's Day

The International Proletarian Women's Day, held each year between 1911 and the outbreak of World War I, focused on the issue of women's suffrage. The day was first suggested by Clara Zetkin, a leading member of the Sozialdemokratische Partei Deutschlands (SPD) [German Social Democratic Party] at the International Socialist Women's Congress in 1910. She proposed that women's demonstrations should be held on a fixed day every year all over the world to show the solidarity of socialist women as they fought for the emancipation of working-class women. It is likely that she was seeking to regain some of the

influence that she had lost within the women's organization of the SPD, which was now run by Luise Zietz. However, Zietz took over the organization of the International Proletarian Women's Day in Germany and ensured that it would become a series of mass demonstrations for women's suffrage. At the first demonstration, held on 19 March 1911, hundreds of meetings were held throughout Germany (there were 41 in Berlin alone) where resolutions were passed in favor of votes for women. The event was less successful in the following year, but in 1913 there was an even greater emphasis on women's suffrage and meetings were better attended than ever before.

Similar Women's Days were organized in other countries, although on a smaller scale, including even Russia in 1913, where the meetings were quickly suppressed by the police. They were all held under the slogan of universal suffrage and gave socialist women a sense that they were part of an international movement working toward the same goal. They also enabled and encouraged working-class women to take part in the suffrage campaign.

See also Socialism in Europe; Stuttgart Congress of the Second International; Zetkin, Clara.
Reference Evans, Richard J. *Comrades and Sisters: Feminism, Socialism and Pacifism in Europe, 1870–1945* (1987).

International Woman Suffrage Alliance

The International Woman Suffrage Alliance, founded in Berlin in 1904, enabled suffragists from different countries to share experiences, to give each other support, and to gain a sense that they were part of an international movement. The alliance consisted of women's suffrage groups from around the world who were pledged to secure the enfranchisement of the women of all nations. It grew out of the International Council of Women

(ICW), founded in the United States in 1888, which sought to achieve a broad range of reforms. At the ICW's 1899 congress, the leadership permitted antisuffragists to take part in a session on women's political rights, prompting the German suffragists Lida Gustava Heymann and Anita Augspurg to call for the formation of a new international organization devoted to women's suffrage. In 1901 Carrie Chapman Catt, president of the National American Woman Suffrage Association, proposed that an international suffrage congress should be held to coincide with her organization's annual meeting in Washington, D.C., in 1902. Delegates from 10 countries attended the new congress and agreed that they would form a permanent organization at the next meeting of the ICW in Berlin. This led to the formation of the IWSA in 1904.

The IWSA was made up of national women's suffrage auxiliaries that had suffrage as their sole objective. The definition of a national group was ambiguous, and this was to cause controversy in later years when there were splits in various national suffrage movements. The purpose of the IWSA was to act as a central bureau to collect, exchange, and disseminate information about suffrage work. The alliance also aimed to stimulate national suffrage activities and held congresses roughly every two years in different countries until war was declared in 1914. The meetings were held in Copenhagen in 1906, Amsterdam in 1908, London in 1909, Stockholm in 1911, and Budapest in 1913. Before World War I, the alliance was dominated by Western European and white colonial countries. The first six auxiliaries to join in 1904 were Australia, Germany, the Netherlands, Sweden, the United States, and Great Britain. By 1913 the number had grown to 26. This number included China, although a banner presented at the Congress of 1913 was the only evidence of the existence of a Chinese

suffrage group and no Chinese women ever attended the international meetings.

Under the leadership of Carrie Chapman Catt, who was president from 1904 to 1923, the IWSA did provide an important forum for suffragists from different countries to inspire each other and to forge friendship links across national boundaries. In countries such as Russia, where a struggling women's movement faced government repression, the alliance could be a lifeline to the support of like-minded women. Those who could not attend IWSA congresses were able to keep abreast of international events through reading *Jus Suffragii* (The right of suffrage), the IWSA journal, launched in 1906. Suffrage presses showed an intense interest in the women's movement abroad, focusing particularly on those countries where women had already gained the vote and reported at length on international developments.

Emphasizing solidarity between women, the IWSA tried to overlook national controversies about methods of campaigning or the basis on which suffrage should be demanded. Nonetheless, it was difficult to avoid conflict, in particular because the alliance allowed only one organization from each country to affiliate. In 1906, for example, Millicent Fawcett, leader of the British constitutionalist group the National Union of Women's Suffrage Societies, challenged the credentials of Dora Montefiore, a delegate to the conference who was a member of the militant Women's Social and Political Union (WSPU). Montefiore was allowed to speak only after the Dutch and Hungarian delegates wrote to the president asking that she should be heard on behalf of the "insurgent women of England." The IWSA never passed a resolution condemning militancy, and on many occasions it praised such tactics for the publicity they generated, but its moderate stand was apparent when the WSPU was admitted as a fraternal association rather than as an affiliated group. There was an even greater gulf between the IWSA, with its largely moderate, educated, middle-class membership, and the Socialist Women's International, which called for adult suffrage and sought cooperation with socialist parties rather than with the "bourgeois women's movement." Nonetheless, individual socialist women such as Isabella Ford from Britain and Martina Kramers from the Netherlands, who attended IWSA congresses, sought to bridge the gap, and in Budapest in 1913 a radical group from the Hungarian movement invited Sylvia Pankhurst to talk about her brand of suffrage and socialist campaigning among workers in the East End of London.

At the end of World War I, so many women had gained enfranchisement and so many of those with votes were anxious to take up other causes that there was some discussion about whether the IWSA should be disbanded. The 1920 Congress, however, divided into enfranchised and nonenfranchised sections and agreed that the alliance would continue to work to achieve suffrage and any other reforms that would establish equality. The war had stimulated the development of women's movements in countries that had once been dependent or colonized, and the main struggle for the vote was now in Latin America, Asia, and Africa. This encouraged the IWSA to link with women throughout the world, and by 1929 the list of national affiliates had grown to 51, including Brazil, Argentina, Egypt, India, Cuba, Puerto Rico, and Japan. It was not easy, however, to find common ground. Those who already had the suffrage took up other campaigns, particularly peace, and the alliance began to lose its distinctiveness. On the other hand, it managed to survive World War II, and in 1946 it adopted the new title of the International Alliance of Women, with a program of peace, democracy, women's rights, and support for the United Nations.

Despite its later difficulties, the IWSA succeeded as a transnational organization that had enabled suffrage campaigners from different countries to share experiences and to support each other. Starting as a European- and American-centered movement, it gained new life in the interwar years as women's movements emerged in the developing, less industrialized world. There was a complex relationship, however, between notions of international sisterhood, women's involvement in their own national politics, and the colonial and imperialist rhetoric employed when suffragists from Western Europe and the United States sought to make links with women elsewhere. For many members of the IWSA, the rhetoric of internationalism sat uneasily alongside a strong national identity that was reinforced at congresses by the use of flags, national anthems, costumes, and songs.

Although IWSA affiliates were constitutionalist in their outlook, the alliance positioned itself between the conservative International Council of Women and the more radical Women's International League for Peace and Freedom, managing to maintain its own identity in a changing world.

See also Augspurg, Anita, and Lida Gustava Heymann; Catt, Carrie Chapman; Fawcett, Millicent Garrett; Ford, Isabella; Imperialism; International Council of Women; International Links; Kramers, Martina; Montefiore, Dora; National American Woman Suffrage Association; National Union of Women's Suffrage Societies; Nationalism; Pankhurst, (Estelle) Sylvia; Women's Social and Political Union.

References Bosch, Mineke, with Annemarie Kloosterman, eds. *Politics and Friendship: Letters from the International Woman Suffrage Alliance, 1902–1942* (1990); Hurwitz, Edith J. "The International Sisterhood" (1977); Rupp, Leila J. *Worlds of Women: The Making of an International Women's Movement* (1997); Wiltsher, Anne. *Most Dangerous Women: Feminist Peace Campaigners in the Great War* (1985).

Iran

In Iran's first constitution, promulgated in 1906, women were not granted the right to vote, but during the debates of the *Majlis* (the Iranian Parliament) in 1911, the issue of female suffrage was raised by the deputy for Hamadan Hadji Vakil el Rooy (or el Roaya) and later that year, the Persian Women's Society sent a telegram to the "Women Suffrage Committee, London," requesting help against Russian intervention in the internal affairs of Iran. They received a sympathetic but noncommittal reply from the Women's Social and Political Union (WSPU).

The collapse of constitutional government in 1912 and the chaos caused by World War I suspended debate, but by 1920 there were again clear signs of a women's movement in Iran, confined admittedly to Tehran and other major cities and comprising only upper- and middle-class women. Numerous feminist periodicals were founded between 1920 and the 1941 abdication of the ruler of Iran, Reza Shah Pahlavi, focusing in general on the necessity of education for women, the reform of Muslim personal law, and child and maternal welfare. Internal evidence indicates that whenever a women's periodical addressed political questions, such as the right to vote, it came under severe attack, particularly from clerical circles, and the suffrage question received little overt support, even after Reza Shah abolished veiling in 1935 and cracked down on the power of the clerics.

With the accession of Reza Shah's son, Mohamed Reza Pahlavi in 1941, political parties were again allowed to operate and many of these opened women's branches. However, although politically active women lobbied for the vote (particularly during the early 1950s), the first two decades of the new Shah's reign brought no major changes in women's issues; in fact, the veil was openly worn again and members of the clergy reestablished themselves as a political force. The reform program introduced in the early 1960s, known collectively as the White Revolution, did eventually provide the platform needed to enfranchise women. The main plank of the White Revolution was land reform, but subsidiary aims were to improve literacy and to give workers and peasants better representation on supervisory committees. To these ends, a referendum was called for early in 1963, and although women's participation was strongly opposed by the clergy (Imam Khomeini described the potential extension of the suffrage as an instrument for the moral corruption of women in particular and of society in general), women set up and staffed their own polling stations. Although the ballot papers cast by women were initially going to be excluded from the count, enough publicity was generated to reverse the situation. A month after the vote, the Shah announced that he was granting women the right to vote and to stand for office. Later, in 1978–1979, in an ironic reversal of fortune, women played such a powerful role in the movement to depose the Shah, with the full backing and encouragement of the Muslim clergy, that neither Ayatollah Khomeini nor his fellow clerics have felt able to repeal the changes introduced by the Shah. Indeed, in the elections of February 2000 huge numbers of women turned out to vote, and the preliminary results indicated that a record number of women deputies would be elected to the *Majlis*.

References Bayat-Philipp, Mangol. "Women and Revolution in Iran, 1905–1911" (1978); Esfandiari, Haleh. *Reconstructed Lives: Women and Iran's Islamic Revolution* (1977); Sanasarian, Eliz. "Characteristics of Women's Movement in Iran" (1985).

Ireland

The founding moment of Irish women's campaign for suffrage was in 1876, when Anna Haslam formed the Dublin Women's Suffrage Association. She and her husband, Thomas Haslam, were the backbone of the first stage of Irish suffragism, which remained confined to a small, middle-class group, most of whom were Quakers. In 1896 the association's membership remained under 50, its activities confined to drawing-room meetings and petitions to the Westminster Parliament. Anna Haslam was also active in campaigns for the Married Women's Property Acts and for the repeal of the Contagious Diseases Acts, and she maintained close links with various British feminist organizations. Politically, she supported the maintenance of the union with Britain.

In Belfast, the Scots-born Isabella Tod founded the lesser-known North of Ireland Society for Women's Suffrage in 1871, linking it to the London Women's Suffrage Society. Tod, one of the few women to speak on the platform of Ulster Unionists during the campaign against Gladstone's Home Rule Bill of 1886, was a pioneer for women's education and well-known as a contributor to the *Englishwoman's Review*. Her premature death in 1896 deprived women in the north of Ireland of an important leader.

In 1898 the Local Government (Ireland) Act gave Irish women the local government franchise and made them eligible for election as urban and rural councillors (only in 1911 did they win the right to become county councillors). In recognition of this milestone in women's citizenship, the Haslam group changed its name in 1901 to the Irish Women's Suffrage and Local Government Association (IWSLGA). Members of the association began to win election as councillors and as Poor Law Guardians. New recruits to the cause were found, many from the newly emergent Catholic middle class.

The Irish cultural revival of this period also enabled nationalist women to undertake a political role. The nationalist-feminist organization Inghinidhe na hEireann (Daughters of Ireland), formed in 1900, refused to campaign for votes from an "alien government," but individual members argued strongly for the rights of women to full citizenship in an independent Ireland. In 1908, in response to the potential of the changing situation, Hanna Sheehy Skeffington and Margaret Cousins, both members of the IWSLGA, broke with that organization in order to form the Irish Women's Franchise League (IWFL). This avowedly militant and nonparty group broke new ground in the Irish campaign for the vote through its heckling of politicians, its open-air mass meetings, and its later campaign of physical violence in the destruction of public property. Significantly, the IWFL also declared itself to favor Irish home rule.

Between 1912 and 1914, Irish suffrage was at its strongest, with an estimated 3,000 members. Sheehy Skeffington claimed that, in proportion to population, this made it comparable to the British movement. The IWFL, with over 1,000 members, was the largest group; the IWSLGA had between 600 and 700; the Irish branch of the Conservative and Unionist Women's Suffrage Association (established in 1909) had 660; and the Irish Women's Suffrage Society, Belfast, a former branch of the IWSLGA, had several hundred. The Munster Women's Franchise League (MWFL) had 300 members in its Cork branch, with other branches in Limerick and Waterford. Its members held a variety of views on the constitutional question, although its president and vice president, Edith Somerville and Violet Martin, came from landowning Protestant Unionist backgrounds. The majority of suffragists were still middle-class and Protestant, but the Catholic to non-Catholic ratio had narrowed to approximately one to two.

In 1911 Louie Bennett, a middle-class Dublin woman from a Protestant background, set up the Irish Women's Reform League to promote the rights of working women. In the same year she and her partner, Helen Chenevix, established the Irish Women's Suffrage Federation as an umbrella group to give some cohesion to the numerous small groups representing different political, religious, and geographical divisions scattered around the country. By 1914 it had 26 affiliated societies, although the larger organizations insisted on retaining their independence by remaining outside. The IWFL did not take part because the federation insisted on following a nonmilitant and constitutional line, but members of both groups spoke regularly from common platforms.

Throughout this period, unsuccessful attempts were made to have a woman's suffrage bill introduced at Westminster. In 1912 the Irish Parliamentary Party, anxious to keep the Liberal government in power so that a bill providing for home rule would be enacted, voted against Philip Snowden's suffrage bill. In response, the IWFL declared war on the Irish Party and embarked on a campaign of militancy that resulted in the imprisonment of many of its members over the next two years. Frank Sheehy Skeffington and James Cousins, husbands of leading IWFL figures, established the *Irish Citizen* in May 1912 in order to provide Irish suffragists with a paper of their own and to explain their situation and distinguish it from that of their British counterparts.

As the home rule situation grew more serious, Ulster unionists, determined to retain the constitutional link with Britain, organized a paramilitary force, the Ulster Volunteer Force, and threatened to establish a secessionist Ulster parliament, separate from the rest of Ireland. Initially, as women in Ulster were promised the vote, unionists were congratulated on their progressive intent. However, when Sir Edward Carson, leader of the Ulster unionists, made plain his hostility to female enfranchisement, Christabel Pankhurst declared war on the Ulster unionists. The Women's Social and Political Union (WSPU) established a branch in Belfast, despite the expressed misgivings of Irish suffragists, who argued that the delicacy of the Irish situation required mediation from Irish women alone. The WSPU's campaign of militancy, which was becoming increasingly difficult to pursue in Britain, was transferred to the north of Ireland as British women moved to Ireland. Although a mixture of unionist and nationalist women in the north did join the WSPU, it would appear that the majority of recruits were unionist. In 1914, at the outbreak of war, the WSPU closed down its Ulster operations, despite protests that the home rule question remained to be settled. Margaret McCoubrey, a Scots trade unionist living in Belfast, attempted to establish a branch of the IWFL that would cater to the militants of the former WSPU, but the sectarian divisions of Belfast ensured that this was a short-lived initiative.

The *Irish Citizen* took an antimilitarist stance at the outbreak of World War I, and the IWFL, unlike many other suffrage groups, refused to engage in any relief work that might prolong the war. During 1915 the IWFL continued to organize speaking tours and suffrage meetings, but the divisions caused by the war had a detrimental effect upon the feminist cause. Those who supported the war withdrew their subscriptions from the *Irish Citizen,* and nationalist members of the MWFL resigned in protest over its decision to raise funds for the war effort.

During the Easter Uprising of 1916, some members of the IWFL carried supplies and messages to the insurgents' outposts. The Proclamation of the Republic, the Irish declaration of independence, was noteworthy for its promise to grant equal rights and opportunities to all citizens. The most serious blow to the Irish suffrage movement was the execution of Francis Sheehy Skeffington, arrested by a British army officer while attempting to organize a citizen's militia to prevent mobs from looting the Dublin shops. His widow took over the editorship of the *Irish Citizen* before traveling to the United States to publicize her husband's murder and to win support for Ireland's fight for independence. In her absence, Louie Bennett, now secretary of the Irish Women Workers' Union (IWWU), took over. From 1918 onwards, both women worked for the paper, which became a vehicle for the IWWU. In 1920, during the War of Independence, it ceased publication.

In 1918 Constance Markievicz, a leading figure in the Easter Uprising, became the first woman to be elected to Westminster. The IWFL and the nationalist women's organization, Cumann na mBan, campaigned on her behalf, but other leading figures from the suffrage movement took different political routes. Louie Bennett refused a nomination from the Irish Labour Party; Hanna Sheehy Skeffington (now a Sinn Fein member) refused a Sinn Fein nomination for a seat in an unwinnable constituency; Anna Haslam supported the Conservative and Unionist Party; and others supported the constitutional nationalists of the Irish Parliamentary Party. The War of Independence began in 1919 and ended in 1922 with the treaty between Britain and Ireland that established the Irish Free State. Irish women between the ages of 21 and 30, in recognition of their contribution to that war, were granted the vote in the Free State Constitution of 1922. The IWSLGA, now renamed as the Irish Women Citizens and Local Government Association, was one of a number of women's organizations to continue to lobby the government on legislation affecting women and children.

See also Bennett, Louie; Citizenship; Cousins, Margaret; Haslam, Anna; Irish Women's Franchise League; Militancy; Nationalism; Pankhurst, Christabel; Skeffington, Hanna Sheehy; Women's Social and Political Union.
References Cullen, Mary, and Maria Luddy, eds. *Women, Power and Consciousness in Nineteenth-Century Ireland* (1995); Cullen Owens, Rosemary. *Smashing Times: A History of the Irish Women's Suffrage Movement, 1889–1922* (1984); Murphy, Cliona. *The Women's Suffrage Movement and Irish Society in the Early Twentieth Century* (1989); Ryan, Louise. *Irish Feminism and the Vote: An Anthology of the* Irish Citizen, *1912–1920* (1996); Ward, Margaret. "Conflicting Interests: The British and Irish Suffrage Movements" (1995).

Irish Women's Franchise League

The Irish Women's Franchise League (IWFL), formed in 1908, was the most active and militant of all the suffrage groups in Ireland. It was modeled partly on the Women's Social and Political Union (WSPU), a militant suffrage organization formed in England by the Pankhursts in 1903 that inspired feminists all over the world. Many feminists in Ireland were dissatisfied with the genteel nature of the long-established Irish Women's Suffrage and Local Government Association, which deplored the new strategy of militancy. An important impetus behind the formation of the IWFL was the County Council Bill of 1907, which made English and Scottish, but not Irish, women eligible to sit on County and Borough Councils. It was believed that the existence of a strong campaigning body in Ireland would have ensured the extension of that legislation to Ireland.

In contrast to the great majority of women in Ireland, the leaders of the IWLF were well educated, including three professors and many writers, poets, and academics among its membership. Its secretary, Hanna Sheehy Skeffington, and its treasurer, Margaret Cousins, both had university degrees. The IWLF was also supported by a number of well-known and influential men. The group began by holding weekly meetings in Dublin and organizing speaking tours throughout the country. It also held mass public meetings. By 1912 its membership had risen to 1,000, although it has been estimated that only about 50 were actively involved in campaigning.

The IWFL was open to women of all political persuasions. Its main aim was to obtain the franchise for women on the same terms as men; its chief objective was to ensure that this measure was incorporated into the Home Rule Bill proposed by the Liberal government elected in 1910. The IWFL slogan, "Suffrage first before all else," indicated its determination that all other issues should be subordinated to this goal. The argument that there should be home rule for Irish women as well as Irish men placed the league, in practice, on the nationalist side of Irish political life.

The IWFL aimed to get the maximum publicity for its activities. These included holding meetings and debates, performing suffrage plays such as *How the Vote Was Won,* harassing visiting English politicians, and resisting the 1911 census. The league also set up a newspaper, the *Irish Citizen,* which was edited by Frank Sheehy Skeffington and James Cousins. The paper provided a platform for all suffrage organizations in Ireland, running from 1912 to 1920. The IWFL did not initially resort to militancy, attempting rather to persuade members of the Irish Parliamentary Party to support its goals. When by 1911 it was clear that this strategy had failed, the league followed the WSPU in arguing for antigovernment measures that would, if necessary, bring down the government, even though this policy would put the Home Rule Bill in jeopardy. In 1912 the IWFL began to adopt militant tactics, including smashing windows of public buildings, for which many IWFL women were arrested and sent to jail.

Although the IWFL was criticized for jeopardizing home rule through its critique of the Irish Party's capitulation to the Liberal government, its members argued that the terms under which a home rule Ireland would be governed were to be fixed for the first three years, denying women a voice in the vital early years of independence. In attempting to steer a "suffrage first" path through the complexities of the Irish constitutional crisis, the league also appeared

to favor Ulster unionism because it had praised Ulster unionists for their promise to give women the vote in a secessionist Ulster parliament. The league was partly motivated by the hope that the enfranchisement of women would provide a unifying force within Irish political life, helping to heal some of the existing divisions. As nationalists, IWFL members resisted strongly the imperialist designs of the WSPU in setting up branches in Belfast and Dublin, and they had no desire to work under English women leaders. They distanced themselves from their more extreme acts of WSPU militancy in Ireland and were relieved when the latter withdrew in 1914 to support the war effort.

During the war, in contrast to the WSPU, the IWFL retained an antimilitarist stance, aiming to unite women of all nations. However, members also hoped that the war would provide the opportunity for Ireland to be recognized as a small nation in the final peace settlement following the end of war. After women over 30 received the vote in 1918, the IWFL joined with Cumann na mBann (the Irish Women's Council) to campaign for the election of Constance Markievicz, the first woman to be elected to Westminster as a Sinn Fein member even though she boycotted the British Parliament. Irish women over 30 were granted the vote while Ireland was still part of Britain. After independence the Free State granted the vote to women between 21 and 30 in 1922.

See also Britain; Cousins, Margaret; *How the Vote Was Won;* Imperialism; Ireland; Militancy; Nationalism; Skeffington, Hanna Sheehy; Women's Social and Political Union.
References Murphy, Cliona. *The Women's Suffrage Movement and Irish Society in the Early Twentieth Century* (1989); Murphy, Cliona. "'The Tune of the Stars and Stripes': The American Influence on the Irish Suffrage Movement" (1990); Ryan, Louise. "Traditions and Double Standards: The Irish Suffragists' Critique of Nationalism" (1995); Ward, Margaret. "'Suffrage First—Above All Else!' An Account of the Irish Suffrage Movement" (1982).

Israel

At the beginning of the twentieth century, the small number of Jewish women in Ottoman Palestine were more active in debating labor issues on their agricultural settlements than in making demands for political rights. The defeat of the Ottoman forces in World War I and the entrance of the British Army into Palestine in 1917, however, changed the situation radically. Initially, the British established a military government, but this was replaced by a civilian administration in July 1920, and the British set about establishing all the organs of government required for administering the territory. Two years later, in 1922, British de facto rule was transformed into an official League of Nations mandate.

The Yishuv (the pre-independence Jewish community in Palestine) responded to British rule by setting up its own political institutions. Among the issues debated by the Yishuv was how the community should be governed and who should be allowed to choose the representatives. Strongly in favor of women's suffrage were the women who had settled in Palestine in the Ottoman period and who had already formed their own Conference of Women Agricultural Workers in 1914. They were joined by the more middle-class Hebrew Women's Organization for Equal Rights in Palestine. However, both were opposed by the ultraorthodox, who feared that they would be underrepresented in any legislative assembly if women were given the vote, given that conservative religious women would not participate in elections. In a compromise, women were given the vote on a temporary basis in the elections to the first Elected Assembly in April 1920, and ultraorthodox men were compensated by a double vote to count for both themselves and their wives.

Women were eventually given the franchise on a permanent basis in 1925 in the elections to the second Elected Assembly, when the orthodox party, Hamizrachi, withdrew its opposition to women's suffrage. However, the principle of one person, one vote was not adopted until the fourth Elected Assembly, chosen in August 1944, and it was the electoral arrangements for this assembly that formed the basis of the constitution of the State of Israel, which attained independence in 1948 on the basis of full adult suffrage for all its citizens, both Jews and Arabs.

See also Citizenship; Middle East and North Africa
References Horowitz, Dan, and Moshe Lissak. *Origins of the Israeli Polity: Palestine under the Mandate* (1978); Sharfman, Daphna. "Israel: Women and Politics in Israel" (1994).

Italy

Women did not receive the vote in Italy until 1945, although the demand for women's enfranchisement had been raised from early in the nineteenth century. Women took an active part in the struggle to democratize and unify Italy, giving considerable support to Giuseppe Mazzini and his liberal ideals, and they saw women's right to vote as an integral part of this movement. The unification of Italy and the establishment of a new kingdom in 1861 were welcomed by feminists, although their hopes for enfranchisement were not realized. They were further disappointed by the sex inequalities embedded in the Civil Code, introduced in 1865, and this led feminists to concentrate on improving women's legal and educational status. The first major criticism of these legal inequalities was Anna Maria Mozzoni's book, *Woman and Her Social Relationships,* published in 1864, which undermined the view that women should concern themselves solely with home and family. Mozzoni, a fervent supporter of Mazzini, was later to gain an international reputation for her feminism. Women's rights activists were also able to disseminate their views on legal and social reforms, in particular the state regulation of prostitution, in the pages of *La Donna,* a periodical published between 1868 and 1892 by Gualberta Alaide Beccari that helped to promote a sense of common sisterhood.

It was not until the 1870s, however, that women's suffrage received attention. The liberal politician and friend of Mozzoni, Salvatore Morelli (1824–1880), raised the issue of women's enfranchisement in Parliament in 1871, but with little success. Mozzoni, who translated John Stuart Mill's *On the Subjection of Women* into Italian, also organized a petition in favor of women's suffrage in 1877. However, in the late nineteenth century the organized women's movement concentrated on economic reforms and the secularization of women's education. A female suffrage movement did not develop until the decade preceding World War I, a period in which politics was liberalized under the Giolitti government, which gave votes to all men in 1912.

The Comitato Nazionale per il Voto alla Donna (National Committee for Women's Suffrage) was formed in 1905, uniting a number of small, local committees that were mainly in the industrializing north. The movement remained very small, collecting only 600 signatures for a petition in 1907. Women's suffrage did receive some support, however, in socialist circles. Anna Kuliscioff (1854–1925), a co-founder of the Italian Socialist Party, was responsible for raising the issue of women's suffrage after 1910 in the annual party congresses. In 1911 she became editor of the *Difesa delle lavoratrici* (Defense of Women Workers), a supplement to the main party newspaper, and she used this as a means of propagandizing for women's suffrage. In the process, her arguments shifted from the need to support women's suffrage in order to strengthen the party, to the importance of the vote for women themselves.

Women's suffrage received support from the conservative wing of the socialist movement and from some liberal intellectuals, but fears that most women would vote Catholic meant that the bulk of Italian politicians opposed the measure. Moreover, the Catholic Church organized its own women's movement that emphasized women's maternal mission and philanthropic activities. After the upheavals of war, the lower house of Parliament did vote to enfranchise women in 1919, but this was not ratified by the Senate despite the fact that the Pope spoke in favor of women's suffrage as a way to halt the spread of socialism. Most of the feminist groups supported Mussolini during the 1920s because he promised to introduce reforms outside the parliamentary system. Both the Associazione per la Donna (Association of Women), founded in 1898, and the National Council of Women, formed in 1903, had emphasized educational and voluntary work rather than women's suffrage and were anxious to see the demise of socialism. Nonetheless, fascism was to set back the women's cause all over Europe, and in 1925 the Association of Women was suppressed. It was not until the end of World War II, with the introduction of a new constitution, that women finally received the right to take part in elections.

See also Mozzoni, Anna Maria.
References De Grazia, Victoria. "How Mussolini Ruled Italian Women" (1994); Evans, Richard J. *The Feminists: Women's Emancipation Movements in Europe, America and Australasia, 1840–1920* (1977); Howard, Judith Jeffrey. "The Civil Code of 1865 and the Origins of the Feminist Movement in Italy" (1977); LaVigna, Claire. "The Marxist Ambivalence toward Women: Between Socialism and Feminism in the Italian Socialist Party" (1978).

Jacobs, Aletta

Aletta Jacobs (1854–1929) was a prominent Dutch suffragist. The daughter of a Jewish physician, she became the first female doctor in the Netherlands and opened a birth control clinic in 1882 in Amsterdam. She was involved throughout her life in a wide range of feminist activities, including fighting for the rights of working women, and described herself as an equal rights feminist who sought political and legal emancipation for women. Although in many respects moderate in her outlook, she refused to accept some of the conventions of the day and lived for over 10 years with Carel Victor Gerritsen, the son of a businessman, who shared her views on women's emancipation and was elected as a radical MP in 1893. Jacobs finally married Gerritsen when she was 38 but retained her own name and kept a separate bank account and living quarters in their shared home. They were both actively involved in the left-liberal Radical Union, which was the first Dutch political party to admit women to membership and to support universal suffrage. They were also founding members in 1901 of the Liberal Democratic Union, the successor to the Radical Union.

Despite the range of Jacobs's activities, the cause that took up most of her energies was the fight for women's suffrage. It was her attempt to register as a voter in 1883 that led the government to formally declare that only men could exercise the franchise. She was a founding member of the Vereeniging voor Vrouwenkiesrecht (VVVK) [Woman Suffrage Association], established in 1894, and helped to design its constitution. In 1895 she became president of the Amsterdam section and in 1903 was chosen as national president, a post that she held until votes for women were won. Over the ensuing years she threw herself into the campaign, traveling all over the Netherlands and elsewhere on lecture tours. However, she was never at ease giving speeches and preferred to put forward her views in articles and pamphlets. She was responsible, for example, for translating Charlotte Perkins Gilman's *Women and Economics* (in 1900) and Olive Schreiner's *Woman and Labour* (in 1910) into Dutch. Although she was keen to encourage women to express their views in the public arena through processions and demonstrations, at the same time she ensured that the VVVK based its campaign on moderation and legality.

Throughout her life, Jacobs, who could speak English, German, and French, was eager to make contact with men and women across national boundaries. From the beginning of her career she attended international conferences and accompanied her husband to meetings of the Interparliamentary Union, an occasion she used to make suffrage contacts. She was thrilled by the conference of the International Council of Women that was held in London in 1899, and she then became actively involved in the International Woman Suffrage Alliance (IWSA). She ensured that the Netherlands was one of the founding members of the IWSA and played an important part in organizing the 1908 congress that was held in Amsterdam. Although she never held office in the IWSA, Jacobs often carried out activities on its behalf and published all the news she received from abroad in the VVVK monthly magazine. She used the international congresses to make contact with suffragists from other countries and then maintained these links through an extensive correspondence. Jacobs formed a close friendship with the IWSA president, the American suffragist Carrie Chapman Catt, and the two women toured the world for suffrage in 1911, visiting countries as diverse as South Africa, Sri Lanka, Indonesia, China, and Japan. There is little evidence that they had much success in gaining new affiliations for the IWSA, but Jacobs's travel letters, which view women in other lands through a Dutch colonial perspective, have proved to be a rich source for understanding the complex relationship between feminism, colonialism, and race.

Although suffrage was her main priority, Jacobs's international outlook was also expressed through her commitment to peace. She was responsible for organizing the International Congress of Women at the Hague in 1915 and played a leading part in the establishment of the Women's International League, a group that lobbied for peace. After women had achieved the vote in the Netherlands, Jacobs continued to work for world peace and also wrote a detailed account of her own role in the struggle for the vote, *Memories* (1924). A strong personality, she inspired affection from close friends but was seen as irritable and difficult to get along with by others. She provides a good example of those "first wave" feminists who saw themselves as part of an international women's movement and who, through conferences and close friendships, sought to link their national suffrage campaigns with like-minded individuals and groups in other lands.

See also Catt, Carrie Chapman; International Congress of Women, The Hague; International Council of Women; International Woman Suffrage Alliance; The Netherlands; Peace Movement; Race and Ethnicity.
References Bosch, Mineke. "Colonial Dimensions of Dutch Women's Suffrage: Aletta Jacobs's Travel Letters from Africa and Asia, 1911–12" (1999); Jacobs, Aletta. *Memories: My Life as an International Leader in Health, Suffrage and Peace* ([1924] 1996).

Japan

Although Japanese women started to organize for social and political reform in the late nineteenth century, they did not gain the vote until after World War II under American occupation. The history of Japan's suffrage campaigns cannot be viewed in isolation from women's other political activities and must be set in the context of women's position in relation to the state.

After the Meiji government was restored in 1868, women were not initially singled out as a political category. In a few towns and villages they could vote in local elections and hold office if they fulfilled the same taxpaying requirements as men. By 1884, legal loopholes were closed, and in 1888 it was decreed that only adult males could be a citizen with the right to vote and serve on local assemblies. In 1887 women were also barred from joining political associations and sponsoring and attending political meetings, measures that were carried into Article 5 of Police Law in 1900.

These prohibitions meant that the state played a major role in defining what constituted political activity, thereby shaping the strategies of the early women's movement. The earliest groups supporting women's rights during the 1900s, such as the socialist Heiminsha (Commoners Society), were led by men who hesitated to raise the issue of women's suffrage in the current political climate. Rather than supporting political parties and radical activity, politically conscious middle-class women were pushed into moral reform causes such as temperance and antiprostitution drives.

The state continued to invoke Article 5 to block the development of a politicized women's movement. For example, in 1920, 200 women were forced to leave a meeting of Kakuseika (the Purity Society), which aimed at abolishing licensed prostitution, when the chairman mentioned universal male suffrage. State bureaucrats justified their exclusion of women from politics on the grounds that women were ill educated and temperamentally nervous and might be harmed by hearing political speeches. Their involvement with politics would also have a bad effect on home management.

After World War I, the expansion of women's education and the emergence of women into new areas of employment and professional life encouraged the development of new women's associations demanding suffrage and gender equality. For example, Shin Fujin Kyōkai (the New Woman's Association), started by Hiratsuka Raichō and Japan's most famous early feminist, Ichikawa Fusae, campaigned strongly for a revision of Article 5 to allow women to attend and sponsor political meetings, a measure finally achieved in 1922.

A new climate of opinion among political elites was apparent in the 1920s, influenced by the mobilization of women and the patriotic behavior of suffragist groups in Western countries during World War I. This change was marked by a growing belief that the inclusion of women in the political process could have positive benefits for the state and by a recognition of women's importance to the state in their new role as consumers and housewives. However, state bureaucrats preferred to integrate women into state structures without acceding to their demands for the vote.

With the exception of the radical Fusen Kakutôku Dômei (League for Woman's Suffrage), led by Ichikawa Fusae, most women's organizations saw the vote as only one of a range of social and political issues. They tended to cooperate with rather than oppose the state in its program of social management as the best means of gaining an improved position in public life. Yet they still criticized the government for denying them the vote. The largest group to support women's suffrage, Zen Kansai Fujin Rengö Kai (Federation of Women's Associations of Western Japan), which claimed 3 million members in 1927, consisted largely of local groups started through official patronage. The federation presented suffrage petitions to the Diet in 1930 and 1931, each with 100,000 signatures. Officials tacitly recognized the legitimacy of the suffrage movement, and in exchange the women lent their support to state campaigns for moral reform, diligence, and thrift.

By 1929 the majority of the lower house endorsed legislation granting women rights to vote at both the municipal and prefectural levels, but bills in 1929 and 1930 were rejected by the House of Peers. The 1931 Suffrage Bill introduced by the Japanese government offered women civil rights only at the local level. It also failed to overcome conservative opponents who refused to recognize women's new civic role, still seeing them as a subordinate element in the traditional family.

Supporters of women's suffrage in the 1920s and 1930s came from a variety of political, religious, occupational, and class positions and varied in their reasons for wanting the vote. The New Women's Association emphasized liberal ideas such as individual development and access to higher education and professional careers. By contrast, the earliest and most prominent pre–World War I women's group,

Nihon Kirisutokyo Fujin Kyofukai (Japanese Woman's Christian Temperance Union), which in 1921 set up the Japanese Woman Suffrage Association, argued for suffrage as a means to upgrade social morality, its chief campaigns being against prostitution. Similarly the Federation of Women's Associations of Western Japan stressed women's role as nurturing mothers and guardians of public welfare.

Women leaders within working-class organizations, such as Yamakawa Kikue, reluctantly subordinated women's suffrage to wider socialist aims, but they were influential in changing male leaders' views about women's subordination in the freer political climate after World War II. Finally, some conservative supporters of suffrage bills within the Diet, looking to British and American precedents, saw women as a politically conservative group whose voting power would prevent radical social change.

Following Japan's occupation of Manchuria in 1931–1932, increasingly illiberal governments continued to block civil rights legislation, forcing suffrage groups to turn their attention to other causes. The increased cooperation between government and women's groups culminated in the formal integration of women into government structures during the China and Pacific Wars (1937–1945), with the appointment of 11 women leaders, including Ichikawa Fusae. All independent women's groups were merged into Dai Nihon Rengo Fujinkai (the Greater Japan Federated Women's Association).

Universal suffrage was finally achieved in 1945 as part of the development of a democratic constitution imposed by occupying authorities. By 1952, Japanese women had been guaranteed equal political, economic, and social rights in law, but they have since made little progress in challenging male prerogatives within government.

See also Citizenship; Ichikawa Fusae; Suffrage Bill; Woman's Christian Temperance Union.

References Garon, Sheldon. "Women's Groups and the Japanese State: Contending Approaches to Political Integration" (1993); Nester, William. "Japanese Women: Still Three Steps Behind" (1992); Nolte, Sharon H. "Women's Rights and Society's Needs: Japan's 1931 Suffrage Bill" (1986).

Kauffmann, Caroline

Caroline Kauffmann (c. 1840s–1926) was one of a small group of French suffrage campaigners who advocated the use of militant methods. From a Jewish background, Kauffman embraced feminism after difficulties in her marriage. She was active in the physical culture movement and was a republican with socialist sympathies. In 1898 she became the leader of the feminist group La Solidarité des femmes (Women's Solidarity), which had links with the socialist movement, and transformed the group by putting more emphasis on the vote. After meeting with foreign militants in Berlin in 1904, Kauffmann became dissatisfied with the polite protests that were characteristic of the French movement and, with Hubertine Auclert, tried to organize a series of marches and parades during the centenary celebrations of the promulgation of Napoleon's Civil Code. Only a small number of women turned up for the marches, but they were faced with a large police presence and were treated roughly. Undeterred, Kauffmann attended ceremonies at the Sorbonne, where she released golden balloons inscribed with the slogan "The Code crushes women." After shouting slogans she was arrested although found innocent of the charge of "injurious disturbance."

Kauffmann was responsible for introducing Madeleine Pelletier to Solidarité and the two women took part in a number of actions during 1906, including demonstrations and rallies in which leaflets were distributed. They also staged a protest at the Chamber of Deputies on 3 June 1906 when they showered the chamber with women's suffrage leaflets. This led to their arrest, but because of the government's fear of the publicity that would surround a trial, they were not charged. In 1908 Kauffmann traveled to London with Pelletier to take part in a large demonstration in Hyde Park, organized by the National Union of Women's Suffrage Societies, which attracted 25,000 women.

Although Kauffmann admired the actions of British suffragettes, her own militancy was mild by comparison; the clash with police in 1904 had convinced both Auclert and Kauffmann that they needed a more legal way to make public protests. Nonetheless, even marches were considered to be extreme in France, and Kauffmann's individual protests alienated moderate suffragists. During World War I, Kauffmann took less interest in politics and became involved in spiritualism. She died in obscurity in 1924, and only six mourners attended her funeral procession.

See also Auclert, Hubertine; France; National Union of Women's Suffrage Societies; Pelletier, Madeleine.
References Gordon, Felicia. *The Integral Feminist: Madeleine Pelletier, 1874–1939* (1990); Hause, Steven C., with Anne R. Kenney. *Women's Suffrage and Social Politics in the French Third Republic* (1984).

Kenney, Annie

Annie Kenney (1879–1953) was a well-known speaker and organizer for the mil-

Annie Kenney was the only working-class woman to become a senior leader of the Women's Social and Political Union; her three sisters and brothers were also suffrage campaigners. (Museum of London)

itant suffrage movement in Britain. Born in Lancashire, England, the fifth of 11 children of a cotton spinner, she worked in a textile mill. By the age of 20 she had become interested in the labor movement and joined her local branch of the socialist group the Independent Labour Party. It was at one of their meetings, in 1905, that she first met Christabel Pankhurst, who had been engaged as a speaker. Kenney was soon a frequent visitor to Christabel's home and joined the Women's Social and Political Union (WSPU), which had been founded by the Pankhursts. In September 1905 Kenney took part with Christabel Pankhurst in the first militant action of the WSPU. The two women disrupted an election meeting and, after refusing to pay a fine, served a short sentence of imprisonment.

Shortly afterward Kenney left her job in the mill in order to give all of her time to suffrage campaigning. After trying to interest working women in the East End of London in the suffrage campaign, she moved to Bristol, where she worked as a district organizer for the WSPU in the west of England between 1907 and 1909. Annie Kenney is usually portrayed as one of those faithful followers who worshipped Christabel Pankhurst and rarely took any initiative of her own. This impression is partly based on the assessments of contemporaries in their autobiographies, including the one written by Kenney in which she describes herself as Christabel's blotting paper. Nonetheless, the diaries left by Mary and Emily Blathwayt, suffragettes from Bath in the west of England, give a different impression. Annie Kenney may have been devoted to Christabel and ready to follow her lead, but in the Blathwayt diaries she emerges as someone who was strong-minded and capable of taking initiatives, a charismatic platform speaker who inspired local women to take up the cause. She also managed to attract her own devoted following of middle-class women who were willing to give her practical support so that nothing would interrupt her suffrage work.

As militancy escalated, however, Kenney moved back to London, where she was arrested and imprisoned on numerous occasions. When Christabel Pankhurst fled to Paris in 1912, Kenney visited her every weekend in disguise in order to receive her instructions and acted as a medium of communication between Christabel and the WSPU in London. Kenney remained loyal to the WSPU, despite the defection of other leaders, and during World War I she followed the Pankhursts in supporting the government war effort. In 1917, when the WSPU was renamed the Women's Party, with a program combining a xenophobic foreign policy with proposals for social reform affecting women and children, she became its secretary.

After her marriage to James Taylor in

1918 and the birth of a son, Annie Kenney no longer took an active part in politics, but she wrote a book about her suffrage experiences, *Memories of a Militant,* which was published in 1924.

See also Pankhurst, Christabel; Women's Social and Political Union.
References Banks, Olive. *The Biographical Dictionary of British Feminists,* Vol 1. *1880–1930* (1985); Hannam, June. "'Suffragettes Are Splendid for Any Work': The Blathwayt Diaries as a Source for Suffrage History" (2000); Rosen, Andrew. *Rise Up Women! The Militant Campaign of the Women's Social and Political Union* (1974).

Kramers, Martina

Martina Kramers (1863–1934), a journalist, was a prominent member of the Dutch Vereeniging voor Vrouwenkiesrecht (Woman Suffrage Association) and was also active at an international level. In 1895 she had been a founding member of the Vereeniging ter Behartiging van de Belangen der Vrouw (Association to Promote Women's Interests) in Rotterdam, which organized community clubs and lectures. Two years later she was asked by several Dutch women's organizations to attend meetings to prepare for the next International Council of Women (ICW) congress. In 1899 she delivered a report at the ICW congress in London about the struggles and achievements of Dutch women over the last half century and was made a member of the council's board, a post she had until 1909. Inspired by what she found in London, Kramers was instrumental in ensuring that a Dutch National Council of Women was established. She also, however, took an active part in the affairs of the International Woman Suffrage Alliance (IWSA), joining the association's board in 1906 and acting as one of its secretaries until 1911. Kramers was a propagandist for the IWSA and in 1905 and 1906 made a lecture tour through Belgium, accompanied by Rachel Foster Avery, a member of the National American Woman Suffrage Association, with the aim of establishing a branch there. This was not the immediate outcome, but the tour did lay the groundwork for the foundation of a suffrage society a few years later.

Under the influence of Bobbie, the man with whom she shared her life, Kramers became a socialist and was particularly active before World War I in trying to bring the women's movement and the socialist movement together. She found that this was an uphill struggle and wrote in 1911 that Social Democratic women refused to take a socialist propaganda leaflet written by August Bebel from the hands of a woman who wore a suffrage badge. Kramers also edited *Jus Suffragii,* the newspaper of the IWSA, between 1904 and 1913, which gave her considerable influence. In the spring of 1913, however, the IWSA planned to establish a new headquarters in London, with an international press office, and Carrie Chapman Catt asked Kramers to give up her position as editor. When she did not agree to this immediately, Catt, with the agreement of Aletta Jacobs, raised the issue of Kramers's irregular personal life (she lived with a married man whose wife would not divorce him). Faced with the possibility that her private life would be made public, Kramers resigned from the editorship and during the IWSA congress in Budapest in 1913 reported that she was unwell and left the meeting. This incident provides an example of the way in which personal friendships and loyalties were sacrificed for what was seen as the good of the suffrage cause.

See also Catt, Carrie Chapman; International Council of Women; International Woman Suffrage Alliance; Jacobs, Aletta; The Netherlands.
References Bosch, Mineke, with Annemarie Kloosterman. *Politics and Friendship: Letters from the International Woman Suffrage Alliance, 1902–1942* (1990); Jacobs, Aletta. *Memories: My Life as an International Leader in Health, Suffrage and Peace* ([1924] 1996); Rupp, Leila. *Worlds of Women: The Making of an International Women's Movement* (1997).

Krog, Gina

Gina Krog (1847–1916) was a leader of the Norwegian suffrage movement and edited the feminist periodical *Nylaende* (New Frontiers) from its first edition in 1887 until her death. When manhood suffrage was extended in Norway in 1885, Krog raised the issue of women's suffrage among members of the Norsk Kvinnesaksforening (Norwegian Feminist Society), but she was not supported because most of the members felt that Norwegian women had not shown sufficient interest in participating in politics. Krog therefore formed a separate group, Kvinnestemmeretsforeningen (Female Suffrage Union), which worked for municipal suffrage, but it had very few members and soon collapsed. In 1895, however, when the Radical Liberals were active in putting forward women's suffrage bills, Krog became leader of a new group, Landekvinnestemmeretsforeningen (LKSF) [National Female Suffrage Union].

Krog was a moderate who advocated a property-based franchise, even after universal suffrage for men had been achieved, because she believed that the middle-class parties of the Norwegian parliament, the Storting, would be more likely to enfranchise women of their own class. Under her leadership, the LKSF achieved a breakthrough in 1901 when, after years of petitioning, the government was finally persuaded to extend voting rights to women at a municipal level as long as they owned property or were married to a property owner.

Krog also played a key role in forging links between Norwegian suffragists and the international women's movement. She admired the American suffragists Elizabeth Cady Stanton and Susan B. Anthony, and *Nylaende* was full of reports about the U.S. movement. Moreover, Norwegian Americans were encouraged to keep in touch with events in Norway by subscribing to the magazine. In 1904 Krog brought Norway into the International Council of Women (ICW) with the formation of Norske Kvinners Nasjonalrad (Norwegian Women's National Council). In 1909, after attending a meeting of the ICW in Toronto, she finally managed to visit the United States, where she gave numerous speeches about the progress of women's suffrage in Norway and had a brief meeting with President Taft. Krog was involved in the formation of all the main feminist organizations in Norway. She worked consistently to achieve women's suffrage and other reforms for women until her death in 1916.

See also Anthony, Susan B.; International Council of Women; Norway; Stanton, Elizabeth Cady.
References Blom, Ida. "The Struggle for Women's Suffrage in Norway, 1885–1913" (1980); Evans, Richard J. *The Feminists: Women's Emancipation Movements in Europe, America and Australasia, 1840–1920* (1977); Rasmussen, Janet E. "Sisters across the Sea: Early Norwegian Feminists and Their American Connections" (1982).

Kuwait

Kuwait gained its independence from Britain in 1961. Since that time it has been ruled directly by the Al-Sabah family, with most legislation being debated by the National Assembly, which is still currently elected by restricted male suffrage.

The first calls for the enfranchisement of women were made shortly after independence by young Kuwaiti male nationalists, who played the role of the opposition both inside and outside the National Assembly. Soon after, Kuwaiti women also made their voices heard, most notably at the Kuwait Women's Conference of 1971; this was organized by Nuriyah al-Saddani (Nouria al-Sadani), the founder of the Jam'iyat al-Nahdah al-'Arabiyah al-Nisa'iyah (Arab Women's Development Society)—later renamed the Jam'iyat al-Nahdah al-Usriyah (Arab Society for the Advancement of the Family). At this conference, the unconditional right of women to contest elections was put forward as one of its seven demands. The first major parliamentary discussion of women's right to vote took place during the passage of the Equal Rights Bill in 1973, which, although it failed, is reported to have provoked the most stormy debates in the history of the National Assembly.

In 1974, the Arab Women's Development Society joined the al-Jam'iyah al-Thaqafiyah al-Ijtima'iyah al-Kuwaytiyah (Women's Cultural and Social Society) to form the Kuwaiti Women's Union (KWU). This new unified organization continued to press for women's suffrage until the government clamped down on opposition bodies, dissolving the National Assembly in 1976 and closing down the KWU itself in 1977. Soon after the reopening of the National Assembly in 1980, the issue of the enfranchisement of women was taken up again; in 1981 a bill to change the electoral law in favor of women was defeated by 27 votes to 7, and in 1985, despite hard work by the Organizing Committee for the Political Rights of Kuwaiti Women, a similar bill was blocked and subjected to a legal ruling, which declared that the nature of the electoral system was suitable for men alone.

Kuwait women resumed their campaign for equal rights immediately after the liberation of Kuwait from the Iraqi occupation of 1990–1991. As before, they grounded their demands for the vote in the constitution, this time arguing in addition that their participation in the resistance to Iraq deserved political recognition, and that all restrictions on second-class citizens, male and female, should be lifted. However, the National Assembly refused to discuss the matter, and in 1992, its secretary-general ruled that women possessed inadequate capabilities for participating in the political field. Various women's groups, including the *diwaniyah* (open house for political discussion) led by Rasha' al-Sabah from the ruling family, reiterated their demands for the right to vote. However, class and kinship interests and pressure by Islamist groups from within, as well as from Saudi Arabia, denied the women's campaign any success, until, in a surprise move, the emir issued a decree in the summer of 1999 enfranchising women. The decree was issued while the National Assembly was not sitting, and when it reconvened it refused to ratify the emir's decision, rejecting the call for women's suffrage twice in the late autumn of 1999. In 2000, the Kuwaiti Constitutional Court rejected the claim by women suffragists that the 1962 Election Law, restricting the franchise to men alone, was unconstitutional. However, the matter is still hotly debated in Kuwait and with Shaykhah al-Nisf, the head of al-Jam'iyah al-Thaqafiyah al-Nisa'iyah al-Kuwaytiyah (Kuwaiti Women's Cultural Society), encouraging women to register for the next election (due in 2003), the question of women's right to vote will remain an active political issue for the foreseeable future.

See also Citizenship; Nationalism.
References Badran, Margot. "Gender, Islam and the State: Kuwaiti Women in Struggle, Preinvasion to Postliberation." (1998); al-Mughni, Haya. *Women in Kuwait: The Politics of Gender* (1993).

Langham Place Circle

The organized British women's suffrage movement could be said to have begun with the founding of the Langham Place Circle in London in the 1850s. Led by two women from middle-class, radical, Unitarian families, Barbara Bodichon (née Leigh-Smith) and Bessie Rayner Parkes, this group of women activists decided to begin a campaign to improve female rights in such areas as marriage, education, employment, and the law.

In March 1865 another group, the Kensington Society, was formed by women who wanted to gain public speaking experience by presenting papers on important political and social questions. A number of women from the Langham Place Circle were also members of the Kensington Society, and in November 1865 Barbara Bodichon submitted a paper to the society calling for women's suffrage. The proposition was overwhelmingly supported, and this led to the idea of forming a committee to work for the enfranchisement of women. At the same time, women from the Langham Place Circle began to collect signatures for a petition asking that women be included in the extension of the franchise to be proposed in a new Reform Bill due to be introduced in March 1866. The bill was to fail, but a petition signed by 1,499 women was presented to Parliament by the Liberal MP John Stuart Mill in June 1866.

During that year, Bodichon continued to discuss the formation of a women's suffrage committee with her colleagues from the Langham Place Circle and the Kensington Society. The first official London committee was formed in November 1866, with the prominent Langham Place campaigner, Emily Davies, as acting secretary. However, from the beginning the committee was divided, and disagreements between conservative and radical members and their supporters over such issues as whether or not married women should be specifically included in any suffrage demand led to the decision to dissolve it in June 1867.

A new London committee was set up shortly afterward by Mentia Taylor, the wife of a radical MP, but none of the members of the old committee joined it, which meant that the Langham Place women were no longer involved in the running of the women's suffrage campaign. By the 1870s, most of the women of the Langham Place Circle had gone their separate ways into such areas as writing, education, and social work.

See also Britain; Mill, John Stuart.
Reference Lacey, Candida Ann, ed. *Barbara Leigh Smith Bodichon and the Langham Place Group* (1987).

Lanteri, Julieta

Julieta Lanteri (1873–1932) was one of the first Argentine feminists to campaign actively for women's suffrage and to challenge the legal restrictions on women's citizenship. Since 1906 Lanteri had been associated with the *librepensadores* (freethinkers), a Masonic-type group, who had endorsed women's suffrage at their national conference in 1908. In 1909 she and María Abella de Ramírez founded the Liga Nacional de Mujeres Librepensadores (the National League of Women Freethinkers) and in 1910 began publishing *La Nueva Mujer* (The new woman). Its radical anticlerical tone was shocking to many, and Lanteri's flamboyant style and willingness to challenge the establishment brought her national notoriety. In 1911 she formed the Liga para los Derechos de la Mujer y el Niño (League for the Rights of Mothers and Children), based in Buenos Aires. Although this group's key objective was to achieve protective legislation for women and children, Lanteri went further, showing herself willing to break rules of propriety and femininity to promote the vote for women.

Lanteri's most significant achievement was to challenge the basis of Argentine citizenship, which from 1916 obliged all citizens to register for military service, thus excluding women. Although most feminists ignored this issue, Lanteri put it to the test. Although she was married to an Argentine and had lived in Buenos Aires for most of her life, she was born in Italy. Her appointment as a lecturer in the Faculty of Medicine in 1911 had required her to be naturalized as a citizen in order to accept the post. On the basis of her acquired citizenship, Lanteri had voted in every election between 1911 and 1916 but was subsequently disqualified. After reviewing her case, the judicial ruling established that the Argentine constitution made no distinction between the sexes in the definition of rights and that, in principle, women had the same political rights as men. Following this very important clarification of the law, confirmed in 1921, women's suffrage supporters knew that they were dependent entirely on the will of Congress to change the electoral law. Having achieved theoretical citizenship,

Lanteri attempted to register for military service in order to be able to vote. On being turned down, she pursued her case all the way to the Supreme Court. Her lawyers pointed out that male citizens exempted from military service were not excluded from voting and argued, unsuccessfully, that Lanteri's case was no different.

In 1920 Lanteri founded the Partido Feminista Nacional (the National Feminist Party), with a 16-point program of legal and political reform. In March 1920 she joined other feminist leaders to hold a mock women's election in which over 4,000 women participated. Standing as a candidate, she polled between 1,300 and 1,730 votes and, although she did not win, received nearly as many votes as some male candidates in the official municipal election. The exercise was repeated on the same day as the municipal elections in November 1920, but as before, Lanteri was denied any official recognition of her candidacy because she was not on any electoral list.

By 1932, when the women's suffrage bill approved by the House of Deputies was shelved by the Senate, Lanteri had died. Yet in the wake of this setback, feminists invoked her memory and recalled her tenacity as they reaffirmed their commitment to the cause for which she had fought with such determination.

See also Argentina; Citizenship; Latin America and the Caribbean.
References Carlson, Marifran. *Feminismo! The Woman's Movement in Argentina from Its Beginnings to Eva Perón* (1988); Lavrin, Asunción. *Women, Feminism and Social Change in Argentina, Chile and Uruguay, 1890–1940* (1995).

Latin America and the Caribbean

Although relatively little has been written in English about suffrage campaigns in Latin America, this does not mean that women's struggles for the vote were insignificant or generally of short duration in this region. From the turn of the twentieth century onwards, inspired by suffrage victories in New Zealand and Australia, men and women in many Latin American and some Caribbean countries began discussing the possibility of achieving a similar goal. Organized women's groups came a little later, and by the 1920s these were expanding in number. Though the vote may not have been a central concern for most Latin American feminists, many groups cited it as one of their objectives. The push toward women's suffrage was visible all over Latin America in the 1920s and early 1930s. Even in countries that denied the vote to women until after World War II, such as Argentina and Chile, public attention was drawn to the issue in this period.

The extent to which women became involved in suffrage campaigns in Latin America varied greatly from country to country. In some countries, such as Bolivia, women gained the vote following the overthrow of autocratic regimes as a part of a wider movement for popular democracy after World War II. In others, like Brazil, the suffrage movement was conducted mainly by women who had close ties with leaders of political elites. The early achievement of the vote in Brazil, in 1932, was facilitated by this relationship. By contrast, in Puerto Rico calls for the vote were first made by working women in the trade union movement. Here the suffrage movement remained irrevocably split between groups representing elite women, who succeeded in 1929 in confining the vote to educated women, and working women's associations, who fought for and achieved universal suffrage six years later. Countries with the most broad-based suffrage movements in the 1930s were those such as Mexico and Chile where women from different social and political backgrounds joined together to form umbrella groups that could recruit a wider membership. Yet in neither of these countries were these umbrella or-

ganizations powerful enough to overcome resistance from male opponents in the ruling parties. And some, like the Mexican teachers who attended feminist congresses, viewed the vote with suspicion, believing that women should not become involved with corrupt masculine regimes.

In more traditional societies such as Peru, Chile, and Colombia, the Catholic Church was a strong force, limiting the possibilities for left-wing and liberal individuals to recruit women's groups focused on reform. In 1920s Chile, concern over the influence of the Catholic Church among women voters caused liberal feminists to deliberately refrain from campaigning for the women's vote. Despite their belief in women's suffrage, they feared it might "sink the country" by enabling the clergy to dominate politics. Yet it was in the deeply conservative pro-Catholic country of Ecuador that the first women in Latin America received the vote, albeit only limited suffrage. Here women were seen as compliant and loyal to the establishment; their votes were needed by the ruling coalition, which faced a threat from young socialists who had staged a military coup in 1925.

One of the problems for suffragists throughout Latin America was to challenge but not entirely undermine traditional cultural values. These values defined women within the family as being under the authority of the male head of household and saw political activity as incompatible with women's "natural" functions within the home. For many reformers, establishing the rights of women, as wage earners as well as mothers, to equality under the law, to education, and to basic health care was perceived to be more important than achieving the vote. They argued that women's position as wives and mothers could be extended to give them more productive roles within society, particularly in education, in establishing higher moral standards, and in forming social legislation. Thus for many women's organizations, suffrage was perceived as a means to involve women in wider social reforms rather than as an end in itself. For example, in 1929 the program of the Uruguayan Alliance of Women for Suffrage had a range of different objectives, with legal equality at the top of its list and suffrage ranked fifth.

To counter arguments that women would become too masculine if they moved into the sphere of politics, some feminists, such as Delia Ducoing of Chile, consciously distanced themselves from the Anglo-American suffrage movement and conformed to traditional gender stereotypes. Yet the International Woman Suffrage Alliance, led in the 1920s by the U.S. feminist Carrie Chapman Catt, was still an important influence in many Latin American countries. Catt visited some of these countries in the early 1920s, offering inspiration and friendship to suffrage leaders such as María Jesús Alvarado Rivera of Peru and Paulina Luisi of Uruguay. Pan-American conferences such as the one held in Baltimore in 1922 were also useful in fostering links between suffrage leaders and, as happened in Costa Rica and Brazil, in stimulating the formation of new suffrage organizations.

Detailed information on the circumstances of women's enfranchisement in every Latin American and Caribbean country cannot be given here, although many do have their own entries elsewhere in the book. The years when women gained the vote in most countries in this area are outlined below.

The first Latin American country to grant women limited suffrage was Ecuador in 1929, although not all women were able to vote there until 1946. During the 1930s a number of other countries followed suit. Brazil and Uruguay enfranchised women in 1932, Cuba in 1934, and El Salvador in 1939. The Dominican Republic, in 1942, and Jamaica, in 1944, were unusual in that they granted the vote

to women during World War II. At the end of the war, a more liberal climate of opinion encouraged other countries to extend the vote to women. Guatemala, Panama, and Trinidad and Tobago gave women the vote in 1945, Argentina and Venezuela in 1947, Chile in 1948, and Costa Rica in 1949. Women in other countries in this region were granted the vote in the 1950s. Haitian women gained the vote in 1950, and the smaller Caribbean islands of Antigua, Barbados, Dominica, Saint Kitts-Nevis, Saint Lucia, Grenada, and Saint Vincent and the Grenadines followed in 1951. Women received the vote in Bolivia in 1953; in Belize, Colombia, and Mexico in 1954 (though for the latter country not on the same terms as men until 1958); in Nicaragua and Peru in 1955; in Honduras in 1957; and finally in Paraguay in 1958. There was often a gap between legislation that granted women the right to vote and an opportunity to exercise that right. For example, in 1932, Uruguay was one of the earliest countries to enfranchise women, but another six years was to pass before, in 1938, they first went to the polls.

See also Argentina; Bolivia; Catholicism; Catt, Carrie Chapman; Chile; Colombia; Costa Rica; Cuba; International Woman Suffrage Alliance; Luisi, Paulina; Mexico; Nicaragua; Pan-American Women's Conference; Peru; Puerto Rico; Uruguay.

References Ehrick, Christine. "*Madrinas* and Missionaries: Uruguay and the Pan-American Women's Movement" (1998); Jaquette, Jane S., ed. *The Women's Movement in Latin America: Participation and Democracy* (1994); Lavrin, Asunción. "Suffrage in South America: Arguing a Difficult Cause" (1994); Miller, Francesca. *Latin American Women and the Search for Social Justice* (1991); Newhall, Beatrice. "Women Suffrage in the Americas" (1936).

Lawson, Louisa

Louisa Lawson was a passionate advocate of women's suffrage in Australia, who saw herself as the mother of the suffrage movement in New South Wales. She promoted the cause through her editorship of her journal, the *Dawn,* which she ran from 1888 until 1905, claiming in 1890 to have recruited 2,000 subscribers.

Lawson grew up in the country town of Mudgee and when she was 15 moved to the Gulagong goldfields, where she helped in the family hotel and store. She experienced poverty, misery, and cultural deprivation in an unhappy contracted marriage to a Norwegian sailor when she was 18. This experience contributed to her recognition of the injustice faced by women who had little control over their lives. After leaving her husband, she set up the *Dawn* in May 1888 as a magazine to be edited, printed, published, and read by women, and this became her life's project. She stopped publication after 17 years only because she was failing in health and trusted no one else to promote her views.

The main subject of the journal was women's suffrage, with coverage including her own and other people's views of the movement within New South Wales and in other states and countries all over the world. In 1889 she formed the Dawn Club, which appears to have been synonymous with the Woman's Franchise Association whose address was at Lawson's office. However, when in 1891 Rose Scott joined with others to set up the Womanhood Suffrage League (WSL), she persuaded Lawson to discontinue the Dawn Club and transfer her allegiance to the new group. Lawson was elected onto the council of the WSL, and for two years she lent her offices for council meetings and gave the group free printing until the late 1890s. However, by the end of 1893 she had resigned from the council and no longer lent her offices for meetings. It appears that her temperament was incompatible with the image of the WSL. In 1901 she joined a newly formed rival group, the Women's Progressive Association, and gave it coverage in the *Dawn.*

After the vote was won in 1902, Lawson felt slighted at not being asked to sit on the platform at the WSL's celebratory meeting, even though she was a member of a rival society. A place on the platform was quickly found and Scott presented Lawson with flowers and gave her credit for her early work in the movement in her speech. Scott also later sent Lawson a letter to soothe her feelings that was subsequently printed in the *Dawn.*

See also Australia; Scott, Rose.
Reference Oldfield, Audrey. *Woman Suffrage in Australia, A Gift or a Struggle?* (1992).

Lebanon

Women's demand for the suffrage in Lebanon was hampered by the struggle for national independence and by religious conservatism. Lebanon was created by the European powers after the defeat of the Ottoman Empire in World War I and was ruled under a French mandate. Women who had taken part in the war effort and in struggles against the French began to demand changes in their own social and political position. A number of women's magazines were established in the 1920s, including *al-Mar'ah al-jadidah* (The New Woman), which contained articles on women's suffrage. Women activists were influenced by news of the postwar suffrage victories in parts of Europe and the United States and also by the prominent role played by women in the 1919 Egyptian revolution. In 1923 women's suffrage was raised by the Lebanese Representative Council during a debate on women's work. Supporters referred to women's work for governments in Europe, India, and elsewhere, but opponents claimed that women had no place in the public world. It was accepted, however, that women should have greater work and educational opportunities. In the following year, women's suffrage was discussed again when Shaykh Yusuf al-Khazin, a member of the Lebanese Representative Council and a prominent newspaper owner, on behalf of women's leaders, proposed that educated women should be enfranchised, but only 3 out of the 30 deputies gave their support.

In 1928 Lebanese women joined with their counterparts in Syria to hold a conference that marked a new departure for the women's movement. They demanded a wide range of social and civic reforms but excluded political rights from the agenda. Elizabeth Thompson argues that the conference introduced a new ethos of patriotic motherhood that praised women's domestic work and philanthropy as national service and called for social rights in order to be able to carry out that task. This tactic was designed to broaden the appeal of women's organizations and to strengthen support for the growing nationalist movement. It was assumed that women who supported nationalist struggles would then achieve political rights once independence had been won, but these hopes were not fulfilled.

In 1935 a new group, the Women's Committee for the Defense of Lebanese Women's Rights, petitioned the government to allow women to work as mayors and judges so that they could prepare themselves for their future role as voters. The government, controlled by French sympathizers, turned down the request. In 1936 women's hopes grew as the French negotiated independence treaties and a new government was installed, led by Emile Eddé, a Francophile. When a draft treaty was prepared in 1935, women claimed that a clause guaranteeing citizens' political and civil rights without discrimination meant that women should have equal rights, and they drew up a petition to that effect. Eddé, who had no sympathy for the women's cause, rejected the petition and did the same to another that was presented in 1937.

In 1943 elections brought victory to nationalists. The Lebanese Women's Union had petitioned the president, Ayyub Thabit, to include a referendum on female suffrage in the summer ballot. He had refused, but agreed that women's suffrage would be raised by the newly elected government—a promise that was not carried out. In 1944 Lebanese women formed the Lebanese-Arab Women's Union to demonstrate solidarity with other Arab women and sent delegates to the first Arab Women's Conference organized by the Egyptian suffragist Hudá Sha'rawi, in Cairo. This conference had political rights at the top of its agenda. One of the Lebanese leaders, Rose Shafa', used the fact that women had taken an extensive role in the political uprising against the French in 1943 to justify the demand for the vote, although she asked only for partial suffrage. She formally presented the resolutions of the Cairo conference, including demands for political and social equality, to the prime minister, who agreed to establish a committee to study them. Although independence was achieved in 1946, women did not gain the vote. The National Pact between Christians and Muslims, formed in 1943, had militated against the introduction of women's suffrage, which was seen as a threat to traditional gender roles and religious teaching.

It was only with the introduction of a new government under Camille Chamoun that women were granted full suffrage in 1953 and the right to hold office. This was part of an electoral law designed to reduce sectarianism and to set Chamoun's regime apart from that of Bisharah al-Khuri who, before he was deposed, attempted to expand the power of religious courts. Women's political rights in Lebanon had been delayed by French influence, which had emphasized gender divisions, a strengthening of conservative Islamic traditions when faced with foreign rule, and the subordination of women's needs to the movement for independence.

See also Citizenship; Middle East and North Africa; Nationalism; Sha'rawi, Nur al-Hudá; Syria.

Reference Thompson, Elizabeth. *Colonial Citizens: Republican Rights, Paternal Privilege and Gender in French Syria and Lebanon* (2000).

Lee, Mary

Mary Lee (1821–1909) was a leading figure in the suffrage movement in South Australia, which in 1894 became the first Australian colony to grant women the vote. A founding member of the Women's Suffrage League of South Australia, she went on to become the movement's best known publicist in the campaigns that led to this early suffrage victory.

Lee had emigrated from Ireland in 1879 as a 58-year-old widow who had borne seven children. On arrival from Ireland, she threw her energies into causes that promoted the welfare of women and children. In 1888 she moved from her initial work with the Social Purity Society into the Women's Suffrage League, for which she became secretary.

Aided by a fiery temperament, a strong intellect, and a professed religious faith, Lee rapidly developed her skills as an orator and letter writer, employing often devastating logic. In 1890 she extended her influence by becoming secretary of the Working Women's Trade Union. Drawing partly on this experience, in March 1890 she published "Letters to Women" in the *Register,* where she presented all the major arguments for the women's vote. These included its value for working women as a means to improve their conditions and its use as an industrial weapon. She can be distinguished from most middle-class suffragists in her commitment to working women's causes. This is indicated by her disclaimer that she was not a women's rights woman. The link forged by Lee between the labor movement and the suffrage movement was vital in the early achievement of the vote in South Australia.

In a spirited response to MP Robert Caldwell's proposal in 1891 for a suffrage bill limited to women property holders (which the Women's Suffrage League opposed), Lee retorted: "We are not asking for the vote, we are demanding it" (Oldfield, 1992, 33). She was equally dismissive in 1893 of a proposed complex and divisive referendum on women's suffrage. Lee called the Labour Party "nincompoops" for supporting the referendum and pointed out that no referendum had been suggested for manhood suffrage. Such forthright speeches earned her a reputation indicated by the couplet:

Mary had a temper hot that used to
    boil and bubble
And e're the suffrage she had got it
    landed her in trouble. (Oldfield,
    1992, 36)

In February 1896, on her 75th birthday two years after the vote was won, Lee was presented with a testimonial acknowledging the work she had done for women's suffrage. She also received a purse of sovereigns raised by public subscription: two Labour Party members had launched a fund to support her in her old age. Yet shortly before her death, she told fellow suffragist Rose Scott that her public work had left her impoverished, with few friends. The importance of the suffrage issue in Lee's life is suggested by the inscription on her tombstone: "Secretary of the Women's Suffrage League."

See also Australia; Nicholls, Elizabeth; Scott, Rose.
References Margarey, Susan. "'Why didn't they want to be members of Parliament?' Suffragists in South Australia" (1994); Oldfield, Audrey. *Woman Suffrage in Australia, A Gift or a Struggle?* (1992); Spearitt, Katie. "New Dawns: First Wave Feminism, 1880–1914" (1992).

Liberalism

Liberal political ideas had an important influence on the way in which suffragists expressed and justified their demand for

Victoria Claflin Woodhull, sometimes known as "the terrible siren," was an early American liberal who espoused "free love"; here, she testifies before a congressional committee on behalf of woman suffrage on January 11, 1871. Wood engraving from Frank Leslie's Illustrated Newspaper, *February 4, 1871. (Library of Congress)*

the vote. They had a considerable impact on the development of the suffrage movements in parts of Europe and America in the nineteenth century, and a liberal perspective continued to inform suffrage ideas in the twentieth century in countries such as Uruguay. Liberalism was based on concepts of individual human rights; equal opportunities on the basis of merit, intellectual, and economic independence; and self-sovereignty, and suffragists were quick to apply these concepts to women. The Americans Susan B. Anthony and Ida Husted Harper, for instance, claimed that "the right of suffrage is simply the right to govern one's self" (Eisenstein, 1987, 83). However, recent studies of liberalism have argued that it cannot be understood simply in terms of individualism, but that it also used the language of duty and obliga-

tion, which assumed that the development and progress of civil society rested on the improvement of individual character and behavior as well as on institutional political change. These personal qualities would encompass altruism and the desire to work for the good of the nation, as well as self-development, and this side of liberal ideology was welcomed by suffragists who sought a moral transformation of society.

One of the key texts that linked liberalism with women's emancipation was John Stuart Mill's *On the Subjection of Women* (1869), which was translated into several languages and stimulated discussion about women's rights in countries as far afield as Russia and Czechoslovakia. Mill believed that self-development was all-important and that only educated citizens, participating in political affairs, would be able to achieve their full human potential. He claimed that there was nothing in women's nature that should disqualify them from playing a part in politics and therefore argued that they should be admitted on an equal basis to public functions and to employment.

Although Mill's work was highly valued by many leading suffragists, others were critical of its shortcomings, in particular of Mill's emphasis on marriage as the normal lot of women and his neglect of the position of the single woman. Arguments around his work reveal the different ways in which liberalism could be interpreted, both in theory and in practice, by male and female contemporaries. Mill believed that women who were immersed in domesticity were unsuited to take part in public life, and that only involvement in the latter would enable women to participate fully in politics. Many female suffragists argued, however, that it was the qualities that women exercised within the home that made them particularly suited to exercise a public role. Such contradictions lay at the heart of nineteenth-century liberalism. Liberalism's rhetoric of formal equality operated within a set of ideas that described men as naturally suited to the public world of work and politics and women as equally suited to the private domain of the family. This "separate spheres" ideology meant that the family was seen as "a private realm beyond the reach of politics" (Caine, 1992, 39). Women attempted to challenge the separation of the public and the private, but in doing so they drew attention to sexual difference. They argued that women needed to be represented in the public world because they had a distinct point of view and specific needs. This argument could empower women while at the same time confirming the continuance of gender divisions in the workplace and in the home.

In terms of practical politics, liberal parties were seen as a likely source of support for the women's suffrage campaign. In practice, however, they proved to be unreliable allies. They frequently opposed specific demands for women's suffrage on pragmatic grounds when it was feared that women's enfranchisement might benefit their political opponents. This was the case in France, for example, where members of the Third Republic assumed that women would vote for Catholic parties and for monarchism. Nonetheless, the opposition was also underpinned by the strength of the separate spheres ideology, in which the public world was associated with a masculine culture that assumed that women needed protection within the confines of the home and that politics were unwomanly.

The relationship between liberalism and women's suffrage, therefore, was complex. Women used the language of individual rights, independence, and duty in arguing for the vote, but they also criticized liberalism when it failed to address sexual oppression. In the process, they sought to modify some of the ideas of liberalism and to add new concerns.

See also Catholicism; Citizenship; Mill, John Stuart; *On the Subjection of Women.*
References Caine, Barbara. *Victorian Feminists* (1992); Caine, Barbara. *English Feminism, 1780–1980* (1997); Eisenstein, Zillah. "Elizabeth Cady Stanton: Radical-Feminist Analysis and Liberal-Feminist Strategy" (1987); Rendall, Jane. "Citizenship, Culture and Civilisation: The Languages of British Suffragists, 1866–1874" (1994).

La Liga Feminista (Costa Rica)
See Acuña, Angela, and
La Liga Feminista.

Limited Suffrage
See Universal Suffrage.

Local Franchise
The local or municipal franchise was often granted to women before they achieved the parliamentary, federal, or national

These Boston women could vote only in their city elections. "Mixed" polling places were considered slightly scandalous, however. (Ann Ronan Picture Library)

vote. During the second half of the nineteenth century, more and more women (mainly, but not exclusively, from the middle class) became involved in organizations concerned with philanthropic and social reform. Their involvement helped them to develop administrative and organizational skills that enabled them to enter the political sphere at the local level. Although they were denied a national franchise, women voted for and were elected to such public bodies as school boards, poor law boards, and municipal councils. This participation enabled women to exercise their influence over social policy at the local level, and very often they were able to institute important reforms in such areas as education, child welfare, and sanitation.

Politically active women believed that they could bring the skills of good household management to the running of local services, and this idea conformed with the accepted notion of women's sphere being the local and the domestic. Where women were allowed to run for election, they usually stood as independent candidates because they wanted to represent women's interests. The entry of party politics into local government, however, meant that it became harder for women to stand because male selection committees did not usually choose female candidates. Nonetheless, once women had exercised a municipal vote and had achieved success at the local level, it was inevitable that they would want to extend that influence to national government and demand women's suffrage.

In newly created British colonies of Australia and New Zealand, female philanthropists and moral reformers worked to ameliorate the effects of frontier society, and gaining the local vote was often part of their reforming campaigns. Women taxpayers in New Zealand, many of whom were involved in the temperance movement, voted in municipal elections from 1867, and all women had the local vote by 1885. For New Zealand women, the local vote was a stepping-stone to the rapid achievement of full parliamentary suffrage in 1893. Similarly, in Australia, the municipal vote was also given to women early on, with South Australia being the first to grant it in 1861. Canada, another frontier society, followed the same pattern. Women in many provinces gained the local vote early, well before 1900. In the United States, Kansas gave women the school vote as early as 1861, and the municipal vote in 1887, but it was difficult for many American women to exercise their rights, as they were often subject to party pressure and were heckled and jeered at when they went to vote.

In Britain the municipal vote was first gained in 1869, but only for unmarried women. Gradually the franchise was extended to school and poor law boards, and by 1900 over 1 million women had a local government vote. The success of women's work at the local level often persuaded male politicians to support the campaign for the parliamentary franchise for women, but antisuffragists argued that although women had exercised their influence for good at the local level, they were not ready to have the "imperial vote" because they could not understand matters of economic and foreign policy. In most Nordic countries, women enjoyed the municipal vote from an early stage, although generally it was only for propertied women. In Sweden, women had the local vote by 1862, but it was only after a campaign by the Association for Married Women's Property Rights that they started to use it. In Iceland, after an attempt to gain the local vote in 1882 that was vetoed by the Danish king, a local suffrage measure was introduced in 1908, and this rapidly led to full suffrage only seven years later.

Some European countries were slow to grant women the local vote. In France, for example, very few municipalities and departments supported it, the first local vote being granted by the First Seine Department in 1907. In Austria the situation was complex; the government removed the right of propertied women to vote in local elections in 1890, and the meeting held by Auguste Fickert to protest the loss of the franchise led to the beginning of a serious feminist movement in Austria.

In some of the other countries under British colonial rule, women did achieve the local franchise, usually with property qualifications. In India, women entered provincial councils from the 1920s onwards, and in Nigeria, women were able to vote in regional elections in the 1950s. In the independent state of Turkey, the nationalist leader and modernizer Mustafa Kemal Atatürk pushed through the municipal vote for women in 1931, and this was followed by the granting of full suffrage in 1934.

The progression from gaining the local vote to achieving full national suffrage was not always inevitable, but in many countries the local vote did provide a stepping-stone by demonstrating that women were more than capable of successfully entering political life. However, some governments did use the municipal vote to appease women's demands in the belief that the local sphere was the best area for women to exercise their political aspirations.

See also Australia; Austria; Britain; Canada; France; Iceland; Imperialism; India; New Zealand; Nigeria; Sweden; Turkey; United States of America.
References Evans, Richard. *The Feminists: Women's Emancipation Movements in Europe, America and Australasia, 1840–1920* (1977); Flexner, Eleanor. *Century of Struggle: The Woman's Rights Movement in the United States* ([1959] 1975); Forbes, Geraldine. *Women in Modern India* (1996); Hollis, Patricia. *Ladies Elect: Women in English Local Government, 1865–1914* (1987); Mba, Nina Emma. *Nigerian Women Mobilized: Women's Political Activity in Southern Nigeria, 1900–1965* (1982).

Lowe, Annie
See Dugdale, Henrietta, and Annie Lowe.

Luisi, Paulina
Paulina Luisi (1875–1950) was the most influential leader of the women's movement in Uruguay, dominating campaigns for women's rights and women's suffrage for two decades. She was the first woman to receive a *bachillerato* or preuniversity degree in 1899 and went on to become the first woman to graduate as a doctor in Montevideo in 1909.

In 1916 Luisi founded the Consejo Nacional de Mujeres (Uruguayan National Council of Women), which in 1917 became the first women's group to initiate a suffrage campaign. Realizing that a specialist suffrage group was needed, in 1919 she formed the Alianza Uruguay de Mujeres para Sufragio (Uruguay Alliance of Women for Suffrage), under the umbrella of the National Council. However, after the failure of the alliance to get congressional approval of a municipal suffrage bill, the group felt obliged to broaden its agenda. Luisi drew up a 10-point social program for the group that would benefit women and children. She did this on the grounds that they would strengthen their case for political rights by showing interest in social problems. The National Council of Women also continued campaigning for the vote. It appears that Luisi's involvement with both groups meant that their agendas were very similar.

Luisi's interest in feminism was sustained by her energy, organizational skills, and strong belief in social justice and was strengthened by her travels to Europe and her links with feminists outside Uruguay. She was much in demand as a speaker on suffrage and other feminist issues abroad. However, her temperament could be abrasive, and this contributed to internal splits within the movement. She was described by a friend as a rough character who talked loudly and could make people feel uncomfortable. During the 1920s, tensions between Luisi and other feminist leaders led her to distance herself from the

National Council of Women and to speak disparagingly of their "antiquated ideas."

Luisi's disaffection with the National Council also instigated the change of name of the Alianza Uruguay de Mujeres para Sufragio to the Alianza Uruguay de Mujeres in line with the policy of the International Woman Suffrage Alliance. She retained her domination of the alliance, which became the most significant feminist group in the late 1920s and early 1930s, and in 1926 she was named president for life. However, she continued to represent both the alliance and the National Council of Women abroad, attending the third Congreso Internacional Femenino (International Women's Conference) in Buenos Aires in 1928.

Luisi saw the vote (which was granted to Uruguayan women in 1932) as the means to make reforms rather than as an end in itself. In 1919 she wrote that "within feminism, suffrage is one of the elements for solving the problem, but it is itself insufficient to find all the answers."

See also International Woman Suffrage Alliance; Latin America and the Caribbean; Uruguay.
Reference Lavrin, Asunción. *Women, Feminism and Social Change in Argentina, Chile and Uruguay, 1890–1940* (1995).

Lutz, Bertha

Bertha Lutz (1894–1976) was the main leader of the Brazilian women's suffrage movement from 1918 until after the vote was achieved in 1932, and she remained politically active during most of the 1930s. She was born into a family of activists in 1894. Her Swiss-Brazilian father, Adolf Lutz, was a pioneer of tropical medicine, and her English mother, Amy Fowler, had nursed lepers and later set up the first free school for neglected boys in Brazil. Lutz was educated in Europe, gaining a degree in science at the University of Paris.

Following a visit to London before World War I, she began to take a strong interest in the suffrage movement in England. Shortly after her return home to Rio to study law in 1918, she published an important article in a Rio newspaper calling for the establishment of a league of Brazilian women. Lutz argued that women in Brazil should eschew the violent politics of British suffragettes but rather be prepared to take on political responsibilities and "become valuable instruments in the progress of Brazil" (*Revista de Semana*, 28 December 1918). By 1922, when she attended the Pan-American Women's Conference in Baltimore, she had become the leading advocate for women in Brazil.

In 1922, Lutz founded an organization in Rio known as Federação Brasileira pelo Progresso Feminino (FBPF) [the Brazilian Federation for the Advancement of Women], of which she became president, whose membership consisted mainly of elite women with political connections. She remained in this prominent position throughout the 1920s and early 1930s until the vote was achieved, using her personal and political contacts to rally support and exploiting her position as a government employee in the National Museum in Rio. In 1929 she expanded her activities, founding three new women's organizations, including a woman's electoral league, and working to establish FBPF sections in every state of Brazil.

When a draft electoral code recommended a restricted women's franchise, Lutz led a delegation to President Getúlio Vargas and persuaded him to grant women the vote on the same terms as men. After the vote was won in 1932, Lutz stood for election but was initially unsuccessful. She finally gained election as an alternate candidate, and following the death of a senator in 1936, she entered the Chamber of Deputies where she served for a year. Sadly, in 1937 the advent of the right-wing regime Estado Nôvo restricted her and all other Brazilian women's political aspirations until after World War II.

Lutz remained interested in women's rights until her death, attending the United Nations–sponsored Women's Year Conference in Mexico City at the age of 81 in 1975.

See also Brazil; Pan-American Women's Conference.

References Hahner, June E. *Emancipating the Female Sex: The Struggle for Women's Rights in Brazil, 1850–1940* (1990); Rachum, Ilan. "Feminism, Woman Suffrage, and National Politics in Brazil, 1922–1937" (1977).

Malaysia

Because of Malaysia's almost 200-year status as a British colony, Malaysian women, unlike women in most Western nations, did not have to fight men from their own country to get the vote. Rather, they received the franchise at the same time as Malaysian men. Women's suffrage was written into the constitution when Malaysia achieved independence from Britain in 1957.

However, this did not mean that all Malaysian women were inactive politically in the years before independence. Rather, they subsumed the issue of equal rights under a wider nationalist objective and fought for democracy and freedom from British rule alongside men. It was only after achieving independence that women's groups started to turn their attention to the issue of equal rights. As in many other countries within and outside Asia, the growth of women's representation in the Malaysian legislature has been very slow; from zero women in the state assemblies in the 1950s, the number had risen to only 8 percent of the total number of legislators by 1995. Thus women's interests are still largely underrepresented, given that nearly half of Malaysia's population of 18 million is female and over 50 percent of women in the population have voted in past general elections.

See also Nationalism.
Reference Ariffin, Rohana. "Feminism in Malaysia: A Historical and Present Perspective of Women's Struggles in Malaysia" (1999).

Masaryk, Tomas

Tomas Masaryk (1850–1937), who became president of the Czech Republic, was a strong supporter of women's rights, including suffrage. In the 1890s he joined other deputies in the Young Czech (National Liberal) Party in taking up the cause of women's education in the Reichsrat and helped to influence the development of the Czech women's movement from his position as a professor at the Charles Ferdinand University in Prague. In his writings and speeches, he linked women's emancipation to his theories about the social transformation of the Czech nation. He argued that throughout Czech history a series of religious and political leaders had struggled for freedom, equality, and humanity, which characterized the spirit of the Czech nation.

For Masaryk, gender equality was an integral part of this struggle. He advocated equal rights for women while at the same time sharing the view of many contemporary feminists that women would play an important role in moralizing society and would help in the struggle against the double standard of sexual morality, which he abhorred. Masaryk's views were influenced by his wife, the American Charlotte Garrigue Masaryková, who translated John Stuart Mill's *On the Subjection of Women* into Czech in 1890. Masaryk ensured that a commitment to placing women on an equal footing with men, culturally, legally, and politically, was part of the program of the Progressive

Party, which cooperated with the women's suffrage campaign. Between 1905 and 1915 his journal, *Our Era,* ran a column devoted to women's issues, covering topics such as the women's movement abroad and suffragette militancy, which was written by the feminist journalist Olga Stranska-Absolonova after 1909. Masaryk's influence, through his students, his journal, and his political position, contributed to the close relationship between the women's suffrage movement and Czech nationalism and helped to ensure that women immediately gained voting rights when the republic was established under his presidency.

See also Czechoslovakia; Mill, John Stuart; Nationalism; *On the Subjection of Women.* *Reference* David, Katherine. "Czech Feminists and Nationalism in the Late Habsburg Monarchy: 'The First in Austria'" (1991).

McClung, Nellie

An important campaigner for women's suffrage in Canada, Nellie Letitia McClung (née Mooney) (1873–1951), was born in Ontario, but moved west to Manitoba with her family in 1880. She was a teacher until 1896, when she married Robert McClung. Nellie McClung became a committed worker for the Woman's Christian Temperance Union (WCTU) and for political equality for women, and she was well known as a gifted and witty public speaker on the question of women's suffrage. She played an important role in the Manitoba suffrage campaign, leading the delegation that went to see Sir Rodmond Roblin, the Conservative antisuffrage premier, in January 1914, and the next evening acting the part of the premier in an amusing staging of the prosuffrage satire *Women's Parliament.* Toward the end of 1914, McClung moved to Alberta, where she participated in the province's suffrage campaign through her membership in the Edmonton Equal Franchise League. In 1916 women's suffrage was

achieved in Alberta, and McClung went on to sit in the provincial legislature from 1921 to 1926.

Like her fellow suffragist Dr. Emily Howard Stowe, McClung was a maternalist who believed in the value of women's role within the family. However, she always recognized women's need to achieve political equality and economic independence, and she was arguably the most significant leader of the women's suffrage movement in the "prairie" provinces.

See also Canada; Stowe, Emily Howard. *References* Cleverdon, Catherine L. *The Woman Suffrage Movement in Canada* (1974); McClung, Nellie. *In Times Like These* ([1915] 1972).

Men's League for Women's Suffrage

The Men's League for Women's Suffrage (MLWS) was founded in 1907 by Herbert Jacobs, a London barrister who was also vice president of the Jewish League for Women's Suffrage and a director of the International Women's Franchise Club. The MLWS was open to any man regardless of his political and religious views, and membership was comprised largely of academics, writers, clergymen, solicitors, and lawyers. *A Declaration of Representative Men in Favour of Women's Suffrage,* published by the league in 1909, listed prominent men in favor of women's suffrage, including 83 officeholders past and present in the Liberal and Conservative parties, 86 academics and writers, and 49 church leaders. By 1910 there were ten branches, including Manchester, Edinburgh, Inverness, and Birmingham, and an overseas branch was also established in the United States. International connections were reinforced through membership in the Men's International Alliance for Woman Suffrage, formed in 1912, which had member societies in several European countries and whose secretary and treasurer were based in the Netherlands.

The MLWS concentrated on propaganda work; it held public meetings, distributed literature, and pressured members of Parliament and candidates through letters and deputations. The league also fielded its own parliamentary candidates, and in 1908 a Welsh solicitor, Walter Roch, was the first MLWS member to become an MP. League members, including Frederick Pethick-Lawrence and Tim Healy, MP, often linked their professional and political practice by defending suffragist campaigners in court. Given that many of its members were academics and writers, it is hardly surprising that the MLWS also gave support to the women's cause by publishing books, pamphlets, and newspapers. At first the league's activities were publicized in the *Women's Franchise,* but it later established its own paper, the *Men's League Monthly Paper.* In 1912 the league published C. V. Drysdale's pamphlet, *Why Men Should Work for Women's Suffrage,* and in the same year it brought out a *Handbook on Women's Suffrage,* which provided a comprehensive account of the suffrage issue at that time.

Members of the league argued that because they already had the vote, they could exert a different kind of pressure on politicians and that this provided the rationale for the establishment of a separate men's society. Although a minority of members saw the vote as part of a broader process of change in gender identities and relationships, the majority of male suffragists, as Angela John argues, were not "prepared to rethink their own sense of manhood even if they believed women's lives should change" (John, 2000, 149). They claimed that they were seeking franchise reform for others, rather than themselves, out of a sense of duty and natural justice and that this was part of a progressive movement toward greater democracy.

The MLWS had its closest links with the Women's Freedom League and constitutional militancy. The cautious methods of the MLWS, however, alienated some of its

younger members, who helped to form a new organization, the Men's Political Union for Women's Enfranchisement (MPU) in 1910. There was some overlap between the two; writer and journalist Henry Nevinson, for example, sat on the MLWS executive committee and also chaired the MPU. Although the MLWS took a nonparty political stand, it was forced by events to change policy. When Prime Minister H. H. Asquith made it clear that he was going to prevent discussion of the Conciliation Bill, which was then before Parliament, the league passed a resolution that put it in opposition to the government, although this led to the resignation of some members. In December the MLWS opposed all government candidates in the general election except those who had been active in the Conciliation Committee.

The work of groups such as the MLWS reveals how men actively supported the women's suffrage campaign. Studying the league provides insights into men's motivation to work for women's enfranchisement and also points out that they were as divided in their methods, political strategies, and ideas as female campaigners for women's suffrage.

See also Conciliation Bill; Fawcett, Millicent Garrett; Men's Political Union for Women's Enfranchisement; Men's Support; National Union of Women's Suffrage Societies; Women's Freedom League; Women's Social and Political Union.
References Crawford, Elizabeth. *The Women's Suffrage Movement: A Reference Guide, 1866–1928* (1999); John, Angela V., "Between the Cause and the Courts: The Curious Case of Cecil Chapman" (2000); John, Angela V. and Claire Eustance, eds. *The Men's Share? Masculinities, Male Support and Women's Suffrage in Britain, 1890–1920* (1992).

Men's Political Union for Women's Enfranchisement

The Men's Political Union for Women's Enfranchisement (MPU) was established in 1910, initially using the title Men's Federation for Women's Suffrage. It was founded by some members of the Men's League for Women's Suffrage (MLWS), a group that was close to the Women's Freedom League (WFL). The founders of the MPU had become impatient with the moderate outlook of the MLWS and wished to show their support for the militant Women's Social and Political Union (WSPU). The MPU adopted the WSPU colors of purple, white, and green, and its members spoke on WSPU platforms and also contributed articles to the official WSPU newspaper, *Votes for Women*. Some men, such as the writers Laurence Housman and Henry Nevinson, retained important positions in both men's groups and helped to provide a bridge between the WFL and the WSPU.

The MPU had radical policies from the start. It claimed that its policy was action and that it would oppose whichever government was in power. It also sought to carry out propaganda through public meetings, demonstrations, the sale of literature, and deputations to politicians. Some of its leading members, including Hugh Franklin, the nephew of a Liberal cabinet member, took direct action that led to their arrest and imprisonment. Franklin was first arrested in 1910 when he tried to strike Winston Churchill with a dogwhip. During subsequent imprisonments, Franklin was forcibly fed over 100 times and eventually escaped to France to avoid rearrest. A number of men broke windows, and Harold Laski, at the time an Oxford University student, tried to destroy a railway station by arson in 1913. Such actions raised questions, however, about the nature of male support for women's suffrage. Men claimed that they were incensed by the violence encountered by women activists, which contradicted notions of fair play. Nonetheless, such ideas drew on traditional masculine characteristics and generated a debate in the suffrage press on the meaning of chivalry.

At first, the WSPU welcomed men's willingness to take direct action, but as women's own militant activity escalated after 1912, relationships between the two groups grew more strained. The WSPU became far more unwilling to work with men and also feared that male violence could harm the legitimacy of their cause, given that men could express their views through the vote. Moreover, the WSPU emphasized the heroic female campaigner fighting with other women against male aggression, an image that did not fit well with active support from men. On the other hand, many male suffragists, such as Housman, became increasingly worried about the growing level of violence. Nonetheless, the MPU continued to expand and by 1914 over 20 branches, including two in Scotland, had been formed. As it became increasingly dangerous to undertake militant activities, the MPU organized a Speakers' Defence Corps in July 1914. There is some evidence that the MPU remained active during World War I; a new branch in North London was opened in 1915.

See also Men's League for Women's Suffrage; Men's Support; *Votes for Women;* Women's Freedom League; Women's Social and Political Union.
References Bartley, Paula. *Votes for Women, 1860–1928* (1998); Crawford, Elizabeth. *The Women's Suffrage Movement: A Reference Guide, 1866–1928* (1999); John, Angela V. "Between the Cause and the Courts: The Curious Case of Cecil Chapman" (2000); John, Angela V., and Claire Eustance, eds. *The Men's Share? Masculinities, Male Support and Women's Suffrage in Britain, 1890–1920* (1992).

Men's Support

Men gave support to the women's suffrage campaign in a variety of different ways, but they faced the unusual situation of being auxiliaries rather than leaders of a major political movement. Most women's suffrage organizations were open to men who attended meetings, gave speeches,

May 2, 1885.]   PUNCH, OR THE LONDON CHARIVARI.   215

INTERIORS AND EXTERIORS. No. 9.

"PLACE AUX DAMES!" A TURN-HIM-OUT MEETING AT ST. JAMES'S HALL.

Many men attended women's suffrage meetings, like this one in St. James Hall, London, 2 May 1885, lampooned by Harry Furness in Punch. *(Ann Ronan Picture Library)*

and distributed literature. In France, for example, men accounted for approximately 10–15 percent of the membership of feminist societies in 1900–1901, and there were three times as many men's signatures as women's on Hubertine Auclert's suffrage petition of 1909.

Male supporters tended to come from professional backgrounds or from middle-class families with a history of involvement in reform campaigns, and their values and political ideas were similar to those of their female relatives. It was also very common for husbands and wives to work together for women's suffrage, including the Pethick-Lawrences and Ursula and Jacob Bright in England, and Nazik 'Abid and Muhammad Jamil Bayhum in Syria. Not all such couples were from middle-class backgrounds. Sam Robinson, a working-class member of the British socialist group the Independent Labour Party, supported women's suffrage both before and after his marriage to Annot Wilkie, a schoolteacher and suffragette. The views of some men were reinforced by their marriage to feminists from countries with strong suffrage movements. The Czech professor and nationalist politician Tomas Masaryk, for instance, was married to an American, and the Sinhalese lawyer George E. De Silva, who later took a leading role in liberal nationalist politics, was married to a British woman, Agnes Nell, whose grandfather had been colonial solicitor general.

Men not only joined into day-to-day campaigning, but they also helped to strengthen the case for women's suffrage and to give the movement publicity through their writings. A particularly influential text for liberal reformers was John Stuart Mill's *On the Subjection of Women* (1869), which was translated into several languages and provided the stimulus for the suffrage movement in a number of countries. In European socialist circles, August Bebel's book, *Woman in the Past Present and Future* (1885), originally published in 1879 under the title *Woman under Socialism,* was widely read and used as a starting point for debates on the "woman question." In the East, many male writers were influenced by the image of the Westernized, emancipated woman. They equated this with progress and wrote novels and political texts that advocated women's rights. In Egypt, for example, Qasim Amin's book, *al-Mar'ah al-Jadidah* (The New Woman), caused considerable controversy because he based his arguments for women's emancipation on natural rights rather than religious grounds; in Turkey, Halil Hamit, Celal Nuri, and Ahmet Agaoglu wrote books in the early twentieth century on the subject of women's rights.

Male editors of newspapers could play a key role in giving favorable publicity to women's suffrage and in helping to promote the cause. Tom Johnston, editor of the Scottish socialist newspaper *Forward,* and Tomas Masaryk, who edited the Czech paper *Our Era,* both gave sympathetic coverage to the suffrage campaign and included regular women's columns written by suffrage activists. Other men were involved in owning and editing suf-

frage newspapers, often alongside their wives. Henry Blackwell and his wife Lucy Stone established and edited the American suffrage paper the *Woman's Journal,* and Frederick and Emmeline Pethick-Lawrence edited *Votes for Women,* the official newspaper of the militant British suffrage group the Women's Social and Political Union (WSPU).

Given that women were excluded from representative political institutions, they needed sympathetic men to present their case and to introduce suffrage bills. In some cases, political groups or parties gave women their official backing; for example, in 1918 both the All-India Muslim League and the Indian National Congress announced their support for women's enfranchisement when the British Montagu-Chelmsford proposals announced that it was not the right time to widen the electorate. It was more usual, however, for individual politicians, many of whom were in leadership positions, to show a willingness to take up the cause. They included Sir John Hall in New Zealand; the British socialist MP, Keir Hardie; Hadji Vakil el Rooy (or el Roaya) from Iran, who in 1911 proposed in parliament that women should be able to vote because they were human beings; Ibrahim al-Khatib and Sa'dauah al-Jabiri, delegates to the Syrian Congress who proposed a limited form of women's suffrage in debates on the state constitution in 1920; and José Batlle y Ordóñez, president of Uruguay in 1903– 1907 and 1911–1915. In Russia, Lev Petrazhitskii, professor of jurisprudence and a member of the Kadets, was prepared to sacrifice his reputation as a serious politician in the Duma in order to argue that women should have political rights.

On one level, men's support was based on a set of liberal or socialist beliefs in equal rights, but they also expressed a variety of different ideas about women's suffrage that were related to the broader context of their own politics. Hardie, for instance, was unusual among European socialists in giving consistent support to the demand for a limited franchise; he believed that it was a matter of principle that there should be no sex disqualification from voting, and that the removal of the sex disability should take priority. Masaryk, on the other hand, as a liberal nationalist, supported his case for women's suffrage by highlighting the Czech democratic tradition and contrasting it with the autocracy of the Austrians. Batlle y Ordóñez believed that women should be liberated from old-fashioned ideas and the influence of the Church.

All of these men had a strong personal conviction about the right of women to exercise the vote. There were other politicians and political parties, however, who gave support to women's suffrage only as a matter of expediency. In Sweden prior to World War I, both the Liberal Party and the Social Democrats thought that championing voting rights for women would strengthen them against conservative groups, and Karen Offen suggests that the socialists were the only group to endorse women's suffrage in France before 1900 because they were so weak that they had nothing to lose.

In any case, the support of individual male politicians and political groups could not guarantee that the women's cause would be successful. Women's claims often took second place to nationalist, anticolonial, or revolutionary struggles, and the fears of political parties, in particular liberal and socialist groups, that women's enfranchisement might benefit their opponents meant that political expediency often took precedence over principles.

A few women's suffrage groups were closed to men, such as the WSPU in Britain and the Kvinnestemmeretsforeningen (the Female Suffrage Union) in Norway, and in a number of countries men decided to make a contribution by establishing their own groups. They may have recognized that through the suffrage campaign, women were developing their own form of political activism and therefore the position of men was to play a secondary and supportive role rather than to take the lead. In the Netherlands for example, the Mannenbond voor Vrouwenkiesrecht (Men's League for Women's Suffrage) was formed in 1909, and in Britain the Men's League for Women's Suffrage was established in 1907 and the Men's Federation for Women's Suffrage, later renamed the Men's Political Union, was established in 1910. Men's groups from the Netherlands, France, Sweden, Britain, Hungary, the United States, Denmark, and France came together to form the Men's International Alliance for Woman Suffrage in 1912. The alliance held its first congress in London in the same year, and its honorary secretary and treasurer were both from Holland.

It is only in recent years that historians have paid greater attention to the scale and importance of male support for women's suffrage. New questions have been raised about the way in which the practice of suffrage politics was gendered. In a study of political partnerships between husbands and wives, for example, June Balshaw examines how such joint activities were affected by gender roles in politics and in the family and the extent to which suffrage work challenged and transformed these roles. What is clear is that men supported the women's suffrage movement in a variety of ways and that their contribution needs to be the subject of more extensive study.

See also Citizenship; Hall, Sir John, Independent Labour Party; Men's League for Women's Suffrage; Men's Political Union for Women's Enfranchisement; Mill, John Stuart; Nationalism; *On the Subjection of Women*; Pethick-Lawrence, Emmeline; Pethick-Lawrence, Frederick; Stone, Lucy; *Votes for Women*; The *Woman's Journal*; Women's Social and Political Union.
References Crawford, Elizabeth. *The Women's Suffrage Movement: A Reference*

Guide, 1866–1928 (1999); Holton, Sandra Stanley. "From Anti-Slavery to Suffrage Militancy: The Bright Circle, Elizabeth Cady Stanton and the British Women's Movement" (1994); Jayawardena, Kumari. *Feminism and Nationalism in the Third World* (1986); John, Angela V., and Claire Eustance, eds. *The Men's Share? Masculinities, Male Support and Women's Suffrage in Britain, 1890–1920* (1992); Lavrin, Asunción. *Women, Feminism and Social Change in Argentina, Chile and Uruguay, 1890–1940* (1995); Mumtaz, Khawar, and Farida Shaheed. *Women of Pakistan: Two Steps Forwards, One Step Back?* (1987); Offen, Karen. "Women, Citizenship and Suffrage with a French Twist, 1789–1993" (1994).

Mexico

Mexican women finally gained full voting rights in 1958 after suffrage campaigns lasting 40 years. Before the revolution of 1910, politics in Mexico were dominated by a narrow male elite. Although at the end of the nineteenth century the issue of women's rights was raised by the government's political opponents, it was not until after the revolution that a feminist movement began to emerge. The fact that women had participated in support roles during the armed struggle was important in that it gave them a moral justification to make political and social demands. Calls for the vote came initially from a small group of radical feminists, including Hermila Galindo. She presented their demands to an all-male constitutional convention in 1917 using the liberal argument for the rights of individuals to equality before the law.

The 1917 Constitution allowed all married residents of the republic over 18 and all single residents over 21 to vote, run for office, and participate in political activities, but this loophole, which could have enfranchised women, was closed by the 1918 National Election Law. This law limited both the vote and the selection of candidates for national office to men. Despite this setback, women continued to move into the workforce during the 1920s and to join women's organizations campaigning for political rights. Some states granted women limited political participation, giving them the right to vote in state and local elections, and in 1925 the state of Chiapas gave women complete political equality. However, other states failed to follow this example. Mexican women who had made political gains toward civil reform were also the subject of attack, especially by members of the Catholic Church. Virulent cartoons regularly appeared in the press depicting the terrible consequences of feminism for the family.

The women's movement at this time was fractured by class allegiances. Most feminist organizations campaigning for suffrage recruited from the urban middle class. By contrast, working-class and peasant women formed groups associated with labor unions or the Communist Party and were more concerned with economic issues. They considered class to be more important than gender and accused suffrage groups of promoting bourgeois interests. A further weakness was the lack of continuity in leadership over time. Very few women who had been feminist leaders in the 1920s continued to be active during the 1930s.

By the mid-1930s alliances between groups resulted in the formation of a broad-based front for women's rights called the Frente Único Pro-Derechos de la Mujer (Sole Front for Women's Rights), which had the vote as its main campaigning issue. At its height, Frente Único had 50,000 members from 800 women's groups whose energies coalesced around the fight for women's suffrage.

In 1936, 2,753 women affiliated with labor unions and peasant organizations voted in primary elections known as *elecciones internas,* and in 1937 victory seemed to be in sight. The Senate and Chamber of Deputies approved an amendment to the constitution proposed by President Cárdenas to allow women full rights of citizenship, and by 1939 this had been ratified by all 28 states. However, despite mass demonstrations, Congress refused to give a formal declaration that the amendment had been ratified. Members of Congress argued that women would vote against government reforms and might support the conservative opposition party.

Following this unfortunate defeat, the feminist movement in Mexico became progressively weaker during the next two decades and mainly concerned itself with domestic issues. However, new economic opportunities opening up for women after World War II coincided with the formation of a reformed ruling party, the Partido Revolucionario Institucional (PRI) [Institutional Revolutionary Party], which was more sympathetic to women's rights and put women in high-profile positions.

The overall weakness of the feminist movement in the 1940s is suggested by the fact that although women received the municipal franchise in 1946, they did not immediately build upon this gain. In 1954, when the confidence of the PRI was high and it no longer feared displacement by the opposition, women were allowed to vote in congressional elections. Yet full political rights that enabled women to vote in presidential elections were deferred until 1958. Further, women's enfranchisement did little to advance the cause of women's issues or broaden the class base of Mexican politics. Those women who did obtain political office were from elite groups who obtained their position through family connections or links to powerful men.

See also Citizenship; Frente Único Pro-Derechos de la Mujer; Latin America and the Caribbean.
References Macías, Anna, Against All Odds: The Feminist Movement in Mexico to 1940 (1982); Miller, Francesca. Latin American Women and the Search for Social Justice (1991); Ramos Escandón, Carmen. "Women's Movements, Feminism and Mexican Politics" (1994).

Middle East and North Africa

Although female suffrage was discussed in the Arabic press in the nineteenth century and debated in the Iranian Parliament before World War I, in general, votes for women have not formed a major part of the political agenda for Middle Eastern women, with a few notable exceptions.

There are several reasons for this. One is that women's attention has been distracted from political issues by questions of equality within the household. Factors that have weighed (and, in some cases, still weigh) heavily on women are veiling, purdah (public seclusion), polygamy, unilateral divorce, and child custody, and as a result, reforming family law has often seemed a higher priority than gaining the vote. In addition, in historical terms almost the entire region was subject to direct or indirect colonial rule until after the end of World War II, and consequently women have often subordinated political discourse and action to the struggle for national independence.

Once independence was gained, many countries considered universal suffrage an essential element of a new state. Among countries that followed this pattern were Algeria (1962), Israel (1948, although Jewish women had voted in the National Assembly from 1920 onwards), Mauritania (1961), Tunisia (1959), and, most recently, the Palestine National Authority, where the first elections were held in 1996. This followed the commitment to universal suffrage outlined in the Protocol of the Declaration of Principles on Interim Self-Government Arrangements for Palestinians issued in 1993–1994.

Syria granted women a limited franchise by decree in 1949, two years after independence; this was confirmed by the constitution of 1950, and an electoral law guaranteeing full adult suffrage was introduced in August 1953. However, President Adib al-Shishakli was overthrown early in 1954, and the country reverted to the

Constitution of 1950, when once again women's right to vote was subjected to an educational qualification. The franchise remained in confusion in Syria following the country's temporary union with Egypt in 1958 and the seizure of power by the Ba'th Party in 1963, and women were not fully enfranchised until 1973, when a new constitution reintroduced universal adult suffrage.

In Yemen, the road to the vote was similarly complex in that the country was originally divided in two and has only recently been united. The northern half of Yemen emerged as the modern, independent state of the Yemen Arab Republic in 1970, and the constitution of the same year granted women the vote, although elections were not held until 1988. The southern half of Yemen was a British colony until 1967, with Aden as its capital. After gaining independence, the country was renamed the People's Democratic Republic of Yemen, and it, too, granted women the vote in 1970. Twenty years later, in 1990, the two separate countries of North and South Yemen came together to form the Republic of Yemen. Here women were enfranchised in 1992, following the principles of the Interim Constitution of 1990.

Although not all countries in the region granted enfranchisement on independence, a phenomenon shared by almost all Middle Eastern countries was the drive for economic growth. Many states saw both the improvement of the lot of women and the introduction of more democratic forms of government as prerequisites for modernization, and so, in many cases, the enfranchisement of women was the by-product of general programs of economic and social advancement. Countries that granted female suffrage as part of development programs or as a result of constitutional reform were Afghanistan (1964), Egypt (1956), Iran (1963), Iraq (1967), Lebanon (1953), Morocco (1959), and

Turkey (1934). In Jordan, women were not given the vote until 1974, although the Ittihad al-Mar'ah al-'Arabiyah (Arab Women's Federation) had raised the issue of women's suffrage as early as 1954. In Sudan, women were fully enfranchised in 1964, although the British had granted the vote to women having at least a secondary school education in 1953, following pressure from the Sudanese Women's Union. Libya, with its unique political system of elected people's committees and congresses, has granted women full representation and voting rights since 1977.

There remain five countries of the Arabian Peninsula where full suffrage has not been granted to either sex—Bahrain, Oman, Qatar, Saudi Arabia, and the United Arab Emirates—and only male suffrage exists in Kuwait. It is worth noting that some progress has taken place in these countries. In Oman, women have been allowed to compete for nomination to the Consultative Council (which, however, is selected rather than elected). In Qatar in 1999, the emir, Hamad ibn Khalifah al-Thani, announced that a commission was being established to draw up a national constitution, which would include provision for an elected assembly. In Bahrain, over 300 women signed a petition in 1995 demanding parliamentary democracy. Finally, Kuwait is locked in a dispute between the emir, Jabir al-Ahmad al-Sabah, who issued a decree in 1999 granting women the vote, and the National Assembly, which refused to ratify the decree. Only in the United Arab Emirates and Saudi Arabia has little progress been made toward full enfranchisement.

See also Egypt; Iran; Israel; Kuwait; Lebanon; Shafiq, Durriyah; Sha'rawi, Nur al-Hudá; Syria; Turkey.
References There is no single book or article that provides a comprehensive overview of women's suffrage in the Middle East. However, two works explore women's growing political participation on a regional basis. Badran, Margot, and Miriam Cooke, eds. *Opening the Gates: A Century of Arab Femi-*

nist *Writing* (1990); Beck, Lois, and Nikki R. Keddie, eds. *Women in the Muslim World* (1978). For a bibliographical survey of the women's movement in the Middle East and beyond, see Kimball, Michelle R., and Barbara R. Von Schlegell. *Muslim Women throughout the World: A Bibliography* (1997).

Militancy

The term *militancy* was first applied to the activities of the British suffrage group the Women's Social and Political Union (WSPU) to distinguish them from the more constitutional methods, including lobbying, petitioning, and letter writing, which were used by older suffrage organizations such as the National Union of Women's Suffrage Societies (NUWSS). Historians have tended to associate militancy with the destruction of property, imprisonment, hunger striking, and forcible feeding, a view that derives in part from the autobiographies of former suffragettes in the interwar years, which emphasized such activities as representing "authentic militancy." More recent studies, however, have drawn attention to the diverse nature of militancy and the changes in militant activity that took place over time.

In the period 1905 to 1908, protests that involved direct action or disruption of any kind were labeled militant. Thus, the beginning of militancy is dated from October 1905, when Christabel Pankhurst and Annie Kenney interrupted an election meeting by standing up and shouting "Votes for women!" They were subsequently arrested when Christabel spat at a policeman. Members of the WSPU then continued to find ingenious ways to gain entry to election meetings so that they could interrupt speakers, or else they carried out mass lobbies of the House of Commons. During this early stage the WSPU and the NUWSS had many members in common, and the NUWSS was inspired to change its own methods—soon its members were distributing propaganda material in public places and holding large demonstrations, pageants, and processions. In turn, after 1908 the militancy of the WSPU escalated to include symbolic acts, such as women chaining themselves to the Ladies Gallery in Parliament, and threats to public order, such as groups of women rushing the House of Commons and destroying property. At first, the destruction of property involved breaking windows, but by 1913 it also involved arson attacks on public buildings. This led to a greater gulf between the constitutionalist wing and the militant wing of the suffrage movement. However, not all militants engaged in actions that led to arrest and imprisonment. They could, for example, choose to confine their actions to disrupting meetings, including interrupting cinema audiences, or to raising money for the cause. Moreover, the Women's Freedom League, which described itself as a militant group, carried out less violent acts, such as tax resistance or refusing to fill in the 1911 census forms.

It is difficult, therefore, to be precise about a definition of militancy although contemporaries were clear in their own minds about who should be labeled a militant. It was less a question of whether a specific activity was undertaken, and more a matter of the spirit in which women approached their political activism. Hilda Kean suggests that it was the intensity of feeling and the daring of suffragettes, encapsulated in their motto "Deeds, Not Words," that inspired women to give up everything for the cause. She quotes from the autobiography of Evelyn Sharp, a former WSPU member, who claimed that "either you saw the vote as a political influence, or you saw it as a symbol of freedom. The desire to reform the world would not alone have been sufficient to turn law abiding and intelligent woman of all ages and all classes into ardent rebels. Reforms can always wait a little longer, but freedom, directly you discover you

Flora Drummond, who engaged in militant tactics with other leaders of the Women's Social and Political Union, being arrested in Hyde Park, 1914. (Ann Ronan Picture Library)

haven't got it, will not wait another minute" (Kean, 1994, 63).

This is why British militancy had such an impact on the international suffrage movement in the decade before World War I. Well-known militants such as Emmeline Pankhurst and Emmeline Pethick-Lawrence addressed meetings in the United States, and news of their exploits was spread through the suffrage press. In Ireland, Hanna Sheehy Skeffington organized the Irish Women's Franchise League, which held demonstrations, harassed politicians, and broke windows. Alice Paul, who had been arrested while living in London, used militant methods when she returned to the United States, including a picket of the White House, and in France, Madeleine Pelletier and Caroline Kauffmann, who had attended demonstrations in England, disrupted political meetings by showering delegates with leaflets. Although militancy was largely confined to Europe and North America in this period, there are examples of militant actions being taken further afield. In 1912 in Nanking, China, members of the Women's Suffrage Alliance armed themselves with pistols and stormed the parliament building for three days when they feared that their petition on women's right to vote might be ignored.

Through their direct action and sense of adventurousness, therefore, the British suffragettes captured the imagination of women both at home and in other countries and generated a great deal of publicity for the suffrage campaign. They challenged contemporary notions of what constituted appropriate political behavior for women and transformed the lives and outlook of the women who took part in the struggle for the vote. On the other hand, militancy was a controversial method of protest. Moderate suffragists feared that militancy would alienate politicians and public opinion and would make it more difficult for women to achieve their goals, and historians continue to argue about the effectiveness of militant methods.

See also Autobiography; Hunger Strikes; Irish Women's Franchise League; Kauffmann, Caroline; Kenney, Annie; National Union of Women's Suffrage Societies; Pankhurst, Christabel; Pankhurst, Emmeline; Paul, Alice; Pelletier, Madeleine; Pethick-Lawrence, Emmeline; Skeffington, Hanna Sheehy; Women's Freedom League; Women's Social and Political Union.

References Holton, Sandra Stanley. "Women and the Vote" (1995); Kean, Hilda. "Searching for the Past in Present Defeat: The Construction of Historical and Political Identity in British Feminism in the 1920s and 1930s" (1994); Mayhall, Laura E. Nym. "Creating the 'Suffragette Spirit': British Feminism and the Historical Imagination" (1995); Purviss, June. "'Deeds, Not Words': Daily Life in the Women's Social and Political Union in Edwardian Britain" (2000).

Mill, Harriet Taylor

An influential British writer on the subject of women's suffrage, Harriet Taylor Mill (née Hardy) (1807–1858) was born in London to a well-connected Unitarian family. In 1826 she married John Taylor, but four years later she was introduced to the philosopher and women's rights sympathizer John Stuart Mill, and the two immediately formed a deep intellectual and emotional attachment to each other. Mill and Harriet Taylor were almost constantly in each other's company until her husband's death in 1849, and after waiting two years, the couple decided to marry and establish a home together.

John Stuart Mill had always been interested in the notion of sexual equality, but his partnership with Harriet Taylor enabled them both to explore and develop their ideas together. Taylor's views were perhaps stronger than Mill's; for example, in the essays they wrote for each other in 1832 on "Marriage and Divorce," she supported the idea of easier divorce for women and advocated women's economic independence. In 1851 Taylor published an article in the *Westminster Review* on "The Enfranchisement of Women" in which she explored the idea of female claims to equality, especially in the field of political rights. In this essay she articulated the Unitarian belief in the equality of the sexes before God, and she maintained that women should be allowed to attain their full potential, free of the social restrictions that had always been placed on them. Both she and Mill believed that women had been given an artificial education that had forced them into a position subordinate to men, and only their freedom from legal and social disabilities would reveal their real nature.

There has always been an unresolved debate about how much Harriet Taylor influenced Mill's thinking and how much she contributed to his published work. Mill always admitted that they had both worked on his major work of political philosophy, *On Liberty* (1859), and that they had collaborated in writing *On the Subjection of Women* (1869), the key text of Victorian liberal feminism, but Taylor was never given authorial status equal to Mill's. There is no doubt that her intellectual influence on Mill was considerable and that her contribution to the Victorian women's suffrage debate was of great importance.

See also Britain; Mill, John Stuart; *On the Subjection of Women.*
References Rossi, Alice, ed. *Essays on Sex Equality: John Stuart Mill and Harriet Taylor Mill* (1970); Spender, Dale. *Women of Ideas (and What Men Have Done to Them)* (1983); Taylor, Harriet. "Enfranchisement of Women" (1851).

Mill, John Stuart

John Stuart Mill (1806–1873) was born in London, the eldest son of the philosopher and economist James Mill. Under his father's influence John became one of the most eminent liberal philosophers of nineteenth-century Britain. His early support of the principle of women's suffrage was considered vital to the progress of the cause during the 1860s and 1870s in Britain and inspirational for suffragists in many other countries.

In 1830 he met a married woman, Harriet Taylor, whose intellect he much admired, and during their long friendship she came to exert a considerable influence on Mill's thinking about the condition of women. After her husband's death, the couple married in 1851, and in the same year she published an article in the *Westminster Review,* entitled "The Enfranchisement of Women." Although his wife died in 1858, it was her influence that led Mill to write his groundbreaking work proposing the political and legal emancipation of women, *On the Subjection of Women,* which was published in 1869 and was translated into many different languages.

Mill's practical involvement in the early women's suffrage campaign began when he

John Stuart Mill was an early advocate of women's rights with his publication On the Subjection of Women *(1869). (Ann Ronan Picture Library)*

was elected the Liberal member of Parliament for Westminster in 1865. He had raised the issue of women's suffrage in his election address, which encouraged Barbara Bodichon of the Langham Place Circle to ask him to present a petition to Parliament, asking for the enfranchisement of women to be included in the 1866 Reform Bill.

The 1866 bill failed, but Mill was determined to introduce a women's suffrage amendment to a second Reform Bill to be introduced the following year. Mill's amendment proposed that the word *man* be replaced by the word *person,* but although he made an eloquent speech in the House of Commons on 20 May 1867, his proposal was defeated by 123 votes. The bill itself was passed.

After his wife's death, Mill's stepdaughter, Helen Taylor, became his intellectual companion, and although the two were not directly involved in setting up the first London women's suffrage committee in November 1866, they played an important and sometimes controversial role behind the scenes. Mill insisted that the committee be composed only of people of whom he approved, and he had strong views about what policies they should adopt. For example, he believed that the suffrage campaign should not associate itself with any controversial activities such as the agitation against the Contagious Diseases Acts, a cause for which he had some personal sympathy.

Mill lost his parliamentary seat in 1869, and in 1872 he became the nominal president of the London National Society for Women's Suffrage, which was the direct successor to the London women's suffrage committee. The following year Mill died, but his advocacy of the suffrage cause and his contribution to liberal feminist thinking continued to be influential among suffragists throughout the nineteenth century.

See also Britain; Langham Place Circle; Liberalism; Mill, Harriet Taylor; *On the Subjection of Women*.
Reference Caine, Barbara. "John Stuart Mill and the English Women's Movement" (1978).

Mitchell, Hannah

Hannah Mitchell (1871–1956) was a working-class English suffragist who campaigned for the militant Women's Social and Political Union (WSPU). Born on a small farm in Derbyshire, she was employed as a servant and later as a seamstress. Her introduction to politics was through the Independent Labour Party (ILP), and she was elected as an ILP candidate to the Ashton Board of Guardians in 1904. In 1905 she joined the Pankhursts' campaign to publicize the suffrage cause in the north of England, often deputizing for them as a speaker at meetings and rallies while they were in London. She was paid a small salary by the WSPU as a part-time organizer in Oldham.

Disillusioned with what she saw as the fanatical and undemocratic outlook of the Pankhursts' leadership, Mitchell joined the breakaway Women's Freedom League after the WSPU split in 1907. She was also hurt by the Pankhursts' apparent lack of interest in her poor health. During World War I, Mitchell's pacifist stance distanced her from many in the suffrage movement but heightened her commitment to socialism. She refounded a local branch of the ILP in 1918 and remained active in labor politics during the interwar years.

Mitchell is best known through her autobiography, *The Hard Way Up*, written in her seventies. In it she stressed the hardships faced by working women involved in active politics. Pointing out that women were forced to juggle paid work with domestic responsibilities and were often opposed by their husbands, she argued that "most of us who were married had one hand tied behind us."

See also Britain; Independent Labour Party; Pankhurst, Christabel; Pankhurst, Emmeline; Pankhurst, (Estelle) Sylvia; Peace Movement; Socialism in Europe; Women's Freedom League; Women's Social and Political Union.
References Liddington, Jill, and Jill Norris. *One Hand Tied Behind Us: The Rise of the Women's Suffrage Movement* (1978); Mitchell, Hannah. *The Hard Way Up* (1977).

Montefiore, Dora

Dora Montefiore (1851–1933) was a British suffrage campaigner, a socialist, and an internationalist. Born into a large middle-class family in Surrey, England, and privately educated, she went to Australia in 1874 to keep house for her brother. In 1881 she married George Barrow Montefiore, a merchant, and had two children. When her husband died at sea in 1889, she realized that she had no rights of guardianship over her children because her husband had not willed them to her.

Montefiore met other women in the same position and began to make connections between the legal inequalities faced by women and their lack of a vote. The first meeting of the Womanhood Suffrage League of New South Wales took place in her home in 1891, and she became its recording secretary. In the following year she returned to England, where she helped those who were attempting to persuade the Liberal Party to change its policy on women's suffrage. In the late 1890s, however, she became more interested in socialist politics and joined the Marxist group the Social Democratic Federation, becoming a member of its executive committee in 1903.

While her politics were changing from liberalism to socialism, Montefiore continued to be active in the suffrage movement. At first she was a member of the National Union of Women's Suffrage Societies (NUWSS), but her main friendships were with women who were impatient with the cautious methods of the NUWSS and were disillusioned with the Liberal Party, such as Elizabeth Wolstenholme-Elmy. Montefiore was attracted, therefore, to the Women's Social and Political Union (WSPU) and formed a branch of the union in London, where she worked enthusiastically alongside Sylvia Pankhurst and Annie Kenney to build up support. In 1906 she gained notoriety by refusing to pay her taxes. This led to a six-week siege by bailiffs of her home, known in the press as Fort Montefiore. In the same year she was among a group of WSPU members who were sent to prison for disruptive behavior. Montefiore had always seen the attainment of limited women's suffrage as a stepping-stone toward her goal of votes for all men and women over the age of 21. In 1907, therefore, she joined the Adult Suffrage Society, becoming its honorary secretary in 1909.

Montefiore also tried to pursue her suffragist and socialist goals through transnational organizations, attending conferences of the International Woman Suffrage Alliance (IWSA) and the International Bureau for Socialist Women. She was often at the center of controversy and her credentials were challenged on a number of occasions, both because of her private life and because of her politics. Margaret MacDonald of the British socialist group the Independent Labour Party, sought to have her removed from the position of recording secretary at the 1899 International Congress of Women because of the rumor that she had had an improper relationship with a married, working-class man. In 1906 there was an attempt by NUWSS delegates to stop her from speaking at the IWSA Congress because she was a member of the militant WSPU, but on this occasion she was allowed to address the audience for 20 minutes.

Montefiore's attempt to work for both women's suffrage and for socialism, her unconventional outlook, her emphasis on class conflict, and her eventual support of the adult suffrage movement meant that she faced hostility within both the socialist and the women's movement at home and abroad. Nonetheless, she played an important role in suffrage politics through her journalism, her international contacts, and her willingness to initiate militant activities. She continued to work for the Adult Suffrage Society until the vote was won in 1918 and was later to be a founding member of the British Communist Party. Dora Montefiore returned to Australia in 1921 and despite failing health still attended international communist conferences. She wrote an account of her life, *From a Victorian to a Modern*, which was published in 1927.

See also Independent Labour Party; International Woman Suffrage Alliance; Kenney, Annie; National Union of Women's Suffrage Societies; Pankhurst, (Estelle) Sylvia; Wolstenholme-Elmy, Elizabeth; Women's Social and Political Union.

References Hunt, Karen. *Equivocal Feminists, The Social Democratic Federation and the Woman Question, 1884–1911* (1996); Montefiore, Dora. *From a Victorian to a Modern* (1927).

Mott, Lucretia Coffin

Quaker minister and abolitionist Lucretia Coffin Mott (1793–1880) was one of the pioneers of the American women's rights movement and an architect of the Seneca Falls Convention. As the daughter of a Nantucket whaling master, Mott was born into a community with a tradition of female equality. However, she soon discovered the financial disadvantages women suffered when she became a schoolteacher and received lower pay than her male colleagues. Following her ordination at the age of 28, she had ample practice in public speaking and became actively involved in the abolitionist movement, founding the first female antislavery society.

Mott met Elizabeth Cady Stanton in 1840 at the World Anti-Slavery Convention in London, where both women were excluded from the proceedings. This proved to be an influential meeting. Inspired by the ideas of the early feminist Mary Wollstonecraft, whose book, *A Vindication of the Rights of Woman,* she revered, Mott exercised a strong influence on the younger Stanton. The two women joined together again eight years later to call the first Women's Rights Convention at Seneca Falls. Yet despite her key position at the convention, Mott was not initially in favor of women's suffrage. She discouraged Stanton from drafting a resolution on the franchise, warning her: "Thou will make us ridiculous. We must go slowly" (Flexner, 1975, 76). She was influenced here by the Quaker boycott of involvement in electoral politics.

Mott subsequently modified this view, becoming an active campaigner for women's rights. In 1850 she published *Discourse on Women,* in which she high-

Lucretia Mott, abolitionist and suffragist, was one of the five women who called the Seneca Falls Convention that began the women's rights movement in the United States. (Library of Congress)

lighted women's educational and political disadvantages and their restricted professional opportunities. Following the abolition of slavery, she joined the Equal Rights Association, formed in 1866, which attempted unsuccessfully to create a joint platform for black and woman suffrage. However, as a strong supporter of the African American vote she expressed her disapproval when Stanton enlisted the support of the racist Democrat George Train.

Mott continued to be an important moral force in the women's rights movement until her death in 1880. Her last two years were spent trying to reconcile the two rival suffrage societies, the National Woman Suffrage Association, led by Susan B. Anthony and Elizabeth Cady Stanton, and the American Woman Suffrage Association, led by Lucy Stone and Henry Blackwell.

See also Anthony, Susan B.; Antislavery Movement; Fourteenth and Fifteenth Amendments; National American Woman Suffrage Association; National Woman Suffrage Association; Protestantism; Stanton, Elizabeth Cady; Stone, Lucy; United States of America; Women's Rights Convention, Seneca Falls.
References Banks, Olive. *Faces of Feminism: A Study of Feminism as a Social Movement* (1981); DuBois, Carol Ellen. *Feminism and Suffrage: The Emergence of an Independent Women's Suffrage Movement in America, 1848–1869* (1978); Flexner, Eleanor. *Century of Struggle: The Woman's Rights Movement in the United States* ([1959] 1975).

Mozzoni, Anna Maria

Anna Maria Mozzoni (1837–1920) was the most prominent feminist and suffragist in Italy in the nineteenth century. She came from an impoverished upper-class family in Milan that sympathized with Giuseppe Mazzini's liberal republican and nationalist ideas. In 1864 Mozzoni gained recognition for her feminist politics when she published *La Donna e i suoi rapporti sociali* (Woman and Her Social Relationships), which called for middle-class women to look beyond their domestic world. She translated John Stuart Mill's *On the Subjection of Women* into Italian, wrote numerous pamphlets on feminist themes, and contributed regularly to the feminist newspaper *La Donna*. Mozzoni was the friend of leading Italian politicians who were sympathetic to women's enfranchisement, such as Salvatore Morelli, and in 1877 she organized a women's suffrage petition.

It was difficult to make progress, however, without a strong feminist organization that could back up her demands. When the first congress of Italian feminists was held in Rome in 1908, Mozzoni found that women were divided among themselves and lacked a clear program of action. She turned for support to other political groups, notably the socialists. Her effectiveness was limited, however, because of her strong commitment to a liberal feminist outlook. This meant that she was almost alone among feminists and socialists in opposing protective legislation for female workers on the grounds that it implied an acceptance of inequality between the sexes. Nonetheless, through her writings she played an important part in introducing feminist ideas to Italy and ensuring that women's rights, including suffrage, received attention in political circles.

See also Italy; Mill, John Stuart; Nationalism; *On the Subjection of Women*.
Reference LaVigna, Claire. "The Marxist Ambivalence toward Women: Between Socialism and Feminism in the Italian Socialist Party" (1978).

Mud March (1907)

The so-called Mud March, which took place in London on 9 February 1907, was the first major outdoor women's suffrage procession to be held in Britain. The march was staged by the National Union of Women's Suffrage Societies (NUWSS), and over 40 different women's organizations took part, although the militant Women's Social and Political Union (WSPU) was not sent an official invitation because of objections from the Women's Liberal Federation. Led by Millicent Fawcett, Lady Frances Balfour, and Lady Jane Strachey, 3,000 women marched with colorful banners and massed bands from Hyde Park Corner to Exeter Hall in the pouring rain—hence the name Mud March. There is no doubt that the impact of so many respectable women marching in the streets of London was extremely effective in promoting the suffrage cause, and this remarkable spectacle established a model for future large-scale women's suffrage processions.

See also Fawcett, Millicent Garrett; National Union of Women's Suffrage Societies; Women's Social and Political Union.
Reference Tickner, Lisa. *The Spectacle of Women: Imagery of the Suffrage Campaign, 1907–1914* (1987).

Myanmar (formerly Burma)

Burmese women first gained a very limited franchise in 1923, while the country was still part of India and under British rule. Under the terms of the Constitution of 1923, the franchise was linked to payment of taxes with no distinction of sex. However, because only men became liable to pay a small poll tax at the age of 18, relatively few women actually qualified to vote. At this time the electorate consisted of 2 million men and only 125,000 women.

Although some were now able to vote, women were still barred from becoming members of the legislature under the terms of the Reform Act of 1919. This could only be changed by making resolutions to provincial legislatures to remove the discriminatory clause. In 1927 a resolution was made by a member of the Legislative Council to delete the clause but was opposed by the British administration. To rally support for the resolution, a demonstration in Rangoon was held by the National Council of Women in Burma, which had been formed a year earlier. The council made an appeal to women to join a march from the Municipal Corporation, which did admit women members, to the Legislative Council building in the Secretariat compound, which did not. A hundred women joined the demonstration, including Europeans, Anglo-Burmese, Chinese, Indians, and Burmese, carrying banners with the names of women legislators from other countries, such as Viscountess Astor from Britain. The demonstrators were met by mounted police and locked out of the Secretariat, although a few women were offered tickets to hear the debate in the Visitors Gallery. The women refused and dispersed peacefully, but the defeat of the motion caused considerable concern among Burmese people who resented foreign influences on the government in what should have been solely a domestic issue. The clause was eventually removed in 1929, and the first woman to enter the legislature was the sister of one of the great nationalist leaders, U Chit Hlaing. Yet few women subsequently sat either on the municipal councils or the Legislative Assembly.

When in 1937 the Government of Burma Act came into force, Burma ceased to be a province of India. Although it remained under British rule, it had its own legislative body. Women could now vote for members of the House of Representatives if they passed a basic literacy test. The female electorate was thus raised to 750,000. This constitution was dissolved when the Japanese occupied Burma in 1942 and established an authoritarian and undemocratic, though nominally independent, Burmese state. Women regained the vote and became fully enfranchised in 1948, after the British had reoccupied Burma and subsequently granted the country full independence.

See also Imperialism; India; Nationalism.
References Furnivall, J. S. *The Governance of Modern Burma* (1960); Mya Sein, Daw. "Toward Independence in Burma: The Role of Women" (1972).

Naidu, Sarojini

A leading campaigner for the enfranchisement of Indian women and a prominent nationalist who was imprisoned for her beliefs, Sarojini Chattopadhyaya (1879–1949) was born in Hyderabad, India, into a Brahmin family, at a time when the subcontinent was under British rule. In 1895 she was sent to England to attend King's College, London, and Girton College, Cambridge, and in 1898 she married Dr. G. R. Naidu.

In December 1917, already heavily involved in political life, Naidu led an all-India women's delegation to meet the Montagu-Chelmsford Committee on constitutional reform, to ask for the enfranchisement of Indian women on the same basis as men. In August 1918 she spoke on behalf of the women's suffrage campaign to a meeting of the Indian National Congress held in Bombay, where she gained considerable support, and at about the same time other political organizations, including the All-India Muslim League, declared their approval for the women's campaign.

In 1919 Naidu and Annie Besant, a fellow nationalist campaigner, went to London as representatives of the Women's Indian Association (WIA) to speak to the Joint Parliamentary Committee on the Government of India Bill. In her address to the committee, Naidu asked for female enfranchisement on behalf of all Indian women, whatever their religious affiliation, thus voicing a strong belief in Hindu-Muslim unity that was to remain with her until the end of her life. While they were in London, Naidu and Besant addressed many public meetings and won support for their case from British women's organizations. As a result of their persistent campaigning, small numbers of Indian women were granted the vote by provincial legislatures during the 1920s.

In 1925 Naidu became the second woman president of the Indian National Congress (Besant was the first), and she supported the decision to boycott the Simon Commission set up to review and propose constitutional reforms. However, in 1931 she was the official representative of the Indian women's organizations to the second Round Table Conference in London, where with Mohandas Gandhi, the leader of the home rule movement, she demanded full adult suffrage, but without success. Despite this setback, some progress was made under the 1935 Government of India Act, when 6 million women were enfranchised as part of a limited electorate of 36 million.

Naidu died in 1949, two years after India gained its independence and in the same year that the new constitution granted universal adult suffrage. She is generally considered to be the most influential woman in Indian political life during the fight for independence and a leading figure in the campaign for Indian women's suffrage.

See also India; Nationalism; Sri Lanka.
References Baig, T. A. *Sarojini Naidu* (1974); Forbes, Geraldine. *Women in Modern India* (1996); Sengupta, P. *Sarojini Naidu: A Biography* (1966).

National American Woman Suffrage Association

The National American Woman Suffrage Association (NAWSA) was established in 1890, thus bringing together suffrage campaigners in the United States into a single national organization over 20 years after the movement had split. Unity was possible because the International Council of Women, meeting in 1888, had shown that members of the different groups could work together, and the National Woman Suffrage Association had narrowed its aims to concentrate on suffrage. Nonetheless, it took three years of discussion before a merger was achieved between the National Woman Suffrage Association and the American Woman Suffrage Association. The first two presidents of NAWSA, Elizabeth Cady Stanton, 1890–1892, and Susan B. Anthony, 1892–1900, were pioneer suffragists with a great deal of experience, but little progress was made at the national level. The leaders disagreed about the best tactics to use, and no central direction was given to state campaigns. Moreover, pressure for a federal amendment was less effective when NAWSA decided to meet biennially in Washington rather than annually.

Some improvements were introduced by Carrie Chapman Catt, who tried to make membership and financial arrangements more systematic when she ran the Organization Committee and then acted as president between 1900 and 1904. Unfortunately, her successor, Dr. Anna Shaw, had far less administrative ability. She was an inspiring speaker, and under her leadership membership of NAWSA grew from 17,000 to 200,000, but the organization had no permanent home and lacked a clear strategy. This led to numerous resignations at the leadership level, and the organization struggled to maintain any stability. After 1910, however, things began to improve. NAWSA gained a permanent home in New York in 1910 and began to take an interest in the labor struggles of working women who were also becoming involved in the suffrage campaign.

There was a revival of interest in a federal women's suffrage amendment after Alice Paul became chairwoman of NAWSA's Congressional Committee. With her friend Lucy Burns, she came to Washington, D.C., and organized a parade the day before Woodrow Wilson's inauguration as president. This event gained considerable publicity for the cause. Paul then established a new group, the Congressional Union, to campaign vigorously for a federal amendment. The NAWSA leadership was not yet ready to endorse these tactics and also disagreed with the Congressional Union's strategy of opposing the Democrats, who were the party in power, and therefore the Congressional Union became independent of the NAWSA.

NAWSA still equivocated about its strategy and suffered from further turnover in its leadership, but a turning point came when Carrie Chapman Catt again assumed the presidency in 1915. She gathered around her a group of women who were committed to working all-out for the suffrage and developed a consistent strategy for achieving the vote. This entailed concentrating on a federal amendment, attempting to persuade President Wilson to give his support, and organizing a detailed plan to mobilize support from all the state suffrage groups. The role of the state groups varied from state to state, depending on the progress of the local campaign and whether or not women already had the vote.

Women did finally gain the vote. Although a number of factors were responsible for this victory, including the publicity generated by the militants and the impact of the war, the NAWSA certainly played its part. The painstaking organization, lobbying, and petitioning carried out by the association at the state and national levels over the next few years were important in ensuring that enough votes were cast, particularly in the Senate, to ratify the Nineteenth Amendment in 1920. After the vote was won, the NAWSA became the League of Women Voters and concentrated on educating women in citizenship, fighting political corruption, and supporting social reforms such as child labor legislation and protective legislation for women.

See also American Woman Suffrage Association; Anthony, Susan B.; Catt, Carrie Chapman; Citizenship; National Woman Suffrage Association; Nineteenth Amendment; Paul, Alice; Stanton, Elizabeth Cady; United States of America.
References Bolt, Christine. *The Women's Movements in the United States and Britain from the 1790s to the 1920s* (1993); Flexner, Eleanor. *Century of Struggle: The Woman's Rights Movement in the United States* ([1959] 1975).

National Council of Women of Canada

Founded in 1893 by Lady Aberdeen (whose husband was governor-general of Canada at the time), the National Council of Women of Canada was arguably the most influential women's organization in Canada during the campaign for women's suffrage. The council was to play a significant part in promoting the suffrage cause, especially among the middle-class and influential women who could give the movement the respectability it needed.

Lady Aberdeen was also the president of the International Council of Women (ICW), which had been founded in the United States in 1888, with the aim of bringing together women from different countries in their own affiliated national councils in order to address questions of political, social, and moral reform. The National Council of Women of Canada carried out its work through a network of Local Councils of Women that were established in many of Canada's towns and cities. The National Council's first concern

was not the suffrage cause, but because all women's organizations were welcome to join the council, it was natural that women's suffrage groups should become affiliated with it. The Dominion Women's Enfranchisement Association (DWEA), founded in 1889 by Dr. Emily Howard Stowe, was a member society of the National Council from its inauguration, submitting its report on women's suffrage activities each year and holding special conferences at the National Council's annual meetings, where women who might never have been exposed to the arguments for women's suffrage were given the opportunity to become involved in the campaign.

In 1904 the National Council of Women established a Standing Committee on Suffrage and the Rights of Citizenship, presided over by Dr. Augusta Stowe-Gullen of Toronto until 1921. Under her leadership, this committee gathered suffrage news from all over Canada and publicized the gains made by women's groups. In 1910, at its annual conference in Halifax, Nova Scotia, the National Council of Women, by a vote of 71 to 51, formally endorsed women's suffrage. It was this act that brought Local Councils of Women from all over the country into the suffrage fold, significantly contributing to the ultimate success of the campaign to enfranchise Canadian women.

See also Canada; Citizenship; International Council of Women; Stowe, Emily Howard.
References Cleverdon, Catherine L. *The Women's Suffrage Movement in Canada* (1974); Strong-Boag, Veronica. *The Parliament of Women: The National Council of Women of Canada, 1893–1929* (1976).

National Union of Women's Suffrage Societies

The National Union of Women's Suffrage Societies (NUWSS) was the largest suffrage group in Britain. After a period of splits and disagreements in the suffrage movement, the formation of the NUWSS

A caravan in Yorkshire, England, bears the banner of the National Union of Women's Suffrage Societies. (Mary Evans Picture Library/Fawcett)

in 1897 brought a new unity to the campaign. The NUWSS was a democratic organization; the membership decided policy at annual conferences and also elected the executive committee, and affiliated groups were able to exercise considerable autonomy. It became identified, however, with Millicent Fawcett, who was formally elected as president in 1907, a post she was to hold until after partial enfranchisement had been achieved.

The union's aim was to obtain votes for women on the same terms as "it is or may be granted to men," and it sought to achieve this end by constitutional methods. These included petitioning Parliament, lobbying political parties, and holding public meetings. The tactics adopted by the NUWSS were radicalized, however, by the militancy of the rival suffrage group, the Women's Social and Political Union (WSPU). The NUWSS began to organize public demonstrations—the first of these, which attracted 3,000 women, took

place in February 1907 and was known as the Mud March because of the torrential rain that accompanied it. Subsequent demonstrations were far larger, and in 1913 the NUWSS organized a pilgrimage, with women marching from all parts of the country to London. Meetings were held in a variety of locations ranging from drawing rooms in private houses to public halls and street corners, and NUWSS speakers visited many towns and villages during the union's suffrage caravan tours, which lasted several weeks.

The extensive propaganda carried out by the NUWSS—including the sale of its own newspaper, the *Common Cause*, established in 1909—coupled with the publicity generated by the militancy of the WSPU, led to a growth in membership; by 1909 the union had 70 affiliated societies with 13,161 members, and in 1914 there were 480 affiliated societies and over 53,000 members. Although its broad, democratic structure enabled women with a variety of views to work together, there were tensions in the NUWSS over tactics and political strategies. The leadership was drawn largely from educated, upper-middle-class women, but working-class women in particular from the textile districts of Lancashire increasingly became involved and demanded a voice. Some of them, notably Selina Cooper and Ada Nield Chew, a tailoress, were employed by the union as organizers.

The strategy of the NUWSS was to support any candidate for election who pledged support for women's suffrage, regardless of party affiliation. In 1912, however, after increasing frustration at the failure of the Liberal government to introduce a suffrage measure, the NUWSS formed an electoral alliance with the Labour Party, which had decided to refuse to support any franchise reform bills that did not include votes for women. An Election Fighting Fund Committee was formed to raise money to support Labour candidates. A number of by-elections were fought, without success, before the outbreak of war in 1914 put an end to suffrage campaigning.

The NUWSS was divided during the war—the union officially gave support to the war effort but a significant group of women from the executive committee resigned to take part in the women's peace movement. Although the union concentrated on relief work, many branches still maintained their interest in the suffrage cause and were well placed to begin campaigning again in 1916 when the government announced its intention to introduce a new franchise bill. A measure of enfranchisement was achieved in 1918, and the NUWSS changed its name a year later to the National Union of Societies for Equal Citizenship. Under the leadership of Eleanor Rathbone, it continued to campaign for equal voting rights for women, alongside a range of other reforms, until success was achieved in 1928.

Often overshadowed by the more dramatic actions of the WSPU, the NUWSS nevertheless continued to attract members up to and beyond World War I. It could be suggested that the union's more conciliatory attitude and eventual links with the labor movement enabled it to gain more widespread support for women's suffrage, making it difficult for the government to omit women from legislation to extend the franchise at the end of the war.

See also Britain; Fawcett, Millicent Garrett; Mud March; Pilgrimage, Suffrage; Rathbone, Eleanor; Women's Social and Political Union. *References* Holton, Sandra Stanley. "Women and the Vote" (1995); Hume, Leslie Parker. *The National Union of Women's Suffrage Societies, 1897–1914* (1982).

National Woman Suffrage Association

The National Woman Suffrage Association was founded in 1869 by Elizabeth Cady Stanton and Susan B. Anthony. It was formed in the wake of an acrimonious split in the U.S. women's rights movement over the Fourteenth and Fifteenth Amendments to the Constitution, which offered the vote to Black men but not to women. Stanton and Anthony felt betrayed by other members of the American Equal Rights Association (formed in 1866 to link the Black and women's suffrage causes) who supported the Fifteenth Amendment. They therefore decided to form a separate association that excluded men and that proclaimed its hostility to the Black male vote while women remained disenfranchised.

The group's main objective was to achieve the national franchise for women, concentrating mainly on federal rather than state politics. It tried to get legal backing for the claim that women already had the vote on the grounds that the Constitution referred to "persons" and, from 1878 onward, it made repeated, unsuccessful attempts to introduce a constitutional amendment in favor of female suffrage. The group's leaders adopted a radical cam-

The National Woman Suffrage Association sent organizers to all major party conventions. They argued that former Negro slaves could vote, so why couldn't women? (Ann Ronan Picture Library)

paigning style, including speaking tours and mass meetings. Their main argument for the vote was based on the rights of women as individuals, and as the century progressed, their appeal was increasingly confined to middle-class women and became less radical in tone. By the late 1880s they had more in common with their moderate rival, the American Woman Suffrage Association led by Lucy Stone, and in 1890 the two groups merged to form the National American Woman Suffrage Association.

See also American Woman Suffrage Association; Anthony, Susan B.; Fourteenth and Fifteenth Amendments; National American Woman Suffrage Association; Stanton, Elizabeth Cady; Stone, Lucy; United States of America.
References Evans, Richard J. *The Feminists: Women's Emancipation Movements in Europe, America and Australasia, 1840–1920* (1977); Flexner, Eleanor. *Century of Struggle: The Woman's Rights Movement in the United States* ([1959] 1975).

National Woman's Party

The National Woman's Party (NWP), formed in the United States in June 1916, adopted militant methods in the struggle for the vote. It was founded by the Congressional Union, an organization led by Alice Paul, who had been influenced by the militancy of the Women's Social and Political Union while staying in England before World War I. The NWP, whose membership was generally drawn from well-educated, middle- and upper-class women, was established to campaign against Democratic congressional candidates and President Woodrow Wilson in the 12 states that had equal voting rights. The campaign was unsuccessful, but this spurred the NWP on to greater militancy. In January 1917 pickets were set up outside the White House, resulting in the arrest and imprisonment of some women for obstruction. Those who went on hunger strike were forcibly fed and received a great deal of publicity in the press. Further acts of militancy included the burning of the president's speeches and his effigy and the holding of demonstrations, but there was no destruction of property.

By its actions, the NWP did help to bring women's suffrage to the forefront of American politics, but the harassment of Democratic candidates and President Wilson also alienated many potential supporters. The NWP, which contained many Quakers in its ranks, remained single-minded in its pursuit of the vote even after the United States entered World War I, and members were frequently accused of being pro-German and unpatriotic. They were astute, however, in making the connection between their country's claim to be fighting a war for democracy abroad and the lack of democracy at home. Moreover, the chairman of the Senate Suffrage Committee did visit imprisoned women just before recommending that action should be taken on a suffrage amendment. The NWP joined with its rival, the National American Woman Suffrage Association, in a joint lobby of members of the House to ensure that the suffrage amendment would be passed on 10 January 1918.

After the vote was finally ratified in 1920, the NWP reorganized itself and declared that its new commitment was to achieve an equal rights amendment to the Constitution. In the campaign that was waged throughout the 1920s, the NWP sought to redefine the agenda of American politics to include women's special interests.

See also Hunger Strikes; National American Woman Suffrage Association; Paul, Alice; United States of America; Women's Social and Political Union.
References Bolt, Christine. *The Women's Movements in the United States and Britain from the 1790s to the 1920s* (1993); Patterson, Cynthia M. "New Directions in the Political History of Women: A Case Study of the National Woman's Party's Campaign for the Equal Rights Amendment, 1920–1927" (1982).

Nationalism

National aspirations began to be aroused during the period of the French Revolution and the subsequent establishment of the Napoleonic empire throughout Europe, which lasted until 1815. The people of Europe developed a national consciousness in their struggle against foreign occupation, and supporters of nationalist struggles often expounded a doctrine that saw communities of race, language, culture, and sometimes religion as constituting aspects of "the nation." The encouragement of a strong sense of national identity and a belief in the right to enjoy self-determination gave rise to many nationalist movements in all parts of the world during the nineteenth and twentieth centuries. One of the main planks of any nationalist program was the achievement of political rights in some form, so it was inevitable that women's desire for political equality often worked together with the struggle for independence.

Richard Evans has taken a detailed look at the links between feminism and the nationalist movements in Scandinavia and the Nordic countries and takes the example of Finland to show these connections. Finland had been under Swedish political and cultural domination for most of its history, until, in 1809, it became subject to Russian rule. The conflicts that arose between different language groups resulted in an outbreak of intense nationalist activity. Alexandra Gripenberg, the leading Finnish moderate feminist, made the connection between the call for national self-determination and women's self-assertion, when she observed that the nationalist movement, by encouraging mothers to teach their children the Finnish language, "became also an indirect means of awakening the women to a sense of their rights and responsibilities" (Evans, 1977, 86).

Nationalism also played a role in the growth of the feminist movement in Iceland, under the rule of the Danish crown until 1944. Opposition to the ruling power drove forward the struggle for women's suffrage, and the Kvenréttindafélag Islands (the Icelandic Women's Rights Association) presented women's political rights as a nationalist issue, particularly as the Danish king had delayed women's municipal suffrage until 1902. In Norway, too, nationalism was the key to radicalizing the movement for female enfranchisement, although women had to wait for independence from Sweden before they gained the vote in 1913.

In Czechoslovakia, which was under the rule of the Habsburg Empire, where German was the language of administration, a strongly nationalist women's movement was supported by an influential Protestant minority. In 1912 Czech suffragists refused to send a delegation to a feminist congress in Vienna because only the German language would be used, and in the same year they sought the help of Czech nationalists in an attempt to stop the Habsburg government from removing the existing limited franchise for women. The situation in Hungary was extremely complex because of the mixture of nationalities within its borders. After self-rule was granted in 1867, the aristocratic Magyars gained control of the country and had to fight off the constant threat of dissident rival nationalities within Hungary. Women had a record of being active in both nationalist and feminist movements in Hungary for many years, but women suffrage campaigners were divided by nationalist differences, which made it difficult to make any progress on the women's franchise issue.

One of the most important links between nationalism and women's political rights can be found in India, which was under British imperial rule until 1947. The demand for women's suffrage began in 1917, when a delegation from the Women's Indian Association (WIA) led by Sarojini Naidu, an active nationalist, went to ask a British constitutional committee for equal voting rights with men. From the 1920s onward, women gained a limited vote in the provincial legislatures and continued their fight for wider suffrage measures. However, nationalist leader Mohandas Gandhi, who had launched his campaign of noncooperation with the British, expected women to put the fight for Indian independence first. This caused a genuine conflict of interest for Indian feminists, which was exacerbated by the fact that Muslim women were increasingly concerned that their views on women's suffrage be taken into consideration.

This conflict was repeated in other countries under British colonial rule, particularly in West Africa, where, for example, the women of Ghana and Sierra Leone subdued their interest in political equality to become prominent members of the nationalist movement. All over Africa, women under colonial governments put the fight for independence before their own interests, believing that self-rule would bring them the political rights they needed. This was also true of many of the countries in the Middle East that were under colonial control until after the end of World War II. In Egypt, women played a prominent role in the 1919 revolution against the British, and this gave them the impetus to start a feminist movement that began the demand for a limited franchise. Often Egyptian women were united on the issue of national independence but found it difficult to agree on how to obtain the franchise, and the conflicting demands of both movements caused a number of problems.

The links between movements for women's political rights and nationalist movements were often strong, but many women encountered a conflict of interest, and they had to prioritize one at the expense of the other. A belief that self-determination would bring equal rights spurred many women on, although sometimes the hoped-for political emancipation was slow to take place.

See also Czechoslovakia; Egypt; Finland;
Ghana; Hungary; Iceland; Imperialism; India;
Norway; Sierra Leone.
References Evans, Richard. *The Feminists:
Women's Emancipation Movements in Europe, America and Australasia, 1840–1920*
(1977); Forbes, Geraldine. *Women in Modern India* (1996); Jayawardena, Kumari.
*Feminism and Nationalism in the Third
World* (1986); Nelson, Barbara J., and
Najma Chowdhury, eds. *Women and Politics
Worldwide* (1994); Philipp, Thomas. "Feminism and Nationalist Politics in Egypt"
(1978).

The Netherlands

A strong suffrage movement developed in
the Netherlands after the late nineteenth
century. The Vereeniging voor Vrouwenkiesrecht (VVVK) [Woman Suffrage Association], founded in 1894 and led by
Aletta Jacobs after 1903, had 62 branches
and 6,500 members in 1909 and 108
branches with 14,000 members in 1913.
In 1907 there were internal disagreements
about the basis on which the vote should
be demanded, and these led to the establishment of a second group, the Nederlandsche Bond voor Vrouwenkiesrecht
(Dutch Woman Suffrage League), which
by 1913 had 62 branches and a membership of 4,800.

Both organizations used similar methods and tactics; they mounted poster campaigns, organized demonstrations, lobbied
political parties, and in 1910 held processions in connection with a special
Women's Suffrage Day. Under Aletta Jacobs's influence, the VVVK was extensively involved in the international suffrage movement. It was affiliated with the
International Woman Suffrage Alliance
(IWSA) as soon as it was founded, and
two other Dutch suffragists, Johanna
Naber, a publicist and feminist historian,
and Martina Kramers, a journalist and
leading member of the VVVK, became
members of the IWSA board. The Dutch
Woman Suffrage League also applied for
membership in the IWSA on the grounds
that its split from the VVVK was on ideological grounds. The application was sent
to all affiliated countries for a judgment
and was turned down. It seems likely that
the influence of IWSA President Carrie
Chapman Catt, who was a close friend of
Aletta Jacobs, played an important part in
the decision.

The Dutch movement was given a boost
when the IWSA agreed to hold its 1908
Congress in Amsterdam. Dutch suffragists
had hoped that this would influence the
Borgesius cabinet, which had agreed to introduce a Constitutional Reform Bill, but
by the time the congress took place, the
Heemskerk government, openly opposed
to women's suffrage, was in power.
Nonetheless, the IWSA congress, which
was reported widely in the press, led to an
increase in membership for the Dutch suffrage groups—the VVVK increased from
2,500 to 6,000—and to the formation of
the Mannenbond voor Vrouwenkiesrecht
(Men's League for Women's Suffrage). By
1911 the Netherlands was one of only
seven member countries of the IWSA that
had a suffrage movement with over 2,500
members. It has been suggested that this
strength derived from the Netherlands'
liberal parliamentary system and also
from the predominance of Protestantism.

With the general election of 1913, constitutional reform once more became an
issue for debate. Three of the liberal political groups decided to form an antigovernment coalition in June and supported the
proposal that there should be universal
male suffrage. Jacobs proposed that suffragists should hold a demonstration at
The Hague to show that Dutch women desired the vote. This alarmed many women
who feared that it would lead to militancy,
but a compromise was reached to enable
women to choose whether or not to join
the march from the train station to the
hall, and hundreds of women turned up
for the demonstration. After the election a
minority government was formed with a

prime minister who was not sympathetic to the women's cause, but for the first time, the queen's speech included a reference to women's suffrage. She announced that the government would seek constitutional reform to allow all men to vote and would remove legal obstacles to women's enfranchisement. When the prime minister claimed that he wished to govern according to public opinion and that women's suffrage was like a leap into the unknown, suffragists organized a national petition calling for equal voting rights between the sexes, obtaining 165,000 signatures. They also wrote to countries that had already introduced women's suffrage to find out how this had worked in practice.

The campaign intensified during 1913, when suffragists distributed pamphlets in working-class districts and made speeches at local markets. This activity was brought to a halt at the outbreak of World War I, although the Netherlands remained neutral, and many suffragists became involved in the peace campaign. Nonetheless, the introduction of a Constitutional Reform Bill in 1916 led to renewed agitation for women's suffrage. Demonstrations were held in Amsterdam and The Hague and women maintained a vigil outside the Parliament Building. Women were not successful in gaining voting rights, but the unusual step was taken of allowing them to stand for office. In the election held under the revised constitution, which had granted universal male suffrage, only one female candidate, Suze Groeneweg, a Social Democrat, was elected, but women used the opportunity to speak to large audiences and to draw attention to the anomalies of their position. By the end of 1918 the government was faced with demands from organized labor and socialists for the eight-hour day and women's suffrage, both of which were conceded by the conservative government that was composed of Christian parties. The leader of the Liberal Democrats, Hendrik Pieter Marchant, had introduced a bill in September 1918 that proposed that women should have the vote on the same terms as men. This was passed by a large majority and received royal assent on 18 September 1919.

See also International Woman Suffrage Alliance; Jacobs, Aletta; Kramers, Martina. **References** Bosch, Mineke, with Annemarie Kloosterman, eds. *Politics and Friendship: Letters from the International Woman Suffrage Alliance, 1902–1942* (1990); Evans, Richard J. *The Feminists: Women's Emancipation Movements in Europe, America and Australasia, 1840–1920* (1977); Jacobs, Aletta. *Memories. My Life as an International Leader in Health, Suffrage and Peace* ([1924] 1996).

New Zealand

In 1893, New Zealand became the first nation state in the world to give women the franchise, allowing all its female citizens to vote in parliamentary elections. Although parliaments in New Zealand during the 1880s and early 1890s generally looked more favorably on the woman's vote than in other Western countries, universal suffrage was not achieved without a struggle. It was aided by the campaigns of a strong and well-organized suffrage movement, with feminist members who had been working to transform the status of women in society over the preceding decades.

By the 1870s and 1880s, New Zealand society was becoming increasingly egalitarian. The principles of democracy and liberalism were generally accepted and the vote was widely extended to all classes of men, including Maoris. Women had made considerable strides toward equality with men in areas such as education, employment, and sport and, inspired by European and American movements for women's rights, feminists were challenging the double moral standard in marriage.

In light of these developments, women's political exclusion appeared increasingly anomalous, and individuals from within and outside Parliament called for a greater degree of representation long before an organized women's suffrage movement was formed. From 1877, most adult women could vote on school boards, and by 1885 women taxpayers gained representation on borough and county councils, on hospital and charitable aid boards, and on liquor licensing committees. Yet despite their enthusiastic participation in politics at a local level, women continued to be denied the right to vote for the national Parliament.

There were three main strands of opinion in Parliament on the suffrage issue: conservatives who disapproved of any woman voting, moderates who favored the enfranchisement of women taxpayers, and radicals who demanded complete emancipation for all women. During the passage of the first suffrage bill, introduced in 1878 by a Liberal government under Sir George Grey, radicals and moderates combined forces in an attempt to gain the vote for women taxpayers. This bill was thrown out over a disagreement connected with the Maori vote. Subsequent bills introduced under John Hall's ministry in 1879, 1880, and 1881 also failed. This was mainly because radicals were no longer prepared to countenance anything other than total democracy and refused to allow the vote to be given to propertied women only. Another negative factor was a widespread anxiety, which cut across all three strands of suffrage opinion, about the prospect of women standing for election and the consequent disruptions this would cause to parliamentary proceedings in the House. There was a tendency among politicians at this time to see women's suffrage as an abstract question unworthy of prolonged debate.

The government was forced to take the suffrage issue more seriously when an organized women's movement emerged in the mid-1880s to spearhead a suffrage campaign. This movement was led by the Woman's Christian Temperance Union (WCTU), formed in 1885 from an American parent body. For many women subjected to the authority of drunken husbands, temperance was a popular cause. Participation in temperance work developed women's practical, organizational, and administrative abilities and gave them opportunities to participate in public activities outside the home, such as lobbying and petitioning. It also enabled them to recognize women's basic rights as citizens. Comparisons between hardworking, clean-living women and disreputable male drunkards made a mockery of ideas about women's inferiority to men and acted as a spur for demands for female political representation.

The WCTU was completely independent of male assistance and acted as a focus for New Zealand women's aspirations and interests more generally. Its main suffrage leader, Kate Sheppard, ensured that every branch elected a member to be responsible for suffrage agitation. Sheppard promoted vigorous press campaigns and produced suffrage literature, such as *Ten Reasons Why the Women of New Zealand Should Vote,* which attracted considerable interest and was used to promote discussion in debating societies and adult education groups. WCTU groups put strong pressure on Parliament, sending in regular petitions and resolutions that had been passed at political meetings. Increasing numbers of women were becoming politically active, attending meetings and canvassing members known to be sympathetic to the cause, such as John Hall, who became leader of the prosuffrage politicians.

The WCTU drew considerable support from working women. It also promoted nationwide petitions that would reach women isolated from suffrage activity in rural areas or who were confined in the home by domestic responsibilities. The group's aim here was to demonstrate that ordinary women wanted the vote. Its most successful petition, carried out in 1893, was the largest ever presented to a New Zealand Parliament, with 30,000 signatures. In 1892 the WCTU encouraged the formation of the Women's Franchise League in order to attract feminists to the campaign who were not in sympathy with temperance. This would show the extent to which women outside the WCTU desired the vote. The league branches were led by union leaders and new recruits, including the wives of politicians.

Despite increasing external pressure from the suffrage campaign, two more bills introduced by Liberals into Parliament in 1887 and 1890 failed to become law. Although politicians made positive speeches and there were impressive majorities in favor of suffrage, many who supported it in public had private reservations. They were therefore willing to allow antisuffrage minorities to get their way. By the early 1890s, there was much speculation about which way women would vote. The majority of the opposition party believed that women would vote Conservative, and this went a long way to converting them to the suffrage cause. Although most Liberals believed that women would never vote Conservative, some were influenced by opposition propaganda and feared that the women's vote would bring about the demise of the Liberal ministry. Thus support for and opposition to women's suffrage cut across party lines. Divisions of this kind played into the hand of a small faction known as "the publican's ring," who feared that giving women the vote would ruin the drink trade.

In 1891 and 1892 Liberal ministries led by John Ballance, who was worried that he might lose power if women were given the vote, ostensibly supported suffrage bills but allowed them to be narrowly de-

feated. In 1893 suffragists redoubled their efforts to convert members of Parliament to their cause. Once again the government, now under Richard Seddon, regarded by suffragists as their worst enemy in the cabinet, privately tried to engineer the defeat of the new suffrage bill. He was foiled by two opponents of suffrage who switched sides at the last minute and enabled the safe passage of the bill into law. These tactics led the *New Zealand Herald* to suggest that "it is hardly too much to say that the enfranchisement of women has been accomplished by her enemies."

The passing of the 1893 Act, which despite opposition from some Maori members of Parliament, enfranchised Maori as well as European women, was greeted with great rejoicing by suffragists throughout the world. The influence of women's vote has been seen as responsible for the growth of humanitarian and social reforms after 1893. Yet, as in other Western countries, women's enfranchisement did not lead to any immediate change in women's role in New Zealand society. New Zealand women did not gain the right to sit in Parliament until 1919. However, many former opponents of suffrage later admitted their mistake; it soon became apparent that their fears of domestic discord and the "unsexing" of women, with the consequent neglect of home and children, were unfounded.

See also Citizenship; Hall, Sir John; Race and Ethnicity; Sheppard, Kate; Woman's Christian Temperance Union.
Reference Grimshaw, Patricia. *Women's Suffrage in New Zealand* (1987).

Newspapers and Journals

Newspapers and journals played a crucial role in the campaign for women's suffrage. During the nineteenth and early twentieth centuries, as education and literacy spread throughout the world, journals and newspapers developed alongside and were a part of a growing women's movement. These publications covered a wide range of issues affecting women's social position, including suffrage, and reported on developments in other countries. Examples include the *Englishwoman's Journal* (1858); the Spanish journal *La Voz de la Mujer* (Woman's Voice); *Nylaende* (New Frontiers), published in Norway in 1887; *La Nueva Mujer* (The New Woman) in Argentina in 1910; the *Chinese Women's Journal,* founded in 1907; the Iranian women's journal *Knowledge;* the Korean journal *Yoja Chinam* (Women's Guide), founded in 1909; and *Nu Gioi Chung* (Women's Bell), first published in Vietnam in 1918. These publications were all unique in style and in political perspective—for instance, the *Chinese Women's Journal* was revolutionary as well as feminist, and *Nylaende* reflected the views of the politically moderate Norwegian Feminist Society—but they all sought to recognize and to challenge aspects of women's subordination.

A number of journals and newspapers were established and edited by individual women who were either active in the women's movement or took an interest in its concerns, and others were associated more closely with a particular organization. In both cases, the editors tended to stamp their own interests and personalities on the content and style of the publications. Julieta Lanteri, for instance, began publishing *La Nueva Mujer* in 1910, and her flamboyant style and anticlericalism gave the journal national notoriety. For her part, Delia Ducoing, editor and director of *Nosotras,* journal of the Unión Femenina de Chile (Women's Union of Chile), was keen to reassure her readers that suffrage would not overturn the existing social order.

As the suffrage movement grew stronger, the number of journals and newspapers devoted largely to the campaign for the vote also grew in quantity and importance. In Britain, for example, the *Women's Suffrage Journal,* established in 1870 and edited by

Women's suffrage organizations countered the popular antisuffrage press with editorial cartoons of their own. This poster by the Artist's Suffrage League was praised by the Common Cause (4 November 1909) for its sense of humor. (Library of Congress)

Lydia Becker, was the first journal to deal specifically with women's suffrage. The intensification of the suffrage campaign and its fragmentation into different groups in the decade before World War I led to a significant increase in the number of suffrage newspapers and journals, which were usually linked to a specific organization. The *Common Cause* (1909), *Votes for Women* (1907), and the *Vote* (1909), for example, were the official newspapers of the National Union of Women's Suffrage Societies, the Women's Social and Political Union (WSPU), and the Women's Freedom League, respectively. Some suffrage newspapers and journals, on the other hand, were produced by the leaders of suffrage organizations, including *La Suffragiste* (The Suffragist), edited by Madeleine Pelletier; *The Revolution,* published between 1868 and 1870 and edited by Elizabeth Cady Stanton; and the *Woman's Journal,* a long-lasting publication established by Lucy Stone and her husband, Henry Blackwell, in 1870. When Emmeline and Frederick Pethick-Lawrence were expelled from the WSPU, they took with them the organization's newspaper, *Votes for Women,* which they edited and largely financed. They used the newspaper to form the basis of a new group, Votes for Women Fellowship.

There was a complex relationship, therefore, between individual and organizational ownership, and questions of finance and editorial control were ever present. It was difficult for suffrage publications that were not owned by suffrage groups to remain solvent through subscriptions and advertising alone, and therefore wealthy backers were often needed. Sources of financing could then influence the content of the paper. For example, the *Revolution* was initially financed by George Train, a financier, speculator, and Democrat who was a controversial figure. He wrote articles on his pet subjects, currency questions, and Fenianism, and Stanton dutifully included these in the newspaper. Madeleine Pelletier's journal was financed from public subscriptions and the private fortune of an associate, Louise Dupont. Pelletier disagreed with Dupont's brand of feminism but found that she had to allow her to publish articles in the journal and always feared losing editorial control.

Newspapers and journals played an integral part in the struggle for women's right to vote. It was assumed that the message that they contained would attract new members to the cause, but it was also thought that they would reinforce an existing commitment to the campaign. To that end, they contained news of the latest events affecting the suffrage movement, publicity about forthcoming meetings, and debates around suffrage questions. Thus, as Antoinette Burton suggests, these publications acted as "workshops for suffrage ideas and strategies" (Burton, 1991, 49). Newspapers and journals enabled women to communicate with each other and to reinforce a sense of solidarity at a time when the written word was paramount. They made it easier for women to find out about the successes and failures of the movement in other countries—information that could then help to strengthen their own campaign. The Norwegian publication *Nylaende,* for instance, had special subscription rates for Norwegian Americans and received numerous foreign journals, including the American publication the *Woman's Journal,* from which it took many news items. British women living abroad had copies of suffrage newspapers sent to them, which was seen as an important way to spread the suffrage message from a British point of view.

Suffrage groups used their publications to demonstrate the strength of their own specific strategies and to justify their position. When *Votes for Women* ceased to be the official organ of the WSPU, for example, Christabel Pankhurst immediately established another newspaper, the *Suffragette,* which became a mouthpiece for her views. Women often subscribed to a variety of suffrage newspapers and journals, but their choice could represent a conscious decision about how they wished to identify themselves. Newspapers and journals, in particular those related to militant groups, were seen not only as a means of communication but also as an integral part of the struggle itself. Women sold them to the public on the street, both as a campaigning method and also as a way to raise funds to ensure the survival of suffrage groups and their publications. It was not always easy to find outlets that would distribute suffrage papers, and therefore women were under even greater pressure to sell their publications at meetings, on the streets, or in the suffrage shops that were a feature of the British movement in the pre-war years. Christabel Pankhurst had difficulty in finding a printer for the *Suffragette* when the Home Office tried to suppress the paper. It was subsequently printed by the presses of the socialist papers, the Glasgow *Forward* and the *Socialist,* and although circulation of the paper was at first 17,000, it fell to 10,000 as the police intimidated shopkeepers who stocked it.

The publication of suffrage newspapers and journals went hand in hand with the growth of the women's suffrage movement and could be seen as a sign of its success. In the United States, for instance, the number of state-based publications such as the New York paper *American Suffragette* increased in the prewar years, attesting to the vitality of the campaign. There was often an uneasy relationship between the political reform objectives of the suffrage press and its business objectives, although it was important for the campaign that its newspapers increase sales and remain solvent. Suffrage newspapers and journals provided new opportunities for a minority of members to gain skills as editors, journalists, and financial managers. Experience with these publications could counter the stereotypes of suffrage activists so often found in the mainstream press, giving women who had been isolated a sense of support and solidarity and an identity as "torchbearers," bringing the light of knowledge and progress to countries throughout the world.

See also Becker, Lydia Ernestine; *The Common Cause*; Lanteri, Julieta; National Union of Women's Suffrage Societies; Pankhurst, Christabel; Pethick-Lawrence, Emmeline; Pethick-Lawrence, Frederick; The *Revolution;* Stanton, Elizabeth Cady; Stone, Lucy; *Votes for Women;* The *Woman's Journal;* Women's Freedom League; Women's Social and Political Union.
References Burton, Antoinette. "The Feminist Quest for Identity: British Imperial Suf-

fragism and 'Global Sisterhood,' 1900–1915" (1991); Crawford, Elizabeth. *The Women's Suffrage Movement: A Reference Guide, 1866–1928* (1999); Finnegan, Margaret. *Selling Suffrage: Consumer Culture and Votes for Women* (1999). Jayawardena, Kumari. *Feminism and Nationalism in the Third World* (1986); Rasmussen, Janet E. "Sisters across the Sea: Early Norwegian Feminists and Their American Connections" (1992); Rendall, Jane. "'A Moral Engine'? Feminism, Liberalism and the *English Woman's Journal*" (1987).

Nicaragua

Women were given the vote in Nicaragua in 1955 during the political reign of Anastasio Somoza García. The constitution under his rule has been described as "a hollow sham, to be alternately flouted, rewritten or given lip service as circumstances demanded" (Black, 1981, 28). Somoza's control over the electoral and legislative process meant that the granting of the vote to women had little real significance in increasing democratization. Under Somoza, quotas of seats in the national legislature were guaranteed to the Conservative and Liberal Parties irrespective of the number of votes cast. By this means Somoza could maintain a dictatorship under the cloak of an apparently representative government. In 1950 the two parties signed a pact that guaranteed Somoza a Liberal majority. The Conservative Party was offered one-third of the seats in Congress in exchange for freedom from economic restrictions.

Although women in the Feminine League of Somoza's Liberal Party had called for the vote in 1932, they had little political clout. In 1939 an "equal protection" clause in the constitution explained women's inferior legal position thus: "All Nicaraguans are equal before the law, except as regards women for the differences that result from her nature and for the good of the family" (Michelle, 1993, 124). However, increased international pressure on Somoza in the mid-1950s, coupled with his desire to gain women's votes for the Liberal Party, led him eventually to give them the franchise. Other legal disadvantages were left unchanged. It was not until after the Sandinista revolution of 1979 that a Statute of Rights and Guarantees secured the unconditional equality of women.

See also Latin America and the Caribbean.
References Black, George. *Triumph of the People: The Sandinista Revolution in Nicaragua* (1981); Saint German, Michelle A. "Paths to Power of Women Legislators in Costa Rica and Nicaragua" (1993).

Nicholls, Elizabeth

Elizabeth Webb Nicholls (1850–1953; née Bakewell) was the president of the Woman's Christian Temperance Union (WCTU) in South Australia for 21 years, from 1889 to 1910, and the WCTU Australasian president for nine years. In this capacity she was a strong voice for the women's suffrage movement throughout Australia.

Nicholls was born into one of Australia's earliest settler families and became an active working member of a Wesleyan church in Adelaide. She took on the South Australian WCTU presidency at the age of 39, when she had seven children at home. During her years as Australian WCTU president, she traveled throughout Australia, offering inspiration to each colonial branch and reinforcing the union's prosuffrage position. In addition to her involvement in colonial campaigns, she argued strongly for the adoption of federal female suffrage and maintained that all Australian women should have a voice in any referendum on the proposed constitution. In her capacity as WCTU Australasian president, Nicholls ensured that the franchise for women was raised at all official meetings between the colonies.

Nicholls was nicknamed the Chieftain and was attributed with many virtues, including tact, dignity, calmness, and wisdom. In 1949, in extreme old age, she pointed out that although they had the vote, women still found it hard to achieve positions of political power and were still organizing to win elections for men.

See also Australia; Woman's Christian Temperance Union.
Reference Oldfield, Audrey. *Woman Suffrage in Australia, A Gift or a Struggle?* (1992).

Nigeria

Nigeria is one of the few African countries south of the Sahara with a strong women's movement and a commitment to female enfranchisement. Women have always played a vital role in Nigeria's economy, but their work has not always been given recognition, with the result that they have had to organize to achieve economic and political rights.

During the precolonial period, Nigerian women were part of the political process, and they often belonged to women's associations that made it possible for them to express their approval or disapproval of the conduct of their political leaders. Although men generally had greater authority and control over political life, women were able to participate in decision making and expected to be heard. However, during the period of British rule (1900–1960), the colonial authorities brought their policies of sexual discrimination with them, and as a result, there were considerable inequalities in education, employment, and political rights. Although many men were offered an education that would enable them to enter the colonial civil service, women were expected to become "good" wives and mothers and were relegated to the margins of Nigerian society.

While Nigeria was under British rule, the constitution changed on a number of occasions. The colonial power created a Legislative Council in 1922, but the franchise for electing the four African members was restricted to wealthy adult males in Lagos and Calabar. Regional assemblies for the Eastern, Western, and Northern Regions were created by the Richards Constitution of 1947, and a new Federal House of Assembly was established by the Macpherson Constitution of 1952, but because the franchise for these legislatures was based on the payment of taxes, few women had a vote.

Most prominent among the women frustrated by their lack of political rights was Funmilayo Ransome-Kuti from western Nigeria. A member of the newly formed nationalist political party, National Council of Nigeria and the Cameroons (NCNC), she set up the Abeokuta Ladies' Club in March 1944, with the aim of teaching women to read. By 1946 the club had expanded to become a political organization, the Abeokuta Women's Union (AWU), committed to promoting the social, economic, and political rights of women, including the right to vote. On 15 May 1949, Ransome-Kuti founded and became president of the Nigerian Women's Union (NWU), with the aim of creating a national organization dedicated to obtaining political equality for all Nigerian women. By 1950 there were branches of the NWU in many areas of Nigeria, especially in the predominantly Muslim Northern Region, where women found it particularly difficult to assert their claims to equality.

In May 1944, shortly after the Abeokuta Ladies' Club was formed, another women's organization, the Women's Party, was set up by Oyinkan Abayomi. The Women's Party sought by "constitutional means the rights of British citizenship in its full measure for the people," and at its first general meeting on 20 September 1944, it had a membership of 358 women, all from the Lagos area. The main objective of the political committee of the Women's Party was to obtain the franchise for women, but it never conducted a formal campaign for this purpose and it did

not have a political manifesto as such. The Women's Party saw itself as a moderate group seeking to protect women's interests, and many of its members agreed that colonialism had provided some positive safeguards for women, despite the lack of political autonomy. Another women's pressure group was started in December 1952 in Ibadan, in the Western Region of Nigeria, by Chief Elizabeth Adekogbe, a political opponent of Ransome-Kuti. She led a delegation to the governor-general, advocating universal suffrage and arguing that the electoral college system made it difficult for women to get beyond the first stage of any elections.

The next development in the women's campaign took place in August 1953, when Ransome-Kuti invited women's organizations to a conference in Abeokuta, where the delegates resolved to form the Federation of Nigerian Women's Societies (FNWS), in order to campaign for universal adult suffrage, dedicated seats in all the regional assemblies, and the right to be consulted when new laws were about to be introduced. At a second annual conference held in July 1954, the FNWS welcomed the fact that the Eastern Region government had introduced universal adult suffrage for regional elections and demanded that the other assemblies do the same.

In 1954 the new Lyttleton Constitution was introduced, which resulted in the first direct federal elections and provided the basis for the Nigerian constitution on independence. Ransome-Kuti stood as the only woman candidate in the elections, and she was unsuccessful. In 1958 the Western House of Assembly followed the example of the Eastern Region and introduced universal adult suffrage on a regional basis, and in 1959 the Southern Cameroons House of Assembly followed suit.

In 1960 Nigeria became independent, and the constitution provided for universal adult suffrage for all federal elections, except in the Northern Region, where, in

The Nineteenth Amendment goes to the states. Suffragists with Speaker of the House Gillette as he signs the resolution. (Library of Congress)

deference to Muslim sensibilities, women did not gain the vote either regionally or federally until 1976, when it was imposed by military decree. Although Ransome-Kuti and the FNWS had approached the governor-general in August 1959 asking for the franchise for Northern Region women, the constitutional conference had rejected their demand. Finally, under the new constitution of 1979 all adult Nigerians were given the vote.

The NWU and the FNWS had articulated the demands of Nigerian women for political and social equality, but after independence the FNWS became a local organization based in Abeokuta and centered around Ransome-Kuti. The organization that was more successful in retaining its membership was a new rival women's group, the National Council of Women's Societies (NCWS), which was formed in 1959 and whose early members included Elizabeth Adekogbe and Oyinkan Abayomi. The NCWS proclaimed itself nonpolitical and won government support and recognition, but the real work in the field of political rights for women had been carried out by the NWU and the FNWS, who had managed to keep the issue of women's suffrage on the political agenda in Nigeria.

See also Africa South of the Sahara; Citizenship; Imperialism; Nationalism; Ransome-Kuti, Funmilayo.
References Johnson-Odim, Cheryl, and Nina Emma Mba. *For Women and the Nation: Funmilayo Ransome-Kuti of Nigeria* (1997); Mba, Nina Emma. *Nigerian Women Mobilized: Women's Political Activity in Southern Nigeria, 1900–1965* (1982).

Nineteenth Amendment (United States)

The Nineteenth Amendment to the Constitution, which gave women in the United States the right to vote, was finally ratified in 1920 after over half a century of campaigning. The wording was the same as that of the "Anthony Amendment," named after Susan B. Anthony, which had been introduced into Congress in 1878 by

Senator A. A. Sargent of California. It read: "the right of citizens of the United States to vote shall not be denied or abridged by the United States or by any state on account of sex." The women's suffrage movement put a great deal of energy into achieving a federal amendment from 1913 onwards, when it became clear that progress at the state level was too slow. Concerted pressure from the suffrage movement, a victory in the New York suffrage referendum in 1917, and women's contribution to the war effort finally persuaded President Woodrow Wilson to declare in favor of the amendment one day before the vote was due to be taken in the House. On 10 January 1918, Congress passed the amendment by exactly the two-thirds majority that was needed, with the bulk of the opposition coming from the South and the industrial states of Massachusetts, Pennsylvania, New Jersey, and Ohio. It took longer to gain the acceptance of the Senate, and over the next few months suffragists had to work hard, particularly at the state level, to increase the number of their supporters. It was not until August 1920 that the Nineteenth Amendment was finally ratified by a margin of two votes, thereby enfranchising 26 million women.

See also Anthony, Susan B.; Citizenship; United States of America.

Norway

Norway was one of the first countries to give women the vote, introducing universal female suffrage in 1913. As in other Nordic countries, notably Finland and Iceland, this development was closely tied to the growth of nationalism. In 1884, after a long struggle with the Swedish crown, Norway managed to establish its own political institutions. Women played a part in this struggle and as a result of their politicization established their own organization, the Norsk Kvinnesaksforening (NKS) [the Norwegian

Feminist Society]. This was a moderate group, open to both sexes, that concentrated on economic and educational reforms. When one of the society's leaders, Gina Krog, proposed that attention should be given to women's suffrage, members showed little interest, and therefore in 1885, with a small group of other women, she established a new association, Kvinnestemmeretsforeningen (KSF) [the Female Suffrage Union], which excluded men.

It was not until the 1890s, however, that women's suffrage became a key political issue, and again this resulted from developments in Norwegian nationalism. Radical Liberals sought complete independence from Sweden, whose king also ruled Norway, and they linked their nationalism with moral questions such as social purity, a sexual code that applied to both men and women, and temperance. Women were thought to be natural supporters of such aims, and Radical Liberals therefore took up the cause of women's suffrage. They introduced suffrage bills in the early 1890s that demanded votes for women on the same terms as men because the Norwegian Liberal Party included universal suffrage for men only in its 1891 program. In 1893 a women's suffrage bill gained a majority in the Storting, the Norwegian Parliament, but did not achieve the two-thirds majority necessary for a constitutional change. In 1894, 12,000 signatures were collected for a women's suffrage petition.

Despite these efforts, women were not included in the franchise reform of 1896 that increased the number of men eligible to vote in local elections. This led to a split within the KSF. Moderate members advocated a property-based franchise and a gradual approach to achieving votes for women, whereas the more radical members sought women's suffrage on equal terms with men and formed a new group, Landekvinnestemmeretsforeningen (LKSF) [National Female Suffrage Union]. Under the able leadership of Frederikke Marie

Qvam, the LKSF grew to double the size of its rival and also attracted women from rural areas. Women associated with the Labor Party also took an interest in votes for women, but demanded a universal franchise. Nonetheless, all of the groups tended to adopt similar methods of pressuring the government, including petitioning, processions, and pamphleteering, while emphasizing that they sought cooperation between the sexes.

After manhood suffrage for national elections was achieved in 1898, the women's cause gained greater support from the Social Democrats, whose suffrage procession, held on 17 May, was devoted exclusively to female suffrage. Growing fears that universal male suffrage might undermine its position also led the Conservative Party to take an interest in a limited suffrage measure for women, and in 1901 women who were property owners or were married to property owners were finally entitled to vote in local elections. When in 1905 the Swedish king was deposed as king of Norway, a referendum that excluded women was held about the future of the monarchy. The LKSF then organized its own plebiscite, and almost 300,000 female votes were cast, compared with 400,000 male votes. The seriousness with which women approached the plebiscite and their loyalty to nationalism impressed the politicians in the Storting. In the 1906 election, women suffragists supported the Radicals, and a Radical victory led to a suffrage measure in 1907 that enfranchised women who already held the municipal vote. This satisfied many suffragists, but the LKSF and socialist women continued to present proposals for a universal franchise to the Storting. Through their newspaper, *Kvinden,* established in 1909, socialist women also sought to persuade women to work for a universal franchise and to use their vote if they had one. The campaign for women's right to exercise the vote on the same terms as men was hampered by the return of a Conservative government in 1909. It was not until the victory of the Radicals in 1912 that a measure of universal women's suffrage was introduced and passed into law in 1913.

The transformation of Norway from a rural to a semi-industrial country, coupled with the willingness of women to take part in nationalist struggles, helped to provide the context for the early achievement of women's suffrage. Nonetheless, the organized suffrage movement also played an important role in keeping the issue in the forefront of national politics and in countering the argument of opponents that women were uninterested in the franchise. Equal voting rights, however, did not ensure that women would play an equal role in formal politics. They were still identified primarily with home and family and for the most part lacked the confidence to enter the political arena. Further, women's groups could not agree about whether there should be a separate Women's Party or a quota of places for women on the electoral lists of political parties. During the interwar years, women never held more than 2.5 percent of seats in local councils and 3 out of the 150 seats in the Storting, and it was not until the 1970s that there were a significant number of female representatives at the local and national levels.

See also Krog, Gina; Nationalism.
References Blom, Ida. "The Struggle for Women's Suffrage in Norway, 1885–1913" (1980); Evans, Richard, J. *The Feminists: Women's Emancipation Movements in Europe, America and Australasia, 1840–1920* (1977).

On the Subjection of Women (1869)

British philosopher John Stuart Mill's classic statement of liberal feminism, *On the Subjection of Women,* was first drafted in 1861 and published in 1869. In writing this work, Mill was certainly influenced by his long-standing relationship with Harriet Taylor, who had written an article entitled "The Enfranchisement of Women" in the *Westminster Review* in 1851.

The book made an immediate impression on educated women and men in many countries. In the same year that it was first published in Britain, it appeared in the United States, Australia, and New Zealand, and in translation in France, Germany, Austria, Sweden, and Denmark. In 1870 it appeared in Polish and Italian, and copies were circulated in Russia, and later, in Finland.

Mill began his book with an attack on the legal and social position of women, which, he contended, subordinated them to men and hindered their development as self-sufficient individuals. As a Victorian liberal, Mill believed in the progress of humankind toward a just society, and the achievement of equal rights for women was part of this gradual improvement in the human condition.

Mill believed that what was called "women's nature" could only be an artificial construct because the sexes had always been viewed in relation to one another and had never been left to develop on their own. The result was an excessive self-abnegation on the part of women, particularly within marriage, where they were legally, and often practically, nothing better than slaves to their husbands. Mill's critique of the existing state of marriage was a powerful one, and he claimed that only equality within marriage in terms of rights and education would lead to "the moral regeneration of mankind." In one of the most significant passages in the book, he asserted that there was no reason why women should not have the suffrage, both parliamentary and municipal, on the same terms as men; women required legal protection, and only possession of the vote would ensure just and equal consideration of their interests.

There have been criticisms of Mill's apparent disregard of the position of single women, his acceptance of the existing division of labor within the family, and his lack of references to the activities of British women who were already beginning to campaign for the changes he advocated. Yet there is no doubt that *On the Subjection of Women* was an important expression of the link between the emancipation of women and liberal political theory. Mill's status as an intellectual and public figure meant that his book was widely read, and his ideas were to influence women's rights campaigners all over the world.

See also Britain; Mill, Harriet Taylor; Mill, John Stuart.
References Mill, John Stuart. *On Liberty and Other Essays* ([1869] 1991); Rossi, Alice S., ed. *Essays on Sex Equality: John Stuart Mill and Harriet Taylor Mill* (1970).

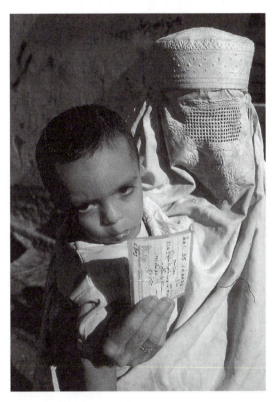

Pakistan and Bangladesh

In 1947 India gained its independence, and as a result of partition, Pakistan became a separate and independent Islamic state. Prior to independence and despite many differences of opinion, Muslim women had worked with their Hindu colleagues in the Indian women's organizations to achieve not only the enfranchisement of women, but also the final goal of universal suffrage for India. However, those Muslim women who became citizens of the new state of Pakistan had to wait a number of years before gaining the vote.

After independence, the Government of India Act of 1935 became the working constitution of Pakistan, which meant that communal electorates were retained and a proportion of women could vote for provincial and central legislatures. The first Constituent Assembly (1947) had two women representatives, Shaista Ikramullah and Jahanara Shah Nawaz of the Muslim League, a seasoned campaigner for women's political rights.

The first Constituent Assembly set up a number of committees to assist in the drawing up of a new constitution. These committees included the Talimaat-i-Islamia, which advised on matters of Islamic law that had to be taken into account when drawing up any new legislation. The members of this committee raised objections to women's suffrage on the grounds that the participation of women in elections could conflict with the requirements of Islam. In

During constitutional discussions after independence from India, conservative Muslims tried to deny Pakistani women the vote but failed. Here a woman exercises her right to vote. (Gamma)

1953, in response to the constitutional debate, a suggestion that 10 seats be reserved for women in the national and provincial assemblies for 10 years came from the All-Pakistan Women's Association (APWA)—which had been founded in 1949 to improve women's welfare and status and had a membership of predominantly urban women from the middle and upper classes.

On 23 March 1956, after years of debate, Pakistan's first constitution was adopted, and it provided for universal adult suffrage. Both men and women could vote for both provincial and national assemblies if they were at least 21 years old and fulfilled a six-month residency qualification. The advice of the APWA was incorporated into the constitution, and 10 seats were reserved for women in the new National Assembly for 10 years, thus giving dual voting rights to women, who could vote for both general seats and reserved women's seats. However, before a general election could be held, the new constitution was abrogated on 7 October 1958.

The Constitution of 1962 only allowed for a system of indirect elections, and although the first general elections in Pakistan were held in 1970, it was not until the Constitution of 1973 that the principle of universal suffrage for all adults 21 years of age and older was reaffirmed. Even this constitution has been amended and, on occasion, suspended.

The state of Bangladesh came into being as a result of the secession of East Pakistan from Pakistan in 1971. The constitution of the new state was promulgated in December 1972, and it provided for universal adult suffrage for all citizens of 18 years and over.

See also Citizenship; India; Shah Nawaz, Jahanara.
Reference Mumtaz, K., and F. Shaheed. *Women of Pakistan: Two Steps Forwards, One Step Back?* (1987).

Pan-American Women's Conference (1922)

The primary aim of the Pan-American Women's Conference, held in Baltimore in 1922, was to further the cause of women's suffrage in the Western Hemisphere. It was sponsored by the Pan-American International Women's Committee, a forum for women who were active in politics throughout North, South, and Central America to meet and work together. The conference, called by Carrie Chapman Catt, the president of the International Woman Suffrage Alliance, was much larger than any previous meeting of women in the Americas, with approximately 2,000 delegates. Women's groups from the United States and Canada were well represented, as were women who were to provide political leadership in Latin America over the next two decades, including Bertha Lutz, the leading women's suffrage activist in Brazil, and Amanda Labarca from Chile.

A number of new suffrage groups were formed in Latin American countries in the wake of this conference, including the Brazilian Woman Suffrage Alliance. The conference also produced the Pan-American Association for the Advancement of Women, whose stated aims included the intention to educate public opinion in favor of granting the vote to women and to secure their political rights. The formation of this association was instigated by the Latin American delegates from Uruguay, Brazil, and Chile. A well-known Mexican activist, Elena Torres, was elected as the Pan-American Association's vice president for North America, and Bertha Lutz became the vice president for South America.

See also Latin America and the Caribbean; Lutz, Bertha.
References Miller, Francesca. "The International Relations of Women in the Americas, 1890–1928" (1983); Miller, Francesca. *Latin American Women and the Search for Social Justice* (1991).

Pan-American Women's Movement

The pan-American women's movement grew out of a conference held in Baltimore in 1922 that was called by the international feminist leader Carrie Chapman Catt. The Pan-American Association for the Advancement of Women was created at the meeting, a group with a broad range of aims relating to women's rights and improved communications among all American countries, including furtherance of the cause of women's suffrage. Catt became its first president and subsequently embarked on a lecture tour of Latin American countries in 1922 and 1923, visiting Brazil, Argentina, Uruguay, Chile, and Peru. Her justification for the tour was the discovery at the conference that many of the women present were not representing any groups and that few or no women's organizations existed in their countries. She believed that for the Pan-American Association to be practical and effective, it must be a federation of national organizations.

Scholars have taken different views of the pan-American women's movement, disagreeing particularly on its benefits for Latin American women and the merits of Carrie Chapman Catt's motives. Francesca Miller claims that by 1922 "the essential components for a formal international exchange among women of the Americas were in place" and that "a political Platform had been enunciated and agreed upon" (Miller, 1986, 182). She cites as evidence the impact of representatives of pan-American women's groups from many nations on the International Conferences of American States held in the 1920s. By 1928, at the sixth conference in Havana, women attendees who were unofficial delegates at the conference had successfully lobbied for the creation of an official body, the Inter-American Commission of Women (IACW), whose task was to investigate the status of women in the 21 member nations. With this entry to the diplomatic community, Miller argues, "women of the Americas could now begin to realize their common goals" (Miller, 1986, 182).

June Hahner has pointed out that links between international suffrage leaders and Latin American feminists had been important in the formation of formal women's rights organizations in Latin American countries. Yet because women's suffrage in Latin America was a middle-class movement that aimed to give the vote only to women with the same qualifications as men, there was little attempt to revolutionize the position of women in those societies. Carrie Chapman Catt desired cooperation and exchange of ideas, but she had little understanding of cultural differences and was unrealistically optimistic about Latin American prospects for achieving the vote.

Christine Ehrick argues that the pan-American movement has generally been viewed from an American perspective and that Carrie Chapman Catt's main interest was in civilizing neighboring states and strengthening the image of the United States in Latin America. She saw herself as a missionary and did not consider Latin American feminists to be her equals. Attitudes of this kind helped to create a gulf between U.S. and Latin American feminist leaders, some of whom were also influenced by nationalist, anti-American propaganda from within their countries. For example, Paulina Luisi, the leading suffragist in Uruguay, became the second vice president of a rival international group, the Liga Internacional de Mujeres Ibéricas e Hispanoamericanas (International League of Iberian and Hispanic-American Women). This offered an alternative to the IACW, which remained under the control of North American women.

See also Argentina; Brazil; Catt, Carrie Chapman; Chile; Latin America and the Caribbean; Luisi, Paulina; Pan-American Women's Conference; Peru; Uruguay.
References Ehrick, Christine. "*Madrinas* and Missionaries: Uruguay and the Pan-American Women's Movement" (1998); Hahner, June, ed. *Women in Latin American History, Their Lives and Voices* (1980); Miller, Francesca. "The International Relations of Women in the Americas, 1890–1928" (1983).

Pankhurst, Christabel

Christabel Pankhurst (1880–1958) was a coleader of the British militant suffrage group the Women's Social and Political Union (WSPU). As the eldest daughter of Richard Pankhurst, a radical lawyer, and Emmeline Pankhurst, a women's rights activist, Christabel grew up in London in a household committed to women's rights and socialist politics. The family moved back to Manchester in 1893, and it was here, at the age of 21, that she met Eva Gore Booth and Esther Roper, members of the North of England Women's Suffrage Society, who were attempting to organize women into trade unions and to interest working-class women in the campaign for the vote. Christabel joined them in their work and also took part in the WSPU, a group founded by her mother and other members of the Manchester Independent Labour Party (ILP) in 1903 to concentrate on women's suffrage. Impatient with the slow progress of the campaign, Christabel sought to develop new methods of protest. In 1905, she and former textile worker Annie Kenney disrupted a Liberal Party election meeting by standing up and asking if a Liberal government would give women the vote. In the confusion that followed, the two women were arrested—Christabel ensured that this would happen by spitting at a policeman. The resulting publicity ensured that WSPU membership increased rapidly.

After this incident, Christabel concentrated on studying for a law degree, which she obtained in 1907. She then moved to London with her mother and took over the leadership of the WSPU campaign. Both women resigned their membership in the ILP and began to distance the WSPU from its roots in the labor movement. Christabel was a persuasive speaker whose charismatic personality attracted many women to the WSPU. She commanded great personal loyalty from leading figures such as Emmeline and Frederick Pethick-Lawrence and Annie Kenney. On the other hand, her autocratic style of leadership alienated many women, and there were frequent splits and resignations in the years leading up to World War I.

Christabel was imprisoned in 1908, but as militancy escalated, she avoided arrest and in 1912 fled to Paris, where she could direct the affairs of the WSPU in safety. While there, she wrote a series of articles on the theme of venereal disease for the *Suffragette;* these were later published as a pamphlet, *The Great Scourge and How to End It* (1913). She argued that women were economically, politically, and sexually subordinate to men and that their lack of a vote was responsible for prostitution, venereal disease, and other forms of social degradation. Her emphasis on male power over women prefigured the arguments made by radical feminists decades later.

At the outbreak of war, however, Christabel stopped campaigning for the suffrage and along with her mother gave wholehearted support to the war effort. In 1917 they founded a Women's Party, and in 1918 and 1919 Christabel stood as a candidate for Parliament. She was unsuccessful on both occasions, and this marked the end of her active involvement in feminist politics. She joined the Second Adventists and spent several years lecturing in America. She lived in England for most of the 1930s but returned to the United States in 1939, where she remained until her death.

Christabel Pankhurst still remains a controversial figure. Her style of leadership and her support for the escalation of militancy, her critique of male power, and her hostility to the labor movement have received little sympathy from historians, in particular labor historians. In recent years, however, her contribution to feminist theory and practice has been reassessed, and she has been reclaimed as a foremother of radical feminism.

"A Conference of the Women's Franchise League, lasting three evenings, was held at the Russell Square house of Dr. and Mrs. Pankhurst." Christabel Pankhurst grew up with many suffrage meetings such as this one held in her home (1891). (Ann Ronan Picture Library)

See also Independent Labour Party; Kenney, Annie; Pankhurst, Emmeline; Pethick-Lawrence, Emmeline; Pethick-Lawrence, Frederick; Sexuality; Women's Social and Political Union.
References Rosen, Andrew. *Rise Up Women! The Militant Campaign of the Women's Social and Political Union, 1903–1914* (1974); Sarah, Elizabeth. "Christabel Pankhurst: Reclaiming Her Power" (1983).

Pankhurst, Emmeline

Emmeline Pankhurst (1858–1928) was one of the most well-known British suffrage campaigners. The daughter of a manufacturer, Robert Goulden, she married radical lawyer Richard Pankhurst in 1879. Both Emmeline and Richard were committed to women's rights and were increasingly drawn to socialist politics, in particular after they had moved to London in 1885. Here they became active in the Women's Franchise League, a group that campaigned for married women's right to vote as well as a range of social reforms. In the early 1890s they moved back

to Manchester and became involved in the Independent Labour Party (ILP), a socialist group that became the focus of Emmeline's activities. She had an early taste of political militancy when she was arrested for taking part in a free speech campaign and she also served as a Poor Law Guardian.

Richard Pankhurst's sudden death in 1898 left Emmeline with five children to support, and she withdrew from politics for a time in order to earn a living, at first opening a small shop and then working as a registrar for births and deaths. She was still a member of the ILP but became increasingly dissatisfied by what she saw as its lukewarm support for women's suffrage and its lack of interest in the needs of working-class women. In 1903, therefore, she joined with other members of the Manchester branch of the ILP in forming the Women's Social and Political Union (WSPU), which aimed to focus on issues of interest to working-class women and the demand for suffrage.

Emmeline Pankhurst, one of Britain's most famous suffragettes. (Ann Ronan Picture Library)

In 1907 Emmeline gave up her paid employment, resigned from the ILP, and moved to London in order to give full-time commitment to the suffrage campaign. Although her daughter Christabel had carried out the first act of suffrage movement militancy when she disrupted an election meeting in 1905, it was Emmeline who was to suffer most for her beliefs. Between 1908 and the outbreak of World War I, she took part in numerous demonstrations, deputations, and lobbies of the House of Commons that led to her repeated arrest and imprisonment. She suffered forcible feeding on many occasions, and her physical courage inspired many other women to join the movement. In 1914 she published an autobiography, *My Own Story,* which was dictated to Rita Child Dorr during a visit to the United States.

Emmeline Pankhurst's single-mindedness in pursuit of the vote, coupled with her physical courage, won her many devoted admirers and "helped to give militancy a heroic quality" (Banks, 1980, 152).

But it also caused tensions with those who disagreed with her, including her closest colleagues, Emmeline and Frederick Pethick-Lawrence, who were expelled from the WSPU in 1912. She was always closest to her daughter Christabel but grew even more distant from her other daughters, Adela and Sylvia, when they remained committed to socialism.

Despite the intensity of her activity on behalf of women's suffrage, Emmeline Pankhurst ceased campaigning for the vote when war was declared and gave wholehearted support to the government's war effort. Although she took little interest when the question of suffrage was raised toward the end of the war, in 1917 she and Christabel formed the short-lived Women's Party, which stood for a mixture of women's rights, racial purity, and the abolition of trade unions. In the 1920s she joined the Conservative Party and was adopted as a candidate for the East End of London, but she did not live to take part in the election. After her death a bronze statue was erected in Victoria Tower Gardens in memory of her contribution to the suffrage campaign that she had come to symbolize.

See also Independent Labour Party; Militancy; Pankhurst, Christabel; Pankhurst, (Estelle) Sylvia; Pethick-Lawrence, Emmeline; Pethick-Lawrence, Frederick; Women's Social and Political Union.

References Banks, Olive. *The Biographical Dictionary of British Feminists*. Vol. 1, *1880–1930* (1980); Pankhurst, Emmeline. *My Own Story* (1914); Purvis, June. "Emmeline Pankhurst (1858–1928) and Votes for Women" (2000).

Pankhurst, (Estelle) Sylvia

Sylvia Pankhurst (1882–1960) was a militant suffrage campaigner in Britain before World War I. She was born in Manchester, the second of five children of Dr. Richard Pankhurst, a barrister, and his wife, Emmeline, who were both involved in women's rights campaigns and socialist politics.

Sylvia also became active in the socialist movement as a member of the Manchester branch of the Independent Labour Party, but she then moved to London to study for two years at the Royal College of Art in Kensington. She gave up her studies in 1906 so that she could devote more time to the suffrage group the Women's Social and Political Union (WSPU), founded in 1903 by her mother and her sister Christabel. She was arrested and imprisoned on numerous occasions and suffered hunger and thirst strikes as well as forcible feeding.

Sylvia always tried to combine her socialist and her feminist politics, and in 1912 she established the East London Federation of Suffragettes (ELFS) in order to interest working women in the campaign for the vote. Her involvement in labor struggles included support for men and women involved in the lockout of 1913 in Dublin, Ireland, in which the city's entire organized workforce had been locked out of work by a federation of employers. This commitment to labor caused a split with Emmeline and Christabel, who had grown increasingly hostile to the labor movement. By 1914 the ELFS was no longer part of the WSPU, and Sylvia had established her own newspaper, the *Women's Dreadnought*.

Sylvia expressed her socialist and feminist ideas in her art, in her journalism, and in her books. She designed the membership card of the WSPU, which depicted working women, and her "trumpeting angel" was used as a design on banners and letterheads. She is best remembered for her suffrage militancy and for writing *The Suffragette Movement* (1931), a lively and vivid account of the militant campaign that has been used extensively by historians.

In 1927, at the age of 45, Sylvia had her first and only child, Richard Keir Pethwick, but refused on principle to marry his father, Silvio Corio, an Italian exile. Although the focus of her activities changed over time, Sylvia Pankhurst supported socialist and revolutionary politics and campaigns for women's political and social freedom throughout her life. In the interwar years, she continued to be politically active in the cause of peace, antifascism, and Ethiopian independence. She moved to Ethiopia in 1954, where she lived until her death.

See also Independent Labour Party; Pankhurst, Christabel; Pankhurst, Emmeline; *The Suffragette Movement;* Women's Social and Political Union.
References Bullock, Ian, and Richard Pankhurst, eds. *Sylvia Pankhurst: From Artist to Anti-Fascist* (1992); Romero, Patricia E. *Sylvia Pankhurst: A Portrait of a Radical* (1986); Winslow, Barbara. *Sylvia Pankhurst: Sexual Politics and Political Activism* (1996).

Paul, Alice

Alice Stokes Paul (1885–1977) was the leader of the militant wing of the suffrage movement in the United States. The daughter of upper-middle-class Quakers, Alice Paul was born in Moorestown, New Jersey. She was highly educated, gaining a doctorate from the University of Pennsylvania and, in the 1920s, a series of law degrees culminating in a Doctorate of Civil Law in 1928. She became involved in settlement work, and it was while she was pursuing graduate work in social studies in England, between 1907 and 1910, that she first took part in the suffrage movement. She joined the militant group the Women's Social and Political Union, led by Emmeline and Christabel Pankhurst. She was imprisoned twice in London and once in Dundee, Scotland, where she went on a three-day hunger strike, and she was later arrested, but not imprisoned, for taking part in a militant demonstration in Glasgow. When she returned to the United States, Paul addressed a series of meetings on the lessons that could be learned from the British suffragettes. While studying for her doctorate, she worked with suffragists in Pennsylvania, where she took part in launching open-air meetings.

Alice Paul, radical leader of the U.S. National Woman's Party, used militant tactics such as White House protests and jailhouse hunger strikes to win the vote for women. (Library of Congress)

During this period the suffrage movement in the United States was concentrating on achieving the vote on a state-by-state basis, and there was little interest in the federal women's suffrage amendment that was presented annually to Congress. Moreover, the National American Woman Suffrage Association (NAWSA) used cautious methods, lacked strong leadership, and appeared ineffective. It was in this context that Paul persuaded the NAWSA, which had its headquarters in New York, to appoint her as cochair of its Congressional Committee in Washington along with Lucy Burns, an American who had also been involved in militant activities in England. The two women had in fact met in a London police station. In 1913 they organized a suffrage parade of 5,000 women in Washington on the day before the inauguration of the new president, Woodrow Wilson. This gained a great deal of publicity and revived the Congressional Committee; pilgrimages were organized to Washington from all over the country and a suffrage petition of nearly a quarter of a million signatures was presented to senators.

In April 1913 Paul and Burns formed a new organization, the Congressional Union, with its own weekly newspaper, the *Suffragist,* to work exclusively for the federal amendment. Paul was chairwoman of both the union and the NAWSA's Congressional Committee, but tensions grew between the union and the NAWSA over issues of control and political tactics, and in 1914 there was a formal split between them. Paul continued to chair the Congressional Union and in 1915 established a Woman's Party for those women in the western states who had obtained the vote; both groups joined together late in 1916 in the National Woman's Party (NWP) under her leadership.

Despite the NWP's campaign against Woodrow Wilson, he was reelected to the presidency, after which Paul's organization stepped up its militancy. The NWP organized parades and demonstrations, conducted automobile petition drives throughout the West, and in 1917 picketed the White House. Many women were arrested for obstruction and imprisoned in very harsh conditions, leading them to go on a hunger strike and suffer forcible feeding. Paul was arrested three times, but she continued to campaign until the Nineteenth Amendment, giving women the vote, was finally ratified by three-quarters of the states in 1920.

In the same year, Paul and the NWP commissioned Adelaide Johnson to create a statue to present to Congress to commemorate the passage of the amendment and to celebrate those women who had devoted their lives to the women's suffrage struggle. Paul continued to fight for women's equality, writing the first version of the Equal Rights Amendment, which was proposed to Congress in 1923, and later forming the World Woman's Party in 1938. In its active period between 1938 and 1953, the World Woman's Party was headquartered in Switzerland and worked with the League of Nations to promote equality for women around the world.

There has been considerable debate about the role played by Alice Paul and militant tactics in the achievement of women's suffrage. Nonetheless, there can be no doubt that she helped to revive the suffrage movement and brought the federal amendment back to the forefront of feminist campaigning.

See also Hunger Strikes; National American Woman Suffrage Association; National Woman's Party; Nineteenth Amendment; Pankhurst, Christabel; Pankhurst, Emmeline; United States of America; Women's Social and Political Union.
References Bolt, Christine. *The Women's Movements in the United States and Britain from the 1790s to the 1920s* (1993); Flexner, Eleanor. *Century of Struggle: The Woman's Rights Movement in the United States* ([1959] 1975).

Peace Movement

The strongest links between pacifism and woman suffrage were forged during World War I. Although the majority of suffragists supported their nations' military programs, others split off from the main suffrage movement and committed themselves to a major international peace initiative.

However, the roots of the connection between peace and suffrage can be found much earlier. The first was the British Quaker pioneer of women's suffrage, Anne Knight, who, speaking at the 1849 peace conference in Paris, linked women's suffrage directly with the cause of peace. More than two decades later American suffragist author and lay preacher Julia Ward Howe was prompted by the Franco-

Prussian War in 1872 to call for an international women's peace congress, but she could not get enough support from Europe to achieve her vision. Although her ideas were taken up by a few equal rights feminists in Britain, Howe was refused permission to address Peace Society meetings when she visited Britain. It was not until the 1878 Peace Congress in Paris that women peace campaigners were allowed to speak out in public.

By the 1880s and 1890s women peace campaigners became involved in new international initiatives that prompted the formation of the International Council of Women (ICW) in 1888. The ICW held meetings every five years, and by 1900 the United States, Canada, Germany, Sweden, Britain, Denmark, and the Netherlands were all affiliated members. The ICW had originally been planned as a suffrage organization, but this idea was rejected by the majority of women involved. The group's organizers adopted a neutral position toward suffrage, concentrating instead on promoting maternal values and upholding women's purifying moral authority as peacemakers.

By the end of the century, peace was high on the ICW agenda, prompted by hostilities in the South African Boer War. At the 1899 ICW conference in London, a resolution was passed "to take steps in every country to further and advance by every means in its power the movement toward International Arbitration." It was at this meeting that the international movement split over the suffrage issue and a new organization was planned, linking the causes of internationalism with a commitment to suffrage and equal rights for women. This was the International Woman Suffrage Alliance, which held its first meeting in Berlin in 1904 and which by 1909 had 21 affiliated countries and its own journal, *Jus Suffragii*. Initially, this organization pledged to observe absolute neutrality on all questions that were strictly national, but the network of friendships and international contacts forged at the many congresses held in European cities encouraged women to take an interest in reducing international tensions and promoting peaceful cooperation between nations.

In the years leading up to World War I, the peace movement in Britain was relatively weak and suffragists who had spoken out against the Boer War 10 years earlier now concentrated their energies on gaining the vote. But the groundwork for an international peace initiative was being laid by influential writers elsewhere, such as Americans Charlotte Perkins Gilman and Jane Addams and South African novelist Olive Schreiner. These women were making powerful connections between maternalism, antimilitarism, and the vote. For example, in her essay "Women and War" published in *Women and Labour* in 1911, Schreiner argued that mothers were inherently antiwar as they "paid the first cost on all human life." She believed peace could only be brought about by women's suffrage: "on that day when the woman takes her place beside the man in governance . . . of her race will also be the day that heralds the death of war as a means of arranging human differences." In other parts of Europe, too, feminists were reacting to the buildup of international tensions by making similar connections between peace and feminism. In 1912 the Russian League for Women's Equality drew up a petition that claimed that the woman's vote would bring about an end to militarism and international tensions, and in 1913 the French Union of Women's Suffrage declared that the women's vote would establish social legislation that would prevent wars and submit conflicts among nations to a court of arbitration.

The IWSA Congress at Budapest in 1913, organized by the Hungarian suffragist and peace campaigner Rosika Schwimmer and attended by both Gilman and Addams, laid the foundations for a more organized initiative to challenge militarism. Peace was one of the main items on the congress agenda, which stressed the "enfranchisement of women as a bulwark against war." Following this in July 1914, Schwimmer tried unsuccessfully to warn British Premier Lloyd George of the dangers lying ahead. She also joined with British suffragists Millicent Fawcett, Chrystal Macmillan, and Mary Sheepshanks (editor of *Jus Suffragii*) to draw up a manifesto signed on behalf of 12 million women asking the government "to leave untried no conciliation or arbitration for arranging international differences that may help to avert deluging half the world in blood." Finally, in a last-ditch attempt to preserve British neutrality, a women's anti-war rally with speakers from five European countries, including Germany, was held at Kingsway Hall in London on 4 August, hours before the British ultimatum expired and the country was plunged into war.

However, almost as soon as hostilities began a major split became apparent between women members of the IWSA, who in Budapest had been united in their calls for an end to war. Some women previously committed to peace, such as Carrie Chapman Catt in the United States and Millicent Fawcett in Britain, now saw participation in their countries' war effort as a means to winning the vote. Others, such as Schwimmer of Hungary and Emmeline Pethick-Lawrence from Britain, turned their attention away from suffrage to commit themselves to the cause of world peace. Matters came to a head in Britain when members of the leading suffrage organization, the National Union of Women's Suffrage Societies (NUWSS), refused to send women to the International Women's Peace Congress, organized by the IWSA at The Hague in April 1915. This led 14 members of the NUWSS executive to resign. The Hague Congress, which pledged to persuade governments of all neutral and hostile nations to sue for peace, was attended by women from 12 nations. However, IWSA members from some countries, such as France, declined to attend on the grounds that they were united with those who were dying in battle and did not know how to talk about peace.

As a result of events at the Hague Congress, a new organization was formed, the Women's International League for Peace and Freedom (WILPF). The British branch was led by many of those who had resigned from the executive of the NUWSS, and its members were drawn from the ranks of both suffrage and socialist organizations. On a practical level, it was argued that women needed to organize separately for peace because, without the vote, they had no part in bringing about the war, and as noncombatants, they had greater freedom to speak their mind.

Women in the WILPF continued in their peacemaking efforts at an international level throughout the war, but they paid a high price for involvement in what was a very unpopular cause. For example, in the United States, Jane Addams was regarded as a traitor to her country, and it was not until 1931 that her work was recognized—with the award of the Nobel Peace Prize. She was the third woman to ever receive this honor.

See also Addams, Jane; Fawcett, Millicent Garrett; Gilman, Charlotte Perkins; International Congress of Women, The Hague; International Woman Suffrage Alliance; National Union of Women's Suffrage Societies; Pethick-Lawrence, Emmeline; Schwimmer, Rosika; Socialism in Europe.
References Costin, Lela B. "Feminism, Pacifism, Internationalism and the 1915 International Congress of Women" (1982); Evans, Richard J. *Comrades and Sisters: Feminism, Socialism and Pacifism in Europe, 1870–1945* (1987); Flexner, Eleanor. *Century of Struggle: The Woman's Rights Movement in the United States* ([1959] 1975); Liddington, Jill. *The Long Road to Greenham: Feminism and Anti-Militarism in Britain since 1820* (1989); Vellacott Newbury, Jo. "Anti-War Suffragists" (1977).

Pelletier, Madeleine

Madeleine Pelletier (1874–1939) took a leading role in the French suffrage movement before World War I. The daughter of a Parisian fruit and vegetable seller and a former domestic servant, she managed to qualify as a doctor in 1903, becoming the first woman to enter the state psychiatric service. She joined the Socialist Party in the same period and spent the rest of her life campaigning for socialist and feminist causes.

Between 1906 and World War I, Pelletier concentrated on the struggle for the vote, using her talents both as a journalist and as a political organizer. In 1906 she became secretary of La Solidarité des femmes (Women's Solidarity), a small group with fewer than 100 members. Pelletier was critical of the moderate outlook of Solidarité members and, influenced by the tactics of large public demonstrations and civil disobedience adopted by the British suffrage movement, sought to institute a number of radical actions. In 1906, for example, with the help of Caroline Kauffmann and Hubertine Auclert, she climbed into the gallery at the Chamber of Deputies and showered the chamber with leaflets. In June 1908 she attended, with Caroline Kauffmann, the women's suffrage demonstration in London's Hyde Park and returned to France even more determined to draw attention to the suffrage cause. Later in the year she supported reporter Jeanne Laloë, who stood as a candidate in the municipal elections in Paris in order to gain publicity for the suffrage campaign. Pelletier broke a window with a stone when refused admittance to the polling booth and received a fine.

Although Pelletier had attempted to unite the very divided feminist movement in France around the cause of women's suffrage, in part by founding a journal, La Suffragiste (The Suffragist), in 1908, moderate suffragists were reluctant to espouse her call for direct action and found both her socialism and her support for sexual liberation far too radical. Pelletier was also disappointed by her failure to gain wholehearted support from the socialist movement for women's suffrage, and after World War I she turned to anarchism.

Through her writings and her practical campaigning Madeleine Pelletier gave publicity to the suffrage cause and tried to link together socialism and feminism. However, her unconventional life—she always dressed as a man to make the point that she lived in a man's world—and her controversial views on sexual questions meant that she was often marginalized in suffragist and socialist circles. At the end of her life, she was arrested for carrying out illegal abortions and was imprisoned in a mental asylum, where she died in 1939.

See also Auclert, Hubertine; France; Kauffmann, Caroline.
Reference Gordon, Felicia. *The Integral Feminist: Madeleine Pelletier, 1874–1939* (1990).

Peru

Peru has a very limited history of organized women's rights campaigns and in 1955 was one of the last Latin American countries to grant women the vote. Ideas about women's emancipation were first discussed in the 1870s by a group of influential women writers in the *tortillas* (salons), where they were able to have a direct exchange of ideas with the male political leaders of their day. However, the isolation of these mainly upper-class women from women in other classes meant that they were unable to influence many of their contemporaries or launch any significant feminist political or social movements.

A suffrage movement formed in the 1920s was pioneered by María Jesús Alvarado Rivera, a young schoolteacher who had previously championed the cause of indigenous people and workers. Alvarado had studied with the feminist writer Elvira García y García at a private secondary school. In 1915 Alvarado started Peru's first women's rights organization, Evolución Femenina (Women's Evolution). It had few supporters. In a largely conservative society that maintained traditional gender roles, people were concerned that this new organization would put the family in jeopardy by taking women out of the home and precipitating a battle between the sexes. Members of Evolución Femenina were also accused of being Protestant, a terrible indictment for Catholic women at that time. Women attending one of Alvarado's lectures in 1924 had to hide their faces to avoid being recognized and photographed by the press.

In 1922 Evolución Femenina won the right for women to act as directors on Public Welfare Committees. These committees, from which women had previously been excluded, dispensed charity to hospitals, orphanages, and other needy groups. Women's inclusion was a significant victory, as these bodies had vast properties at their disposal and a seat on the Directing Committee often conferred more political power than a seat in Congress or on a departmental or municipal council.

After the president of the International Woman Suffrage Alliance, Carrie Chapman Catt, visited Peru in 1923, other groups joined with Evolución Feminina to fight for women's enfranchisement. However, the National Council of Women in Peru, formed through this alliance, was divided in its views. Although the council supported women's suffrage in principle, many members opposed Alvarado's proposal that the civil code be reformed to give all women, both married and single, equality before the law. Moreover, Alvarado was seen by many men as dangerous and inflammatory. In December 1924 she was arrested as a political prisoner, imprisoned, and deported to Argentina for 12 years.

The National Council of Women made little concerted effort to pursue women's suffrage as a policy, although individual women's groups made sporadic and ineffective attempts to gain the vote over the next three decades. Peru, unlike Brazil and Uruguay, was primarily a rural, agricultural society and did not contain a middle-class, urban, educated elite who could support a democratic reform movement. The Constitution of 1933 allowed propertied women to vote in elections but did not identify them as citizens, this term being reserved for men with property.

Peruvian women were finally enfranchised in 1955 by President General Manuel Odría. He did this primarily for his own political ends, hoping to gain women's support in the polls. Thus the vote, when it finally came, was perceived as a gift, one that surprised many women, rather than as a reward for a successful suffrage campaign. Neither of the leading daily papers in Peru covered the debate leading up to the act, suggesting it was not a topic of general interest. After emancipation, women's participation in elections was substantially lower than men's (in the 1960s they formed only 37 percent of the electorate). This was mainly because women's very low rates of literacy meant that large numbers found it impossible to qualify for a voting card.

See also Argentina; Brazil; Citizenship; Latin America and the Caribbean; Uruguay.
References Chaney, Elsa M. *Supermadre: Women in Politics in Latin America* (1979); Hahner, June E. *Emancipating the Female Sex, The Struggle for Women's Rights in Brazil, 1850–1940* (1990); Miller, Francesca. *Latin American Women and the Search for Social Justice* (1991).

Pethick-Lawrence, Emmeline

Emmeline Pethick-Lawrence (1867–1954) was a leading member of the British militant suffrage group the Women's Social and Political Union (WSPU). The daughter of a businessman, she, like other women of her class and generation, wanted to help those less fortunate than herself and at the age of 24 offered her services to the

West London Mission, where she became the leader of a club for working-class girls. This gave her greater confidence in her abilities and also led her to an interest in socialism.

In 1895 Emmeline established the Esperance Girls Club with her friend Mary Neal, and together they carried out educational work and lived among the working-class girls who were members of the club. It was during this time that Emmeline met Frederick Lawrence, who was also involved in settlement work, and they married in 1901, taking the surname Pethick-Lawrence to acknowledge Emmeline's independence. At first they gave all their energies to the labor movement and showed little interest in the suffrage campaign. Then, on a visit to South Africa in 1905, they read about the arrest of Christabel Pankhurst and Annie Kenney for disrupting a political meeting. On their return to England, Annie Kenney persuaded Emmeline to meet with members of the WSPU, and in February 1906 both Emmeline and Mary Neal joined the organization, with Emmeline in the post of treasurer.

Emmeline was arrested in 1906 when she took part in a lobby at the House of Commons, and over the next six years she was imprisoned five times. It was her first brief imprisonment that brought her husband into the movement, for while she was away he took her place as treasurer of the WSPU. In 1907 they both founded and edited *Votes for Women*, the newspaper of the WSPU. They were loyal supporters of the Pankhursts and played a crucial role in strengthening the WSPU. Emmeline was a charismatic speaker and skillful fundraiser, and for a number of years the union's office was in their London home, where Christabel Pankhurst also lived.

In 1912, after a spate of window breaking carried out by members of the WSPU, the Pethick-Lawrences were arrested along with other leaders for conspiracy to damage property and were sentenced to nine months in prison, although public protests led to their early release. They had to pay the costs of the trial and in the following year were sued successfully by those who had experienced damage to their property. Both Emmeline and Frederick were unhappy with the turn that militancy seemed to be taking and argued that large public demonstrations should be held rather than individual militant acts. Christabel refused to accept their arguments, and in 1912 they were expelled from the WSPU. Although they continued to edit *Votes for Women*, it no longer represented the policies of the WSPU.

Emmeline and Frederick continued to be active in suffrage politics. In 1913 they formed a new group, the Votes for Women Fellowship, and in 1914 they became founding members of the United Suffragists, a mixed-sex organization. With the outbreak of war, Emmeline put most of her energies into the women's peace movement, but she still found time to take part in the Council for Adult Suffrage, which aimed to ensure that the new Franchise Bill would include women on the same terms as men. In the interwar years she remained active in feminist politics; she was vice president of the Six Point Group and president of the Women's Freedom League, where among other campaigns, she helped to pressure the government to introduce equal voting rights for women. She also played a part in the Suffragette Fellowship and left a record of her suffrage activities in her autobiography, *My Part in a Changing World* (1938).

Ill health brought Emmeline's political activities to an end at the outbreak of World War II, and she died after a series of heart attacks in 1954. Throughout her life she had attempted to bring together her socialism and her feminism and had campaigned for a wide range of causes, including the welfare of working-class mothers, birth control, and equal pay. She is best remembered, however, for her involvement in the militant suffrage movement and for the role she played in the day-to-day work of gaining support for the WSPU.

See also Newspapers and Journals; Pankhurst, Christabel; Pethick-Lawrence, Frederick; *Votes for Women;* Women's Freedom League; Women's Social and Political Union.
References Banks, Olive. *The Biographical Dictionary of British Feminists.* Vol. 1, *1880–1930* (1985); Pethick-Lawrence, Emmeline. *My Part in a Changing World* (1938).

Pethick-Lawrence, Frederick

Frederick Pethick-Lawrence (1871–1961) was unusual in that he was the only man to have an official position in the British militant suffrage organization the Women's Social and Political Union (WSPU). Educated at Cambridge, Lawrence acted as treasurer for Mansfield House University settlement while he read for the bar. He put himself forward as a Liberal Unionist parliamentary candidate, but his political views moved to the left when he met his future wife, Emmeline Pethick, a voluntary social worker and a socialist. To acknowledge Emmeline's independence, they adopted the name of Pethick-Lawrence, but they showed little interest in women's suffrage until meeting Annie Kenney, who persuaded Emmeline to take over as treasurer of the WSPU.

When Emmeline was arrested during a demonstration at the House of Commons, Frederick was drawn into the movement. He took over as treasurer and used his legal training to help the prisoners. Christabel Pankhurst was very close to the Pethick-Lawrences, and their home in London became the headquarters of the militant movement. Frederick financed and coedited a journal, *Votes for Women,* which became the official organ of the WSPU, and he also published *Women's Fight for the Vote* (1910). In 1912, when the WSPU adopted a strategy involving the destruction of property, Frederick Pethick-Lawrence was arrested along with the other leaders on a charge of incitement to violence. He was imprisoned and then forcibly fed. Until this point, Emmeline and Frederick had been loyal supporters of the Pankhursts, but they were not happy with the destruction of property. Christabel Pankhurst would not countenance opposition and dismissed the Pethick-Lawrences from the WSPU. Frederick continued to finance and control the journal *Votes for Women* until 1914, when he handed it over to the United Suffragists, a group of men and women committed to women's suffrage, which he and Emmeline had helped to form. During World War I, Frederick was a conscientious objector and in 1923 was elected as a Labour MP—the beginning of a long parliamentary career.

Frederick maintained his connections with the suffrage movement in later life. In 1957, three years after the death of his wife, he married Helen Craggs, a former suffragette who was 20 years his junior. He wrote an autobiography, *Fate Has Been Kind* (1945), and helped in the publication of Christabel Pankhurst's autobiography, *Unshackled* (1959).

See also Kenney, Annie; Men's Support; Pankhurst, Christabel; Pethick-Lawrence, Emmeline; Suffragette; *Votes for Women;* Women's Social and Political Union.
References Banks, Olive. *The Biographical Dictionary of British Feminists.* Vol. 1, *1800–1930* (1985); John, Angela V., and Claire Eustance, eds. *The Men's Share? Masculinities, Male Support and Women's Suffrage in Britain, 1890–1920* (1992).

Petitioning

Petitioning was one of the most widespread campaign methods used by suffragists throughout the world as a way of demonstrating the strength of their support from ordinary women and men. Petitions demanding the vote for women were repeatedly presented to legislative bodies

Elizabeth Cady Stanton petitions a Senate committee on the merits of the National Woman Suffrage Association's Sixteenth Amendment proposal. Wood engraving in New York Daily Graphic, *January 16, 1878. (Library of Congress)*

throughout the world and, though generally unsuccessful, they did help to bring pressure to bear on members of the legislature and to raise the profile of the suffrage movement. A particularly dramatic gesture that provoked press attention occurred in New Zealand in 1893. On this occasion, liberal politician Sir John Hall unrolled a petition of signatures 300 yards long, signed by 25,000 women, on the floor of the House of Parliament, for which gesture he was humorously dubbed "the Carpet Knight."

See also Hall, Sir John; New Zealand.
References Grimshaw, Patricia. *Women's Suffrage in New Zealand* (1987).

Philippines

Women in the Philippines were granted the vote in 1937, three decades after the Philippine Legislature established by the Americans in 1907 gave men the vote. The female franchise was not achieved without a struggle. Filipina women were influenced by their links with America, particularly in the spread of education and the decline of beliefs in female subservience that had been encouraged by their earlier Spanish colonizers, and suffrage proved to be one of the key issues around which women activists organized.

The first women's groups in the Philippines were formed soon after the U.S. occupation in 1899, but they did not take up the franchise issue until 1905, when Concepción Félix formed the Asociación Feminista Filipina. Félix had made contact with Fiske Warren from the Anti-Imperialist League in Boston, who, having heard her speak in a debate on women's place in Filipino society, encouraged her to form a women's political party. However, at this stage Félix preferred to include the suffrage as only one in a range of social issues taken up by the group. A year later another group was formed, the Asociación Feminista Ilonga, aimed specifically at women's suffrage, and by 1907 the two groups had gained enough support to get a bill introduced into the House of Representatives. In 1912, two leading international suffragists, Carrie Chapman Catt and Aletta Jacobs, visited Manila and tried unsuccessfully to unite the groups. However, they did succeed in initiating a new organization, named the Women's Club of Manila, which reinvigorated the suffrage movement. Between 1912 and 1918 four franchise bills were introduced into the legislature, all of which were unsuccessful.

From 1920 the movement began to broaden its previously bourgeois membership base and to move outside Manila. Leaders of the Women's Club of Manila organized a countrywide convention of women's organizations, and from this base the National League of Filipino Women was formed with the primary goal of fighting for the vote. Yet although the 1921 bill gained support from the governor-general, it suffered the same fate as its predecessors.

As the movement grew, it attracted the support of the first woman doctor in the Philippines, Dr. Maria Paz Mendoza-Guazon, who in 1928 formed the Women Citizens League. This group was more successful than any other in broadening the class and regional base of the movement, holding rallies throughout the country and launching propaganda to attract the press, most of whom supported women's suffrage by 1931. Success seemed in sight in 1933, when the House of Representatives passed a bill giving women the vote, effective from January 1935. However, before women actually went to the polls, the decision was overturned by the Constitutional Convention, which in 1934 drafted a new constitution to reflect the change of status of the Philippines as a commonwealth within the United States.

Suffragists joined together to form a General Council of Women, and appeared before the Constitutional Convention to plead their cause. The convention decided that a plebiscite on the female franchise should be held within two years of the adoption of the new constitution. It would be passed only if 300,000 women voted yes. Feminists redoubled their efforts over the next two years to persuade women to register for the plebiscite and to support the suffrage. They held rallies and lectures, made house-to-house visits, and conducted a press and poster campaign. As a result of their work, 500,000 women registered, out of which number less than 60,000 declined to support the suffrage, an overwhelming victory for the cause.

See also Catt, Carrie Chapman; Jacobs, Aletta; United States of America.
References Jayawardena, Kumari. *Feminism and Nationalism in the Third World* (1986).

Pilgrimage, Suffrage (1913)

In 1913 the National Union of Women's Suffrage Societies (NUWSS) organized the Women's Pilgrimage to try to gain more support for the suffrage cause and at the same time to counter the growing criticism of militancy within the movement. In June and July 1913, thousands of women took part in a peaceful pilgrimage to London from all over Britain, holding meetings on the way and raising more than £8,000 for the cause. On 26 July the pilgrimage ended in Hyde Park, where there was a great demonstration attended by well over 50,000 people. One important result of this impressive show of support was that H. H. Asquith, the Liberal prime minister, agreed to meet a deputation from the NUWSS on 8 August. There is no doubt the pilgrimage did achieve a great deal of positive publicity for the nonmilitant suffrage campaign, and it was arguably the most important demonstration for women's suffrage ever held in Britain.

See also Britain; National Union of Women's Suffrage Societies.
References Hume, Leslie Parker. *The National Union of Women's Suffrage Societies, 1897–1914* (1982); Tickner, Lisa. *The Spectacle of Women: Imagery of the Suffrage Campaign, 1907–1914* (1987).

Plamínková, Františka F.

Františka Plamínková (1875–1942) was a leading women's rights campaigner and suffragist in Czechoslovakia. She founded the Women's Club of Prague in 1901 and the Committee for Women's Suffrage in 1905, both of which were positioned on the radical wing of the women's movement and were nationalist in outlook. As a Jew with a radical political perspective, Plamínková was particularly anxious to express national loyalty; in the early years of the century, for example, she organized a "buy Czech" campaign through the Women's Club. When the Habsburg Empire sought to extend male suffrage even as it removed women's right to vote for the Bohemian Diet, a suffrage already limited by property ownership, the Committee for Women's Suffrage attempted to persuade the Czech political parties to defy Vienna by running a female candidate in Bohemia. When this was unsuccessful, the committee put up its own female candidate, Marie Tumova, in the elections of 1908 and 1909. Plamínková played an active part in both election fights and used the occasion of a visit by American activist Carrie Chapman Catt to announce the second candidacy. She demanded universal equal suffrage, and as a member of the committee she continued to work to convince other parties to nominate female candidates. Over the years many did, but no female candidates were successful in the elections. Plamínková became a senator after the establishment of the republic and was executed by the Nazis in 1942.

See also Catt, Carrie Chapman; Czechoslovakia.
Reference David, Katherine. "Czech Feminists and Nationalism in the Late Habsburg Monarchy: 'The First in Austria'" (1991).

Plural Vote

The term *plural vote* refers to the power held by individual citizens to cast multiple votes in an election. This practice was widespread in the early electoral systems of countries that used property ownership as the basis of the franchise, such as Britain and Australia. Thus, it was possible for an individual who owned property of the requisite value in a number of different electoral constituencies to qualify for a separate vote in each location. The working-class suffrage movement in Australia campaigned vigorously to abolish the plural vote, but not all suffragists agreed on the matter, and the issue created a dilemma for the women's suffrage movement. For example, in Queensland, the earliest demands that women be enfranchised on the same basis as men came from conservative politicians. These men saw the advantage of extending the vote to propertied women, some of whom would be able to cast multiple votes and many of whom were likely to be conservative voters. They hoped by this means to counter the growing influence of gold miners, who were demanding universal male suffrage. The labor movement, on the other hand, refused to support women's suffrage until the principle of one man, one vote had been achieved. In this instance, two rival women's suffrage societies were formed, one demanding the vote on the same terms as men (whether or not the plural vote was retained), the other insisting on the abolition of the plural vote and full adult suffrage.

In Britain before World War I, there were several unsuccessful attempts by the Liberal government to abolish plural voting. They believed it favored the Conservative Party with its preponderance of propertied voters, and furthermore, if women obtained a limited franchise based on property, it would only add to conservative power. The Liberals were anxious, therefore, to combine any limited suffrage bill with the abolition of plural voting. However, although all British women were fully enfranchised by 1928, plural voting was not abolished until 1948.

See also Australia; Britain; Universal Suffrage.
References Blewitt, Neal. "The Franchise in the United Kingdom, 1885–1918" (1965); Oldfield, Audrey. *Woman Suffrage in Australia, A Gift or a Struggle?* (1992).

Popp, Adelheid

Adelheid Popp (1869–1939) was a leader of the Austrian socialist women's movement and a supporter of women's suffrage. She came from a poor, working-class family in Vienna and worked as a factory girl. After attending a socialist meeting with her brother, she joined the Social Democratic Party because of its concern for what she saw as the most exploited groups, women and the urban poor. She married the party treasurer, Julius Popp, who was 20 years older, and when he died after seven years of marriage she had to bring up their two sons on her own.

As a member of the party, Adelheid Popp encouraged other women to take on organizing work and to join in strikes, and in 1892 she was made editor of the *Arbeiterinnenzeitung* (Working Women's Newspaper). During the 1890s and early 1900s, the paper carried numerous articles about women's suffrage that were aimed at working-class women. Popp linked women's enfranchisement to broader feminist questions. She argued that once women had the vote they would develop their intellectual abilities and would become far more independent in their outlook and personalities.

Popp and other socialist women faced a conflict of loyalties in 1905–1906. The Russian Revolution of 1905 encouraged the Social Democratic Party to step up its demand for a universal male franchise. Women members were asked to support this campaign and to put their own demands to one side for the time being. Socialist women did put party loyalty first, although Popp argued that this was a temporary situation and that the demand for women's suffrage had not been abandoned. She came under attack, along with her colleagues, from the German socialist Clara Zetkin, who claimed that it was a mistake to postpone the struggle for women's suffrage and that such a move was against the policy of the socialist umbrella group, the Second International. Popp argued, however, that Austrian tactics had not delayed women's achievement of the vote, because if socialist deputies were elected to Parliament they would be able to support the women's cause.

At the Austrian socialist women's conference of 1908, a resolution was passed that emphasized the urgent need to fight for women's suffrage now that men had achieved their aims. Popp joined others in taking an assertive stand and encouraged women to be less cautious in their approach. She helped to develop a system of female cadres that brought more women into the Social Democratic Party, so that female membership reached 15,000 by 1910. When women achieved the suffrage after World War I, Popp was one of seven women to be elected to Parliament. Throughout the 1920s, she continued to be active in movements to improve women's work conditions both inside and outside the home and helped revive the international socialist women's movement. Ill health led her to withdraw from active politics in the early 1930s.

Popp was seen as the undoubted leader of the Austrian socialist women's movement, which played an important role in the suffrage campaign. She gained an international reputation through her *Autobiography of a Working Woman* (1909), which had gone through six editions by 1930, and also because of her prominence at international socialist women's conferences. An enthusiastic organizer and energetic speaker, Adelheid Popp was a conciliator who tried to smooth over differences in order to maintain party unity. Yet she never forgot that the purpose of socialism was to free women as well as men from their subordinate position, and she campaigned for women's issues throughout her life.

See also Austria; Zetkin, Clara.
Reference Lafleur, Ingrun. "Five Socialist Women: Traditionalist Conflicts and Socialist Visions in Austria, 1893–1934" (1978).

Portugal

Women's rights in Portugal were secured with great difficulty, particularly because of the long rule of the right-wing dictator, Antonio Salazar, who was premier from 1932 to 1968. During his time in office, a great deal of legislation was passed that was detrimental to the rights and freedom of women in Portugal. Although a very limited number of highly educated women obtained the vote in 1931, it was not until 1968 that women gained political equality with men (based on a literacy qualification), and finally, under the democratic Constitution of 1976 all electoral restrictions were lifted.

The first steps toward the achievement of political and social rights for Portuguese women began in the early 1900s, when women started to ask for voting rights, educational reforms, and improved economic conditions. In 1905, Ana de Castro Osório wrote the first feminist manifesto, *As Mulheres Portuguesas* (Portuguese Women), and in 1909 she joined with Adelaide Cabete to found the Liga das Mulheres Republicanas (League of Republican Women), the first women's

rights organization in Portugal. One of the league's first demands was that women be given the vote.

Shortly after the establishment of the First Republic in 1910, a number of laws improving the rights of women within marriage were introduced, but the demand for the vote was still denied. In 1911, Dr. Carolina Beatriz Ângelo set out to register to vote for the forthcoming elections. She fulfilled all the voting requirements, being a widowed head of the household, 21 years of age, and able to read and write. When she was denied the right to register, she took the case to court and won, and on election day she became the first Portuguese woman to vote, much to the delight of many women. However, this victory was short-lived, and soon afterward the government changed the law so that only male heads of household could vote.

In 1914 there was another important development in the campaign for women's rights. Cabete founded the Conselho Nacional das Mulheres Portuguesas (National Council of Portuguese Women), the Portuguese branch of the International Council of Women, which was to become the most important and long-lived women's organization in Portugal. Among the objectives of this moderate association was to obtain the enfranchisement of women and to secure an improvement in women's legal rights; to pursue these ends they held two conferences—the First Portuguese Feminist Congress in 1924 and the Second Feminist Congress in 1928.

Although some Portuguese women had made a considerable contribution to the war effort during World War I, women received little tangible recognition for their services beyond progress in women's education in the 1920s. In 1926, Antonio Salazar's right-wing dictatorship was installed, and much of the progress that women had made began to be reversed. The new regime was committed to keeping women at home carrying out purely domestic duties, and some of the opportunities for education were withdrawn. Surprisingly, in 1931, Salazar granted the vote to the small minority of women with university degrees or secondary school qualifications (male voters only had to be able to read and write).

After World War II, the National Council of Portuguese Women, led by Maria Lamas, allied itself with the opposition to the Salazar regime. As a result, the organization was closed down in 1948 and Lamas came under considerable official pressure. After being forced out of her job as a journalist she fled to Paris, but not before she had written one of the most important books on women in Portugal, *As Mulheres do Meu País* (The Women of My Country), published in 1948. Legislation continued to restrict women's freedom of action, particularly within marriage, but in 1968, during a relatively liberal period after Salazar fell ill and was replaced by Marcello Caetano, women gained the right to vote on the same terms as men, that is, with a literacy qualification. Salazar died in 1970.

During the early 1970s, despite a weakened government, new restrictions were imposed on political action and women activists came under attack once again. It was during this period that Maria Velho da Costa, Maria Isabel Barreno, and Maria Teresa Horta wrote their important and controversial feminist text, *Novas Cartas Portuguesas* (New Portuguese Letters), which was published in 1972. In this best-selling book, the authors attacked the patriarchy and the conditions of oppression under which women in Portugal had to live.

In 1974, after a relatively bloodless revolution, democracy was restored to Portugal and new laws came into effect that considerably improved the position of women, including improved working conditions and access to divorce. A new constitution was voted on in 1975 by all citizens over 18 years of age, and in 1976 it was adopted, confirming universal adult suffrage.

See Also International Council of Women. *References* Guimarães, Elina. *Portuguese Women Past and Present* (1987); Sadlier, Darlene J. "The Struggle for Women's Rights in Portugal" (1991).

Propaganda

Propaganda became increasingly important for suffrage campaigners, particularly in Britain and the United States, as they sought to develop a mass movement in the early twentieth century. Traditional methods of propaganda had included the establishment of a suffrage press, holding public meetings, and gathering signatures for petitions. However, the militant movement in Britain, led by the Women's Social and Political Union (WSPU), developed new forms of propaganda that involved far more direct action on the street and a greater emphasis on spectacle. Large demonstrations and processions were held in which women were encouraged to wear the colors of their organization. These events were carefully organized for maximum visual impact, as when women were all expected to wear white. Carefully embroidered banners represented the many different organizations and occupations that supported women's suffrage, and posters and postcards provided an image of suffrage campaigners that countered the stereotypes put forward by opponents. The militant campaign had an impact on the suffrage movement in the United States, which also organized processions and poster parades in the years just before the war.

Suffrage campaigners spread their message by traveling around the country in vehicles that they covered in suffrage posters; in Britain they used "caravans" (covered wagons) and a suffragette bus, and in the United States women toured on tramcars and "suffrage special" trains.

The "Appeal of Womanhood" poster (left), published in the Suffrage Atelier in 1912, was designed in response to Harold Bird's poster (right) published by the National League for Opposing Women's Suffrage the same year. Both are examples of propaganda about gender roles in relation to the suffrage movement. (Museum of London)

Commodities made in suffrage colors were sold at demonstrations and in suffrage shops, and all the main suffrage groups had their own newspapers, which served as an integral part of the campaign. Various other methods were used to attract attention: militants in France showered deputies with leaflets and distributed balloons covered in suffrage slogans, and in Britain they interrupted cinema audiences by advertising meetings on the screen. The emphasis on spectacle, pageantry, and direct action on the street helped to give the suffrage movement a high profile and to attract support. It also gave campaigners a sense of solidarity and a way to express their commitment at a time when they faced opposition from the government and a hostile press.

See also Advertising; Imagery; Militancy; Newspapers and Journals; Women's Social and Political Union.
References Atkinson, Diane. *The Purple, White and Green: Suffragettes in London, 1906–14* (1992); Tickner, Lisa. *The Spectacle of Women: Imagery of the Suffrage Campaign, 1907–1914* (1987).

Protestantism

The Protestant Reformation in Europe, which arguably began with the publication of Luther's reforming theses in Germany in 1517, was founded on the belief that salvation is based not on works but on the individual's faith in God, and that the relationship between the individual and God is a direct one with no need for mediation by either the priest or the Church. In theory, this belief recognized men and women as equal before God, although in practice women were usually expected to be submissive to men, as ordained in such familiar biblical texts as Ephesians 5:22, "Wives, submit yourselves unto your own husbands . . ." Protestantism gave rise to a number of religious sects with more advanced progressive beliefs about the position of women. These included groups such as the Quakers and the Unitarians, whose members often dominated the nineteenth-century movements for social and political reform, including the early campaigns for women's suffrage.

The evangelical revival that swept through Protestant Europe and the United States in the late eighteenth and early nineteenth centuries was based on a mission to regenerate and reform a corrupt society, and many women responded to the call. Evangelical writers often identified women as the prime movers in the movement for renewal, arguing that their superior moral qualities gave them the vital role of religious and moral educator in the family and in society at large—a role that was often called "woman's mission." Despite its emphasis on women's role in the home, evangelical religion gave rise to numerous philanthropic associations and missionary societies, often dominated by women, and gave them experience in public speaking, administration, and association. This experience was to be invaluable for those women who went on to become involved in the nineteenth-century antislavery, temperance, and moral reform movements. Protestant sects that were sympathetic to female emancipation, such as the Quakers and the Unitarians, were influenced by the moral imperatives of the evangelical revival, and many women from these religious traditions became prominent in the early women's suffrage movement, particularly in Britain and the United States.

The Unitarians formally established congregations in Britain and the United States in the late eighteenth century. Their reliance on rational and scientific thought led Unitarians to reject the Trinity, the divinity of Christ, and the doctrine of original sin; to accept women's equality with men before God; and to believe that women should receive a good education. Of all the Protestant groups, Unitarians were one of the most radical, in political as well as religious matters, and it is not surprising that a number of prominent women suffragists emerged from their ranks. In late eighteenth-century Britain, feminist writer Mary Wollstonecraft was deeply influenced by a Unitarian minister and supporter of the American and French Revolutions, Dr. Richard Price, who believed in the application of reason to religious and political thinking to achieve a reformation of society. There were a number of Unitarian women in the Langham Place Circle, which was set up in the 1850s to campaign for educational and employment opportunities for women and circulated the petition asking for women's suffrage that was presented to Parliament in 1866 by John Stuart Mill. Two of the founders of the circle, Barbara Leigh Smith Bodichon and Bessie Rayner Parkes, came from Unitarian backgrounds, as did Harriet Taylor Mill, who used the rational language of Unitarianism in her article "The Enfranchisement of Women" (1851) to argue for women's political equality. Family networks of Unitarian women were prominent in the campaigns to improve women's legal and political rights, and they contributed significantly to the development of feminist thought in Britain.

Quaker women also played an important part in political and social reform movements in Britain, and they were active in the early nineteenth-century antislavery campaign. Quaker women were used to participating fully in religious worship and in the administrative meetings of their sect, and their belief in female equality soon led them into the women's suffrage movement. Anne Knight (1786–1862), a Quaker and the aunt of Barbara Bodichon, became an antislavery campaigner, a Chartist, and an early advocate of women's suffrage. In 1851 she helped to form the short-lived Sheffield Female Political Association, which published an "Address to the Women of England," asking for the enfranchisement of women. Networks of Quaker women, usually from leading manufacturing families, were often involved in antislavery, temperance, and moral reform movements, as well as in the growing campaign for women's suffrage. The Brights of Manchester were among the most influential Quaker families involved in these activities. Jacob Bright (1821–1899) was a radical Liberal member of Parliament, and his wife, Ursula; his sisters, Priscilla Bright McLaren and Margaret Bright Lucas; and his nieces, Lilias Ashworth Hallett and Anne Ashworth, all signed the 1866 petition for women's suffrage instigated by Bodichon. All the Bright women went on to varying degrees of involvement in the British women's suffrage movement. In the United States, Unitarian women were active in the antislavery and women's suffrage campaigns, and their concern for natural rights certainly influenced the language of the Declaration of Sentiments that emerged from the Seneca Falls Convention of 1848 and included a demand for women's enfranchisement. However, there is little doubt that many of the most influential women in the American suffrage movement came from Quaker backgrounds. Like Unitarians, Quakers believed in the equality of men and women before God—another belief reflected in the wording of the Seneca Falls Declaration. It is no coincidence that the women who featured most prominently in the events at Seneca Falls were Quakers, including Lucretia Mott, who joined with her friend Elizabeth Cady Stanton to lead the call for women's rights. As Stanton ar-

ticulated it, women based their claims to equality on two ideas, "our Protestant idea, the right of individual conscience and judgment, [and] our republican idea, individual citizenship" (Evans, 1977, 23). Mott and Stanton were joined by another Quaker, Susan B. Anthony, and a Unitarian, Lucy Stone, and together these women formed the bedrock of leadership in the U.S. women's suffrage movement during the nineteenth century. Quaker involvement in the women's suffrage campaign was continued into the twentieth century by Alice Paul, who founded the Congressional Union in 1913 to campaign for the federal vote for women.

Quakers and Unitarians were not the only Protestant groups to become involved; there was also a strong Methodist presence in the U.S. women's suffrage movement. Among Methodist suffragists were the early temperance and suffrage campaigner, Frances Willard, and the Methodist minister and orator, Anna Howard Shaw, who became president of the National American Woman Suffrage Association (NAWSA) in 1904.

The predominantly Protestant countries of Australia and New Zealand gained the vote very early on, thanks in part to the support of many male migrants, often politically radical, who had arrived in the colonies looking for political and social change. Middle-class female migrants were more anxious to promote a stable, moral society in these new, developing countries; this reforming zeal was responsible for the rapid growth of temperance societies, inspired by Protestant evangelical religion. In Australia, the temperance movement supported the cause of women's suffrage, as it had done in the United States and Canada, and in New Zealand temperance also played a major role in the struggle for the vote, which was achieved as early as 1893. The campaign for women's suffrage in New Zealand was assisted by women like the Unitarian Harriet Morison, who had helped to found the Women's Franchise League in 1892 and was an active member of the Woman's Christian Temperance Union (WCTU).

In Canada, the enfranchisement of women took longer to achieve. The WCTU became a powerful supporter of the suffrage movement in the hope that the female vote would bring in prohibition and "help defend Protestant morality and sobriety" (Bacchi, 1983, 70). Interestingly, in the mainly French-speaking Catholic province of Quebec, women's demand for the provincial vote faced considerable opposition from the Catholic Church, and the movement did not achieve success until 1940, more than 20 years after most of the other, predominantly Protestant provinces had granted women the suffrage.

In Europe, the picture of Protestant women's involvement in the women's suffrage movement is more complex. Chief among the factors influencing the establishment of women's suffrage organizations in European countries were the political and social structures in each individual country, which ranged from authoritarian, semifeudal societies in Central and Eastern Europe; to countries with liberal political constitutions aligned with a strong Catholic Church, like France, Italy, and Belgium; to the Nordic countries, which were predominantly Protestant and had liberal legislatures. Commenting on the success of feminist movements in Europe, Richard Evans has observed that "at an intellectual or ideological level, the most striking contrast is between Catholicism and Protestantism, the one a major obstacle to feminism, the other an almost essential precondition of its emergence" (Evans, 1977, 237). There is no doubt that campaigners for women's suffrage in the Protestant Scandinavian countries achieved the vote after comparatively short campaigns, even though in Norway, as well as in the Nordic countries of Finland and Iceland, there was the additional element of a struggle for national self-determination. Women in the Protestant Netherlands, too, achieved women's suffrage relatively quickly, after a campaign that began in the 1890s and ended in 1919. Germany, which had a predominantly Protestant culture with a strong Catholic minority, might have been expected to be progressive on questions of women's rights, but a military aristocracy, combined with a very conservative Protestant Church, meant that the embryonic women's suffrage movement was not able to function publicly until the beginning of the twentieth century, when a number of suffrage organizations began to campaign in earnest.

In France, although women undertook philanthropic activities as part of the Catholic revival during the first half of the nineteenth century, there appeared to be little enthusiasm for taking the participation of women in public life any further. With the spread of secularism in France, women were seen as the last bastion of Catholicism and were subject to legal and social restrictions that were strongly supported by both the state and the Catholic Church. It is not surprising, therefore, that many nineteenth-century French feminists came from a predominantly republican, liberal, Protestant background, with a tradition of involvement in voluntary philanthropic activities. One woman in this category was Eugénie Niboyet, who was a member of the Protestant "Société de la morale chrétienne," a liberal reforming group founded in 1821 that was involved in philanthropic and antislavery activities. Niboyet, who was active in the 1848 revolution, published in the same year a short-lived journal, La Voix des femmes (Women's Voice), which asked for improved legal, political, and educational rights for women, including the right to vote. Anne Knight, the British Quaker suffragist, was a contributor to the journal, which had a broadly international outlook and was sympathetic to the antislavery movement. It is a matter of irony that the movement for women's suffrage in France suffered from being a predominantly Protestant, anticlerical pressure group that was opposed by republican politicians who believed that giving women the vote would only strengthen the influence of the Catholic Church. As a result of this conflict, French women did not gain the vote until 1945. Indeed, women's suffrage came late to many European countries where Catholicism was the religion of the majority—in France, Italy, Belgium, and Switzerland women did not receive the vote until after World War II, compared to most Protestant countries, where women had gained the vote by 1920.

Although the suffrage movement encountered considerable opposition in most cases, there is no doubt that the early granting of women's suffrage in some countries coincided with the existence of a strong Protestant reforming religion and was often linked with such evangelical causes as temperance and moral reform. Radical Protestant sects, such as Quakers and Unitarians, had a strong tradition of equality between men and women and a long involvement in the antislavery movement; these combined to produce women activists who took up the cause of women's suffrage with some success, particularly in Australasia, Britain, and North America.

See also Australia; Britain; Canada; Catholicism; Citizenship; France; Germany; Langham Place Circle; Mill, John Stuart; Mott, Lucretia Coffin; National American Woman Suffrage Association; New Zealand; United States of America; Wollstonecraft, Mary; Women's Rights Convention, Seneca Falls.
References Bacchi, Carol Lee. *Liberation Deferred? The Ideas of the English-Canadian Suffragists, 1877–1918* (1983); Evans, Richard. *The Feminists: Women's Emancipation Movements in Europe, America and Australasia, 1840–1920* (1977); Gleadle, Kathryn. *The Early Feminists: Radical Unitarians and the Emergence of the Women's Rights Movement, 1831–51* (1995); Rendall, Jane. *The Origins of Modern Feminism: Women in Britain, France and the United States, 1780–1860* (1985).

Puerto Rico

Women in Puerto Rico began calling for the vote in the late nineteenth century, but they had to wait more than three decades before a bill granting universal suffrage was approved in 1935. Women's political progress in Puerto Rico has been intimately bound up with their country's relationship to the United States. Placed under U.S. control as a nonincorporated territory in 1898, Puerto Rico subsequently underwent a rapid transformation from an agrarian to a capitalist economy, and this change had a profound effect on women's lives. Their increased participation in the labor market and the labor movement gave working women a heightened awareness of gender inequalities and highlighted the lack of political rights for women.

Thus, although some educated women had spoken out for the suffrage since before the U.S. invasion, it was working women in the trade union movement who started the first organized suffrage campaign. In 1908 a group associated with the Federación Libre de Trabajadores (Free Federation of Workers) lobbied to get a bill presented to the legislature demanding for women "all the rights of any kind or nature granted by law to male citizens." This bill, though unsuccessful, was a landmark for Puerto Rican feminism.

From this point suffrage became a central issue for both upper- and working-class feminists, although they remained divided by class and campaigned from separate platforms. In 1917 upper-class women organized a separate group, the Liga Femínea, which sought only limited suffrage, influenced by educated women who had spent time in the United States.

Suffragists hoped that when the Nineteenth Amendment was passed in 1920 enfranchising women in the United States, women's suffrage would be extended to Puerto Rico. But their hopes were dashed by a test case brought by a Puerto Rican labor leader, who had emigrated to the

United States and returned to Puerto Rico to register her vote. The Puerto Rican government's request to Washington, D.C., to clarify the matter resulted in a decision that the amendment did not apply on the island, thereby confirming its inferior colonial status. During the following decade, new suffrage organizations were formed and further links were made with U.S. suffrage leaders. However, attempts at cooperation between working women and upper-class women were doomed to failure by the controversy over whether suffrage groups should be pushing for limited or universal suffrage, and this conflict proved a major obstacle to the passage of legislation. Conservative leaders were concerned that the enfranchisement of working women would lead to the victory of the Socialist Party. Thus, despite public approval for the suffrage, 10 suffrage bills between 1917 and 1927 failed to pass the legislature.

By the late 1920s, feminist leaders in the United States were successful in lobbying the U.S. Congress Committee on Territories and Island Possessions to recommend universal suffrage for Puerto Rican women. Meanwhile, the Puerto Rican legislature passed a bill in 1929 that gave the vote only to literate women, excluding thereby most Puerto Rican working women. Despite strong protests and campaigns by feminist leaders and working women, it took another six years before a bill submitted by the president of the Socialist Party for universal suffrage was finally passed. Although women turned out in large numbers at the first election, their interests still remained largely unrepresented. The first woman legislator was not a feminist, nor was she interested in addressing working women's concerns.

See also Latin America and the Caribbean; Nineteenth Amendment; United States of America; Universal Suffrage.
Reference Azize-Vargas, Yamila. "At the Crossroads: Colonialism and Feminism in Puerto Rico" (1994).

R

Race and Ethnicity

Suffragists campaigning for women's right to vote during the nineteenth and twentieth centuries often used racist arguments to claim that white women should have full rights to citizenship at the expense of women of other ethnic groups, especially indigenous Americans and Australians and women of African and Asian origins. By the early twentieth century, these arguments can be linked to imperialist and eugenicist ideas about the superiority of Anglo-Saxon races and fears about the security of European empires.

The issue of "race" permeated the suffrage campaigns in the United States from its earliest phases. (The term *race* is problematic and divisive. Some scholars have questioned whether races exist—or whether they are political constructs—since there is as much variation within racial groups as between them.) In 1868, when the Fourteenth Amendment introduced the word *male* into the U.S. Constitution for the first time, supporters of women's suffrage were faced with the prospect of Black men being enfranchised before white women. Whereas the movements for Black and women's suffrage had previously been linked together in one campaigning body, the women's suffrage movement now split over this issue. The National Woman Suffrage Association, led by Elizabeth Cady Stanton and Susan B. Anthony, argued that women had subordinated their own interests during the Civil War for the cause of abolition and

that they should now be rewarded with the vote. Stanton maintained that illiterate African American and immigrant men should not be given the rights to citizenship before educated white women.

Thereafter, the suffrage movement in the United States remained substantially divided along race lines. Although some African American women identified with mainstream white suffrage organizations, others developed their own agendas in separate Black women's suffrage groups. By the 1890s and early 1900s their aims included fighting to regain the vote for Black men who had been disenfranchised in the southern states and lobbying white women's groups, some of which were acceding to white supremacist strategies that would write Black women out of suffrage proposals and limit the ballot to educated white women. Attempts to keep Black women without a vote continued until the passage of the Nineteenth Amendment enfranchised all women. However, within 10 years, Black women in southern states lost the vote, and their plight was largely ignored by white women voters.

The Woman's Christian Temperance Union (WCTU), the largest organization in the world to fight for women's suffrage, also has a racist record. With the exception of New Zealand, where Maori women were included in its campaigns, the WCTU concurred with prevailing views about the political incapacity of Black peoples and often forced them to form separate branches of the union.

Journalist Ida Wells-Barnett founded the Alpha Suffrage Club, the first African American women's suffrage organization, and wrote editorials against the practice of lynching. (Courtesy: University of Chicago)

While on a tour of England, African American suffragist Ida B. Wells criticized this prejudice, claiming that, by accepting the view of Black people as amoral, WCTU president Frances Willard was abetting the epidemic of lynchings in the U.S. southern states.

In South Africa, WCTU members and other suffragists avoided getting involved in racial politics by arguing that women there should have the vote on the same basis as men. Yet they had little difficulty in acceding to the exclusion of Cape Africans (defined as people of mixed descent) from voting rolls in the 1920s. The subsequent enfranchisement only of white South African women by the Nationalist Party in 1930 had more connection to the party's desire to reduce the importance of the Cape African vote than to a genuine conviction that women deserved the franchise. Similar views of the political naiveté

and ignorance of Black people were accepted by Australians. When, in 1902, the Commonwealth Franchise Bill would have enfranchised all Aboriginal men and women along with white women, delegates from western Australia and Queensland objected strongly on the grounds that Aboriginals were the most degraded people in the world. They were horrified that Aboriginal women might have the same privileges as their own wives and daughters: "If any thing could tend to make the concession of female suffrage worse than it is in the minds of some people it would be giving it to any of the numerous gins of the blackfellow" (Oldfield, 1992, 64). A clause was inserted in the bill that excluded Aboriginal Australians and natives of Africa and the Pacific islands (with the exception of New Zealand) from obtaining the federal vote if they did not also possess a state vote. The fact that Maori people living in Australia gained the vote when Aboriginal Australians were excluded illustrates the supposed hierarchy of non-European races. The lighter-skinned, more warlike Maoris, who had put up greater resistance to European invasion of New Zealand than their Australian counterparts, were considered racially superior to Aboriginals and therefore more capable of exercising the rights of citizenship.

New Zealand women had included Maori women in their suffrage organizations and New Zealand had given them the vote at the same time as white women, but this fact was used negatively by British women to assert racial superiority. For example, in 1909, Millicent Fawcett was applauded when she pointed out the injustice of the fact that "Maori women of New Zealand . . . [had] more power in developing and moulding the future of Empire than we have in England. Why should the Maori Women be in a superior position to that held by women in England?" (Dalziel, 1994, 57). This example, among others, supports the view that the European suffrage movement drew upon theories of racial superiority and empire, and it bolsters Antoinette Burton's argument that there was a conflict between British suffragists' vision of a universal movement linking women through the world in sisterhood and their belief in British superiority. British white women's claims to the vote were often established with reference to the racial inferiority of their Indian "sisters," whom they sought to rescue and whose interests they sought to represent.

Such colonial racism was not confined to British suffragists. The letters of the Dutch suffrage leader Aletta Jacobs, who traveled in 1911 to South Africa and Asia with the International Woman Suffrage Alliance leader Carrie Chapman Catt, show that her feminist meetings can be divided by color. White men and women, whom she usually met in the context of suffrage activities, were almost always mentioned by name, whereas women of color were nameless and meetings with them were less obviously politically motivated, even though they were usually with high-caste or aristocratic women. In this way Jacobs makes clear racial demarcations within her feminist politics between "them" and "us."

Challenges to notions of Anglo-Saxon racial superiority can be found within the suffrage movement, coming not only from Black American suffragists but also from Latin American suffrage leaders. For example, the views of the Chilean feminist Delia Ducoing, from Uruguay, were based on a kind of racial stereotyping that valued the Latin American tradition above the Euro-American. She stressed the ideal of "conscious order" within Latin culture and contrasted it with the ideas of Anglo-Saxon feminists in England and America, which she did not see as a positive model for Chilean feminists to imitate.

See also Antislavery Movement; Australia; Britain; Catt, Carrie Chapman; Citizenship; Ducoing, Delia; Fawcett, Millicent Garrett; Fourteenth and Fifteenth Amendments; Imperialism; Jacobs, Aletta; New Zealand; Nineteenth Amendment; South Africa; Stanton, Elizabeth Cady; United States of America; Wells-Barnett, Ida Bell.
References Bosch, Mineke. "Colonial Dimensions of Dutch Women's Suffrage: Aletta Jacobs's Travel Letters from Africa and Asia, 1911–1912" (1999); Burton, Antoinette. "The Feminist Quest for Identity: British Imperial Suffragism and 'Global Sisterhood,' 1900–1915" (1991); Dalziel, Raewyn. "Presenting the Enfranchisement of New Zealand Women Abroad" (1994); Dubois, Ellen. "Woman Suffrage Around the World: Three Phases of Internationalism" (1994); Hine, Darlene Clark, Elsa Barkley Brown, and Rosalyn Terborg-Penn, eds. *Black Woman in America: An Historical Encyclopaedia.* Vols. 1 and 11 (1993); Oldfield, Audrey. *Woman Suffrage in Australia, A Gift or a Struggle?* (1992).

Ransome-Kuti, Funmilayo

The most prominent campaigner for women's suffrage in Nigeria, Frances Abigail Olufunmilayo Thomas (1900–1978) was born in Abeokuta, in what was then the British-ruled colonial protectorate of Southern Nigeria. A member of the Egba group of the Yoruba people, she was educated locally and in England and became a teacher at Abeokuta Girls' Grammar School. In 1925 she married the Rev. I. Ransome-Kuti, a teacher and politician.

In 1932 Funmilayo Ransome-Kuti founded a Ladies' Club, which consisted of a group of educated, charitable women who worked to eradicate illiteracy and improve living conditions in the community. In March 1944 the Abeokuta Ladies' Club (ALC) began to expand to include local market women, and its members became more politically conscious when Ransome-Kuti led a successful campaign to stop rice sold by the market women from being seized by the authorities, who claimed that it was needed for the war effort. In March 1946 the ALC became the Abeokuta Women's Union (AWU), with a new commitment to political action. Under Ransome-Kuti's leadership the

AWU became more anticolonial and adopted the cause of the enfranchisement of women, as well as seeking to promote women's social and economic rights.

On 15 May 1949, Ransome-Kuti proposed the founding of the Nigerian Women's Union (NWU), with the long-term aim of becoming a nationally based organization dedicated to obtaining the vote for all Nigerian women. In the same year she was appointed by the British administration to represent Abeokuta at the Western Provinces conference on a new constitution. The only female representative present, she argued strongly for women's enfranchisement and against the indirect electoral system. The resulting Macpherson Constitution set up regional assemblies and a new federal legislature to be elected by an electoral college, but the voting system was based on the payment of taxes, thus excluding the vast majority of women. In 1951 Ransome-Kuti stood as a candidate for the Western House of Assembly on behalf of the nationalist party, the National Council of Nigeria and the Cameroons (NCNC), but she was defeated.

During the early 1950s Ransome-Kuti visited a number of communities to call on women to form their own branches of the NWU. Gradually, the organization became a federation of autonomous branches, each one concerned primarily with the problems of local women, with a national executive committee that concentrated on national issues. With Ransome-Kuti as its president and Margaret Ekpo as national secretary, the NWU proclaimed itself unattached to any political party and decided on a number of specific objectives. These included women's suffrage, the abolition of electoral colleges, and the allocation of a definite proportion of political representation to women, with women having the right to nominate their own representatives on the local councils.

The next development in the campaign occurred in 1953, when Ransome-Kuti organized a two-day conference in Abeokuta, which was attended by 400 delegates and was called a "parliament of the women of Nigeria." It was decided that the conference should become known as the Federation of Nigerian Women's Societies (FNWS), and the gathering passed a resolution asking for universal adult suffrage. The federation's policies were essentially the same as those of the NWU, placing great emphasis on achieving equal opportunities for women, particularly in the field of education. At its second annual conference in July 1954, the FNWS congratulated the Eastern Region government for introducing universal adult suffrage for regional elections and called on the other assemblies to follow suit. In December 1954 Ransome-Kuti stood as the only woman candidate in the first direct federal elections held as a result of the new Lyttleton Constitution, but she was not elected.

Like the NWU, the FNWS never became affiliated with any political party, despite the fact that most of its leaders, including Ransome-Kuti, were members of the nationalist party, the NCNC. Ransome-Kuti had always been a nationalist and a socialist as well as a feminist, but she was never an unthinking party politician, and she was prepared to be critical of any organization that discriminated against women and oppressed the Nigerian people. The NCNC put tremendous pressure on the FNWS to affiliate with it, but Ransome-Kuti refused on the grounds that the FNWS wished to remain independent and able to support any party that worked for women's rights and the welfare of all Nigerian citizens. From 1956 to 1959, Ransome-Kuti was simultaneously president of the NWU, the FNWS, and the women's wing of the Western Region of the NCNC, and there is no doubt that it was difficult for her to keep the roles separate and distinct, although she always insisted that her loyalty to the women of Nigeria came first. In 1959 Ransome-Kuti was about to stand as an NCNC candidate for a seat in the Federal Assembly, but because of disagreements with the national executive committee of the party, she stood as an independent instead, and as a result, the NCNC lost the election and she was expelled from the party.

With Nigeria's independence in 1960, universal adult suffrage was introduced under the new constitution, except in the predominantly Muslim Northern Region, where women did not get the vote until it was granted by military decree in 1976. Ransome-Kuti had always been committed to improving the political and social rights of women in northern Nigeria, and she was involved in numerous campaigns for their enfranchisement over a number of years.

In February 1977 Ransome-Kuti was thrown from a window when soldiers sent by the military junta raided the family home. She was seriously injured and never fully recovered. The following year, on 12 April 1978, she died in Lagos. During the later years of her life, Ransome-Kuti received a number of national and international honors, including the Lenin Peace Prize, in recognition of her services to the women of Nigeria. She was one of the few nationalists who attempted to bridge ethnic and class divides in order to lead Nigerian women in the struggles for equal political rights and national independence.

See also Africa South of the Sahara; Nationalism; Nigeria.
Reference Johnson-Odim, Cheryl, and Nina Emma Mba. *For Women and the Nation: Funmilayo Ransome-Kuti of Nigeria* (1997).

Rathbone, Eleanor

The British suffragist Eleanor Rathbone (1872–1946) was born in Liverpool, the daughter of a wealthy industrialist and Liberal member of Parliament, William Rathbone. Shortly after leaving Somerville College, Oxford, she joined the women's suffrage movement in Liverpool and be-

came the first woman to serve on Liverpool City Council, which she did from 1909 to 1910. At the same time, Rathbone became a member of the national executive committee of the National Union of Women's Suffrage Societies (NUWSS), where she used her public speaking abilities to promote the suffrage cause.

After the failure of successive Conciliation Bills between 1910 and 1912, proposing a limited parliamentary franchise for women, the NUWSS felt betrayed by the Liberal government and decided to change its strategy. Despite its nonparty stance, Millicent Fawcett and the NUWSS executive explored the idea of a temporary alliance with the Labour Party because it was the only political party that had made women's suffrage part of its official program. Although the majority of NUWSS members were Liberals (including Rathbone), there was reluctant agreement among the executive committee that a partnership with the Labour Party might be the best way forward.

Rathbone warned Fawcett that such an alliance would alienate many Liberal supporters, and she spoke against the proposal at the NUWSS council meeting held in May 1912. However, the council agreed to the new policy, which would mean that financial support would be given to Labour candidates in parliamentary elections where there were no prosuffrage Liberal candidates. Rathbone continued to object to the alliance, believing it would split the vote of progressive suffrage sympathizers, possibly leading to a win for the Conservatives in any future general election. Amidst much acrimony Rathbone and several of her colleagues on the NUWSS executive resigned in protest some time afterwards, although she did return to the fold when World War I broke out.

In 1919, after women had gained a limited measure of parliamentary suffrage in the 1918 Representation of the People Act, Rathbone succeeded Fawcett as president of the NUWSS. The organization was renamed the National Union of Societies for Equal Citizenship (NUSEC), and its primary objective was to campaign for equal voting rights for women, although it also fought for other measures, including equal pay, fairer divorce laws, and family allowances. Finally, in 1928, the objective of full and equal suffrage was achieved. The following year Rathbone became an Independent member of Parliament and continued her fight for family allowances, which were introduced just before her death in 1946.

> See also Britain; Citizenship; Conciliation Bill; Fawcett, Millicent Garrett; National Union of Women's Suffrage Societies; Representation of the People Act; Representation of the People (Equal Franchise) Act.
> References Alberti, Johanna. *Eleanor Rathbone* (1996); Stocks, Mary. *Eleanor Rathbone: A Biography* (1949).

Representation of the People Act (1918)

The Representation of the People Act, passed in February 1918, entitled some women in Britain to vote in parliamentary elections for the first time. Women could be registered as voters if they had reached the age of 30 and were local government electors or were married to local government electors. The latter had to occupy land or premises of a yearly value of not less than five pounds or a dwelling house. Approximately 8.5 million women were enfranchised by the act, leaving 5 million women still excluded. Because the demographic imbalance between the sexes had been exacerbated by losses during World War I, the age limit was introduced to ensure that men still made up a majority of the electorate.

Politicians had first raised the possibility of franchise reform in 1916 when they were under pressure to ensure that soldiers returning from the front would be able to vote in postwar elections. Many would have been disenfranchised under the existing residential and property qualifications, and the Representation of the People Act enabled all men over the age of 21 to vote.

There is considerable debate about why, after so many years of struggle, women were finally included in the franchise. Women's contribution to the war effort made it more difficult to leave them out, and in the absence of militant campaigning, Prime Minister H. H. Asquith could move away from his long-standing opposition without losing face. On the other hand, it has also been suggested that women had already won the argument before the outbreak of war and that the majority of MPs in 1914 were in favor of granting women the vote. This support was reinforced by the continued lobbying by nonmilitant women's suffrage societies in 1916 and 1917. Representatives of at least 12 such groups worked together to put pressure on Asquith to ensure that women were included in the new legislation. The main debate was then over which categories of women would be enfranchised. On pragmatic grounds, the suffrage societies accepted that women should be enfranchised on different terms than men—a reversal of their position before the war. It was not until 1928 that women received the vote on the same terms as men.

> See also Britain; Representation of the People (Equal Franchise) Act.
> References Law, Cheryl. *Suffrage and Power: The Women's Movement, 1918–1928* (1997); Pugh, Martin. *Women and the Women's Movement in Britain, 1915–1959* (1992); Summerfield, Penny. "Women and War in the Twentieth Century" (1995).

Representation of the People (Equal Franchise) Act (1928)

The 1928 Representation of the People Act at last gave equal voting rights to women in Britain, 10 years after a limited franchise had been granted to women over 30. The women's suffrage groups had never been happy with the restrictions of the 1918 act, but they were initially optimistic that the age differential between men and women would soon be removed. The manifesto of the postwar government coalition, signed by Prime Minister Lloyd George and Conservative Party leader Bonar Law in November 1918, pledged that the government would remove legal inequalities between men and women, and both the Liberal and Labour Parties made similar promises.

In practice none of the political parties gave priority to women's suffrage in the 1920s, and women's groups had to continue their campaign for full voting rights. In the early 1920s several private members' bills on the subject were introduced in Parliament, and the National Union of Societies for Equal Citizenship (NUSEC), which had replaced the National Union of Women's Suffrage Societies, used familiar prewar methods, including sending deputations to ministers, holding meetings, and publicizing the cause in the press. This cautious approach was criticized by another feminist organization, the Six Point Group, which threatened to reintroduce more militant methods.

The election of eight female MPs in 1923 and the return of a Labour government made success seem more likely. Feminist groups stepped up their campaign to pressure the government, holding large rallies and demonstrations as well as lobbying MPs. A private member's bill was introduced, but its passage was delayed by complicated amendments introduced by Conservative MPs and it ran out of time. Further prevarications by the incoming Conservative government after 1924 gave further impetus to the women's suffrage campaign, which staged a procession in London in July 1926. This was followed the next year by a mass protest rally in Trafalgar Square arranged by the Equal Political Rights Campaign Committee. The opening of Parliament in 1928 was preceded by a women's motorcade, and members of the Young Suffragists delivered a petition to Prime Minister Stanley Baldwin in his home. In March 1928 Baldwin finally introduced a bill that enfranchised over 5 million more women.

The Conservative Party was preoccupied with recession, foreign affairs, and the general strike in the 1920s, and therefore women's suffrage was low on its agenda. Moreover, the party feared that women, in particular younger women, would be radical in their politics. It was crucial, therefore, for women's groups to use their influence to keep women's suffrage at the forefront of parliamentary politics. They undoubtedly played an important part in ensuring that a measure for equal voting rights between the sexes was passed in 1928.

See also Britain; Citizenship; Flapper Vote; National Union of Women's Suffrage Societies; Rathbone, Eleanor; Representation of the People Act.
Reference Law, Cheryl. *Suffrage and Power: The Women's Movement, 1918–1928* (1997).

The *Revolution*

The *Revolution*, founded in 1868 by Elizabeth Cady Stanton and Susan B. Anthony, was one of the most well-known suffrage newspapers in the movement, despite its short life. It gained notoriety partly because it was backed financially by George Francis Train, a Democrat and railroad promoter known for his racist views who contributed articles on his own pet causes, in particular financial questions and Fenianism. More importantly, however, the *Revolution* aroused interest because it covered a wide range of women's rights causes besides the struggle for the suffrage.

Edited in the first year by Elizabeth Cady Stanton, with Susan B. Anthony acting as publisher and business manager, the *Revolution* discussed conditions of employment for women, prostitution, the double standard of morality, and legal in-

The first issue of the Revolution *was published in New York on 6 January 1870. (Sophia Smith Collection)*

See also Anthony, Susan B.; Stanton, Elizabeth Cady; United States of America; The Woman's Journal.
Reference Flexner, Eleanor. *Century of Struggle: The Woman's Rights Movement in the United States* ([1959] 1975).

Robins, Elizabeth

Elizabeth Robins (1862–1952) was a well-known actress and popular novelist who took a prominent part in the British suffragette movement. Born in Kentucky in the United States, she spent her childhood on Staten Island, New York. After the breakdown of her parents' marriage, she lived with her grandmother in Ohio and was then educated at Vassar, where she studied medicine. Instead of pursuing a career as a doctor, however, she decided to become an actress, playing a wide variety of roles and traveling all through the United States. In 1888, after the suicide of her husband, she went to live in England, where she enjoyed a successful acting career. She was largely responsible for introducing Ibsen to an English audience and claimed that her struggle to produce his plays and to free actresses from the actor-manager system had made her a feminist.

In 1902 Robins retired from the stage so that she could concentrate on journalism and writing fiction. She had begun to write popular fiction in the 1890s under the pseudonym C. E. Raimond, and after a visit to Alaska to visit her brothers, she wrote a novel, *The Magnetic North* (1904), which became a best-seller. She moved in artistic and intellectual social circles, where she came into contact with suffrage supporters but she had not yet been convinced to support their cause. In 1905, however, she declared that she was in favor of votes for women, and in the following year she began to write suffrage dramas that were performed by suffrage supporters both in Britain and the United States. Her play *Votes for Women!* was completed in the au-

equalities in marriage. Eleanor Flexner claims that it not only carried news, but gave the suffrage movement "a forum, focus and direction," with lively editorials that railed against injustices of every kind. Running through all the editorials and leading articles was the argument that although the vote provided the essential basis for real equality and was therefore of key importance, the fight for women's rights was a broader cause than the suffrage alone.

In 1870 the *Revolution* faced competition from the recently established and more conservative *Woman's Journal*. Despite valiant efforts by Susan B. Anthony to increase the number of subscribers and advertising revenue, the debts became so great that the paper was forced to close in May 1870.

tumn of 1906 and was later turned into a novel, *The Convert* (1907).

Robins drew her material from a series of suffrage meetings that confirmed her own commitment to the suffrage cause. Although she admired Millicent Fawcett, leader of the National Union of Women's Suffrage Societies, she began to feel that constitutional methods were not inspiring enough, and after attending the Women's Parliament, where she was almost trampled by police horses, she decided to support the militant group the Women's Social and Political Union (WSPU).

Emmeline Pankhurst, a leader of the WSPU, saw the value of having such a well-known figure associated with the militant campaign. In 1907 she persuaded Robins to join the WSPU executive committee, a position she retained for five years. Robins joined a wide variety of activities, including demonstrations, deputations to government ministers, and election campaigning. Although she disliked making speeches, she took part in public meetings all over the country and was clearly able to inspire an audience. Her greatest contribution, however, was through her writing, which interpreted and justified militancy to an often hostile world. She published numerous articles in *Votes for Women* and other newspapers and was president of the Women Writers' Suffrage League, which was founded in 1908. Many of her speeches and articles were published in a collection called *Way Stations* (1913), which was distributed in the United States as well as Britain. It presented the women's suffrage campaign as a railway journey, and as Angela John notes, it was the second history of the WSPU from within, following Sylvia Pankhurst's *The Suffragette* (1911).

In 1912, in the context of escalating militancy and the expulsion from the WSPU of her friends, Emmeline and Fred Pethick-Lawrence, Robins resigned from the executive committee of the union. She continued, however, to give active support to the suffrage campaign and remained a committed feminist for the rest of her life. In the 1920s, for example, she wrote regularly for the feminist journal *Time and Tide* and was a member of the Six Point Group, which campaigned for sex equality in all spheres.

Robins played an important role as a political propagandist for the militant suffrage cause between 1907 and 1912. She did not put herself in a position to be arrested and imprisoned, but through her writings she provided a defense of militant tactics and a positive portrayal of suffragettes that countered the negative images put forward by their opponents.

See also *The Convert*; Fawcett, Millicent Garrett; National Union of Women's Suffrage Societies; Pankhurst, Emmeline; Pankhurst, (Estelle) Sylvia; Pethick-Lawrence, Emmeline; Pethick-Lawrence, Frederick; *Votes for Women!*; Women Writers' Suffrage League; Women's Social and Political Union.
Reference John, Angela V. *Elizabeth Robins. Staging a Life, 1862–1952* (1995).

Russia

An organized movement for women's suffrage did not begin in Russia until 1905. Conditions in Russia in the nineteenth century were unfavorable to the development of a women's movement; the Tsar governed autocratically, the population was predominantly rural, and there was only a small middle class. The main critique of social and political life came from an intelligentsia based in the major cities, and the first expression of interest in feminism was a literary one. The "woman question" was widely discussed in the 1860s after the publication of a series of articles on the issue by the poet and radical publicist M. L. Mikhailov. He did not mention political rights for women in any direct way, but he raised the possibility of women's ultimate right to representation through his translation of an article by the

English liberals John Stuart Mill and Harriet Taylor Mill on the enfranchisement of women. As Edmondson notes, however, there was little interest in voting rights in Russia since "there was no national legislature and, for much of the period, no freedom to campaign for one." Nonetheless, there was also little pressure from women to "gain access to the newly created zemstvos and municipal councils. Finally, in the 1870s, many women left the women's movement to take part in radical, oppositional politics" (Edmondson, 1992, 79).

After the turn of the century, a younger generation of feminists, who were dissatisfied with the emphasis of their predecessors on charity work, began to take more interest in women's suffrage. A number of zemstvos had been advocating a limited franchise for women in local government for a number of years, but the liberals had still not embraced this goal. In the political banquets held by liberals in the autumn of 1904 to demand citizenship rights, women's enfranchisement was not mentioned. The more revolutionary parties, however, were adopting the goal of universal suffrage, and women factory workers began to join the women's sections of Father Gapon's Assembly of Russian Factory Workers, a group that sought to foster trade unionism, in the autumn of 1904. The assembly did not address the question of suffrage, but it did encourage factory women to see themselves as active participants in a political struggle. They in turn may have encouraged other women to set up their own organization to achieve equal rights.

Feminists were inspired to demand the suffrage both by the success of the women's suffrage movement in Finland (which achieved the vote in 1906) and by the political upheavals in Russia in 1904–1905. In response to demands made during the 1905 Revolution, the Tsar had to proclaim civil liberties and call a parliament (Duma) with a wide electorate that included only men. Women were so infuriated by their exclusion that they formed the All-Russian Union of Equal Rights for Women (SRZh), led largely by Moscow women with professional and literary backgrounds. Its general aim was to achieve equality before the law, regardless of sex, and its first act was to petition the City Duma and other local representative bodies for voting rights. Branches were formed all over Russia, with the strongest located in Moscow and St. Petersburg.

By 1907 the SRZh had 80 branches and approximately 12,000 members. The leadership had close ties with the Kadets (Constitutional Democrats), the most important party in the Duma. Ariadna Tyrkova, for example, was on the central committee of the Kadets, and Anna Milyukova was married to a Kadet leader. The union's activities also radicalized the older, more moderate RZhVBO, which sent a petition to the Duma with 7,000 signatures that demanded votes for women. In 1908 the RZhVBO organized an All-Russian Women's Congress, attended by over 1,000 delegates.

The congress marked the end of a liberal period that had enabled a women's suffrage movement to develop. As early as 1906, the Tsar had already begun to undermine the powers of the Duma and to repress opposition through the use of force. By 1908 the membership of the SRZh had fallen to 1,000. Most of its members then joined the government-sponsored but inactive Russian League for Equal Rights, taking it over and using it to maintain a women's suffrage presence and to pressure the Duma for reform up to the outbreak of World War I. The league took a more moderate stance than the All-Russian Union had, however, demanding equal suffrage for both sexes under existing electoral laws, rather than universal suffrage. These were difficult years for the women's movement. Not only did feminists face interference from the police and local authorities, but they also met hostility from social democratic parties. The Bolsheviks in particular condemned the league as bourgeois, in part to bolster its support from working-class women. The Bolsheviks participated in a variety of activities in support of working-women's issues, including the first Russian celebration of International Proletarian Women's Day, on 8 March 1913.

With the outbreak of war in 1914, feminists concentrated on supporting the war effort, but the downfall of the Tsar early in 1917 brought constitutional questions to the fore once again. The Provisional Government that was established after the February Revolution promised to introduce civil equality, but sex inequality was not mentioned. This prompted the League for Equal Rights to organize a campaign to ensure that women were included in the franchise, a campaign that was met with support from all over Russia. In March, a procession attended by over 40,000 women lobbied the new government in Petrograd, and two days later the prime minister, Georgy Yevgenyevich L'vov, gave a firm commitment to a deputation of all the main feminist leaders that women would be included in the proposed electoral law. The government hoped to establish a Western-style liberal democracy and to ward off the threat posed by the more revolutionary Bolsheviks. The law that finally emerged in May gave Russian citizens over the age of 20 the right to vote for the Constituent Assembly. This gain was short-lived, however; in the Bolshevik takeover of power in the revolution of November 1917, the old-style elected bodies were replaced by a communist regime.

See also All-Russian Women's Congress; Citizenship; International Proletarian Women's Day; Mill, Harriet, Taylor; Mill, John Stuart.
References Edmondson, Linda Harriet. *Feminism in Russia, 1900–1917* (1984); Edmonson, Linda Harriet, ed. *Women and Society in Russia and the Soviet Union* (1992); Evans, Richard J. *The Feminists: Women's Emancipation Movements in Europe, America and Australasia, 1840–1920* (1977).

Samoa (formerly Western Samoa)

The islands that constitute Samoa are part of a much larger and socially complex geographical region known officially as the Pacific Islands, which are divided into 22 politically dependent and independent countries and territories. Australia, Britain, France, New Zealand, and the United States all have dependencies in the area.

Western Samoa, which became Samoa in 1997, was the first South Pacific island group to achieve full political independence in 1962, after previously being administered by New Zealand. From 1962 to 1990 the franchise was restricted to titled heads of families or clans, known as *matai*, with only two members of the Legislative Assembly (Fono) out of a total of 49 being elected by universal suffrage.

The great majority of *matai* have always been male, although women's success in attaining higher education qualifications, which are rewarded with titles, has increased the number of female *matai* since the 1960s and a small number of women have been elected to the Legislative Assembly since 1962.

Universal suffrage was introduced in Western Samoa after a referendum in October 1990, and the first elections under the reformed system were held in April 1991. In May 1991 the government appointed the country's first female cabinet member, Fiame Naomi, the daughter of Western Samoa's first prime minister, Fiame Mata'afa Fuamui Mulinuu. She became the minister of education, youth, sport, culture, and labor.

The cautious progress of Western Samoa to full universal suffrage demonstrates the restricted nature of political society encountered by women in the whole Pacific Islands region, due to the patrilineal nature of society, with its hierarchical systems of rank, and the complexity of its kinship and ethnic groups.

See also Citizenship; Universal Suffrage.
Reference Meleisea, Penelope Schoeffel. "Women and Political Leadership in the Pacific Islands" (1994).

Schneiderman, Rose

Rose Schneiderman (1882–1972) was one of the many working-class women who were active in the U.S. suffrage movement. Born in a village in Russian Poland, she came to the United States in 1891 and later worked as a cap-maker. In 1904 she was elected to the executive committee of the Cap Makers' Union, and during a lengthy strike she attended her first meeting of the Women's Trade Union League (WTUL), an umbrella group that aimed to promote female trade unionism. Schneiderman was to work with and for the WTUL for most of her life, becoming president of the New York chapter and then of the national organization.

After 1905 the WTUL began to take a greater interest in the vote, emphasizing the importance of suffrage for working-class women, who could use it to improve their conditions of employment. The WTUL worked closely with a new suffrage organization, the Equality League of Self-Supporting Women, established in New York in 1907 by Harriot Stanton Blatch. Schneiderman became a member and was soon one of the most popular suffrage speakers in the league.

In 1912 Schneiderman took a leave of absence from the WTUL to work for women's suffrage. She was hired by the National American Woman Suffrage Association to help in the suffrage campaign in Cleveland. Her job was to speak at street meetings and to persuade trade unionists to support a women's suffrage amendment to the state constitution. She then went back to trade union organizing, but in 1917 she was offered the post of chairwoman of the industrial section of the Women's Suffrage Party of New York City, where she succeeded her friend Leonora O'Reilly, who had also been active in the WTUL. Schneiderman joined the campaign for a suffrage amendment that was being waged in New York City, again concentrating on gaining the support of trade unionists by attending meetings and distributing literature, including a series of open letters. The campaign was successful and Rose then returned to the WTUL as an organizer.

Rose Schneiderman was one of the many working-class women who were dedicated to socialist principles and active in the labor movement and who helped to broaden the social base and the methods of the women's suffrage movement after the turn of the century. She was keen to point out the relevance of the vote for working-class women and sought to strengthen links between trade unions and the women's movement. She wrote about her experiences in an autobiography, *All for One*, published in 1967.

See also Blatch, Harriot Stanton; National American Woman Suffrage Association; United States of America; Women's Trade Union League.

References DuBois, Ellen Carol. "Working Women, Class Relations and Suffrage Militance: Harriot Stanton Blatch and the New York Woman Suffrage Movement, 1894–1909" (1987); Schneiderman, Rose, with Lucy Goldthwaite. *All for One* (1967); Wertheimer, Barbara Mayer. *We Were There: The Story of Working Women in America* (1977).

Schwimmer, Rosika

Rosika Schwimmer (1877–1948) was a leading member of the Hungarian suffrage movement and also took an active part in the International Woman Suffrage Alliance (IWSA). She was born in Budapest, the eldest of three children of an upper-middle-class Jewish family, but because of her father's business failures, she had to work as a bookkeeper from the age of 18. Her family background helped to foster an interest in reform—her mother was a freethinker and one of her uncles helped to form the Hungarian Peace Society. It is hardly surprising, therefore, that in 1897 Rosika Schwimmer began to work for the National Association of Women Office Workers in Budapest, soon becoming its president. She also founded the first Hungarian Association of Working Women in 1903.

It was soon after this, however, that Schwimmer began to take a greater interest in women's suffrage. In 1904 she attended the inaugural congress of the IWSA in Berlin as a reporter, and she returned to Hungary determined to fight for the vote in her own country. She founded the Munkásnő Egyesülete (Council of Women) in 1904, and in the same year, with her friend, the teacher Vilma Glücklich, she established the Feministák Egyesülete (Hungarian Feminist Association). The association fought for women's suffrage as well as a range of other reforms, including equal education, employment rights, and access to birth control. Influenced in her outlook by the German suffragists Anita Augspurg and Lida Gustava Heymann, Schwimmer ensured that the association was radical in its methods, which included distributing leaflets, making speeches from the floor at political meetings, and holding demonstrations. In 1913 Schwimmer helped to organize the annual IWSA Congress in Budapest, which attracted 3,000 participants.

Because of the complex political situation in Hungary, which was part of the Habsburg Empire, the suffrage campaign made little progress before World War I. Nonetheless, Schwimmer moved on to play a more international role in the suffrage movement in 1914, when she was asked to become international press secretary at the headquarters of the IWSA in London. Schwimmer was well qualified for such employment. She had worked as a journalist, spoke nine languages, and had become familiar with European suffrage affairs after undertaking a lecture tour through Europe in the prewar years. A well-known figure in international suffrage circles, she was in great demand as a speaker, and audiences enjoyed her scathing attacks on men, her clever use of satire, and her dramatic hand gestures.

A flamboyant and forceful personality, Schwimmer was a controversial figure who inspired either fierce dislike or great affection. She was particularly close to Aletta Jacobs, a leading Dutch suffrage campaigner. She smoked and wore loose-fitting dresses, and her black, frizzy hair, dark eyebrows, and aristocratic gold pince-nez gave her a striking appearance. Schwimmer had been married in 1911 but was divorced two years later, a fact that she kept secret throughout her life.

With the outbreak of war, Schwimmer turned her attention to peace campaigning. She resigned from her post with the IWSA because she believed that her nationality was an embarrassment to her coworkers. She sought to convince anyone who would listen, including national branches of the IWSA, to support her plan to persuade neutral governments to mediate in order to bring a speedy end to the conflict. She traveled to the United States, where she lectured all over the country on the need for a conference of neutral nations. Her eloquence inspired the formation of a number of peace groups, including the Women's Peace Party, with Jane Addams as president and Schwimmer as international secretary.

When Hungary became a democratic republic in November 1918, Schwimmer was appointed as ambassador to Switzerland. The appointment of a woman to a diplomatic post was unprecedented but also short-lived. Schwimmer opposed the subsequent communist takeover of Hungary and in 1920 escaped to Vienna, after which she emigrated to the United States. She spent the rest of her life working for peace as a member of both the Women's International League for Peace and Freedom and the Campaign for World Government, which she founded with her friend Lola Maverick Lloyd in 1937.

See also Augspurg, Anita, and Lida Gustava Heymann; Hungary; International Woman Suffrage Alliance; Jacobs, Aletta; Peace Movement.
References Bosch, Mineke, with Annemarie Kloosterman. *Politics and Friendship: Letters from the International Woman Suffrage Alliance, 1902–1942* (1990); Wiltsher, Anne. *Most Dangerous Women: Feminist Peace Campaigners of the Great War* (1985).

Scotland

Scotland played an important part in the British suffrage movement from its very beginning. Edinburgh was one of the first cities in Britain to form a suffrage group, the Edinburgh National Society for Women's Suffrage, in the period 1866–1867, and the group's president, Priscilla McLaren, wife of the Edinburgh MP Duncan McLaren and sister of John Bright, had close family ties with many of the leading English and Scottish suffragists of the period. By the 1870s branches of the National Society for Women's Suffrage

Scottish suffragettes welcoming Mary Phillips (standing third from left) on her release from prison on 3 August 1908. (Museum of London)

had been formed all over Scotland, and between 1867 and 1876, 2 million signatures were collected for suffrage petitions.

In the late nineteenth century, Scottish branches of the auxiliary groups associated with the Conservative and Liberal Parties took up the suffrage cause. For example, members of the Scottish Women's Liberal Federation, which was formed in 1892, were unequivocal from the beginning about including women's equal franchise as one of their objectives. This attitude contrasted with the protracted struggle over the issue that had caused problems for their English counterparts. After the turn of the century, there was a further increase in the number of local suffrage groups. One of the most important of these was the Glasgow and West of

Scotland Association for Women's Suffrage, established in 1902. The association had representatives from groups such as the Women's Liberal Federation and the Women's Cooperative Guild on its executive committee, and it worked closely with the Edinburgh suffrage group. In 1903 it affiliated with the National Union of Women's Suffrage Societies (NUWSS). As a general election became more imminent during 1904 and 1905, suffrage societies set up committees in a wide range of constituencies, and both Glasgow and Edinburgh had full-time organizing secretaries.

The greater publicity generated by the suffrage movement after 1906 attracted more women to take part in the cause, in Scotland as well as in England. New societies were formed under the auspices of the NUWSS, and existing groups grew in size; in 1909–1910 membership of the Edinburgh Society, for example, increased from 384 to 854. In 1910 the Scottish Federation of Women's Suffrage Societies was formed to coordinate local activities. Despite opposition, in particular from the Liberal-dominated Glasgow branch, the Scottish Federation endorsed the policy of the NUWSS to ally with the Labour Party and supported the Labour candidate in the by-election at Midlothian in September 1912. The election received a great deal of publicity, and activists with labor sympathies came from England to take part in the campaign. Among them was the Scotswoman Annot Robinson, née Wilkie, who had been the secretary of the Dundee Women's Social and Political Union (WSPU) before moving to the north of England on her marriage. Robinson later switched her allegiance to the NUWSS.

After 1906, branches of the militant groups, the WSPU and the Women's Freedom League (WFL), were also established in Scotland. The WSPU targeted Scotland because it was a Liberal stronghold, and it sent Teresa Billington-Greig as an organizer to drum up support. She had married a Scot, Frederick Greig, and had subsequently made her home in Scotland. It is not surprising that when she left the WSPU in 1907 to become one of the leaders of the breakaway WFL, she was followed by many local WSPU members, such as Anna Munro of Dunfermline, and the WFL maintained a strong presence in Scotland. Others, however, remained loyal to the WSPU and carried out militant activities that paralleled those of their English counterparts. A number of Scottish women, including Helen Crawfurd, Janie Allan, Mary Phillips, and the McPhun sisters, Margaret and Frances, were active members of the WSPU, and their reputation for militancy went beyond Scotland. Mary Phillips was imprisoned in Holloway in 1908 and was a very active campaigner in Scotland until 1909, when she went to England to work for Sylvia Pankhurst's East London Federation of Suffragettes. Helen Crawfurd, who did not join the WSPU until 1910, was a regular speaker for the union up to World War I. She was arrested on several occasions, including March 1914, when she was imprisoned in Glasgow for breaking windows at an army recruiting office.

There were close links between the WSPU and the socialist movement, particularly in Glasgow, where Tom Johnston, a committed supporter of women's suffrage and member of the socialist group the Independent Labour Party (ILP), edited an influential newspaper called *Forward*. Helen Crawfurd, Mary Phillips, and Margaret McPhun were all contributors to the paper, which had a regular suffrage column and was far more sympathetic to the militant suffragettes than the ILP's national newspaper, *Labour Leader*.

Scottish suffrage societies and individual campaigners played an integral role in the British suffrage movement. English suffrage activists made a point of touring Scotland for support, and Scottish women held leadership positions in the main suffrage organizations; Chrystal Macmillan, for example, was vice president of the Edinburgh National Society for Women's Suffrage and was also an active member of the NUWSS executive committee where she represented Scottish views. Leah Leneman notes that the Scottish and English movements were very similar in their largely middle-class composition and in the range of views put forward. Scottish suffrage activists did draw on a sense of national identity, using the thistle in their imagery and making reference to William Wallace fighting for Scottish liberties. Nonetheless, as Leneman points out, Scotland was different from Ireland, where the independence issue led to the establishment of separate groups. She concludes that "Scottish suffragists were proud to be part of Britain and part of the British movement, without ever losing their parallel sense of being Scottish" (Leneman, 1991, 219).

> *See also* Billington-Greig, Teresa; Britain; Independent Labour Party; Local Franchise; National Union of Women's Suffrage Societies; Pankhurst, (Estelle) Sylvia; Women's Freedom League; Women's Social and Political Union.
> *References* King, Elspeth. *The Scottish Women's Suffrage Movement in Glasgow* (1978); Leneman, Leah. *A Guid Cause: The Women's Suffrage Movement in Scotland* (1991).

Scott, Rose

Rose Scott (1847–1925) was one of the central figures in the suffrage movement in Australia. Not only was she instrumental in gaining the vote for women in New South Wales in 1903, but she also supported women's suffrage movements throughout Australia and corresponded frequently with suffragists in Europe and America. Her gracious manner hid an unflinching determination to achieve her goals. For her, gaining the vote was the road to all other reforms in the legal and economic position of women.

Born in Glendon, New South Wales, in 1847, Scott gained some financial independence after her father died, but she was also left with the care of her mother and two-year-old nephew, whom she adopted after the death of her sister. Despite these domestic responsibilities, she became a prominent social figure in Sydney, where her home was the site of regular salons. This allowed her to make important political, religious, artistic, and literary contacts. After founding the Women's Literature Society in 1889, she established a further network of contacts with feminists, writers, and journalists; these relationships would be essential in her campaign for women's suffrage in New South Wales.

Scott founded the Womanhood Suffrage League in New South Wales in 1891 and imposed her philosophy on the league throughout its life. In 1901 she survived a challenge from members of a breakaway group, the Women's Progressive Association, who were unhappy at the concentration of power in the central branch. She maintained control of the league's organization and activities and used her diplomatic skills to get prospective candidates for the legislature to sign declarations for women's suffrage before they were elected. She constantly sought support for suffrage, bringing together a variety of groups and organizations in support of her cause. She also organized deputations to the premier of New South Wales and a series of petitions to Parliament.

Scott was a compulsive letter writer, often sending 50 to 100 letters a day. Although most of her own letters have not survived, she preserved the replies to her letters and these offer us an interesting view of the relationship between women suffragists and male politicians during the New South Wales suffrage campaign. After the vote was won, Scott received congratulations from throughout Australia and the world, and thereafter she was frequently asked to address meetings and write articles on women's political responsibilities.

> *See also* Australia; Goldstein, Vida; Lawson, Louisa; Lee, Mary; Nicholls, Elizabeth.
> *Reference* Oldfield, Audrey. *Woman Suffrage in Australia, A Gift or a Struggle?* (1992).

Seneca Falls Convention

See Women's Rights Convention, Seneca Falls.

Sexuality

Many late nineteenth- and early twentieth-century feminists made direct connections between women's sexual exploita-

"The Age of Iron. Man as He Expects to Be," an 1869 lithograph by Currier and Ives, depicts many men's fears of women's rights, including the vote. (Library of Congress)

tion by men, both within and outside marriage, and their political powerlessness. Campaigns for the vote in some countries arose out of women's involvement in feminist campaigns to end the sexual double standard by changing men's sexual behavior and giving women greater control over their own bodies. Women claimed the vote on the basis of their moral authority over men. They believed they had higher spiritual and moral values, which should be extended to society as a whole, and they linked this reform with an attack on male sexuality, encapsulated in the British suffragette slogan "Votes for women, chastity for men."

The best known of the sexuality campaigns was the movement to repeal the Contagious Diseases (CD) legislation that was enacted across the British Empire and in parts of Europe in the mid-nineteenth century. In 1864 the British government had established secured hospitals in garrison towns throughout the empire to protect their troops from infection from venereal disease. The CD Acts allowed the forcible medical inspection and detention of prostitutes but had no jurisdiction over their male clients. In Australia and New Zealand, campaigns against the CD Acts were coordinated by the Woman's Christian Temperance Union (WCTU), which also became the main national organization agitating for the vote in both countries. In fact, the issue of prostitution in relation to the vote had first been raised in Australia by antisuffragists who were concerned that giving the vote to women would enfranchise prostitutes. Suffragists pointed out the double standard in this argument: the men who hired prostitutes were not denied the vote. The WCTU went on to make direct links between giving women the vote and repealing the CD Acts, declaring that women, who had higher moral standards than men, would use their votes to abolish measures they saw as "obnoxious" and "iniquitous."

The vote was also linked to social purity movements (coordinated in some countries by the WCTU), which sought to close down brothels, reform male sexual behavior, and raise the age of sexual consent. This last issue was of particular concern to suffragists who were worried about illegitimacy rates and other problems associated with the seduction of young girls by older men. For example, in Australia, Jessie Ackerman pointed out how difficult it was for a young, pregnant girl to prove paternity and how pitifully low the enforceable rates of maintenance were if paternity could be proved.

Women joining the anti-CD campaigns often moved on to become involved with suffrage groups. For example, Millicent Fawcett, leader of the British National Union of Women's Suffrage Societies, was told by many of her supporters that their interest in the suffrage stemmed from their involvement with or knowledge of Josephine Butler. Butler was leader of the British anti-CD campaigns and became the world superintendent of the Moral Purity Department of the WCTU. Yet Fawcett also saw the necessity of keeping campaigns against the sexual double standard separate from the suffrage campaign for fear the latter would be tainted by sensational and prurient press reports. Concerns of this kind can also be found in other countries and in relation to other sexual campaigns. For example, in 1904 women in Germany founded the Bund für Mutterschutz (League for the Protection of Mothers), which sought reproductive freedom for mothers, including legalized birth control and state maternity insurance for unmarried mothers. Its members also campaigned for the vote. Yet by 1910 the group's sex radicalism had alienated women in the mainstream feminist and suffrage organization Bund Deutscher Frauenvereine (BDF) [Federation of German Women's Associations]. In the more sexually conservative United States, Carrie

Chapman Catt was determined to sever connections between the vote and the transformation of sexual standards, anxious to rid the movement of any association with free love.

Another central concern for feminists in this period was the unequal position of women in marriage, which they regarded as legalized prostitution, often likened to slavery. In most countries, men's rights over women within marriage were absolute, extending even to legalized rape. For example, in nineteenth-century Britain, women became the property of their husbands on marriage and could be imprisoned or sued if they refused their husband conjugal rights. Furthermore, although women could be sued for divorce if they committed adultery, men could have extramarital affairs without fear of divorce action. The vote was widely viewed as the means to achieve equality within marriage and enable women's special moral influence to be extended into the sphere of legislation. Thus, laws could be passed in the area of sexual conduct that were equally stringent for men and women. Some suffrage leaders even advised women not to marry until the vote had been achieved. The most outspoken writer on this issue was British suffragette Christabel Pankhurst, who wrote a series of articles entitled "The Great Scourge and How to End It," published in the *Suffragette* in 1913. She claimed that 75 to 80 percent of all men in England had venereal disease and risked infecting their wives. Thus, she warned, the dangers of marriage for women would persist until they got the vote.

Feminists in Latin America also criticized the sexual double standard, although there the links between sexuality and suffrage were less explicit and the discourse on sexuality tended to be dominated by men. Nevertheless, feminist organizations often included both the suffrage and sexual issues on their list of objectives. For example, the National Council of Women in Uruguay was founded by suffragist leader

Paulina Luisi, who was a doctor with a strong interest in promoting sex education. Although suffrage remained a central goal, Luisi also encouraged the council to become involved in the campaign against the white slave trade, which imported prostitutes from Europe to Montevideo and Buenos Aires.

Antisuffragists saw the links between sexual campaigns and the suffrage movement as deeply threatening. Women's active participation in these campaigns heightened their fear of women's move into the political sphere, a move, they felt, that might lead to a more general rebellion of women against male domination. A British MP concerned with women's activities in the anti-CD movement "looked upon their conduct respecting that movement as a foretaste of what the country might expect of women who were engaged largely in politics" (Walkowitz, 1980, 88).

See also: Australia; Britain; Catt, Carrie Chapman; Fawcett, Millicent Garrett; Germany; Latin America and the Caribbean; Luisi, Paulina; National Union of Women's Suffrage Societies; New Zealand; Pankhurst, Christabel; United States of America; Uruguay; Woman's Christian Temperance Union.
References Cott, Nancy. "Early-Twentieth Century Feminism in Political Context: A Comparative Look at Germany and the United States" (1994); Jackson, Margaret. *The Real Facts of Life: Feminism and the Politics of Sexuality, 1850–1940* (1994); Kent, Susan Kingsley. *Sex and Suffrage in Britain, 1860–1914* (1990); Lavrin, Asunción. *Women, Feminism and Social Change in Argentina, Chile and Uruguay, 1890–1940* (1995); Oldfield, Audrey. *Woman Suffrage in Australia, A Gift or a Struggle?* (1992); Walkowitz, Judith. *Prostitution and Victorian Society: Women, Class and the State* (1980).

Shafiq, Durriyah (Shafik, Doria)

An influential Egyptian suffragist, Durriyah Shafiq (1908–1975) was born into a middle-class Muslim family in the Egyptian province of Tanta in 1908. She won a scholarship to the Sorbonne in 1928 and also obtained her doctorate in France in 1940 but she was refused a post at the University of Cairo on her return home. As a result, she decided to channel her energies into creating a dynamic new women's movement, with the object of winning full political rights for women. In 1945 she founded the magazine *Bint al-Nil* (Daughter of the Nile), and in 1948 she established Ittihad Bint al-Nil (the Bint al-Nil Union), which became a full political party in 1951.

Despite disputes with other feminist organizations, Ittihad Bint al-Nil was successful in placing women's suffrage and women's rights on the political agenda. In 1951, Shafiq led an invasion by 1,500 women of the Egyptian Parliament, demanding the right to vote; in 1952, she submitted her electoral registration papers in a bid to run as a candidate in the forthcoming elections; and in 1954, she and eight other women went on a hunger strike when they discovered that the Egyptian Revolutionary Command Council had appointed no women to its constitutional committee. This act, together with a multitude of demonstrations, lectures, debates, and articles, helped to persuade the constitutional committee to change its mind and give all Egyptian women the vote in 1956 (although women still had to register to vote, whereas men's voter registration was automatic). However, Shafiq's outspoken championing of the freedom of the individual and of secular (though not anti-Islamic) liberalism was deeply antipathetic to President Gamal Abdel Nasser, who placed her under house arrest in Cairo in 1957. Thereafter, she disappeared from the political stage, until, prey to depression, she committed suicide in 1975, at age 66.

See also Egypt; Sha'rawi, Nur al-Hudá.
References Nelson, Cynthia. "Biography and Women's History: On Interpreting Doria Shafik" (1991); Nelson, Cynthia. *Doria Shafik, Egyptian Feminist: A Woman Apart* (1996).

Shah Nawaz, Jahanara

A leading suffragist and worker for Muslim women's rights in preindependence India, and later a prominent politician in independent Pakistan, Jahanara Shah Nawaz (1896–1979) was born into a highly politicized Punjabi Muslim family from Lahore. From the beginning, she was an active member of Indian women's organizations, following the example of her mother and other women in her family, and by 1915 she was participating in the All-India Muslim Women's Conference.

Shah Nawaz first became prominent in the suffrage debate when, in 1930, she went with her father to the first Round Table Conference in London, set up by the British to discuss the future constitution of India. The Indian women's organizations had boycotted the event in support of the nationalists, but Shah Nawaz was nominated as a representative by the British, together with Mrs. Radhabai Subbarayan. The two women advocated an interim measure of reserved seats for women as a prelude to universal adult suffrage, but the women's organizations disagreed, favoring the complete equality of the universal franchise.

At the second Round Table Conference in 1931, Shah Nawaz and Subbarayan were again appointed as representatives by the British, but this time there was an official delegate from the women's organizations—the suffragist Sarojini Naidu. On this occasion Shah Nawaz decided to support the call from Naidu and the Indian National Congress for universal adult suffrage, but because of her allegiance to the Muslim minority in India, she faced a conflict of loyalties over the question of the franchise. This conflict surfaced when the British government made a communal award in 1932, which allocated communal electorates and reserved seats for Muslims and other special groups, including women. When the Indian women's organizations denounced the award as divisive, Shah Nawaz and a number of other Muslim women disagreed, believing that this was the only way that Muslim women could be adequately represented. To preserve a united front and to support the nationalist stance on a unified electorate, the All-India Women's Conference (AIWC) and the other women's organizations appeared to ignore the views of Shah Nawaz and her Muslim colleagues.

The new constitution for India was enshrined in the 1935 Government of India Act, a compromise measure that enfranchised 6 million women out of a total electorate of 36 million and allowed for special electorates and reserved seats for women. By this time, Shah Nawaz had become disillusioned with the Indian women's organizations, and she turned instead to the Muslim League, which had been formed in 1906 to advance the political rights of the Muslim community. She became active in the movement for an independent Pakistan and, following partition in 1947, she was one of two women members of the first Constituent Assembly of Pakistan.

See also India; Naidu, Sarojini; Pakistan and Bangladesh.
References Forbes, Geraldine. *Women in Modern India* (1996); Shahnawaz, Jahan Ara. *Father and Daughter: A Political Autobiography* (1971).

Sha'rawi, Nur al-Hudá (Shaarawi, Huda)

The most influential figure in the early Egyptian feminist movement and a leading suffragist, Hudá Sha'rawi (1879–1947) was born in Al Minya in Upper Egypt in 1879. The daughter of a wealthy landowner and provincial administrator, she received a traditional upper-class upbringing and was married at age 13 to 'Ali Sha'rawi, who later became an important figure in the Wafd (Egyptian Nationalist) Party. During the 1919 revolution, Hudá, as wife of the provisional leader of the Wafd Party, was called upon to play a leading role in organizing resistance to British rule. She was instrumental in forming and becoming first president of the Lajnat al-Wafd al-Markaziyah lil-Sayyidat (Ladies' Central Committee of the Wafd Party) in 1920. The committee became the main channel of Egyptian women's political views, until Sha'rawi herself, in conjunction with other upper-class women, founded the Jam'iyat al-Ittihad al-Nisa'i al-Misri (Egyptian Feminist Union, or EFU) in 1923, a year after the declaration of Egyptian independence and the death of her husband.

After attending the 1923 Congress of the International Woman Suffrage Alliance (IWSA) in Rome, where she spoke eloquently about the lack of political rights suffered by Egyptian women, Sha'rawi turned her attention to the suffrage question in Egypt. Bitterly disappointed by the electoral law of April 1923, which restricted the universal suffrage promised by the new constitution to men alone, Sha'rawi led women of the EFU and other organizations in picketing the Egyptian Parliament when it opened in 1924, demanding the enfranchisement of women, among many other issues.

Thereafter, until her death in 1947, Sha'rawi and the EFU pursued the question of women's political rights with varying degrees of vigor. Low points were the period between 1926 and 1934, when the EFU dropped its suffrage demands and concentrated on legal and educational issues, and the late 1930s, when the Palestine question dominated the agenda. High points were, first, the period around 1934–1935, when the return of liberalism in Egyptian politics coincided with the IWSA Congress in Istanbul, and Sha'rawi was granted an audience with Turkish President Kemal Atatürk, who had just granted Turkish women the vote in 1934; and second, in 1944, when Sha'rawi made an impassioned speech for the political rights of all Arab women at the Arab Women's Congress held in Cairo in 1944.

By the 1940s, however, the mostly upper-class EFU was beginning to lose its dominance in Egyptian feminism, as new organizations with middle-class roots were formed. Sha'rawi did not live to see Egyptian women gain the vote in 1956, but because of her determined and energetic leadership of the EFU, the suffrage question was never allowed to die. The success of the campaigns of the 1950s rests in large measure on her efforts to win political rights for women for almost a quarter of a century.

See also Egypt; Shafiq, Durriyah.
References Abdel-Kader, Soha. *Egyptian Women in a Changing Society, 1899–1987* (1987); Badran, Margot. *Feminists, Islam and Nation: Gender and the Making of Modern Egypt* (1995); Sha'rawi, Nur al-Hudá. *Harem Years: The Memoirs of an Egyptian Feminist, 1879–1924* (1986).

Sheppard, Kate

Kate Wilson Sheppard (1848–1934) was the most influential suffrage leader in the New Zealand Woman's Christian Temperance Union (WCTU) from the start of its campaigns in the mid-1880s until the vote was achieved in 1893. Born in Britain to Scots parents and emigrating to New Zealand in 1868, she became interested in feminist causes from an early age, particularly equality in marriage. Her petitions for the protection of women and children were ignored, and this heightened her awareness of women's political exclusion. That she was relatively well off and had a husband who was sympathetic with the cause and only one child made her public activities as WCTU leader easier.

Sheppard became national franchise superintendent in 1887. From this position, she put pressure on the WCTU to take action, arousing interest in the outside community and making allies in Parliament, including the influential politician Sir John

Hall. Initially she made use of American WCTU leaflets but later produced her own. In *Ten Reasons Why the Women of New Zealand Should Vote,* she drew upon the arguments of John Stuart Mill and found a receptive audience. She also pressured newspaper editors to print suffrage articles. In 1891 she rented a page of the temperance journal the *Prohibitionist* and wrote under the pseudonym "Penelope." Her column informed women of national and international suffrage news and activities.

Sheppard made friends with suffrage leaders in other countries, including the leader of the International Woman Suffrage Alliance, Carrie Chapman Catt, and in 1894 and 1908 she visited England and the United States, where she was a popular speaker. She also wrote letters to the editors of national newspapers on the suffrage debate. In 1904, poor health kept her from attending the Congress of the International Council of Women in Berlin, but her paper was read to the assembly.

Sheppard saw the enfranchisement of women as the outcome of "a larger vision of rights and duties." Although fought for by women, suffrage could not have been accomplished without the support of "earnest men who preached the gospel of government by all for the good of all." It has been said that without her work, the women's vote in New Zealand would certainly have taken many more years to accomplish.

Sheppard's first husband, Christchurch businessman and councillor Walter Sheppard, died in 1915. In 1925, when Sheppard was 78, she married the author of *Outlines of the Women's Franchise Movement in New Zealand,* William Sydney Smith (later known as W. Lovell Smith). She died in July 1934 at age 87 in Christchurch.

See also Catt, Carrie Chapman; Hall, Sir John; International Woman Suffrage Alliance; Mill, John Stuart; New Zealand; Woman's Christian Temperance Union.

References Grimshaw, Patricia. *Women's Suffrage in New Zealand* (1972); Malcolm, Tessa K. "Katherine Wilson Sheppard, 1847–1934" (1993).

Sierra Leone

Although some qualified women had the vote in Sierra Leone before independence in 1961, universal adult suffrage did not come until the country had self-rule.

The capital of Sierra Leone, Freetown, was founded by the British in 1787 as a colony for former slaves. Thereafter, British control gradually extended into the interior, over which a protectorate was proclaimed in 1896. A new ethnic group emerged within the colony of freed slaves, known as the Krios (Creoles), and this Western-influenced population and their British rulers had many of the conventional Victorian attitudes toward women, that is, although women had some education, they played little part in political life. The women of the protectorate were mostly illiterate, but many of them did play a part in tribal administration, rising to the position of paramount chief in some cases.

In 1930 elections were held in the colony only, with an electorate based on literacy and income qualifications. Both men and women were enfranchised, but because of the qualifications, fewer than 2,000 Black Africans voted. After World War II, elections for the colony continued as before, with the franchise based on income and property qualifications, and in the protectorate the vote was given to taxpayers only, which meant that virtually no women qualified.

In 1951 a Krio woman, Constance Cummings-John, who had been the first woman to be elected to the Freetown Municipal Council before the war, returned from the United States, where she had been a political activist. Cummings-John joined with Lottie Hamilton-Hazeley and Mabel Dove, who was involved in nationalist politics in Ghana, to found the Sierra

Leone Women's Movement (SLWM). The main goals of the SLWM were to improve the status of all women in Sierra Leone and to seek female representation in government bodies that were concerned with education, welfare, and economic issues. The organization adopted a nonpolitical stance and set out to eradicate class barriers and unify the country; all women were welcome at meetings, and each addressed each other as "comrade." The SLWM organized a number of demonstrations against inflation, and it set up adult literacy classes, nursery schools, and health care classes. By 1954 the SLWM had a total membership of 5,000 and had begun to publish a regular newspaper, the *Ten-Daily News*. At this stage the SLWM was the only mass-based organization in Sierra Leone that united ethnic groups, and whenever it held a demonstration it attracted considerable support. This provided a considerable contrast to the male-dominated political parties, which exploited ethnic tensions and encouraged political rivalry between the colony and the protectorate.

Although she was a Krio, Cummings-John was a member of the protectorate-based Sierra Leone People's Party (SLPP) because she believed that it represented the majority of the people. In 1955 she helped to establish a women's section of the SLPP to bring women into political life and to provide a base for women candidates who wished to stand for election.

Throughout the 1950s, women of protectorate origin began to join the SLWM, encouraged by the self-improvement programs it offered, and soon political awareness among Sierra Leonean women from all kinds of different backgrounds began to grow. In the 1957 elections, Cummings-John and Patience Richards successfully stood as SLPP candidates in Freetown, but they did not take up their seats because election petitions had been entered against them. The only woman to enter Parliament was Ella Koblo Gulama, who was elected to one of the 12 seats that were reserved for chiefs and later became Sierra Leone's first woman minister.

As preindependence constitutional talks began, the women of the SLWM decided to stay loyal to the SLPP, because they wanted a unified campaign to help obtain self-government as soon as possible. In 1960, when it was announced that the final constitutional discussions would be held in London in April, Sierra Leonean women expected to be members of the delegation, as the women of Ghana and Nigeria had been. When they heard that no women were included, they published a petition in the *Daily Mail* of 16 March, presenting their views on the issues to be discussed in London. They demanded that a new constitution should clearly define the status of women under the law and establish safeguards for their economic, social, and political rights. Cummings-John and Etta Harris were included in the delegation at the last minute, and after difficult negotiations, the date for independence was set for 27 April 1961—the year that Sierra Leone achieved universal adult suffrage.

See also Africa South of the Sahara.
Reference Denzer, LaRay. "Women in Freetown Politics, 1914–61: A Preliminary Study" (1987).

Skeffington, Hanna Sheehy

Hanna Sheehy Skeffington (1877–1946) was an Irish suffrage leader, cofounding member of the Irish Women's Franchise League. She was born Johanna Sheehy in Kanturk, County Cork; her father, David Sheehy, came from a prosperous milling family, her mother from a Limerick farming background. Both parents had supported the revolutionary nationalist group the Fenians, and her father and uncle suffered imprisonment for their participation in the Irish Land War of 1879–1882. In 1885 David Sheehy became an MP for the Irish Parliamentary Party and the family moved to Dublin. Hanna's secondary education was with the Dominican Convent in Eccles Street, Dublin, followed by attendance at a Dominican school, St. Mary's University College, the first Catholic women's college in Ireland. Hanna received her bachelor's degree, with honors, in modern languages in 1899 and was awarded a master's degree in 1902. On graduation she was employed as a teacher of French and German, but the religious monopoly of education made it impossible for women outside religious orders to find full-time or permanent teaching positions. Concern with gender equality in education led to the founding of the Women Graduates' and Candidate Graduates' Association in 1902, in which Hanna played a leading part in campaigning for parity of rights in education.

In 1903 Hanna married Francis Skeffington, a fellow student who had become university registrar at the National University. Both were members of the Young Ireland Branch of the United Ireland League, the constituency organization of the Irish Parliamentary Party, which had accepted women with reluctance. They resigned membership in 1912, in protest at the Irish Party's refusal to support women's suffrage. Francis had resigned his post as registrar in 1904, refusing to compromise his right to protest against the university's unequal treatment of women, and thereafter he earned a living through journalism. His wife, still a part-time teacher, was often the primary wage earner. Both became members of the Irish Women's Suffrage and Local Government Association (IWSLGA) in 1902, and in 1904 Hanna became a member of its committee. She remained a member of the IWSLGA until 1908, when she and her husband cofounded, with Gretta and James Cousins, the Irish Women's Franchise League (IWFL)—a militant, nonparty campaigning organization. Men were accepted as associate members of the IWFL.

Hanna was an important propagandist for the suffrage cause, contributing articles to many of the leading journals of the time and engaging in debate over a variety of political opinions. On 13 June 1909, she was among the first group of IWFL members to undertake militant action. For smashing windows in Dublin Castle, she received two months' imprisonment. She was dismissed from her teaching post at Rathmines College and devoted herself to the path of "militant militancy" as a full-time political activist. Her effectiveness was noticed by the authorities. In 1913 she was imprisoned for one month on a fabricated charge of assaulting a policeman. This was in retaliation for her participation in protests against Sir Edward Carson's refusal to keep his promise of prosuffrage votes in an Ulster parliament.

Both Sheehy Skeffingtons opposed World War I. Hanna was an Irish delegate to the Hague Women's Peace Congress in 1915. After her husband's murder during the Easter Uprising in 1916, she toured the United States from December 1916 to August 1918, publicizing conditions in Ireland. She declared herself to be a Sinn Feiner and was granted an audience with President Woodrow Wilson. She was forbidden by the British to return to Ireland and, following her secret return, was arrested and returned to Holloway Jail, where she went on a hunger strike and won her release.

Hanna refused a nomination for the 1918 elections on the grounds that she could not win the seat allocated, becoming instead an executive member of Sinn Fein. She continued, together with Louie Bennett, to publish the *Irish Citizen*, which had formerly been edited by her husband. It provided an outspoken assessment of women's progress in Ireland until its demise in 1920. In 1943 Hanna stood as an independent candidate in the general election, hoping that a woman's party would emerge, but she received only 917 votes. She died in 1946.

See also Bennett, Louie; International Congress of Women, The Hague; Ireland; Irish Women's Franchise League; Militancy.
References Levenson, Leah, and Jerry H. Natterstad. *Hanna Sheehy Skeffington, Irish Feminist* (1986); Luddy, Maria. *Hanna Sheehy Skeffington* (1995); Ward, Margaret. *Hanna Sheehy Skeffington, A Life* (1997).

Socialism in Europe

Socialist parties that developed in Europe in the late nineteenth century were unusual among political parties of the time in that they opened their membership to women as well as men and often included an explicit demand for women's suffrage in their programs. For example, the Austrian socialists included women's suffrage in their Hainfeld Program of 1888–1889, Lenin and the Bolsheviks wrote it into their program at the Party Congress of 1903, and it formed part of the aims of the German Sozialdemokratische Partei Deutschland (SPD), the Swedish Social Democrats, and the British Independent Labour Party (ILP). With a few exceptions, socialist men rarely spoke in opposition to women's suffrage, and in specific contexts, socialist parties could be relied upon to support proposals to extend voting rights to women.

However, in the context of the practical politics faced by socialists in their own countries, this commitment to women's suffrage often broke down. Socialists emphasized the importance of class solidarity and, in practice, focused on the needs of the male worker. This meant that issues involving sex inequalities tended to be marginalized or looked on with suspicion. Although the British ILP worked closely with women's suffrage groups, the German socialists, who dominated the Second International, were hostile to cooperation with the "bourgeois" women's movement. This policy was confirmed at the 1907 Congress of the International at Stuttgart.

This poster published by the Artists' Suffrage League (1909) realistically depicts the hard work of a seamstress and argues for her right to vote; socialist and labor union women were integrally involved in the fight for suffrage. (Library of Congress)

One difficult issue for socialists was the support given by the women's movement to limited suffrage measures, which would have enfranchised propertied women. It was argued that this would do little to help working-class women and could damage the prospects of socialist groups in elections. Further, in some instances, as in Belgium and France, women's commitment to Catholicism made socialists unwilling to champion any kind of women's suffrage measure. Because of the socialists' emphasis on the male worker, they were sometimes willing to support manhood suffrage—for example in Belgium, Austria, and in some local legislatures in Germany—and in these cases they did not press for the inclusion of women, lest this jeopardize the male cause.

Nonetheless, socialists did play an important part in the struggle for the women's vote, a part that has often been neglected in histories of the suffrage campaign. They enabled working-class women to take part in a movement that was usually associated with middle-class women, and where socialist women had a strong organization, as in Austria and Germany, they were able to mobilize thousands of women in street demonstrations in favor of the vote. This often contrasted, at least outside Britain, with the very moderate tactics employed by mainstream suffrage groups. Socialist women, particularly in Britain, Austria, Germany, and Italy, were able to put pressure on their socialist parties to give support to women's suffrage. This was a matter of some importance when the achievement of manhood suffrage increased the electoral support of those parties.

See also Independent Labour Party; Stuttgart Congress of the Second International; Zetkin, Clara.
References Boxer, Marilyn J., and Jean H. Quataert, eds. *Socialist Women: European Socialist Feminism in the Nineteenth and Twentieth Centuries* (1978); Evans, Richard J. *Comrades and Sisters: Feminism, Socialism and Pacifism in Europe, 1870–1945* (1987); Gruber, Helmut, and Pamela Graves, eds. *Women and Socialism, Socialism and Women: Europe between the Two World Wars* (1998).

South Africa

Women's suffrage began in South Africa with the foundation of a Franchise Department within the Woman's Christian Temperance Union in 1895. This was followed by the founding of several more suffrage societies, all of them tiny, and all of them dominated by women from the white, mainly English-speaking leisured class. These organizations focused their attention on Parliament, but they had little effect at first. Then, after World War I,

the examples of other countries and the greater prominence of white women in public employment and higher education caused the main political parties to reevaluate their attitudes.

In 1921, the Women's Enfranchisement Association of the Union (WEAU), which had been founded in 1911, presented a petition of over 50,000 signatures to Prime Minister Jan Christiaan Smuts in favor of white women's suffrage, and although the general principle was conceded, no action was taken. The issue became really significant only after the Afrikaner-dominated National Party organized by General James Hertzog came to power in 1924. One of Hertzog's chief aims was to eliminate the limited colored vote in the Cape (*colored* was defined constitutionally as people of mixed descent, Cape Malays, Bushmen, and Hottentots). Frustrated in his attempts to change the constitution, he saw the introduction of white women's suffrage as a means of diluting the importance of the nonwhite electorate. With his support, the Women's Enfranchisement Bill was passed into law in 1930. Because it applied to white women only, the colored vote in the Cape was halved. It can be argued that the desire to eliminate nonwhite rights in the Cape was not the only factor behind support for white women's suffrage, and it is certain that without this factor, women's suffrage would have been achieved in due course. However, the timing and nature of the legislation were bound up more with the National Party's attitude toward the colored vote than with its conviction that women were entitled to the franchise.

With the passing of the 1930 Act, the WEAU lost interest in extending the vote to nonwhites. There were sporadic attempts to initiate new franchise organizations—Cissy Gool founded the League for the Enfranchisement of Non-European Women in 1938 and a Non-European Women's League was formed in 1948 to fight for the vote for Black women—but these bodies were small and ineffectual, and the few Black and Indian women interested in politics were more concerned with discriminatory laws and the cost of living than with obtaining the vote. The banner of women's suffrage was really carried forward only by the African National Congress (ANC), the Communist Party of South Africa (CPSA), and part of the trade union movement. The CPSA declared itself in favor of women's suffrage in 1941, but the party was suppressed in 1950. In 1943, the ANC committed itself to universal adult suffrage, and for the first time, it included women in its definition of the word *adult*. The ANC Women's League was set up in the same year, but it does not appear to have been a dynamic organization until it was affiliated with the Federation of South African Women (FSAW), which held its inaugural conference in 1954. The FSAW was a small group; it is estimated that it never had a membership of more than 10,000, of whom only a few hundred were activists. Nonetheless, its leaders were veteran campaigners for women's rights, including Ray Alexander, Helen Joseph, Hetty McLeod, and Ida Mtwana of the ANC Women's League. In 1955 the ANC issued its Freedom Charter, which guaranteed universal adult suffrage, but the campaign for women's suffrage was derailed to a great extent by the increasingly oppressive anti-Black legislation and the suppression of opposition movements.

Colored men in the Cape finally lost the vote in 1956, and at the same time, Helen Joseph and other leaders of the FSAW were put on trial for treason. The persecution of its most prominent members created major difficulties for the FSAW, and it gradually lost the ability to organize itself. Its final meeting of any significance was held in 1962, two years after the banning of the ANC and the other major Black opposition group, the People's African Congress (PAC).

For the next 30 years, the struggle against apartheid dominated South African politics. Worsening economic conditions and pressure from abroad brought about a new constitution for South Africa in 1983 and the creation of a Tricameral Parliament in 1984; this set up a House of Assembly (for whites), a House of Representatives (for coloreds), and a House of Delegates (for Indians). Every white, colored, or Indian person who was a South African citizen and who was over 18 was entitled to vote for these bodies, thus including new groups of women within the franchise for the first time. This new structure deliberately excluded all Black South Africans and was unsuccessful among most middle-class Indians and coloreds, with as few as 5 percent of the colored electorate voting in the 1984 elections. It was only with the decisive break with white supremacy in 1990 and the end of the ban on the ANC in the same year that suffrage for Black women returned to the political agenda. After discussions lasting two years, a new constitution was promulgated in 1994, and in April of that year, South Africa's first multiracial election was held, based on universal adult suffrage. South Africa's Black women had finally won the right to vote, 64 years after their white compatriots.

See also Africa South of the Sahara; Citizenship; Nationalism; Race and Ethnicity; Woman's Christian Temperance Union.
References Walker, Cherryl. *Women and Resistance in South Africa* (1991); Walker, Cherryl. *The Women's Suffrage Movement in South Africa* (1979).

Spain

At the beginning of the twentieth century, Spanish women probably had fewer rights and privileges than any of their counterparts in Western Europe. They were subject to the authority of their fathers or husbands, had almost no access to higher education and the professions, and were confined by numerous other legal impediments. It is therefore somewhat surprising to find that women's suffrage was debated on several occasions in the Spanish Parliament before World War I.

The first mention of the subject was in the Madrid daily newspaper, *La Unión Liberal,* which in 1854 published an anonymous manifesto for political reform, the first article of which was a demand for universal suffrage, specifically including women "of good repute" *(mujeres de probidad).* Much more serious, however, was a bill to give the vote to female heads of families, which was introduced into the Spanish Chamber of Deputies in 1877 by a right-wing MP in an attempt to strengthen the family. However, the bill was heavily defeated. Two more bills were debated in 1907, both introduced by Republican MPs and both influenced by recent European legislation. One sought to give women over 23 the vote in municipal elections; the other wished to grant parliamentary suffrage to taxpaying widows. In the end, Parliament combined the question of municipal and national suffrage and held a debate on whether only men of 25 years and over could vote in national elections; this proposition was decisively won by 54 votes to 9. The issue surfaced again in 1908, when a Republican MP, Francisco Pi y Arsuaga, introduced another bill to give the right to vote in municipal elections to women who were not subject to marital authority. For the first time, critics publicly voiced the anticlerical argument that maintained that giving the vote to the widow was like handing it over to the priest *("Dar el voto a la viuda es entregarlo al cura").* Ironically, this argument persuaded some right-wing deputies to vote in favor of the bill. Nonetheless, it was lost by 64 votes to 35.

During this period before World War I, women themselves played little part in the debate; there were no significant women's organizations, and only a few publications of the women's press, like *La Mujer, El Álbum del Bello Sexo, El Pensamiento Femenino,* and the daily *El Heraldo de Madrid* supported even the limited enfranchisement of women. The *Heraldo* was the most vocal of these in the person of its columnist "Columbine," the pen-name for the divorced journalist Carmen de Burgos Seguí.

The first serious efforts by women to gain the franchise took place in 1920, when a petition was presented to the government in favor of women's unrestricted suffrage by the Valencia-based Liga Española para el Progreso de la Mujer (Spanish League for the Progress of Women). Later the same year a similar petition was handed in by La Cruzada de Mujeres Españoles (Crusade of Spanish Women) from Madrid. In 1921, La Cruzada organized a street demonstration where pamphlets were distributed calling for the vote. La Cruzada's founder, Carmen de Burgos, considered this to be the first public act of Spanish suffragists, and whether this is true or not, it shows how far Spain was behind other Western nations in demanding political rights.

Other women's organizations and periodicals had also sprung up in the postwar period, stimulated by the recent enfranchisement of women in many countries. The most important of these were the nonmilitant Asociación Nacional de Mujeres Españolas (ANME) [National Association of Spanish Women], founded in 1918 by María Espinosa de los Monteros, a divorced businesswoman from Málaga, and the Unión de Mujeres Españolas (UME) [Union of Spanish Women] led by the Marquesa del Ter and María Martínez Sierra. ANME and UME competed for the right to lead the small group of educated and independent-minded Spanish women who were willing to defy tradition and fight for rights in the political arena. ANME was probably the more effective, presenting a series of proposals to the

Ministry of Justice in 1921 and beginning to organize a serious campaign for suffrage in 1924, when Benita Asas Manterola took over as president from María Espinosa. Both Clara Campoamor Rodríguez and Victoria Kent, who later became Spain's first women MPs, were early members of ANME.

Unfortunately, the infighting between the ANME and the UME caused confusion, particularly regarding international representation. For example, in 1926, when the secretary of the International Woman Suffrage Alliance (IWSA) wished to compliment Spanish women on obtaining the right to vote in municipal elections, she was obliged to send her message to the umbrella organization, the Consejo Supremo Feminista de España (Supreme Feminist Council of Spain), rather than to UME or ANME. Other important associations of women in Spain in the 1920s were the Lyceum Club of Madrid; Acción Femenina (Feminine Action), founded in Barcelona in 1921 by Carmen Karr; and the Juventud Universitaria Feminista (Young University Women), led by Elisa Soriano Fischer, all of which campaigned for women's equality before the law, as did feminist periodicals, such as *La Voz de la Mujer* (Woman's Voice).

Despite the best efforts of these organizations, the right to vote in municipal elections had been granted to female heads of families, not as a result of pressure from women's groups, but unilaterally by the Spanish dictator Miguel Primo de Rivera, in 1924, as a means of strengthening the right-wing, Catholic vote. In fact, this right was never exercised during Primo de Rivera's rule; he allowed no elections to be held and ruled merely with the aid of a National Assembly, a consultative body inaugurated in 1927, to which 13 women had been nominated. It was only with Primo de Rivera's resignation in 1930 and the formation of a provisional government bent on reform that genuine democracy reentered Spanish political life.

As a result of the law of 8 May 1931, the franchise was widened to include all males over 23, and the impediment on priests, public employees, and women standing for election to the National Parliament was lifted, although, ironically, women were still denied the vote. As a result, three women were elected to the first Parliament of the Second Republic: Clara Campoamor Rodríguez, Victoria Kent Siano, and Margarita Nelken y Mansbergen. Both Campoamor and Kent were well educated (indeed, they were the only female lawyers practicing in Madrid), and both participated vigorously in the debates on Spain's new constitution, which was passed into law on 9 December 1931.

One of the most contentious areas in the constitutional debates was the question of female suffrage. In general, the liberal parties and their allies opposed extending the suffrage to women, and the socialists and many members of the Catholic parties favored it, although many individuals voted against party lines or simply abstained. The hostility of the Radical Party and its factions was based on the belief that Spanish women were ill-educated and would vote however their confessors told them to vote. Victoria Kent spoke out against female suffrage on the grounds that women had not become imbued with the republican ideal and required time to understand the value of citizenship. She was answered on this issue by Campoamor of the Radical Party, who argued that Spain must provide an example of the best form of constitutional democracy, and that the Spanish Parliament was "the first chamber in a Latin country to have raised the women's voice."

Campoamor faced considerable hostility, being heckled in Parliament and insulted and attacked in private. Nevertheless, she maintained a dignified, intelligent stance during the debates, emphasizing the need for universal rights to be enshrined within the new constitution, without antagonizing either the Catholic conservatives or the

Liberal anticlericals. Even after Article 36, giving women the vote, had been passed on 1 October by 40 votes, she faced a renewed attack from Kent, who put forward an amendment on 1 December that would have required women to have voted in two municipal elections before being entitled to the national vote. Because the Catholic parties who had supported Article 36 had withdrawn by then from Parliament, all of Campoamor's ability was required to fight against the amendment. In the end, the amendment was defeated by four votes, and the battle for women's suffrage was won, as much due to Campoamor's efforts as to any other cause.

Many historians have seen the extension of the franchise to women in 1931 as principally the result of constitutional reform, rather than as a consequence of pressure exerted by feminist organizations, and it is true that the desire for a new, liberal constitution was undoubtedly the most significant factor in winning women the vote. Yet, without these pro-suffrage groups, dedicated to improving the rights of Spanish women, activists like Campoamor would not have had an opportunity to develop the political contacts, organizational ability, and skill in public debate that enabled them to influence the course of Spanish parliamentary life.

Unfortunately, the achievement of Campoamor and women like her lasted only a few years, as Spain was engulfed by a civil war from 1936 to 1939 and did not emerge from the dictatorship of General Francisco Franco until 1975. During Franco's rule, universal suffrage was suppressed, and although some political rights for women were gradually introduced (heads of families and married women, for example, could elect deputies to the Parliament as part of family representation from 1957), it was only with the restoration of democracy in the mid-1970s that women fully regained the franchise. Women voted in the referendum of 1976 and the elections of 1977, and full adult suffrage was guaranteed by the new constitution of 1978.

See also Campoamor Rodríguez, Clara; Citizenship.
References Capel Martínez, Rosa María. *El Sufragio Femenino en la Segunda República Española* (Women's Suffrage and the Second Spanish Republic) (1992); Fagoaga, Concha. *La Voz y el Voto de las Mujeres: El Sufragismo en España, 1877–1931* (The Women's Vote: Suffrage in Spain, 1877–1931) (1985); Keene, Judith. "'Into the Clean Air of the Plaza': Spanish Women Achieve the Vote in 1931" (1999).

Sri Lanka

Sri Lanka (formerly Ceylon) was one of the first Asian countries to grant women the vote. In 1931, while it was still under British rule, all women over 21 were enfranchised as part of the Donoughmore Constitutional Reforms.

The women's suffrage movement in Ceylon was mainly middle-class in character, although it had the support of some male radicals and trade union leaders. Women's groups started campaigning for the vote in 1912, after the suffrage had been granted to middle-class men. Women were inspired to lobby Congress by the visit of Indian suffrage campaigner Sarojini Naidu in 1922. In 1925 Agnes De Silva and Aseline Thomas of the Mallika Kulangana Samitiya (Women's Society), a women's organization that was affiliated with Congress, put forward a motion for limited women's suffrage. The motion failed.

In 1927 the Women's Franchise Union (WFU) was formed by middle-class and professional women, some of whom were related to nationalist and labor leaders. The public meeting they organized to demand voting rights in December 1927 had the support of prominent native and foreign women, including teachers and theosophists, some of whom had been pioneers in Buddhist female education. The meeting was chaired by Lady Dias Bandaranaike, mother of future Sri Lankan

Prime Minister Solomon Dias Bandaranaike. A delegation from the WFU subsequently gave evidence at the Donoughmore Commission on Constitutional Reform that met in 1928. On 21 September 1928, the WFU passed a resolution requesting the Legislative Council "to consider the granting of Franchise to women on equal terms with men and to make recommendations accordingly to the Imperial Government." Although the Donoughmore Commission recommended a limited franchise to women over 30, the Legislative Council accepted the WFU's resolution, and in 1931 all women over 21 were granted voting rights.

Despite Sri Lankan women's early victory in achieving the vote, they did not make much headway in local or national politics. In the national legislature, their levels of representation never exceeded 4 percent, and those women who did go into politics were generally members of political dynasties, taking up office on the death of a husband or father.

See also Imperialism; India; Naidu, Sarojini; Nationalism.
Reference Jayawardena, Kumari. *Feminism and Nationalism in the Third World* (1986).

Stanton, Elizabeth Cady

Elizabeth Cady Stanton (1815–1902) was a leading figure in the early women's suffrage movement in the United States. She was the first woman in the country to recognize fully that women's access to equal rights was contingent on a change in their political status. As such, she is widely regarded as the founder of political feminism.

Elizabeth Cady was born in 1815 in New York State, the daughter of a judge. Her recognition, even as a child, of the legal disadvantages suffered by women spurred her to involvement in feminist politics. This sensitivity was compounded by her personal experiences of frustration and isolation as a wife and mother, following her marriage to abolitionist leader Henry Stanton.

Elizabeth was moved to action by her experiences at the World Anti-Slavery Convention in London in 1840, where she and Lucretia Mott were excluded from the proceedings on the grounds of their sex. In 1848 she and Mott organized the first Women's Rights Convention at Seneca Falls. At this meeting, Stanton strongly promoted what proved to be the convention's most controversial resolution: "that it is the duty of the women of this country to secure for themselves their sacred right of elective franchise."

Stanton was strongly influenced by Enlightenment ideas and particularly the writings of Mary Wollstonecraft. She initially based her argument for the vote on a belief that the natural rights of the individual are "as necessary to man under government, for the protection of person and property, as are air and motion to life." Although Stanton had supported the abolitionist cause during the Civil War, her position shifted after 1867, with the issue of the Black vote. In opposition to Lucy Stone and Henry Blackwell, Stanton joined with Susan B. Anthony to oppose the Fifteenth Amendment, which prohibited disenfranchisement on the grounds of race but excluded women. In 1869 she and Anthony formed the National Woman Suffrage Association, excluding men on the grounds that they had betrayed the movement. In taking up this position, Stanton changed the basis of her argument for the franchise, claiming women's right to vote *as a sex* rather than *as individuals*. By taking this position, she was also led into racist and elitist arguments that were to typify the later U.S. women's suffrage movement.

In 1868, with Anthony's assistance, Stanton started a journal called the *Revolution*. Although it only lasted two years, the *Revolution* became very well-known, partly because of its association with racist Democratic Senator George Francis Train, who backed it financially. In the

Elizabeth Cady Stanton with her daughter Harriet Stanton Blatch on the right and her grand-daughter Nora on the left, c. 1890. (Library of Congress)

early 1880s Stanton embarked on a major literary project; between 1883 and 1886, she worked with Anthony and another feminist leader, Matilda Joslyn Gage, to publish the first three volumes of a *History of Woman Suffrage*, documenting the achievements of women in the movement.

When rival suffrage groups joined again in 1890 to form the National American Woman Suffrage Association, Stanton was elected as the group's first president, but by this time her influence was waning. During her later years, her chief concern was the responsibility of organized religion for women's inferior position, which she propounded in *The Woman's Bible*, published in 1895. When the Suffrage Convention of 1896 disassociated itself from her work on the grounds that it would alienate religious believers from supporting the cause, she was undeterred and continued writing on this subject until her death in 1902.

See also Antislavery Movement; Anthony, Susan B; *History of Woman Suffrage*; Mott, Lucretia Coffin; National American Woman Suffrage Association; National Woman Suffrage Association; Race and Ethnicity; The *Revolution*; Stone, Lucy; United States of America; Women's Rights Convention, Seneca Falls.

References Banks, Olive. *Faces of Feminism: A Study of Feminism as a Social Movement* (1981); DuBois, Ellen Carol. "Outgrowing the Compact of the Fathers: Equal Rights, Woman Suffrage and the United States Constitution, 1820–1878" (1987); Flexner, Eleanor. *Century of Struggle: The Woman's Rights Movement in the United States* ([1959] 1975).

Stone, Lucy

Lucy Stone (1818–1892) was a prominent campaigner in the early women's suffrage movement in the United States and one of its most gifted speakers. She is best known as leader of the American Woman Suffrage Association, formed in 1869.

Stone was born in 1818 into a farming family in western Massachusetts. In 1843 she graduated from Oberlin College, the first coeducational college in the nation. She began her career as a public speaker in 1847, when she gave her first speech on women's rights from the pulpit of her brother's church. Although employed as an agent for the Anti-Slavery Society, she saw her strongest commitment as the "elevation of my sex." She promoted her beliefs in a lecture series that included the subject of women's legal and political handicaps. In 1855 Stone married Henry Blackwell, retaining her maiden name, and converted him to the cause of women's rights. She returned to politics a decade later, following the birth of her daughter, Alice Stone Blackwell, who also became a suffragist. In 1865, after the ratification of the Thirteenth Amendment conferred citizenship on Blacks and women without granting them political rights, Stone became a prominent figure in the American Equal Rights Association. This group attempted to link the two causes and campaigned for universal suffrage.

In 1867 Stone went on an intensive three-month speaking tour as part of the campaign for the Kansas state referendum on Black suffrage and women's suffrage. It was during this campaign that the suffrage movement split, with Black suffrage but not women's suffrage being adopted by the Republican Party, in opposition to the Democrats, who supported women's suffrage at the expense of the Black vote. Stone felt betrayed by Elizabeth Cady Stanton and Susan B. Anthony's alliance with racist Democratic leader George Train, and she blamed the small size of the woman's vote in the referendum on his in-

Lucy Stone, well-known U.S. abolitionist and suffragist, founded the American Woman Suffrage Association in 1869. (Library of Congress)

volvement with the campaign. Stone disagreed with Stanton and Anthony's anti-Republican stance, believing that most supporters of women's suffrage were still Republican in sympathy.

Despite her disappointment at the Republican Party's refusal to support women's suffrage, Stone accepted the Fifteenth Amendment granting Black men the vote, in the mistaken belief that the women's cause would receive Republican support in the future. In 1868 she became an executive member of the New England Woman Suffrage Association, the first major political society with women's suffrage as its chief goal. After Stanton and Anthony formed the National Woman Suffrage Association in 1869, Stone and Blackwell set up a rival organization, the American Woman Suffrage Association. This group, which had support from Republican and abolitionist men, attempted to attract conservative women who had not yet converted to the cause. To achieve this goal, the association presented suffrage as an abstract concept, a single issue unconnected to other feminist causes.

In 1872 Stone and her husband started publishing one of the most influential women's rights papers, the *Woman's Journal*. Stone remained active in the movement until after the two main suffrage societies were brought together again in 1890, a merger organized by her daughter Alice. Her last public appearance was at the Suffrage Convention in 1892; she died the following year.

See also American Woman Suffrage Association; Anthony, Susan B.; Citizenship; Fourteenth and Fifteenth Amendments; National Woman Suffrage Association; Race and Ethnicity; Stanton, Elizabeth Cady; United States of America; The *Woman's Journal*.
References Banks, Olive. *Faces of Feminism: A Study of Feminism as a Social Movement* (1981); DuBois, Carol Ellen. *Feminism and Suffrage: The Emergence of an Independent Women's Suffrage Movement in America, 1848–1869* (1978); Flexner, Eleanor. *Century of Struggle: The Woman's Rights Movement in the United States* ([1959] 1975).

Stowe, Emily Howard

A remarkable pioneering suffragist and doctor, Emily Howard Stowe (née Jennings) (1831–1903) was born in Upper Canada into a prosperous Quaker family. In 1854 she graduated with first-class honors, and shortly afterward she became the first female principal of a public school in Ontario, leaving the position on her marriage to John Stowe in 1856. After the birth of her third child, Stowe decided to enter the medical profession, but after being refused admission to the University of Toronto School of Medicine, she went to train in New York, graduating in 1867 and setting up a practice in Toronto shortly afterward.

Stowe is probably best known for her contribution to the cause of women's suffrage in Canada. After attending a meeting of the American Society for the Advancement of Women in 1876, she decided to form the Toronto Women's Literary Club in order to generate an interest in women's rights, including the right to vote; in 1883 this group became the Toronto Women's Suffrage Association. After some initial vigorous campaigning, the association lost its momentum, and in January 1889 Stowe revived the crusade, helping to found the Dominion Women's Enfranchisement Association (DWEA). Although the DWEA aspired to a national presence, in reality it was more local than national in scope. Stowe became the first president and held that position until her death in 1903.

As president of the DWEA, Stowe led an unsuccessful deputation to the Ontario legislature in February 1889, demanding passage of a suffrage bill about to be introduced by a Liberal member, John Waters. In 1896 she played a lead part in the "mock parliament" held in Toronto, which had been organized to publicize the political and legal inequalities suffered by Canadian women. Stowe also helped to foster close and profitable connections between the DWEA and the National Council of Women of Canada and the Woman's Christian Temperance Union (WCTU).

Like many other Canadian suffragists, Stowe advocated equal rights for women at least in part because she believed that women's maternal and domestic duties were of the greatest importance to society, even though her own most notable achievements took place in the public sphere. Stowe always adopted a low-key style of campaigning, but she proved to be a persistent pioneer of the Canadian women's suffrage movement. After her death, she was succeeded as president of the DWEA by her daughter, Dr. Augusta Stowe-Gullen.

See also Canada; National Council of Women of Canada.
References Cleverdon, Catherine L. *The Woman Suffrage Movement in Canada* (1974); *Dictionary of Canadian Biography.* Vol. 13, *1901–1910* (1994).

Stuttgart Congress of the Second International (1907)

The Stuttgart Congress helped to clarify the question of women's suffrage for groups affiliated with the Second International. The Second International enabled representatives from socialist parties throughout the world, but primarily from the United States and Europe, to meet and formulate guiding policy. As early as 1900, at the congress in Paris, a resolution had been passed that proclaimed that women's suffrage was a "necessity for both sexes." Faced with their own national political circumstances, however, not all affiliated groups felt able to keep to this policy. The Belgian and Austrian socialist parties in particular supported manhood suffrage bills; their situation provided the immediate context for the Stuttgart Congress and its emphasis on the suffrage question.

The first Socialist Women's International met just before the full congress and passed a resolution, proposed by the influential leader of the German women's socialist movement, Clara Zetkin, which stated that "the socialist parties of all countries have a duty to struggle energetically for the introduction of universal suffrage for women." Zetkin went on to put a resolution to the full congress that declared that "wherever a struggle is to be waged for the right to vote, it must be conducted only according to socialist principles, that is, with the demand for universal suffrage for both women and men." Victor Adler, the leader of the Austrian socialists, proposed an amendment that would have left each national section with freedom to decide when to campaign for women's suffrage, but this amendment was defeated. After 1907 any national group subordinating women's suffrage to the fight for men's suffrage would be going against the formal policy of the International.

As a result of the resolution, an International Bureau for Socialist Women was established, led by Zetkin, in order to maintain communication between national sections and to promote the implementation of the International's decisions. The bureau helped to stimulate the demand for women's suffrage among socialist women, in particular in Austria, Italy, and Germany in the immediate prewar years.

See also International Proletarian Women's Day; Socialism in Europe; Zetkin, Clara. *Reference* Sowerwine, Charles. "The Socialist Women's Movement from 1850–1940" (1998).

Suffrage Atelier

The Suffrage Atelier began with a group of artists meeting in London in February 1909 "with the special object of training in the arts and crafts of effective picture propaganda for the Suffrage." Although most of the members of its sister organization, the Artists' Suffrage League, had trained in the fine arts, the Suffrage Atelier was crafts-based, using processes such as engraving, hand-printing, stenciling, and woodcuts to produce posters and decorative schemes. The Atelier was run by women, with a formal constitution and weekly committee meetings, and its members were mainly employed producing banners, posters, and postcards for the Women's Freedom League (WFL) and the Women's Social and Political Union (WSPU). The Atelier also provided training for women in modern as well as traditional printing methods, so that they could earn their living as commercial artists.

Two of the cofounders of the Atelier were Laurence and Clemence Housman; Laurence was an influential illustrator and member of the Men's League for Women's Suffrage, and his sister Clemence, a member of the WSPU, was a commercial engraver for weekly journals such as the *Illustrated London News*. Another prominent member of the Atelier was Edith Craig, a costume designer and daughter of the actress Ellen Terry. An active member of the Actresses' Franchise League and the WFL as well as the Suffrage Atelier, Craig designed banners and themes for suffrage processions and pageants.

The Suffrage Atelier was best known for its striking woodcut posters, which harked back to the political material of previous centuries and succeeded in conveying a sense of urgency and popular protest. Like many other suffrage organizations, the Atelier ceased its activities on the outbreak of war in 1914.

> See also Actresses' Franchise League; Artists' Suffrage League; Britain; Imagery; Men's League for Women's Suffrage; Men's Political Union for Women's Enfranchisement; Women's Freedom League; Women's Social and Political Union.
> Reference Tickner, Lisa. *The Spectacle of Women: Imagery of the Suffrage Campaign, 1907–1914* (1987).

Suffrage Bill (1931)

In 1931 the cabinet of Hamaguchi Osachi of the ruling Minseitō Party in Japan introduced a civil rights bill that offered women a limited suffrage. They would be able to vote and hold office in local government at the level of towns, cities, and villages but not at the prefectural level (earlier bills introduced in 1929 and 1930 had extended the vote to the prefectural level, but these had been rejected by the House of Peers). The 1931 bill permitted women to be elected to local assemblies and to serve as mayors and other appointed officials, but only with the permission of their husbands. The voting age for women was set at 25, and it was proposed that the age for men be reduced to 20. This legislation arose in part as a response to the growth of a vigorous and highly politicized women's suffrage movement during the 1920s. This movement, which peaked in 1931, had been stimulated partly by the enactment of universal manhood suffrage in 1925.

However, many middle-class women's organizations were disappointed by the limits on women's enfranchisement in the 1931 bill; women were by no means united in their opposition. Thirteen major women's organizations expressed absolute opposition to the bill at the second All-Japan Women's Suffrage Convention in 1931. Yet only two groups pressed for a complete civil rights bill. These were the Fusen Kakutôku Dômei (League for Women's Suffrage), led by Ichikawa Fusae, which had only 1,511 members in 1930, and the even smaller Fujin Sansei Dômei (Women's Suffrage League). The absence of an effective opposition to the government's bill indicates that although by 1930 most bureaucrats, politicians, and middle-class women's organizations in Japan agreed that women possessed special attributes that would improve political life, they generally saw local rather than national government as the natural place for women.

In March 1931 the lower house passed the bill. However, conservative opposition was strongly represented in the House of Peers, which was composed primarily of older Japanese elites, including titled nobles, retired bureaucrats, and military men. These men believed that women's suffrage would "undermine the family system that was the basis of our national polity," and this older, conservative gender ideology proved too resilient to overcome (Garon, 1993, 34). On 24 March 1931, a slightly modified version of the women's suffrage bill was decisively defeated in the House of Peers by a vote of 184 to 61. This crushing defeat marked the end of realistic hopes for the achievement of women's suffrage in prewar Japan.

> See also Ichikawa Fusae; Japan.
> References Garon, Sheldon. "Women's Groups and the Japanese State: Contending Approaches to Political Integration" (1993); Nolte, Sharon H. "Women's Rights and Society's Needs: Japan's 1931 Suffrage Bill" (1986).

Suffrage Pilgrimage

See Pilgrimage, Suffrage.

This illustration from Le Petit Journal Supplement Illustrated *shows Edith New and Mary Leigh being carried triumphantly through London streets after being released from Holloway prison, 22 August 1908. (Ann Ronan Picture Library)*

Suffragette

The term *suffragette* was first used on 10 January 1906 in the British newspaper the *Daily Mail* to describe members of the Women's Social and Political Union (WSPU) who were disrupting the election meetings of Winston Churchill, a prospective Liberal cabinet minister. The term was soon used more widely to describe those who engaged in militant activities and was adopted by the WSPU itself; one of the union's newspapers, published between 1912 and 1915, was entitled *Suffragette*. The term has been employed by historians, as well as by contemporaries, and has been seen as a useful way to refer to militants as distinguished from those who used more legal or constitutional methods to obtain the suffrage.

See also Suffragist; Women's Social and Political Union.

The Suffragette Movement (1931)

The Suffragette Movement, written by Sylvia Pankhurst and published in 1931, is one of the most extensively quoted early histories of the campaign for the vote in Britain. It can only be understood, however, in the context of the development of Pankhurst's own politics and the period in which it was written. Sylvia Pankhurst, whose mother and sister, Emmeline and Christabel Pankhurst, were the leaders of the militant suffrage group the Women's Social and Political Union (WSPU), had taken an active part in the militant campaign before World War I. In contrast to her mother and sister, Sylvia retained her commitment to socialist politics and in the interwar years took up the struggle against fascism.

In the 1920s and 1930s many former suffrage campaigners wrote autobiographical

The National American Woman Suffrage Association organized parades like this one in New York City to advance their cause, 1908. (Library of Congress)

accounts that celebrated their part in the achievement of the vote. In a similar vein, Pankhurst used her own autobiography to tell the history of the militant suffrage movement from her perspective as a socialist feminist. This provided an alternative account to Ray Strachey's *The Cause* (1928), which characterized both the WSPU and the socialist movement as "undemocratic" and "uncivilized." Rather than producing a straightforward history in reply, Sylvia "wrote about the experience of being a socialist-feminist from below" (Dodd, 1991, 21).

Pankhurst's account provides vivid descriptions of people and events, but it must also be seen as a forum in which she could work out her own troubled relationship with Emmeline and Christabel. It is interesting to compare her description of Christabel with the one in her earlier, less well-known book, *The Suffragette,* published in 1911, just before militancy escalated and when Sylvia was still closely involved with her family and the WSPU. In *The Suffragette,* Christabel is seen as an inspiring leader, whereas in *The Suffragette Movement,* written long after Sylvia had been expelled from the WSPU, Christabel is criticized for her autocratic leadership. Like *The Cause,* therefore, this absorbing account must be viewed through the lens both of the period in which it was written and of the changing priorities and political perspectives of its author.

See also The Cause; Pankhurst, Christabel; Pankhurst, Emmeline; Pankhurst, (Estelle) Sylvia; Women's Social and Political Union.
References Dodd, Kathryn, ed. *A Sylvia Pankhurst Reader* (1991); Pankhurst, E. Sylvia. *The Suffragette Movement: An Intimate Account of Persons and Ideals* (1931).

Suffragist

The term *suffragist* is applied to men and women who supported the movement for women's suffrage. In Britain, it was employed by contemporaries, and later by historians, to describe those who used constitutional or legal methods to obtain the vote, such as the National Union of

Women's Suffrage Societies, in contrast to those who used more militant tactics, who were described as *suffragettes*.

See also National Union of Women's Suffrage Societies; Suffragette.

Sweden

The campaign for women's suffrage in Sweden, as in neighboring Denmark, was closely linked to the struggles of middle-class liberals and socialists to achieve more representative government. It was not until the 1870s, when Sweden experienced rapid industrial growth, the emergence of middle-class liberalism, and the growth of a strong temperance movement, that an organized feminist movement developed. However, the groups formed in the late nineteenth century still concentrated on the achievement of economic opportunities, married women's property rights, and moral reforms such as temperance, taking little interest in women's suffrage. Under the Municipal Laws of 1862, unmarried women who fulfilled certain property qualifications were able to vote in local elections, but very few exercised this right. Such apathy was common wherever women had voting rights but lacked an organized feminist movement that could stimulate an interest in political participation. Therefore the Association for Married Women's Property Rights, established in 1873, mounted a campaign to encourage women to vote in municipal elections. In the 1890s it sought to register women and to persuade them to vote in elections in Stockholm. In 1889 the group was successful in generating widespread support for the idea that women should be eligible to stand for school boards and poor law boards.

Women's right to vote for the Swedish Parliament, the Riksdag, was raised in 1884, when Frederick Borg introduced a bill to that effect, but it was greeted with laughter by the deputies and was not successful. This may have been partly because

women had shown little interest in using the municipal vote and partly because so few men had been enfranchised by the constitutional reforms of 1865 that had created a bicameral parliament. The demand for women's suffrage did not become a key issue, therefore, until after the more general movement to extend the male franchise had gathered momentum in the 1890s. As industrialization increased in pace, radical liberals and socialists organized petitions, people's parliaments, and a general strike in 1902 to support their demands. It was in this context that the first women's suffrage group was formed, the Landsföreningen för Kvinnans Politiska Rösträtt (Swedish Women's Suffrage Association), led between 1903 and 1913 by journalist and educator Anna Whitlock. By 1912 the association had 13,000 members, organized in 187 local associations. This growth reflected changes in the wider political context that led to more demands to broaden the franchise. The Liberal Union Party, formed in 1900, united progressive, middle-class parties behind the demand for universal manhood suffrage; in 1905 it became the largest party in the Riksdag and the Social Democrats also gained 13 seats. One of the new government's first acts was to introduce a bill for manhood suffrage, leading to a long controversy about the principles on which the vote should be based. Women's suffrage bills were introduced by individual members of the Riksdag but had little success until 1907, when the Liberal Union finally included women's suffrage into its program.

During this period, suffragists maintained pressure on members of the Riksdag by organizing petitions, questioning individual candidates, and publicizing their cause through the press. They also tried to mobilize women to use their municipal vote, and by 1910 over a third of those eligible had voted in a sample of 50 towns. This was very close to voting figures for men and reflected the increased publicity given to the suffrage campaign. Another factor may have been the fact that after 1909 women were eligible to stand as candidates.

For most of the period suffragists maintained a position of political neutrality, but they identified closely with the Liberal Union Party. Although the party had backed a manhood suffrage bill in 1908–1909, it managed to keep a good relationship with the women's suffrage movement by introducing a separate women's suffrage bill. The narrow defeat of the bill convinced suffragists that they should abandon their position of neutrality and seek to defeat the Conservative Party. To that end, they worked hard to support Liberal and Social Democratic candidates. The Social Democrats were reluctant at first to give support to women's suffrage because their movement was dominated by workers in heavy industry and women formed only a small minority of the membership. There was some cooperation with suffragists, but socialist women generally followed Clara Zetkin's position, expressed at Stuttgart in 1907, that socialists should avoid cooperation with bourgeois women and should work for voting rights for both sexes. Nonetheless, as advances were made in manhood suffrage, Social Democrats gave greater support to the demand for the enfranchisement of women.

In 1911 a Liberal victory led to the introduction of a Government Bill to enfranchise women, but this was defeated by the First Chamber. Faced with a king and a Conservative Party who were reluctant to accept parliamentary government, the Liberal Union Party worked with the Social Democrats to gain a working majority. Both believed it was in their interests to support women's suffrage. This political alliance, however, alarmed middle-class voters who feared labor unrest, and the Liberals were heavily defeated in

1914. The return of a Conservative government ruined any possibility that a women's suffrage measure would be passed in the near future.

Women in Sweden had to wait until after World War I to receive the franchise. In common with many other European countries, Sweden faced food riots and an economic crisis in 1918, fueling fears of a Bolshevik-style revolution. Thus, all constitutional parties agreed to strengthen parliamentary democracy in 1919, and women's suffrage was included in a package of measures that were ratified in 1921.

See also Denmark; Liberalism; Zetkin, Clara.
References Evans, Richard, J. *The Feminists: Women's Emancipation Movements in Europe, America and Australasia, 1840–1920* (1977); Qvist, Gunnar. "Policy towards Women and the Women's Struggle in Sweden" (1980).

Switzerland

Switzerland was exceptional among industrialized Western European countries in taking so long to grant women the right to vote, passing a women's suffrage measure as late as 1971. This can partly be explained by the country's complex political system, in particular the role of direct democracy, including initiatives and referenda. The popular initiative enables citizens to propose changes to the constitution as long as they can obtain sufficient signatures. Although rarely successful, initiatives have been used by opposition groups to put pressure on the government and to raise new political questions. Referenda, on the other hand, have to be used whenever changes to the constitution are proposed, or they can be used by voters who wish to protest federal laws. Any women's suffrage measures, therefore, could be subject to the veto of male voters.

Local autonomy also hampered the achievement of women's suffrage. Switzerland is a confederation of autonomous cantons that limits the power of the Federal Assembly. This consists of two councils with identical powers: the National Council, or Nationalrat, is filled by popular election under proportional representation, and the Council of States, or Ständerat, has two members for each canton serving at the discretion of their canton. The executive group, the Federal Council, is elected by the Federal Assembly. Political parties, therefore, tend to be strong in the cantons but weak at a federal level, where they operate as umbrella groups for regional interests. Any attempt to pass federal legislation involves complex negotiations between interest groups, and coalitions are constantly changing. In this context, it was very difficult for women to achieve the right to vote.

After the National Congress of Women in Geneva in 1896, women from the cantons established the first national women's organization, the Bund Schweizerischer Frauenorganisationen, or Union of Swiss Women's Organizations (USO). The USO concentrated on achieving legal and social reforms rather than political equality, and it emphasized women's importance to society as wives, mothers, and temperance campaigners. It was not until 1909 that a number of suffrage groups that were active in the cantons founded the Schweizerischer Frauenstimmrechtsverband (Swiss National Organization for Women's Suffrage) in order to pursue the suffrage at a national level. The organization did not have a clear policy, however, and was reluctant to interfere in the affairs of cantonal groups. The National Organization for Women's Suffrage then divided into three groups, weakening the suffrage movement. There was the traditional USO, the Arbeiterinnenvereine (Working Women's Associations), and the Katholischer Frauenbund (Catholic Women's Organization). Suffragists were cautious in their tactics and focused on organizing petitions or general letters to the government rather than demonstrating, lobbying, or disrupting election meetings. They were usually from middle-class backgrounds and were reluctant to be associated with progressive or left-wing ideas.

After World War I, only the Social Democrats demanded women's suffrage. One radical member and one Social Democrat member formulated a resolution in 1919 asking for a constitutional change, but this was ignored by the government. In 1921 popular votes on women's suffrage were held in six of the cantons, but these were all unsuccessful, with considerable opposition coming from local Social Democrats who did not follow the official policy of the party. It was not until 1928, following a national exhibition relating to women in the professions, that a petition in favor of women's suffrage, signed by 250,000 people, was presented to the Federal Assembly. Again, this had no success, and after World War II, eight cantons also rejected demands for women's suffrage in local referenda.

It was not until 1957 that the Federal Council organized a national referendum on women's suffrage for the first time. International pressure for women's rights had been mounting, and in this context both chambers of the government finally accepted women's suffrage in 1959. Despite this success at the federal level, a mandatory referendum had to take place and 69 percent of male voters opposed giving women the vote. A new women's organization had been formed just before this vote, the Arbeitsgemeinschaft der Schweizerischen Frauenverbände für die Politischen Rechte der Frau (Working Group of the Swiss Women's Associations for the Political Rights of Woman), providing an umbrella group for most women's organizations in the country. They worked together to pressure for the suffrage until there was a breakthrough in 1959, when Geneva gave women the right to vote on local affairs. Geneva was followed in 1960 by Vaud and Neuenburg, and in 1966 by the German-speaking canton Basel-City. This helped to familiarize the Swiss with the idea that women could exercise the vote.

Switzerland's membership in the Council of Europe in 1963 also exposed some of the anomalies in its constitutional position. The absence of women's suffrage left Switzerland unable to sign the European Human Rights Convention in 1968, so it sought a separate clause that would exempt it from the women's suffrage requirement. This infuriated a broad range of women's organizations, who organized a march to Bern in 1969, using the slogan "Women's suffrage is a human right." The Council of Europe did not accept Switzerland's petition for an exemption, and in 1971 a referendum on women's suffrage at last received the necessary majority. Although women could now vote in national elections on the same terms as men, the new legislation did not interfere with the power of the states to deny women the vote at the local level. The German-speaking canton of Appenzell refused to allow women to vote or to stand as candidates in local elections. Finally, the canton was challenged by a woman who took the issue to the Supreme Court at Lausanne. The court declared that in the light of the Equal Rights Amendment of 1981, it was illegal to restrict women's voting rights. Thus, since 1990, all Swiss women have been able to vote and to stand for office.

Reference Stämpfli, Regula. "Direct Democracy and Women's Suffrage: Antagonism in Switzerland" (1994).

Syria

The issue of women's suffrage was first raised in Syria when women became involved in the nationalist struggle. Syria was created by the European powers after the defeat of the Ottoman Empire in World War I and was ruled under a French mandate. In April 1920 the Syrian Congress debated a proposal to give women the vote. Several developments had given rise to the question. Women had taken part in the war effort and, inspired by nationalist ideas, sought to participate more directly in politics. They were keen to join in struggles against the French and also aimed to achieve greater equality by changing the personal status laws. In Damascus a small number of women, including Nazik 'Abid (1887–1960), who was related to Syria's first president, and Mary 'Ajami (1888–1969), a teacher and publisher of a women's magazine, established women's groups that pursued a wide range of interests, such as promoting Arabist schools and protecting women's traditional handicrafts. They were also aware of suffrage gains in postwar Europe, were inspired by the role that women had played in the Egyptian rebellion against the British, and raised the subject of women's suffrage in their magazines.

Several members of the Syrian Congress, including the Lebanese Igrahim al-Khatib and Sa'dallah al-Jabiri, who later became a leader of the Syrian National Bloc, supported a proposal that women who held a secondary school certificate (approximately 2 percent of the population) should have the vote. The resolution was opposed by conservative and landowning politicians with religious and French sympathies who argued that the suffrage posed a revolutionary threat to traditional gender relationships that were rooted in religious doctrines. A vote on the question was postponed while Syria faced a crisis in its relationship with France. Nonetheless, the issue was kept alive during the 1920s in several women's magazines, including *al-Fajr* (The Dawn), founded by Najla Abi al-Lama', which carried articles on women's suffrage and asserted women's patriotism. However, women suffered in the 1920s as the reform movement shifted away from more radical interpretations of Islam to an emphasis on women's exclusion from politics. This in turn reflected a broader anxiety about the threat to the civil order if gender boundaries were blurred, a view that was also upheld by the French.

In 1928 a conference was held in Beirut that brought together women's groups from Syria and Lebanon. The conference marked a departure from previous activism; although a wide range of reforms were demanded, political rights were not. In the following year, Nazik 'Abid, who had presided over the conference, rejected the change of emphasis and called on women to continue to demand political rights. In the 1930s, however, other leaders of the women's movement, such as Mary 'Ajami, repudiated their earlier support for women's suffrage and claimed that it had been premature. They had been unable to attract popular support for the suffrage campaign in the 1920s and may have seen the demand for social and civil rights as easier to achieve. By moving away from more controversial questions that alienated religious leaders, such as veiling and the vote, they hoped to gain support for other reforms affecting women's social position. Elizabeth Thompson suggests that in the 1930s, therefore, the women's movement emphasized "patriotic motherhood," in which social reforms were seen as a stepping-stone to political rights, rather than the other way around. She claims that this was also a way to mobilize mothers and to give them an influence in the growing nationalist movement. In Syria in particular, leaders of the women's movement agreed in the early 1930s to put off their own demands until independence had been won.

In 1944, when independence appeared likely, women's groups in Syria renamed themselves the Syrian-Arab Women's Union and agreed to emphasize solidarity among all Arab women. Delegates were sent to the first Arab Women's Conference, organized by Egyptian suffragist Nur al-Hudá Sha'rawi in Cairo, which had women's political rights at the top of the agenda. Nonetheless, Syrian women were careful to demand the vote only for educated women. In 1945 they turned out in large numbers in battles against the French, but when independence was achieved in 1946, women were still denied the suffrage. President Shukri Quwatli argued that only those who performed military service should have full citizen rights and that women's "natural" role, as defined by religious law, was in the home. He praised women as mothers and patriots but warned that education and ambition could be dangerous. Women finally achieved the vote when a coup by Colonel Husni al-Za'im in 1949 overthrew Quwatli. The new regime decreed a limited suffrage for educated women as part of a range of other political and social reforms. Full suffrage was achieved in 1953, but after another coup in the same year, enfranchisement returned to the 1949 basis. Women did not regain full suffrage rights until 1973.

See also Citizenship; Lebanon; Middle East and North Africa; Nationalism; Sha'rawi, Nur al-Hudá.
Reference Thompson, Elizabeth. *Colonial Citizens: Republican Rights, Paternal Privilege, and Gender in French Syria and Lebanon* (2000).

Tang Junying and the Chinese Suffragette Society

Tang Junying was the leader of the Chinese Suffragette Society, one of the earliest suffrage organizations in China, which she founded in Beijing soon after the revolution of 1911 had removed the Manchu dynasty from power and brought in a republic.

Tang Junying had studied in Japan and developed a strong interest in the militant British suffragette movement. Therefore she modeled her organization directly on the Women's Social and Political Union in Britain. The Chinese Suffragette Society established schools staffed almost exclusively by members, and it published papers that included news of women's movements abroad. The constitution of the society included 10 aims, only one of which related to political rights, but its activities were limited almost entirely to agitation for the vote.

Tang Junying was a strong platform speaker in Beijing and Tientsin and had a far-reaching reputation as a woman of her word; one story has it that she destroyed a newspaper office that had slandered her good name. One of her first militant acts was to lead a deputation of women to an early meeting of the National Assembly in Nanking to demand the vote. When the assembly refused to recognize the equality of women and men in the constitution, Tang Junying and her followers joined with the Women's Suffrage Association to launch a violent attack lasting three days. After having forced an entry into the House, the women were still not allowed to see the president, so they smashed windows and attacked constables, obliging the government to bring in troops the following day for protection.

After the accession of a militarist government in 1913, Tang Junying was arrested and it was rumored that she had been executed. Laws were passed that forbade women to join political groups, and the Chinese Suffragette Society and its sister suffrage organizations were suppressed.

See also Britain; China; Japan; Militancy; Women's Social and Political Union.
Reference Croll, Elizabeth. *Feminism and Socialism in China* (1978).

Truth, Sojourner

Sojourner Truth (née Isobel Baumfree) (c. 1797–1883) was one of the most famous African American woman to speak out for the rights of Black women to get the vote. She was born about 1797 into slavery on an estate south of New York, owned by Dutch settlers. After gaining her freedom in 1827, she successfully sued for the return of her son, who had been sold illegally, becoming the first Black woman to win a lawsuit against a white man.

In 1843 she changed her name to Sojourner Truth and traveled around New England as an itinerant preacher, often calling her own prayer meetings. During her travels, Truth made links with female abolitionists, and after publishing her autobiography (written by a white woman friend, Olive Gilbert), she went on to

I SELL THE SHADOW TO SUPPORT THE SUBSTANCE.

Sojourner Truth, born a slave in New York, became an influential leader in the U.S. abolitionist and women's suffrage movements. (Library of Congress)

woman." Her speech electrified the audience. It enabled Frances Gage (who later wrote down her view of the event) to take back control of the meeting and continue presiding over the convention.

After the abolition of slavery, Truth became an active campaigner in the American Equal Rights Association, whose aim was universal suffrage, linking Black rights with women's rights. She opposed those abolitionist men in the association who supported the Fourteenth Amendment, excluding women. Truth commented: "There is a great stir about colored men getting their rights but not a word about colored women; and if colored men get their rights and not colored women theirs, the colored men will be masters over the women and it will be just as bad as before."

Truth continued to lecture on women's and Black rights throughout the 1870s until she was stopped by her failing health. She died at her home in Battle Creek, Michigan, in 1883.

See also Antislavery Movement; Fourteenth and Fifteenth Amendments; Race and Ethnicity; United States of America.
References DuBois, Ellen, and Karen Kearns. *Votes for Women: A 75th Anniversary Album* (1995); Truth, Sojourner. *Narrative of Sojourner Truth* (1991).

champion Black freedom and women's rights, including female suffrage, in her speaking tours.

Her most famous speech was made at a women's rights convention in 1851 in Akron, Ohio. In the face of male heckling that white women seemed unable to challenge, Truth took over the meeting. Although many of the white women present tried to stop her for fear that she would harm their cause, Truth was able to challenge male ministers' claims that women were too weak for equality and should not be allowed the vote. Baring her arm, she cried: "Look at my arm! I have ploughed and planted and gathered into barns and no man could head me—and a'nt I a

Turkey

Turkey arose as an independent state from the ashes of the Ottoman Empire after World War I. Kemal Atatürk (1881–1938), Turkey's first president, followed in the footsteps of earlier Ottoman intellectuals, who combined the radical modernization of society on the Western model with a fierce Turkish nationalism. Central to the aims of Atatürk and his followers was a determination to raise the status of women, a campaign that culminated in women being granted full suffrage in 1934.

Turkish women, particularly the urban elite, were not slow to take advantage of the changing political climate toward the end of the Ottoman period. Women's magazines flourished in the aftermath of the Young Turk Revolution of 1908, and organizations like the Ottoman Association for the Defence of the Rights of Women (founded in 1913) and activists like Halide Edib Adivar (1885–1964) were prominent in promoting women's issues. The most comprehensive change in attitudes, however, came after Turkey's entry into World War I. Women played an important part in public life during the war and the struggle for independence that followed, a role publicly acknowledged by Atatürk, who led a campaign to give them equal rights. His early attempts were unsuccessful; supporters of women's suffrage in the Turkish Grand Assembly were not even allowed to speak during debates on the electoral law bill of 1921–1922, and in 1924, the National Assembly resembled a battlefield during the debate on women's role in the constitution. The 1927 elections, however, tilted the balance against the conservative forces in the assembly, and supported by the Türk Kadin-lari Birligi (Turkish Women's League), Atatürk was able to force franchise legislation through. Women won the right to vote in municipal elections in 1931 and in parliamentary elections in 1934.

It has been argued that Atatürk used the women's issue not only as part of his modernization program but also as both a calculated attack on the Turkish religious establishment and a means of distinguishing the Turkish single-party state from its European counterparts like Italy and Germany. Whatever his ulterior motives, there is little doubt that, despite the best efforts of some energetic and talented female activists, the major political rights conferred on Turkish women were "a product of the unrelenting efforts of a small revolutionary [male] elite, rather than of large-scale demands by Turkey's female population" (Abadan-Unat, 1991, 179).

See also Middle East and North Africa.
References Abadan-Unat, Nermin. "The Impact of Legal and Educational Reforms on Turkish Women" (1991); Sirman, Nükhet. "Feminism in Turkey: A Short History" (1980); Tekeli, Sirin. "Women in Turkish Politics" (1981).

Union française pour le suffrage des femmes

The Union française pour le suffrage des femmes (UFSF) [French Union for Women's Suffrage] was the largest women's suffrage organization in France. It was formed in 1908 by suffragists who were concerned that France was not represented in the International Woman Suffrage Alliance (IWSA), which was organizing its next meeting to be held in London in 1909. Jeanne Schmahl took a leading role in setting up the UFSF. She was influenced by the insistence of the IWSA that suffrage should be a nonparty issue, and she sought to establish an organization that would attract a wide range of women, although she saw the core of the membership as "active, moderate, bourgeois" women. Her ideas were given publicity in Jane Misme's newspaper, *La Française* (The Frenchwoman), formed in 1906, and 300 women attended the inaugural meeting of the UFSF in 1909.

Suffrage was to be the sole aim of the UFSF. Its statutes stressed moderate methods, including publications, posters, and lectures, although demonstrations were not ruled out. Within a year the union was the largest suffrage organization in France, with over 1,000 members, and it was accepted as a member of the IWSA. The UFSF continued to grow, particularly in the provinces, and by 1914 it had 12,000 members distributed through 75 departments. One of the reasons for this growth was the energetic propaganda work of Ce-cile Brunschwicg, who ousted Schmahl from the leadership of the union in 1910. The aim of the UFSF to build a moderate consensus was tested in 1914, when younger members, discontented with its methods, sought to engage in direct actions that might attract working-class women to the cause. At the same time, a number of rival militant groups were established. Nonetheless, the union remained optimistic that the vote would soon be won. An increasing number of deputies had pledged their support for women's suffrage, and in July 1914, the UFSF held a suffrage rally that attracted approximately 6,000 demonstrators, the largest group yet assembled in favor of the vote.

The outbreak of war, however, brought a halt to the suffrage work of the UFSF, and its members were diverted to other causes. After the war was over, the union no longer concentrated only on the vote, as many of its members were drawn to work for peace movements and other causes. The UFSF continued to grow and to campaign for suffrage in the interwar years (it had 100,000 members in 1928), but it faced an unsympathetic Senate. Its influence on the achievement of the vote in 1944 is difficult to determine, but it did apply pressure when it mattered, kept the issue before the public, and won the argument so completely that there was little opposition to the measure when it was finally passed.

See also Brunschwicg, Cecile; France; International Woman Suffrage Alliance.

References Hause, Steven C., with Anne R. Kenney. *Women's Suffrage and Social Politics in the French Third Republic* (1984); Reynolds, Siân. *France between the Wars: Gender and Politics* (1996).

United States of America

At the Seneca Falls Convention in 1848, women in the United States became the first in the world to develop an organized movement to demand the vote, but they would have a very long fight ahead of them until they were finally granted full voting rights at a federal level in 1920. Women had been able to vote in some states, notably New Jersey, in the late eighteenth century, when property owners were given the franchise with no restrictions on the basis of sex. Concerted attempts were made to change this, however, and in 1807 suffrage in New Jersey was restricted to adult male property owners. It was not until the 1840s that women began to raise the issue of their exclusion from the franchise. They were inspired to do this by their involvement in antislavery work. The refusal of the British and Foreign Anti-Slavery Society to grant women delegate status at the World Anti-Slavery Convention held in London in 1840 infuriated male and female followers of U.S. abolitionist William Lloyd Garrison. After prolonged debate, Lucretia Mott and Elizabeth Cady Stanton pledged to hold a convention when they returned home and to "form a society to advocate the rights of women."

The convention was finally held eight years later at Seneca Falls, New York, in July 1848 with 300 people in attendance. Mott and Stanton were among the organizers and former slave and abolitionist leader Frederick Douglass was a key speaker. Resolutions were passed on married women's rights, divorce, and greater educational and employment opportunities. Stanton's resolution that it was a duty of women to secure the franchise was only barely successful because many women feared that it would harm their other causes. However, it was included in the Declaration of Sentiments and Resolutions that was later signed by 100 women and men.

Over the next few years, the women's movement held conventions around the country and argued for a broad range of reforms, in particular the improvement of married women's legal and property rights. Some of the best-known speakers were committed to women's suffrage, including Lucy Stone, a graduate and lecturer for Garrison's American Anti-Slavery Society; Sojourner Truth, a former slave who toured New England as a public speaker and preacher; and Susan B. Anthony, a Quaker, abolitionist, and temperance advocate. In 1851 Anthony and Stanton met for the first time, beginning their 50-year collaboration as campaigners for women's rights and the suffrage.

During the Civil War, feminists worked for Black emancipation and began to see that enfranchisement would be required if they were to have an effective political voice. They were bitterly disappointed, however, when the Fourteenth and Fifteenth Amendments extended the franchise to Black men but continued to exclude women. In 1869 the movement split over the Fifteenth Amendment and strategies to promote women's suffrage.

Two of the resulting organizations concentrated on the suffrage. The National Woman Suffrage Association (NWSA), led by Anthony and Stanton, was an all-female group that opposed the Fifteenth Amendment but called for a Sixteenth Amendment that would enfranchise women. The New York–based NWSA focused on gaining the suffrage through federal action. It promoted a variety of feminist reforms through its journal, the *Revolution,* which adopted a radical tone. Stanton's pronouncements were often elitist: she called for an educated franchise

Suffrage parades like this one in New York City advanced the progress of the vote for women, 1913. (Library of Congress)

that would counter the influence of "ignorant" immigrants and Black people. A rival, mixed-sex group centered in Boston, the American Woman Suffrage Association (AWSA), was led by Lucy Stone and endorsed the Fifteenth Amendment while also supporting women's suffrage. It concentrated on gaining the vote on a state-by-state basis and expressed its ideas through the *Woman's Journal,* a conservative publication that pointed out how feminist reforms were consistent with widely held American beliefs.

Both groups sought the support of the state suffrage societies that had developed during the Civil War and were largely white and middle-class in composition. A majority of the small number of Black women who took part in the campaign at this stage worked with the AWSA; in the 1870s, for instance, Frances Harper of Pennsylvania, Caroline Remond Putnam of

Massachusetts, and Lottie Rollin of South Carolina all attended national AWSA conventions as delegates from their states.

Over the next few years, suffrage campaigners tried a number of different tactics, including petitions, meetings, speeches, and pamphlets, as well as lobbying sympathetic politicians. They also sought links with the labor movement and attempted to use the courts to challenge their exclusion from the franchise. In 1868, for example, Anthony tried to involve working-class women in the fight for the suffrage by forming a Working Women's Association, with a membership made up largely of newspaper typesetters, but this failed to attract widespread support. Women also tried to vote in state elections, but their efforts were deemed invalid by the Supreme Court in 1874.

At a state level, women did make gains during this period, but this was largely in the western states. In 1869, Wyoming was the first state to adopt women's suffrage, followed by Utah in 1870. It appears that this had little to do with feminist agitation or the less rigid traditional gender roles of frontier states, but rather was a matter of political expediency. For instance, in Utah, Mormons hoped that women's suffrage would tip the balance of power in their favor against non-Mormons. Women also gained partial suffrage in a number of states where they were able to vote for members of school committees or gained the right to vote on questions submitted to taxpayers.

Women also took part in other political movements and organizations, many of which gave support to women's suffrage while also providing women with experience in political campaigning. The Populist Party, for example, gave rural women an outlet for political activism and included women's suffrage in its program, and the Woman's Christian Temperance Union (WCTU) also supported women's suffrage as a way to achieve the goal of temperance. The WCTU tended to argue that women should have the vote because of their special qualities as wives and mothers, rather than because of natural rights, and similar arguments were increasingly used in the suffrage movement as a whole toward the end of the nineteenth century.

Meanwhile, the NWSA was still campaigning to secure a Sixteenth Amendment to the Constitution, drafted by Susan B. Anthony, which proposed that the right to vote should not be denied on the basis of sex. The amendment was brought before Congress on several occasions during the 1880s and was supported by petitions, and meanwhile, annual suffrage conventions lobbied politicians and tried to gain publicity in the press. Stanton and Anthony also sought to strengthen their links with suffrage groups in other countries, and after a visit to Britain in 1883, they set up a committee of correspondence with the aim of forming an international association. The NWSA arranged an International Council, which met in Washington in 1888, 40 years after the Seneca Falls Convention, and attracted delegates from Europe, India, Canada, and the United States. A new group, the International Council of Women, was established, but women's suffrage was such a controversial issue that initially it was not included as one of the council's aims.

By the late 1880s, suffrage activists seemed no closer to obtaining their goal at either a federal or a local level. Attempts to gain the ballot were often thwarted by the liquor interests, which were alarmed by the growth of the WCTU, and by social and political conservatism. Indeed, Carrie Chapman Catt referred to the liquor industry as the "invisible enemy" that had helped to delay the coming of women's suffrage. Although smaller groups such as the Populist Party were willing to endorse women's suffrage, no major political party could be relied on for support, particularly when party officials felt that their own political interests might be undermined. Nonetheless, women had gained invaluable political experience during these years, and the suffrage movement had spread from the Northeast and the Midwest into the West and to some extent the South as well. The campaign produced very able leaders, including Julia Ward Howe in Massachusetts and Ellen Clark Sargent in California and Washington, D.C. Their activities were chronicled in detail in the *History of Woman Suffrage*, the early volumes of which were written in the 1880s by the suffrage pioneers Elizabeth Cady Stanton, Susan B. Anthony, and Matilda Joslyn Gage.

In 1890 unity was achieved at the national level when the NWSA and the AWSA merged to form a new organization, the National American Woman Suffrage Association (NAWSA). It was led after 1892 by Susan B. Anthony and then by Carrie Chapman Catt between 1900 and 1904. When Catt left for personal reasons and to play an active role in the International Woman Suffrage Alliance, her place was taken by Dr. Anna Shaw, who acted as president from 1904 to 1915. It has been suggested, in particular by Eleanor Flexner and William O'Neill, that whereas the suffrage pioneers had a liberal view of social progress, the new generation of suffrage activists were narrower in their interests, and that fear of immigrants led them to demand an educational qualification for voting. It has also been argued that these later suffragists argued for the vote on grounds of expediency and the special qualities that women could bring to politics rather than on the grounds of equal rights and natural justice. More recent studies, however, suggested that this was not a conflict between generations of activists, but an ongoing argument within the movement. Some scholars claim that suffragists continued to disagree—first, about whether to emphasize equality between the sexes or difference, and second, about the basis on which women should claim citizenship rights.

What is more certain is the fact that women's suffrage made no progress during these years at a national level. Anna Shaw was an inspiring speaker and under her leadership NAWSA membership rose from 17,000 to 200,000, but she was a poor organizer and strategist and she alienated a number of leading figures. Her concentration on suffrage also led to criticism that she was not interested enough in the needs of working-class women. Moreover, no effective campaign was mounted in support of a federal suffrage amendment until after 1912. Given this context, it is not surprising that the main developments occurred at a local level, with uneven results. When Wyoming and Utah were admitted to the Union in 1890 and 1896, respectively, their commitment to women's suffrage

was upheld, and the vote was also won after a referendum in Colorado in 1893 and Idaho in 1896. There was a further spate of victories in the period just before World War I, when women's suffrage was granted in Washington in 1910; California in 1911; Arizona, Kansas, and Oregon in 1912; Alaska and Illinois in 1913; and Montana and Nevada in 1914. These gains resulted from a combination of local campaigning and specific political and social conditions; there was little overall direction from the NAWSA, which simply gave help when needed.

Other changes took place at the state level in the suffrage campaign in the first decade of the new century. The movement became more broadly based, as more Black and working-class women became involved. Moreover, inspired by the example of the British Women's Social and Political Union, the American suffrage movement adopted more militant tactics. A nationally organized Black women's club movement, led by Ida B. Wells-Barnett, developed in the 1890s. Its leaders not only encouraged Black women to participate in the suffrage movement but also sought to counter the tendency of northern white suffragists to support restrictions such as literacy qualifications on the grounds of political expediency. Such restrictions would limit voting rights for Black women and also suggested a tacit acceptance of the anti–Black suffrage views of many women in the South.

The politics of race and class caused divisions in the U.S. suffrage movement, but after the turn of the century there was a greater attempt to involve working-class women. In New York, for example, the Women's Trade Union League worked closely with the suffrage movement, and working-class trade union leaders such as Rose Schneiderman and Leonora O'Reilly made speeches for the suffrage cause. New York suffrage leader Harriot Stanton Blatch, a friend of British suffragette Emmeline Pankhurst, helped to introduce new tactics such as parades, open-air meetings, pickets, and speeches by members of the working class at suffrage hearings before the state legislature.

A change of tactics could also be seen at the national level after 1912, when there was a new drive to gain a federal amendment. The two women who were instrumental in pushing this forward, Alice Paul and Lucy Burns, had both gained experience in the British militant movement and were keen to ensure that the American suffrage campaign adopted a more activist approach. Paul became chairwoman of the Congressional Committee of NAWSA in 1913 and organized a suffrage march in Washington, D.C., the day before the inauguration of Woodrow Wilson as president. The marchers were overwhelmed by a mob and it took the combined forces of the police, army, and militia to restore order, all of which generated considerable publicity for the suffrage cause. Although the leaders of NAWSA welcomed the new interest in the suffrage, they were alarmed that militancy might lead to destruction of property, as it had in Britain. They also disagreed with Paul's tactic of opposing the party in power, assuming that, unlike in Britain, the support of both parties would be necessary to gain success for a congressional bill.

In 1913 Paul had formed her own organization, the Congressional Union, which was affiliated at first with the NAWSA. However, differences between the two organizations had grown so great that the Congressional Union became an independent organization in 1914. In that year, it sent organizers to nine states to work against Democratic candidates and by 1915 had extended its work into most other parts of the country. It kept a high profile in Washington by organizing petitions, demonstrations, and meetings as well as sending deputations to the president. This helped to breathe life into the

movement, although there was no immediate success for the union's tactics; Democratic candidates continued to be elected to Congress, a congressional vote on the women's suffrage amendment by both houses was defeated, and Wilson pledged to support women's suffrage as a private citizen, but not on behalf of his party. In 1915, after failure to make headway on women's suffrage in the industrial states of New York, Pennsylvania, Massachusetts, and New Jersey, the NAWSA, under the dynamic and able leadership of Catt, also began to focus on the federal amendment. Nonetheless, the methods of the Congressional Union and the NAWSA continued to diverge.

In 1915 the Congressional Union had amalgamated with Harriot Stanton Blatch's Women's Political Union, and in the following year the leadership founded a new group, the National Woman's Party (NWP), to campaign in the 12 states that already had equal suffrage against Wilson and other Democratic candidates. This strategy was unsuccessful against the Democrats, but it did lead to increased militancy. In 1917 the NWP set up pickets outside the White House, and consequently some women were arrested and subsequently imprisoned for obstruction. When the prisoners went on a hunger strike, they were forcibly fed. The NWP then went on to stage further pickets, burning the president's speeches and writings and also his effigy. On their release from prison, the women hired a railroad car, named the "prison special," and toured the country to give an account of their experiences.

As in Britain, the militants believed that their campaign had done more in a short time to raise the profile of women's suffrage than had decades of sedate lobbying and petition gathering. It was certainly the case that the chairman of the senate Suffrage Committee had visited the women in prison and recommended that action should be taken on the federal amendment. Yet adverse publicity could also work against the women's cause; many Democrats were alienated by the political tactics that the NWP had used.

Catt adopted a different range of methods. Rather than attacking President Wilson, she sought to gain his support by persuasion and also encouraged the states with the greatest commitment to women's suffrage to keep the pressure on Washington. When America entered World War I, the NAWSA offered its services to the president, whereas the NWP continued to concentrate on the suffrage. Meanwhile, nationwide support for women's suffrage grew, and when both the NAWSA and the NWP lobbied members of the House to pass a suffrage amendment in January 1918, they were successful. It took longer to gain the support of the Senate, but the winning of suffrage referenda in several more states provided the context for the passing of the Nineteenth Amendment by both houses in 1919. The necessary ratification by two-thirds of the states was finally achieved in August 1920, albeit by the narrowest of margins.

It cannot be assumed that the vote was gained simply because the arguments in favor of women's suffrage had won the day. There was still considerable opposition, in particular from big business and from the South, where there was fear about the Black woman's vote. On the other hand, support had been growing in many states during the war, and evidence that arguments based on expediency, that is, claims that women's suffrage would lead to a better kind of society, had become influential. The changes brought by the war also provided a new context that enabled President Wilson to give official support to women's suffrage in 1918 in gratitude for their war services.

It has been estimated that at least 2 million women had taken part at some stage in this very lengthy political movement, which fragmented once the vote had actu-ally been achieved. Black women in particular felt let down by white women voters when they were disenfranchised in the South in the late 1920s. Once they were enfranchised, women activists tended to pursue their goals through the different political parties, although women's organizations continued to act as pressure groups. The NAWSA became the League of Women Voters and concentrated on educating women in their new role as voters, and the NWP worked for an equal rights amendment to the Constitution. It passed Congress but feminists were not able to get enough states to ratify it before the deadline in 1981.

The United States suffrage movement had provided inspiration to women in the rest of the world, in particular in the nineteenth century before militancy brought the British campaign to center stage. Women in other countries envied the personal freedoms that American women seemed to enjoy, were impressed by the size and vitality of the suffrage movement, and looked up to the able and charismatic leaders produced by the campaign. Suffragists from abroad were eager to visit the United States, and their suffrage organizations kept their countrywomen informed about the U.S. movement through their newspapers. It is hardly surprising, then, that women from the United States played key leadership roles in transnational organizations such as the International Woman Suffrage Alliance and exerted an influence that mirrored the growing power of their country on the world stage.

See also Addams, Jane; American Woman Suffrage Association; Anthony, Susan B.; Antislavery Movement; Blatch, Harriot Stanton; Catt, Carrie Chapman; Citizenship; Fourteenth and Fifteenth Amendments; International Council of Women; International Links; International Woman Suffrage Alliance; Mott, Lucretia Coffin; National American Woman Suffrage Association; National Woman Suffrage Association; National Woman's Party; Nineteenth Amendment; Pankhurst, Emmeline; Paul, Alice; Race and

Ethnicity; The *Revolution;* Schneiderman, Rose; Stone, Lucy; Truth, Sojourner; Wells-Barnett, Ida Bell; The *Woman's Journal;* Women's Rights Convention, Seneca Falls; Women's Social and Political Union.

References Bolt, Christine. *The Women's Movements in the United States and Britain from the 1790s to the 1920s* (1993); DuBois, Ellen Carole. *Feminism and Suffrage: The Emergence of an Independent Women's Movement in America, 1848–1869* (1978); DuBois, Ellen Carol. *Harriot Stanton Blatch and the Winning of Woman Suffrage* (1997); Flexner, Eleanor. *Century of Struggle: The Woman's Rights Movement in the United States* ([1959] 1975); Hine, Darlene Clark, Elsa Barkley Brown, and Rosalyn Terborg-Penn, eds. *Black Women in America: An Historical Encyclopedia,* Vol. 11 (1993); O'Neill, William L. *The Woman Movement: Feminism in the United States and England* (1969); Terborg-Penn, Rosalyn. *Afro-Americans in the Struggle for Woman Suffrage* (1998).

Universal Suffrage

Universal suffrage is the enfranchisement of all adult men and women. Another term for this is *adult suffrage*. Women's suffrage activists often suspected that those who campaigned for universal or adult suffrage might support measures that would enfranchise all adult men only, excluding women, thereby achieving *manhood suffrage*. Thus, they sought to pass resolutions that made it explicit that the demand for universal suffrage included women as well as men.

In many countries during the nineteenth and early twentieth centuries, the franchise was restricted to certain groups of men, such as property owners or taxpayers. Women suffragists then had to decide whether to demand votes for women on the same terms as men, a stance described as a *limited suffrage* position. This was a controversial question because with limited suffrage, the majority of women, in particular married women, would continue to be excluded. Many socialist women argued that such a measure would enfranchise propertied women, for the most part, which would be of little help to

working-class women. They therefore fought for the achievement of universal suffrage. Limited suffragists, on the other hand, claimed that removing a restriction based solely on the sex of the voter was all-important and that a campaign for limited suffrage was also more likely to succeed. Some wished to avoid a universal franchise, whereas others thought that a limited suffrage would be a first step toward a broader, more democratic suffrage. Such disagreements about suffrage strategy led to splits within the women's suffrage movement in individual countries and also caused tensions between suffrage campaigners and mainstream political parties, sometimes weakening support for the enfranchisement of women.

Uruguay

Uruguay was one of the first countries in Latin America to grant the vote to women. Following in the path of Brazil and Ecuador, the Uruguayan legislature approved female suffrage in 1932. However, it was not until the reform of the Civil Code in 1946 that women were elected to Congress and could play a part in forming legislation. This achievement ended a period of 40 years of feminist activity.

Women's suffrage first emerged as a topic of political debate in Uruguay in 1912 as part of a broader platform to expand popular participation in government, a measure that had the support of socialists and the Colorado Party. In 1914 a bill to grant women the national suffrage was introduced by Colorado Party Deputy Héctor Miranda, who was convinced that politics, which he saw as a "dirty business," would be elevated by the higher moral sense of women. These arguments were subsequently taken up by suffragists in the 1920s and 1930s. The Catholic and conservative press opposed the bill on the grounds that women needed to conserve energy for motherhood and lacked men's leadership skills. Miranda's argument that the constitution did not specifically exclude women was countered by jurist Jiménez de Araéchaga, who insisted that the term *free men* referred only to biological males.

The issue of women's suffrage was taken up again at the 1916 Constitutional Convention. Socialists argued that women needed the vote to protect their rights and prevent exploitation as workers and that the suffrage would not jeopardize their family obligations. They were opposed by conservatives who saw the vote as subversive and refused to acknowledge women's role as workers, believing they should remain in the home as wives and mothers. They dismissed the 66 women who signed a petition in support of constitutional reform as "intellectuals" whose views were not shared by other women. Although the convention failed to approve women's suffrage, it did leave the door open. The Constitution of 1917 acknowledged the right of women to vote and hold office in the nation or the municipality, but this could only come into effect through a bill passed by a two-thirds majority in both chambers.

The most significant event for women at this time was the foundation of the Uruguayan Consejo Nacional de Mujeres (National Council of Women) in 1916 by Paulina Luisi. In December 1917, after the failure of the Constitutional Convention to grant women political rights, the National Council launched a campaign for female suffrage. Although its members were primarily educated women, it campaigned on behalf of working women and linked suffrage to the issue of alcoholism on the grounds that countries where women voted had effectively reduced alcohol consumption through legislation. In 1919 Luisi formed the Alianza Uruguay de Mujeres para el Sufragio (Uruguay Alliance of Women for Suffrage) under the umbrella of the National Council of Women.

Despite a considerable degree of support from prominent politicians, suffrage proved a harder cause to win than suffrage campaigners had anticipated. Feminists were vulnerable to party political maneuvering. Their cause was weakened by the growing opposition of the conservative Nationalist Party, and the fact that socialists supported the suffrage alienated antisocialists from feminist causes. Although the Colorado Party restated its commitment to civil and political equality of men and women in 1925, it still failed to get a majority in Congress to pass a reform bill. Luisi's domination of the feminist movement also encouraged internal splits and conflicts between women's organizations, although she remained a high-profile speaker abroad.

After the centenary of the republic in 1928, the debate was reignited, influenced in part by pan-American women's conferences and by suffrage victories for women elsewhere, including Ecuador. By this time, both the Colorado Party and the Blancos of the Nationalist Party (who had a majority in the Senate) hoped to improve their position by a liberal reform that would deflect attention away from the worsening economic situation. Then in March 1929, the request of a woman, Elda Orona, for the "citizens certificate" that was required to hold a public service debate sparked a legal discussion. It was concluded by the electoral court that her request was in fact a request for the qualification of citizenship, not the exercise of citizenship, and this qualification was granted without giving her the right to vote.

At the end of 1929 the Alianza launched a new women's rights campaign, which called for equality for women in a number of different arenas, including education and the family, but which put suffrage at the end rather than the head of its list of demands. This rhetoric of social justice was attractive to male politicians. Aided by intensive press coverage over the next two years, this campaign helped to effect a change of heart among many former opponents of women's suffrage, including Luis Alberto Herrera, the leader of the Nationalist Party. It has been argued that this shift in perspective on women's suffrage came only when women voters could be perceived as allies of the ruling elite rather than as dangerous feminists whose allegiances lay with the Socialist or Anarchist Parties (Miller, 1991, 98). Influenced also by the example of women voters in the United States, the Nationalist Party adopted women's suffrage at its 1930 convention, and a congressional committee was set up to study women's suffrage.

Tactics used by feminists in this period included the production of propaganda, letters to politicians, and the organization of cells in provincial areas. In March 1932 the Alianza created an umbrella group for all organizations that favored suffrage called Comité Pro-Derechos de la Mujer, which recruited members outside the capital. The propaganda campaign was invigorated by the leadership of a new feminist leader, Rey Alvarez, who had established links with feminists in Belgium and England.

By the end of the year, the Senate had approved a suffrage bill without discussion. So widespread was support for the measure by this time that the Chamber of Deputies used their debate on the bill as a forum for political leaders to score political points and claim that they had each been long-standing supporters of women's suffrage. The bill was finally approved by the deputies on 14 December 1932, but women were unable to cast their vote until the elections of 1938.

See also Catt, Carrie Chapman; Citizenship; Latin America and the Caribbean; Luisi, Paulina.
References Lavrin, Asunción. *Women, Feminism and Social Change in Argentina, Chile and Uruguay, 1890–1940* (1995); Miller, Francesca. *Latin American Women and the Search for Social Justice* (1991).

Vérone, Maria

Maria Vérone (1874–1938) was a leading member of the militant wing of the French suffrage movement. The daughter of an accountant and a shopworker, both of whom were left-wing republicans, she took on a variety of occupations after the death of her father, including teaching and singing in a chorus line. She married and had children, and after her divorce she undertook legal studies and in 1907 became only the fifth Frenchwoman to be admitted to the bar.

While still a student, Vérone became secretary-general of the Ligue française pour le droit des femmes (LFDF) [French League for Women's Rights]. Her enthusiasm helped to revive the league, and as a committed suffragist, she ensured that the struggle for the vote became one of its main objectives. Although she concentrated on women's rights, Vérone was also active in the socialist movement and tried to disseminate her ideas through her journalism. For example, she edited the journal *Le Droit des femmes* (Women's Rights), founded in 1906, and also edited a women's suffrage column in the left republican newspaper *L'Oeuvre*.

Maria Vérone stood somewhere between the radical militancy of those who considered the use of violence and the moderation of those who opposed direct action in public. In December 1913 her frustration with the suffrage movement's lack of progress led her to declare that there must be a "new phase" to reopen the question of strategy. Which forms of collective action were most appropriate and effective? She opened a "suffragette kiosk" in Paris where she disseminated suffrage literature and then sponsored the registration of women during the annual revision of electoral lists. Vérone and her second husband, Georges L'Hermite, undertook litigation on behalf of women who were refused registration, but the cases were lost and little was achieved.

Vérone was bitterly disappointed when women failed to gain the vote after World War I, but she continued to organize demonstrations, parades, and an invasion of the floor of the Senate. Nonetheless, "these actions remained small, rare and ineffective; they produced more police harassment than political support" (Hause with Kenney, 1984, 249) because the majority of feminists were still reluctant to take direct action to achieve their goals. Vérone died in 1938, before women achieved the vote in France.

See also France.
References Hause, Steven C., with Anne R. Kenney. *Women's Suffrage and Social Politics in the French Third Republic* (1984); Reynolds, Siân. *France between the Wars: Gender and Politics* (1996).

Votes for Women

Votes for Women, published between 1907 and 1918, was until 1912 the official newspaper of the militant suffrage group the Women's Social and Political Union. It was edited and partly financed by Emmeline and Frederick Pethick-

Lawrence and played an important role in publicizing and justifying the actions of the suffragettes. *Votes for Women* became an integral part of the campaigning methods of the Women's Political and Social Union. Members were encouraged to increase the circulation of the paper, both to raise money and to spread propaganda and to make new recruits for the cause. After 1909 the WSPU made a more determined effort to increase the circulation of the paper. It was sold on the street and in suffrage shops and was advertised on the sides of lorries and carts that toured the streets, both in London and in the provinces. The paper used powerful imagery to draw attention to the courage and heroism of suffragettes, particularly in the face of the torture of forcible feeding. Circulation rose steadily, from 5,000 a month in 1908 to over 22,000 a week in 1909 and to 30,000 a week early in 1910.

In October 1912, however, the Pethick-Lawrences were ousted from the WSPU. They retained control of *Votes for Women,* which was replaced as the official organ of the WSPU by the *Suffragette,* edited by Christabel Pankhurst. The Pethick-Lawrences used *Votes for Women* to promote a new organization, the Votes for Women Fellowship, which attracted militants who could no longer accept the leadership and policies of the WSPU. In 1914 they also helped to found another organization, the United Suffragists, which was open to men and women regardless of their views on militancy. In August Emmeline and Frederick Pethick-Lawrence helped to ensure the survival of the United Suffragists when they handed over *Votes for Women* to the new group. The paper had been in financial difficulties since the editors had been expelled from the WSPU and they believed that the backing of an organization would ensure its survival. However, it continued to have financial problems and became a monthly rather than a weekly publication in 1917. When some women were at last enfranchised in 1918, *Votes for Women* ceased publication.

See also Newspapers and Journals; Pankhurst, Christabel; Pethick-Lawrence, Emmeline; Pethick-Lawrence, Frederick; Suffragette; Women's Social and Political Union. *References* Cowman, Krista. "'A Party between Revolution and Peaceful Persuasion': A Fresh Look at the United Suffragists" (1998); Crawford, Elizabeth. *The Women's Suffrage Movement: A Reference Guide, 1866–1928* (1999).

Votes for Women!

The play *Votes for Women!,* written in 1906 by the American actor and producer Elizabeth Robins, was the earliest suffrage drama to be written and performed in Britain. Designed as a rallying call to feminists, it was an immediate success. It inspired a new genre of theater that itself became part of the suffrage cause and led to the formation, in 1908, of two new suffrage leagues, one for writers and one for actors.

By the time Robins wrote the play, she had already joined the WSPU, delivered her first suffrage speech, and become a committed supporter of the women's movement. She described the three-act play as a dramatic tract. The play subverted many of the conventions of Edwardian theater, manipulating them for feminist ends. Robins did much more than simply argue for women's suitability for public life. More radically, she offered her heroine, a woman with an unhappy sexual past, a future of political activity in the service of women's emancipation rather than a conventional "happily ever after" marriage.

The play was first performed at the Court Theatre. A number of male writers, including Henry James, Bernard Shaw, and the theater manager Harley Granville-Barker, exerted some influence on the composition and title of the play. However, Robins maintained final control over its shape and direction. She also expanded it into a novel, *The Convert.*

Robins donated part of her fee for *Votes for Women!* to the two leading suffrage societies, pointing out that this redistribution of royalties was one of the only rights that women already had. Though some critics doubted the wisdom of mixing suffrage with other feminist issues, the play was extremely popular; ticket-seekers were turned away each night. *Votes for Women!* was also produced in New York and Rome in 1909, and a reading of the play sponsored by the Political Equality League in Chicago attracted an admiring audience.

See also Artists' Suffrage League; Britain; *The Convert;* Drama, Novels, Poetry, and Film; *How the Vote Was Won;* Women Writers' Suffrage League; Women's Social and Political Union.

References John, Angela. *Elizabeth Robins: Staging a Life, 1862–1952* (1995); Stowell, Sheila. *A Stage of Their Own: Feminist Playwrights of the Suffrage Era* (1992).

Wales

The movement for women's suffrage was slow to develop in Wales, but after 1906, branches of both the National Union of Women's Suffrage Societies (NUWSS) and the Women's Social and Political Union (WSPU) were formed and attracted increasing support. Two ingredients for a collective organizational base from which to support a suffrage movement were missing in nineteenth-century Wales: a strong middle class and a strong union presence among women. The middle class, which in many other countries provided the backbone of the women's suffrage movement, was weak, and there were few opportunities for paid employment among working-class women. Consequently, any suffrage activity was usually stimulated from outside Wales. In 1874, for example, the Manchester National Society for Women's Suffrage organized a campaign in north and central Wales in favor of the vote for single and widowed women who, aside from their sex, met the franchise qualifications.

During the 1890s the women's suffrage movement in Wales was given an organizational focus with the establishment of branches of the Women's Liberal Federation, and by 1895 the Welsh Union of Women's Liberal Associations had 9,000 members. The associations numbered women's suffrage as one of their aims, as did Cymru Fydd (Young Wales), a cultural and political pressure group for home rule. By emphasizing Welsh traditions of liberty, both groups drew a link between Welsh identity and women's right to vote.

Women's Liberal Associations were less active after the turn of the century, and the campaign for women's suffrage lost momentum temporarily. The growing publicity generated by the suffrage campaign in England after 1905, however, restimulated the movement in Wales, and well-known suffrage leaders such as Millicent Fawcett, Charlotte Despard, and Mary Gawthorpe made speaking tours of the country. Branches of the NUWSS were established in Llandudno in 1907 and Cardiff in 1908. The Cardiff Society, which covered most of southeast Wales, was the largest NUWSS branch outside London in 1912–1913. NUWSS branches spread through north and south Wales, and members were active in holding meetings and distributing literature. Branches of the militant WSPU were also established in south Wales, and leading figures such as Emmeline Pankhurst spoke at meetings throughout the country. Suffragettes disrupted meetings and harassed Liberal candidates. The most notorious incident took place toward the end of 1912 at Llanystumdwy when suffragettes interrupted David Lloyd George, Chancellor of the Exchequer in the Liberal government, who had come to open the village hall. This led to violent scenes, with the women being attacked by the crowd, and it helped to stimulate an antisuffrage movement.

There was also evidence of support for women's suffrage from sections of the labor movement. Socialists and trade unionists in the borough of Rhondda supported a series of meetings held by the WSPU in 1913 and claimed that only the labor movement was in favor of an equal franchise for women. Other trade union branches, influenced by the Labour Party's alliance with the NUWSS, gave the constitutionalist suffrage activists a more sympathetic hearing. As in England, militancy in Wales began to escalate just before World War I, when, for example, there was a series of attacks on mailboxes in Bridgend and Newport. In the same period, Welsh branches of the NUWSS took part in the 1913 Suffrage Pilgrimage organized by the NUWSS, and some women made the long trip all the way to London.

When a limited women's suffrage was achieved in 1918, many suffrage branches were dissolved, although others, such as the Cardiff Society, worked to get women elected to local councils. In 1921 the society turned itself into the Cardiff and District Women's Citizen Association and aimed to foster a sense of citizenship in women.

In many respects the women's suffrage movement in Wales followed and was stimulated by developments in England. However, as Neil Evans and Kay Cook note, the commitment to building up support for women's suffrage from a grassroots level remained even after charismatic speakers from England had gone. The nature of Welsh politics also gave the movement distinctiveness; Welsh branches generally remained loyal to the Liberals when the NUWSS formed its alliance with the Labour Party in 1912, and suffragette attacks on the Liberal Party, which was associated with national culture and pride, tended to be counterproductive. Suffrage campaigners also displayed a strong sense of national identity. They wore national costumes to demonstrations in London, used the red dragon on their banners, and drew on traditions of Welsh liberty in

their speeches. Nonetheless, it was difficult for them to link their feminism with their sense of Welsh identity in a context in which the Liberal government, and Lloyd George in particular, were so actively opposed to their cause.

See also Britain; Citizenship; Despard, Charlotte; Fawcett, Millicent Garrett; Gawthorpe, Mary; National Union of Women's Suffrage Societies; Pankhurst, Emmeline; Pilgrimage, Suffrage; Women's Social and Political Union.
Reference Cook, Kay, and Neil Evans. "'The Petty Antics of the Bell-Ringing Boisterous Band'? The Women's Suffrage Movement in Wales, 1890–1918" (1991).

Ward, Mary Augusta (Mrs. Humphry)

A leader of the British antisuffrage campaign, Mary Augusta Ward (née Arnold) (1851–1920) was born in Hobart, Tasmania, but she and her family went to live in Britain in 1856. In 1872 she married Thomas Humphry Ward, an Oxford don, and she went on to become a prominent author and philanthropist.

Ward first came to prominence as an antisuffragist when she organized a petition entitled "Appeal against the Extension of the Parliamentary Franchise to Women," which was published in the *Nineteenth Century* in June 1889. The petition was signed initially by 104 women, and later by a further 1,200 female antisuffragists. In July 1908 Ward became a member of the executive committee of the newly formed Women's National Anti-Suffrage League, and in December she launched the *Anti-Suffrage Review*. The following year, she embarked on a round of speaking engagements, including a much publicized public debate with suffragist Millicent Fawcett, which ended in Ward's defeat by a large majority.

In January 1910, Ward's son Arnold became the Conservative MP for West Hertfordshire, and between 1910 and 1912, Ward involved him in her vigorous campaign against the Conciliation Bill, a com-

Mary Augusta Ward, English novelist, social worker, and antisuffragist. (Ann Ronan Picture Library)

promise measure that aimed to give a limited franchise to women. In December 1910 the women's antisuffrage organization was amalgamated with the Men's League for Opposing Women's Suffrage, to become the National League for Opposing Women's Suffrage (NLOWS), led by Lord Cromer. In an effort to expand women's role in local rather than national politics, Ward founded the Local Government Advancement Committee in 1911, but its attempt to support antisuffragist woman candidates in municipal elections led to friction among other women's groups.

Ward continued her antisuffrage work until the outbreak of World War I in 1914, when she became a war reporter and propagandist, sending her dispatches to the U.S. press. During the war years, support for the antisuffrage cause began to decline, and when women finally obtained a limited parliamentary franchise in 1918, the NLOWS was dissolved, and the *Anti-Suffrage Review* ceased publication. Despite her own involvement in political life, Ward always believed that women were not constitutionally suited to participate directly in national politics and that their influence was stronger when it was indirect, in the home and in the local community. However, she failed to see that the distinction between local and national politics was becoming unrealistic, and that once governments began to interfere through legislation in all aspects of family life, the need for women's participation at a national level became increasingly important.

See also Antisuffrage Campaign, British; Britain; Conciliation Bill; Fawcett, Millicent Garrett; Representation of the People Act.
References Harrison, Brian. *Separate Spheres: The Opposition to Women's Suffrage in Britain* (1978); Sutherland, John. *Mrs Humphry Ward: Eminent Victorian, Pre-eminent Edwardian* (1990).

Wells-Barnett, Ida Bell

Ida Bell Wells-Barnett (1862–1931) was a leading member of the movement to enfranchise all African Americans in the United States, and she also worked for civil, women's, and economic rights. Born in Holly Springs, Mississippi, in 1862, Ida Bell Wells was the eldest of eight children of a carpenter and a plantation cook, both of whom had been slaves. When Ida was 16 her parents died of yellow fever, and she assumed responsibility for the family. She later moved to Memphis, Tennessee, where she worked as a teacher and became editor of the *Evening Star* and then the *Living Way*. In the *Living Way* she wrote a column under the name Iola, in which she tried to reach rural, uneducated people, and she grew so popular that she was soon writing articles for a variety of local and national newspapers.

In 1889 Wells bought a one-third interest in the Memphis *Free Speech and Headlight* and later became editor. She used the paper to publicize her views against lynching, which led to the destruction of the newspaper's office and threats on her life. Wells therefore moved to New York and worked on the *New York Age,* where she continued to expose lynching. Her tour of England and Scotland in 1892 led to the establishment of organizations to fight segregation and lynching. After attending the Chicago World's Fair in 1893, she remained in the city, where she helped to set up Black women's and reform organizations, including the Ida B. Wells Club and the Negro Fellowship League. In 1895 she married Ferdinand Barnett, owner of the *Chicago Conservator* and a widower with two children. They both shared a commitment to Black equality and had four children together.

Ida Wells-Barnett always believed that the vote was crucial for the achievement of equality and reforms for African Americans, and the Ida B. Wells Club supported the suffrage campaign. She lobbied Susan B. Anthony to gain her support against northern white suffragists who, on grounds of political expediency, were advocating a restricted educational franchise that would have excluded many Black women. In 1913, with her white colleague Belle Squire, she formed the Alpha Suffrage Club, the first Black female suffrage club in Illinois. Its aim was to politicize Black women in Chicago, who in June 1913 had gained the right to vote for all offices not mentioned in the state constitution, such as mayors, aldermen, and municipal court judges. The Alpha Suffrage Club attracted 200 members, who canvassed neighborhoods and organized weekly meetings on the rights and duties of citizenship. The club also aimed to counter the racism inherent in most predominantly white suffrage groups, and it sent Wells-Barnett as a delegate to the National American Woman Suffrage Association suffrage parade held on 3 March 1913 in Washington, D.C. White Illinois delegates asked her not to march with them, but to join Black marchers at the back of the procession instead. Wells-Barnett refused to accept this, and once the march had got under way, she stepped out from a crowd of spectators to join the Illinois contingent, thereby ensuring that the procession would be integrated.

The political activities of the Alpha Suffrage Club did encounter skepticism from some Black men, but when canvassers achieved high registration numbers in their districts, politicians began to use their techniques and to work with them. Wells-Barnett played a key role in 1915 by ensuring that the Suffrage Club, through its newsletter, the *Alpha Suffrage Record,* gave support to Oscar DePriest's candidacy for alderman. He won the election, becoming the first Black alderman in Chicago. This strengthened the role of Black women in local politics; they expected the Republicans to commit to reform and economic equality in exchange for their support.

Wells-Barnett continued to be active in politics during the 1920s, and in 1930 she stood unsuccessfully as an independent candidate for the Illinois Senate. Her emphasis on direct action and protest, along with her hostility to Booker T. Washington and her support for Timothy Thomas Fortune and Marcus Garvey, ensured that she was always a controversial figure. Through her writings and organizing work, she played an important part in a range of movements for African American rights, including the demand for women's suffrage. She died in Chicago in 1931 of a kidney disease, and her autobiography, *Crusade for Justice* (1970), edited by her daughter Alfreda Duster, was published after her death.

See also Anthony, Susan B.; Citizenship; National American Woman Suffrage Association; Race and Ethnicity; United States of America.

References Duster, Alfreda, ed. *Crusade for Justice: The Autobiography of Ida B. Wells* (1970); Hine, Darlene Clark, Elsa Barkley Brown, and Rosalyn Terborg-Penn, eds. *Black Women in America: An Historical Encyclopaedia*, Vol. 11 (1993).

Wollstonecraft, Mary

Often considered to be the pioneer thinker of the British women's suffrage movement, Mary Wollstonecraft (1759–1797) was born in London. She spent her early life as a teacher and governess, but in 1790 she went to London to work for publisher Joseph Johnson as a writer, translator, and critic. Johnson introduced Wollstonecraft to an influential group of radical thinkers that included Thomas Paine, the author of *Rights of Man* (1791–1792), and William Godwin, who was to become her husband in 1797. Wollstonecraft spent some time in France in 1792, during the height of the French Revolution, and although she was critical of the worst excesses of the Terror, she was deeply influenced by the founding document of the revolution, the Declaration of the Rights of Man.

During her brief writing career, she produced two novels and a number of political and educational texts, but the work with which she is most associated is the classic feminist text, *A Vindication of the Rights of Woman* (1792). One of the main themes that Wollstonecraft examined in *A Vindication* was the state of women's education, which she believed was only designed to please men and which created an unhealthy weakness and dependency. She believed that if women were given the same educational opportunities as men, they would become enlightened citizens, rational mothers, better intellectual companions to their husbands, and if they were single, more able to find employment.

The principles of female citizenship and equality of rights were important to Woll-

Mary Wollstonecraft, Anglo-Irish author and feminist. (Ann Ronan Picture Library)

stonecraft, although in her writing she only hinted at the idea of the enfranchisement of women—"women ought to have representatives, instead of being arbitrarily governed without having any direct share allowed them in the deliberations of government" (Wollstonecraft, 1975, 259–260). Although *A Vindication* contained only this brief reference to the idea of political representation, Wollstonecraft's book was seen by some leaders of the campaign for women's suffrage as the founding text of the women's movement.

Wollstonecraft's private life challenged conventional sexual morality (she lived with Gilbert Imlay outside marriage and bore him an illegitimate daughter), but her reputation was partly rehabilitated when Millicent Fawcett, the British constitutional suffragist, wrote a sympathetic preface to a new edition of *A Vindication*, published in 1891. Fawcett believed that

Wollstonecraft had "started the demand of women for political liberty in England." The militant suffragette Sylvia Pankhurst went further to write in 1931 that women's claim to emancipation was "wrought into comprehensive form by Mary Wollstonecraft."

See also Britain; Citizenship; Fawcett, Millicent Garrett; French Revolution; *The Suffragette Movement* (1931).
References Tomalin, Claire. *The Life and Death of Mary Wollstonecraft* (1974); Wollstonecraft, Mary. *A Vindication of the Rights of Woman* ([1792] 1975).

Wolstenholme-Elmy, Elizabeth

Elizabeth Wolstenholme-Elmy (1833–1918) was a controversial figure in the British suffrage movement because of her radical political views and her unconventional private life. The daughter of a cotton spinner and a Methodist minister in Lancashire, she was orphaned while still a child, but she was able to use her small inheritance to open a boarding school for girls near Manchester when she was only 19. She took part in the campaign for women's suffrage from the beginning, collecting 300 signatures for the petition presented to Parliament in 1866 by John Stuart Mill. In 1865 she was the honorary secretary of a small group, the Manchester Committee for the Enfranchisement of Women, which later became the Manchester National Society for Women's Suffrage, with Lydia Becker as its secretary. The two women worked closely together and also with other radical Liberals from Manchester, such as Richard Pankhurst and Ursula Bright. They argued for women's suffrage to be granted to married as well as to single women, seeing the franchise as just one of a wide range of reforms that were needed for the emancipation of women. These included improvements in women's access to higher education and employment, changes in the marriage laws, the double standard of morality, and sexual relations.

The Conservative Party victory in the 1874 election led some suffragists, including Becker, to narrow their focus on pragmatic grounds to the enfranchisement of single women. This was unacceptable to Wolstenholme and her friends, who continued to demand the vote for married women. Political tensions were exacerbated by Wolstenholme's personal life. She lived with Benjamin Elmy and became pregnant. Friends feared her unwed pregnancy would damage the women's movement, and they pressured her to marry Elmy, which she did in 1874.

After her marriage, Wolstenholme-Elmy retained a radical outlook; in 1889, along with her husband, she joined Richard and Emmeline Pankhurst in forming the Women's Franchise League, which worked for married women's rights, including equal divorce laws, as well as the franchise. She was paid secretary to the league, but she resigned after disagreements with members of the committee. In 1891 the Wolstenholme-Elmys founded another group, the Women's Emancipation Union (WEU), which campaigned for women's suffrage as an integral part of a broader set of demands, including married women's rights to sexual and legal autonomy. Wolstenholme-Elmy was also close to the labor movement, and when the WEU disbanded in 1899 after internal disagreements, she supported the suffrage campaigning of Lancashire textile workers and worked with the socialist group the Independent Labour Party.

Wolstenholme-Elmy was always impatient at the cautious approach of groups such as the National Union of Women's Suffrage Societies, and it is not surprising that she was attracted to the "insurgent women" of the Women's Social and Political Union. In 1905 she joined a protest with Emmeline Pankhurst outside the House of Commons and subsequently became a well-known figure in processions and demonstrations, remaining loyal to the Pankhursts despite splits in the organization. During World War I, however, she did not follow their lead in supporting the war effort but continued with her lifelong commitment to internationalism and pacifism. She died in 1918, after seeing women achieve the parliamentary vote.

Sandra Holton suggests that because Wolstenholme-Elmy has been neglected in histories of the suffrage movement, historians have been unable to recognize continuities between radicalism in the nineteenth century and militant suffragism in the twentieth. Recovering her story makes it possible to look at the British suffrage movement with a new perspective.

See also Becker, Lydia Ernestine; Independent Labour Party; Mill, John Stuart; National Union of Women's Suffrage Societies; Pankhurst, Emmeline; Women's Social and Political Union.
Reference Holton, Sandra Stanley. *Suffrage Days: Stories from the Women's Suffrage Movement* (1996).

Frances Willard, president of the Woman's Christian Temperance Union and suffragist leader, between 1880 and 1898. (Library of Congress)

Woman's Christian Temperance Union

The Woman's Christian Temperance Union (WCTU) was founded in 1874 in the United States and was led from 1879 to 1898 by its founding secretary, Frances Willard. Under her direction, the WCTU became a very important pressure group for women's suffrage, growing into an international organization with branches in many parts of the world, including Canada, Australia, New Zealand, and Japan. It was a powerful force in colonial societies where men were notoriously heavy drinkers and where the woman's vote was viewed by many as the means to achieving prohibition. The WCTU campaigns were opposed in these countries by the liquor trade, which financed antisuffragist campaigns.

The WCTU's particular strength in Australasia and in the midwestern United States can be explained partly by the lack of established institutions against which

women had to fight; feminist campaigns were free to focus narrowly on the vote and on moral reform. Rather than using rights-based arguments, Willard recruited women to the movement by offering them protection in the home. She stressed the importance of their role as mothers, pointed out that the liberal assumption that men necessarily protected women was false, and argued that only the vote would guarantee them security. A narrow focus on suffrage as a means to an end rather than as the key to wider political participation for women is suggested by the WCTU's continuing opposition to women electoral candidates.

The WCTU played an important part in the struggle for the vote in the United States, partly because of the sheer numbers of women it recruited, including many working-class women. Following its official endorsement of suffrage in 1880, the WCTU created a Department of Franchise that encouraged local groups to support the suffrage cause and to distribute suffrage literature. By 1890 it had recruited 150,000 American members. This contrasts with the National American Woman Suffrage Association, with only 13,000 members. By 1912 the number had risen to 250,000, many of whom became converts to feminism. However, by this time the mainstream U.S. suffrage movement had begun to turn away from temperance, which many saw as old-fashioned. Besides, the WCTU's antagonism toward the liquor industry was perceived as a hindrance to the cause.

By contrast, in Canada the temperance movement maintained its position as the most popular route by which both men and women became involved in the suffrage movement. The popularity of the temperance cause among reform politicians gave the movement powerful allies, and the WCTU worked in tandem with other suffrage societies throughout the history of the Canadian campaigns. The close connections between the two movements helped to convince men in positions of power that suffrage was not a threat. However, the connections also contributed to the conservatism of the Canadian suffrage movement and its acceptance of traditional roles for men and women.

The WCTU took root in New Zealand and Australia after Mary Clement Leavitt, a WCTU envoy from the United States, visited the area in 1885. In Australia the WCTU was first established in Victoria and grew rapidly, thanks to the efforts of another U.S. visitor, Mary Love, who became president of the Colonial WCTU in 1888. Love traveled 200,000 miles across the country, forming many new branches. Her work was consolidated by Jessie Ackerman, the first Australasian WCTU president, and Elizabeth Nicholls, who became involved in suffrage activities throughout the colony. The WCTU was instrumental in setting up suffrage organizations or coordinating suffrage campaigns in nearly every Australian state. It was only in large cities that separate suffrage organizations existed, and women in these groups often had a similar outlook to WCTU members, being for the most part Protestant Christians and teetotalers. Leavitt also founded the New Zealand WCTU in 1885, and in 1887 Kate Sheppard was appointed as superintendent of the WCTU's Franchise and Legislation Department. The WCTU single-handedly organized the campaign for the vote in New Zealand, where its objective was achieved before any other nation state.

As it had in New Zealand and Australia, the WCTU founded a branch in Tokyo in 1886 in the wake of Leavitt's world tour. Here as elsewhere, the WCTU supported the suffrage movement, and in 1921 it set up the Japanese Women's Suffrage Association as a branch within the union. The WCTU also took the lead in 1924 in setting up an umbrella suffrage organization, campaigning vigorously across the country for legislative change and collecting signatures on suffrage petitions. However, the WCTU was much less successful in Japan than in Australasia. Japan was not a Christian country, and membership was low, peaking at 800 members in 150 branches in 1926. Nevertheless, the WCTU did have an important impact on suffrage, giving impetus to the movement and teaching women organizational and campaigning skills.

See also Australia; Canada; Japan; National American Woman Suffrage Association; New Zealand; Nicholls, Elizabeth; Sheppard, Kate; United States of America.
References Bacchi, Carol Lee. *Liberation Deferred? The Ideas of the English-Canadian Suffragists, 1877–1918* (1983); Evans, Richard J. *The Feminists: Women's Emancipation Movements in Europe, America and Australasia, 1840–1920* (1977); Grimshaw, Patricia. "Presenting the Enfranchisement of New Zealand Women Abroad" (1994); Matsukawa, Yukiko, and Kaoru Tachi. "Woman's Suffrage and Gender Politics in Japan" (1994); Oldfield, Audrey. *Woman Suffrage in Australia, A Gift or a Struggle?* (1992).

Alice Stone Blackwell continued publication of Lucy Stone and Henry Blackwell's (her parents') suffrage newspaper, the Woman's Journal; *photo dated between 1905 and 1917. (Library of Congress)*

The *Woman's Journal*

The *Woman's Journal*, edited by Lucy Stone, her husband Henry Blackwell, and Mary Livermore (who gave up her own paper in Chicago to join the editorial team), championed the suffrage cause over a very long period and only ceased publication in 1931. Soon after forming the American Woman Suffrage Association in 1869, Stone and Blackwell used their own money, along with financing provided by benefactors, to establish a joint stock company to publish a suffrage paper. The first issue of the *Woman's Journal* came out in January 8, 1870 (on the anniversary of the founding of the *Revolution*).

In contrast to the *Revolution*, edited by Elizabeth Cady Stanton, the *Woman's Journal* avoided controversial issues within the women's movement and concentrated instead on news about the women's suffrage campaign, on fundraising techniques, and on topics that appealed to women interested in reform, thereby becoming the mouthpiece for moderate suffragists. The editors sought to raise revenue through subscriptions and advertising, but circulation figures remained low (around 2,500) in the early twentieth century.

By 1906 Alice Stone Blackwell, the daughter of the founders, owned and edited the *Woman's Journal*. She introduced new strategies that improved the finances of the paper. In 1910 she was approached by the leaders of the National American Woman Suffrage Association (NAWSA), who wished to adopt the paper as an official publication. Thereafter, circulation rose rapidly, reaching over 15,000 by 1911. Readers were encouraged to sell the paper on the streets as a method of campaigning and fundraising, although there was some opposition to this from conservative suffragists who thought it unwomanly.

Disagreements over finance and the style and content of the paper led to the end of the partnership between Blackwell and the NAWSA. Blackwell continued to publish the paper, however, publicizing the suffrage movement from a position of independence. As the struggle for the vote increased in popularity, the paper played an important propaganda role, provided advice to activists, and served as a means of communication among them. However, there continued to be tension between Blackwell and her business manager. Blackwell always put the suffrage movement first; for her, the rationale for the paper's existence was the campaign for women's enfranchisement. Her manager, on the other hand, was concerned about it as a commercial venture. In 1917 Blackwell finally relinquished ownership and control to a group set up by the NAWSA, and the *Woman's Journal* merged with other publications to form the *Woman Citizen,* which in turn was renamed the *Woman's Journal* in 1928.

See also American Woman Suffrage Association; National American Woman Suffrage Association; The *Revolution;* Stanton, Elizabeth Cady; Stone, Lucy.
References Finnegan, Margaret. *Selling Suffrage: Consumer Culture and Votes for Women* (1999); Flexner, Eleanor. *Century of Struggle: The Woman's Rights Movement in the United States* ([1959] 1975).

Women Writers' Suffrage League

The Women Writers' Suffrage League (WWSL), formed in 1908, was the first professional organization of women writers in Britain. It was the suffrage movement that inspired women writers to organize and develop a new degree of professionalism, as had been the case with the WWSL's sister organizations, the Artists' Suffrage League (1907) and the Actresses' Franchise League (1909). The criterion for membership in the WWSL was simply that applicants should have published a book, article, story, poem, or play for which they had received payment; the group included both male and female writers of all classes and political persuasions.

The WWSL was formed by feminist author Cicely Hamilton, whose suffrage pamphlet *How the Vote Was Won* was subsequently turned into a very popular play. The group's stated aim was to achieve equal franchise by changing public opinion; its methods focused on journalism, especially publishing articles and engaging in public correspondence in the press. The high profile of suffragettes in issues such as militancy and force-feeding made suffrage front-page news in popular newspapers. Thus, in addition to writing regular pieces for suffrage journals such as *Votes for Women* and the *Common Cause,* WWSL members attempted to reach unconverted audiences in conservative papers with antisuffragist editorial views. Among the best-known pieces was a defense of the cause by the league's first president, Elizabeth Robins, against well-known antisuffragist Mrs. Humphry Ward in the *Times* in 1912.

The WWSL joined in pageants and processions and sent delegates to conferences with other suffrage organizations. It cooperated with the Actresses' Franchise League to produce plays and pageants. League members were also very successful as fundraisers, selling their literature at public meetings, including fiction, sketches, plays, and poems. Competitions and prizes held for first-time authors also encouraged more women to write. Much of their mate-

Women's Freedom League caravan in the summer or autumn of 1908. (Mary Evans Picture Library/Fawcett)

rial was published anonymously because members were much more concerned with effective rhetoric than with authorship or literary style.

Without fully achieving its goal, the WWSL disbanded in 1919, a year after the 1918 Representation of the People Act enfranchised 8.5 million women over 30.

See also Actresses' Franchise League; Advertising; Artists' Suffrage League; Britain; The *Common Cause*; Drama, Novels, Poetry, and Film; *How the Vote Was Won*; Imagery; Militancy; Representation of the People Act; Robins, Elizabeth; *Votes for Women*; Ward, Mary Augusta.
Reference Park, Sowon S. "The First Professionals: The Women Writers' Suffrage League" (1997).

Women's Freedom League

The smallest of the three main British women's suffrage organizations, the Women's Freedom League (WFL) was set up in 1907. It arose out of a split within the militant women's suffrage organization the Wom-

en's Social and Political Union (WSPU). In 1907 Emmeline Pankhurst set aside the draft constitution of the WSPU and canceled the annual conference, due to be held in October, arguing that what was needed to achieve the vote was military-style organization rather than a democratic consensus. Charlotte Despard, Teresa Billington-Greig, and Edith How Martyn, all WSPU executive committee members, resented the autocratic leadership of the Pankhursts, and with a substantial number of other members, they left the organization to form the WFL in 1907.

Despard was president of the league until 1918 and was instrumental in fostering its links with the Labour Party. However, she also became somewhat autocratic and had to fight off an attempt to oust her from the leadership in 1912. There has always been some debate over the size of the WFL, but it is estimated that there were 53 branches in England, Scotland, and Wales in 1908, and 4,000 members in 1914.

The WFL offered a more democratic, nonviolent approach to suffrage campaigning than the WSPU, and it allowed local branches to be more independent in their choice of activities. Using the motto "Dare to be Free," the league adopted militant but nonviolent tactics to achieve its aims. In addition to petitioning and picketing the House of Commons, WFL members recruited support on street corners and outside factory gates, sent out a WFL caravan on propaganda tours, distributed leaflets by balloon, and even used a boat on the river Thames to harangue MPs who were sitting on the terrace of the Houses of Parliament. The league also embarked on a campaign of tax resistance, and it led a boycott of the census held in 1911.

In 1909 the WFL launched its own weekly paper, the *Vote*. In addition to reporting suffrage events and branch news, it included reviews of plays, poetry, and art, and it devoted space to news from groups concerned with other women's issues, such as prostitution and child welfare. The WFL's official object was not only to secure the vote for women, but also "to establish equality of rights and opportunities between the sexes." Although most WFL members accepted that women had important domestic and maternal roles, they were concerned about the wider economic and social issues that affected them in the home and the workplace.

On the outbreak of World War I, the WFL decided to concentrate on the home front, organizing the Women's Suffrage National Aid Corps to aid mothers and children in the poorer areas of the country. Once partial women's suffrage had been achieved in 1918, the WFL expanded its campaigning program to demand further rights for women, including equal pay and access to all the professions. Despite its relatively small membership, the WFL continued to campaign on a broad range of feminist issues until 1961.

See also Billington-Greig, Teresa; Britain; Despard, Charlotte; Pankhurst, Emmeline; Representation of the People Act; Women's Social and Political Union.
References Frances, Hilary. "'Dare to be Free!': The Women's Freedom League and Its Legacy" (2000); Garner, Les. *Stepping Stones to Women's Liberty: Feminist Ideas in the Women's Suffrage Movement* (1984).

Women's Rights Convention, Seneca Falls (1848)

The first Women's Rights Convention, held at Seneca Falls in July 1848 and attended by 300 people, marked the birth of the organized feminist movement in the United States. The convention was planned and executed by a small group of women led by Elizabeth Cady Stanton and Lucretia Mott. Both women had been excluded from the World Anti-Slavery Convention in London in 1840 on the grounds of their sex, and this indignity inspired them to organize a convention for women.

The convention's principal achievement was to ratify a Declaration of Sentiments and Resolutions, drawn up by Stanton and Mott and modeled on the American Declaration of Independence. This new declaration, which anticipated most of the demands of the nineteenth-century feminist movement, identified women's suffrage as a key issue. Resolution 9 of the declaration stated that it was women's duty to secure their right to the elective franchise. This proved to be the most controversial part of the declaration; it was the only resolution that did not pass unanimously. Stanton's husband had refused to attend the conference if suffrage formed part of the program, and many of the women present were wary of making overt declarations about sexual equality. In the end, the resolution was passed by a small majority. Only 1 woman out of the 68 who signed the declaration, Charlotte Woodward, survived to cast her vote for president after universal suffrage was achieved in 1920.

See also Antislavery Movement; Mott, Lucretia Coffin; Stanton, Elizabeth Cady; United States of America.
References DuBois, Ellen Carol. "Outgrowing the Compact of the Fathers: Equal Rights, Woman Suffrage and the United States Constitution, 1820–1878" (1987); Flexner, Eleanor, *Century of Struggle: The Woman's Rights Movement in the United States* ([1959] 1975).

Women's Social and Political Union

The militant suffrage organization the Women's Social and Political Union (WSPU) was founded on 10 October 1903 in Manchester, England, by a small group of women led by Emmeline Pankhurst and her daughter Christabel, all of whom belonged to the Manchester branch of the Independent Labour Party (ILP). After some discussion, the new group was named the Women's Social and Political Union, with an exclusively female membership and the sole objective of securing social and political equality with men.

The WSPU was committed to the franchise for propertied women, which belied its ILP origins but may have been a reflection of the middle-class background of their leaders and of the belief that a limited female franchise would be easier to obtain than full adult suffrage. The initial policy of the WSPU was to try to persuade the Labour Party to include women's suffrage in its program, but many ILP members were hostile to the idea, preferring instead to campaign for an adult suffrage measure, which would include all working-class men and women.

During the next two years, the WSPU worked with the ILP and alongside the constitutional suffrage organization the National Union of Women's Suffrage Societies (NUWSS) to campaign for the enfranchisement of women. However, the WSPU began to adopt a more aggressive approach to campaigning when, in October 1905, WSPU members interrupted a Liberal political meeting at which Sir Edward Grey was speaking, and Christabel Pankhurst and Annie Kenney were both arrested and given a prison sentence. This incident attracted a great deal of publicity, receiving the kind of attention that decades of petitioning had failed to achieve, and the motto of the organization, "Deeds, not words," took on a new meaning.

In 1906 the Liberal Party, always sympathetic to the idea of the female franchise, won a landslide victory in the general election, and the women's suffrage movement was optimistic about the prospects of gaining the vote in the near future. The WSPU decided to move its headquarters from Manchester to London, in the belief that it was important for the suffrage fight to be conducted in the capital, where they could exert the most influence on central government. Disappointed with the absence of Liberal commitment to women's suffrage in the King's Speech of February 1906, the WSPU began to hold protest meetings that aimed to persuade members of Parliament to support the suffrage cause. Typical of this early phase of WSPU militancy was the holding of a "Women's Parliament" at Caxton Hall at the beginning of every parliamentary session, with a subsequent march to the Houses of Parliament to demand the vote. The clashes with police that resulted from these demonstrations resulted in many arrests, and often imprisonment. Such events attracted a great deal of publicity and gave the "suffragettes," as they came to be called, the chance to argue their case in court. Millicent Fawcett, the leader of the NUWSS, praised the "courage, endurance and self-sacrifice" of the suffragettes, and she admitted that "far from having injured the movement, they have done more in the last twelve months to bring it within the region of practical politics than we have been able to accomplish in the same number of years."

It was during 1906 that the WSPU began a long-running campaign to oppose

Liberal candidates at by-elections. Christabel Pankhurst, who was beginning to dictate the policy of the organization, indicated that candidates from other parties would be treated impartially, including those from the ILP. This new policy was intended to attract more middle- and upper-class women to the WSPU so that it did not have to rely on the support of working-class women, but the move was opposed by paid organizers Mary Gawthorpe and Teresa Billington-Greig, among others, who still felt a loyalty to their socialist roots.

This split with the ILP was exacerbated when, in January 1907, the Labour Party Conference decided to campaign for adult suffrage rather than support a measure that would only enfranchise propertied women. Emmeline and Christabel Pankhurst indicated their displeasure by resigning from the ILP in April 1907. This move away from the original principles of the WSPU, together with an increasing lack of democratic decision making, led to a rift in the organization in the autumn of 1907, when important members like Teresa Billington-Greig, Charlotte Despard, and Edith How Martyn left to form their own suffrage group, the Women's Freedom League (WFL).

By early 1907 the WSPU had 47 branches, and it was felt that the organization needed a monthly newspaper to motivate and inspire the membership and to spread the suffrage message. *Votes for Women* was founded in October 1907 by Emmeline and Frederick Pethick-Lawrence, two of Emmeline Pankhurst's closest supporters, and it grew from an initial circulation of 2,000 copies to 16,000 copies by 1909. During 1908 the WSPU concentrated on holding large public meetings, and its most striking demonstration was held on 21 June, when a crowd of over 250,000 people witnessed 30,000 women in seven processions march to Hyde Park, with bands playing, banners flying, and the marchers wearing white dresses with accessories in the WSPU colors of purple, white, and green. In the park, the crowd was addressed by 20 speakers on different platforms, and at the end of the demonstration a resolution calling for the enfranchisement of women was put to the audience, which responded enthusiastically. The next day, most newspapers had to admit that it was one of the most spectacular political events ever held in England.

Despite this impressive demonstration, Liberal Prime Minister H. H. Asquith refused to change his policy of opposition to women's suffrage, and this led the WSPU to adopt a more aggressive approach. Later that month, on 30 June, after a group of women led by Emmeline Pankhurst had tried unsuccessfully to see Asquith, there were serious disturbances in Trafalgar Square, and a number of suffragettes were treated with some brutality before being arrested by the police. Two WSPU members who were outraged by these events, Edith New and Mary Leigh, went to Asquith's residence at 10 Downing Street and smashed two windows, an act for which they were immediately arrested and later imprisoned. This act not only represented an escalation of militant activities by the suffragettes, but it also fueled the beginning of an antisuffrage campaign by those who believed that it was time to express their opposition to women's suffrage in a more public way.

One of the last major WSPU events of 1908 was held on 13 October, when groups of suffragettes tried to "rush" the House of Commons in order to confront the prime minister. Emmeline and Christabel Pankhurst, with Flora Drummond, were charged with inciting public disorder and were sentenced to terms of imprisonment. Their trial attracted enormous publicity, with two government ministers called as witnesses and Christabel Pankhurst delivering a two-hour speech that was published in the newspapers the following day. Militancy had gained more publicity for the suffrage movement than had ever been achieved during the earlier years of the campaign, and this lesson was not lost on the leaders of the WSPU.

During 1909 the WSPU tried to increase its pressure on the government, but with little tangible result. However, one campaigning event was to change for the worse the already difficult relationship between the suffragettes and the Liberal government. On 29 June, when Asquith refused to see a deputation from the WSPU, serious disorder broke out, and a number of windows in government buildings were broken. This resulted in a number of arrests, and when the authorities refused to accord the suffragettes the status of political prisoners, the women announced that they were going on a hunger strike. At first the government decided to release the hunger strikers before the end of their sentence to avoid any adverse publicity that might bolster the suffrage cause, but after a few months the authorities changed their policy, announcing that the women would be forcibly fed if they continued to refuse to eat. This painful and violent practice gave rise to much public criticism, and eventually, in 1913, the government brought in the Prisoners' Temporary Discharge for Ill Health Act, commonly called the Cat and Mouse Act. This legislation allowed the authorities to release a suffragette prisoner whose health had deteriorated from hunger striking and then to rearrest her once she had recovered.

At the beginning of 1910 a cross-party group of politicians came together to form the Conciliation Committee for Women's Suffrage, with the object of framing a women's suffrage bill that would be acceptable to all. The WSPU decided to call a truce on its militant activities, and on 12 July the Conciliation Bill (which allowed for a limited parliamentary franchise for women) passed its second reading by a large majority. However, the government shelved the measure, and on 18 November the WSPU resumed its campaign and sent a deputation of about 300 women to the House of Commons to protest the killing of the bill. The women attempted to rush past the police lines, but on this occasion the officers acted with particular brutality, and many women were kicked, punched, and even sexually molested. Black Friday, as the day later came to be called, resulted in over 100 arrests, but charges against the women were later dropped. In anticipation of the introduction of a second Conciliation Bill in 1911, the WSPU announced a new truce, but when the government shelved the measure yet again and announced in November that it intended to bring in a new Reform Bill that could be amended to include the enfranchisement of women, WSPU members were deeply suspicious and announced a resumption of militancy.

From 1912 onward militancy entered into a more violent phase, with window-smashing campaigns, attacks on public and private property, burning of mailboxes, and vandalism against works of art. By now the constitutional suffragists of the NUWSS had become extremely critical of the escalating violence of the suffragettes and were concerned that these activities could seriously reduce the chances for the Conciliation Bill. Their fears were confirmed when the bill was presented to the House of Commons for a third time on 28 March 1912 and was defeated by 14 votes. It is likely that the measure was lost not only because the Irish Nationalists voted against it for tactical reasons, but also because suffragette militancy had given the politicians the excuse they needed to get rid of the bill entirely. The promised Reform Bill never got beyond a second reading and was eventually withdrawn by the Liberal government in January 1913.

After further outbreaks of militant activities, the authorities decided to raid the headquarters of the WSPU on 5 March 1912, with warrants for the arrest of Christabel Pankhurst, who had fled to Paris; Emmeline Pankhurst, who was already in prison; and Frederick and Emmeline Pethick-Lawrence. On 5 May 1912 Emmeline Pankhurst and the Pethick-Lawrences were sentenced to nine months' imprisonment for conspiracy, and a few months later the Pethick-Lawrences were asked to leave the WSPU after expressing their concern about the increasingly violent tactics being advocated by the Pankhursts. Emmeline and Christabel Pankhurst now took over complete control of the WSPU, and a new official paper called the *Suffragette* was established to replace *Votes for Women,* which the Pethick-Lawrences continued to publish on their own.

During 1913 and 1914 the suffragette violence continued, and private houses, public buildings, and churches were damaged or destroyed by arson or bombing, including the house of Lloyd George, the Liberal minister, in February 1913. However, the most dramatic protest was that of Emily Wilding Davison, who ran out onto the Derby racecourse on 4 June 1913 and was struck down by the king's horse and seriously injured. Davison died in the hospital a few days later, and on 14 June the WSPU staged a spectacular martyr's funeral, with 2,000 suffragettes following the coffin through London streets that were lined by silent spectators.

By the beginning of 1914 Christabel Pankhurst was facing considerable internal criticism of her policies. In January, with her mother's support, she expelled Sylvia Pankhurst from the organization, on the grounds that her links with the Labour Party were contrary to WSPU policy. Sylvia Pankhurst left to form the East London Federation of Suffragettes, and the following month some discontented WSPU members broke away to form the United Suffragists. Both groups included

male supporters who had become alienated by the recent WSPU policy of discouraging male participation. By the middle of 1914, the WSPU was losing popular support and was becoming less effective as a campaigning organization, and the police were constantly harassing its members and raiding its meetings in an attempt to quell its activities.

On the outbreak of war in August 1914, the government granted all WSPU prisoners an amnesty, Christabel Pankhurst returned from her exile in France, and Emmeline Pankhurst announced a suspension of all suffrage agitation so that the war effort could take priority. Many members of the WSPU were extremely critical of this change of policy and left the organization to continue the campaign for women's suffrage. In November 1917 the WSPU changed its name to the Women's Party and founded a newspaper called *Britannia,* which supported the war and condemned pacifism. The following year, in February 1918, the Representation of the People Act gave a limited parliamentary vote to British women.

Although in the latter years of its campaign the WSPU was severely criticized for its use of violent action, its members had taken the campaign for women's suffrage from the stage of polite petition gathering and personal lobbying to one where the issue of the women's vote dominated newspaper headlines and became a subject of public debate, both in Parliament and in the country at large. At the same time, the militant campaign gave many women a feeling of self-respect and a determination to stand up for themselves; some might even say it became the inspiration for many future feminist struggles. The WSPU was a relatively small organization compared to the nonviolent NUWSS, and yet its militant activities have, until recently, dominated much of the debate about the British women's suffrage movement. Recent academic work has helped to acknowledge the enormous contribution made by other suffrage organizations, but the militant campaign of the WSPU continues to fascinate all students of women's suffrage history.

> *See also* Britain; Cat and Mouse Act; Independent Labour Party; Kenney, Annie; Militancy; National Union of Women's Suffrage Societies; Newspapers and Journals; Pankhurst, Christabel; Pankhurst, Emmeline; Pankhurst, (Estelle) Sylvia; Representation of the People Act; Suffragette; *Votes for Women;* Women's Freedom League.
> *References* Marcus, Jane, ed. *Suffrage and the Pankhursts* (1987); Purvis, June. "'Deeds, Not Words': Daily Life in the Women's Social and Political Union in Edwardian Britain" (2000); Rosen, Andrew. *Rise Up, Women! The Militant Campaign of the Women's Social and Political Union* (1974).

The logo of the Women's Trade Union League, at a convention in New York City, 1924. (Courtesy: University of Florida, Gainesville)

Women's Trade Union League

The Women's Trade Union League (WTUL), formed in Boston in 1903 as an umbrella group bringing together working women to improve their conditions of employment, helped to provide a link between trade unionism and women's suffrage in the United States. Middle-class leaders of the league, known as "allies" if they were not union members, such as Margaret Dreier Robins, president of the WTUL, Florence Kelley, and Jane Addams, tried, on the one hand, to convince working women that the vote was relevant to their needs because it would enable them to influence legislation and, on the other hand, to persuade the suffrage movement that it needed the support of working-class women and their unions. The middle-class leadership intended from the start that the league should eventually be run by working women. Robins in particular was successful in recruiting working-class women to take office in the organization.

Members of the WTUL worked closely with Harriot Stanton Blatch when she established the Equality League of Self-Supporting Women in New York, and working-class leaders of the WTUL soon

became popular as suffrage speakers. Rose Schneiderman of the Cap Makers' Union, Agnes Nestor of the International Glove Workers' Union, and Pauline Newman, an experienced organizer, were among the most active suffrage campaigners. The WTUL also organized a special suffrage division, the Wage Earners' Suffrage League, which was chaired by Leonora O'Reilly, a garment worker, experienced organizer, and popular speaker. Membership was open only to working women "to preserve harmony of purpose and . . . freedom of discussion at meetings"—a statement that hints at the tensions that could exist between union women and middle-class women's organizations.

WTUL members traveled widely in support of the suffrage. In 1910, for example, Agnes Nestor joined the "suffrage special," a train going from Chicago to Springfield to pressure legislators to pass the state suffrage bill. Nestor spoke along the way wherever industrial workers were in the audience. WTUL members also distributed literature, took part in demonstrations, and spoke outside factory gates

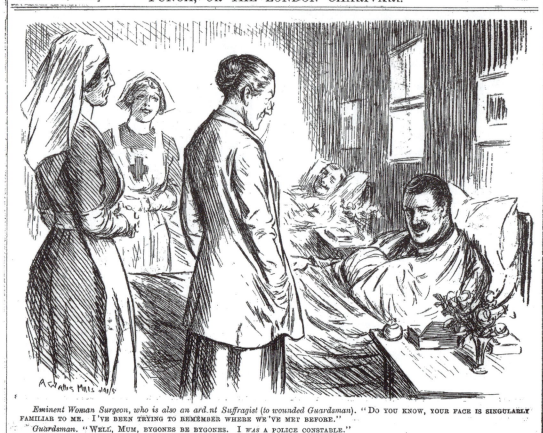

Eminent Woman Surgeon, who is also an ard.nt Suffragist (to wounded Guardsman). "DO YOU KNOW, YOUR FACE IS SINGULARLY FAMILIAR TO ME. I'VE BEEN TRYING TO REMEMBER WHERE WE'VE MET BEFORE."
Guardsman. "WELL, MUM, BYGONES BE BYGONES. I WAS A POLICE CONSTABLE."

Woman surgeon and suffragist treating soldiers during World War I, *from* Punch, *London, 4 August 1915. (Ann Ronan Picture Library)*

and on street corners, contributing to a more direct-action, radical approach to suffrage campaigning.

See also Addams, Jane; Blatch, Harriot Stanton; Schneiderman, Rose.
References DuBois, Ellen Carol. "Working Women, Class Relations and Suffrage Militance: Harriot Stanton Blatch and the New York Woman Suffrage Movement, 1894–1909" (1987); Wertheimer, Barbara Mayer. *We Were There: The Story of Working Women in America* (1977).

World War I

In the immediate aftermath of World War I, from 1918 to 1920, women gained the vote in several countries, although in many cases on a restricted basis; all of these, except for Rhodesia (now Zim-babwe) and Kenya, were in Europe or North America. There has been considerable debate about the role of the war in women's enfranchisement. It has often been assumed that women were enfranchised as a reward for their services in the war effort, but this correlation does not stand up when various countries are compared. Women did not achieve the suffrage in some countries that took part in the war, such as Italy and France, whereas they did gain the vote in the Netherlands, which remained neutral. Steven Hause and Anne Kenney suggest that in France, the war was actually a setback for women's suffrage in that it "truncated a political campaign that had apparently reached its takeoff stage in 1914 but could not recover so well in 1919" (Hause with Kenney, 1984, 202). Many French suffragists diverted their energies to other issues during wartime, and the movement was further weakened when different attitudes toward the war produced splits between suffrage campaigners. Moreover, the Bolshevik Revolution led to the development of a greater rift between socialists and "bourgeois feminists."

The relationship between World War I and women's suffrage, therefore, was a complex one and can only be understood in the overall political context of individual countries. In some areas, such as Germany, Austria, and Czechoslovakia, the upheavals brought by the war led to the downfall of authoritarian regimes and the introduction of more radical or democratic governments. In these cases it was the changed political context, rather than women's contribution to the war effort, that was responsible for the introduction of women's suffrage. In Britain, Prime Minister Asquith saw women's suffrage as a reward for war work, but it has been suggested that this was an expedient that allowed him to save face and reverse a long-standing opposition to the female vote.

In any case, too much emphasis on the role of the war in obtaining women's suffrage tends to overshadow the organized campaign by women to place the question of sex inequality at the forefront of debate. World War I did have an impact on the extension of voting rights to women, but it was only one of many factors, which varied from country to country, and its influence should not be exaggerated.

References DuBois, Ellen Carol. "Woman Suffrage and the Left: An International Socialist-Feminist Perspective" (1991); Hause, Steven C., with Anne R. Kenney. *Women's Suffrage and Social Politics in the French Third Republic* (1984); Summerfield, Penny. "Women and War in the Twentieth Century" (1995).

Z

Zetkin, Clara

Clara Zetkin (1857–1933) was a leading theoretician and political activist in the Sozialdemokratische Partei Deutschland (SPD) [German Social Democratic Party]. She was responsible for developing policy on women's suffrage specifically and the "woman question" more generally, first for the party and then for the Second International. Born Clara Eissner, the daughter of a housewife and a teacher in a small weavers' village in Saxony, she was introduced to the ideas of the women's rights movement by her mother and then by Auguste Schmidt, a leader of the women's movement and founder of the teacher training college that Eissner attended. By the time she graduated, Eissner had also become closely associated with the SPD.

When the party was outlawed in 1881, Eissner went into exile in Paris, where she lived with her companion, Ossip Zetkin, and their two children. She assumed Zetkin's name, and when he died in 1889 she had to support the family, gaining firsthand experience of poverty. After delivering a key speech on the woman question at the founding conference of the Second International in 1889, Clara Zetkin became well known and influential in international socialist circles. Returning to Germany, she became the leader of the socialist women's organization and editor of its journal, *Die Gleichheit* (Equality).

In her writings and speeches, Zetkin argued that socialism and feminism were inextricably linked, but she emphasized that the causes of women's inferior social position were their economic dependence and their class oppression and she opposed any attempts to cooperate with the bourgeois women's movement. After the 1890s Zetkin did shift her emphasis to acknowledge noneconomic causes of women's oppression, although she still gave primacy to class issues if gender questions threatened socialist unity.

Nonetheless, Zetkin also fought sex discrimination within the SPD and encouraged women to participate fully in socialist politics. She stressed the importance of suffrage for women as well as men, arguing that the SPD should fight for the enfranchisement of both sexes with equal commitment. As the chief speaker on suffrage at the 1907 Congress of the Second International at Stuttgart, Zetkin argued that whenever socialist parties campaigned for suffrage, women's suffrage should be "vigorously advocated in the agitation as well." She attacked Austrian socialist women for refusing to press the cause of female enfranchisement for fear that it might harm the cause of manhood suffrage. When she became secretary of the International Bureau of Socialist Women, she was responsible for instituting International Proletarian Women's Day, a celebration that involved yearly demonstrations between 1911 and 1914 in a number of European countries in support of women's suffrage.

Zetkin was one of a small minority of the SPD membership who opposed Germany's entry into World War I, and she advocated pacifism. Disillusioned with the socialists, she became a founder of the German Communist Party and spent much time in the 1920s in Moscow, although she returned to represent the communists in the German Reichstag. She became honorary president of the Reichstag and made her last speech in August 1932 before the Nazis took over the government.

Although Zetkin held ambivalent views toward the women's movement, she was instrumental in raising the question of women's rights, including women's suffrage, both inside and outside the SPD, the most influential socialist party in Europe before World War I.

See also Germany; International Proletarian Women's Day; Stuttgart Congress of the Second International.

References Honeycut, Karen. "Clara Zetkin: A Socialist Approach to the Problem of Women's Oppression" (1981); Quataert, Jean H. *Reluctant Feminists in German Social Democracy* (1979).

Appendix: Web Resources in English on Women's Suffrage

The World Wide Web has been with us for less than ten years, but it has grown to be a major source of information on every possible subject. Although Web sites rarely provide original data and their content is sometimes superficial or occasionally misleading or inaccurate (particularly in sites that attempt to list when women first won the vote in various countries), their format is convenient and they are excellent at providing concise, well-illustrated information that is accessible 24 hours a day.

Web sites on women's suffrage can be divided into three types: those that describe and permit access to major library collections on women's studies; those that provide the text of an important document (or series of documents), usually with commentary; and those that provide a combination of types of information, such as biographical, illustrated, and chronological material. This listing of Web resources organizes sites into these three categories, plus a section on material about suffrage movements outside the United States. It is neither comprehensive nor definitive; it is simply an introductory list of sites we have found helpful.

Collections

Duke University, Durham, NC, available at:
http://scriptorium.lib.duke.edu/women

Fawcett Library, London, available at:
http://www.lgu.ac.uk/fawcett/main.htm

Schlesinger Library, Radcliffe College, Cambridge, MA, available at:
http://www.radcliffe.edu/schles

Sophia Smith Collection, at Smith College, Northampton, MA, available at:
http://www.smith.edu.libraries/ssc

Documents

Documents about women's struggle for the vote in the United States available on the Web include:

National Woman's Party and the Enfranchisement of African American Women, available at: http://womhist.binghamton.edu/nwp/introduc.htm

This is a collection of 23 documents dealing with the question "How did the National Woman's Party address the issue of African American women in connection with the passage of the Woman Suffrage Amendment?" This site forms part of the *Women and Social Movements in the United States, 1830–1930* program.

Other useful sites in the series are:
Booker T. Washington and W. E. B. Du Bois and Woman Suffrage, available at:
http://womhist.binghamton.edu/webdbtw/Intro.htm

and *Lobbying for Passage of the National Suffrage Amendment,* available at:
http://womhist.binghamton.edu/lobby/bigintro.htm

The seminal text of the Declaration of Sentiments of the Seneca Falls Convention can be found on two sites:
http://www.rochester.edu/SBA/declare.html
http://lcweb.loc.gov/exhibits/treasures/trr040.html

The U.S. National Archives and Record Administration Web site includes documents on *Woman Suffrage and the Nineteenth Amendment,* available at:
http://www.nara.gov/education/teaching/woman/home.html

General U.S. Suffrage

These sites usually combine biographical information with illustrations and chronological information. Some also include documentary material.

Sites devoted to individual American suffragists include:

Carrie Chapman Catt Childhood Home site, available at:
http://catt.org

Travels for Reform: The Early Work of Susan B. Anthony and Elizabeth Cady Stanton, 1852–1861, available at:
http://mep.da.sc.edu/sa/sa-table.html
This is an introduction to the U.S. women's suffrage movement, including a mini-edition of some of the formative texts of the movement.

More information on the *Stanton and Anthony Papers Project* at Rutgers University, New Brunswick, NJ, is available at:
http://ecssba.rutgers.edu

Matilda Joslyn Gage site, available at:
http://www.pinn.net/~sunshine/gage/mjg.html

Lucretia Coffin Mott Project, available at:
http://www.mott.pomona.edu/index.htm

Suffragists Oral History Project, based at the University of California at Berkeley, can be found at:
http://library.berkeley.edu/BANC/ROHO/ohonline/suffragists.html
This contains interviews with 12 leaders and participants in women's struggle for the vote in the United States (including an interview with Alice Paul).

Motherhood, Social Service and Political Reform: Political Culture and Imagery of American Woman Suffrage, available at:
http://www.nmwh.org/exhibits/exhibit_frames.html
A fascinating exhibition describing women's suffrage in the United States based at the National Museum of Women's History in Washington, D.C.

Votes for Women: Suffrage Pictures, 1850–1920, available at:
http://memory.loc.gov/ammem/naw/nawshome.html
This splendid collection of portraits, photographs, and cartoons comes from the National American Woman Suffrage Collection (NAWSA), 1848–1921, held by the Library of Congress in Washington, D.C. Found at the same site are details from NAWSA's collection of 167 books, pamphlets, and other artifacts highlighting the suffrage campaign, which is a subset of the larger collection donated by Carrie Chapman Catt, and a chronology of events in the U.S. women's suffrage movement by E. Susan Barber.

History of the Suffrage Movement, available at:
http://www.rochester.edu/SBA/hisindx.html
A brief overview of the U.S. suffrage movement containing documents, biographies, a chronology, and a bibliography, this site is maintained by the Susan B. Anthony Center at the University of Rochester, NY.

Votes for Women, available at:
http://www.huntington.org/vfw
A superb chronicle of the American suffrage movement, this site includes a vivid and informative exhibition of photographs, imagery, and artifacts held at the Huntington Library in San Marino, CA.

Suffrage Movements outside the United States

Information on suffrage movements outside the United States is sparse.

A History of the Vote in Canada, available at:
http://www.civilization.ca/membrs/canhist/elections/el_000_e.html
Focusing on the movement in Canada, this site has disappointingly little to say about women's fight for the vote at either the provincial or the federal level.

The Suffragists: Women Who Worked for the Vote, available at:
http://www.nzhistory.net.nz/Gallery Frameset.html

This site on the New Zealand suffrage movement contains illustrated biographies of eight women who fought for women's suffrage in New Zealand, taken from the book *The Suffragists: Women Who Worked for the Vote: Essays from the Dictionary of New Zealand Biography* (Wellington, NZ: Bridget Williams Books/Dictionary of New Zealand Biography, 1993). At the same site is an illustrated essay on the New Zealand suffrage movement by Roberta Nicholls, taken from her book *The Women's Parliament: The National Council of Women of New Zealand, 1896–1920* (Wellington, NZ: Victoria University Press, 1996).

British History, 1700–1920: The Emancipation of Women, 1780–1920, available at:
http://www.spartacus.schoolnet.co.uk/women.htm

This is the best, indeed almost the only, site on the British suffrage movement. Based on the *Spartacus Internet Encyclopedia,* this excellent site contains numerous biographies of suffragists, suffragettes, and pioneers of women's rights, along with entries on suffrage campaigns and tactics, parliamentary reform acts from 1832 to 1928, suffrage organizations and pressure groups, and important background information on related issues in the nineteenth century, including birth control, marriage, and careers and professions for women.

References Miller, Heather Lee. "Getting to the Source: The World Wide Web of Resources for Women's History" (1999); National Women's History Project at: http://www.nwhp.org/links.html.

Chronology

This chronology lists the years when women in individual countries (not provinces, states, or regions within countries) were granted full adult suffrage. Only in exceptional cases is it noted when a partial or restricted franchise was given to women earlier, or conversely, where particular minority groups were excluded from full political rights at the time of enfranchisement. The chronology only deals with the countries covered in this encyclopedia; the reader interested in other countries can consult Joni Seager, *The State of Women in the World Atlas* (New Revised Edition, London: Penguin, 1997), and Caroline Daley and Melanie Nolan, eds., *Suffrage and Beyond* (New York: New York University Press, 1994).

It is sometimes difficult to establish the exact year when women's suffrage was achieved because often considerable time passes between the promulgation of a new constitution or electoral law, its formal ratification by the legislature, and its implementation in the first election to include female voters. With these factors in mind, this chronology attempts to identify the year when women's suffrage became actual law. Other problems arise in cases such as those former sub-Saharan African colonies where the colonial power enfranchised the female population shortly before independence, for example, the French *loi-cadre* (framework law) of 1956. In these cases, for the sake of clarity, the year of the achievement of universal suffrage on independence has been given. Because of these complex issues, chronologies of women's suffrage rarely agree in all respects; however, this list is as accurate as current research permits.

1893	New Zealand
1902	Australia (Aboriginal women excluded until 1962)
1906	Finland
1913	Norway
1915	Denmark, Iceland
1917	Russia
1918	Austria, Canada (although minority groups such as the Inuit and registered Indians were excluded until after World War II), Germany
1919	Czechoslovakia, the Netherlands
1920	United States of America
1921	Sweden
1922	Republic of Ireland
1928	Britain (limited franchise granted in 1918)
1931	Sri Lanka
1932	Brazil, Uruguay
1934	Cuba, Turkey
1935	Puerto Rico
1937	Philippines
1939	El Salvador
1942	Dominican Republic
1944	France, Jamaica
1945	Bulgaria, Guatemala, Hungary (franchise gained in 1919, restricted in 1921), Indonesia, Italy, Japan, Panama, Trinidad and Tobago
1946	Ecuador (limited franchise in 1929)

1947	Argentina, Venezuela
1948	Belgium, Chile, Israel, Myanmar (Burma)
1949	China, Costa Rica, India
1950	Haiti
1951	Antigua, Barbados, Dominica, Grenada, St. Kitts and Nevis, St. Lucia, St. Vincent and the Grenadines
1953	Bolivia, Lebanon
1954	Belize, Colombia
1955	Ethiopia, Peru, Nicaragua
1956	Egypt, Pakistan (first elections not held until 1970)
1957	Ghana, Honduras, Malaysia
1958	Mexico, Paraguay, Togo
1959	Mauritius, Morocco, Tunisia
1960	Benin, Burkina Faso, Cameroon, Central African Republic, Chad, Comoro Islands, Republic of the Congo, Democratic Republic of the Congo (Zaire), Equatorial Guinea, Gabon, Gambia, Guinea, Ivory Coast, Madagascar, Mali, Niger, Nigeria (Northern Region in 1976), Senegal
1961	Burundi, Rwanda, Mauritania, Sierra Leone, Somalia (Northern Region in 1963), Tanzania
1962	Algeria, Uganda
1963	Iran, Kenya (white women enfranchised in 1919, Asian women in 1923)
1964	Malawi, Sudan, Zambia
1965	Botswana, Lesotho
1967	Iraq, Swaziland

1971	Switzerland
1972	Bangladesh
1973	Syria (full suffrage granted briefly in 1953, restricted franchise in 1949)
1974	Guinea-Bissau, Jordan
1975	Angola, Cape Verde Islands, Mozambique, São Tomé and Principe
1976	Portugal (restricted suffrage in 1931), Seychelles, Spain (full suffrage granted in 1931, suffrage virtually lost in 1936)
1977	Djibouti, Libya
1980	Zimbabwe (white women enfranchised in 1919)
1986	Liberia (suffrage by property qualification in 1947)
1989	Namibia
1990	Samoa (Western Samoa)
1992	Yemen (while separate countries, both North Yemen and South Yemen gave women the vote in 1970)
1994	South Africa (white women given the vote in 1930)
1996	Palestine National Authority
1997	Eritrea (1955 while part of Ethiopia)
No Female Suffrage	Kuwait
No Suffrage	Bahrain, Oman, Qatar, Saudi Arabia, United Arab Emirates

Bibliography

Books and Journal Articles

Abadan-Unat, Nermin. 1991. "The Impact of Legal and Educational Reforms on Turkish Women." In *Women in Middle Eastern History: Shifting Boundaries in Sex and Gender,* edited by Nikki R. Keddie and Beth Baron. New Haven, CT: Yale University Press.

Abdel-Kader, Soha. 1987. *Egyptian Women in a Changing Society, 1899–1987.* Boulder, CO: Lynne Rienner.

Alberti, Johanna. 1996. *Eleanor Rathbone.* London: Sage.

Amin, Qasim. 1992. *The Liberation of Women: A Document in the History of Egyptian Feminism.* Translated by Samiha S. Peterson. Cairo: American University in Cairo Press.

Anderson, Bonnie S., and Judith P. Zinsser. 1988. *A History of Their Own: Women in Europe from Prehistory to the Present.* Vol. 2. Harmondsworth, England: Penguin.

Ardaya, Gloria Salinas. 1994. "Women and Politics: Gender Relations in Bolivian Political Organizations and Labor Unions." In *Women and Politics Worldwide,* edited by Barbara J. Nelson and Najma Chowdhury. New Haven, CT: Yale University Press.

Arhin, Kwame, ed. 1991. *The Life and Work of Kwame Nkrumah.* Accra, Ghana: Sedco. (First American edition, Trenton, NJ: African World Press, 1993).

Ariffin, Rohana. 1999. "Feminism in Malaysia: A Historical and Present Perspective of Women's Struggles in Malaysia." *Women's Studies International Forum* 22, 4 (1999): 417–423.

Atkinson, Diane. 1992. *The Purple, White and Green: Suffragettes in London, 1906–14.* London: Museum of London.

Ayoade, John A. A., Elone J. Nwabuzor, and Adesina Sambo, eds. 1992. *Women and Politics in Nigeria.* Lagos: Malthouse Press for the Centre for Democratic Studies.

Azize-Vargas, Yamila. 1994. "At the Crossroads: Colonialism and Feminism in Puerto Rico." In *Women and Politics Worldwide,* edited by Barbara J. Nelson and Najma Chowdhury. New Haven, CT: Yale University Press.

———. 2000. "The Emergence of Feminism in Puerto Rico, 1870–1930." In *Unequal Sisters: A Multicultural Reader in U.S. Women's History,* 3d ed. Edited by Vicki L. Ruiz and Ellen Carol DuBois. New York: Routledge.

Bacchi, Carol Lee. 1983. *Liberation Deferred? The Ideas of the English-Canadian Suffragists, 1877–1918.* Toronto: University of Toronto Press.

Badran, Margot. 1995. *Feminists, Islam and Nation: Gender and the Making of Modern Egypt.* Princeton, NJ: Princeton University Press.

———. 1998. "Gender, Islam and the State: Kuwaiti Women in Struggle, Pre-invasion to Postliberation." In *Islam, Gender and Social Change,* edited by Yvonne Yazbeck Haddad and John L. Esposito. New York: Oxford University Press.

Badran, Margot, and Miriam Cooke, eds. 1990. *Opening the Gates: A Century of Arab Feminist Writing.* London: Virago.

Baig, T. A. 1974. *Sarojini Naidu.* New Delhi: Publications Division, Ministry of Information and Broadcasting.

Baker, Paula. 1994. "The Domestication of Politics: Women and American Political Society, 1780–1920." In *Unequal Sisters: A Multicultural Reader in United States*

Women's History, 2d ed. Edited by Vicki L. Ruiz and Ellen Carol DuBois. New York: Routledge.

Balshaw, June. 1992. "Sharing the Burden: The Pethick-Lawrences and Women's Suffrage." In *The Men's Share? Masculinities, Male Support and Women's Suffrage in Britain, 1890–1920*, edited by Angela V. John and Claire Eustance. London: Routledge.

Banks, Olive. 1981. *Faces of Feminism: A Study of Feminism as a Social Movement*. New York and Oxford: Basil Blackwell.

———. 1985. *The Biographical Dictionary of British Feminists*. Vol. 1, *1880–1930*. Brighton, England: Harvester Wheatsheaf.

Bartley, Paula. 1998. *Votes for Women, 1860–1928*. London: Hodder and Stoughton.

Bayat-Philipp, Mangol. 1978. "Women and Revolution in Iran, 1905–1911." In *Women in the Muslim World*, edited by Lois Beck and Nikki R. Keddie. Cambridge, MA: Harvard University Press.

Beck, Lois, and Nikki R. Keddie, eds. 1978. *Women in the Muslim World*. Cambridge, MA: Harvard University Press.

Beddoe, Deirdre. 1989. *Back to Home and Duty: Women between the Wars 1918–1939*. London: Pandora Press.

Black, George. 1981. *Triumph of the People: The Sandinista Revolution in Nicaragua*. London: Zed Press.

Blackburn, Helen. 1902. *Women's Suffrage: A Record of the Women's Suffrage Movement in the British Isles with Biographical Sketches of Miss Becker*. London: Williams and Norgate.

Blewitt, Neal. 1965. "The Franchise in the United Kingdom, 1885–1918." *Past and Present* 32: 27–56.

Blom, Ida. 1980. "The Struggle for Women's Suffrage in Norway, 1885–1913." *Scandinavian Journal of History* 5: 3–22.

Bolt, Christine. 1993. *The Women's Movements in the United States and Britain from the 1790s to the 1920s*. Hemel Hempstead, England: Harvester Wheatsheaf, 1993.

Bosch, Mineke. 1999. "Colonial Dimensions of Dutch Women's Suffrage: Aletta Jacobs's Travel Letters from Africa and Asia, 1911–12." *Journal of Women's History* 11 (2): 8–34.

Bosch, Mineke, with Annemarie Kloosterman, eds. 1990. *Politics and Friendship: Letters from the International Woman Suffrage Alliance, 1902–1942*. Columbus, OH: Columbus University Press.

Boxer, Marilyn J., and Jean H. Quataert, eds. 1978. *Socialist Women: European Socialist Feminism in the Nineteenth and Twentieth Centuries*. New York: Elsevier.

Braker, Regina. 1995. "Bertha Von Suttner's Spiritual Daughters: The Feminist Pacifism of Anita Augspurg, Lida Gustava Heymann, and Helene Stöcker at the International Congress of Women at the Hague, 1915." *Women's Studies International Forum* 18 (2): 103–111.

Bullock, Ian, and Richard Pankhurst, eds. 1992. *Sylvia Pankhurst: From Artist to Anti-Fascist*. Basingstoke, England: Macmillan.

Burton, Antoinette. 1991. "The Feminist Quest for Identity: British Imperial Suffragism and 'Global Sisterhood,' 1900–1915." *Journal of Women's History* 3 (2): 46–81.

———. 1994. *Burdens of History: British Feminists, Indian Women and Imperial Culture, 1865–1914*. Chapel Hill, NC: University of North Carolina Press.

Bush, Julia. 2000. *Edwardian Ladies and Imperial Power*. London: Leicester University Press.

Caine, Barbara. 1978. "John Stuart Mill and the English Women's Movement." *Historical Studies* 18 (70): 52–67.

———. 1992. *Victorian Feminists*. Oxford: Oxford University Press.

———. 1993. "Vida Goldstein and the English Militant Campaign." *Women's History Review* 2 (3): 363–376.

———. 1997. *English Feminism, 1780–1980*. Oxford: Oxford University Press.

Campbell, Beatrice. 1987. *The Iron Ladies: Why Do Women Vote Tory?* London: Virago.

Campoamor Rodríguez, Clara. 1936. *Mi Pecado Mortal: El Voto Feminino y Yo*. Madrid: Beltrán. Reprinted with introduction by Concha Fagoaga and Paloma Saavedra, Barcelona: LaSal, 1981.

Candy, Catherine. 1994. "Relating Feminisms, Nationalisms and Imperialisms: Ireland, India and Margaret Cousins' Sexual Politics." *Women's History Review* 3 (4): 581–594.

Capel Martínez, Rosa María. 1992. *El Sufragio Femenino en la Segunda República Española*. Madrid: Mujeres en Madrid.

Carlson, Manifran. 1988. *Feminismo! The Woman's Movement in Argentina from Its Beginnings to Eva Perón*. Chicago: Academy Chicago Publishers.

Casgrain, Thérèse. 1972. *A Woman in a Man's World*. Toronto: McClelland and Stewart.

Chaney, Elsa M. 1979. *Supermadre: Women in Politics in Latin America*. Austin, Texas: University of Texas Press.

Cleverdon, Catherine L. 1974. *The Woman Suffrage Movement in Canada*. 2d ed. Toronto: University of Toronto Press.

Cockburn, Katharine. 1998. "Woman's Suffrage Drama." In *The Women's Suffrage Movement, New Feminist Perspectives,* edited by Maroula Joannou and June Purvis. Manchester: Manchester University Press.

Cook, Kay, and Neil Evans. 1991. "'The Petty Antics of the Bell-Ringing Boisterous Band?' The Women's Suffrage Movement in Wales, 1890–1918." In *Our Mothers' Land: Chapters in Welsh Women's History, 1830–1939,* edited by Angela V. John. Cardiff: University of Wales Press.

Costin, Lela B. 1982. "Feminism, Pacifism, Internationalism and the 1915 International Congress of Women." *Women's Studies International Forum* 5 (3/4): 301–315.

Cott, Nancy. 1987. *The Grounding of Modern Feminism*. New Haven, CT: Yale University Press.

———. 1994. "Early-Twentieth Century Feminism in Political Context: A Comparative Look at Germany and the United States." In *Suffrage and Beyond: International Feminist Perspectives,* edited by Caroline Daley and Melanie Nolan. New York: New York University Press.

Cousins, James H., and Margaret E. Cousins. 1950. *We Two Together*. Madras, India: Ganesh.

Cowman, Krista. 1998. "'A Party between Revolution and Peaceful Persuasion': A Fresh Look at the United Suffragists." In *The Women's Suffrage Movement: New Feminist Perspectives,* edited by Maroula Joannou and June Purvis. Manchester: Manchester University Press.

Crawford, Elizabeth. 1999. *The Women's Suffrage Movement: A Reference Guide, 1866–1928*. London: UCL Press.

Croll, Elizabeth. 1978. *Feminism and Socialism in China*. London: Routledge and Kegan Paul.

Crowder, Michael, ed. 1984. *The Cambridge History of Africa*. Vol. 8, *From c. 1940 to c. 1975*. Cambridge: Cambridge University Press.

Cullen, Mary. 1995. "Anna Maria Haslam." In *Women, Power and Consciousness in Nineteenth-Century Ireland,* edited by Mary Cullen and Maria Luddy. Dublin: Attic Press.

Cullen, Mary, and Maria Luddy, eds. 1995. *Women, Power and Consciousness in Nineteenth-Century Ireland*. Dublin: Attic Press.

Cullen Owens, Rosemary. 1984. *Smashing Times: A History of the Irish Women's Suffrage Movement 1889–1922*. Dublin: Attic Press.

Daley, Caroline, and Melanie Nolan, eds. 1994. *Suffrage and Beyond: International Feminist Perspectives*. New York: New York University Press.

Dalziel, Raewyn. 1994. "Presenting the Enfranchisement of New Zealand Women Abroad." In *Suffrage and Beyond: International Feminist Perspectives,* edited by Caroline Daley and Melanie Nolan. New York: New York University Press and Auckland, New Zealand: Auckland University Press.

David, Katherine. 1991. "Czech Feminists and Nationalism in the Late Habsburg Monarchy: 'The First in Austria.'" *Journal of Women's History* 3 (2): 26–45.

Davis, Tricia, Martin Durham, Catherine Hall, Mary Langan, and David Sutton. 1982. "'The Public Face of Feminism': Early Twentieth Century Writings on Women's Suffrage." In *Making Histories: Studies in History-Writing and Politics,* edited by the Centre for Contemporary Cultural Studies. London: Hutchinson.

De Grazia, Victoria. 1994. "How Mussolini Ruled Italian Women." In *A History of Women in the West*. Vol. 5, *Towards a Cultural Identity in the Twentieth Century,* edited by Françoise Thébaud. Cambridge, MA: Belknap Press of Harvard University Press.

Denzer, LaRay. 1987. "Women in Freetown

Politics, 1914–61: A Preliminary Study." *Africa* 57: 439–452.

Dictionary of Canadian Biography. Vol. 13, *1901–1910.* 1994. Toronto: University of Toronto Press.

Dodd, Kathryn. 1990. "Cultural Politics and Women's Historical Writing: The Case of Ray Strachey's *The Cause.*" *Women's Studies International Forum* 13 (1/2): 127–137.

———, ed. 1991. *A Sylvia Pankhurst Reader.* Manchester: Manchester University Press.

DuBois, Ellen Carol. 1978. *Feminism and Suffrage: The Emergence of an Independent Women's Movement in America, 1848–1869.* Ithaca, NY: Cornell University Press.

———. 1987. "Working Women, Class Relations and Suffrage Militance: Harriot Stanton Blatch and the New York Woman Suffrage Movement, 1894–1909." *Journal of American History* 74 (1): 34–58.

———. 1987. "Outgrowing the Compact of the Fathers: Equal Rights, Woman Suffrage and the United States Constitution, 1820–1878." *The Journal of American History* 74 (December): 836–861.

———. 1991. "Woman Suffrage and the Left: An International Socialist-Feminist Perspective." *New Left Review* 186 (March/April): 20–45.

———. 1994. "Woman Suffrage around the World: Three Phases of Internationalism." In *Suffrage and Beyond: International Feminist Perspectives,* edited by Caroline Daley and Melanie Nolan. New York: New York University Press.

———. 1997. *Harriot Stanton Blatch and the Winning of Woman Suffrage.* New Haven, CT: Yale University Press.

DuBois, Ellen, and Karen Kearns. 1995. *Votes for Women: A 75th Anniversary Album.* San Marino, CA: Huntington Library Press.

Duster, Alfreda, ed. 1970. *Crusade for Justice: The Autobiography of Ida B. Wells.* Chicago, IL: University of Chicago Press.

Edmondson, Linda Harriet. 1984. *Feminism in Russia, 1900–1917.* Stanford, CA: Stanford University Press.

———. 1992. *Women and Society in Russia and the Soviet Union.* Cambridge: Cambridge University Press.

Ehrick, Christine. 1998. "*Madrinas* and Missionaries: Uruguay and the Pan-American Women's Movement." *Gender and History* 10 (3): 406–424.

Eisenstein, Zillah. 1987. "Elizabeth Cady Stanton: Radical-Feminist Analysis and Liberal-Feminist Strategy." In *Feminism and Equality,* edited by Anne Phillips. Oxford: Blackwell.

Esfandiari, Haleh. 1977. *Reconstructed Lives: Women and Iran's Islamic Revolution.* Washington, DC: The Woodrow Wilson Center Press.

Eustance, Claire, Joan Ryan, and Laura Ugolini. 2000. *A Suffrage Reader: Charting Directions in British Suffrage History.* London: Leicester University Press.

Evans, Richard J. 1977. *The Feminists: Women's Emancipation Movements in Europe, America and Australasia, 1840–1920.* London: Croom Helm; New York: Harper and Row.

———. 1987. *Comrades and Sisters: Feminism, Socialism and Pacifism in Europe, 1870–1945.* Brighton, England: Harvester Wheatsheaf.

Fagoaga, Concha. 1985. *La Voz y el Voto de las Mujeres: El Sufragismo en España, 1877–1931.* Barcelona: Icaria.

Fagoaga, Concha, and Paloma Saavedra. 1986. *Clara Campoamor: La Sufragista Española.* 2d ed. Madrid: Ministerio de Cultura, Instituto de la Mujer.

Finnegan, Margaret. 1999. *Selling Suffrage: Consumer Culture and Votes for Women.* New York: Columbia University Press.

Flexner, Eleanor. [1959] 1975. *Century of Struggle: The Woman's Rights Movement in the United States.* Revised edition, London and Cambridge, MA: Harvard University Press.

Forbes, Geraldine. 1996. *Women in Modern India.* New Cambridge History of India, vol. 4, part 2. Cambridge: Cambridge University Press.

Fowler, Robert Booth. 1986. *Carrie Catt: Feminist Politician.* Boston, MA: Northeastern University Press.

Fox, R. M. 1958. *Louie Bennett.* Dublin: Talbot Press.

Frances, Hilary. 2000. "'Dare to be Free!': The Women's Freedom League and Its Legacy." In *Votes for Women,* edited by

June Purvis and Sandra Stanley Holton. London: Routledge.

Furnivall, J. S. 1960. *The Governance of Modern Burma*. New York: International Secretariat, Institute of Pacific Relations.

Garner, Les. 1984. *Stepping Stones to Women's Liberty: Feminist Ideas in the Women's Suffrage Movement, 1900–1918*. London: Heinemann.

Garon, Sheldon. 1993. "Women's Groups and the Japanese State: Contending Approaches to Political Integration." *Japanese Studies* 19 (1): 5–41.

Gawthorpe, Mary. 1962. *Up Hill to Holloway*. Penobscot, ME: Traversity Press.

Gleadle, Kathryn. 1995. *The Early Feminists: Radical Unitarians and the Emergence of the Women's Rights Movement, 1831–51*. Basingstoke, England: Macmillan.

González-Suárez, Mirta. 1994. "With Patience and without Blood: The Political Struggles of Costa Rican Women." In *Women and Politics Worldwide*, edited by Barbara J. Nelson and Najma Chowdhury. New Haven, CT: Yale University Press.

Gordon, Felicia. 1990. *The Integral Feminist: Madeleine Pelletier, 1874–1939*. Cambridge, England: Polity Press.

Graves, Robert, and Alan Hodge. 1941. *The Long Weekend: A Social History of Great Britain, 1918–1939*. London: Faber and Faber.

Grimshaw, Patricia. 1987. *Women's Suffrage in New Zealand*. Auckland, New Zealand: Auckland University Press.

———. 1994. "Presenting the Enfranchisement of New Zealand Women Abroad." In *Suffrage and Beyond: International Feminist Perspectives*, edited by Caroline Daley and Melanie Nolan. New York: New York University Press.

Gruber, Helmut, and Pamela Graves, eds. 1998. *Women and Socialism. Socialism and Women. Europe between the Two World Wars*. New York and Oxford: Berghahn Books.

Guimarães, Elina. 1987. *Portuguese Women Past and Present*. 2d ed. (revised). Lisbon: Commission on the Status of Women.

Gullett, Gayle. 2000. *Becoming Citizens: The Emergence and Development of the California Women's Movement, 1880–*

1911. Champaign: University of Illinois Press.

Hahner, June E. 1990. *Emancipating the Female Sex: The Struggle for Women's Rights in Brazil, 1850–1940*. Durham, NC: Duke University Press.

Hahner, June, ed. 1980. *Women in Latin American History, Their Lives and Voices*. Rev. ed. UCLA Latin American Studies, No. 51. Los Angeles: UCLA Latin American Center.

Hannam, June. 1989. *Isabella Ford, 1855–1924*. Oxford, UK: Blackwell.

———. 1992. "Women and the ILP, 1890–1914." In *The Centennial History of the Independent Labour Party*, edited by David James, Tony Jowitt, and Keith Laybourn. Halifax, England: Ryburn Publishing.

———. 2000. "'Suffragettes Are Splendid for Any Work': The Blathwayt Diaries as a Source for Suffrage History." In *A Suffrage Reader: Charting Directions in British Suffrage History*, edited by Claire Eustance, Joan Ryan, and Laura Ugolini. London: Leicester University Press.

———. 2000. "'I had not been to London': Women's Suffrage—A View from the Regions." In *Votes for Women*, edited by June Purvis and Sandra Stanley Holton. London: Routledge.

Hansen, Emmanuel, and Kwame A. Ninsin, eds. 1989. *The State, Development and Politics in Ghana*. London: Codesria.

Harrison, Brian. 1978. *Separate Spheres: The Opposition to Women's Suffrage in Britain*. London: Croom Helm.

Hause, Steven C., with Anne R. Kenney. 1984. *Women's Suffrage and Social Politics in the French Third Republic*. Princeton, NJ: Princeton University Press.

Hazlekorn, Ellen. 1988. "The Social and Political Views of Louie Bennett, 1870–1965." *Saothar* 13: 32–44.

Hine, Darlene Clark, Elsa Barkley Brown, and Rosalyn Terborg-Penn, eds. 1993. *Black Women in America: An Historical Encyclopaedia*, Vols. 1 and 11. Bloomington and Indianapolis, IN: Bloomington University Press.

Hirschfield, Claire. 1995. "The Woman's Theatre in England 1913–1918." *Theatre History Studies* 15: 123–137.

Hollis, Patricia. 1987. *Ladies Elect: Women in English Local Government, 1865–1914.* Oxford: Clarendon Press.

Holton, Sandra Stanley. 1986. *Feminism and Democracy: Women's Suffrage and Reform Politics in Britain, 1900–1918.* Cambridge: Cambridge University Press.

———. 1994. "From Anti-Slavery to Suffrage Militancy: The Bright Circle, Elizabeth Cady Stanton and the British Women's Movement." In *Suffrage and Beyond. International Feminist Perspectives,* edited by Caroline Daley and Melanie Nolan. New York: New York University Press.

———. 1995. "Women and the Vote." In *Women's History: Britain, 1850–1945,* edited by June Purvis. London: UCL.

———. 1996. *Suffrage Days: Stories from the Women's Suffrage Movement.* London: Routledge.

Honeycut, Karen. 1981. "Clara Zetkin: A Socialist Approach to the Problem of Women's Oppression." In *European Women on the Left: Socialism, Feminism and the Problems Faced by Political Women, 1880 to the Present,* edited by Jane Slaughter and Robert Kern. Westport, CT: Greenwood Press.

Horowitz, Dan, and Moshe Lissak. 1978. *Origins of the Israeli Polity: Palestine under the Mandate.* Chicago: University of Chicago Press.

Howard, Judith Jeffrey. 1977. "The Civil Code of 1865 and the Origins of the Feminist Movement in Italy." In *The Italian Immigrant Woman in North America,* edited by Betty Boyd Caroli, Robert F. Harney, and Lydio F. Tomasi. Toronto: The Multicultural History Society of Ontario.

Hume, Leslie Parker. 1982. *The National Union of Women's Suffrage Societies, 1897–1914.* New York: Garland Publishing.

Hunt, Karen. 1996. *Equivocal Feminists. The Social Democratic Federation and the Woman Question, 1884–1911.* Cambridge: Cambridge University Press.

Hurwitz, Edith F. 1977. "The International Sisterhood." In *Becoming Visible: Women in European History,* edited by Renate Bridenthal and Claudia Koonz. Boston, MA: Houghton Mifflin.

Jackson, Margaret. 1994. *The Real Facts of Life: Feminism and the Politics of Sexuality 1850–1940.* London: Taylor and Francis.

Jacobs, Aletta. [1924] 1996. *Memories. My Life as an International Leader in Health, Suffrage and Peace.* 2d ed. Edited by Harriet Feinberg. New York: The Feminist Press.

Jallinoja, Riitta. 1980. "The Women's Liberation Movement in Finland." *Scandinavian Journal of History* 5: 37–49.

Jaquette, Jane, ed. 1994. *The Women's Movement in Latin America: Participation and Democracy.* Boulder, CO: Westview Press.

Jayawardena, Kumari. 1986. *Feminism and Nationalism in the Third World.* London: Zed Books.

———. 1995. *The White Woman's Other Burden: Western Women and South Asia during British Colonial Rule.* London and New York: Routledge.

Joannou, Maroula. 1998. "Suffragette Fiction and the Fictions of Suffrage." In *The Women's Suffrage Movement: New Feminist Perspectives,* edited by Maroula Joannou and June Purvis. Manchester: Manchester University Press.

Joannou, Maroula, and June Purvis, eds. 1998. *The Women's Suffrage Movement: New Feminist Perspectives.* Manchester: Manchester University Press.

John, Angela V. 1995. "Radical Reflections? Elizabeth Robins: The Making of Suffragette History and the Representation of Working-Class Women." In *The Duty of Discontent: Essays for Dorothy Thompson,* edited by Owen Ashton, Robert Fyson, and Stephen Roberts. London: Mansell.

———. 1995. *Elizabeth Robins: Staging a Life, 1862–1952.* London: Routledge.

———. 2000. "Between the Cause and the Courts: The Curious Case of Cecil Chapman." In *A Suffrage Reader: Charting New Directions in British Suffrage History,* edited by Claire Eustance, Joan Ryan, and Laura Ugolini. London: Leicester University Press.

John, Angela V., and Claire Eustance, eds. 1992. *The Men's Share? Masculinities, Male Support and Women's Suffrage in Britain, 1890–1920.* London: Routledge.

Johnson-Odim, Cheryl, and Nina Emma Mba. 1997. *For Women and the Nation: Funmi-*

layo Ransome-Kuti of Nigeria. Urbana and Chicago: University of Illinois Press.

Jones, Mary. 1988. *These Obstreperous Lassies: A History of the Irish Women Workers' Union.* Dublin: Gill and Macmillan.

Kean, Hilda. 1994. "Searching for the Past in Present Defeat: The Construction of Historical and Political Identity in British Feminism in the 1920s and 1930s." *Women's History Review* 3 (1): 57–80.

Keene, Judith. 1999. "'Into the Clean Air of the Plaza': Spanish Women Achieve the Vote in 1931." In *Constructing Spanish Womanhood: Female Identity in Modern Spain,* edited by Victoria Lorée Enders and Pamela Beth Radcliff. Albany, NY: State University of New York Press.

Kent, Susan Kingsley. 1990. *Sex and Suffrage in Britain 1860–1914.* London: Routledge.

Kimball, Michelle R., and Barbara R. Von Schlegell, eds. 1997. *Muslim Women throughout the World: A Bibliography.* Boulder, CO: Lynne Rienner.

King, Elspeth. 1978. *The Scottish Women's Suffrage Movement in Glasgow.* Glasgow: People's Palace Museum.

Klingshirn, Agnes. 1971. *The Changing Position of Women in Ghana: A Study Based on Empirical Research in Larteh, a Small Town in Southern Ghana.* Ph.D. diss., Philipps-Universität, Marburg, Germany.

Kraditor, Aileen, S. 1965. *The Ideas of the Woman Suffrage Movement.* New York: Columbia University Press.

Lacey, Candida Ann, ed. 1987. *Barbara Leigh Smith Bodichon and the Langham Place Group.* London: Routledge and Kegan Paul.

Lafleur, Ingrun. 1978. "Five Socialist Women: Traditionalist Conflicts and Socialist Visions in Austria, 1893–1934." In *Socialist Women: European Socialist Feminism in the Nineteenth and Early Twentieth Centuries,* edited by Marilyn J. Boxer and Jean H. Quataert. New York: Elsevier.

LaVigna, Claire. 1978. "The Marxist Ambivalence toward Women: Between Socialism and Feminism in the Italian Socialist Party." In *Socialist Women: European Socialist Feminism in the Nineteenth and Early Twentieth Centuries,* edited by Marilyn J. Boxer and Jean H. Quataert. New York: Elsevier.

Lavrin, Asunción. 1994. "Suffrage in South America: Arguing a Difficult Cause." In *Suffrage and Beyond: International Feminist Perspectives,* edited by Caroline Daley and Melanie Nolan. New York: New York University Press.

———. 1995. *Women, Feminism and Social Change in Argentina, Chile and Uruguay 1890–1940.* Lincoln: University of Nebraska Press.

Law, Cheryl. 1997. *Suffrage and Power: The Women's Movement, 1918–1928.* London: I. B. Tauris.

Lazreg, Marnia. 1990. "Feminism and Difference: The Perils of Writing as a Woman on Women in Algeria." In *Conflicts in Feminism,* edited by Marianne Hirsch and Evelyn Fox Keller. London: Routledge.

Leneman, Leah. 1991. *A Guid Cause: The Women's Suffrage Movement in Scotland.* Aberdeen: Aberdeen University Press.

Lerner, Gerda. 1979. *The Majority Finds Its Past: Placing Women in History.* Oxford: Oxford University Press.

Levenson, Leah, and Jerry H. Natterstad. 1986. *Hanna Sheehy Skeffington, Irish Feminist.* Syracuse, NY: Syracuse University Press.

Levine, Philippa. 1990. "Love, Feminism and Friendship in Later Nineteenth-Century England." *Women's Studies International Forum* 13 (1/2): 63–78.

Levy, Darlene Gay, and Harriet B. Applewhite. 1977. "Women and Political Revolution in Paris." In *Becoming Visible: Women in European History,* edited by Renate Bridenthal, Claudia Koonz, and Susan Stuard. Boston, MA: Houghton Mifflin.

Liddington, Jill. 1989. *The Long Road to Greenham: Feminism and Anti-Militarism in Britain since 1820.* London: Virago.

Liddington, Jill, and Jill Norris. 1978. *One Hand Tied Behind Us: The Rise of the Women's Suffrage Movement.* London: Virago.

Light, Alison. 1991. *Forever England: Femininity, Literature and Conservatism between the Wars.* London: Routledge.

Luddy, Maria. 1995. *Hanna Sheehy Skeffington.* Dundalk, Ireland: Dundalgan Press.

Macías, Anna. 1982. *Against All Odds: The Feminist Movement in Mexico to 1940.* Westport, CT: Greenwood Press.

Maguire, G. E. 1998. *Conservative Women: A History of Women and the Conservative Party, 1874–1997*. Basingstoke, England: Macmillan.

Malcolm, Tessa K. 1993. "Katherine Wilson Sheppard 1847–1934." In *The Suffragists: Women Who Worked for the Vote: Essays from the Dictionary of New Zealand Biography*. Wellington, New Zealand: Bridget Williams Books/Dictionary of New Zealand Biography.

Marcus, Jane, ed. 1987. *Suffrage and the Pankhursts*. London: Routledge and Kegan Paul.

Margarey, Susan. 1994. "'Why didn't they want to be members of Parliament?' Suffragists in South Australia." In *Suffrage and Beyond: International Feminist Perspectives*, edited by Caroline Daley and Melanie Nolan. New York: New York University Press.

Matsukawa, Yukiko, and Kaoru Tachi. 1994. "Woman's Suffrage and Gender Politics in Japan." In *Suffrage and Beyond: International Feminist Perspectives*, edited by Caroline Daley and Melanie Nolan. New York: New York University Press.

Mayhall, Laura E. Nym. 1995. "Creating the 'Suffragette Spirit': British Feminism and the Historical Imagination." *Women's History Review* 4 (3): 319–344.

Mba, Nina Emma. 1982. *Nigerian Women Mobilized: Women's Political Activity in Southern Nigeria, 1900–1965*. Berkeley, CA: University of California, Berkeley, Institute of International Studies.

McClung, Nellie. *In Times Like These*. [1915]. 1972. New York: Appleton. Reprint, with an introduction by V. Strong-Boag, Toronto: University of Toronto Press.

Meleisea, Penelope Schoeffel. 1994. "Women and Political Leadership in the Pacific Islands." In *Suffrage and Beyond: International Feminist Perspectives*, edited by Caroline Daley and Melanie Nolan. New York: New York University Press.

Midgley, Clare. 1992. *Women against Slavery: The British Campaigns, 1780–1870*. London: Routledge.

———, ed. 1998. *Gender and Imperialism*. Manchester: Manchester University Press.

Mill, John Stuart. 1991. *On Liberty and Other Essays*. Oxford: Oxford University Press.

Miller, Francesca. 1983. "The International Relations of Women in the Americas 1890–1928." *The Americas* 43: 171–182.

———. 1991. *Latin American Women and the Search for Social Justice*. Hanover, NH, and London: University Press of New England.

Miller, Heather Lee. 1999. "Getting to the Source: The World Wide Web of Resources for Women's History." *Journal of Women's History* 11 (3): 176–187.

Mitchell, Hannah. 1977. *The Hard Way Up*. London: Virago.

Montefiore, Dora. 1927. *From a Victorian to a Modern*. London: E. Archer.

Moore, Sarah J. 1997. "Making a Spectacle of Suffrage: The National Woman Suffrage Pageant, 1913." *Journal of American Culture* 20: 89–103.

Morgan, David. 1984. "Woman Suffrage in Britain and America in the Early Twentieth Century." In *Essays in Comparative History: Economy, Politics and Society in Britain and America, 1850–1920*, edited by Clive Emsley. Milton Keynes, England: Open University Press.

al-Mughni, Haya. 1993. *Women in Kuwait: The Politics of Gender*. London: Saqi Books.

Mulvihill, Margaret. 1989. *Charlotte Despard: A Biography*. London: Pandora.

Mumtaz, Khawar, and Farida Shaheed. 1987. *Women of Pakistan: Two Steps Forwards, One Step Back?* Lahore, Pakistan: Vanguard Books.

Murphy, Cliona. 1989. *The Women's Suffrage Movement and Irish Society in the Early Twentieth Century*. New York and London: Harvester Wheatsheaf.

———. 1990. "'The Tune of the Stars and Stripes': The American Influence on the Irish Suffrage Movement." In *Women Surviving: Studies in Irish Women's History in the Nineteenth and Twentieth Centuries*, edited by Maria Luddy and Cliona Murphy. Dublin: Poolbeg Press.

Murray, Patricia. 1975. "Ichikawa Fusae and the Lonely Red Carpet." *Japan Interpreter* 10 (2): 171–189.

Mya Sein, Daw. 1972. "Toward Independence in Burma: The Role of Women." *Asian Affairs* 59 (3): 288–299.

Nelson, Barbara J., and Najma Chowdhury,

eds. 1994. *Women and Politics Worldwide.* New Haven, CT: Yale University Press.

Nelson, Cynthia. 1991. "Biography and Women's History: On Interpreting Doria Shafik." In *Women in Middle Eastern History: Shifting Boundaries in Sex and Gender,* edited by Nikki R. Keddie and Beth Baron. New Haven, CT: Yale University Press.

———. 1996. *Doria Shafik, Egyptian Feminist: A Woman Apart.* Gainesville, FL: University of Florida Press.

Nester, William. 1992. "Japanese Women: Still Three Steps Behind." *Women's Studies* 21: 457–478.

Nestorova, Tatyana. 1996. "Between Tradition and Modernity: Bulgarian Women during the Development of Modern Sisterhood and Society, 1878–1945." *Women's History Review* 5 (4): 513–524.

Newhall, Beatrice. 1936. "Women Suffrage in the Americas." *Pan American Bulletin* 70: 424–428.

Nicholls, Roberta. 1996. *The Women's Parliament: The National Council of Women of New Zealand, 1896–1920.* Wellington, New Zealand: Victoria University Press.

Nolan, Melanie, and Caroline Daley. 1994. "International Feminist Perspectives on Suffrage: An Introduction." In *Suffrage and Beyond: International Feminist Perspectives,* edited by Caroline Daley and Melanie Nolan. Auckland, New Zealand: Auckland University Press.

Nolte, Sharon H. 1986. "Women's Rights and Society's Needs: Japan's 1931 Suffrage Bill." *Comparative Studies in Society and History* 28 (October): 5–41.

O'Barr, Jean. 1984. "African Women in Politics." In *African Women South of the Sahara,* edited by Margaret Jean Hay and Sharon Stichter. London: Longman.

Offen, Karen. 1988. "Defining Feminism: A Comparative Historical Approach." *Signs* 14 (1): 119–157.

———. 1994. "Women, Citizenship and Suffrage with a French Twist, 1789–1993." In *Suffrage and Beyond: International Feminist Perspectives,* edited by Caroline Daley and Melanie Nolan. New York: New York University Press.

Oldfield, Audrey. 1992. *Woman Suffrage in Australia, A Gift or a Struggle?* Cambridge: Cambridge University Press.

O'Neill, William L. 1969. *The Woman Movement: Feminism in the United States and England.* London: George Allen and Unwin.

Pankhurst, Emmeline. 1914. *My Own Story.* London: Eveleigh Nash.

Pankhurst, E. Sylvia. 1931. *The Suffragette Movement: An Intimate Account of Persons and Ideals.* London: Longman.

Pankhurst, Richard. 1954. "Anna Wheeler: A Pioneer Socialist and Feminist." *Political Quarterly* 25: 132–143.

Park, Sowon S. 1997. "The First Professional: The Women Writers' Suffrage League." *Modern Language Quarterly* 58(2): 185–200.

Pateman, Carole. 1992. "Equality, Difference, Subordination: The Politics of Motherhood and Women's Citizenship." In *Beyond Equality and Difference: Citizenship, Feminist Politics and Female Subjectivity,* edited by Gisela Bock and Susan James. London: Routledge.

———. 1994. "Three Questions about Womanhood Suffrage." In *Suffrage and Beyond: International Feminist Perspectives,* edited by Caroline Daley and Melanie Nolan. New York: New York University Press.

Patterson, Cynthia M. 1982. "New Directions in the Political History of Women: A Case Study of the National Woman's Party's Campaign for the Equal Rights Amendment, 1920–1927." *Women's Studies International Forum* 5 (6): 585–597.

Pethick-Lawrence, Emmeline. 1938. *My Part in a Changing World.* London: Victor Gollancz.

Philipp, Thomas. 1978. "Feminism and Nationalist Politics in Egypt." In *Women in the Muslim World,* edited by Lois Beck and Nikki R. Keddie. Cambridge, MA: Harvard University Press.

Pugh, Martin. 1992. *Women and the Women's Movement in Britain, 1915–1959.* London: Macmillan.

———. 2000. *The March of the Women: A Revisionist Analysis of the Campaign for Women's Suffrage 1855–1914.* Oxford: Oxford University Press.

Purvis, June. 1995. "The Prison Experiences of the Suffragettes in Britain." *Women's History Review* 4 (1): 103–133.

————. 2000. "'Deeds, Not Words': Daily Life in the Women's Social and Political Union in Edwardian Britain." In *Votes for Women*, edited by June Purvis and Sandra Stanley Holton. London: Routledge.

————. 2000. "Emmeline Pankhurst (1858–1928) and Votes for Women." In *Votes for Women*, edited by June Purvis and Sandra Stanley Holton. London: Routledge.

Purvis, June, and Sandra Stanley Holton, eds. 2000. *Votes for Women*. London: Routledge, 2000.

Quataert, Jean H. 1979. *Reluctant Feminists in German Social Democracy*. Princeton, NJ: Princeton University Press.

Qvist, Gunnar. 1980. "Policy towards Women and the Women's Struggle in Sweden." *Scandinavian Journal of History* 5 (1): 51–74.

Rachum, Ilan. 1977. "Feminism, Woman Suffrage, and National Politics in Brazil 1922–1937." *Luso-Brazilian Review* 14: 118–134.

Ragan, John David. 1998. "French Women Travellers in Egypt: Discourse Marginal to Orientalism?" In *Travellers in Egypt*, edited by Paul Starkey and Janet Starkey. London: I. B. Tauris.

Ramos Escandón, Carmen. 1994. "Women's Movements, Feminism and Mexican Politics." In *The Women's Movement in Latin America: Participation and Democracy*, edited by Jane S. Jaquette. Boulder, CO: Westview Press.

Ramusack, Barbara. 1990. "Cultural Missionaries, Maternal Imperialists, Feminist Allies: British Women Activists in India, 1865–1945." *Women's Studies International Forum* 13 (2): 309–321.

Rasmussen, Janet E. 1982. "Sisters across the Sea: Early Norwegian Feminists and Their American Connections." *Women's Studies International Forum* 5 (6): 647–654.

Rendall, Jane. 1985. *The Origins of Modern Feminism: Women in Britain, France and the United States, 1780–1860*. Basingstoke, England: Macmillan.

————. 1987. "'A Moral Engine'? Feminism, Liberalism and the *English Woman's Journal*." In *Equal or Different: Women's Politics, 1800–1914*, edited by Jane Rendall. Oxford: Blackwell.

————. 1994. "Citizenship, Culture and Civilisation: The Languages of British Suffragists, 1866–1874." In *Suffrage and Beyond: International Feminist Perspectives*, edited by Caroline Daley and Melanie Nolan. New York: New York University Press.

————, ed. 1987. *Equal or Different. Women's Politics, 1800–1914*. Oxford: Blackwell.

Reynolds, Siân. 1986. "Marianne's Citizens? Women, the Republic and Universal Suffrage in France." In *Women, State and Revolution*, edited by Siân Reynolds. Brighton, England: Harvester Wheatsheaf.

————. 1996. *France between the Wars: Gender and Politics*. London: Routledge.

Richardson, Mary. 1953. *Laugh a Defiance*. London: Weidenfeld and Nicolson.

Romero, Patricia E. 1986. *Sylvia Pankhurst: A Portrait of a Radical*. New Haven, CT: Yale University Press.

Rosen, Andrew. 1974. *Rise Up Women! The Militant Campaign of the Women's Social and Political Union, 1903–1914*. London: Routledge and Kegan Paul.

Rossi, Alice S., ed. 1970. *Essays on Sex Equality: John Stuart Mill and Harriet Taylor Mill*. Chicago: University of Chicago Press.

————. 1974. *The Feminist Papers: From Addams to de Beauvoir*. New York: Bantam.

Rover, Constance. 1967. *Women's Suffrage and Party Politics in Britain, 1866–1914*. London: Routledge and Kegan Paul.

Rubinstein, David. 1991. *A Different World for Women: The Life of Millicent Garrett Fawcett*. Brighton, England: Harvester Wheatsheaf.

Rupp, Leila J. 1997. *Worlds of Women: The Making of an International Women's Movement*. Princeton, NJ: Princeton University Press.

Ryan, Louise. 1995. "Traditions and Double Standards, the Irish Suffragists' Critique of Nationalism." *Women's History Review* 4 (4): 487–503.

————. 1996. *Irish Feminism and the Vote: An Anthology of the Irish Citizen, 1912–1920*. Dublin: Folens Publishers.

Sadlier, Darlene J. 1991. "The Struggle for Women's Rights in Portugal." *Camões Center Quarterly* 3 (1–2): 32–36.

Saint German, Michelle A. 1993. "Paths to Power of Women Legislators in Costa Rica and Nicaragua." *Women's Studies International Forum* 16 (2): 119–138.

Sanasarian, Eliz. 1985. "Characteristics of Women's Movement in Iran." In *Women and the Family in Iran,* edited by Fathi Asghar. Leiden, the Netherlands: Brill.

Sarah, Elizabeth. 1983. "Christabel Pankhurst: Reclaiming Her Power." In *Feminist Theorists: Three Centuries of Women's Intellectual Traditions,* edited by Dale Spender. London: The Women's Press.

Scheck, Raffael. 1997. "German Conservatism and Female Political Activism in the Early Weimar Republic." *German History* 15 (1): 34–55.

Schneiderman, Rose, with Lucy Goldthwaite. 1967. *All for One.* New York: Paul Erikson.

Scott, Joan. 1988. "Deconstructing Equality-Versus-Difference: Or the Uses of Post-Structuralist Theory for Feminism." *Feminist Studies* 14: 33–50.

Seager, Joni. 1997. *The State of Women in the World Atlas.* Rev. ed. London and New York: Penguin.

Sengupta, P. 1966. *Sarojini Naidu: A Biography.* London and Bombay: Asia Publishing House.

Shahnawaz, Jahan Ara. 1971. *Father and Daughter: A Political Autobiography.* Lahore, Pakistan: Nigrashat.

Sha'rawi, Nur al-Hudá. 1986. *Harem Years: The Memoirs of an Egyptian Feminist (1879–1924).* Translated by Margot Badran. London: Virago.

Sharfman, Daphna. 1994. "Israel: Women and Politics in Israel." In *Women and Politics Worldwide,* edited by Barbara J. Nelson and Najma Chowdhury. New Haven, CT: Yale University Press.

Sharratt, Sara. 1997. "The Suffragist Movement in Costa Rica 1889–1949: Centennial of Democracy?" In *The Costa Rican Women's Movement: A Reader,* edited by Ilse Abshagen Leitinger. Pittsburgh: University of Pittsburgh Press.

Sheppard, Alice. 1994. *Cartooning for Suffrage.* Albuquerque: University of New Mexico Press.

Showalter, Elaine. 1992. *Sexual Anarchy: Gender and Culture at the Fin de Siècle.* London: Virago.

Sirman, Nükhet. 1980. "Feminism in Turkey: A Short History." *New Perspectives on Turkey* 3: 1–34.

Smith, Paul. 1997. "Political Parties, Parliament and Women's Suffrage in France, 1919–39." *French History* 11 (3): 338–358.

Sowerwine, Charles. 1998. "The Socialist Women's Movement from 1850–1940." In *Becoming Visible: Women in European History,* 2d ed. Edited by Renate Bridenthal, Claudia Koonz, and Susan Stuard. Boston: Houghton Mifflin.

Spearitt, Katie. 1992. "New Dawns: First Wave Feminism, 1880–1914." In *Gender Relations in Australia: Domination and Negotiation,* edited by Kay Saunders and Raymond Evans. Sydney, Australia: Harcourt Brace Jovanovich Group.

Spender, Dale. 1983. *Women of Ideas (and What Men Have Done to Them).* London: Ark.

Spender, Dale, and Carol Hayman, eds. 1985. *How the Vote Was Won and Other Suffrage Plays.* London: Methuen.

Stämpfli, Regula. 1994. "Direct Democracy and Women's Suffrage: Antagonism in Switzerland." In *Women and Politics Worldwide,* edited by Barbara J. Nelson and Najma Chowdhury. New Haven, CT: Yale University Press.

Stanley, Liz, with Ann Morley. 1988. *The Life and Death of Emily Wilding Davison.* London: Women's Press.

Stanton, E. Cady, Susan B. Anthony, Matilda Joslyn Gage, and Ida Husted Harper. 1881–1922. *History of Woman Suffrage,* Vols. 1–6. Rochester, NY: Susan B. Anthony. Reprinted Salem, NH: Ayer, 1985.

Stocks, Mary. 1949. *Eleanor Rathbone: A Biography.* London: Gollancz.

Stoner, Lynn. 1991. *From the House to the Streets: The Cuban Women's Movement for Legal Change, 1898–1940.* Durham, NC: Duke University Press.

Stowell, Sheila. 1992. *A Stage of Their Own: Feminist Playwrights of the Suffrage Era.* Manchester: Manchester University Press.

Strachey, Ray. 1928. *The Cause: A Short History of the Women's Movement in Great Britain.* London: G. Bell and Sons.

Strobel, Margaret. 1987. "Gender and Race in the Nineteenth- and Twentieth-Century British Empire." In *Becoming Visible: Women in*

European History, 2d ed. Edited by Renate Bridenthal, Claudia Koonz, and Susan Stuard. Boston: Houghton Mifflin.

Strong-Boag, Veronica. 1976. *The Parliament of Women: The National Council of Women of Canada, 1893–1929.* Ottawa: National Museums of Canada.

The Suffragists: Women Who Worked for the Vote: Essays from the Dictionary of New Zealand Biography. 1993. Wellington, New Zealand: Bridget Williams Books/Dictionary of New Zealand Biography.

Summerfield, Penny. 1995. "Women and War in the Twentieth Century." In *Women's History: Britain, 1850–1945,* edited by June Purvis. London: UCL.

Sutherland, John. 1990. *Mrs Humphry Ward: Eminent Victorian, Pre-eminent Edwardian.* Oxford: Oxford University Press.

Taylor, Barbara. 1983. *Eve and the New Jerusalem: Socialism and Feminism in the Nineteenth Century.* London: Virago.

Taylor, Harriet. 1851. "Enfranchisement of Women." *Westminster Review* 55.

Tekeli, Sirin. 1981. "Women in Turkish Politics." In *Women in Turkish Society,* edited by Nermin Abadan-Unat. Leiden, the Netherlands: Brill.

Terborg-Penn, Rosalyn. 1998. *Afro-Americans in the Struggle for the Vote, 1850–1920.* Bloomington: Indiana University Press.

Thompson, Elizabeth. 2000. *Colonial Citizens. Republican Rights, Paternal Privilege and Gender in French Syria and Lebanon.* New York: Columbia University Press.

Thompson, William. 1825. *Appeal of One-Half of the Human Race, Women, against the Pretensions of the Other Half, Men, to Retain Them in Political, and Thence in Civil and Domestic Slavery.* London: Longman, Hurst, Rees. Reprinted London: Virago, 1983.

Tickner, Lisa. 1987. *The Spectacle of Women: Imagery of the Suffrage Campaign, 1907–1914.* London: Chatto and Windus.

Tims, Margaret. 1961. *Jane Addams of Hull House, 1860–1935.* London: Allen and Unwin.

Tomalin, Claire. 1974. *The Life and Death of Mary Wollstonecraft.* London: Weidenfeld and Nicolson.

Truth, Sojourner. 1991. *Narrative of Sojourner Truth,* edited by Jeffrey Stuart. Oxford: Oxford University Press.

Tyler-Bennett, Deborah. 1998. "Suffrage and Poetry: Radical Women's Voices." In *The Woman's Suffrage Movement, New Feminist Perspectives,* edited by Maroula Joannou and June Purvis. Manchester: Manchester University Press.

Uglow, Jennifer. 1989. *Macmillan Dictionary of Women's Biography.* London: Macmillan.

Vavich, Dee Ann. 1967. "The Japan Woman's Suffrage Movement: Ichikawa Fusae: A Pioneer in Woman's Suffrage." *Monumenta Nipponica* 22 (3/4): 401–436.

Vellacott Newbury, Jo. 1977. "Anti-War Suffragists." *History* 62: 411–425.

Walker, Cherryl. 1979. *The Women's Suffrage Movement in South Africa.* Cape Town: University of Cape Town, Centre for African Studies.

———. 1991. *Women and Resistance in South Africa.* 2d ed. Cape Town: D. Philip; New York: Monthly Review Press.

Walkowitz, Judith. 1980. *Prostitution and Victorian Society: Women, Class and the State.* Cambridge: Cambridge University Press.

Ward, Margaret. 1982. "'Suffrage First—Above All Else!': An Account of the Irish Suffrage Movement." *Feminist Review* 10: 21–36.

———. 1995. "Conflicting Interests: The British and Irish Suffrage Movements." *Feminist Review* 50: 127–147.

———. 1997. *Hanna Sheehy Skeffington: A Life.* Cork: Attic Press.

Weiner, Gaby. 1993. "Vida Goldstein: The Woman's Candidate." In *Feminist Theorists: Three Centuries of Women's Intellectual Traditions,* edited by Dale Spender. London: Women's Press.

Wertheimer, Barbara Mayer. 1977. *We Were There: The Story of Working Women in America.* New York: Pantheon Books.

Wiltsher, Anne. 1985. *Most Dangerous Women: Feminist Peace Campaigners of the Great War.* London: Pandora.

Winslow, Barbara. 1996. *Sylvia Pankhurst: Sexual Politics and Political Activism.* London: UCL.

Wolchik, Sharon J. 1996. "Czech and Slovak Women and Political Leadership." *Women's History Review* 5 (4): 525–538.

Wollstonecraft, Mary. 1975. *A Vindication of the Rights of Woman*, edited by Miriam Brody. Harmondsworth, England: Penguin.

———. 1993. *Mary Wollstonecraft: Political Writings*. Edited by Janet Todd. Toronto: University of Toronto Press.

Woollacott, Angela. 1998. "Inventing Commonwealth and Pan-Pacific Feminisms: Australian Women's Internationalist Activism in the 1920s–30s." *Gender and History* 10 (3): 425–448.

Yeo, Eileen Janes, ed. 1997. *Mary Wollstonecraft and 200 Years of Feminisms*. London and New York: Rivers Oram Press.

Yihong, Pan. 1997. "Feminism and Nationalism in China's War of Resistance against Japan." *The International Review of History* 19: 115–130.

Videocassettes

Give the Ballot to the Mothers. Springfield, MO: Southwest Missouri State University, 1996. 1 videocassette (28 minutes). Narrated by Francie Wolff. On the music of the U.S. women's suffrage movement.

Not for Ourselves Alone: The Story of Elizabeth Cady Stanton and Susan B. Anthony. Alexandria, VA: American Lives Film Project; PBS Video, 1999. 2 videocassettes (210 minutes) plus book. Narrated by Sally Kellerman.

One Woman, One Vote. Sydney, Australia: ABC, 1996. 1 videocassette (84 minutes). Narrated by Susan Sarandon. On the U.S. women's suffrage movement; originally produced as part of *The American Experience*. Also produced in a version for the hearing impaired. Annandale, VA: Educational Film Center; Santa Monica, CA: Direct Cinema Limited, 1995. 1 videocassette (106 minutes).

Shoulder to Shoulder. London: BBC Television, 1974. 3 videocassettes (348 minutes). Directed by Midge Mackenzie, Waris Hussein, Moira Alexander. Dramatizations of the stories of the Pankhursts (cassette 1), Annie Kenney (cassette 2), and Lady Constance Lytton (cassette 3).

Six Generations of Suffragettes. Princeton, NJ: Films for the Humanities and Sciences, 1999. 1 videocassette (15 minutes). On the Stanton family.

Votes for Women. Sherman Oaks, CA: Wild West Women, distributed by Ishtar Films, 1996. 1 videocassette (20 minutes) plus list of images. Written by Kay Weaver.

The Women Get the Vote. Del Mar, CA: CRM McGraw-Hill Films, 1986. 1 videocassette (25 minutes). A production of CBS News, featuring Walter Cronkite.

The Women's Suffrage Movement and the Nineteenth Amendment, 1919–1920. New York: New York Times Company, 1995. 1 videocassette (17 minutes) plus 10 articles from the *New York Times*, one poster, and a teacher's guide.

The Women's Vote. Princeton, NJ: Films for the Humanities, 1988. 1 videocassette (24 minutes). On Elizabeth Cady Stanton and Susan B. Anthony.

Index

JUNE HANNAM is principal lecturer in history at the University of the West of England, Bristol.

MITZI AUCHTERLONIE is a graduate student at the University of Exeter.

KATHERINE HOLDEN is a research associate at the University of the West of England, Bristol.